THE PAPERS
OF
JOHN MARSHALL

Sponsored by
The College of William and Mary
and
The Institute of Early American History and Culture
under the auspices of
The National Historical Publications and Records
Commission

Mary Willis Ambler Marshall

by an unknown artist (ca. 1799)

THE PAPERS

OF

JOHN MARSHALL

Volume II

Correspondence and Papers, July 1788—December 1795
Account Book, July 1788—December 1795

Editors

CHARLES T. CULLEN
HERBERT A. JOHNSON

Assistant Editors

JOANNE M. WOOD
SUSAN H. ELIAS

The University of North Carolina Press, Chapel Hill
in association with the
Institute of Early American History and Culture,
Williamsburg, Virginia

*The Institute of Early American History and Culture
is sponsored jointly by The College of William and Mary in Virginia
and The Colonial Williamsburg Foundation*

*The ornament on the title page is based upon John Marshall's personal seal, as it appears on
a gold watch fob that also bears the seal of his wife, Mary Willis Marshall. It was drawn
by Richard J. Stinely of Williamsburg, Virginia, from the original, now owned by the Association for the Preservation of Virginia Antiquities, Richmond, Virginia, and is published with
the owner's permission.*

Library of Congress Cataloging in Publication Data

Marshall, John, 1755–1835.
   The papers of John Marshall.
   "Sponsored by the College of William and Mary and the Institute of Early American History
and Culture under the auspices of the National Historical Publications Commission."
   Includes bibliographical references and index.
   CONTENTS: v. 1. Correspondence and papers, November 10, 1775–June 23, 1788. Account
book, September 1783–June 1788. v. 2. Correspondence and papers, July 1788–December 1795.
Account book, July 1788–December 1795.
      1. Marshall, John, 1755–1835. 2. United States—Politics and government—Revolution,
1775–1783—Sources. 3. United States—Politics and government—1783–1865—Sources. 4.
Statesmen—United States—Correspondence. 5. Judges—United States—Correspondence. I. John-
son, Herbert Alan, ed. II. Cullen, Charles T., 1940–   ed. III. Institute of Early American
History and Culture, Williamsburg, Va.
E302.M365   347'.73'2634   74–9575
ISBN 0–8078–1233–1 (Vol. I)
ISBN 0–8078–1302–8 (Vol. II)

CONTENTS

CORRESPONDENCE AND PAPERS
July 1788—December 1795

1788

1789

ACCOUNT BOOK
July 1788—December 1795

FOREWORD

John Marshall was almost thirty-three years old when the Virginia ratifying convention adjourned and he returned to his law practice and other matters of local and personal concern. He had been married five years, had seen three of his children born, and was about to begin construction of the house that he and his family would occupy for the rest of his life. By July 1788 he had established a professional and civic position of leadership in Richmond that continued to grow during the years covered in this volume.

Although Marshall continued to concentrate his professional activities in the city of Richmond and its vicinity, the nature of his law practice was substantially altered by two events: the reorganization of the Virginia court system and the establishment of the federal courts. The 1787 General Assembly had adopted a new court system to take effect July 1, 1788, but the Court of Appeals had declared it unconstitutional in May. A special session after the ratifying convention and more prolonged deliberation at the fall 1788 session produced a new system of district courts that began in 1789. Marshall decided to limit his practice to the district courts in Fredericksburg, Petersburg, and Richmond, and to the High Court of Chancery and the Court of Appeals in Richmond. That decision is clearly reflected in this volume of his papers. Extant correspondence, legal papers, and his Account Book between 1788 and 1795 reveal an active professional career. Correspondence with John Breckinridge, Archibald Stuart, and William Branch Giles provides information about Marshall's practice because he transferred to these attorneys the cases that were to be tried in the districts in which he chose not to practice. At the same time, he received from them referrals of cases they wanted filed in the High Court of Chancery or the Court of Appeals.

Even though Marshall's law practice became increasingly concentrated in the state capital, it was never provincial in its subject matter. As an attorney who frequently represented residents of other states in Virginia courts, Marshall was preeminently qualified for practice in the federal courts established under the new Constitution. Litigation in the U.S. Circuit Court for Virginia, which met in Richmond after 1789, quickly assumed a major position in his professional career. He was particularly active in the defense of Virginians against the multitude of actions and suits brought against them for the collection of pre-Revolutionary British debts.

Personal inclination as well as professional and financial reasons reinforced Marshall's determination to limit his activities to the Richmond area. By 1788 he had established a position of leadership in the city that only increased by 1795. His close relationship with the Council of State, the House of Delegates, the Richmond City Common Council, and the important courts located in the capital made his residence there useful when he was asked to plead political or legal causes before those bodies. Occasionally the Council of State and the city council asked his advice on matters before them. In one opinion for the city council of *ca.* July 15, 1793, Marshall wrote, "I am . . . inclined to construe [legislative] Acts literally," an interesting indication of his early attitude toward the interpretation of laws. When James Innes left the state in late 1794, Marshall acted as attorney general of Virginia until his return. His continued residence in the state capital became essential as he assumed professional responsibility for defending Denny Martin Fairfax's claim to the Northern Neck in order to buy a portion of it from him. When the federal militia was established in 1792, Marshall accepted a commission to head a new Richmond regiment, and soon thereafter the General Assembly elected him a brigadier general. Afterward he became active in enforcing and supporting the national government's official policy of neutrality during the first Napoleonic War. During 1793 and 1794 Marshall became the most important spokesman for Federalism in the state. He not only wrote resolutions for adoption by a public gathering of area citizens but also strongly supported President Washington's policies in the House of Delegates and wrote a series of letters signed Aristides or Gracchus in response to those published by James Monroe as Agricola.

Throughout the early years of the new Republic, Marshall continued to decline offers of federal office ranging from U.S. attorney in Virginia to U.S. attorney general. Because he had no special desire to hold federal office, the decision to remain in Richmond was as easy as it was important for his career. A move to Philadelphia would have prevented Marshall from maintaining his voluminous legal practice before the state courts, and his position of influence with state officials would have been lost.

Concern with law practice dominated Marshall's life during the seven and a half years covered in this volume. It is noteworthy, however, that his activities ranged far beyond the realm of law, bringing him back into a military role as brigadier general in the new militia and into prominence as grand master of Freemasons in the state. His papers also reveal his concern for the financial security of his family not only in the successful compromise of the Fairfax lands title controversy but also in his investments in military pay certificates and federal bonds. Marshall's involvement in a wide variety of events offers new information about the Old Dominion, in addition to presenting a closer look at law practice and the legal system in this important period.

Every document that Marshall wrote or signed between July 1788 and 1795 is printed, summarized in a calendar entry, or listed in this volume. All extant letters to Marshall as well as documents called to his attention, such as wills, are also printed or calendared here. More than 90 percent of the documents in this volume have never appeared in print.

A departure from a policy described in Volume I should be noted. Marshall's arguments before various courts as recorded in printed reports have not been summarized in calendar entries in this volume. (Notes on his arguments taken by St. George Tucker, presently available only in manuscript, have been printed here, however.) A complete list of reported cases in which Marshall appeared will be appended to the volume devoted to his law practice. The editors emphasize, however, that all Marshall documents, legal or otherwise, known to exist from July 1788 through 1795 are recorded here as described above. Faced with a plethora of such routine legal documents as declarations and answers, and not wanting to omit documents with potential significance to scholars, the editors decided to list routine legal papers at the end of each month for which papers are extant. Some of these bear exact dates, but in the interest of clear organization all are grouped together under month and year only.

The editors were fortunate throughout the work on this volume to have had the assistance of several individuals and institutions that helped make the finished book more valuable and complete. Especially noteworthy has been the contribution of the project's research associate, George M. Curtis III, whose research on the

Fairfax lands controversy led the editors to a much better understanding of that important segment of Marshall's professional and
personal life in the 1790s. Curtis's knowledgeable criticism of that
and several other editorial notes was of great value. Joanne M.
Wood and Susan H. Elias provided essential assistance with research on a wide variety of topics covered in this volume. Ms.
Wood's work on the Freemasons, the Smithfield expedition, and
the Account Book was especially helpful. She also supervised the
copy editing with assistance from Lucy Brown, Elizabeth Fried-
berg, Sharon Middleberg, and Leslie Tobias, editorial apprentices
at the Institute of Early American History and Culture. Before Ms.
Elias resigned in January 1975, she surveyed Virginia newspapers
for information that added greatly to the Account Book annotation.
She also did background research on the William Constable correspondence and Marshall's stock certificates. The project's secretary, Lee H. Ellis, has typed and retyped scores of notes with a
patience the editors respect and appreciate. This volume could not
have been edited without the skills of each member of the staff.
Several people not on our staff provided special assistance. The
editors wish to recognize and express appreciation to C. Harper
Anderson, Joy Dickinson Barnes, Gerald Cowden, John W. Dudley, William H. Gaines, Jr., George E. Kidd, Louis H. Manarin,
W. Warner Moss, William Ray, and Susan Agee Riggs. Although
many people contributed to this volume, the editors accept responsibility for any shortcomings or mistakes that might remain.

Each private collector and institution that provided copies of
their manuscripts for inclusion in this volume has been identified
in the source line preceding the text of the document. Nevertheless, the editors wish to express special appreciation to them here.
In addition to the Association for the Preservation of Virginia Antiquities, and the Mt. Vernon Ladies' Association, the following
individuals permitted their Marshall items to be printed here:
Robert W. Carver, Summit, New Jersey; Justice George M. Cochran, Staunton, Virginia; Louis L. Croland, Paterson, New Jersey;
Henry N. Ess III, New York, New York; Mrs. Kenneth R. Higgins, Richmond, Virginia; Philip Gardiner Nordell, Ambler, Pennsylvania; and Matthew W. Paxton, Lexington, Virginia. Private
collections at the Grand Lodge A.F. & A.M. of Virginia, Richmond, and Marshall Lodge No. 39, A.F. & A.M., Lynchburg,
Virginia, were also made available.

Many documents came from the following institutions and academic libraries: College of William and Mary, Swem Library, Williamsburg, Virginia; Colonial Williamsburg Foundation Research Department, Williamsburg, Virginia; Dartmouth College, Baker Memorial Library, Hanover, New Hampshire; Duke University Library, Durham, North Carolina; The Filson Club, Louisville, Kentucky; Free Library of Philadelphia, Philadelphia, Pennsylvania; Historical Society of Pennsylvania, Philadelphia, Pennsylvania; Huntington Library, San Marino, California; Library of Congress, Washington, D.C.; Minneapolis Public Library, Minneapolis, Minnesota; National Archives, Washington, D.C.; New York Public Library, the Astor, Lenox, and Tilden Foundations, New York, New York; Panhandle Plains Historical Society, Canyon, Texas; Pennsylvania Historical and Museum Commission, Harrisburg, Pennsylvania; Rutgers University Library, New Brunswick, New Jersey; University Court of the University of Glasgow, Glasgow, Scotland; University of Minnesota Library, Minneapolis, Minnesota; University of Virginia, Alderman and Law Libraries, Charlottesville, Virginia; and The Virginia Historical Society, Richmond, Virginia.

Public records were provided by the clerks of the following courts: Circuit Court, Warrenton, Virginia; Superior Court, Frederick County, Winchester, Virginia; Circuit Court, Fredericksburg, Virginia; Hardy County Court, Moorefield, West Virginia; Henrico County Court, Richmond, Virginia; Chancery and Hustings Court, Richmond, Virginia; and the Circuit Court, Farmville, Virginia. Important documents were made available to the editors by the Land Office of the Office of the Secretary of State, Frankfort, Kentucky. Again the editors have been the beneficiaries of the outstanding archival collections of the Commonwealth of Virginia, maintained at the Virginia State Library, Richmond, Virginia. The editors also wish to acknowledge, with special thanks, the permission of the Keeper of Her Majesty's Public Record Office for the publication of Marshall documents found in the collections of the Public Record Office, London, England.

Finally, the editors wish to express their thanks to the project's two sponsoring institutions, the College of William and Mary and the Institute of Early American History and Culture, for their continuing support of this editorial endeavor. Funding for the project has been obtained from the National Historical Publications and Records Commission, the General Assembly of the Commonwealth of Virginia, and the National Endowment for the Humanities. In addition, the following contributors provided matching funds that permitted the project to take full advantage of the matching funds grant from the National Endowment for the Humanities: Association for the Preservation of Virginia Antiquities; Association for the Preservation of Virginia Antiquities, Colonial Capital Branch; James C. Ambler; Charles N. Cresap; William D. Doeller; S. Douglas Fleet; Friends of the College of William and Mary; Hon. Thomas C. Gordon, Jr.; Henry C. Hofheimer Family Foundation; John Stewart Bryan Memorial Foundation; National Society of the Daughters of Colonial Wars; James Marshall Plaskitt; Society of the Cincinnati in the Commonwealth of Virginia; Sons of the American Revolution, Virginia Society; Braxton Harrison Tabb, Jr.; and the Langbourne Williams Foundation.

EDITORIAL APPARATUS

RENDITION OF TEXT

In accordance with modern editorial standards, the editors have attempted to render the text as faithfully as possible. However, the dateline on each letter and document has been modernized and standardized to indicate the place and date of composition. The editors have also made a standard practice of bringing the signatures to letters flush with the right margin, wherever those signatures may appear upon the original. Should a letter contain the designation "private," or bear a dispatch number, or both, this material has been placed at the left margin above the salutation and in line with the place and dateline of the letter. Likewise acknowledgments or jurats to a document have been arbitrarily brought to the left margin, as have the signatures of witnesses or notaries. Postscripts also have been placed at the left margin, regardless of where they might appear on the face of a letter.

Each document and calendared synopsis has been given a heading, composed by the editors to provide a brief key to the nature of the document. These headings also make up the table of contents and are designed solely for the convenience of the reader in locating particular classes of documents. Letters are identified by the name of the individual who wrote to John Marshall or the person to whom Marshall wrote. In the case of multiple authors or addressees, the editors have tried to identify the group to which these individuals belonged and to use this group identification in heading the letter. Documents other than letters are, as a rule, identified by the category of document that is being printed or synopsized, such as "Petition," "Speech," or "Legislative Bill." For printed or calendared legal documents the heading has been expanded to include not only the category of the document but also the title of the case.

Within the text of documents copy has been followed as far as modern printing methods would permit. In most cases superscript letters have been lowered to the line, and omitted letters in a word have been inserted only when necessary to preserve the meaning of the word as written in the original. The ampersand (&) has been retained, but the editors have expanded "&c" and "&ca" to "etc." to conform to modern usage and typography. The tailed "p" (ꝑ) has been rendered as either "pro" or "per," depending upon the context in which it appears in the original. Finally, the editors have followed the tradition that all sentences begin with capital letters and terminate with periods, question marks, or exclamation points, and these corrections have been silently inserted in the text as necessary to preserve the original intention of the writer. All dashes at the end of sentences and paragraphs have been silently omitted from documents other than those that reproduce a previous imprint. Where punctuation was needed for clarity, the editors have added it in square brackets, except at the end of sentences.

Signatures to documents have been uniformly rendered in large and small capitals, regardless of their appearance on the original. However, where the editors have not examined the original signature or have no reason to believe that the signature on the edited document was copied from an original signature, the signature has been rendered as it appears in the text being copied. Usually, this situation occurs only in the case of printed documents where the original manuscript copy and all contemporary copies and later transcripts from the original manuscript have been lost.

Where interpolation has become necessary, the editors have been sparing and cautious in their exercise of imagination. If the meaning of a word was clear, although some letters may have been illegible or missing because of mutilation, up to four missing letters have been supplied silently, that is, without the use of brackets. However, if the meaning was unclear, or more than one meaning was possible, the editors have inserted their preferred choice in square brackets ([ ]) and, if necessary, have supplied the explanation in a footnote. Where more than one word was missing, or the text was supplied through editorial conjecture, this has been indicated by brackets and the inserted matter rendered in italics rather than roman. Where material in a manuscript text appears to have been inserted through a slip of the pen, the editors have followed the text and explained the error by means of a footnote. However, in the case of typographical errors in printed matter, which are more likely to reflect the compositor's mistake than the author's, the editors have made a silent correction.

Matter deleted by the writer has, as a general rule, been deleted from the text as printed in this edition. In those circumstances where the editors believe that the significance of the material deleted is sufficient to justify an exception to this general policy, however, the canceled word or passage has been placed *before* the matter that replaced it, and enclosed in angle brackets (⟨ ⟩). A deletion within a deletion has been indicated by double angle brackets (⟨⟨ ⟩⟩), and the preceding rule concerning its placement in the text has been applied.

Throughout, the editors have avoided interpreting the text for the reader with excessive insertions of conjectural material. All insertions of a word or more in length appear in italics within brackets. Where necessary, additional information has been supplied in a footnote. The editors have tried generally to limit the use of brackets, thereby permitting easier reading of the text.

The presentation of seals in a printed edition is a matter of some difficulty. For purposes of clearer rendition, the editors have divided seals into two categories. One group covers the official and corporate seals, which are rendered [SEAL], provided the document indicates that such a seal was at one time attached to the original. The other seal, be it a wafer seal or simply a signature followed by "L.S.," has been considered a hand seal and rendered "L.S." The editors have treated variations in hand seals as follows:

J. Marshall L.S.	is shown as	J. Marshall L.S.
J. Marshall (LS)	is shown as	J. Marshall (LS)
J. Marshall (Seal)	is shown as	J. Marshall [LS]
J. Marshall (SEAL)	is shown as	J. Marshall [LS]
J. Marshall (L.S)	is shown as	J. Marshall (L.S)

In presenting documents containing seals, the editors have attempted to conform the appearance of the seal on the printed page to its place on the original manuscript.

ANNOTATION OF DOCUMENTS

While the editors have preferred a policy of sparse annotation, they have attempted to provide the reader with some guidance in interpreting Marshall's papers, including essential explanations and a reasonably complete identification of individuals upon their first mention in the text of the papers. (The volume index will facilitate cross-reference to the first mention of a given name or individual.) Biographical references to well-known individuals who are listed in the *Dictionary of American Biography* or *Dictionary of National Biography* are intentionally brief, and the editors similarly have not expansively discussed individuals of slight importance to Marshall's career or those whose identity is not material to an understanding of the text of the document. When the editors have been unsuccessful in identifying a person mentioned in the text, they upon occasion have advanced a supposition based upon knowledge of Marshall's activities and associations, but in most cases they have chosen the safer policy of leaving it to the reader to speculate upon the identity of an unknown person.

In identifying individuals and business firms the editors have frequently relied on several basic reference works and have used information from them without citation in each instance. In addition to the *DAB* and the *DNB*, these include Lyon G. Tyler's *Encyclopedia of Virginia Biography* and Earl Gregg Swem's *Virginia Historical Index*. Information derived from the periodicals indexed in the latter has been used without naming the specific source. To identify military figures the editors have similarly depended on Frederick B. Heitman's *Historical Register of the Officers of the Continental Army* and two publications of the Daughters of the American Revolution, the *DAR Patriot Index* and the *Lineage Book*.[1] Definitions of little-used or archaic terms taken from the *Oxford English Dictionary* have not been given a citation, nor have definitions of legal terms obtained from *Black's Law Dictionary*. For all other sources, the editors have provided a full bibliographic citation in the appropriate footnote. Whenever possible, book-length biographies have been cited at the first mention of a given individual in one of Marshall's papers.

The source of each document is identified in full in the line immediately below its heading. In cases where this description is not adequate, the first footnote gives further information and also identifies the writer or recipient if he has not been previously identified. In the case of a particularly delicate problem of documentary analysis, there is, of course, no substitute for viewing the original document, but the editors believe that their annotation policy will reduce to a minimum the researcher's need to consult the original documents.

In preparing calendared synopses of documents not printed in this edition the editors have tried to summarize concisely the con-

---

1. Lyon G. Tyler, *Encyclopedia of Virginia Biography* (New York, 1915); E[arl] G. Swem, *Virginia Historical Index* (Richmond, 1934); Frederick B. Heitman, *Historical Register of the Officers of the Continental Army during the War of the Revolution, April, 1775, to December, 1783* (Washington, D.C., 1893); the *DAR Partiot Index* (Washington, D.C., 1966); *Lineage Book, National Society of the Daughters of the American Revolution* (Harrisburg, Pa., 1895; Washington, D.C., 1896–1939).

tents of the manuscript or printed source. As a general rule the synopsis includes a notation concerning John Marshall's connection with the document, and an attempt has been made to identify individuals mentioned in the synopsis. Additional details, if available, have been provided by way of footnote annotations, but in the interest of economy of space, these have been kept to a minimum. Synopses dealing with Marshall's law practice include, if possible, sufficient information for the reader to identify the case involved, the nature of the litigation, and the court in which the case was pending when the calendared document was prepared.

The decision to include every identifiable Marshall document in these volumes led to the accumulation of a large number of legal documents that are routine except that they were written or signed by John Marshall. Summaries of most of these would demand excessive space and produce little useful information. The editors decided to list them together at the end of the appropriate month, thereby providing the reader with a description of the document and its present location.

When a document or group of documents has required more extended discussion than could be conveniently included in a footnote, an editorial note has been added immediately preceding the document to which it pertains. Although these notes are intended to be definitive discussions, they obviously are limited in scope to a consideration of the basic document and the situation that gave rise to the documentary material. The editorial notes also contain editorial commentary about interpretive difficulties that have arisen concerning the paper or papers being edited.

ABBREVIATIONS AND SHORT TITLES

The editors have tried to avoid ambiguous abbreviations and have made short titles in citations sufficiently complete to permit ease in bibliographic reference. The following lists contain, first, explanations of abbreviations that may not be readily understood and that have a special meaning in this series and, second, full citations for short titles that are used frequently throughout this volume. Generally accepted abbreviations, such as months of the year, have not been listed, nor have short titles that occur in a limited section of the volume. The latter can easily be expanded by going to the first reference to a work in each document or editorial note; there a full citation is provided.

ABBREVIATIONS

AD   Autograph Document
ADS   Autograph Document Signed
AL   Autograph Letter
ALS   Autograph Letter Signed
DS   Document Signed
LS   Letter Signed

SHORT TITLES

Blackstone, *Commentaries*

Sir William Blackstone, *Commentaries on the Laws of England . . .* (Oxford, 1765–1769)

CVSP

William P. Palmer *et al.*, eds., *Calendar of Virginia State Papers and other manuscripts . . .* (Richmond, 1875–1893)

Dove, *Proceedings*

John Dove, *Proceedings of the M.W. Grand Lodge of Ancient York Masons of the State of Virginia . . .* (Richmond, 1874)

JVCS

Wilmer L. Hall *et al.*, eds., *Journals of the Council of the State of Virginia . . .* (Richmond, 1931–1967). These volumes cover meetings of the Council from July 12, 1776, to November 10, 1788.

JVCS

Journals of the Council of the State of Virginia, manuscript, available on microfilm, Virginia State Library

JVHD

Journal of the House of Delegates of the Commonwealth of Virginia. . . . This short title will be followed by the month and year in which the General Assembly convened.

Tucker, *Blackstone's Commentaries*   St. George Tucker, [ed.], *Black-stone's Commentaries: With Notes of Reference, to the Constitution and Laws, of the Federal Government of the United States; and of the Commonwealth of Virginia* (Philadelphia, 1803)

In addition to the foregoing abbreviations and short titles, the editors have followed the policy of using legal form citations when discussing or citing the reports of cases in courts and statutes passed by legislative bodies in England or the United States. These generally conform to *A Uniform System of Citation*, 11th ed. (Cambridge, Mass., 1967), adopted for use by several law reviews. All other legal citations follow the Institute of Early American History and Culture's *Style Sheet for Authors*, with the following exceptions:

Hening   William Walter Hening, ed., *The Statutes at Large; Being a Collection of All the Laws of Virginia . . .* (Richmond, 1809–1823)

Shepherd   Samuel Shepherd, ed., *The Statutes at Large of Virginia, from October Session 1792, to December Session 1806 . . .* (Richmond, 1835–1836)

Stat.   *Statutes at Large of the United States of America, 1789–1873* (Boston, 1845–1873)

Wythe   George Wythe, *Decisions of Cases in Virginia in the High Court of Chancery . . .* (Richmond, 1795)

MARSHALL CHRONOLOGY

1788–1795

December 20, 1788	Elected charter member of Amicable Society of Richmond.
April 1789	Admitted to practice before district courts at Fredericksburg, Petersburg, and Richmond.
October 19–December 19, 1789	Served as member of the House of Delegates representing city of Richmond.
November 26, 1789	Admitted to practice before U.S. Circuit Court, Virginia.
December 17, 1789	Admitted to practice before U.S. District Court, Virginia.
October 18–December 29, 1790	Served as member of the House of Delegates representing city of Richmond.
May 30, 1791	Commissioned colonel, Richmond Regiment (Nineteenth), Virginia militia.
October 29, 1792–October 28, 1793	Served as deputy grand master, Grand Lodge of Ancient Free and Accepted Masons of Virginia.
June 7, 1793	Argued *Ware v. Hylton* before U.S. Circuit Court, Virginia.
June 10, 1793	Commissioned lieutenant colonel, Richmond Regiment (Nineteenth), Virginia militia.
September 8–November 20, 1793	Wrote Aristides and Gracchus letters.
October 28, 1793–November 23, 1795	Served as grand master, Grand Lodge of Ancient Free and Accepted Masons of Virginia.
December 2, 1793	Elected brigadier general, Second Brigade, Virginia militia.

February 1, 1794	Purchased South Branch Manor from Denny Martin Fairfax.
July 12, 1794– *ca.* 1796	Served as member of the Richmond City Common Council.
July 23–27, 1794	Led militia expedition to Smithfield, Virginia.
October 1794– March 1795	Served as acting attorney general of Virginia.
February 2, 1795	Admitted to practice before the Supreme Court of the United States.
November 10– December 29, 1795	Served as member of the House of Delegates representing city of Richmond.

CORRESPONDENCE AND PAPERS
July 1788—December 1795

To George Chapman

ALS, Marshall Papers, Swem Library, College of William and Mary

Dear Sir[1]   Richmond, July 23, 1788

I send you another subpoena—the first not being returnd must I presume have miscarried. It had better I think be returnd by the sheriff of Fauquier, if Mr. Chapman shoud not be in the state, as the land lies in that county.[2] Take care that it is returnd before the next court. You will also please to send me an affidavit made by some disinterested person that the defendant lives out of the state.[3] The exr. or admr. of your brother shoud also be a party. As I do not know who may be exr. or admr. you will please to insert the name in the spa.[4] The same affidavit must be made as to him or her as is before directed with respect to the young gentlemen. If there is to be a controversy concerning the 91 Acres the tenant in possession shoud also be added to the subpoena.

If you wish to take any depositions you must make an affidavit that the person whose deposition you wish to take is an aged & infirm witness & is material, or that he or she is a single witness to a material fact, in the suit depending between yourself plaintiff & George Chapman an infant & others defendants.[5] Send me such an affidavit & I will procure you a commission. I shall be glad to hear from you on the receipt of this.[6] I am Sir, respectfully, your obedt. Servt.

J MARSHALL

1. Addressed to Chapman at "Summer hill near Alexandria" and postmarked at Fredericksburg on Aug. 19. According to JM's Account Book, he was in Richmond from July 23 to Aug. 9; he made a trip to Winchester, via Fredericksburg, between Aug. 9 and Aug. 25.

2. At issue was a suit in chancery concerning title to real property.

3. The plaintiff could serve papers by publishing a notice in the *Virginia Gazette* only after obtaining an affidavit that the defendant was not residing in the state. See 11 Hening 343 (1783).

4. Subpoena.

5. This paragraph obviously applies to a parallel case at common law pending in the General Court; the rule concerning a single witness to a material fact applied to open commissions from the General Court but not to open commissions from the High Court of Chancery. Compare 9 Hening 394 (1777) with 9 Hening 410 (1777).

6. A fee in the case Chapman v. Chapman appears in JM's Account Book, Receipts, Sept. 26, 1790.

Assignment

ADS, Land Office, Kentucky Secretary of State's Office[7]

[Richmond, *ca.* July 1788]

By virtue of a power of attorney[8] to me given & herewith filed I do assign the within survey & tract of land, the one moity to Abraham Foe & his heirs forever the other moity to Christopher Greenup[9] & Humphrey Marshall as tenants in common & to their heirs forever.

J MARSHALL
for Charles Tyler

Certification

ADS, Executive Papers, Virginia State Library

[Richmond, *ca.* August 4, 1788]

[Petition.] "To his Excellency the Governor and the Members of the Privy Council, The Petition of Robert Means humbly sheweth;

That in May last he was fined by the Judgment of the Court of Henrico County sixty pounds for keeping a disorderly house, suffering unlawful Gaming therein, and selling liquors contrary to Law. Your Petitioner humbly shews that at the time he was charged with keeping a disorderly house etc. he kept a Billiard-table; that he entered it and paid a Tax upon it according to Law; the tax upon it amounting to fifteen pounds Specie, for one year, and five pounds specie tax to the Corporation. Your Petitioner understood and believed that nothing further was payable. It was the practice at every table in Town to play for punch or some other liquor, and to take it from the Keeper of the table, who, in no one instance, took out a Tavern licence on that account: Your petitioner who came a stranger to this place, believing it to be right did the same; nor has he yet been informed that it was wrong. His house was an orderly house, the Gaming charged in the presentment was only playing at Billiards.

After Issue was joined for which your Petitioner employed no Lawyer, he was compelled to go to Philadelphia on business; making no doubt of

7. JM wrote this on the verso of a survey for Charles Tyler. It is among other documents in the bundle for Survey 8118, Virginia Land Grants.

8. See Vol. I, 250.

9. Greenup was a lawyer in Fayette County and had represented that county in the House of Delegates in 1785. He later moved to Frankfort, represented Kentucky in Congress from 1792 to 1797, and served as governor of Kentucky from 1804 to 1808.

returning before the trial, he deferred engaging an Attorney 'till then. He was kept back by contrary winds so that he did not reach Virginia, 'till the Judgment had passed against him, and therefore no proof of the circumstances above mentioned, and especially that the table was legally entered, and the Tax paid, was made to the Jury. Your Petitioner humbly shews, that if he has committed an Offence against the Laws by selling liquors at his table, it was ignorantly committed. Your Petitioner therefore humbly prays that the fine may be remitted to him.

And your Petitioner will humbly pray etc.

ROBERT MEANS."[1]

We the subscribers certify that we have been several times at the billiard table of Robert Means & that we always considered it as an orderly table never having seen anything to give us a contrary opinion either at the table or in the house.[2]

J MARSHALL
JOHN STEWART.
JOHN BECKLEY.
GEO PICKETT
ROBT. MITCHELL
FRIEDRICK THOMAS[3]

From George Washington

Letterbook Copy, Washington Papers, Library of Congress

Sir,   Mount Vernon, August 15, 1788

Your letter of the 10th. Uto. to Doctr. Stuart enclosing a Summons for L. Washington etc. did not come to my hand till lass Night.[4]

I am at a loss what step to take in this matter, and should be glad of your advice. Luther Martin is the Attorney Genl. of Mary-

1. Means, or Minns (d. 1808), accompanied his petition with a May 5, 1788, recommendation of the Henrico County Court that £50 of his fine be remitted. The Council of State decided to remit that amount on Aug. 4, 1788. *JVCS*, IV, 275. See Account Book, Receipts, Aug. 2, 1788, for Means's payment to JM for his services.

2. The certification in JM's hand is on a separate sheet of paper included with the petition and the recommendation of the Henrico County Court.

3. Thomas (b. *ca.* 1744) was a baker in Richmond in 1784. "Return of the Inhabitants," 1784, Richmond City Common Hall Records, I, 345, Virginia State Library.

4. David Stuart was an Alexandria physician and close friend of George Washington; Lund Washington (1737–1796) was a cousin of Washington residing in Fairfax County. JM's letter has not been found.

land and lives in Baltimore. Elizabeth and Sarah Cresap I have always understood live with one Jacobs who Married there Mother, and is said to be a resident of Hampshire County; but two or three summons having been already Sent to the Sheriff thereof and no return of them made, the presumption I think is that there must have been either a Miscarriage—or that *these* Daughters of Michl. Cresap are not residents of that County. Possibly they are Married, and living in Maryland where their Father did.[5]

I should be glad to know whether, the issuing of the Patent, if the summons now sent is not executed and returned, or good reason assigned for the non execution is *merely* an *Officis* actor—will be in consequence of application from the heirs of Michael Cresap or any person in their behalf and who? My reason for it is, I have been informed and I believe from good authy. that Jacobs *was* so well convinced of the legality and *equity* of my Title as to declare he should cease all further prosecution of the claim in behalf of the Childrin to whom I have heard he was guardian. This however may not be true nor may it be the case with Mr. Martin. The dismission of the Caveat will not invalidate my title to the land but may involve me in a more letigeous and expensive prosecution, or defence of it[6]—and on this principle it was that Mr Randolph[7] ad-

5. Washington had been trying to summons the heirs of Michael Cresap (1742–1775) to the General Court at Richmond in order to settle a dispute over a parcel of western land. Luther Martin (1748–1826) had married Cresap's eldest daughter, Maria. The other daughters presumably lived with John Jeremiah Jacobs (1757–1839), who had married Cresap's widow.

6. The dispute between Washington and the Cresaps began in 1773 when Washington learned that Michael Cresap had taken possession of a tract of land along the Ohio River, known as the Round Bottom, that Washington had claimed and had surveyed in 1770 and 1771. Washington immediately wrote Cresap, defending his prior right to the land.

After the Revolution, Washington attempted to secure his title to the Round Bottom. He received a patent from the governor of Virginia in 1784 and, after talking with John Jeremiah Jacobs, believed Cresap's heirs would not continue to claim title. John Harvie, register of the Land Office, informed Washington in 1785, however, that the Cresap heirs had in fact entered a survey and claim for the Round Bottom. Washington immediately entered a caveat against their claim and began his attempt to get the case into court. After the Cresap heirs failed to appear, Washington's claim seemed secure in 1791. Another Cresap heir reopened the dispute in 1796, and it was not until 1834 that the Virginia Court of Appeals ruled against the Cresaps' claim, thus ending the dispute. For a detailed account of this affair, see Roy Bird Cook, *Washington's Western Lands* (Strasburg, Va., 1930), 88–89; and correspondence with Michael Cresap, William Crawford, John Harvie, Thomas Lewis, and Edmund Randolph, in the Washington Papers, Library of Congress.

See also Washington to JM, Mar. 17, and Apr. 5, 1789.

7. JM became involved in this case as a consequence of assuming the law practice of Edmund Randolph in 1786. See Vol. I, 378, n. 90.

vised the Caveat. Under this relation of the matter I shall be very glad to hear from you. With very great esteem and regard I am, Sir, Yrs. etc.

Go. WASHINGTON

To George Washington

ALS, Henry E. Huntington Library

Sir,   Richmond, September 5, 1788

I have been some time absent from Richmond[8] or your letter of the 15th. of August woud not have remaind unanswered. On proof that the parties defendants to the caveat are out of the state, or that they reside in a different county from that in which they had been supposed to reside, or of any other fact which woud shew to the court that there has been no negligence on the part of the caveator but that the non service of the process is to be ascribed to accident, the caveat will be continued & new process be issued, but if no cause iss[9] assignd why the process is not servd, the law directs a dismission which is certified by the clerk of the court to the Register of the land office who immediately makes out the patent which is deliverd to any applicant authorized to receive it unless it be retained for office fees.[1]

The dismission of the caveat can in no sort impair your title. As your patent is the eldest & comprehends within its lines the land caveated the junior patentee can only establish a claim against you by a suit in chancery. To this he may resort shoud the caveat be determind in your favor. I remain Sir with the highest respect & veneration, Your obedt. Servt.

J: MARSHALL

8. JM had been to Winchester. See Account Book, Disbursements, Aug. 25, 1788.

9. JM clearly wrote a double *s*; perhaps he intended to write "issue" or some other word.

1. See 11 Hening 292, for the appropriate section of "An act for giving further time to enter certificates for settlement rights, and to locate warrants upon preemption rights, and for other purposes," passed by the May 1783 General Assembly.

Law Papers, September 1788

General Court

McHaney v. George, declaration, AD, Term Papers, Office of the Clerk of the Circuit Court, Fredericksburg, Va.[2]

Montgomery v. Mason's Executors, replication and demurrer, AD, Term Papers, Office of the Clerk of the Circuit Court, Fredericksburg, Va.

Construction Account

AD, Marshall Papers, Swem Library, College of William and Mary

[Richmond], October 1788–[November 1790]

Money paid for my house[3]

October		£			
88	Paid Mr. B. Lewis[4]		80		
Novr. 88	Paid Mr. Sydnor (specie)		6	17	4
Jany. 4th.					
89	Paid for plank		3	9	
	paid Keeting & Smith		1	15	5
Jany. 8th.	paid Mr. Lewis		29	8	2
Jany. 22d.	Paid Keeting & Smith		10	5	
	Paid Mr. Sydnor (in specie)		16		8
	Paid Mr. Sydnor in warrants		49	19	4
	Paid Mr. Lewis		38	10	5

2. See JM's notes on argument, May 4, 1791, and Account Book, Receipts, May 1791.

3. These entries represent the expenditures for building or finishing the house that JM occupied the rest of his life, located at what is now Ninth and Marshall streets in Richmond. Construction obviously began before the deed to the property was transferred to JM, suggesting he held an option to buy the land. See Deed, July 7, 1789, and entry in Account Book, Disbursements, July 5, 1789. For information on JM's previous houses, see Vol. I, 332, n. 97.

The account is recorded in JM's law notes and accounts, beginning in the law notes portion of the book near where he stopped heading pages for legal commonplacing. He began on a page headed "Legacies" and continued on pages headed "Libel," "Mayhem," "Maintenance," "Mandamus," and "Master & Servant." A page marked "Limitation of actions" contains law notes, although he crossed through them as he turned the page to begin recording expenditures in June 1790. For a physical description of JM's law notes and accounts, see Vol. I, 289.

4. Benjamin Lewis.

March				
14th.	Paid Mr. Goode	24		
	Paid Keeting & Smith	12		
	Paid do.	8	1	8
Apl. 4th.	Paid Mr. Goode	16	2	1
do.	Paid Mr. Sydnor (specie)	18		
	paid do. (int. warrants)	27	3	8
May 9th.	Paid Mr. Lewis (specie)	51		
	Nails		5	9
	Paid Keating & Smith	1	3	7
16	Paid Mr. Sydnor	25		
	Paid do. (specie)	12	6	3½
		428	8	4½
	Paid Mr. Duke			
	for levelling the cellar	0	18	0
June 11th.				
89	Paid Mr. Goode	6		
	for nails		6	
June 25	paid Mr. Lewis (specie) £14	14		
June 29th.	Paid Mr. Keating & Smith	12	7	
	nails £1-4-6, oil & paint £4-5-6	5	10	
July 6th.	paid Mr. Sydnor through			
	Mr. Winston	6		
July 20th.	paid Mr. Duke altering a window		6	
July 20th.	paid Mr. Lewis	20		
23d.	freight for nails 6/, carriage for			
	do. 2/		8	
29th.	paid Keating & Smith	16	4	8
	Paid Mr. Lewis	8	4	3
Augt.	paid Mr. Goode	6		
	paid for glue		6	
	Locks for vault	1		
31st.	paid Mr. Lewis	30		2½
Septr. 1st.	Paid for 4 douzen pullies	1	14	
8th.	Paid Mr. Lewis through			
	D. Cockran[5]	5		
15th.	Paid Mr. Duke for the window			
	arches	1	12	
26th.	paid Keating & Smith	4		
Oc. 12	paid for 26 gallons of oil	4	11	
	Paid for Hinges	1	16	
		145	5	1½
Oc. 15th.	Paid Keating & Smith	8	17	4

5. See Account Book, Receipts, Sept. 8, 1789, where JM also entered the receipt of the money from D. Cochran.

Date	Item	£	s	d
	Paid for hinges	1	5	
	for brads		9	
Novr. 9th.	Paid Mr. Goode £14-18	14	18	
16th.	Paid Mr. Lewis in full	39	11	0½
Decr. 2	Paid Mr. Sydnor	9	8	
4th.	Mr. Keating	2	5	6
6th.	Paid Mr. Goode in full	8	0	11
	Glass & nails (to Mr. Morris)	56	0	5
22d.	To Mr. Keating	21	5	
Jany. 90				
7th.	To Mr. Heron[6] for nails & paint	5	6	3
	Glue 3 dollars		18	
Feb. 9th.	4d. nails—10000	2		
	Paid Keating	6		
March 7th.	Paid Keating	5	0	9
13.	paid do. in int. war.	10	1	6
26th.	pd. do. in do.	9	10	9
May 12	pd. do. in do.	9	1	6
15	pd. Mr. Booker for scantling	2	5	
20	nails	1	1	
24th.	Paid Keating	7	4	
		220	8	11½
June[7]	leads for windowns £	12	11	
	Nails	1	18	
	lead for house	1	18	9
	plank	1	10	
	Nails		12	
	nails		12	
	Shingles 12/			
	Paid Keating	9		
	Paid Mr. Kays for plaistering	33		
	Cord for windows		12	
July	paint	1	3	6
	nails		12	
	plank	1	12	6
July [14]	Paid Mr. Keating (specie)	10	0	10
	Paid Mr. Keating (warrants)	13	19	1
	plank to Mr. Burton	4	11	
	drayage plank from Rockets[8]		5	

6. James Heron, Richmond merchant.

7. These entries begin on a page intended for entries on "Mayhem," but JM crossed out that legal term and wrote "Money Paid for my house," as he began recording expenditures on this page. The page immediately preceding contains law notes on "Limitation of actions."

8. Rocketts warehouse and landing.

		To Mr. Lipscomb for putting in	£		
		grates etc. & cellar door	6	12	
Augt.		paint & nails		16	
		Hinges	2	8	
		painting roof	1	4	
		£	104	18	8
Augt.		Hinges bought in Alexandria	1	17	6
Sep.		paint 10/6, do. 24/	1	14	6
		blacksmith for crowbars	1	16	
		paid Voss for plaistering etc.	55	6	2¾
		Hinges Glue Skews[9]		19	
		Pd. Keating	2	8	
		paint 18/, do. 6	1	4	
		Pd. Doctor McClurg[1] for grate	5	5	2
		nails		9	
	26	Paid Mr. Keating	16	1	4
Oc.		Paid do. in warrants	18	12	9
		Paid Mr. Allen for painting	3	12	
		Paper etc.	12	2	5
		iron for porch		7	
		nails	1	4	
	16	Paid Mr. Burton for scantling to			
		porches etc.	6	12	
		Painter £3-12, do. £2-8, 42/	8	2	
		brick work £3-11, £3	6	11	
		putting up paper	1	1	
		laying marble slabs	1	11	3
		paint 36/	1	16	
		nails	1	2	6
		three brass locks	3	4	
			151	18	7¾
	27th.	Glazing windows	1	4	
No.	3d.	Paid Mr. Keating	7		
	6	pd. Do.	6	0	8
	8th.	pd. Mr. Burton for scantling for			
		porches in full	8	10	9
		brick work	3	4	3
		iron for porch etc.		2	9
		Paid Mr. McKim for banisters	2	17	6
		paid for latches		12	
		paint	1	8	
		shingles etc.	3	8	
		Mr. Keating	29		

9. Skews are stones especially made for joining with other similar stones to form the sloping head or coping of a gable, rising slightly above the level of the roof.
1. James McClurg.

Grates & Franklin	19	1	7
Glass		12	
Paid Keating warrants	2	11	
Paid do. specie	26	19	2
Paid Do. in bonds[2]	36	7	3
paint & nails	12	10	2
iron for cellar windows	2	19	9
	164	[18]	10
Lock	0	7	6
Making end window	3	10	

Law Papers, October 1788

General Court

Vest v. Fore, declaration, record book copy, District Court Records at Large, Office of the Clerk of the Prince Edward County Circuit Court, Farmville, Va.[3]

West v. King, declaration, record book copy, District Court Records at Large, Office of the Clerk of the Prince Edward County Circuit Court, Farmville, Va.[4]

Law Papers, 1788

High Court of Chancery

Griffin v. Alexander & Co., bill in chancery, printed extract, Kenneth W. Rendell, Inc., Catalog No. 97 (Newton, Mass., 1974), 35.

Morris v. Alexander & Co., bill in chancery, ADS, Marshall Papers, Swem Library, College of William and Mary.

2. This entry is in a hand other than JM's.
3. See JM to John Breckinridge, *ca.* Mar. and Apr. 3, 1790.
4. See JM to John Breckinridge, Mar. 28, 1790, and Vol. I, 398, n. 67.

Deed of Trust

Deed Book Copy, Office of the Clerk of the Henrico County Circuit Court, Richmond

Richmond, January 10, 1789

THIS INDENTURE made this tenth day of January in the year of our Lord one thousand seven hundred and eighty nine BETWEEN George Webb Junior of the County of Buckingham[5] of the one part and John Marshall and John Beckley[6] of the City of Richmond of the other part WITNESSETH that for and in consideration of the sum of five shillings Current Money of Virginia to him in hand paid by the said John Marshall and John Beckley, the receipt whereof he doth hereby acknowledge, and thereof doth acquit the said John Marshall and John Beckley. He the said George Webb junior Hath granted bargained and sold and by these presents doth bargain and sell unto the said John Marshall and John Beckley their Heirs and assigns the nine negro slaves following to wit, John Abraham, Mingo, Tempe, Billy, Hannah, Louisa, Fanny, and Phil, To HAVE AND TO HOLD the said Slaves to the said John Marshall and John Beckley their Heirs and assigns in Trust, that they the said John Marshall and John Beckley will apply the hire and profits of the labor of the said Slaves to the sole and seperate use of Hannah Webb wife of George Webb senior[7] during her life and after her death then to the use of George Webb Senior during his life and after the death of the said Hannah Webb and of the said George Webb her husband, then to the use of the said George Webb junior his heirs and assigns forever IN WITNESS whereof the said George Webb junior hath hereunto set his hand and seal the Day and year first above written.

Signed Sealed and Delivered
in presence of   GEO. WEBB jr: (LS)
CHARLES TALLEY.[8]
BD. WEBB.[9]

---

5. Webb (d. 1803) subsequently lived in Goochland and Henrico counties but at the time of his death was a resident of Richmond.

6. For information on Beckley, see Vol. I, 243, n. 4, 249.

7. George Webb, Sr. (b. 1729), married Hannah Fleming in 1756. She was his second wife and stepmother of George Webb, Jr.

8. Talley (ca. 1755–ca. 1816) was a resident of Hanover County.

9. Bernard Webb was the son of George Webb, Sr., and Hannah Webb. This deed of trust apparently arose from a family settlement designed to provide financial security

At a Montly Court continued and held for Henrico County at the Courthouse on Tuesday the 7th: of April 1789 This Indenture of Trust was proved by the Oaths of Charles Talley and Bernard Webb the Witnesses thereto and Ordered to be Recorded.

Test ADAM CRAIG C.C.

From Beverley Randolph

Copy, Executive Letterbooks, Virginia State Library

Gentlemen,[1]   Richmond, January 29, 1789

It having been suggested to the Executive that Catharine Chrull[2] now under sentence of death is disordered in her mind, they have thought proper to reprieve her until the 6th. of next month. And in order that the best information may be obtained of the truth of this suggestion, I must beg the favour of you to examine her and report as soon as convenient your opinion as to the present state of mind of this unhappy Woman. I am etc.

B R[3]

To Beverley Randolph

LS, Executive Papers, Virginia State Library

Sir   Richmond, February 4, 1789

In obedience to the request of Your Excellency, we have visited Catherine Crull: She appears to us to be almost in a state of entire

---

for Hannah Webb. It created a trust in which she was entitled to income for her life from the hire of the slaves, and upon her death her husband became entitled to a similar income if he survived her. Upon the expiration of the two life estates the remainder vested in the grantor, George Webb, Jr.

1. The letter was addressed to Rev. John Buchanan, William Foushee, and JM. The procedure for committing insane persons, adopted in 1769, required examination by three members of the local government. 8 Hening 379. See Vol. I, 193, for a similar request.

2. Mrs. Crull (b. *ca.* 1772), of Monongalia County, was convicted at the Dec. 1788 General Court of murdering her husband. Attorney General Joseph Jones wrote Gov. Randolph on Jan. 9, 1789, suggesting the insanity of Mrs. Crull, whereupon the governor requested the examination. *CVSP*, IV, 528, 554; JVCS, Dec. 29, 1788, Jan. 29, 1789; *Virginia Gazette and Weekly Advertiser* (Richmond), Oct. 30, and Dec. 18, 1788.

3. Beverley Randolph was elected governor by the General Assembly on Dec. 3, 1788.

ideotcy. Her Mind seems so Much disordered that we think her totally incapable of distinguishing right from wrong, or even of knowing what is said to her.[4] We have the honer to be, with great respect, Your Excellencies Most Obt Servts

JOHN BUCHANAN[5]
JOHN MARSHALL
W: FOUSHEE

Petition of John Peter Cauvy

AD, Executive Papers, Virginia State Library[6]

Richmond, February 12, 1789

To his Excellency the Governor & the Honble. the members of the Privy Council of State the petition of John Cauvy humbly sheweth

That in observance of the act "for the protection & encouragement of the commerce of nations acknowleging the independence of the United States of America"[7] your Honble. board hath directed that the consul of France shall be aided in carrying into execution two judgements he has renderd against your petitioner the one in favor of a Mr. Peter Barthes, the other in favor of Messrs. Cagneau & Subercaseaux. To the first sentence your petitioner has submitted, but with respect to the second he begs leave humbly to state that when their contest was decided by the consul of France it was actually depending before the court of Dinwiddie county in which Messrs. Cagneau & Subercaseaux had instituted a suit against your petitioner. Considering the subject as appropriated to the courts of law of this commonwealth by the act of the plain-

4. Randolph presented this report to the Council of State on Feb. 5, whereupon Mrs. Crull was pardoned and committed to the state hospital in Williamsburg. While she was in the hospital, the state provided for the care of her infant daughter. On Dec. 9, 1789, Mrs. Crull was declared sane, released from the hospital, and reunited with her daughter. The following month, however, she abandoned her child, and the state resumed paying for the child's care. CVSP, IV, 559, 589, VII, 453; JVCS, Dec. 29, 1788, Feb. 5, Mar. 28, and Dec. 9, 1789, and Jan. 21, 1790.

5. Apparently Buchanan signed JM's name as well as his own; JM did not sign.

6. The petition is in JM's hand and is signed by Cauvy. See JM's entry in Account Book, Receipts, Feb. 4, 1789.

7. 10 Hening 202–203 (1779).

tiff himself, being unwilling for many reasons to submit this case to the decision of a single man whose will was his only law, & supposing that the laws of Virginia afforded their protection to every resident of the state, more especially to one possessd of real property within the commonwealth, and that the act giving jurisdiction to the consul, being designed to favor foreigners, only comprehended those who were willing to submit their cases to his cognizance. Your petitioner refusd to appear before the consul & chose to continue his cause in the court of Dinwiddie county. Your petitioner humbly shews that in his absence the consul proceeded to render judgement against him. With this judgement your petitioner has much cause to be dissatisfied, as it is for more than the plaintiffs own account shews to have been due & as he is to pay instantly for a lott to which no title has been made him.

Your petitioner humbly states that the act aforementioned leaves it entirely to the discretion of the Honble the executive to aid the consul in executing his decrees or to withhold that aid. Your petitioner therefor humbly hopes that under the circumstances of this case, he having originally disclaimd the jurisdiction of the consul, & sought the protection of the laws of Virginia, your Excellency & the Honble. the members of the council will resume the consideration of this subject & withdraw all aid from the consul of France so far as respects the enforcement of this decree.[8] And your petitioner will ever pray etc.

JOHN CAUVY

8. On Jan. 31, 1789, Martin Oster, consul of France in Norfolk, requested the aid of the governor and Council in executing a judgment he had made in a dispute between Cauvy and Henry Cagneau, Jean Alexis Subercaseaux, and Pierre Barthis, all merchants and French subjects living in Petersburg. The Council of State ordered the Dinwiddie County sheriff to see that Oster's judgment was executed according to the provisions of the 1779 act of Assembly regarding foreign consuls. This led to Cauvy's petition, accompanied by certification that his cause with Cagneau and Subercaseaux was pending before the Dinwiddie County Court, whereupon the Council suspended its Jan. 31 order. On Mar. 2, Oster asked the Council to reconsider its latest action. In the meantime, Cauvy had not only sworn allegiance to the United States but also become a Virginia citizen. Because of this development, the Council of State ruled on Mar. 10 that Cauvy was "no longer subject to the Consular power." *CVSP*, IV, 558, 563, 572, 581; *JVCS*, Jan. 31, Feb. 12, and Mar. 10, 1789. The Dinwiddie County Court certificate is dated Feb. 8, 1789, and is filed with Cauvy's petition in Executive Papers, Virginia State Library.

To Anthony Walton White

ALS, Collection of Louis L. Croland, Paterson, N.J.

Dear Sir[9]   Richmond, March 15, 1789
  I have held up your certificate & warrants till now in hopes of
getting a better price for them. I have sold them to Mr. John Hopkins,[1] the certificate for 4/6 in the pound, the interest warrant issued in 88 at 17/ in the pound & that issued in 89 for 15/ in the
pound. I had hopd to have sold the warrants on better terms but
I coud not. I transmit you a bill for the proceeds. Tis drawn on
ten days sight but Mr. Hopkins has engagd to write to his correspondent requesting him to pay it on sight. As it was impossible
for me to see Mr. Greenhill & settle with him in time I thought it
best to transmit you the whole money.
  I hope to receive something from Hughes or Scott which will be
in time for any expenses on your military land. I am dear with
great esteem, Your obedt. Servt.

                                   J Marshall

£597.16.1 Military certificates at 4/6 in the pound	is	£132.16.11
£ 35.17.3 int. issued in 88 at 17/	is	30. 9. 6
£ 35.17.3 int. issued in 89 at 15/	is	26.17. 9
		£190. 4. 2

From George Washington

Letterbook Copy, Washington Papers, Library of Congress

Sir,   Mount Vernon, March 17, 1789
  I have taken the liberty to enclose a protested bill of Exchange
drawn in 1763 by the Exts. of William Armsted Esqr.[2] in my favor

9. Addressed to White at Sans Souci, N.Y., the letter was postmarked in Richmond
on Mar. 15.
1. Hopkins had been Virginia commissioner of continental loans since 1780. See
William T. Hutchinson and William M. E. Rachal, eds., *The Papers of James Madison*,
III (Chicago, 1963), 325, n. 2.
2. William Armistead (d. *ca.* 1755), the son of Henry and Martha Burwell Armistead, had owned extensive holdings in Prince William, Culpeper, and Caroline counties. Washington had been trying to collect this debt since the 1770s. Washington
Papers, Ser. 5, Accounts Ledger, A, 150, 192, B, 14, Library of Congress (microfilm ed.,
reel 115); John C. Fitzpatrick, ed., *The Writings of George Washington from the Original*

—which I will thank you to take the necessary steps to recover; and as a compensation for your trouble therewith I will allow you ten per Cent upon whatever you may obtain of the debt. The letters etc. whh. accompany the bill will serve to shew that the matter has not been totally neglected by me between the time of its being protested and the present period; Applications have been also made by Colo. Fielding Lewis[3] & Lund Washington on my behalf in my absence during the war—but without effect. If this Debt can be recovered without a suit it will be infinitely the most agreeable to me.[4]

I have been frequently troubled with applications to serve summonses in the dispute (which was supposed to exist) between the Heirs of Michl. Cresap and myself concerning a piece of Land on the Ohio.[5] I cannot see what prevents this matter from being closed, for, I presume the Heirs never had an idea of a claim to that land after the nature of my right to it had been explained to them. The substance of the matter is this—When I was engaged in the public service, Michl. Cresap had a piece of Land surveyed on the Ohio whh. had been *previously* surveyed on Military claims for me. But in 1784, when I was in the western Country, I met with a Mr. Jacobs who married the widow of the said Michael and upon an explanation of the matter he was fully convinced of the priority of my claim and readily gave up his pretentions—since which I have heard nothing of the claim from the Heirs, neither do I believe that they have the least intention of persisting in it. The person concerned in the Land office, upon finding that a warrent had been taken out for a part of the land contained in my survey and a Survey thereof returned me might think it was done by the party with an intention of disputing my claim thereto—and has therefore advised the entering a caveat—when *I believe* there is no intention on the part of any one to contend the validity of my Patent

---

Manuscript Sources, 1745–1799 (Washington, D.C., 1931–1944), XXVIII, 410, XXX, 94, XXXVII, 499, 509; Douglas Southall Freeman, *George Washington, A Biography* (New York, 1951), III, 111. See Margaret Randolph Cate and Wirt Armistead Cate, *The Armistead Family and Collaterals* (Nashville, Tenn., 1971), 48–49, 61–62.

3. Lewis (1725–*ca.* 1782) was a brother-in-law of Washington and had been married earlier to Washington's cousin. In 1761 Lewis was associated with Washington in organizing the Dismal Swamp Company. He also served as a burgess from Spotsylvania County in the 1760s. During the Revolution, Lewis was in charge of a small arms factory in Fredericksburg. See also Washington to JM, Apr. 5, 1789.

4. Washington soon had second thoughts about collecting this debt. See his letter to JM, Apr. 11, 1789.

5. See Washington to JM, Aug. 15, 1788, for a discussion of the dispute.

which has been granted several years. I will thank you Sir, to have the business finally settled. I am etc.

GO WASHINGTON

From George Washington

ALS, University Court of the University of Glasgow, Scotland

Sir,[6]   Mount Vernon, March 27, 1789
I have reasons for wishing that the enclosed letter[7] could be conveyed with safety and expedition; but no opportunity offering from these parts, I take the liberty of committing it to your care on a supposition that the intercourse between Richmond & the Western District[8] will soon furnish one. With very great esteem & regard I am, Dear Sir, Yr. most Obedt. Hble Servt.

GO: WASHINGTON

From George Washington

Letterbook Copy, Washington Papers, Library of Congress

Sir,   Mount Vernon, April 5, 1789
I have duly received your letter of the 26 Ulto. and am sorry to inform you that it is not in my power to furnish the proof which you require of Mr. Armsteads executors having had *regular* notice of the protest.[9] The only person (Colo Fielding Lewis) who could have been adduced to prove that fact, is dead. Upon my going to Congress in 1774 I left that among other debts, with him to collect for me—and there is not the smallest doubt but that he took the necessary and proper steps to recover it[1]—indeed the several payments which were made by the Executors, or their order upon Acct. of the bill sufficiently proves, in my opinion, that proper

6. Addressed to JM in Richmond.
7. Not found, but probably a letter to Col. Thomas Marshall. See Washington to JM, Apr. 11, 1789.
8. Kentucky.
9. JM's letter has not been found. The subject of Armistead's executors is discussed in Washington to JM, Mar. 17, 1789.
1. See John C. Fitzpatrick, ed., *The Writings of George Washington from the Original Manuscript Sources, 1745–1799* (Washington, D.C., 1939), XXX, 94.

notice was given them—but if this should not be sufficient I can recollect no *absolute* proof of the fact at this time. I will thank you Sir, if you will, at your leisure inform me what will be the consequence of the dismission of my caveat against Cresap's heirs.[2] I am etc.

Go: WASHINGTON

From George Washington

Letterbook Copy, Washington Papers, Library of Congress

Sir,   Mount Vernon, April 11, 1789

I have duly received your letter of the 8 Instt.[3] From a bad memory, I can recollect nothing of the circumstances relating to the payment of the money by Colo Pendleton more than what is stated in my books. The Acct. with the Executors of Mr. Armstead was transmitted to you[4] and I find the entry of the Cash paid by Colo Pendleton to stand thus on my *Cash* Acct.—1765 May 10th To Cash of Mr. Edmd. Pendleton on Acct. of Armsteads Exectrs. protest—£100 Virginia Currency—and the payment made by Mr. Montgomerie[5] was on the same acct. I do not know of any act by which I have discharged the Executors and taken Mr Armsteads for my debtor; if any such thing has been done the Executors will certainly be able to shew it.

I have been lately informed that Mrs. Armsteads Sons are dead and have left their families not in very good circumstances. If this is the case and the payment of the debt due to me would distress them I must beg that you will not proceed any further in the matter, for however pressing my want of money is at present I had much rather lose the debt than that the widow and fatherless should suffer by my recovering it. You will please to accept of my thanks for your attention to the letter which I wrote to your fa-

2. See Washington to JM, Aug. 15, 1788, for a discussion of the dispute with Cresap's heirs. Washington's caveat against Cresap's claim had been dismissed when the summons was returned not executed, a routine procedure in Virginia law. Tucker, *Blackstone's Commentaries*, III, app. B, 34.

3. Not found.

4. See Washington to JM, Mar. 17, 1789.

5. Probably Thomas Montgomerie (d. 1796), of Fairfax County.

ther.[6] And believe me to be, with very great esteem, Sir yours etc.

Go: Washington

To John Dandridge

ALS, Marshall Papers, Swem Library, College of William and Mary

Dear Sir[7]   Richmond, April 25, 1789

I must beg pardon for not having answerd sooner yours of the 10th. I receivd it just as I was going to Petersburg & since my return from thence I have been pretty closely engaged.[8] By the common law when a person died intestate his personal estate went to the ordinary who was not compeld to make distribution among the next of kin. By subsequent statutes the admr. is created & the power of the ordinary has been devolvd on him.[9] The act of distribution[1] seems to me to be directory to the administrator & not to vest in the next of kin the property to be distributed. If I am right then when B. D. took possession of K B's personal estate without administration, as he coud only have a right to do so in the character of exr., he will be considerd as exr. in his own wrong so far as creditors are concerned,[2] I had some doubts whether you

6. See Washington to JM, Mar. 27, 1789.

7. Addressed to Dandridge (1758-1799), "Atty at Law, New Kent." JM received a fee from Dandridge in December. See Account Book, Receipts, Dec. 3, 1789.

8. JM attended the district court session begun at Petersburg on Apr. 15. See Account Book, Disbursements, Apr. 8, 1789. Dandridge's Apr. 10 letter has not been found.

9. This was a general discussion of English legal history. In church court practice before 1357, the ordinary was the bishop of the diocese in which an intestate decedent resided at the time of his death. He took possession of the personal property of the deceased and, after payment of debts, distributed it according to ecclesiastical law among charities and the family of the deceased. By 31 Edw. 3, c. 11 (1357), the power to administer the personal estate of a person who died intestate was required to be granted by the ordinary to an administrator appointed among the deceased's next of kin, or from among his creditors. See Henry Swinburne, *A Treatise of Testaments and Last Wills* . . . , 5th ed. (London, 1728), 207; Alison Reppy and Leslie J. Tompkins, *Historical and Statutory Background of the Law of Wills, Descent and Distribution, Probate and Administration* (Chicago, 1928); Thomas E. Atkinson, *Handbook of the Law of Wills and Other Principles of Succession* . . . , 2d ed. (St. Paul, Minn., 1953), 606-608.

1. The Virginia act of distribution concerning personal property was adopted in 1748. 5 Hening 444-448. In 1785 the intestate descent of real property was altered by a statute that abolished primogeniture, but the distribution of personal property was left unaltered by this 1785 statute or by another passed at the same time that revised probate procedure. 12 Hening 138-154.

2. An executor of his own wrong, also known as an executor *de son tort*, was one who took possession of, or intermeddled with, a decedent's property without court appoint-

as exr. of B D finding the property of K B mixd with that of B D & considerd by B D as his own coud distinguish between them so as to [be] chargeable as exr. of K B for any disposition you may have made of it.[3] I am not yet absolutely clear but I think you woud be considered as exr. in your own wrong because if B. D. had been the real exr. of K.B. you must have distinguishd between the property of B D & K. B. & as that property is subject to the debts of K B it woud appear to me that with respect to the creditors of K. B you must be considerd as exr.[4] of K. B. so far as the personal estate of K B has come to your hands.

Any just debts of K B which you may have paid of equal dignity with the present claim may unquestionably be pled against a suit now to be instituted.[5] With respect to those judgements which have been obtain'd against you as exr. of B. D. the law I think is otherwise.[6] If I understand your [case] rightly I shoud advise you to administer on the estate of K B unadministerd & in the character of Admr. of K B to discharge those bonds before this suit is brought;

---

ment as an administrator or as an executor of the decedent's will. While every such possession and use of a decedent's property would not result in the taker being considered an executor *de son tort*, the use, sale, or disposition of the goods to creditors would in most cases be sufficient. The liability of the executor *de son tort* was a creation of ecclesiastical law to protect the creditors of the deceased by providing them recourse against the individual who held the property of the decedent, even though such possession was not lawful in the eyes of the ecclesiastical courts. William Nelson, *Lex Testamentaria* . . . (London, 1724), 558–559; Swinburne, *Treatise of Wills*, 320–325; Reppy and Tompkins, *Historical and Statutory Background of the Law of Wills*, 141–144.

3. John Dandridge, as executor of B.D., had come into possession of goods of K.B. held by B.D. as executor *de son tort*. Had B.D. been a duly appointed executor of K.B., Dandridge would have been entitled to appointment as executor of K.B.'s estate. In such a case he would have been compelled to distinguish between the assets of K.B., the first decedent, and those of B.D., his testator, in the payment of debts. Nelson, *Lex Testamentaria*, 270. Under Virginia law the debts of first priority in settlement were those arising from the incomplete administration of another's estate by a deceased fiduciary. 12 Hening 152 (1785). As JM's statement implied, however, there was some question whether the actions of B.D. had not so commingled K.B.'s assets with his own that Dandridge might not have had adequate notice of the interests of K.B.'s estate.

4. JM probably meant "executor *de son tort*" in this context. Such an executor was liable to the decedent's creditors to the extent of the decedent's goods in his hands. Swinburne, *Treatise of Wills*, 324.

5. The priority in payment of various categories of obligation incurred by the deceased was an established principle of English ecclesiastical law. See Nelson, *Lex Testamentaria*, 209–213; Thomas Wentworth, *The Office and Duties of Executors* . . . (London, 1728), 32, 116–117, 129–155. Although its connection with this letter is unclear, on June 30, 1789, JM received a fee of £5 in a case entitled Dandridges' Executors v. Lyon. See Account Book, Receipts, June 30, 1789, and the report of the High Court of Chancery's opinion in that case, Wythe 123–129 (1791).

6. In other words, the payment of debts from K.B.'s estate and the payment of debts from B.D.'s estate were to be handled separately. Presumably the action to which this letter refers pertained to an action brought by a creditor of K.B.

for the judgement v B. D's exr. does not discharge the claim against K B until actual payment. I think you may lay down this principle —the whole personal estate of K. B. will be liable to his own debts & to those where he was security for B. D. & you must only hope not to make yourself liable by any act of yours. I shall with great pleasure converse or correspond with you further on this subject & am dear Sir with high esteem, your obedt.

J MARSHALL

Law Papers, April 1789

District Court, Fredericksburg

Allen v. Wilson, declaration, record book copy, District Court Records, Office of the Clerk of the Circuit Court, Fredericksburg, Va.

Graham v. Harrison, declaration, record book copy, District Court Records, Office of the Clerk of the Circuit Court, Fredericksburg, Va.[7]

From Thomas Booth

ALS, Term Papers, Office of the Clerk of the Circuit Court, Fredericksburg, Va.[8]

Gloucester, May 25, 1789

The inclosd is the answers of the Revd. Mr [Davis] & myself in the suit of Shermer[9] against us. [Pleas]e take out commissions for the taking of [the] following depositions James City County Mrs. [   ]rus Henley & Mr. Charles Hankins, in Glos'ter Mrs. Mary Tabb Mrs. Ann Jones & Mrs. Mary Booth. You will also examine the notice sent & make any alteration you may think necssary & give the bearer hereof every instruction he may require. If you should make any alteration in the notice please observe the date & let it be the same. Let me heare from you if any thing should be wanting. I am Sir, Yr. Hble Servt.

THOS. BOOTH

7. See Account Book, Receipts, Apr. 7, 1789.
8. The letter is filed with the case papers of Coleman v. Wyatt, to which it has no apparent relation except that JM was an attorney in both cases.
9. Rev. Pryce Davis, of New Kent County, and Booth were filing answers with the High Court of Chancery in Shermer v. Shermer's Executors, which had been initiated

John Marshall's Case

Argument in the General Court

Extract from Casebook, Tucker-Coleman Papers, Swem Library, College of William and Mary

Richmond, June 10, 1789

Adjourned from the district court of Henrico.[1] The Question was, whether the attornies who qualified in the district courts were liable to any & what tax on Admission to practice in those courts.[2]

Mercer[3] doubted. Parker[4] thought 20/. But the majority of the court were of opinion that no tax on admission is due, but merely the practising tax.[5]

---

on Nov. 5, 1787. For a copy of the record, including many of the depositions requested in this letter, see Treasury 79/36, Public Record Office. The decree of the High Court of Chancery is in Wythe 156-162 (1792); the opinion of the Court of Appeals is in 2 Va. (2 Wash.) 266–272 (1794).

1. St. George Tucker, who took these notes, meant the District Court at Richmond, whose jurisdiction included Henrico County. The case was adjourned by that court for a hearing before the entire General Court. The District Court at Fredericksburg had also adjourned the question when JM and others applied for admission on Apr. 30, 1789. District Court Law Orders, A, 1789–1793, 6, Fredericksburg, Virginia State Library.

2. Upon qualification for admission to the superior courts, attorneys were required to pay a £15 admission tax. Once admitted to any superior court in the state, attorneys could be admitted to either of the other superior courts without paying an additional admission tax. 11 Hening 378, 440 (1784). Although it is not so stated in Tucker's notes, it seems clear that the court was referring to attorneys who had already paid an admission tax in another superior court prior to the court reorganization of 1788. The district courts were new, but in effect they were the old General Court decentralized. JM no doubt made this argument before the court.

3. James Mercer.

4. Richard Parker (1732–1813) was a General Court judge from 1788 to 1813. On the basis of the statutes regulating the admission tax, it is impossible to determine how he arrived at the 20s. assessment.

5. The practicing tax was an assessment computed at 10% of the attorneys' fees included, by statute, in taxation of a bill of costs. Each attorney appearing in an action was required to pay this amount to the clerk of the court before his appearance would be entered in the records of the court. See 9 Hening 409 (1777); 11 Hening 285 (1786); 11 Hening 750 (1788). Unlike the writ tax, which was a small clerk's fee payable for issuance of process, the practicing tax was deducted from attorneys' general earnings and could not be reimbursed by the client.

Conway v. Harrison

Argument in the General Court

Extract from Casebook, Tucker-Coleman Papers, Swem Library, College of William and Mary

Richmond, June 16, 1789

Marshall moved to quash an Exo. which was returned executed, on certain property, which had been restored to deft on a bond to have it forthcoming on the day of sale—but the Bond being evidently insufficient This motion was made to quash the Exo. & proceedings & grant a new Exo.[6]

Motion granted.

To John Breckinridge

ALS, Breckinridge Family Papers, Library of Congress

Dear Sir   Richmond, June 22, 1789

I enclose you[7] my list of causes for Charlottesville & P. Edward.

6. An "Exo," or execution, was a writ issued to the sheriff directing him to seize chattels or realty, or to imprison the judgment debtor, to secure payment of the judgment debt. Colonial practice, continued in the Virginia state courts, permitted a party to retain property that had been levied upon by the sheriff in execution of a judgment. The party executed a "forthcoming bond" in favor of the judgment creditor, which was filed in court, and the bond was considered to have the force of a judgment. Upon the judgment debtor's failure to deliver the property covered by the bond at the request of the judgment creditors or the sheriff, the bond might be reduced to judgment upon 10 days' notice of a motion to the judgment debtor. 8 Hening 326, 327 (1769); 12 Hening 751 (1788). In this case the forthcoming bond was insufficient in amount, leaving JM's client without adequate security if the property was not delivered at the sale date. A motion to quash the execution upon which the bond was based and to issue a new execution against the judgment debtor's property was required to obtain a forthcoming bond with a larger penalty for nonperformance.

In a marginal note, St. George Tucker wrote, "On a similar motion in W[illiamsbur]g D[istrict] Oct. 1789, Tazewell overruld it saying Gen. Court had determined Cole vs Johnson, & several other cases otherwise." Cole v. Johnson was decided sometime before Oct. 27, 1786, because it was cited by Tazewell in a similar case, McRae & Muse v. Bennet, on that day. In that case Tazewell decided against following the precedent set in Cole v. Johnson. Obviously, the law in question was far from being finally determined.

For JM's fee in this case, see Account Book, Receipts, June 15, 1789.

7. Addressed to Breckinridge, "Atty. at law, Albemarle." Enclosures not found. See Vol. I, 292, for a discussion of JM's practice in the district courts following the 1788 reorganization. The reorganization act transferred to the district courts cases of origi-

I have markd where fees are due that you may demand & receive them. I have sent such papers as I have concerning the suits. It is probable that I may have been employd in some causes which are omitted. If so I am markd on the docket & will thank you to attend to them. I wish you to send subpoenas to each of my clients & inform them all that no judgement can be entered in their favor unless they appear & pay the judgement tax. This applies to defts. as well as plfs. Wherever you are or wish to be concerned against me in Charlottesville Colo. Monroe or my brother[8] will take the papers & appear for me. I wish to hear from you & to be advisd of every difficulty which occurs. I am dear Sir, yours etc.

J MARSHALL

Wild v. Ambler

Argument in the General Court

Extract from Casebook, Tucker-Coleman Papers, Swem Library, College of William and Mary

Richmond, June 22, 1789

Upon an Appeal from Henrico.[9] Defts moved for a new trial, assigning as a reason for it, that the Jury had taken away with them a paper which the court had over-ruled as improper evidence, as the witnesses subscribing it were in court: which motion was over ruled.

In the Bill of Exceptions which was tendered to the opinion of the court, it is set forth, that it appeared to the court that there was *no variance* between the Certificate, & the Testimony of the witnesses thereto, as given to the Jury.

Taylor, for plt. in Error, cited Gilbert's Law of Evidence—18, 20; Co. Litt: 227, b; Buller 308.[1]

---

nal jurisdiction then pending before the General Court. 12 Hening 759 (1788). A later act transferred all General Court cases, and JM sent additional business to Breckinridge at that time, having decided not to practice in the western districts. 13 Hening 11 (1789); JM to Breckinridge, Mar. 28, 1790.

8. James Monroe and James Markham Marshall.

9. Henrico County Court.

1. John Taylor's argument for a new trial stressed the irregularity of the jury's having had written evidence in its possession that had not been admitted as evidence in open court. The assertion that a copy of a document given by an officer of the court

Marshall contra—cited a strong Case from Buller 308.[2]

Judgt. affirmed, dissentiente Mercer totis viribus.[3]

Tucker,[4] thought, that the Court having certified in the Bill of Exceptions tendered to them, that there was *no Variance*, that it was good cause to refuse a new trial, since it was no fault of the plt, but perhaps an accidental impropriety of Conduct in the Juror who took the paper.

---

should not be accepted as evidence without a showing that it had actually been examined by the jury, presumably after admission in evidence, is the most pertinent passage in Sir Geoffrey Gilbert, *The Law of Evidence* (Dublin, 1754), 18. Taylor's citation to Sir Edward Coke was more to the point, for that authority asserted that if the jury carried away a writing "which was given in evidence in open court," that action would not void their verdict. Coke, *The first part of the Institutes of the laws of England; or, A commentary upon Littleton*, 16th ed. (London, 1809), II, 227b. An earlier passage indicated that if the plaintiff delivered a paper to the jury that had not been given in evidence, that would be sufficient cause to set aside a verdict for the plaintiff, but not for the defendant. The facts as stated in the notes on appeal do not reflect how the jury in Wild v. Ambler obtained the certificate in question; so it is not clear if this additional argument applied to Taylor's case. Taylor also cited Sir Francis Buller's statement that the jury may not examine a writing without a seal unless they have the consent of the parties and that if a jury carry out an unsealed writing without permission of the court or consent of the parties, that would not necessarily void the verdict. Buller, *An Introduction to the Law relative to Trials at Nisi Prius*, Am. ed. (New York, 1806 [orig. publ. London, 1768]), 308. The distinction seems to be between actual delivery of the paper to the jury by the party for whom the verdict is eventually given, that delivery having been made after the jury retires to deliberate, and the removal of the paper from the courtroom by the jury after the document had been delivered to it by one of the parties in open court.

2. In opposition, JM relied upon the similarity between the contents of the paper and the oral testimony before the jury. Buller presents two cases that support this contention. The case of Vicary v. Farthing, Cro. Eliz. 411–412, 78 Eng. Rep. 653–654 (K.B. 1595), upon objection to the jury's consideration of a church book, held that this would not result in a new trial, because the actual examination of the book during deliberation could not induce the jury any further than the showing of the book in open court had already persuaded them. Graves v. Short, Cro. Eliz. 616–617, 78 Eng. Rep. 857–858 (K.B. 1597), involved an escrow deed carried away by the jury without having been presented by either of the parties. In that case the court held that a new trial need not be awarded, because the deed had not been delivered by either of the parties, and that since the deed had not been examined in court, and hence was not a part of the record, its consideration could not be assigned as error. Buller, *Trials at Nisi Prius*, 308. The second reason for denying a new trial in Graves v. Short would probably have been considered overly technical in JM's day. From the emphasis on the words *no variance* in the text of the argument, it is most likely that JM's "strong case" was Vicary v. Farthing.

3. Judge James Mercer dissented vigorously.

4. St. George Tucker, who took these notes on the argument, was elected a judge of the General Court on Jan. 4, 1788. Charles T. Cullen, "St. George Tucker and Law in Virginia, 1772–1804" (Ph.D. diss., University of Virginia, 1971), 103.

Deed

ADS, Collection of the Association for the Preservation of Virginia Antiquities, on deposit at the Virginia Historical Society

Richmond, July 7, 1789

THIS INDENTURE[5] made this seventh day of July in the year of our Lord one thousand seven hundred & eighty nine BETWEEN Philip Turpin and Caroline his wife of the county of Powhatan of the one part & John Marshall of the city of Richmond of the other part WITNESSETH that for and in consideration of the sum of one hundred and fifty pounds to him the said Philip Turpin in hand paid at & before the sealing & delivery of these presents the receipt whereof he doth hereby acknowlege they the said Philip Turpin & Caroline his wife have granted bargained and sold and by these presents do grant bargain & sell unto the said John Marshall one certain half acre lott of land lying in the city of Richmond & known in the plan of the said town by the number seven hundred & eighty six (786)[6] To HAVE & TO HOLD the said lott of land with all its appurtenances unto the said John Marshall his heirs & assigns forever to the only proper use & behoof of him the said John Marshall his heirs & assigns for ever. And the said Philip Turpin & Caroline his wife for themselves & their heirs & each of them do covenant & agree with the said John Marshall his heirs & assigns in m[anner] following that is to say that they the said Philip Turpin & Caroline his wife & their Heirs shall & will from time to time & at all times when thereunto required by the said John Marshall his heirs or assigns make do & execute at the charge of the said John Marshall his heirs or assigns such further & other assurances for the more perfect conveyance of the premisses hereby bargained & sold as by the said John Marshall his heirs or assigns or his or their counsel learnd in the law shall be required. And the said premisses hereby bargained & sold they the said

5. The indenture is in JM's hand and is endorsed in a clerk's hand on the verso "July 1789, acknowledged (Mrs. Turpin being first privily examd.) & to be Recorded. Recorded and Examd." For information on Turpin, see Vol. I, 339, n. 30.

6. This is the lot on which JM's house was built. The deed is recorded in the Richmond City Hustings Deed Book, I, 29, Virginia State Library. JM paid taxes on this lot on July 5, 1789, indicating that possession and the deed had been transferred some time before this deed was recorded. See Account Book, Disbursements, July 5, 1789. JM recorded payment for the property in Jan. 1790. See Account Book, Disbursements, Jan. 14, 1790.

Philip Turpin & Caroline his wife & their heirs executors & administrators shall & will warrant and for ever defend to the said John Marshall his heirs and assigns for ever. IN WITNESS whereof the said Philip Turpin & Caroline his wife have hereunto set their hands & seals the day & year first above written.

PHILIP TURPIN L.S.

CAROLINE TURPIN, L.S.

At a monthly Court continued and held for Henrico County at the Courthouse on Tuesday the 7th. of July 1789. This Indenture was acknowledged by Philip Turpin and Caroline his wife parties thereto (the said Caroline having been first privily examined as the Law directs) and Ordered to be Recorded. Teste

ADAM CRAIG C.C.

To William Branch Giles

Printed extract, Thomas F. Madigan, Inc., Catalog (New York, n.d.), 62

[*July 8, 1789, Richmond.* "I have received yours enclosing the papers in Constable's suit. I shall endeavor to prepare an answer. Your declaration & bonds are filed. . . ."]

To Thomas Walker

ALS, Page-Walker Manuscripts, University of Virginia Library

Dear Sir[7]   Richmond, July 9, 1789

I enclose you a draught of an answer to Symes bill.[8] You will please to make any alterations you may think proper. I have endeavored to draw it according to your statement of facts. If you have a copy of the account you renderd to Syme I wish you woud send it to me. You will examine it accurately—see whether it contains a credit for the other negroes purchasd at the same time with the two mentiond in the bill. Send me a copy of Mr. Meriwethers

7. Addressed to Walker at Albemarle. "Marshall not usefull" is written on the address leaf in an unknown hand.
8. John Syme. See Vol. I, 240 n. 4, 372.

will.[9] Fill up the blanks in the bill. Depositions cannot be taken till after the answer is fild. I must have the answer in the course of this month. I am dear Sir with high respect, Your obedt. Servt.

J MARSHALL

To William Constable

ALS, Constable-Pierrepont Papers, New York Public Library

Sir[1]   Richmond, July 11, 1789
    I have been engaged by Mr. Harrison[2] as counsel for you in the suit in chancery instituted against yourself & Capt. Sergeant by Hunter Banks & Co.[3] I transmit you a copy of the bill & account,

9. Walker's first wife was Mildred Thornton Meriwether (1721–1778), the widow of Nicholas Meriwether (1699–1739). Her daughter, Mildred, was married to John Syme. Walker had received "Castle Hill" and additional land of the Meriwether estate as dower when he married Mildred in 1741. Some of the Meriwether land passed to other heirs, however. In 1762 Walker bought part of the Meriwether estate from Syme, who had inherited it from his wife. The Meriwether estate is undoubtedly the source of the litigation between Walker and Syme. William Ridgely Griffith, *1631–1899: The Record of Nicholas Meriwether of Wales and Descendants in Virginia and Maryland* (St. Louis, 1899), 83–86. See Account Book, Receipts, July 2, and Oct. 19, 1789, and JM to Francis Walker, Sept. 20, 1792, and Feb. 23, 1793.
    1. Constable (1752–1803) was a New York merchant. Partly in an effort to clear his name from a war-profiteering scandal, Constable joined Lafayette's staff in 1781 as an aide-de-camp. After the Revolution he returned to New York City and set up the company of Constable, Rucker & Co., in which Robert and Gouverneur Morris were partners. He divided his time between supplying tobacco as subcontractor to Silas Deane (1737–1789), Robert Morris, and Thomas Willing for shipment to France; carrying goods independently in his own cargo ships in a triangular trade route between the United States, the West Indies, and France; and speculating in securities. For a number of years he was also a director of the Bank of New York. A cautious and thorough merchant, Constable made much money from his various mercantile activities, which from 1787 onward helped finance his growing interest in land speculation. William A. Davis, "William Constable: New York Merchant and Land Speculator, 1772–1803" (Ph.D. diss., Harvard University, 1957).
    2. Benjamin Harrison, Jr., a Richmond merchant.
    3. William Hill Sargeant, of Petersburg. James Hunter (b. 1746) and Henry Banks were Richmond merchants. "Return of the Inhabitants," 1787, Richmond City Common Hall Records, I, 308, Virginia State Library.
    The suit, Hunter, Banks & Co. v. William Hill Sargeant and William Constable, began in the High Court of Chancery and was removed to the U.S. Circuit Court for Virginia, where an 1801 decree removed Sargeant from the case and ordered Constable to pay 33,325 pounds of tobacco with interest from Apr. 1, 1782, and costs. The case arose from a series of commercial transactions that began in 1780. In 1791 Constable filed a petition to remove the case from the High Court of Chancery to the U.S. Circuit Court by virtue of diversity of citizenship. In 1794 Hunter, Banks & Co. obtained the appointment of commissioners to examine and settle all accounts between the two parties. When Master in Chancery William Hay filed a report in favor of Hunter in 1798, Banks took exception, and a restatement of the account was made by

Mr. Sergeants answer, your statement of facts & some exhibits with a part of an answer for yourself.[4] It was impossible to conclude the answer because I have no information concerning several facts stated in the bill. You will please to alter it where you think proper, complete it, swear to it & send it properly authenticated to me so soon as you can with convenience. The original papers wherever they are mentiond must be sent to me. You will please to answer the items of the account fild against you & draw up an account as you think right which you will annex to your answer. I am Sir very respectfully, Your obedt. Servt.

J MARSHALL

Land Grant

Registry Book, Grants, XX, 480–481, Land Office Papers, Virginia State Library

[*July 12, 1789, Richmond.* JM receives grant of 280½ acres in Nelson County (formerly Jefferson County), Ky., based upon a survey conducted on Jan. 4, 1786, on a tract approximately 10 miles east-southeast of Bardstown.]

From William Constable

Letterbook Copy, Constable-Pierrepont Papers, New York Public Library

[New York], July 13, 1789

Counting upon the introduction of my friends Messrs. B: Harrison & Jno Hopkins I address you on the Subject of a Bill in

---

Hay in 1799. In 1800 it was ordered that the restatement be set aside and sent back to the commissioners, but on Nov. 29, 1800, Hay stated that he found no reason to alter it. Constable finally paid Hunter, Banks & Co. a $2,480 settlement in Sept. 1802. U.S. Circuit Court, Va., Order Book, I, 49, 379, 444, III, 2, 417, IV, 74, and Rule Book, I, 43, 44, Va. State Lib. The case papers are in U.S. Circuit Court, Va., Ended Cases (Restored), 1801, Va. State Lib.

See William Constable to JM, July 13, 1789; JM to Constable, July 23, 1789; Constable to JM, Aug. 8, Aug. 12, and Aug. 19, 1789; fee entered in Account Book, Receipts, July 10, 1789; JM's partial answer listed at Law Papers, July 1789; and JM's stipulation in the case listed at Law Papers, May 1792.

4. JM's draft of a partial answer is in the case papers on file at the Va. State Lib. See this document listed at Law Papers, July 1789.

Chancery filed by Mr H: Banks[5]—the Transactns. upon wh. He founds his claim took place 7 Yrs since, of course many particulars of the Business may have Escaped my Memory. It happens however that I had committed a Narrative of the Affair to writing, when the circumstances were fresh in my Mind previous to my going to the W. Indies in 1782. This Statemt. of Facts was intended to have Explaind my Demand agt. Hunter Banks & Co. in case any Accident shoud have happened to me or to have been laid before Arbitrators in the Event of Mr Banks' agreeing to Refer our Accots. to Arbitration. I transmitted this Paper to Captn. Sar. geant[6] some Short time since, who I suppose has left it with Mr Harrison the Several points there insisted on are Supported by Vouchers & I will pledge my honour to the truth of every thing therein sett forth. I have lately recd. a Copy of Mr Banks' Bill & Accots. upon wh. I have made some Remarks wh. I shall transmit with the Several Vouchers Relative to the Business by the first good oppty. When Mr Banks was here in 1786, I urged him to have our Accots. submitted to arbitration & got him to Enter into Bond,[7] to refer them Accordingly—his Bond I now inclose—this I shoud hope might be used to sett aside his present suit. My Objection to having it tried at Law arises from the impossibility of my attending in person to give in my Answer, & the delay & Expence wh. must be incurred by carrying it on at so great a distance, not that I have the smallest Anxiety of the issue of a Cause which is founded in justice supported by your abilities & submitted to the upright decision of a Wyth[8]—but I shoud suppose that the Accots. might be settled by a Couple of Merchants in half an hour.

Mr Hunter's[9] acknowledgemt. of my Accot. & Mr Banks' letter agreeing to Replace the Tobacco putts the matter on the clearest footing. I will not trespass on your time by Entering into the Business, the Several papers will Explain it fully, & you will then be enabled to judge of the best ground upon wh. to take up my claim-

5. Benjamin Harrison, Jr., John Hopkins, and Henry Banks. See JM to Constable, July 11, 1789, for a description of this case.

6. William Hill Sargeant.

7. An arbitration bond was posted as assurance that the parties would honor an arbitrator's award. See JM to Constable, July 23, 1789, and Constable to JM, Aug. 8, 1789.

8. Chancellor George Wythe.

9. James Hunter.

To John Breckinridge

ALS, Breckinridge Family Papers, Library of Congress

Dear Sir[1]   Richmond, July 17, 1789

I have this instant received yours of the 15th.[2] I thank you for your information concerning my fathers family & congratulate you on your safe arrival. I shoud have transmitted you my docketts e'er this had I known certainly that you had returnd. The bearer will deliver them to you. The question you put concerning the sale of a bond is I beleive undecided. I really cannot tell certainly how it woud be determind, but if the sale of the bond is good the purchaser may use the name of the obligee & the court woud not permit the executor to dismiss the suit nor coud the obligor make a payment to him after notice of the sale. It seems however to be subject to objections, especially if it has sold at less than its nominal value, among others the executor might find some difficulty in shewing he had not committed a devastavit.[3] I am dear Sir, yours etc.

J MARSHALL

To William Constable

ALS, Constable-Pierrepont Papers, New York Public Library

Dear Sir   Richmond, July 23, 1789

Yours of the 13th. inst. reachd me yesterday evening.[4] Before its receipt I had transmitted you through Mr. Harrison a copy of Mr. Banks's bill & of Capt. Sergeants answer, also your statement of your case & an answer drawn as far as, from the materials in my possession, I coud draw it.[5] I repeat my request that you will compleat the answer & insert in it a response to the items of the ac-

1. Addressed to Breckinridge in Albemarle County.
2. Not found.
3. A devastavit is an act of mismanagement of an estate by the executor or administrator whereby a loss occurs.
4. See Constable to JM, July 13, 1789. A cancellation mark on the address leaf of this letter indicates it did not leave Richmond until July 27. Constable wrote, "Received Augt. 4."
5. Benjamin Harrison, Jr., Henry Banks, and William Hill Sargeant. See JM to Constable, July 11, 1789, for a description of this case.

count. It will also be proper to mention the arbitration bond as a paper ready to be producd at the hearing. The accounts will after your answer is fild, be refered to Mr. Hay[6] a gentleman of this town unless you have a particular reason for wishing a reference to some other person. I am Sir very respectfully, Your obedt. Servt.

J. MARSHALL

Law Papers, July 1789

High Court of Chancery

Hunter, Banks & Co. v. Sargeant and Constable, partial answer, AD, U.S. Circuit Court, Va., Ended Cases (Restored), 1801, Virginia State Library.[7]

To George Mason

[*ca. August 3, 1789.* JM requests an answer to a bill in chancery he had filed for William Lee, who was being sued by Mason. JM wrote that he might request the injunction be dissolved, because "as the principal Ground of the Injunction was the Trial by Surprise, it was probable the Cause might be remitted for a new Trial. . . ." Mentioned in George Mason to Benjamin Waller, Aug. 12, 1789, Robert A. Rutland, ed., *The Papers of George Mason, 1725–1792* (Chapel Hill, N.C., 1970), III, 1168–1169. Not found.]

From William Constable

Letterbook Copy, Constable-Pierrepont Papers, New York Public Library

Dear Sir   [New York], August 8, 1789
    I am favoured with yours of the 23d July & shall in the course of the Week send you the Answer agreeably to your Directions. I

6. William Hay, a Richmond merchant, often acted as master in chancery and as such was responsible for examining accounts, taking testimony, assessing damages, and performing other quasi-judicial functions leading to the submission of evidence to the chancellor. See William Constable to JM, Aug. 8 and 12, 1789.
    7. See JM to William Constable, July 11, 1789.

mean to lay peculiar Stress on the Arbitration Bond.[8] I can have no possible objection to Mr Wm Hay as an Auditor of the Accots. if He is in no wise interested in Mr Banks' Affairs. This I suppose will easily be known. I should have sent on the Papers 'ere now but they are too bulky to go by Post. When will this cause come to a hearing & what kind of an Authentication will be Requisite for my Answers? I am Sir

From William Constable

Letterbook Copy, Constable-Pierrepont Papers, New York Public Library

[New York], August 12, 1789

I am indebted for your favr. of the 23rd Ulto.[9] I shall send on my Answer to Messrs H Banks & Co. Bill by Mr Slith who setts off next Week. As there is a Charge in the Accot for Cash paid to Capn. Sargeant wh I deny I presume it will be necssary to await his Return to America before any decission on that point can be had.[1] I only wish if possible that Mr Banks coud be compelled to give Security for the fullfilment of the Award or Decree as I have no doubt of Recovering from Him if He is able to pay, Five Hundred Pounds at least. I woud have sued him long since for this Balce. had I supposed He had any ability. Mr Richard will be back in your Country & I will instruct him fully to concede any points wh. may tend to expedite the Settlement of these Accots. Mr Willm Hay is highly Acceptable to me, if He is in no wise interested in H. Banks & Co.'s Affairs. His knowledge of Accounts is considerable. I am Respectfully

8. For a description of the case Hunter, Banks & Co. v. William Hill Sargeant and William Constable, see JM to Constable, July 11, 1789.
9. See JM to Constable, July 23, 1789.
1. For a description of the case Hunter, Banks & Co. v. William Hill Sargeant and William Constable, see JM to William Constable, July 11, 1789.

To Percival Butler

ALS, Pennsylvania Historical and Museum Commission

Dear Sir[2]   Richmond, August 16, 1789

I receivd your letter of the 15th. of June[3] & wish it was in my power to serve you in the business you mention. I do not practise in the district in which your suit must be brought. This is in consequence of a change made in the arrangements by the last assembly.[4] I woud recommend you to a Mr. Wycomb[5] who resides in Williamsburg & is a young man of great cleaverness. I have written to Mr. Buckner requesting him to inform me in what state your business is & also requesting him to write to you on the subject & transmit the letter to me. When I hear from [him] I shall immediately communicate the information to you. I fear tho' that it will not be favorable as Dixon is dead I beleive insolvent. If however Maury has not conveyed the land I shoud suppose him certainly liable to you. I am Sir very respectfully, Your obedt. Serv.

J. MARSHALL

From William Constable

Letterbook Copy, Constable-Pierrepont Papers, New York Public Library

[New York], August 19, 1789

I wrote you the 8th Inst. per Post since wh. I have been deprived of your favours.[6] I now send you by Mr. Slith, a Draft of an Answer to Mr Banks' Bill to be corrected & Returned cloathed in such form as you may deem requisite. The technical Phrasealogy has already been amended by a Young Gentleman of the Law my Neighbour, but I wish it to have your sanction before I swear to

2. Addressed to Butler (1760–1821) in Kentucky.
3. Not found.
4. JM was referring to the reorganization of the General Court. See 12 Hening 730–763 (1788); 13 Hening 11–17 (1789); and Charles T. Cullen, "St. George Tucker and Law in Virginia, 1772–1804" (Ph.D. diss., University of Virginia, 1971), 100–119.
5. John Wickham (1763–1839) was admitted to the bar in 1786 after studying law at the College of William and Mary.
6. See Constable to JM, Aug. 8, 1789.

it & your Direction as to the Necessary Authentication wh. may be required.

I believe Captn Sargeant will be absolutely essential to us to prove an Accot. wh. I find I Recd. from Him being a Memt. of Accot Recd. from H. Banks & Co.—part of it in Sargeant's handwriting—but I make no doubt dictated by them, in wh. He charges the ¼ of the Brign Wilkes at £520 as in the Accot. alluded to in my Answer made out by their Clerk which differs nearly £400 from that charge made by them in the % new rendered.

I expect Mr Richard will be up shortly & that He will have to Return upon Mr Morris'[7] Affairs. I shall instruct Him fully Respectg. all the points so that He may Represent me with the Auditors or Referrees as I know Mr Banks too well to doubt that He will Assert any thing which may promote his cause.

To Corbin Washington

Copy, Mount Vernon Ladies' Association

Sir[8]   Richmond, August 23, 1789

Your Suit with the Hites is for trial in Octr. next.[9] On inspecting the papers I find a chasm in the Title which it is absolutely necessary to supply. I can find no conveyance from Patrick Mathews to Johnston nor any from Johnston to Russel. That from Mathews to Johnston is probably not on record. I presume it is an assignment of Hites bond to him or some verbal purchase which must be proved. The Title to the land depends on the establishment of this fact. Tis therefore indispensibly necessary to take depositions immediately to prove it. The conveyance from Johnston to Russel is I presume of record in the County Court of Frederick, this must also be procured. There appears to be reason to suppose that there

7. This is either Robert Morris or Gouverneur Morris, who were partners with Constable in the New York firm of Constable, Rucker & Co.

8. Washington (1765–ca. 1800), the son of John Augustine and Hannah Washington, was married to Richard Henry Lee's daughter, Hannah, and lived at "Walnut Farm" in Westmoreland County. John W. Wayland, *The Washingtons and Their Homes* (Staunton, Va., 1944), 318.

9. The suit, brought in the High Court of Chancery by Washington's father, concerned 850 acres of land in Berkeley County affected by the decree in Hite v. Fairfax. See Vol. I, 192; List of Fees, printed at 1791; Account Book, Receipts, May 1790; and JM's stipulation in this case, listed at Law Papers, May 1790.

was a conveyance from Johnston to Templeman for I find one from Templeman to Colo. Washington.[1] This should also be searched for. The transfer from Mathews is so very essential that without it the Cause cannot possibly be maintained. This transfer and the existence of the sale from Hite to Mathews must be proved. I am etc.

JOHN MARSHALL

Law Papers, August 1789

District Court, Fredericksburg

James v. Lillard, plea in bar in justification of slander, AD, Term Papers, Office of the Clerk of the Circuit Court, Fredericksburg, Va.[2]

From Abner Vernon

ALS, Executive Communications, Virginia State Library

Sir   Fredericksburg, September 17, 1789
I[3] take the liberty of introducing the Bearer Mr. Joseph Fant[4] to you, & as He may need your kind advise I beg leave to inform you, that I have been well acquainted with him now between fifteen & twenty Years, During which he has, to my knowledge, been counted an Honest, Sober, Industrious Man. He has Acted Nine Years last past as Inspector at Dixons Ware-House in Falmouth, and generally given as great Satisfaction as any, in attention to Business, & his knowledge of the Quality of Tobacco is In-

1. Frederick County records do not contain any conveyances or other instruments of title connected with this tract of land. There are, however, seemingly unrelated transactions between the executors of George Johnston (d. 1766), an Alexandria attorney, and William Templeman in 1768. Deed Book, XII, 329-331, Office of the Clerk of the Frederick County Court, Winchester, Va.

2. See Account Book, Receipts, Oct. 9, 1788.

3. Vernon had worked as a clerk at the Fredericksburg Arms Manufactory during the Revolution. For additional business with JM, see entries in Account Book, Receipts, Sept. 17, and Oct. 6, 1788.

4. Fant (1738–1812) went to Richmond a few days after the Stafford County Court declined on Sept. 14 to nominate him for another term. His petition to the governor and Council of State, Sept. 15, 1789, is in Executive Communications, Virginia State Library. Fant had first been appointed an inspector on Mar. 12, 1783, not in 1780, as Vernon implies in the next sentence. *JVCS*, III, 230.

disputable. At our Last Court Inspectors were Nominated for an other Year, & without his having the least Notice of any being Dissatisfied, a Motion was made to Displace him, by Frivilous Complaints, without hearing etc.

It is done, beyond doubt, through the prejudice of some few Capricious Persons whom He now wishes to contend the matter with, & either have a rehearing, or redress with the Governour & Council as you may think most proper to advise.[5] On this Occasion I beg refering you to a Letter from Mr. Buchanan to the Honble. James Wood Esqr.,[6] & conclude with assuring you that I think Mr. Fants general Character will be found Superior to those who have so Artfully combined to Injure His, on Which, *with my own*, I would willingly risque the matter, & on his having time to apply for Recommendation, have not the Least Doubt of his producing to your approbation from the most respectable Characters of his Acquaintance. I flatter myself with hopes of the Honor of seeing you at the Circuit Court in Fredg. I am with Respect, Sir, Your very hble Servt.

ABNER VERNON

From Charles M. Thruston

ALS, Term Papers, Office of the Clerk of the Circuit Court, Fredericksburg, Va.

Sir[7]   Winchester, September 24, 1789
On My Way from Glocester, at the request of Mr. John Hatley

5. JM advised Fant against pressing his claim, or the Council of State ignored his plea. On Oct. 15, 1789, the inspectors recommended by the county court were approved. JVCS, Oct. 15, 1789.

6. See Andrew Buchanan to James Wood, Sept. 16, 1789, Exec. Communications, Va. State Lib. Wood was chosen president of the Council of State on Dec. 6, 1788. The president acted as lieutenant governor in the governor's absence. JVCS, Dec. 6, 1788. Buchanan represented Stafford County at the 1788 Virginia ratifying convention and in the House of Delegates from 1786 to 1790 and again in 1795.

7. The letter is addressed to JM, "Atty. at Law, from Richmond, expected at Fredericksburg," and is filed with papers from Corbin v. Norton.

Richard Corbin v. John Hatley Norton and George F. Norton, surviving partners of John Norton & Sons, was a debt action that had been in the General Court since 1784. It was continued until the reorganization of the courts in 1788, when it was transferred to the District Court at Fredericksburg. On Oct. 9, 1794, a demurrer to the plaintiff's plea was overruled. District Court Record Book, 1789–1792, 119–120, Law Orders, A, 1789–1793, 538, and Law Orders, B, 1794–1798, 103, Fredericksburg,

Norton, I waited upon Mr. Francis Corbin,[8] on the business of his, & his Father's claim against the house of John Norton & Sons, late Merchts. of London. Mr. Corbin & Myself settled the accot., and by a statement in his hand writing, the balance due to Mr. Corbin is ascertained to be, nine hundred, fifty five pounds, ten shillings and an half penny sterling Money of Great Britain. Mr. Corbin agreed to accept of a judgment for this Sum the ensuing District Court at Fredericksbg from the house of Norton & sons, to be discharged at three annual instalments, the first to commence in one Year from the time of Settlement, Vizt. 29 August 1789.

A Copy of the accot. as settled between Mr. Fras. Corbin & Myself, and above referred to, is inclosed.[9] This he also promised Me to forward to your hands, with a Recital of the agreement, as above. With great Respect, I am, Sir, Yr Most Obed Servant,

C. M. THRUSTON

I do hereby certify that the within Agreement enterd into by Colo. Charles M: Thruston with M Francis Corbin was done agreable to my directions being one of the Surviving Partners of John Norton & Sons & I further agree that the Judgment be enterd up accordingly.

J: H: NORTON

Virginia State Library. See JM's fee in this case in Account Book, Receipts, Aug. 23, 1789.

Charles Mynn Thruston (1738–1812), originally of Gloucester County, was an Episcopal clergyman who gained fame as a soldier during the Revolution and became known as the "Fighting Parson." After the war he settled in Winchester and represented Frederick County in the House of Delegates from 1782 to 1783 and from 1785 to 1788. He moved to Louisiana in 1809.

8. Norton (1749–1799), son of the founder of John Norton & Sons, was originally from Yorktown but had settled in Winchester by this time. Frances Norton Mason, ed., *John Norton & Sons, Merchants of London and Virginia* (Richmond, 1937), 516.

Corbin (1759–1821), of "Buckingham Lodge" in Middlesex County, represented that county in the House of Delegates from 1784 to 1794. His father, Richard (1708–post 1783) had been a prominent citizen of the colony.

9. Not found.

Commission

Copy, RG 59, National Archives[1]

New York, September 26, 1789

GEORGE WASHINGTON President of the United States of America. To all who shall see these Presents—GREETING.

KNOW YE, That reposing special Trust and Confidence in the Integrity, Ability and Learning of JOHN MARSHALL of Virginia Esquire, I have nominated, and by and with the Advice and Consent of the Senate, do appoint him Attorney of the said United States in and for the Virginia District, and do authorize and empower him to execute and fulfil the Duties of that office according to Law; and to have and to hold the same, together with all the Powers, Privileges, Emoluments thereto of Right appertaining, unto him the said John Marshall during the pleasure of the President of the United States for the time being.

[SEAL]

IN TESTIMONY WHEREOF, I have caused these letters to be made Patent and the Seal of the United States to be hereunto affixed. GIVEN under my hand at the City of New York the twenty sixth day of September in the year of our Lord one thousand seven hundred and eighty nine.

GO. WASHINGTON.

From George Washington

Draft, RG 59, National Archives

Sir   [New York], September 30, 1789

I have the pleasure to inform you that you are appointed [Attorney] of the District of [Virginia] and your Commission is en-

1. Entered in a clerk's hand on p. 39 of Appointment Records, Permanent Commissions, 1789–1802.

JM's appointment was announced in the *Virginia Gazette and Weekly Advertiser* (Richmond) on Oct. 8, 1789, but in an Oct. 14, 1789, letter to Washington he refused the office. Washington had been told JM wanted the appointment. See Washington to JM, Nov. 23, 1789.

closed, accompanied with such Laws as have passed relative to the Judicial Department of the United States.

The high importance of the Judicial System in our national Government, made it an indispensable duty to seclect such characters to fill the several offices in it as would discharge their respective trusts with honor to themselves and advantage to their Country. I am, Sir, Your most Obedt. Servt.

(sign'd) G. WASHINGTON

Law Papers, September 1789

District Court, Fredericksburg

Wayles's Executors v. Lomax, declaration, record book copy, District Court Records, Office of the Clerk of the Circuit Court, Fredericksburg, Va.

Weir v. Elliott & Co., declaration, ADS, Term Papers, Office of the Clerk of the Circuit Court, Fredericksburg, Va.[2]

To George Washington

ALS, Free Library of Philadelphia

Sir   Richmond, October 14, 1789

Not having been in Richmond when your Excellencys letter arrived, enclosing me a commission as Attorney for the United States in the Virginia district, I coud not, sooner, acknowlege the receit of it.[3]

I thank you sir very sincerely for the honor which I feel is done me by an appointment flowing from your choice, & I beg leave to declare that it is with real regret I decline accepting an office which has to me been rendered highly valuable by the hand which bestowed it. Coud a due attention to the duties of the office have consisted with my practice in the superior courts of this state I

2. See Account Book, Receipts, June 4, 1789.
3. See Commission, Sept. 26, 1789, and Washington to JM, Sept. 30, 1789. JM had attended the District Court at Petersburg, which opened on Sept. 15, and the District Court at Fredericksburg, after Sept. 29. He resumed entries in his Account Book on Oct. 14, the day this letter was written and presumably the day he returned to Richmond. See Account Book, Disbursements, Sept. and Oct. 1789.

shoud with great satisfaction have endeavord to discharge them, but the session of the foederal & state courts being at the same time in different places an attendance on the one becomes incompatible with the duties of an Attorney in the other.

With every sentiment of respect & real attachment, I remain Sir, Your most obedt. Servt.

JOHN MARSHALL

Oath

DS, Executive Letterbooks, Virginia State Library[4]

Richmond, [October 19, 1789]

I   do solemnly promise and Swear that I will be faithful and true to the Commonwealth of Virginia, that I will well and truely demean myself as a   of the General Assembly, to which I have been elected, in all things appertaining to the duties of the same, according to the best of my skill & Judgment, and without favour affection or partiality. So help me God.

I   do declare myself a Citizen of the Commonwealth of Virginia; I relinquish and renounce the Character of Subject or Citizen of any Prince or other state whatsoever, and abjure all allegiance which may be claimed by such Prince or other State. And I do Swear to be faithful and true to the said Commonwealth of Virginia so long as I continue a Citizen thereof. So help me God.

J MARSHALL

Receipts

ADS, William Cabell Rives Papers, Library of Congress

[*October 19, 1789, Richmond.* JM signs two receipts for Francis Walker:

4. Laws requiring these oaths of delegates are in 9 Hening 120 (1776) and 10 Hening 22 (1779). This is the only extant record indicating a written oath was required. The signatures of every member of the General Assembly are attached, with JM's appearing on p. 7. This document is attached to the Executive Letterbook dated Aug. 22–Nov. 29, 1781, immediately following the index.

JM had been elected on Apr. 27, 1789, to represent Richmond. See Election Certificate, Election Records, Virginia State Library. See also "expenses at the election," entered at Account Book, Disbursements, Apr. 22, 1789.

one for £4 10s. in *Syme v. Walker* in chancery and one for £1 8s. in *Walker v. Thompson's Executors* in the district court.⁵]

Law Papers, October 1789

District Court, Fredericksburg

Mitchell v. Williams's Executors, plea, AD, Term Papers, Office of the Clerk of the Circuit Court, Fredericksburg, Va.⁶

From George Washington

Letterbook Copy, Washington Papers, Library of Congress

Sir,   New York, November 23, 1789
   Upon my return to this place from a tour through the eastern States, I met your letter of the 14th Ulto. giving me information of your declining the appointment of Attorney for the district of Virginia, and assigning the reasons for so doing.⁷

   Your name was mentioned to me for that Office by Colo. Samuel Griffin⁸ as a request of your own, to which my feelings assented with peculiar pleasure, and I am sorry that circumstances are such as render your acceptance of the appointment incompatible with your business.

   As some other person must be appointed to fill the office of Attorney for the district of Virginia it is proper your Commission should be returned to me. I am, Sir, With great esteem, Your Most Obt. Servant

                                      (Signed) GEORGE WASHINGTON

5. JM entered these fees in his Account Book, Receipts, Oct. 19, 1789. Francis Walker (1764–1818), son of Thomas Walker, represented Albemarle County in the House of Delegates from 1788 to 1791 and from 1797 to 1801. He also served as a U.S. congressman from 1793 to 1795. See JM to Thomas Walker, July 9, 1789.
6. See Account Book, Receipts, Oct. 22, 1788.
7. Washington had toured from Oct. 15 to Nov. 13. Douglas Southall Freeman, *George Washington, A Biography* (New York, 1954), VI, 240–245.
8. Griffin (1739–1810), of Williamsburg, had been a member of the House of Delegates in 1787 and 1788. He was at this time a congressman from Virginia.

Birth of Mary Ann Marshall

Entry, Marshall Family Bible, Collection of Mrs. Kenneth R. Higgins, Richmond

[*November 24, 1789 (Richmond)*. A notation in JM's hand indicates that his daughter, Mary Ann Marshall, was born on this day. See Account Book, Disbursements, Nov. 21, 1789.]

Legislative Bill

AD, House of Delegates Papers, Virginia State Library

Richmond, [*ca*. December 1, 1789]

The omission of the plaintiff ⟨in any⟩ on the return of any writ of supersedeas to issue an ⟨alias supersedeas⟩ other shall not in any case ⟨occasion⟩ work a discontinuance but the district court to which the cause may be sent may issue ⟨an alias⟩ other writs of supersedeas in like manner as such ⟨supersedeas⟩ writs might have been issued by the Genl. court on the return ⟨of the first supersedeas⟩ of any preceding writ.[9]

Legislative Bill

AD, House of Delegates Papers, Virginia State Library

Richmond, [*ca*. December 2, 1789]

Be it enacted that the common Hall for the city of Richmond shall have power to lay & collect a reasonable toll on all vessels

9. Only this section of the 24-page manuscript bill is entirely in JM's hand. JM was a member of the subcommittee of the Committee for Courts of Justice, which was assigned the task of writing the bill on Oct. 23, 1789. Edmund Randolph, as chairman, presented the bill on Dec. 1; it finally passed both houses on Dec. 17. *JVHD*, Oct. 1789, 8, 92, 98, 116, 135, 141. See 13 Hening 11–17 (1789) for a complete copy of the bill; the words in angle brackets were not included in the final version. This bill was part of the difficult attempt by the General Assembly to revise the laws of Virginia. See Charles T. Cullen, "Completing the Revisal of the Laws in Post-Revolutionary Virginia," *Virginia Magazine of History and Biography*, LXXXII (1974), 84–99.

This bill also transferred all cases pending in the General Court to the district courts established by the previous General Assembly. The transferal of cases therefore did not take place until after this act was passed in Dec. 1789. In Vol. I, 291–292, the editors implied that it occurred earlier. See 13 Hening 11 for the section dealing with transferal.

lying at the public wharf at Rockets which wharf shall be as free to other vessels as to those lading with tobo. The money so collected shall be applied first to the payment of a moderate sallery to the harbor Master & afterwards ⟨to the payment of so much⟩ in such manner as the assembly shall direct.[1]

Receipt

ADS, M. H. Loewenstern Collection, Panhandle Plains Historical Society, Canyon, Tex.

[*December 24, 1789* (*Richmond*). JM writes a receipt for £47 8s. 8d. paid by Charles Dabney for Wilson Miles Cary.[2]]

Pay Voucher

AD, Virginia State Library

[*ca. December 31, 1789, Richmond.* JM is paid £29 10s. for 59 days' attendance, Oct. 19 through Dec. 19, at the General Assembly.[3]]

1. On Nov. 14, 1789, a petition from the city officials of Petersburg was presented to the House of Delegates and referred to the Committee of Propositions and Grievances. The petition asked legislative authorization to collect a tax for use of a public wharf in Petersburg, and a bill to this effect was presented by the committee on Dec. 2, 1789. After winning approval in both houses of the General Assembly, the bill was signed on Dec. 19. At some point in the debate, JM offered this amendment to grant the same authority to the city of Richmond. His amendment, slightly altered, became part of the bill that passed. 13 Hening 84 (1789); *JVHD*, Oct. 1789, 62, 96, 97, 115, 120, 135, 141.

2. Dabney (1745–1829) served as a colonel in the Revolution and spent much time after the war pressing the claims of soldiers upon the General Assembly. Cary (1734–1817) had attended the 1776 state constitutional convention and served in the House of Delegates at various sessions in the 1780s and 1790s, representing Warwick and Elizabeth City County. He finally settled in Fluvanna County. For earlier business between Cary and JM, see Vol. I, 413.

3. In Auditor's Item 292, Pay Vouchers, Officers of Government, 1788–1789. On the bottom of the voucher is written in another hand, "Entered, Charles Hay C. H D, 31 Decr 1789." In addition to writing this voucher, JM also entered a copy in the attendance book of the House of Delegates. See House of Delegates Attendance Book, Oct. 1789, Virginia State Library.

To Archibald Stuart

ALS, Collection of Justice George M. Cochran, Staunton, Va.

My dear Sir[4]   [Richmond, *ca.* December 1789]

I have just receivd yours by Mr. Patteson & shall with great pleasure attend to the injunction as you have directed. I forgot I beleive in my former letter to tell you that the suit Syme v Johnston was determind in favor of the latter on which there is an appeal[5] which will I trust yield a few guineas more. I do not think Maeze will prosecute his appeal so that Hambleton may commence his liberality as soon as he pleases.[6] Nothing coud come amiss with me now.

I am not surprizd at the news you tell me about Zach.[7] & yet I do not beleive he has one iota of real esteem for the man he so lavishly praises. The instant that character departs from a slavish observance of every dictum of a particular party he will lose their good opinion & they will think themselves licensd to brand him with what appellations they may chuse to bestow on him. I wish you coud be with us next session but if your interest pronounces a loud & firm negative to your coming you will be right to stay. Notwithstanding the illiberal abuse of contracted prejudice I can tell you that the lawyers of the last assembly preservd the little reputation which is still left to the old dominion.[8]

How comes on McClures business. Certificates are now at 8/ in the pound. I wish he woud pay the certificate itself. I am sure my father woud prefer it to 10/ in the pound. A client is just come

4. JM addressed the letter to Stuart, "Atty at law, Stanton," and wrote on the bottom left corner of the address leaf, "Mr. Patterson."

5. The High Court of Chancery had decreed in favor of the Johnstons in John Syme, Jr., v. Thomas and William Johnston on Nov. 2, 1789. JM's appeal was first heard by the Court of Appeals on June 30, 1790, and the decree was affirmed on Dec. 15, 1790. See additional information in Account Book, Receipts, Oct. 1789.

6. See JM's fees in Maeze v. Hambleton entered in Account Book, Receipts, May 21, 1789, and Mar. 1792. He also entered fees in Maeze v. *Hamilton* in Oct. 1793 and May 1795. If JM misspelled the defendant's name, the additional fees would suggest Maeze did prosecute an appeal.

7. Zachariah Johnston (1742–1800) represented Augusta County in the House of Delegates from 1778 to 1791 and Rockbridge County in 1792 and 1797. He supported adoption of the U.S. Constitution at Virginia's ratifying convention in 1788.

8. Stuart, who had not served in the General Assembly since the session of 1787, did not return until 1797.

The General Assembly session of 1789, which adjourned on Dec. 19, was active and controversial. Patrick Henry had left in disgust midway in the session. Edmund Randolph had emerged as the most important member and had led the attempt to ratify

in—pray heaven he may have money. I wish much to see you & am with sincere esteem & affection Your

J MARSHALL

To Albert Gallatin

ALS, Gallatin Papers, New-York Historical Society

Dear Sir[9]   Richmond, January 3, 1790

I have receivd yours of the 23d of Decr.[1] & wish it was in my power to answer satisfactorily your questions concerning our judiciary system but I was myself in the army during that period concerning the transactions of which you enquire & have not since informd myself of the reasons which governd in making those changes which ⟨governd⟩ took place before the establishment of that system which I found on my coming to the bar. Under the colonial establishment the judges of common law were also judges of chancery, at the revolution these powers were placd in different persons.[2] I have not understood that there was any considerable opposition to this division of jurisdiction. Some of the reasons leading to it I presume were that the same person coud not appropriate a sufficiency of time to each court to perform the public business with requisite dispatch—that the principles of adjudication being different in the two courts, it was scarcely to be expected that eminince in each coud be attaind by the same man.

---

a bill of rights for the U.S. Constitution. Opposition in the state senate prevented approval of amendments at that session, however. See Susan Lee Foard, "Virginia Enters the Union: A Legislative Study of the Commonwealth, 1789–1792" (M.A. thesis, College of William and Mary, 1966), 17–56.

9. Gallatin (1761–1849) immigrated to the United States from his native Switzerland and, after serving in the Revolutionary army, settled in 1780 in Boston, where he taught French at Harvard College. In 1785 he moved to Virginia and settled in Fayette County on a tract of land that later became part of Pennsylvania. He served in Congress from 1795 to 1801 and was appointed secretary of the Treasury in 1802, a post he held until 1814. After completing several diplomatic assignments to France and England, Gallatin settled in New York. A year before his death, he recalled that in 1786 JM had offered to accept him as a law clerk without charging a fee. Gallatin to William Maxwell, Feb. 15, 1848, Carl E. Prince and Helene H. Fineman, eds., The Papers of Albert Gallatin, microfilm ed. (Philadelphia, 1969), reel 39.

1. Letter not found.

2. 9 Hening 389–399 (1777).

That there was an apparent absurdity in seeing the same men revise in the characters of Chancellors the judgements they had themselves renderd as common law judges. There are however many who think that the chancery & common law jurisdiction ought to be united in the same persons. They are actually united in our inferior courts & I have never heard it suggested that this union is otherwise in convenient than as it produces delay to the chancery dockett. I never heard it proposd to give the judges of the genl. court chancery jurisdiction. When the district system was introduced in 82 it was designd to give the district judges the powers of chancellors but the act did not then pass,[3] tho the part concerning the court of chancery formed no objection to the bill. When again introducd it assumd a different form, nor has the idea ever been revived.[4]

The first act constituting a high court of chancery annexd a jury for the trial of all important facts in the cause. To this I presume we were led by that strong partiality which the citizens of America have for that mode of trial. It was soon parted with & the facts submitted to the judge with a power to direct an issue wherever the fact was doubtful. In most chancery cases the law & fact are so blended together that if a jury was impaneld of course the whole must be submitted to them or every case must assume the form of a special verdict which woud produce inconvenience & delay.

The delays of the court of chancery have been immense & those delays are inseparable from the court if the practise of England be observd. But that practise is not necessary. Tis greatly abridgd in virginia by an act passd in 1787 & great advantages result from the reform.[5] There have been instances of suits depending for twenty years but under our present regulations a decision woud

3. Proposals for a district court system were presented by the governor in 1782, but it was not until 1784 that a bill creating assize courts passed. This bill never went into effect, however. In 1788, when a district court system was finally adopted, chancery jurisdiction was withheld from the district court judges. 11 Hening 421–429 (1784); 12 Hening 532–558 (1787), 730–763 (1788). See also Charles T. Cullen, "St. George Tucker and Law in Virginia, 1772–1804" (Ph.D. diss., University of Virginia, 1971), 100–117, for a discussion of the court reorganization in the 1780s.

4. In 1792 the General Assembly gave the district court judges some chancery jurisdiction, but the court, sitting as the General Court, declared the act unconstitutional in Kamper v. Hawkins. 13 Hening 427–449 (1792). See Cullen, "St. George Tucker," 120–127, for a discussion of this problem.

5. 12 Hening 464–467 (1787).

be had in that court as soon as any other in which there were an equal number of weighty causes. The parties may almost immediately set about collecting their proofs & so soon as they have collected them they may set the cause on the court dockett for a hearing.

It has never been proposd to blend the principles of common law & chancery so as for each to operate at the same trial in the same cause & I own it woud seem to me to be very difficult to effect such a scheme but at the same time it must be admitted that coud it be effected it woud save considerable sums of money to the litigant parties. I enclose you a copy of the act you request. I most sincerely condole with you on your heavy loss.[6] Time only aided by the efforts of philosophy can restore you to yourself. I am dear Sir with much esteem, Your obedt. Servt.

J MARSHALL

Deed of Trust

Deed Book Copy, Office of the Clerk of the Henrico County Circuit Court, Richmond

[*January 18, 1790, Richmond.* Henry Banks transfers his property in Richmond to JM to be held in trust until Jan. 1, 1791, as security for a bond that was the subject of litigation in *Clark*[7] *v. Banks* in the District Court at Richmond.]

To William Branch Giles

Printed extract, Walter R. Benjamin Autographs, Inc., *The Collector* (New York, February 1942), 58

[*February 3, 1790, Richmond.* After writing about business matters, JM concludes, "I hope you have met with a continued series of kind looks from consenting widows since you left Richmond."]

6. Gallatin's wife, the former Sophie Allegre, had died in 1789.
7. Macajah Clark (1749–1838) lived in Albemarle County. Edgar Woods, *Albemarle County in Virginia* . . . (Charlottesville, Va., 1901), 165–166.

To William Branch Giles

ALS, Emmett Collection, New York Public Library

My dear Sir[8]   Richmond, February 9, 1790
    Wat brought me last evening your letter with several other papers. I have examind the records in our two suits. The Clerk I perceive has improperly enterd the judgement of the court in the suit against Booker.[9] This ought to be corrected—no judgement was renderd. I think, tho' I am not perfectly master of the subject, that this case is in our favor—at any rate we have a good chance for it. I am afraid we shall lose the action of detinue. If the exception respecting the letters of administration will not save us I fear nothing can. I have fild your bills against Call & directed copies.[1] They appear to me to be well drawn but I have only glancd them over. I will give the copies a serious reading. I send you some declarations in ejectment. You will perceive they are returnable to the Genl. court. This you can easily correct.[2] I am dear Sir, Your

J. MARSHALL

To James Mercer

[*February 29, 1790, Richmond.* JM writes about legal matters. Listed in Charles F. Heartman, Auction Catalog (Metuchen, N.J., June 29, 1926), 41. Not found.]

From John Hatley Norton

LS, Term Papers, Office of the Clerk of the Circuit Court, Fredericksburg, Va.[3]

D. Sr.   Winchester, March 25, 1790
    You will be pleased to dismiss the Suits now depending in the

8. Giles was an attorney practicing in Petersburg.
    9. JM had received a fee in Field v. Booker. See Account Book, Receipts, Sept. 18, 1789.
    1. JM had received a fee in Burwell's Executors v. Call in 1789. See Account Book, Receipts, Sept. 18, 1789, and Apr. 1791.
    2. JM mentioned this because of the Dec. 1789 act that transferred such cases to district courts.
    3. The letter is addressed to JM, "Atty at Law, in Richmond, or in Fredericksburg

Fredericksburg District Court—Viz John Norton & Sons against the Exrs of Colo John Baylor, & Jno. Norton & Sons against John Baylor esqr, being, D. Sir, Your most obedt. Sr.

J: H: NORTON

To John Breckinridge

ALS, Breckinridge Family Papers, Library of Congress

Dear Sir[4]   Richmond, March 28, 1790

The last Assembly having transferd the appeals etc. to the district courts I must beg your attention to those I have been employd in which are transmitted to Prince Edward or Charlottesville.[5] There is but little difficulty in them. I send you a list of those in Prince Edward on which I have markd to save you trouble where there is clearly no error, & where there is probably error I have stated what that error is. I have also markd the few fees which are due. I wish the compensation may be more considerable. I am sensible tis not sufficient & feel myself obliged very much by your engaging in this business for me. Shoud you be disinclind to finish this business, which I hope will not be the case, I will thank you to give the paper to Mr. Carrington[6] or to some other gentle-

---

at the District Court to be held in April next," and is filed with the case papers of John Hatley Norton and George F. Norton, surviving partners of John Norton & Sons, v. John Baylor, and same v. John Armistead and John Baylor, executors of John Baylor. JM had filed declarations in both cases in Aug. 1785, and pleas had been filed in 1786 and 1788. The cases were dismissed on Apr. 29, 1790. District Court Law Orders, A, 1789–1793, 40, 53, 75, Fredericksburg, Virginia State Library.

Col. John Baylor (1702–1772) had lived at "New Market" in Caroline County and served in the House of Burgesses from 1740 to 1760. His wife's sister had married John Hatley Norton, Sr. Frances Norton Mason, ed., *John Norton & Sons, Merchants of London and Virginia* (Richmond, 1937), 507.

4. The letter is marked to be delivered by Mr. West.

5. See 13 Hening 11–17 (1789) for the act transferring appeals to the district courts. Breckinridge lived at "The Glebe" in Albemarle County and practiced law in the district courts meeting at Charlottesville and Prince Edward County Courthouse. Lowell H. Harrison, *John Breckinridge, Jeffersonian Republican* (Louisville, Ky., 1969), 24–27.

6. Paul Carrington, Jr. (1764-1816), lived in Charlotte County and had served in the House of Delegates in 1786 and 1787. He was elected to the state senate for each term from 1791 to 1794, at which time he became a judge of the General Court. He died while still on the bench. His father, Paul Carrington, Sr., was also a judge of the General Court from 1778 to 1788 and is often confused with the son. When the court system was reorganized in 1788, Paul Carrington, Sr., was elevated to the new Court of Appeals, where he served until 1807. In Vol. I, 184, the editors incorrectly stated that these two men were not related.

man of my acquaintance & request him to undertake it for me. The bearer is agent for Mr. West in the suit West v King.[7] No declaration was ever fild as the suit was sent out before any rules were held after the return of the writ. The suit is brought for money had & receivd to the plaintiffs use. The case is that West bought of King some patented land with an entry of 300 acres adjoining. A bond of £50 was payable after £11 was actually paid. The entry is totally lost as will be provd by the surveyor. King obtaind a judgement on the bond. This was injoined. On a hearing the decree was that the injunction shoud be dissolvd on the assignment of the entry for 300 acres to West. The entry was not assignd nor does it exist. King found means to get out an execution on which something more than £40 was paid. To recover this money is the suit brought.

I was concernd formerly in three suits of assault & battery v Hobson & al. One in the name of Ransom or Robinson (I forget which) was by mistake dismissed.[8] I advisd the man to bring it again & told him I woud engage a lawyer to appear for me in the suit. For this purpose I send you a half Joe.[9] Mr. Henry[1] is employd by the man himself. If you are for the defendant speak to Mr Carrington or Mr. Venable.[2] There were three suits brought two remain upon the dockett, the third was dismissed. I am dear Sir with much esteem, your obedt. Servt.

J MARSHALL

7. See Vol. I, 398 n. 67, for details of the case Joseph West v. Edmund King, which was transferred to the District Court at Prince Edward County after the reorganization of the courts in 1788, at which time JM turned it over to Breckinridge. See also JM's declaration listed at Law Papers, Oct. 1788.
8. See Vol. I, 376 n. 83.
9. A half Joe equaled approximately four dollars.
1. Patrick Henry.
2. Abraham B. Venable (1758–1811) practiced law in Prince Edward County. From 1791 to 1799 he represented Virginia in Congress and in 1803 was elected to the Senate to fill the vacancy caused by the death of Stevens Thomson Mason (1760–1803). He resigned in 1804 and became president of the first national bank organized in Virginia. He died in the Richmond theater fire of 1811.

To John Breckinridge

ALS, Breckinridge Family Papers, Library of Congress

Dr Sir   [Richmond, *ca.* March 1790]
    I enclose you the papers in Vest v Fore[3] an action of detinue in
Prince Edward district court. It is one of those cases in which my
fee depended on success. If I faild I was to receive nothing, if I
succeeded I was to have a negroe or £50. I consider you as standing precisely in my situation & as being entitled to the same fee. I
think there is a good prospect of success. I am dear Sir, your obe[*dt.*
Servt.][4]

J MARSHALL

To Archibald Stuart

ALS, Stuart Papers, Virginia Historical Society

Dear Sir[5]   [Richmond, *ca.* March 1790]
    You have heard long since or will soon hear all the news of the
assembly & I shall not therefore pester you with more of it than to
tell you that the appeals etc. go to the districts[6] & that I must be-
speak your attention to those I am concernd in. I receivd for you
last summer two bonds—they were given I think by Clendinnen
or I know not who—perhaps Donnelly to Judge Bullett.[7] Have you

3. This case was transferred to the District Court at Prince Edward County after
the reorganization of the courts in 1788, at which time JM turned it over to Breckinridge. See JM to Breckinridge, Apr. 3, 1790, and JM's declaration listed at Law Papers, Oct. 1788.
    4. The document is torn.
    5. Addressed to Stuart in Staunton, this is item no. Mss1St9102f40 in the society's
collections.
    6. 13 Hening 11 (1789). A district court was to meet in Staunton.
    7. George Clendinen (1746–1797), Andrew Donnally (1745–1824), and Cuthbert
Bullitt. Clendinen had served, along with Donnally, as a delegate to the General Assembly from Greenbrier County. Clendinen, a land speculator and agent, was very
interested in migration to and settlement of western Virginia. He had represented
Greenbrier County at the state ratifying convention in 1788. Later he moved to Kanawha County, became a justice of the peace there, and settled on land that became the
county seat and later Charleston. John Edmund Stealey III, "George Clendinen and
the Great Kanawha Valley Frontier: A Case Study of the Frontier Development of
Virginia," *West Virginia Magazine*, XXVII (1966), 278–295. Bullitt had been elected
a district court judge in Dec. 1788. *JVHD*, Oct. 1788, 126.

receivd them? Do let me know as early as possible. I send you some papers. If you are concernd for Gaston ads. Devier please to speak to my friend Nicholas[8] or to some other person for me. Half the fee is due & tis a plain easy cause. I send you a letter from McClain concerning Bains business.[9] It may be necessary to order out executions immediately. Be careful of the letter as I may want it. With affection & esteem, I am your

J MARSHALL

Law Papers, March 1790

District Court, Fredericksburg

Allason v. Walden's Executors, plea, AD, Term Papers, Office of the Clerk of the Circuit Court, Fredericksburg, Va.[1]

Payne v. Walden's Executors, plea, AD, Term Papers, Office of the Clerk of the Circuit Court, Fredericksburg, Va.[2]

To John Breckinridge

ALS, Breckinridge Family Papers, Library of Congress

Dr Sir   [Richmond], April 3, 1790

Mr. Vest has just shewn me a memorandum of yours in his suit against Fore.[3] I have not been sufficiently attentive to this business & really thought I had sent you the papers till I saw them the other day.[4] I immediately sent them to Charlottesville but suppose they are now there. I hope a continuance may be obtaind. Your

J MARSHALL

8. Wilson Cary Nicholas of Albemarle County.
9. McLain v. Bain, Vol. I, 394.
1. See Account Book, Receipts, Oct. 1, 1789.
2. See *ibid*.
3. See declaration listed at Law Papers, Oct. 1788.
4. JM to Breckinridge, *ca*. Mar. 1790.

Lewis v. Dicken

Declaration

ADS, District Court, Fredericksburg, Abatement and Dismissions, 1791–1796, Virginia State Library

[Fredericksburg, *ca.* April 15, 1790]

Culpeper county to wit.[5]

Henry Lewis[6] complains of Benjamin Dicken in custody and so forth for this to wit; that whereas the said Henry Lewis the plaintiff is a married man & further, is a good, true, honest and faithful citizen of Virginia, and as such, from the time of his birth hitherto hath behaved and carried himself and was reputed to be of a good name, condition and conversation, and free from any crime, and particularly from the crime of adultery or fornication. Nevertheless the said Benjamin Dicken the defendant, well knowing the premises, and maliciously contriving to deprive the plaintiff of his good name, credit, and reputation as aforesaid & of his domestic happiness, and to subject him to the penalties of the law, and to bring him into infamy and disgrace, on the   day of April in the year of our Lord 1789 at the parish of   in the county aforesaid, falsely and maliciously related, spoke, published, proclaimed, and with a loud voice pronounced these feigned, scandalous, and approbious words following, of and concerning the plaintiff in the presence and hearing of divers good and honest people of the commonwealth of Virginia, to wit: Henry Lewis (the plf meaning) is a damnd old negroefucking son of a bitch & his wife beat him off a negroe wench with a poking stick (meaning that he was on a negroe wench in the act of adultery when so beat of) and also these words following to wit Henry Lewis (the plf. still meaning) has fuckd a negroe woman, by reason of the speaking and publishing of which said feigned, scandalous, and opprobrious words by the defendant of and concerning the plaintiff as aforesaid, the plaintiff had the great infamy and scandal of the hurtful and wicked crime of adul-

5. This declaration was a form that had been printed for Edmund Randolph. JM completed the form in his hand and signed his name after marking through Randolph's. It is printed here primarily as an example of the law of slander, wherein the slander had to be set out in exact words in the declaration.

6. Lewis (1733–1804) was a resident of Culpeper County. See his letter to JM, Apr. 28, 1790, asking that the suit be dismissed; see also the fee entered in Account Book, Receipts, Oct. 12, 1789.

tery among very many venerable and creditable persons with whom the plaintiff was before in great honour and esteem & his domestic happiness is [*injured*]; and the plaintiff is farther in danger of a prosecution under the laws of the commonwealth, to the damage of the plaintiff   pounds; and therefore he brings suit, and so forth.

Pledges of prosecution. ⎫
JOHN DOE, and   ⎬   J MARSHALL, for the plaintiff.
RICHARD ROE,   ⎭

To Andrew Reid

ALS, Personal Papers, Marshall, Virginia State Library

Sir[7]   [Richmond], April 26, 1790
I have just receivd yours. Your power of Attorney is with me. Your attendance is not necessary. You may rely on my taking the expeditious steps with your cause.[8] I am Sir your obedt.

J MARSHALL

From Henry Lewis

ALS, District Court, Fredericksburg, Abatement and Dismissions, 1791–1796, Virginia State Library

Sir   [Culpeper County], April 28, 1790
You'll please dismiss the Suit betwixt Mr. Benjamin Dicken & my self.[9]

HENRY LEWIS
33[1]

7. Reid (d. 1837) was clerk of the Rockbridge County Court, having been appointed in 1778. His letter to JM has not been found.
8. JM received fees for Reid v. Burnside, possibly the case in question. See Account Book, Receipts, Mar. 10, 1790, and Oct. 1793.
9. See Lewis v. Dicken, Declaration, *ca.* Apr. 15, 1790. The suit was dismissed June 11, 1790. District Court Rule Book, 1789–1803, Office of the Clerk of the Circuit Court, Fredericksburg, Va.
1. Lewis wrote "33," the year of his birth, beneath his signature to distinguish him from others of the same name.

Law Papers, April 1790

District Court, Fredericksburg

Graham v. Elliott, Hoomes et al., declaration, record book copy, District Court Records, Office of the Clerk of the Circuit Court, Fredericksburg, Va.[2]

Malone v. Carter's Administrator, declaration, record book copy, District Court Records, Office of the Clerk of the Circuit Court, Fredericksburg, Va.[3]

Smith v. Stockdale and Young, declaration, record book copy, District Court Records, Office of the Clerk of the Circuit Court, Fredericksburg, Va.[4]

Law Papers, May 1790

District Court, Fredericksburg

Gray v. Ashton, stipulation as to judgment, AD, Term Papers, Office of the Clerk of the Circuit Court, Fredericksburg, Va.[5]

Martin & Co. v. Strachan, declaration, DS, Term Papers, Office of the Clerk of the Circuit Court, Fredericksburg, Va.

Turner v. Scott, replication, AD, Term Papers, Office of the Clerk of the Circuit Court, Fredericksburg, Va.[6]

High Court of Chancery

Washington v. Hite's Representatives, stipulation, AD, Land Papers, Clark-Hite Papers, The Filson Club.[7]

2. See Account Book, Receipts, Feb. 25, 1790.
3. See Account Book, Receipts, Jan. 12, 1789.
4. See Account Book, Receipts, Oct. 1789.
5. See Account Book, Receipts, Oct. 1789.
6. See Account Book, Receipts, May 1791.
7. See JM to Corbin Washington, Aug. 23, 1789, and Account Book, Receipts, May 1790.

To John Conrad Rhuling

[*July 14, 1790, Richmond.* JM writes about a libel against the ship *Pamela* and about other legal matters and encloses a two-page legal opinion. Listed in American Art Association-Anderson Galleries, Inc., Catalog No. 3916 (New York, October 20, 1931), 41. Not found. See Account Book, Receipts, July 22, 1790, for JM's fee.]

To Charles Simms

ALS, Simms Papers, Library of Congress

Dear Sir[8]   [Richmond], August 3, 1790
I have just receivd a letter from the Gentleman who does my business on the eastern shore informing of a judgement against Wilkins & his wish to discharge it in money. I can give no directions on the subject. The bond was put into my hands by you. Will you say whether you will receive money instead of tobo. & at what price? Your

J MARSHALL

To John Breckinridge

ALS, Breckinridge Family Papers, Library of Congress

Dear Sir[9]   Richmond, August 15, 1790
There were some actions of detinue depending I beleive in the Prince Edward district court brought by the exrs. or admrs. of Custis against different persons I forget their names.
These suits were brought by Mr. Randolph but Doctor Stuart[1] who employd him in them has written a letter of enquiry to me on the subject. If you can by resorting to your dockett give me any inteligence concerning them you will very much oblige me. I wrote to you on the receipt of your Mothers answer to the bill fild against her & shall next time move for a dissolution of the injunc-

8. Addressed to Col. Charles Simms, Alexandria.
9. The letter was addressed to Breckinridge at Albemarle. "Quae: Stuart Exs. &. What was done with Suits" was written on the address leaf in another hand.
1. Edmund Randolph and David Stuart. Stuart's letter to JM has not been found.

tion against her.[2] I shoud have done so [*before*] this but supposd it woud be agreeable to you that I shoud wait till your affidavit or deposition coud be taken. With much esteem, I am dear Sir, your obedt.

J MARSHALL

To Patrick Henry

ALS, Personal Papers, Marshall, Virginia State Library

Dear Sir[3]   Richmond, August 31, 1790

I have receivd yours by Mr. Francisco[4] & am sorry that I cannot furnish you with the paper you request. I have not a copy of Mr. Randolphs[5] will nor do I know where it is unless it be as indeed I suppose it is with Mr Hay[6] from whom I coud not get a copy in the short time Mr. Franisco stays. I have read it tho with attention & think I recollect it well. There is no general clause subjecting his land to the payment of his debts. The devises to his sons are in the usual forms. Mr. Randolph has several bond creditors who will I presume & some of them have brought suits against the devisees. I know of nothing which can possibly bar their success. The law of the land has ever since the year 1748 subjected

2. JM received a fee in Vaughan v. Breckinridge, possibly the case referred to here. See Account Book, Receipts, Dec. 2, 1790.

3. Addressed to Henry in Prince Edward County.

4. Peter Francisco (*ca.* 1760–1831), an orphan, had been cared for by Patrick Henry's uncle, Anthony Winston, and lived in Buckingham County. After the Revolution he operated a tavern and a store in the county and was one of Henry's most ardent followers. He moved to Richmond in 1825 and was appointed sergeant at arms of the House of Delegates. Catherine Fauntleroy Albertson and Nannie Francisco Porter, *The Romantic Record of Peter Francisco, A Revolutionary Soldier* (Staunton, Va., 1929), 42; Robert Douthat Meade, *Patrick Henry, Practical Revolutionary* (New York, 1969), 5. Henry's letter to JM has not been found.

5. This is either John Randolph (1742–1775), of "Bizarre" and "Matoax," whose will is dated July 25, 1774, and is recorded in Will Book, II, 328–333, Chesterfield County Court; or it is Richard Randolph II (*ca.* 1725–1786), the brother of John Randolph, whose will is dated Mar. 21, 1786, and is recorded in Deeds, 1781–1787, 301–308, Henrico County Court.

John Randolph owed a large amount of money, some of it to creditors in Charlotte County, where Patrick Henry practiced law. Richard Randolph was also heavily indebted to both English merchants and Virginians. He had owned land in Cumberland, Prince Edward, and Charlotte counties.

6. This is probably William Hay, a Richmond merchant who sometimes acted as master in chancery.

lands in the hands of a devisee as well as heir to bond creditors in which the heir is expressly bound.[7] There are some suits (I know of one) brought by British creditors in the foederal court under the idea that the act of parliament subjecting lands to the payment of debts which we considerd as obligatory before the revolution will still operate where the debt was contracted under the authority of that act. This is a doubtful question. Some of the ablest men & soundest lawyers in America (I can instance Mr. Jefferson) think that act will still subject lands to the payment of those debts which were contracted while the force of the law was acknowledgd by us. But for such authority I shoud myself have inclind to the contrary opinion.

The court of chancery have made no positive or final decree in the business of Randolphs exrs. & creditors.[8] There is [entered] an interlocutory order directing such a report to be made as will enable the court to form a decree. I have directed the clerk to make a copy of that order which I will send you. With very much respect & esteem, I am Sir your obedt. Servt.

J MARSHALL

From William DuVal

ALS, Term Papers, Office of the Clerk of the Circuit Court, Fredericksburg, Va.

September 18, 1790

I request you'll be pleased to dismiss the suits of John Norton & Sons agt. Mr. Robert Hart surviving Partner of Hart & Marshall; and also the suit of Norton & Sons agt him as surviving Partner of Robert Hart & Co which are now depending in the Fredericksburg District Court Mr Hart having settled the same with me agreeable to Mr. J H. Nortons instructions to, Yr obt. Servt.[9]

WM. DUVAL

7. 5 Hening 560–564 (1748).

8. See Account Book for entries under Randolph. For a possible connection, see JM to St. George Tucker, *ca.* Dec. 1794.

9. Declarations had originally been filed in 1786 in John Hatley Norton and George F. Norton, surviving partners of John Norton & Sons, v. Robert Hart, same v. Robert Hart & Co., and same v. Robert Hart, surviving partner of Hart & Marshall. The cases were dismissed on Oct. 5, 1790. District Court Law Orders, A, 1789–1793, 50, 155, Fredericksburg, Virginia State Library.

The letter, filed with the case papers, is endorsed "Maj. DuVal to John Marshall Esqr respecting Mess Nortons Suits agt Robt Hart." DuVal was an attorney.

Map Subscription

Printed, *Virginia Gazette, and General Advertiser* (Richmond), September 29, 1790, 3

[Richmond, *ca.* September 29, 1790]

BEING requested by Mr. Tatham,[1] to view the Map of the Southern Division of the United States which he has begun, we attended at the Mason's-Hall, and after examining the progress he has made, and being fully informed of the materials he has collected, and the assistance he will derive from both public and private sources, are of opinion——That Mr. Tatham is fully adequate to the work he has undertaken; that he has made considerable progress in the Map, in a very neat and correct manner; and that when finished, we believe it will be the most useful and valuable Map, yet published of the Southern parts of the United States; and in such opinion have each subscribed for a copy.

BEVERLEY RANDOLPH,

JAMES WOOD,

JAMES M'CLURG,

JOHN TYLER,

WILLIAM NELSON, Jun.

WILLIAM HAY,

JOHN HARVIE,

J. MARSHALL,

ALEXANDER MONTGOMERY.

1. William Tatham (1752–1819) came to Virginia in 1769 from his native England. After the Revolution he served briefly as clerk of the Council of State, was admitted to the bar in 1784, moved to North Carolina in 1786, and served in that state's legislature in 1787. After a visit to England he returned to Virginia and organized a state geographical department. On Sept. 30, 1790, in Richmond, Tatham published a broadside, *Proposals for publishing a large and comprehensive Map of the southern division of the United States of America*. In Nov. 1790 he wrote to the House of Delegates in hopes of securing funds to aid him in preparing the map. In 1791 the General Assembly authorized a lottery to enable Tatham to complete his work. Although he published *A Topographical analysis of the Commonwealth of Virginia: compiled for the years 1790–1* (Richmond, 1791), he never completed his map of the South. He traveled extensively from 1792 until his death in 1819, when he walked in front of a cannon as it was fired in celebration of George Washington's birthday. *JVHD*, Oct. 1790, 29, 48–49, 120, 148; 13 Hening 318 (1791); *Virginia Gazette, and General Advertiser* (Richmond), Dec. 28, 1791.

Law Papers, September 1790

High Court of Chancery

Walker v. Cabell, bill in chancery, copy, Page-Walker Manuscripts, University of Virginia Library.[2]

From Samuel Redd

ALS, Term Papers, Office of the Clerk of the Circuit Court, Fredericksburg, Va.

Sir   October 2, 1790
    You are requested to dismist my sute Agst. Colo. Burnley an Oblige.[3]

                                                            SAML REDD
Test
HARDEN DUKE

Petition

AD, Legislative Petitions: Henrico County, Virginia State Library[4]

[Richmond], October 25, 1790
    To the Honble. the speaker & Members of the house of delegates the petition of Benjamin Lewis Alexander McRoberts & John McKean[5] exrs. of the last will of William Coutts & admrs. with the

    2. See Account Book, Receipts, May and Aug. 3, 1790, and JM to Francis Walker, Feb. 23, 1793.
    3. The letter is addressed "John Marshill, Attorney Law." The suit, Samuel Redd v. Zachariah Burnley, was dismissed on this date. District Court Law Orders, A, 1789–1793, 86, 143, Fredericksburg, Virginia State Library.
    4. The entire petition is in JM's hand. A clerk wrote on the verso, "Lewis & al exors of Coutts Peto., 25th. Octr. 1790, Refd. To Courts of Justice, as to Patrick Coutts, Reasonable, [as to] Wm. [Coutts], Rejected."
    JM had been elected to the House of Delegates by the voters of Richmond on Apr. 26, 1790. When the session convened on Oct. 18, JM was appointed to the Committee for Courts of Justice. The petition was introduced and referred to this committee on Oct. 25. Election Certificate, Apr. 26, 1790, and Qualification Certificate, Oct. 18, 1790, Election Records, Virginia State Library; *JVHD,* Oct. 1790, 14.
    5. McKean (1742–1791) was a Richmond merchant who had served as a commissary for the Continental Line during the Revolution. He, Lewis, and McRoberts

will annexd of Patrick Coutts decd. humbly sheweth That Patrick
Coutts made his last will & testament whereby he devisd after
some small bequests his whole estate for the payment of his debts
& after the payment of them to his Brother William who took administration on his estate with the will annexed. Some time in
Jany. 1787 William Coutts departed this life & by his last will subjected the whole estate to the payment first of the debts of Patrick
Coutts & secondly of his own. The debts of the said Patrick are
very considerable—sufficient to swallow up his whole estate. Your
petitioners shew that they were about to sell the said estate when
it was discoverd that almost the whole of the property was purchasd after the date of the will of Patrick Coutts & therefore coud
not pass by that will but descended to his heir at law[6] in the Kingdom of Great Britain whose name is John Coutts. Your petitioners
shew that the said John as a British subject is incapable of holding
lands in this Commonwealth & that upon every principle of Justice the said land ought to be subjected to the payment of the
debts which debts were contracted for the purchase of the lands
themselves, & which the purchaser designd to subject to those
debts but his designs are frustrated by supposing that the lands
woud pass by his will at whatever time they might be purchased.
Upon the credit of these lands too many citizens have become security for the said William for the debts of Patrick to a very great
amount & will be ruind if this estate be not subjected to the payment of these debts. Your petitioners therefore humbly pray that
the said estate may be vested in trustees & sold for the payment of
the debts of the said Patrick & William or that such other thing
may be done in the premises as to your Honble. house may seem
proper and your Petitioners will ever pray.[7]

BENJA: LEWIS
ALEXR. MC:ROBERT
JOHN MCKEND

---

probated William Coutts's will in 1787 and were appointed administrators of Patrick
Coutts's estate in 1788. See Henrico County Court Order Book, II, 608, 664, III, 61,
164, 172, 408, 509, 569, IV, 584, Va. State Lib.

6. In the absence of a republication of a will after the acquisition of real property,
the devises in the will could have no effect. Only realty in the testator's possession at
the time the will was executed and, similarly, in his possession at the date of death,
could pass under the terms of the will. Tucker, *Blackstone's Commentaries*, II, 378.

7. When Patrick Coutts died in 1777, he owned several parcels of land in Henrico
County. This land escheated to the state because his heir was an alien. The petitioners,
having earlier been appointed administrators of Coutts's estate, were arguing that it

Legislative Amendments

AD, House of Delegates Papers, Virginia State Library[8]

Richmond, [*ca.* November 2, 1790]
Provided always that nothing in this act contain shall be construed so as to prohibit any sheriff or collector from selling any land from which taxes may be due to reimburse himself for any ⟨advances of⟩ payments he may have made into the treasury on that account.

That in any case where judgement shall have been rendered against a sheriff or collector for the balance of taxes due from his county he may proceed to sell the lands or part thereof from which taxes may be due for the payment ⟨of the said tax⟩ thereof in like manner as if this act had never passd.[9]

Land Bounty Certificate

ADS, Bounty Warrants, Virginia State Library

[Richmond], November 8, 1790
I do certify that Peter Lee has been in the continental service

---

would be better for the lands to be sold to help satisfy the large debt left by the Coutts brothers than for the proceeds of their sale to go into the public treasury.

On Nov. 29 the Committee for Courts of Justice resolved that the House of Delegates accept the petition as it pertained to the debts of Patrick Coutts but that the debts left by his brother William not be satisfied in this manner. A bill to this effect was introduced on Dec. 2 and, after being approved by the House and amended by the senate, was finally enacted on Dec. 16.

William Coutts had sold part of his brother's estate before he died, and the petitioners had also sold some parcels before the entire estate had escheated to the state. The bill as finally adopted provided that title to these lands should be conveyed to those who had purchased them. 13 Hening 228–230; *JVHD*, Oct. 1790, 14, 99, 106, 109, 128, 132, 138, 139.

8. JM's amendments were written on separate pieces of paper and are filed with drafts of the bill they sought to amend.

9. Neither of these amendments became part of the act that finally passed on Dec. 27, 1790. The act sought to "remedy abuses in the manner of selling lands, for the payment of public taxes." The original act had passed on Jan. 7, 1788, but the House of Delegates had begun attempts to amend it as early as Oct. 1789. After failing to enact an amended law at that session, the 1790 session began consideration on Nov. 2. *JVHD*, Oct. 1789, 10, 42, 51, 87, 114, Oct. 1790, 32, 33, 63, 115, 116, 119–120, 121, 161; 12 Hening 564–566 (1788); 13 Hening 115–117 (1790).

from this State in the third virginia Regt. & in the state service in the artillery Regt. more than three years.[1]

J MARSHALL
late Capt. 11th V.R.

To James Madison

ALS, Madison Papers, Library of Congress

Dear Sir   Richmond, November 29, 1790

My friend Mr. Giles[2] will present you this. He is particularly desirous of being known to you. I shoud not presume so far on the degree of your acquaintance with which I have been honord as to introduce any Gentleman to your attention if I did not persuade myself that you will never regret or change any favorable opinion you may form of him. With much respect & esteem, I am dear Sir, Your obedt.

J MARSHALL

Legislative Bill

AD, House of Delegates Papers, Virginia State Library

Richmond, [ca. December 2, 1790]

Be it enacted by the General Assembly that so much of the act entitled "an act for amending the several acts of the General assembly concerning the high court of chancery as directs the said court to sit ⟨on the four times in every year⟩ on the first or when that shall happen to be sunday, on the second day of August in each year shall be & the same is hereby repeald.

And be it further enacted that ⟨so much⟩ the sessions of the said court directed to be holden on the first or when that shall happen

---

1. Lee (ca. 1759–1823). Certificates were required in order to receive a military land grant. See 9 Hening 179 (1776); 10 Hening 373, 375 (1780); and 11 Hening 559–565 (1784).

2. William Branch Giles had recently been elected to Congress and was en route to Philadelphia, where Congress had convened in November. Giles probably stayed in the same boardinghouse where Madison and other Virginia delegates lived. Irving Brant, *The Fourth President: A Life of James Madison* (New York, 1970), 248–249.

to be sunday on the 2d. day of march in every year shall henceforth continue for eighteen juridical days successively unless the business therein depending shall be sooner dispatchd.[3]

Bracken v. College of William and Mary

EDITORIAL NOTE

John Marshall's appearance as attorney for the board of visitors of the College of William and Mary has directed more attention to *Bracken v. College of William and Mary* in later years than was accorded to it at the time of its argument and decision. A recent commentator, Florian Bartosic, has noted that Marshall's argument in this case and the U.S. Supreme Court opinion he delivered in *Dartmouth College v. Woodward* are similar in their discussion of the private eleemosynary character of the two colleges. "The Chief Justice's reasoning in 1819," Bartosic asserted, "was in certain respects grounded upon premises only one step removed from the reasoning of Marshall, the lawyer, in 1790."[4] Yet the importance of the Bracken case transcends Marshall's involvement with it; as a significant case in the fields of higher education and corporate law, it was a major legal development in this period.

Although the legal issues raised by *Bracken v. College of William and Mary* are quite complex, the facts of the case are relatively simple. The Reverend John Bracken (1745–1818), already installed as rector of Williamsburg's Bruton Parish Church, was appointed master of the grammar school of the College of William and Mary sometime between 1775 and 1777.[5] The grammar school prepared students for admission to the college through training in Latin and Greek grammar and scrupulous attention to their religious discipline. As master of the grammar school, Bracken also held the professorship of humanities at the college, but in the confusion of the first years of the American Revolution, he and the two other remaining professors, James Madison and Robert Andrews, "shared all of the chairs

3. The entire document is in JM's hand. The bill was read first on Dec. 2 and then a second time on Dec. 3. On the third reading, which was on Dec. 4, it passed and was entitled "An act, concerning the sessions of the High Court of Chancery." The final bill, as printed in 13 Hening 121, contained an additional paragraph specifying when chancery bills could be considered confessed. This had been added by the senate and accepted by the House on Dec. 21. *JVHD*, Oct. 1790, 108, 109, 113, 149, 167.

4. Florian Bartosic, "With John Marshall from William and Mary to Dartmouth College," *William and Mary Law Review*, VII (1966), 259–266 (quotation on p. 266).

5. Rutherfoord Goodwin, "The Reverend John Bracken (1745–1818), Rector of Bruton Parish and President of the College of William and Mary in Virginia," *Historical Magazine of the Protestant Episcopal Church*, X (1941), 354–389. Goodwin provides the explanation for conflicting dates of appointment. Bracken's name first appears in faculty minutes on Nov. 1, 1775, but it is possible that he was not formally appointed until the Apr. 1, 1777, meeting of the board of visitors. *Ibid.*, 376. Obituary notice, f. 95, William and Mary College Papers, Swem Library, College of William and Mary; Lyon G. Tyler, *The College of William and Mary in Virginia, Its History and Work. 1693–1907* (Richmond, 1907), 56.

between them."[6] With the exception of the president of the college, the grammar school master had the highest income among the college faculty; in 1758 the emoluments were fixed by college statute at £150 per year in salary plus 20s. from each student.[7]

On December 4, 1779, the board of visitors of the College of William and Mary met in convocation and enacted an extensive revision of the curriculum, creating several new professorships and eliminating the chairs that had existed since shortly after the founding of the college. The board of visitors also abolished the grammar school and concurrently dismissed Bracken as master. For the academic program of the college this marked a shift in emphasis from classical studies to the modern languages, medicine, the natural sciences, and law.[8] One product of this curriculum revision was the establishment of the courses in law under newly appointed professor George Wythe. Thus, John Marshall's first formal training in law was made possible by this change in instruction at the College of William and Mary.[9]

The sweeping 1779 alteration in educational policy was not the result of a precipitate decision by the board of visitors. Rather, it was the product of a longstanding and acrimonious dispute between the visitors and the faculty that had raged intermittently since 1760 and that at times had threatened to undermine the college as an effective educational institution. Although it is not necessary to trace the precise details of that dispute to understand the Bracken case, it is necessary to note that aside from the personality clashes and pedagogical differences between the members of the board of visitors and leaders of the faculty, there was also fundamental disagreement over the division of corporate authority between the visitors and the faculty.[1] With the coming of Independence, the severing of

6. Barbara Wilbur, "The Influence of English and Scottish Universities on the Curriculum of the College of William and Mary" (M.A. thesis, College of William and Mary, 1957), 31; Carra G. Dillard, "The Grammar School of the College of William and Mary, 1693–1888" (M.A. thesis, College of William and Mary, 1951), 66; Tyler, *College of William and Mary*, 58.

7. On the grammar school master's salary, see Tyler, *College of William and Mary*, 62; Goodwin, "John Bracken," *Hist. Mag. P. E. Church*, X (1941), 377; *The Charter, transfer and Statutes of the College of William and Mary in Virginia* (Williamsburg, Va., 1758), 127.

8. The curriculum reorganization is described in [Herbert B. Adams], *The College of William and Mary: A Contribution to the History of Higher Education, with Suggestions for Its National Promotion* (Washington, D.C., 1887), 38–39; and Tyler, *College of William and Mary*, 60. The most thorough discussion of the academic significance of the change and a good discussion of the colonial disputes are in Robert Polk Thomson, "The Reform of the College of William and Mary, 1763–1780," American Philosophical Society, *Proceedings*, CXV (1971), 187–196. See also Richard M. Gummere, *The American Colonial Mind and the Classical Tradition: Essays in Comparative Culture* (Cambridge, Mass., 1963), 55–75, 120–138; and Meyer Reinhold, "Opponents of Classical Learning in America During the Revolutionary Period," Am. Phil. Soc., *Procs.*, CXII (1968), 221–234.

9. Charles T. Cullen, "New Light on John Marshall's Legal Education and Admission to the Bar," *American Journal of Legal History*, XVI (1972), 345–347; JM's legal education is discussed in and a portion of his student law notes are printed in Vol. I, 37–87.

1. Wilbur, "Influence of English and Scottish Universities," 44–45, 59–62; Thomson, "Reform of William and Mary," Am. Phil. Soc., *Procs.*, CXV (1971), 188–190, 192–193, 196. Thomson's observation concerning this point is quite accurate. "No-

ties with the English church and crown left the faculty without recourse to authority higher than the visitors or the Virginia General Assembly.[2] The subsequent ascendancy of the board of visitors resulted in the 1779 curriculum revision, the dismissal of Bracken, and the final attempt by the faculty to contest the board's powers through an appeal to the Virginia courts.

The nonacademic aspect of the colonial dispute, namely deciding who held the policy-making authority in the College of William and Mary, was presented to the Virginia Court of Appeals in *Bracken v. College of William and Mary*. John Marshall's opponent, John Taylor, argued for Bracken that the board of visitors had acted beyond the limits of the Charter of 1693 when they dismissed the incumbents of the established chairs and the master of the grammar school. While Taylor did not use the term, it is clear that his argument depended upon proving the ultra vires nature of the 1779 corporate statutes that revised the curriculum.[3] Bracken's position, based upon strict conformity with the old charter provisions, called for recognition of the faculty's authority over dismissals and championed the classical system of education that had fallen into disfavor with the board of visitors.[4]

The college's 1693 charter was sufficiently ambiguous to encourage various constructions of its terms, thereby adding to the dispute. The charter created a group of trustees, who would hold gifts made to the college and take the steps necessary to establish it as an educational institution. Once the college was in operation, the trustees were to transfer the property of the corporation to the president and masters of the college.[5] The original trustees served a dual function, because each trustee was also a member of the first board of visitors, a body that was to perpetuate itself by electing successors when a vacancy occurred.[6] Commissary James Blair (1655–1743), named in the charter to be president of the College of William and Mary for life, was also a trustee and visitor.[7] Commissary Blair's holding of overlapping offices, coupled with his personal prestige in Virginia ecclesiastical and political affairs, insured mutual cooperation between the trustees and visitors on the one hand and the president and masters on the other. This situation may have produced a tendency to ignore the possibilities for conflict that were inherent in the vague charter provisions concerning the powers of the visitors and the authority of the president and faculty.

According to the 1693 charter provisions, the board of visitors was empowered to make and establish rules, statutes, and orders for the good and wholesome

---

where was the William and Mary charter less clear than in its division of power between the Visitors and the Society [i.e. president and faculty]." *Ibid.*, 190.

2. Rev. John Camm, who had earned the enmity of the board of visitors because of his participation in the Parsons' Cause in 1763, had been reinstated after his dismissal by order of the British Privy Council in 1765. Later that same year his veiled threat to appeal again to the king in council stayed the board of visitors from a second dismissal. Thomson, "Reform of William and Mary," Am. Phil. Soc., *Procs.*, CXV (1971), 190–192.

3. Taylor's argument is in 7 Va. (3 Call) 579–588 (1790).

4. Dillard, "Grammar School," 53, 153.

5. Cls. 2 and 4 of the charter. *Charter*, 15, 17, 19. Transfer of 1729. *Ibid.*, 101.

6. Cls. 1 and 9. *Ibid.*, 9, 29.

7. Cl. 3. *Ibid.*, 17, 19. For biographical details on Blair, see Parke Rouse, *James Blair of Virginia* (Chapel Hill, N.C., 1971).

government of the college and to decide "all Business of great Weight and Consequence especially if the President and Masters cannot agree. . . ." At the same time, the president and masters were to be "maintained and supported" by the board in their exercise of "ordinary Authority" in the College of William and Mary. The visitors were not to "suffer themselves to be troubled, except in matters of great Moment."[8] Unfortunately, the definition of what constituted "Business of great Weight" was not included in the charter, nor was any guidance provided concerning the respective rights and responsibilities of the visitors and faculty for curriculum development.

In 1729 the trustees finally transferred the property of the College of William and Mary to the president and faculty, accomplishing this through an elaborate document known in the college's history as "the transfer." Basically this was a deed in writing transferring the real and personal property of the corporation; it did not confer any additional powers upon the president and masters other than those coincident to the rights of ownership of the physical property conveyed. In one section, however, the transfer referred to the president and faculty as being "subject therein as they are in all their trusts" to the visitation and inspection of the visitors.[9] A college statute enacted before 1758, permitting the faculty to depart from Aristotelian texts in certain fields of learning, indicates that the visitors had already played an important, if not controlling, role in curriculum development during the colonial period. During the last three decades of the colonial history of the college, the visitors had also exercised what they deemed their proper authority to regulate the activities of the president and masters and to dismiss clerics from their professorships for cause deemed sufficiently weighty by a majority of the board of visitors.[1]

John Marshall's argument for the board of visitors stressed the board's prerogative to alter the curriculum even when confronted with direct opposition from the faculty. It also asserted the board's authority over a professor's tenure in office as well as the board's right to dismiss the master of the grammar school and to eliminate that portion of the college's program. In a certain sense it was a plea for the right of the board of visitors to replace the traditional professorships instituted in the seventeenth century with a new academic staff competent to teach subjects that the board emphasized in the new curriculum. Rather than turning to an interpretation of the charter, Marshall supported a principle of flexibility in educational policy that would in most cases not be restricted by the exact terms of the 1693 document. More to the point, Marshall contended on behalf of the board that the right to exercise discretion in policy-making reforms affecting the curriculum was vested in the board of visitors to the exclusion of the college faculty. English corporate law and usage, brought into the argument of the case through the use of English legal terms and concepts in the text of the charter, also tended to support Marshall's contentions for the visitors. In addition, English precedents buttressed Marshall's procedural point that the prerogative

---

8. Cl. 9 of the charter merely established the power to make rules for the good government of the college; statutes passed by the visitors prior to 1758 are the source of the quoted material. *Charter*, 31, 121, 123.

9. *Ibid.*, 93.

1. *Ibid.*, 133; Thomson, "Reform of William and Mary," Am. Phil. Soc., *Procs.*, CXV (1971), 188–190, 196.

writ of mandamus was not available to challenge the acts or compel the actions of a private charitable corporation or the officers of such a corporation. Characteristically, John Marshall's argument ranged widely over the common law and chancery reports of England to obtain support for his client's position. Added to the persuasiveness of his contentions within the courtroom was the weight of public opinion favoring the reform of the college curriculum. For decades the board of visitors had championed Virginians' preferences for utilitarianism in higher education against English clerical preferences for the classical tradition. The Bracken case was therefore not an external assault upon the charter rights of the College of William and Mary; it was rather the legal manifestation of a struggle between the board of visitors and the faculty over internal control of the college and its curriculum.

John Marshall had been associated with the case from the beginning, having been retained by the board of visitors in 1787,[2] but the destruction of the records of the General Court makes difficult any suppositions concerning the case before it reached the Court of Appeals. Daniel Call reported that the matter came before the General Court by an order to show cause served upon the board of visitors, requiring them to appear and assign reasons why a mandamus should not be issued against them and ordering them to restore Bracken to his mastership and professorship of humanities. Arguments were heard on the application in the September 1788 term of the General Court, and the case was adjourned on account of difficulty to the Court of Appeals.[3]

Following the arguments of Marshall and John Taylor, the court, rendering a per curiam opinion, said, "Let it be certified that, *on the merits of the case,* the General Court ought not to award a writ of mandamus to restore the plaintiff to the office of grammar master and professor of humanity in said College."[4] Bracken subsequently began a new action in one of the district courts, this time requesting his arrears in salary. Upon the precedent of the opinion of the Court of Appeals in the first litigation, the trial court entered judgment in favor of the college. Again Bracken appealed to the Court of Appeals, and in the fall term of 1797 the appellate court upheld the college in its dismissal and withholding of salary. In

2. JM had traveled to Williamsburg in July 1786. See Vol. I, 357. A postscript to a letter of Rev. James Madison to St. George Tucker, June 1, 1787, reads, "Mr. Marshall is also engaged in Behalf of the Society." Madison was writing to Tucker, who was practicing law in Richmond at the time, to ask him to assist in the defense. Rutter Collection, Church Historical Society, Austin, Tex.

3. 7 Va. (3 Call) 577 (1790). St. George Tucker may have assisted in preparing the case, although his election to the bench in Jan. 1788 removed him from further participation. There is in his papers a note endorsed "Motion for a rule to shew Cause on the third Saturday in April Term 1788—granted Octo. 27th. 1787." It contains a number of citations later utilized in JM's argument and the statements that "Mandamus does not lie in this Case" and "A writ of Mandamus gives no right." Tucker-Coleman Papers, Swem Library, College of William and Mary.

4. 7 Va. (3 Call) 597 (1790). The original argument in Bracken v. College of William and Mary had been held on July 7 and 8, 1790, and the Court of Appeals reserved judgment. On July 13, the court ordered that the case be continued for reargument at the next term. JM and the opposing counsel argued the matter on Dec. 7, and the court's decision was handed down the following day. Court of Appeals Order Book, II, 22, 29, 43, 46, Virginia State Library. For JM's fee, see Account Book, Receipts, Dec. 2, 1790.

this second case Edmund Randolph argued on behalf of the board of visitors in the Court of Appeals. As far as can be determined, John Marshall did not appear in that case.[5]

Bracken v. College of William and Mary

Argument in the Court of Appeals

Printed, Daniel Call, *Reports of Cases Argued and Adjudged in the Court of Appeals of Virginia*, III (Richmond, 1805), 577–579, 589–597

[Richmond, December 7, 1790]

MARSHALL, for the College. Contended,

1st. That a *mandamus* was not grantable in such a case as this: And,

2dly, If the court could take jurisdiction, still a *mandamus* ought not to be granted, because the visitors or governors had not exceeded the powers given them by the charter.

The court have no jurisdiction of the subject in the form the case now wears, because this is a mere eleemosynary institution, with visitors appointed for its government and direction. 1 *Ld. Raym.* 8;[6] *Comb.* 143;[7] 1 *Black. rep.* 82;[8] *Sir T. Jones* 175;[9] *Hard.* 218;

5. See 5 Va. (1 Call) 161–164 (1797).

6. The minority opinion of Chief Justice Sir John Holt, subsequently upheld in the House of Lords, distinguished between public corporations and private corporations in which visitors had been appointed. Private corporations were entirely subject to the rules, laws, and statutes ordained by the founder, or the visitor appointed by him, Holt contended, and the visitor's authority to deprive or expel scholars "upon just occasions" was not examinable in any court. Philips v. Bury, 1 Ld. Raym. 5–10, 91 Eng. Rep. 900–904 (K.B. 1694); JM's citation was to 1 Ld. Raym. 8, where Holt's opinion appears; the case is also reported in Skin. 477–516, 90 Eng. Rep. 198–230 (K.B. 1689), with a deemphasis of Holt's argument and an extended publication of the argument in the House of Lords.

7. Parkinson's Case, Comb. 143–144, 90 Eng. Rep. 393–394 (K.B. 1689), involved an application for a mandamus to restore a fellow in Lincoln College, Oxford, to his position. The court held that since Lincoln College was a lay corporation, no mandamus would lie, and since a visitor had been appointed, appeal should be made to him, and his decision would not be examinable elsewhere.

8. King v. Bishop of Ely, 1 Bla. W. 71–90, 96 Eng. Rep. 39–49 (K.B. 1756), involved a motion for a prohibition against the bishop of Ely, visitor of St. John's College, Cambridge, where it was held that visitorial power was a *forum domesticum*, which would result in great confusion if the learning, morals, and proprietary qualifications of students were determinable at common law. JM's reference to *ibid.*, 82, indicates that he quoted the opinion in support of the position that the visitor was a summary judge of matters within the corporation and was a judge without appeal from his decisions.

9. King. v. Warden of All Souls College in Oxford, Jones 2, 174–175, 84 Eng. Rep.

Andrews 174;[1] *and* 1 *Bl. Rep.* 24.[2] (Mr. Marshall was here stopped, and the position that a *mandamus* will not lie in the case of a private eleemosynary institution where visitors were appointed, was admitted to be law.)

This is an eleemosynary institution. It comes completely within the description of chief justice Holt in the case of *Philips vs Bury* 1 *Ld. Raym.* 8. It is founded on charity. That the donations proceeded from the King and from the government is perfectly immaterial, as visitors are appointed. Colleges are considered as meer eleemosynary institutions, as entirely as hospitals, *Comb.* 268.[3]

But if the court have jurisdiction, it ought not to issue a *mandamus*, because the visitors have not exceeded the powers given them in the charter.

The charter establishes one President and six masters or professors for divinity, philosophy, languages and other good arts. It is not necessary, under the charter, that a grammar master should form a part of the system. The professor of modern languages satisfies its requisitions. The visitors or governors have power to make such laws for the government of the college, from time to time, *according to their various occasion and circumstances*, as to them should seem most fit and expedient. The restraining clause annexed, serves to shew the extent of the grant. "Provided that the said laws, &c. be no way contrary to our prerogative royal, &c."[4]

1203–1204 (K.B. 1681), involved a mandamus to admit one Ayloffe as a fellow. The warden had returned that visitors had been appointed and mandamus would not lie. The warden's return was upheld as good, since "by the appointment of visitors they are made the sole Judges without Appeal." *Ibid.*, 175.

1. These cases were probably cited to accentuate the difference in law between municipal corporations and private charitable corporations. Dr. Walker's Case, Hardw. 212–219, 95 Eng. Rep. 137–141 (K.B. 1726), involved a mandamus to the vice-master of Trinity College, Cambridge. The court held that if there was a lay foundation, the visitor had sole and entire power to execute justice, and all applications to the Court of King's Bench for a mandamus to admit fellows would be denied. The visitor's authority over the college was a *forum domesticum,* and "in these kinds of eleemosynary bodies, the visitor has the sole power." *Ibid.*, 218. To the contrary was the case of an alderman's request for a mandamus to restore him to office. Kynason and the Corporation of Shrewsbury, And. 174, 95 Eng. Rep. 350 (K.B. 1738).

2. King v. Bishop of Chester, 1 Bla. W. 22–26, 96 Eng. Rep. 12–14 (K.B. 1748), involved a motion for a mandamus to restore a canon removed for "several enormities." While the court upheld visitorial powers, the case is not directly in point with Bracken v. College of William and Mary since it involved an ecclesiastical corporation rather than a private charitable corporation.

3. In another report of Philips v. Bury, Comb. 266–269, 90 Eng. Rep. 469–471 (K.B. 1694), Holt is reported to have said that "there is no difference save only in degree between a college and an hospital, if both incorporated." *Ibid.*, 268.

4. Cl. 9, *The Charter, transfer and Statutes of the College of William and Mary in Virginia* (Williamsburg, Va., 1758), 30, 31 (quotation on p. 31).

Their power of legislation then extended to the modification of the schools in any manner they should deem proper, provided they did not depart from the great outlines marked in the charter; which are divinity, philosophy, and the languages. It was proper that this discretion should be given to the visitors, because a particular branch of science, which, at one period of time would be deemed all important, might at another be thought not worth acquiring. In institutions therefore, which are to be durable, only great leading and general principles ought to be immutable.

If then the visitors have only legislated on a subject upon which they had a right to legislate, it is not for this court to enquire, whether they have legislated wisely, or not, and if the change should even be considered as not being for the better, still it is a change; still the grammar school is lawfully put down; and there can be no *mandamus* to restore a man to an office; which no longer exists. One of the statutes, enacted by the trustees themselves, authorises the visitors to change even those very statutes, one of which creates the grammar school.[5]

MARSHALL in reply.[6] It was shown, in opening the cause, that this court can have no jurisdiction in a case of a private eleemosynary institution where visitors with general powers are appointed. The authorities in support of this position were too numerous to be opposed. But the counsel for Mr. Bracken insists,

1st, That this is a public, not a private institution.

2dly, That the visitors have limited powers.

3dly, That, in putting down the grammar school, they have exceeded those powers.

I shall answer these in their order. And,

5. The statute creating the senate (board of visitors) reads: "As to the Number, Authority, and Power of the College Senate, in chusing the Chancellor, and the President, and Masters, and in appointing and changing of Statutes all of this is sufficiently set forth in the College Charter." *Ibid.*, 119, 121.

6. John Taylor on behalf of Bracken had argued that the college was a corporation created for "purposes of further government," that the visitorial power was defined and limited by the terms of the charter, and that the visitorial act of Dec. 4, 1779, exceeded the powers of the visitors under the charter. He further contended that a master of the grammar school, once nominated to that office, is under the protection of the charter and has an estate for life in his office. He also objected to depriving Bracken of his office without giving notice of a hearing and argued that the college was subject to control by mandamus because it was "a corporation for public government" by virtue of its powers to elect a delegate to the General Assembly and its right to exercise the office of surveyor general of Virginia. 7 Va. (3 Call) 579–588 (1790).

I. This is a private, not a public institution.

In the case of *Philips and Bury* reported by *Lord Raymond*, and *Comberbach*, Lord Holt says, "There are two sorts of corporations agregate, 1st, For public government, 2d, For private charity. That for public government, as Mayor and citizens &c, is subject to the common law; *of such there is neither founder or visitor, nor patron.*"[7] In the case before the court, there is a founder and there are visitors. It bears no resemblance to a corporation of a mayor and citizens, which is the case of a public corporation put by lord Holt. According both to the affirmative and negative parts of the description, this is a private and not a public institution. The persons who compose it have no original property of their own, but it belongs to the corporation. Its funds are meer charitable donations. It is then completely eleemosynary. In many of the cases, colleges and hospitals are classed together as private eleemosynary corporations, subject to the will of the founder. There would seem to be no principle on which this college should be placed in a different class of corporations from all other colleges. I will examine the points of difference made by the counsel for Mr. Bracken. It has been urged that the professors have estates as professors, of which, upon general and correct principles of law, they ought not to be deprived, without a right to resort to this court.

But these estates are the gift of the founder. They are his voluntary gift. To this gift he may annex such conditions as his own will or caprice may dictate. Every individual, to whom it is offered, may accept or reject it; but if he accepts, he accepts it subject to the conditions annexed by the donor. He must take the gift *cum onere.*[8] The condition annexed in private corporations is, that the will of the visitor is decisive; and, as lord Holt says, "if the founder directs no appeal, no appeal lyeth."[9] That the masters have estates, as masters, cannot convert this into a public corporation; for all masters must have salaries as masters; in all charitable institutions something is given, which the professors, if there be any, receive as professors; and if this was the criterion of a public institution, there could be none private in their nature. But that this is not the criterion, I again refer to the cases which have been cited.

7. This sentence is verbatim from Philips v. Bury, Comb. 267, 268. The italicized emphasis was added by JM or by the reporter, Daniel Call.
8. "Cum onere"; that is, subject to the burden or conditions of the gift.
9. From Philips v. Bury, Comb. 268.

But the acts of Assembly giving certain duties to the college are relied on, as giving the government a right, by its courts, to supervise the disposition of those revenues.

The College was founded by William & Mary. Since its foundation, the bounty of Virginia has been added to that of the original founder. It is an established principle, that all annexed foundations follow, and are governed by the rules of the old foundation to which they are annexed,–1 *Black. rep.* 77, 87.[1] The gift of any individual then, to a chartered corporation, is subject to the laws which control the original donation. That this gift was made by the public does not alter the case; because it is decided, that colleges of royal foundation are not different from those of private foundation. Where the king has appointed visitors their power is precisely the same as where a private founder has appointed them. Of consequence, a donation to an old foundation, tho made by the public, is as subject to the fundamental law of the corporation, as the donation of an individual would be. But the charter it is said gives to the corporation a representative in the General Assembly, and the office of surveyor general:[2] Which are subjects of public concern, and would justify the interference of the courts of law.

It is true that these are subjects of public concern; but it does not follow, that they totally change the character of the corporation.

Their power to elect a member was taken from them by the present constitution of Virginia,[3] which was before the abolition of the grammar school.

The office of surveyor general is an emolument given by the founder. Admitting this to be of public concern it cannot affect the case. They have not declined to appoint surveyors. The existence,

1. After the founding of St. John's College, Cambridge, an endowment of two fellowships and two discipleships was granted to the college by Dr. Keton and was subject to special visitation by Keton and Sir Anthony Fitzherbert, or the survivor of them, and thereafter by individuals to be designated in Keton's will. At bar it had been argued that annexed foundations, such as Keton's, should follow the nature of the original foundation of the institution to which they were given and hence be subject to the general visitorial powers created under the original grant. This contention was upheld by the court, which took note of the confusion that would result in the universities if this rule were repudiated. King v. Bishop of Ely, 1 Bla. W. 74, 75, 77, 87–88.

2. The grant of the office of surveyor general is in cl. 16; that of the right to elect a member of the General Assembly is in cl. 18. *Charter*, 57, 59, 61, 63, 65.

3. Art. 6 of the 1776 Virginia Constitution did not include the College of William and Mary among the designated groups authorized to elect a member of the House of Delegates.

or non existence of the grammar school does not affect those appointments. It is unconnected with them. As this mandamus is not applied for to compel the college to proceed to the election of a member to the General Assembly, or to the appointment of a county surveyor, the argument does not touch the case, unless it be intended to prove, that if a case can exist in which a mandamus might be awarded to the college, it may be awarded in any case; that if there be a power annexed to the corporation to do any one act which concerns the public, the whole corporation immediately changes its nature, and, from a private, becomes a public corporation. Unless the argument proves this, it proves nothing. It cannot prove this. There is no reason, in the nature of the thing, why the donation of an individual, subjected by him to particular conditions, shall be subjected to other conditions, because a public office is conferred on the corporation, to whom that donation was made. The interference of the court, so far as concerns the public office, produces no necessity, which I can discern, for their interference in points with which the public have nothing to do.

If the argument which would be drawn from these powers confered on the college be unsupported by reason, it will derive no weight from authority. No decision, no *dictum* asserting the principle, has been adduced. I believe none can be adduced. The contrary is laid down in 1 *Black. rep.* 83, 85, 86.

Then though a mandamus might lie to compel the election of a member of Assembly (had the power to elect one still been retained) or of a county surveyor, yet it will not lie to compel the establishment of a grammar school, or the restoration of its master.

II. The Objection, that the power of the visitors is limited so that they are to be considered as special and not general visitors, is not well founded.

The mere appointment of a visitor, without any description of his power, creates him a general visitor, and gives him the power incident to the office. 1 *Black rep.* 83.[4] There being no set form of words for the appointment of a general visitor let us enquire, whether those used in the college charter are not sufficient. The 9th section contains the appointment. It ordains and appoints Francis Nicolson &c., Gentlemen, and their successors "to be true, sole and undoubted visitors and governors of the said college for

4. The citation is to the statement in the case of King v. Bishop of Ely, 1 Bla. W. 83, that "no precise form of words is necessary to the appointment of a visitor," paraphrased in the following sentence of JM's argument.

ever." It gives them "power to make such rules, laws, statutes orders, & injunctions, for the good & wholesome government of the college, as to them and their successors shall, from time to time, according to their various occasions and circumstances seem most fit and expedient."[5]

Unquestionably then they were general visitors with all the powers incident to that office.

If I have been successful in proving that the college of William and Mary is, so far as concerns the grammar school, like all other colleges, a private corporation, and that its founder has given it general visitors, there is an end of the question concerning the mandamus. This court has clearly no jurisdiction of the case, and from the acts of the visitors there is no appeal.

But if I should be mistaken in this, it will become necessary to enquire,

III. Whether the visitors have or have not exceeded their authority?

I contend that they have not.

Much argument has been used to prove, that the visitors are bound by the college charter.[6]

That is a position I never designed to contravert.

If the acts of the visitors are at all examinable in this court, none can be supported which transcend the limits prescribed for them in the charter which gives them being, and from which their power is drawn. The enquiry is, What are those limits? It is unnecessary to examine the whole statute of 1779. It is only material to defend that part of it which puts down the grammar school. With respect to this, the whole operation of the statute is to commute a school for ancient languages into a school for modern languages. Was this within the power of the visitors?

The charter gives them the power of making such laws for the government of the college as to them shall seem proper. Sect. 9.[7]

But it is contended that this gives them only the power of making laws for the government of the college as constituted, and not, in any manner, to change its organization. I admit that it can give no power to change that which is established by the charter. But the grammar school is not established by the charter. In its first section, power is given to the trustees "to erect, found and

5. *Charter*, 31.
6. Taylor's argument is summarized at n. 6 above.
7. *Charter*, 29, 31.

establish, a certain place of universal study, or perpetual college for divinity, philosophy, languages and other good arts and sciences, consisting of one president, six masters or professors &c. according to the statutes and orders of the said college to be made, appointed and established upon the place by the said Francis Nicholson &c."[8] It is then only made necessary by the charter, that there should be a president and six professors: and, perhaps, that divinity, philosophy and the languages should be taught in the college. This requisition of the charter, if it be one, is as well satisfied by teaching the modern as the ancient languages.

But it is urged, that the trustees, in forming the statutes which shall regulate the president and masters, act as trustees or founders, and not as visitors, because the power is given to them only, and not to their successors. This is true; but I cannot admit the inference which is drawn from it. That inference is, that having once executed their power, by constituting the six professorships, and having made to the college, so constituted, a transfer of the property vested in them, the trust was completely executed, and the professorships, thus constituted, remained immutable.

Whatever might be the force of this argument, if the trustees or founders had merely constituted the professorships without any further declaration on the subject, it seems to me to have lost that force in the case which has actually happened.

The trustees, in the very moment of passing the statute for the organization of the college, declare that the visitors may entirely cut off some salaries, and that they reserve to the visitors the power of making new statutes, or of changing those made by the trustees, as their affairs and circumstances shall, from time to time, require. This declaration precedes the transfer, and the property is taken under the operation of this statute.[9]

The trustees, it is said, could only have designed a change, as to such offices as did not compose one of the six professorships, required by the charter; but the expression of the trustees is general, and is not now to be restrained by this court.

It is said that, having executed the trust, they could not transmit to the visitors the power of altering that, which was established by themselves.

This deserves a serious consideration.

8. *Ibid.*, 7, 9, 11, 13.
9. Cl. 19 of the charter covers this subject; however, JM refers to the recital of the charter clause in the preamble of the Transfer of 1729. *Ibid.*, 19, 73.

The trustees are something more than meer trustees for the conveyance of property to an existing corporation, or to one the crown was about to create. They are empowered to found a college, and are entrusted with property with which to endow the college they shall have founded. They have then the power of founders, subject only to that restriction which the charter imposes on them. As founders, they might authorise the visitors to make any alterations within the limits of the charter. The alteration I contend does not exceed those limits, because languages are still taught in the college.

Let it be true, that a Court of Chancery would have decreed the trustees to have executed their trust by a conveyance of the property to the college, yet a court of equity would not have decreed them to have relinquished any discretion which they possessed as founders, and which was compatible with the charter.

It cannot be admitted to be true, that the masters are independent of the visitors; because they, as well as the visitors, are ordained by the charter. The charter expressly gives to the visitors the power of legislating for, and governing the college. They have, with respect to the professors, the power of appointment and the power of deprivation.

Nor is it to be admitted, that the masters are appointed for life. This is no where declared in the charter or statutes. The first president only is appointed in the charter,[1] and there is no expression which would shew, that the professors are not removable at the will of the visitors. That they vote on their freehold is no proof of it; because an estate which may endure for life, but is subject to be defeated, draws after it, many of the qualities of a life estate. The estate is attached to the office, not to the person; and, as the office may be held for life, the officer, like one who holds an estate during widowhood, has many of the privileges of a tenant for life.[2] But it is contended, that, if they have the power of deprivation, still Mr. Bracken ought to have been summoned, and for this *Bentley's* case is cited, as reported in *Strange*.[3]

1. Cl. 3. *Ibid.,* 17, 19.
2. JM was arguing that there was a determinable life estate, similar to that of a widow during the continuance of her widowhood.
3. "*Bentley's* Case" involved a mandamus requested to restore Richard Bentley to his degrees of Bachelor of Arts, Bachelor of Divinity, and Doctor of Divinity, of which he had been deprived by the action of the University Court of Cambridge because of his verbal denial of the jurisdiction of the court to a beadle who served process upon him in a civil action to recover the sum of £4. The Court of King's Bench held that Bentley was convicted of a contempt without adequate notice of a hearing. King v.

To that corporation there was no visitor. But that is not material as to the point I am now considering. There is however a material difference between the act we are now considering and that of which Doctor Bently complained. He was deprived of his office by a judicial act, the office of Mr. Bracken is put down by a legislative act. He was arraigned for misconduct, and therefore should have had notice that he might have defended his conduct; Mr. Bracken has not been complained of, but the college senate have deemed it for the interest of the college to change his office. If the act was within their power, it could not be necessary to give him notice, that they were about to perform it.

Concerning the case of Mr. Camm I know nothing certain, but am informed that the visitors consented to what was done.[4]

Mr Taylor is incorrect in stating that there were not a sufficient number of members in December 1779, to form a convocation.

I suppose it need not appear, on the proceedings, that every member was summoned, should it even be necessary (which I do not admit) that such should be the fact.

Legislative Bill

AD, House of Delegates Papers, Virginia State Library

Richmond, [ca. December 23, 1790]

Be it enacted by the General assembly that instead of the twentieth day of June & the twentieth day of November the court of appeals shall henceforth be holden on the first day of June & the first day of november in every year or when that shall happen to be sunday on the succeeding day & shall sit each time untill the business depending before them shall be dispatchd.

Whensoever a summons shall issue to the Judge of the High court of chancery or to the Judges of the General court ⟨the same shall⟩ as directed by "an act for amending the acts concerning the court of appeals," passd in the year 1789, the same shall require their attendance on the first day of ⟨June or if that happen on a

---

Chancellor, Masters, and Scholars of the University of Cambridge, 1 Str. 557–567, 93 Eng. Rep. 698–704 (K.B. 1723).

4. Taylor had cited the dismissal of Rev. John Camm as evidence that the visitors could exceed their powers.

sunday, then on the day following, or on the first day of November ⟨⟨&⟩⟩ or if that happen on a sunday then on the day following, whichsoever shall first happen⟩ the following session of the court of appeals.

Each Judge attending in consequence of such summons shall in open court take an oath to ⟨decide⟩ do his duty as a judge of appeals in the case or cases on which he is summond impartially & truely without favor or affection, which oath shall be administerd by the eldest sitting judge & shall then be administerd to him if he shall not before have qualified as a judge of the court of appeals, by ⟨the second judge present⟩ one other of the Judges.[5]

To William Branch Giles

ALS, Bound in Marshall, *Life of Washington*, University of Minnesota Library

Dear Sir[6]   [Richmond, *ca.* 1790]
I receivd yours by Mr. Jones & shall offer the petition to day. If the law is not settled otherwise by former decisions I think it in our favor. I have spoken with McColl. He has no objection to a resignation of all claim on Wrights exr. but says he has none. He cannot consent to try the cause in Chesterfield county because he cannot give Wrights exrs. notice who must defend the suit. We shall stir the subject in the chancery. Your

J MARSHALL

I thank you for the law papers.

5. The entire bill is in JM's hand. On Dec. 20 he was appointed chairman of a committee to prepare this bill "for amending the acts concerning the court of appeals." He presented it on Dec. 23; it was given a second reading on Dec. 24 and was adopted on Dec. 25, at which time JM transmitted it to the senate. *JVHD*, Oct. 1790, 148, 152, 154, 159; and 13 Hening 118 (1790), where the bill is printed as JM wrote it.
6. The letter is addressed "William B. Giles esquire, Atty. at law, Petersburg, Hond by Mr. Jones." Giles practiced law in Petersburg at least until he was elected to Congress. He took his seat on Dec. 7, 1790, having been elected to fill the unexpired term of Theodorick Bland (1742–1790). Although JM entered receipts for fees in several cases that could be the one discussed here, the editors have been unable positively to identify the case or the date of this letter. See entries in Account Book, Receipts, June 1792 and Sept. 1793, for Wright v. Wright's Executors.

Clew & Company v. Donald & Burton

Opinion

DS, Blow Family Papers, Swem Library, College of William and Mary

[Richmond, *ca.* 1790]

Andrew Clew & Co. of Philadelphia brought a foreign Attachment[7] agt. Donald & Burton and some of their debtors in the H. Ct. Chy.:[8] all the partners of Clew & Co. are dead—since which Robert Burton of the House of Donald & Burton has arrived in Virginia where he now is & where he means to continue, til the affairs of the House are wound up.[9]

Does not the suit in Chancery abate by the death of all the partners of Clew & Co.?

If it does abate, can it be ⟨renewed⟩ re[vived] in the name of the Executors of the surviving partner of Clew & Co. as Robert Burton is a resident of Virginia?

Answer the Suit does abate:[1] And I am of Opinion that it can not be revived in the Ct. of Chancery: the remedy of the Execu-

7. Foreign attachment, or garnishment, was a procedure by which a plaintiff might secure the property of a nonresident defendant and subject it to the disposition of the court should the plaintiff be awarded judgment. Normally the foreign attachment issued against tangible personal property that could be sold upon execution; in this instance it appears that the property attached was a credit upon the books of an unnamed Virginia merchant.

The editors have assumed that these actions were concluded prior to the ratification of the Federal Constitution but that this opinion may have been written as late as 1790. JM later assisted Robert Burton in litigation before the U.S. Circuit Court in Richmond. See Account Book, Receipts, Feb. 1, 1791, and Nov. 1793.

8. The 1777 act creating the High Court of Chancery gave it jurisdiction over suits against nonresident defendants who had not appeared but whose property was subject to an attachment. 9 Hening 396–397. For the mode of publication against the absentee defendants and provisions permitting them to appear and reopen the decree within seven years of entry, see *ibid.*, 397–398. This is probably the procedure termed a "chancery attachment" in Patterson v. McLaughlin, 1 Cranch C.C. 352, Fed. Case 10,828 (Cir. Ct. D.C. 1806).

9. In other words, after the commencement of the action and after the death of the last surviving partner of the plaintiff firm, one of the members of the defendant firm became a resident of Virginia and was hence subject to process in the common law courts.

1. In contractual actions, the death of the parties would not cause the action to abate, but it would survive to the executors or administrators of the last surviving partner, who might revive it. See Blackstone, *Commentaries*, III, 302.

tors being at Law as Mr. Burton is in the Country, agt whom they may bring a Suit at Law.[2]

BURWELL STARKE

J MARSHALL

Notice of Estate Auction

Printed, *Virginia Gazette, and General Advertiser* (Richmond), January 12, 1791, 1

Richmond, January 3, 1791

On Saturday the 15th of this month, will be sold to the highest bidder, on 6 *months credit, at the front door of the* EAGLE-TAVERN, THE HOUSE-HOLD FURNITURE of Serafino Formicola,[3] deceased. Also a HORSE and CHAIR. Bond and good security will be required of the purchasers.

J. MARSHALL, *Ex'or.*

2. The chancery suit depended upon the inability of the plaintiff to obtain an adequate remedy at law by virtue of the defendant's nonresidence. In the circumstances enumerated, it is most likely that the inadequacy was connected with the difficulties a plaintiff would experience in collecting his judgment from the merchant who held the attached intangible personal property. For difficulties in procedure at law that would justify resort to equity, see John Norton Pomeroy, *A Treatise on Equity Jurisprudence*, 3d ed. (San Francisco, 1905), IV, 2787–2788; see also the general discussion in Henry L. McClintock, *Handbook of the Principles of Equity*, 2d ed. (St. Paul, Minn., 1948), 103–105, 110–111. Although in this particular case submitted for JM's opinion the High Court of Chancery might have entered an order compelling payment by the stakeholder, it might have declined to do so if it could be shown that the courts of the defendant's domicile would refuse to recognize the Virginia decree and would therefore force the stakeholder to make a second payment to the defendant. Thus, while foreign attachment did confer a species of in rem jurisdiction upon the High Court of Chancery, there was some uncertainty concerning the interstate acceptance of such a decree under the then recognized principles of comity.

The uncertainties of practice in this area were doubtless eased by the ratification of the U.S. Constitution, Art. IV, sec. 1, which accorded full faith and credit in every state to the common law judgments entered by the courts of other states. Thus, where the remedy at law was adequate, the need for such a request for equitable relief would be substantially reduced.

3. Formicola, owner of one of JM's favorite taverns, had died on Oct. 6, 1790. See additional notice at Feb. 20, 1791.

Deed

Copy, Richmond City Deed Book, Office of the Chancery and Hustings Court Clerk, Richmond

[*January 4, 1791, Richmond.* James and Ann Dent Hayes[4] sell to JM for £50 a half–acre lot, no. 787,[5] which they had bought from Philip Turpin.]

Lottery Notice

Printed, *Virginia Gazette, and General Advertiser* (Richmond), January 19, 1791, 3

[*ca. January 19, 1791, Richmond.* The scheme of a lottery, authorized by the General Assembly for the benefit of Nathaniel Twining,[6] is described, and notice is given that the drawing will be held at the capitol on May 16, 1791. The plan called for the sale of 3,000 tickets at $4 each, yielding $10,000 for 893 prizes and $2,000 for Twining. JM signed as one of the trustees of the lottery.]

Law Papers, January 1791

U.S. Circuit Court, Va.

Asselby v. Pleasants, answer, copy, Treasury 79/37, Public Record Office.

Robinson v. Lewis, declaration, ADS, U.S. Circuit Court, Va., Ended Cases (Restored), 1791, Virginia State Library.

---

4. Hayes (*ca.* 1759–1804) and his wife lived in Chesterfield County. He was the printer and publisher who had established the *Virginia Gazette, or the American Advertiser* (Richmond, 1782–1786).

5. This lot was directly behind one JM bought from Philip Turpin on July 7, 1789. It was on the northeast corner of the square, on the corner of present-day Clay and Ninth streets.

6. Twining, a stagecoach operator, had received a franchise to establish a stagecoach line between Alexandria and Richmond in 1784. Soon afterward he attempted to establish an extensive route from the northern to the southern states and met with financial disaster. When the 1790 General Assembly convened, Twining presented a petition requesting permission to obtain relief through a state lottery. The legislature adopted a bill to that effect on Dec. 20, 1790. 11 Hening 395 (1784); *JVHD*, Oct. 1790, 13, 29, 147; 13 Hening 174 (1790). See Account Book, Disbursements, Mar. 1793, for JM's payment "on account of Twinings lottery."

Receipt

Printed extract, Walter R. Benjamin Autographs, Inc., *The Collector* (New York, February 1942), 58

[*February 2, 1791, Richmond.* JM acknowledges receipt of £30 from James Brown.]

Land Grant

Record Book Copy, Land Office, Kentucky Secretary of State's Office

[*February 8, 1791, Richmond.* JM receives grant of 1,000 acres in Bourbon County (formerly Fayette County), Ky., based upon a survey conducted on Aug. 17, 1787. The documents pertaining to this grant are printed in full under the date Sept. 4, 1783, Vol. I, 104–107.]

To James Brown

ADS, Collection of Robert W. Carver, Summit, N.J.

[*February 10, 1791 (Richmond).* JM writes an order to Brown to pay Col. Robert Goode[7] £18 9s. 4d. from his account.]

Notice

Printed, *Virginia Gazette, and General Advertiser* (Richmond), February 23, 1791, 3

[Richmond], February 20, 1791
All persons who are indebted to the estate of SERAFINO FORMI-

7. James Brown (1762–1841) came to Richmond in 1785 from his native Scotland and acted as agent for Donald & Burton, a London mercantile firm. He later formed the partnership of Brown & Burton, which became Brown, Rives & Co. in 1806 after Burton's death. For other examples of Brown paying checks, see Receipt, Aug. 27, 1792; and "St. George Tucker in account with James Brown," Tucker-Coleman Papers, Swem Library, College of William and Mary.

Col. Robert Goode (1743–1809) lived at "Whitby" in Henrico County outside Richmond. Described as a man of "wealth and influence," he served in the Continental army and from 1790 to 1797 was a member of the Council of State. G. Brown Goode, *Virginia Cousins . . .* (Richmond, 1887), 54, 55, 58.

COLA, deceased, are requested to make immediate payment; and those who have claims against that estate, are desired to make them known to the executor.[8]

J. MARSHALL, *Ex'or.*

Law Papers, February 1791

U.S. Circuit Court, Va.

Asselby v. Pleasants, answer, AD, U.S. Circuit Court, Va., Ended Cases (Restored), 1793, Virginia State Library.

Dobson and Daltera v. Crump and Bates, answer, AD, U.S. Circuit Court, Va., Ended Cases (Restored), 1794, Va. State Lib.[9]

Dobson and Daltera v. Eggleston, answer, AD, U.S. Circuit Court, Va., Ended Cases (Restored), 1793, Va. State Lib.[1]

Dobson and Daltera v. Trents and Calloway, answer, AD, U.S. Circuit Court, Va., Ended Cases (Restored), 1795, Va. State Lib.

Donald & Co. v. Hopkins, answer, AD, U.S. Circuit Court, Va., Ended Cases (Restored), 1793, Va. State Lib.

Donald & Co. v. Williamson, answer, AD, U.S. Circuit Court, Va., Ended Cases (Restored), 1793, Va. State Lib.

Donald, Scot & Co. v. Anderson, answer, AD, U.S. Circuit Court, Va., Ended Cases (Unrestored), Va. State Lib.

Donald, Scot & Co. v. Anderson, pleas in bar, AD, U.S. Circuit Court, Va., Ended Cases (Unrestored), Va. State Lib.

Donald, Scot & Co. v. Guy, answer, AD, U.S. Circuit Court, Va., Ended Cases (Restored), 1796, Va. State Lib.

Jones v. Randolph, answer, printed document, U.S. Circuit Court, Va., Ended Cases (Restored), 1791, Va. State Lib.

Jones v. Randolph's Executors, answer (assumpsit for 280 Negroes), AD, U.S. Circuit Court, Va., Ended Cases (Restored), 1797, Va. State Lib.[2]

Jones v. Randolph's Executors, answer (assumpsit for £342 5s. 5d.), AD, U.S. Circuit Court, Va., Ended Cases (Restored), 1797, Va. State Lib.

8. See also Jan. 3, 1791, notice.
9. See Account Book, Receipts, Apr. 15, 1790, and Mar. 10, 1791.
1. See Account Book, Receipts, Jan. 1791.
2. See JM's opinion in this case, Apr. 1, 1791.

Jones's Executors v. Walker, answers, AD, U.S. Circuit Court, Va., Ended Cases (Restored), 1797, Va. State Lib.

Lidderdale's Executor v. Braxton, answer, AD, U.S. Circuit Court, Va., Ended Cases (Restored), 1793, Va. State Lib.

From Joseph Simon

Draft, Library Company Manuscripts, Historical Society of Pennsylvania

Sir   Philadelphia, March 25, 1791
   I am Sorrey to Trouble you So often with my affair Concerning Mr. Richd. Lees Debt.[3] By Mr. Gratz[4] I have Reced. 2 Days agoe 250 Dollrs. for Mr. Lees order on Mr. Seth Barton of Baltemore which he would not pay untill 20 Days Was allowed [to] him, for which you will be pleased to order Crd. Given him on the Execution for the above 250 Dollrs from the 11th. Instant when it [was] pd. at Bartons or[der]. I am Sorry to Inform you that the Bill of Exchange he Sent me Last augt. trough Mr. Gratz is Noted for none acceptince the protest I Reced. yesturday and as it only Mentions for none acciptence Did not think it Necessary to send it on. I Expect shortly now by febry packet to know the faith of it, but in the meantime should you think any Step is Necessary to be taken Now, I must Beg of you to act as you think proper so as I Gett my own from him as he Dosenot Deserve any Indulgince from me by Keeping me out So Long with Desseption. The Indorser on the above bill is one Mr. John Ballentine Lives in Westmoreland County or the County adjoining Mr. Lee, within Seven or Eight miles from him. I Some time agoe Mentioned to you of

3. The letter is addressed at the top to "John Marshall Esqr., attorney at Law, Richmond," but this is written on the verso of an address leaf originally intended for "Mr. Barnard Gratz, in Race Street between 2 & 3 Streets, Philadelphia," which is written in another hand. The paper is filled with mathematical calculations on both sides, some relating to bonds and interest.
   Joseph Simon v. Richard Lee was a debt action on appeal from Westmoreland County. It had been transferred from the General Court to the District Court at Northumberland County after the reorganization of the courts, and judgment had been confessed in Sept. 1789. District Court Order Book, 1789–1793, 30, Northumberland County, Virginia State Library. See Account Book, Receipts, Aug. 5, 1788.
   4. Barnard Gratz (1738–1801) had emigrated in 1754 from London to Philadelphia, where he formed a mercantile firm with his brother, Michael (1740–1811), who later married Joseph Simon's daughter. The Gratz brothers were successful in business and also became large landholders. Michael moved to Virginia during the Revolution,

keeping 4 half Joes[5] for yr. fee which hope will Prove satisfactory when Reced. for what yo have Done, and Now have to Recquest you will urge the payments of the Present Execution as allso the Remaining Bills in the hands of yr. frind Bushard washington[6] Esqr. to Be Brot to Issue as Soone as Possible in the District Court & for which Truble you & he Shall be forther Satisfyde, as his Bills prove allways protested. Must Recquest you to Gett the money on Such Inland Bills as the money may be had Soone. Yr. perticuler Care in this & yr. speedey answer will very Much oblige, Sir Yr. Most obedt. Servt

J. S[7]

Law Papers, March 1791

District Court, Fredericksburg

Isaacs v. Thornley, acknowledgment, AD, Term Papers, Office of the Clerk of the Circuit Court, Fredericksburg, Va.[8]

Opinion

Printed, John E. Oster, ed., *The Political and Economic Doctrines of John Marshall* (New York, 1914), 181

[Richmond], April 1, 1791

We are decidedly of opinion that if any engagement relative to

---

and in 1795 Barnard moved to Baltimore. Simon was obviously referring to Michael Gratz here. See Account Book, Receipts, Dec. 2, 1790.

5. A half Joe equaled approximately four dollars.

6. Bushrod Washington (1762–1829), nephew of the president and a future Supreme Court justice, was practicing law in Richmond at this time.

7. Simon (1712–1804), a merchant who concentrated on frontier trade, settled in Lancaster, Pa., in 1735, and became one of the largest landholders in the colony. As one of the organizers of the Indiana Company, he became involved in the dispute between the company and Virginia over the title to the land deeded the company by Indians in 1768. The land consisted of more than half of western Virginia. Simon traveled to London and to Williamsburg in an unsuccessful attempt to secure title to the land. Virginia finally gave the company land in the northwestern territory in exchange for their original claim. Litigation continued for many years. See H. M. J. Klein, *Lancaster County, Pennsylvania: A History* (New York, 1924), II, 861–863; and Samuel Evans, "Sketch of Joseph Simon," Lancaster County Historical Society, *Historical Papers and Addresses*, III (1898–1899), 165–172.

8. See Account Book, Receipts, Sept. 26, 1790.

the consignment of a Gumeaman[9] to Randolph & Wayler[1] was entered into subsequent to the receipt of Mr. Wayler's letter of the 14th of May 1772,[2] That Messrs Farrel & Jones have a good claim on the writer of that letter for indemnity.

ANDREW RONOLD[3]

J. MARSHALL.

Law Papers, April 1791

District Court, Fredericksburg

Mitchell v. Pendleton, case agreed, DS, Term Papers, Office of the Clerk of the Circuit Court, Fredericksburg, Va.

Mitchell v. Williams's Executors, case agreed, DS ,Term Papers, Office of the Clerk of the Circuit Court, Fredericksburg, Va.[4]

---

9. Probably "guineaman" in the original manuscript, which has not been found. The reference is to the vessel *Prince of Wales* and her cargo of 280 Negro slaves. Correspondence concerning this consignment and other financial transactions between the Bristol firm Farrell & Jones and the Virginia venturers John Wayles (1715-1773) and Richard Randolph (1725-1786) is printed in Julian Boyd *et al.,* eds., *The Papers of Thomas Jefferson,* XV (Princeton, N.J., 1958), 649-677. Litigation in Jones v. Wayles's Executors and Randolph's Executors began in the U.S. Circuit Court for Virginia in Nov. 1790, but on Nov. 27, 1790, the action as it pertained to Randolph's estate was dismissed. In Feb. 1791 judgment by nil dicit had been entered against Wayles's executors, and a writ of inquiry was issued. JM received a fee of nine pounds from the defendants in this case on or about Mar. 9, 1791, probably for his review of the case and participation in the preparation of this legal opinion. The executors, despite the opinion, seem to have vacated the default judgment and subsequently brought the case to trial on the merits. The matter reappeared on the docket of the U.S. Circuit Court in Nov. 1791, and when it was tried in 1797, the jury returned a verdict for the defendants. U.S. Circuit Court, Va., Ended Cases (Restored), 1797, and Rule Book, I, 9-10, 15, 21-22, 68-69, Virginia State Library; Account Book, Receipts, Mar. 1791; Boyd *et al.,* eds., *Jefferson Papers,* XV, 647-648.

1. Probably "Wayles" in the original manuscript. Wayles was the father-in-law of Thomas Jefferson, who served as one of his executors.

2. In this letter Wayles had advised Farrell & Jones that he gave them "every Assurance, that whatever engagement you may be kind enough to enter into on our behalf shall be complied with without inconvenience or prejudice to yourselves, and if you desire it to share in the Profit." Boyd *et al.,* eds., *Jefferson Papers,* XV, 653. This was written in reply to a series of letters from the Bristol merchants that referred to the *Prince of Wales* in a tentative way, at the same time requesting Wayles and Randolph to settle balances outstanding against them on the books of Farrell & Jones. John Wayles's letter of May 14, 1772, may be taken as the date of the contract and also as an assurance of indemnification to Farrell & Jones on behalf of himself and Randolph.

3. Andrew Ronald (*ca.* 1754-1799) had been in practice in Richmond since 1783.

4. See Account Book, Receipts, Oct. 22, 1788.

Mitchell v. Yancey's Executor, case agreed, DS, Term Papers, Office of the Clerk of the Circuit Court, Fredericksburg, Va.[5]

McHaney v. George's Executor

Notes on Argument in the District Court

AD, Term Papers, Office of the Clerk of the Circuit Court, Fredericksburg, Va.

[Fredericksburg, May 4, 1791]

Gave her a fortune
To build her a house
she his child. poverty
Told she left it more destitute than she found [it.]
above labor
other daughters.
Mrs. McHeny said it was a gratuity etc witness thought so attempt the account by that generous conduct[6]

To John Breckinridge

ALS, Breckinridge Family Papers, Library of Congress[7]

Dear Sir   [Richmond, *ca.* May 20, 1791]
Mr. Johnston[8] has informd me that in the suits against Duncan[9]

5. See *ibid.*

6. JM wrote these notes on what was used as a wrapper marked "McHaney vs. George's exr., c. 1.," in a clerk's hand. The clerk also wrote, "1791 Apl. Court, Jud. Accd. to award." JM no doubt used these notes in arguing before the jury or the arbitrator.

JM appeared for the plaintiff in Cornelius McHaney and Mary, his wife, v. Reuben George, executor of John George, before the District Court at Fredericksburg. The action resulted in two hung juries before it was finally submitted to binding arbitration on May 5, 1791, the day after the jury heard arguments. On May 6 an award and judgment for the amount sought were entered for McHaney. District Court Law Orders, A, 1789–1793, 16, 169, 235, 236, 246, Fredericksburg, Virginia State Library. See JM's declaration listed at Law Papers, Sept. 1788, and a fee in Account Book, Receipts, May 1791.

7. Addressed to "John Breckinridge, Atty at Law, Albemarle," the letter bears no date or postmarks. Internal evidence indicates that this was the letter to which Breckinridge replied on May 29. See JM to Breckinridge, June 10, 1791.

8. Lain Johnson, after consulting with his attorney, JM, wrote to Breckinridge on Mar. 31, 1791, informing him that a juror had been withdrawn at trial because an

which I brought there is a defect in the declarations which will prevent a judgement on them. It was the practise in the Genl. court & was founded on an agreement signd by every lawyer, to amend a declaration at any time & on this account I have been less attentive than I ought to have been.[1] I think tho I am not certain that the writ is in case. If so the court will permit the declaration to be amended so as to conform it to the writ. If this is not the case I fear the suits must be dismissd. If you find this absolutely necessary it will be better to bring new suits to the next court if possible. Tho perhaps it may be dangerous to risk even this as they may plead the pendency of a former action. I am dear Sir, Your obedt.

J MARSHALL

---

incorrect declaration had been filed. Johnson advised Breckinridge of JM's opinion that if the defect could not be corrected, presumably by an amended declaration, the pending action would have to be withdrawn and a new writ obtained. Johnson to Breckinridge, Mar. 31, 1791, Breckinridge Family Papers, Library of Congress. Apparently that course of action was adopted, only to be discovered that the statute of limitations had run and might be pleaded in bar to the new action. See JM to Breckinridge, June 10, 1791, and ca. Sept. 1791.

9. Robert Duncan. This case may be related to the case of Watson v. Turner in which JM received a fee in early Jan. 1794. See Account Book, Receipts, Jan. 1794.

1. JM was referring to the following agreement, ca. Apr. 1785, which was recently discovered in the Robinson Family Papers at the Virginia Historical Society:

"We do agree, that at any time before the opening of a cause the declaration may be amended; in any manner whatsoever, correspondent with the nature of the action, expressed in the writ. If upon such amendment, the defendant's defence be changed in his opinion of the case, he shall have it in his power to continue the suit generally; unless four month's previous notice be given to the defendant's counsel of the intended amendment, which may so change his defence.

"By a liberty of amendment we mean a liberty to file even a new declaration either where one has or has not been filed.

"We also assent, that this agreement shall be deposited with the clerk.

"Relying on the honor of each subscriber, that this agreement will never become the instrument of fraud or artifice, we hereto affix our names."

It was signed by Edmund Randolph, Henry Tazewell, John Taylor, Jerman Baker, JM, William DuVal, and Paul Carrington, Jr. St. George Tucker, James Innes, James Monroe, and William Nelson, Jr., signed after 1785 as they were admitted to practice.

Prior to this agreement the practice regarding amendment probably conformed to Bacon's explanation that pleadings were amendable until they were entered upon the record, although they might even then be amendable within the same term. Thereafter they could be amended only by leave of the court and with payment of costs. Matthew Bacon, A New Abridgement of the Law . . . , 3d ed. (London, 1766), I, 107.

Jones v. Hylton and Eppes

Answer

Printed Document, U.S. Circuit Court, Va., Ended Cases (Restored), 1794, Virginia State Library

[*May 24, 1791, Richmond.* An answer is filed on one of JM's printed forms to an action in debt on behalf of Daniel L. Hylton and Francis Eppes.[2] The action was based upon a writing obligatory for £2,926 11s. 6d. sterling, dated July 7, 1774, payable to Farrell & Jones, a British mercantile firm. The answer alleges payment into the Virginia Land Office.

The form is completed in JM's hand, although he crossed out his printed name and wrote, "James Innes" above it. Rejoinders and replications, and then new pleas, were filed later in 1791, and the case was continued until 1793. Apparently JM entered the case in Apr. 1793, one month before the case name was changed to Ware v. Hylton, Jones having died. JM appeared for Hylton in June 1793 and won partial judgment, although the case was continued on the first plea. A verdict for Ware in May 1794 contained a judgment unsatisfactory to the plaintiff, and he sought a writ of error to the U.S. Supreme Court. In addition to the case papers in the Virginia State Library, see Ware v. Hylton, 3 U.S. (3 Dall.) 199–285, and JM's Account Book, Receipts, Apr. 1793.]

Law Papers, May 1791

U.S. Circuit Court, Va.

Donald & Co. v. Crawley, answer, AD, U.S. Circuit Court, Va., Ended Cases (Restored), 1793, Virginia State Library.

Donald & Co. v. Owen, answer, AD, U.S. Circuit Court, Va., Ended Cases (Restored), 1793, Va. State Lib.[3]

Donald, Scot & Co. v. Gilbert's Executors, answer, AD, U.S. Circuit Court, Va., Ended Cases (Restored), 1795, Va. State Lib.[4]

2. Hylton was a prominent Richmond merchant who had served on the Henrico County Committee of Safety in 1775 and was sheriff of the county in 1791. For the Eppes family, see Eva Turner Clark, *Francis Eppes, His Ancestors and Descendants* (New York, 1942).
3. See Account Book, Receipts, May 12, 1791.
4. See Account Book, Receipts, Jan. 1791.

Hanson v. Donald, answer, AD, U.S. Circuit Court, Va., Ended Cases (Restored), 1795, Va. State Lib.

Hanson v. Taylor, answer, AD, U.S. Circuit Court, Va., Ended Cases (Restored), 1793, Va. State Lib.

Jones v. Randolph's Executors, answer (debt for £9,400 sterling), printed document, U.S. Circuit Court, Va., Ended Cases (Restored), 1797, Va. State Lib.

Jones v. Ruffin's Executor, answer, AD, U.S. Circuit Court, Va., Ended Cases (Unrestored), Va. State Lib.

Robinson v. Rumney, declaration, copy, U.S. Circuit Court, Va., Record Book, I, 31–33, Va. State Lib.

Wilson v. Wilson, declaration, AD, U.S. Circuit Court, Va., Ended Cases (Restored), 1792, Va. State Lib.[5]

To John Breckinridge

ALS, Breckinridge Family Papers, Library of Congress

Dear Sir[6]   Richmond, June 10, 1791

I have just receivd yours of the 29th. of May[7] on the subject of the suits against Robert Duncan & Co. I feel myself extremely chagrind at the issue of this business because I feel that I have been extremely culpable in the manner of conducting it. I will be obligd to you to inform me whether the writs were issued from the county or general court & whether they were in case or debt? I had hopd that my faulty declaration might have been amended provided the writ woud have justified a proper one, because at the time it was filed an agreement existed signd by every attorney practising in the Genl. court authorizing such amendments. An over desire for the ten percent[8] inducd me to file a declaration which I intended afterwards to change if I shoud think it necessary.

5. See Vol. I, 403, n. 88.
6. The letter was addressed to Breckinridge at "Albemarle" and was endorsed in his hand "ansd 15 July 1791." Breckinridge's letter of July 15 has not been found. See JM to Breckinridge, *ca.* May 20, and *ca.* Sept. 1791.
7. Letter not found.
8. This does not refer to the statutory fees awarded to attorneys in the taxation of a bill of costs, for these were specified amounts that depended upon the nature of the cause of action. JM was possibly referring to the portion of the fee that would come to him by reason of his referral of the case to Breckinridge.

As things are we must be content with endeavoring to set out rightly the second time & avoid any future similar misfortune.

On the bills which are accepted an action ought be brought on the case against Robert Duncan & Co. If you are satisfied that John Turner & Robert Duncan were the partners it woud be best to name them separately John Turner & Robert Duncan late Merchants & partners under the firm of Robert Duncan & Co., otherwise bring it against Robert Duncan & Co.[9]

With respect to the bills which are not accepted an action on the case must be brought against the drawers. If it appears plainly in proof (& I think it does that Robert Duncan was a partner of John Turner & Co then he may be sued as a drawer of the bill under the firm of John Turner & Co. If this does not appear in proof then bills must be put in suit in chancery.[1]

There is one consideration which I regard more than any other. The act of limitations will I fear run against the bills.[2] Do not whisper this to any person as it may perhaps not be thought of. Shoud it be pleaded we have no reliance but on the former action & that I fear will not protect us. Farewell I am dear Sir, Your obedt.

J MARSHALL

I will draw the declarations & send them when you tell me how you have issued the writs.

9. In pleading, a distinction was made between those acting as partners and those in a principal and agent relationship. In the former case all living partners had to be joined as parties defendant; however, if one of the individuals involved in the transaction was merely an agent of the others, it would not be necessary to join him unless he was otherwise liable. If a living partner was not joined in the action, the other defendants might enter a plea in abatement supported by an affidavit showing his improper omission. J[oseph] Chitty, *A Treatise on the Parties to Actions, Forms of Action, and on Pleading*, 3d Am. ed. (Philadelphia, 1819), I, 19–20, 23, 24–25.

1. The action of debt was not available on a bill of exchange that had not been accepted. Hence, an action on the case in assumpsit was the proper form of action. *Ibid.*, 74–75. Resort to chancery, as opposed to an action at law, would permit the plaintiff to demand information by way of interrogatories to resolve the question of the partnership relationship between the parties defendant.

2. The Virginia statute of limitations was five years on contractual actions and three years on promissory notes. 5 Hening 513 (1748); 3 Hening 377 (1705). Presumably the shorter period of limitations also applied to bills of exchange. JM was uncomfortable with this case, because he had commenced the action and perhaps had done so in a way that made it vulnerable to a plea in abatement. If the action were dismissed, it would be impossible for him to institute another, since the statute of limitations had run during the pendency of the first action and would constitute a bar to the second.

Law Papers, June 1791

U.S. Circuit Court, Va.

Asselby v. Pleasants, rejoinder, AD, U.S. Circuit Court, Va., Ended Cases (Restored), 1793, Virginia State Library.

Buchanan, Hastie & Co. v. Newman's Executors, rejoinder, AD, U.S. Circuit Court, Va., Ended Cases (Restored), 1793, Va. State Lib.

Donald & Co. v. Hopkins, rejoinder, AD, U.S. Circuit Court, Va., Ended Cases (Restored), 1793, Va. State Lib.

Donald & Co. v. Taliaferro and Wiatt, answer, AD, U.S. Circuit Court, Va., Ended Cases (Restored), 1791, Va. State Lib.

Donald, Scot & Co. v. Anderson, rejoinder, AD, U.S. Circuit Court, Va., Ended Cases (Unrestored), Va. State Lib.

Donald, Scot & Co. v. Guy, joinder and rejoinder, copy, U.S. Circuit Court, Va., Ended Cases (Restored), 1796, Va. State Lib.

To John Breckinridge

ALS, Breckinridge Family Papers, Library of Congress

[Richmond, *ca.* July 1791]

I would advise Mr. Harris to institute a suit in chancery against Mr. Watkyns & his wife & those who may be in possession of the land, stating the decree, the payment of the money & asking for an absolute decree for the land & for rents & profits.[3]

J MARSHALL

I see no error in the decree & am persuaded there can be no difficulty in obtaining such a decree as woud enable Mr. Harris to sue out a writ of habere facias possessionem.[4]

3. See Account Book, Receipts, July 1791, where JM received an advice fee from Harris and entered a fee in Watkins v. Harris. JM had also entered a fee in this case in June 1788. See Vol. I, 412. It is likely that JM had handled the original case in the General Court in 1788 but transferred it to Breckinridge when the courts were reorganized.

4. This writ is a process used by the successful party in an ejectment action in order to have the sheriff put the party in actual possession of the land in dispute.

Law Papers, July 1791

U.S. Circuit Court, Va.

Hanson v. Markham, answer, AD, U.S. Circuit Court, Va., Ended Cases (Restored), 1793, Virginia State Library.

Jones's Executor v. Walker, rejoinder, AD, U.S. Circuit Court, Va., Ended Cases (Restored), 1797, Va. State Lib.

To John Breckinridge

ALS, Breckinridge Family Papers, Library of Congress

Dear Sir[5]   [Richmond, *ca.* September 1791]

I transmit you a declaration against John Turner jr. & Co. & one against Robert Duncan & Co. You will perceive that I have laid higher damages in the declaration than in the writ & that they are laid in current money. It was necessary to do so. The damages must be high enough to cover the interest & must be in current money or it woud be error. The variance can only be taken advantage of in abatement[6] & I trust it will not be observd or if observd that the defendant will not give bail until an office judgement when it will be too late to plead in abatement.[7] I dread the act of limitations. Shoud it be offerd insist on its being put in writing & send me a copy of it. Do not let it [be] receivd otherwise than in writing. With much esteem, I am dear Sir, Your

J MARSHALL

5. Addressed to "John Breckinridge esquire, Atty. at law, Albemarle," the letter is endorsed in Breckinridge's hand: "Relates to Suits which I appeard to, for Mr. Marshall in Alb: Dist. Court; but being brought wrong, were obliged to be dissd.; and renewed agreeable to Mr. Marshalls directions; The 4 bills; and declarations I filed in the Dist. Ct. office. Feby. 93." Clearly Breckinridge was anxious about the multitude of errors that plagued the attorneys for Lain Johnson in Johnson v. Duncan & Co. and wished to leave no doubt that his actions were taken at JM's direction.

6. A declaration was required to correspond to the terms of the writ, and if it did not, the defendant might enter a plea in abatement against the declaration. J[oseph] Chitty, *A Treatise on the Parties to Actions, Forms of Actions, and on Pleading*, 3d Am. ed. (Philadelphia, 1819), I, 321.

7. JM hoped that Duncan & Co. would default in appearance, permitting the case to proceed to default judgment. In such a case the variance between the writ and the declaration would be cured by the entry of judgment. In English practice the error was not noticeable by the court without an affidavit of truth appended to the plea in abatement. Blackstone, *Commentaries*, III, 302.

Law Papers, September 1791

District Court, Fredericksburg

Aylar v. Porter, rejoinder, copy, Term Papers, Office of the Clerk of the Circuit Court, Fredericksburg, Va.[8]

U.S. Circuit Court, Va.

Asselby v. Pleasants, demurrer, AD, U.S. Circuit Court, Va., Ended Cases (Restored), 1793, Virginia State Library.

To William Watts

ALS, Irvine-Saunders Collection, University of Virginia Library

Dear Sir[9]   [Richmond, *ca.* October 1791]

I have receivd yours on the subject of your suits in the district of Petersburg. Upon the receipt of your former letter[10] on this subject I had the order of reference set aside so that the referees have now no power over the subject.

I wrote to you, but I suppose the letter has miscarried informing you that the reason why the order was originally made was that Mr. Briggs[11] said you wishd it, & as well as I recollect you desird me to attend to what he said on the subject. I am Sir your obedt.

J MARSHALL

Law Papers, October 1791

U.S. Circuit Court, Va.

Hanson v. Atkinson, bond, AD, U.S. Circuit Court, Va., Ended Cases (Restored), 1793, Virginia State Library.

8. See Account Book, Receipts, Jan. 7, 1790.
9. Watts (*ca.* 1749–1795) was a Dinwiddie County attorney who became a justice of the peace in 1789 and later served as the county's sheriff.
10. Not found.
11. Gray Briggs (1730–1807), of "Wales" in Dinwiddie County, had attended the House of Burgesses from 1754 to 1758 and held various minor public offices thereafter, including Commonwealth's attorney in the 1780s.

Law Papers, November 1791

U.S. Circuit Court, Va.

Bagg v. Galt, answer, AD, U.S. Circuit Court, Va., Ended Cases (Unrestored), 1797, Virginia State Library.[12]

Donald & Co. v. Burton, answer, AD, U.S. Circuit Court, Va., Ended Cases (Restored), 1793, Va. State Lib.[1]

Donald & Co. v. Ware, answer, AD, U.S. Circuit Court, Va., Ended Cases (Restored), 1793, Va. State Lib.

Donald's Executors v. Ogelby, answer, AD, U.S. Circuit Court, Va., Ended Cases (Restored), 1793, Va. State Lib.

Hanson v. Atkinson, answer, AD, U.S. Circuit Court, Va., Ended Cases (Restored), 1793, Va. State Lib.

Jones v. Quarles, answer, AD, U.S. Circuit Court, Va., Ended Cases (Unrestored), Va. State Lib.

Lidderdale's Executor v. Randolph, answer, AD, U.S. Circuit Court, Va., Ended Cases (Unrestored), Va. State Lib.

McCall and Elliott v. Richards's Executors, answer, AD, U.S. Circuit Court, Va., Ended Cases (Unrestored), 1797, Va. State Lib.[2]

To Humphrey Marshall

Printed Extract, *Kentucky Gazette* (Lexington), December 31, 1791, 3

[Richmond, *ca.* December 1, 1791]

I cannot fix the day of your arrival, but this I well recollect we were at dinner when you came, and Col. Brooke the clerk of the Senate dined with me that day. There was some conversation concerning the division of the county (of Woodford) and as well as I remember Col. Brooke informed us of the rejection of the Bill. That day or soon after, I heard you express some satisfaction at not having come down till the Bill was rejected from an idea that its rejection might be ascribed to you. I noticed this business more

12. See Account Book, Receipts, June 1791.
1. See Account Book, Receipts, Feb. 1791.
2. See consent to take deposition in this case listed at Law Papers, 1791, and fee entered in Account Book, Receipts, May 1791.

than I should otherwise have done, because from my father's representation I had in some small degree interested my self in passing the Bill thro the house of Representatives. Col. Brooke probably recollects the circumstances; and if he does can give a more positive certificate than I have done. I can only add that I am sorry to hear such paltry falsehood continue to be told and believed.[3]

J. MARSHALL.

Petition of James Crane

AD, Executive Papers, Virginia State Library

[Richmond, *ca.* December 2, 1791]

To his Excellency the Governor & the Honbles the members of the Privy counsel the petition of James Crane humbly sheweth

That John Crane son of your petitioner was arraignd in the Honble the district court holden at Winchester for killing a certain Abraham Vanhorn in a fight & a special verdict was found thereon which was referd to the Honble. the General court for difficulty. On the hearing of the said special verdict it was by a majority of the court determind to be murder & judgement of death will be pronouncd at the next term unless Your Excellency & your Honors will interpose with mercy. Your petitioner humbly prays that the case may be considerd & if it shall appear to be a proper case for pardon your petitioner prays that your Excellency & Honors will extend your mercy to the son of your petitioner. And your petitioner will ever pray etc.[4]

3. John Craig, a delegate from Woodford County, Ky., had accused Humphrey Marshall of interfering with his efforts to support the passage of a bill to divide Woodford County while it was under consideration by the Virginia Senate in 1790. Marshall published this letter from JM to prove that he did not arrive in Richmond until after the Senate had rejected the bill. He also published a letter from Humphrey Brooke.

Humphrey Brooke, formerly clerk of Fauquier County, had become clerk of the Virginia Senate in 1785.

The House of Delegates had passed a bill for dividing Woodford County on Nov. 9, 1790. The Senate rejected it on Nov. 30, 1790. *JVHD*, Oct. 1790, 14, 31, 44, 47; *Journal of the Senate of the Commonwealth of Virginia* . . . , Oct. 1790 (Richmond, 1828), 12, 14, 28, 30.

4. When Crane was brought before the District Court at Winchester in Sept. 1791, the judges questioned whether the indictment should have been for manslaughter rather than murder and adjourned the decision to a full meeting of the judges in the General Court. JM was retained by payment of £14 and represented Crane before the General Court. On Nov. 22 that court determined that the crime was murder, where-

From Wilson Cary Nicholas

ALS, Nicholas Papers, University of Virginia Library

Dear Sir   [Albemarle County], December 5, 1791
 I have taken the liberty to give Colo. Lindsey[5] an order upon you for twelve pounds. I owed that gentleman a sum of money payable on demand all of which I have paid him except the sum that I have mentioned. You will oblige me very much by paying my order. I shall be in Richmond in eight or ten days when I will either repay the money with thanks, or win it of you at whist as you please. I am ashamed of the liberty I have taken with you. My credit is at stake if the money is not paid. I am my Dear Sir, Your friend

WILSON CARY NICHOLAS

The within mentiond order is mislaid. I have receivd the within mentiond sum of twelve pounds.[6]

RN. LINDSAY

Notice of Public Auction

Printed, *Virginia Gazette, and General Advertiser* (Richmond), December 21, 1791, 2

Richmond, December 11, 1791

Pursuant to a Decree of the Honorable the High Court of Chancery, dated the 8th day of November last, will be sold at public auction, at the Eagle Tavern in this city, on Monday the 20th day of February next, to the

---

upon JM wrote this petition for Crane's father and sent it to the Council of State. On Dec. 2 the Council decided to postpone a decision until final sentencing. In April, after hearing evidence that Crane suffered seizures, the District Court at Winchester sentenced Crane to hang on June 8, 1792. Several inhabitants of Frederick and Berkeley counties petitioned for mercy, and on May 9 the Council of State granted a reprieve until July 6. Crane is not mentioned again in the minutes of the Council, and presumably he was executed. *CVSP*, V, 362, 371–372, 398, 404, 491, 502, 510–513, 541, 597–599, VI, 234–235; JVCS, Dec. 2, 1791, May 9, 1792; Account Book, Receipts, Nov. 1791.

 5. Reuben Lindsay (1747–1831), of Albemarle County, was a wealthy landowner and magistrate who contributed a great deal of money to the Continental Congress during the Revolution. He was married to Sarah Walker, daughter of Thomas Walker, one of JM's clients in Albemarle County.

 6. JM wrote this on the verso for Lindsay's signature. On the address leaf in another hand is written "R. Lindsy for David Rodes tobacco."

highest bidder, The LEAD MINES in the county of Wythe, commonly known by the name of Chissels Mines,[7] together with FOURTEEN HUNDRED ACRES of LAND thereunto belonging, subject to a lease of the same to Moses Austin, & Co. eight years of which are still to run from the first day of October last, at the annual rent of 150 l. for the first three years, and 200 l. for the remaining five years, which said eight years rents the purchaser is to be entitled to. Two years credit will be allowed for one moiety of the purchase money, and three years for the other. Bond and good security must be given to the subscribers, to be held in trust for such person or persons as shall upon the final decree be adjudged to be entitled thereto. The mines and premises are not to be sold unless 5000 l. at least shall be bidden for the same, and no conveyance is to be made until the money is paid, or until the further order of the court therein.

JOHN MARSHALL,⎫ Com'rs.
WILLIAM HAY,⎭

To Richard Bland Lee

Printed extract, Goodspeed's Bookshop, Inc., *The Flying Quill* (Boston, February–March 1954), 3

[*December 25, 1791, Richmond.* "You must pardon the time which has elapsed without answering your letters on the subject of your bonds in my hands. I have been the most busy man in the world but even that is not a sufficient apology, nor can I think of one which is sufficient. I now

7. After discovery of a rich lead deposit on the New River in Augusta County (now Montgomery), Francis Fauquier (1704–1768), royal governor of Virginia, John Robinson, William Byrd III (1728–1777) of "Westover," and John Chiswell formed the Lead Mining Company. Fauquier soon withdrew, and Chiswell actually managed the operation of the mines while his son-in-law, Robinson, furnished most of the money. The company was generally known as Chiswell's Mine. Chiswell murdered a man in May 1766, and when he was sent to Williamsburg for trial, he was bailed under suspicious circumstances that provoked a major controversy over the role of the aristocracy in Virginia. He died just before his trial was to begin in Oct. 1766. In November the General Assembly vested his lands in trustees, who were directed to sell the lands to satisfy the claims of Chiswell's heirs and to clear title to that part of the land previously sold. 8 Hening 270. See Carl Bridenbaugh, "Violence and Virtue in Virginia, 1766: or, The Importance of the Trivial," Massachusetts Historical Society, *Proceedings,* LXXVI (1964), 3–29; and J. A. Leo Lemay, "Robert Bolling and the Bailment of Colonel Chiswell," *Early American Literature,* VI (1971), 99–142. A copy of Chiswell's will is preserved in Box 90 (Lead Mine Papers), Auditor's Papers, Virginia State Library.

enclose you a state of the account and wish most seriously I could tell you that I had an immediate prospect of collecting the balance . . . you have heard all the news of Virginia, and therefore I will not give you the trouble of reading it from me."]

Law Papers, December 1791

U.S. Circuit Court, Va.

Dobson and Daltera v. Trents, rejoinder and demurrer, AD, U.S. Circuit Court, Va., Ended Cases (Restored), 1798, Virginia State Library.

Donald & Co. v. Clarke's Executors, pleas in abatement, AD and copy, U.S. Circuit Court, Va., Ended Cases (Restored), 1792, Va. State Lib.[8]

McCall and Shedden v. Jeffries, answer, AD, U.S. Circuit Court, Va., Ended Cases (Restored), 1793, Va. State Lib.

Snodgrass v. Miller, answer, AD, U.S. Circuit Court, Va., Ended Cases (Restored), 1793, Va. State Lib.[9]

To John Breckinridge

ALS, Breckinridge Family Papers, Library of Congress[10]

Dear Sir   [Richmond, *ca.* 1791]
    I have received yours. The certiorari is obtaind. The court rises to day. By the next post I can send up the certiorari & write to you. Mention to Mr. Harris[1] the necessity of sending some money. I am your

J MARSHALL

I am in court. You will excuse the want of a ⟨paper⟩ wafer.

8. See Account Book, Receipts, Nov. 1791.

9. See Account Book, Receipts, May 12, 1791.

10. The letter is addressed in JM's hand to "John Breckenridge esquire, Atty at Law, Albemarle" and is bound into the Breckinridge Family Papers immediately following the opinion given by JM to Breckinridge concerning the chancery litigation in Harris v. Watkins, *ca.* July 1791.

1. The reference is probably to a bill of certiorari obtained from the High Court of Chancery by JM for reviewing an equity decision of one of the county courts that was adverse to Harris's interests.

Law Papers, 1791

U.S. Circuit Court, Va.

McCall and Elliott v. Richards's Executors, consent to take deposition, ADS, Mss2M3567b1, Virginia Historical Society.[2]

List of Fees

AD, Marshall Papers, Swem Library, College of William and Mary

[Richmond, August 1786–1791][3]

List of fees recd. from Tents. Fairfax ads. Hite[4]

Stroude John,[5] Vanmetre Abm. on same land £	4	17	8
Godwin Swift, Wm. Dark, Jacob Miller, Phillip Ingle, Robt. Lomy, Michael Ingles, Abra-			

2. See Account Book, Receipts, May 1791, and answer listed at Law Papers, Nov. 1791.

3. This list begins at the end of the pages JM had used to write his law notes in 1780, following the blank page originally intended for notes on "Master & Servant." The date assigned to the document and the document's inclusion in this volume deserve explanation. Within the manuscript volume these accounts follow the law notes and JM's list of disbursements for the construction of his Richmond house, completed in 1790 or 1791, which raises the possibility that this fee list was prepared in 1790 or later. The list itself bears earlier dates, however, and it ends with two fees in Nov. 1791, at which time some of the tenants' cases against Hite were argued before the Court of Appeals by JM. In addition, the chronology of the tenant litigation against Hite's representatives supports the *ca.* Aug. 1786 date. Under the May 6, 1786, decision of the Court of Appeals in Hite v. Fairfax, the parties were allowed three months to file petitions in the High Court of Chancery to assert their claims against the Hite estate. Vol. I, 152. In Aug. 1786, JM traveled to Winchester and Fauquier County, just three months after the Court of Appeals decision. None of the fees recorded in his regular accounts for August relates to the Hite v. Fairfax tenant litigation. Given this evidence, this list should have been dated *ca.* Aug. 1786–1791 and included in Vol. I. Because of its bearing on other litigation concerning the Fairfax proprietary, the editors have elected to include it in this volume, under its closing date, rather than to postpone its publication until the addendum volume.

While most of the cases listed in this document are also represented by litigation papers in the Clark-Hite Papers, The Filson Club, Louisville, Ky., there are JM cases in that depository not reflected on this list, and conversely there are cases on this list for which there are no manuscripts in the Clark-Hite Papers. Some of the Clark-Hite Papers relating to these cases have been calendared in Vol. I; those inadvertently omitted will be included in the addendum volume. Cases on this list that have material in the Clark-Hite Papers have been noted.

4. The evidence indicates that these cases were consolidated for purposes of argu-

ham Neale.[6] Neale has paid but	9	17	
one Guinea of this	1	8	
Abraham Neal (relinquishd	2	16	
James Leith (100 acres of this in name of Josiah)[7]	1	8	
Jeremiah Whitson[8]	1	8	
Ebenezer Leith	1	8	
John Yates	1	8	
Edward Snickers, Joseph Anderson, Cornelius Anderson, Jasper Ball, Thomas Shepherd[9]	3	12	
Francis Stribling, John Milton[1]	1	16	
Wm. Booth, Wm. Taylor & John Milton[2]		19	4
Lancelot Lee[3]	2	12	
Jonathan Odle & Samuel,[4] Jonathan proprietor	1	8	
From Fort tract[5]	3	8	
	8	12	
	46	18	
James Odle	1	8	
Genl. G. Washington	1	4	

ment and decision. Extant records indicate that all the decrees of the High Court of Chancery were entered on Aug. 5, 1790, and that most appeals were decided by the Court of Appeals on Nov. 14, 1791. The large number of clients, and JM's apparent willingness to accept fees from individuals rather than groups of petitioners, may have complicated his bookkeeping sufficiently to require this separate account. At least five fees pertaining to this litigation appear in the general accounts, however. See Stribling v. Hite, Vol. I, 406; and Account Book, Receipts, Browning v. Hite, Nov. 11, 1788, Strother v. Hite, Aug. 13, 1789, Washington v. Hite, May 1790, and Stroude v. Hite, Sept. 1792.

5. See Stroude v. Hite, Account Book, Receipts, Sept. 1792.

6. See f. 105, Clark-Hite Papers, Filson Club, for this group of seven clients. Godwin Swift served on the Berkeley County Court from 1773 through 1776 and was still residing in the county in 1792. Gen. William Darke (1736–1801) had served in the Virginia ratifying convention in 1788 and represented Berkeley County in the House of Delegates in 1791. He was later elected a brigadier general at the same time as JM.

7. See Vol. I, 190–191, and additional papers concerning a large tract of land, in f. 105, Clark-Hite Papers, Filson Club.

8. See f. 163, Clark-Hite Papers, Filson Club.

9. See f. 166, ibid., for this group of five clients. Snickers (d. 1791), of Frederick County, was a wealthy merchant. Shepherd was the Thomas Shepherd who founded Shepherdstown, now in West Virginia.

1. See f. 141, ibid., for these two clients.

2. See Vol. I, 192, for these three clients.

3. Lee was a complainant with Walter Clarke, William Grubb, Owen Thomas and Thornton Washington (b. ca. 1760), a nephew of George Washington. See f. 142, Clark-Hite Papers, Filson Club.

4. See f. 105, ibid., for these two clients.

5. Perhaps a reference to Powell's Fort. See Vol. I, 190.

	John A. Washington[6]	I	4
	John Overall, Abraham Keller & Henry Netherton[7]	2	16
	Edmund Clair[8]	I	10
	Mary Clevinger Exx. etc.[9]	I	8
	Humphry Keys	2	16
	Walter Cuninghame[1]	I	
	John & Thomas Lindsay, Albion Throckmorton.[2] no fee paid by A.T.	2	16
	Robert Bull, John Grantham, Nicholas Schull, Simeon Hiat[3]	4	16
	[Coutts] Survey:		
	Simeon Hiatt, George Cloke, John Daniel, John Rees jr. & Adam Livingston[4]		
	Wm. Leman & John Leman, Nicholas & Edward Mercer	5	
	Wm. Morgan & Vandever		
	From Denton & Cockenour[5]	2	16
	Mr. Harrison	3	16
		36	4
	Warner Washington[6] £	I	8
	Mr. Washington jr.[7]	I	8
87/	From Odle	5	2
99	From Layman	I	8
	From Spigle (part of Dentons tract)	I	8
	Mr. Yates	I	16
May 90	Lanncelott Lee	4	10
	Leman	2	10
	Harrison	2	8
		20	2
	Washington[8]	6	
		26	2

6. See *ibid.*, 192.
7. See ff. 105, 162, Clark-Hite Papers, Filson Club, for these three clients.
8. See Vol. I, 191.
9. See f. 141, Clark-Hite Papers, Filson Club.
1. See f. 144, *ibid.*
2. See Vol. I, 191, for these three clients.
3. See f. 139, Clark-Hite Papers, Filson Club, for these four clients.
4. See Vol. I, 192, for these five clients.
5. See *ibid.*, 189, for these two clients.
6. See *ibid.*, 191.
7. Warner Washington, Jr., was a co-complainant with Edward Snickers and his associates.
8. See JM to Corbin Washington, Aug. 23, 1789, and Account Book, Receipts, May 1790.

		36	4
		46	18
		109	4
Augt. 90	E Leith	2	8
	J. Leith	2	8
Sep.	Odel	5	
	Walter Cuninghame (appeal)	5	12
	E. Leith	2	12
	Mr. Hoop[9]	3	
No. 91	Jeremiah Whitson[1]	4	4
	Leman v Hite	6	18

Opinion

Printed, *Opinion of Judge Marshall, in Relation to the Potomac Company; and Agreement by the Potomac Company with General Henry Lee* . . . (Georgetown, D.C., 1817), 3–4[2]

[Richmond], January 31, 1792

I HAVE read and considered the act for opening and extending the navigation of Potomac River.[3] Upon the 11th and 12th sections thereof a question arises, whether lands may be condemned of the width of one hundred and fifty feet, or an acre, at the places of receiving tolls, after the Canal shall have been cut? The 11th section, which relates to the condemnation of land through which the Canal is to be cut, speaks entirely upon the idea that the procedure will be had before the Canal shall be cut. "It shall be lawful to agree with the owners of any land through which the *said Canal is intended to pass.*" In the oath to be administered the juryman swears that he will value the damage the party shall sustain by cutting the said Canal.[4] This is a mode of expression which would arise

9. John Hoop, who was joined in a case with Solomon Matthews. See f. 105, Clark-Hite Papers, Filson Club.

1. Papers relating to Whitson's appeal are in f. 173, *ibid.*

2. The lands involved were the private property of Henry Lee, who was governor of Virginia at this time. Corra Bacon-Foster, "Early Chapters in the Development of the Potomac Route to the West," *Records of the Columbia Historical Society*, XV (Washington, D.C., 1912), 175, 178.

JM's opinion is the only item printed in this pamphlet. The reference to the agreement with Lee is unclear.

3. 11 Hening 510–525 (1784).

4. For the juror's oath, see *ibid.*, 520. Sec. 11 also provides for a later application by the landowner for additional damages "in consequence of the opening of the canal." *Ibid.*, 520–521. Based upon this terminology, JM correctly asserted that the legislative intent was to authorize condemnation of lands only before the construction of the canal.

from the nature of the case, because it would be readily supposed that the Company would ever secure the lands before they cut the Canal. It is true that this expression is by no means decisive; but although the work be of great public utility, yet I conceive that any law which is to wrest from an individual his property without his consent must be construed strictly, and rather narrowed than enlarged.[5] If the clause under consideration meets with that construction, (and on legal principles I think it ought) the land on the sides of the Canal cannot be condemned after the Canal shall be cut.

On the 12th section no doubt arises. There is nothing in the expression of the act or in the nature of the thing to restrain the directors to any point of time. The power given then may therefore be exercised even after the Canal shall have been completed.

If the President and Directors persist in endeavoring to condemn land through which the Canal has passed[6] it will be proper to forbid them to proceed, and if they do so they may be sued as trespassers, and ejectment may be maintained for the land itself if they exercise any act of ownership over it, or if the proprietor chuses to consider himself as dissiezed.

J. MARSHALL.

Receipt

DS, Vol. 1110A, RG 53, National Archives

[*February 8, 1792, Richmond*. JM, for Charles Marshall, signs a receipt of John Hopkins, U.S. commissioner of loans for Virginia, for $1,403.27 in certificates of assumed debt.]

5. Blackstone asserted that even the rights of the community would not justify the taking of private property but that the legislature might "oblige the owner to alienate his possessions for a reasonable price; and even this is an exertion of power, which the legislature can perform." Blackstone, *Commentaries*, I, 135. For an analysis of JM's views on private property, see Robert Kenneth Faulkner, *The Jurisprudence of John Marshall* (Princeton, N.J., 1968), 20–33. JM's statement here indicates he thought either that the acquisition of property by eminent domain was quasi-criminal in nature or that the statute authorizing the acquisition was in derogation of the common law; in either instance it was his view that the statute should have been strictly construed.

6. Under the authority of sec. 11 of the act.

Receipt

DS, Vol. 1110A, RG 53, National Archives

Richmond, February 10, 1792
No. 88   COMMISSIONER'S-OFFICE,
STATE OF VIRGINIA,
RECEIVED of *John Hopkins*, Commissioner of Loans in the State of VIRGINIA, the following Certificates of Funded Debt, viz.[7]

One Certificate, bearing Interest at 6 per cent. per annum, from the first day of January, 1792, payable quarter yearly, and redeemable by payments not exceeding in one year the proportion of eight Dollars upon a hundred, on account of Principal and Interest.   3,174.33

One Certificate, bearing the like Interest from January 1st, 1801, and subject to be redeemed in like manner.   1,587.16

One Certificate, bearing Interest at 3 per cent. per annum, from the first day of January, 1792, payable quarter yearly, and redeemable at the pleasure of the United States.   2,380.75

DOLLARS. 7,142.24

Amounting in the whole to Seven Thousand One hundred & forty two Dollars & 24 Cents being in full of the Certificates of Debt due by the State of VIRGINIA, contained in a statement of this date (No. 88) for which I have signed duplicate Receipts.

J MARSHALL

7. On July 26, 1790, the House of Representatives approved a plan for the federal assumption of the state debts. "An act making provision for the (payment of the) Debt of the United States," of which assumption was part, became law on Aug. 4, 1790. The law stated that holders of state certificates could exchange them before Sept. 30, 1791 (later extended to Mar. 1, 1793), for new federal stock or, more specifically, could subscribe state certificates toward a loan to the United States and receive federal stock in return. Of the total sum subscribed, new federal stock certificates were issued at a rate of four-fifths in stock bearing 6% interest, two-ninths in stock bearing 6% interest, but on which the payment of interest was deferred until Jan. 1, 1801, and the remaining one-third in stock bearing 3% interest. The interest and principal on the state securities was computed to the end of 1791, and interest on the total was paid by the United States starting Jan. 1, 1792. 1 Stat. 138–144 (1790), 281–283 (1792); E. James Ferguson, *The Power of the Purse: A History of American Public Finance, 1776–1790* (Chapel Hill, N.C., 1961), 306–325.

The register for "Subscriptions in Certificates of debt due by the State of Virginia

Birth and Death of John James Marshall

Entry, Marshall Family Bible, Collection of Mrs. Kenneth R. Higgins, Richmond

[*February 13–June 10, 1792 (Richmond)*. Notations in JM's hand indicate that his son John James Marshall was born on Feb. 13 and died on June 10. See Account Book, Disbursements, Feb. and Aug. 1792.]

Orandorf v. Welch's Administrators

Petition of Appeal

AD, University of Virginia Law Library

[*February 18, 1792, Richmond*. JM files a petition of appeal on behalf of Christian Orandorf in the High Court of Chancery, requesting issuance of supersedeas and appellate review of a decree entered in Berkeley County Court. The petition asserts that the complainant's property was taken without notice by the court and that the court set aside a firm contract in the complainant's favor without notice to him. In addition, the decree does not require the complainant there to post a bond in the event the nonresident defendant appears and subsequently sets aside the county court's decree. The petition, entirely in JM's hand, is endorsed by Chancellor George Wythe to award the supersedeas upon the posting of an appeal bond by JM's client. A clerk's endorsement on the document indicates that the matter was continued until Sept. 1792, when an answer

---

towards a Loan to the United States" is detailed and complete, showing both current and original holders of state certificates. From this register it is known exactly which certificates JM exchanged for new federal stocks. By 1790, like many other holders of state certificates, JM was not the original holder of any of the certificates he subscribed. On Aug. 15, 1791, JM "in trust for Wm. Moore of Kentacky" subscribed two military certificates totaling £151 5s. 6d. Vol. 1108, RG 53, National Archives. (JM also received Lt. William Moore's balance of back pay on that date. Record Book, War 4, Virginia State Library.) The rest of the military certificates, totaling £1,861 11s. 2d., were subscribed by JM on Sept. 30, 1791, and included £1,119 16s. 4d. in certificates originally held by Thomas Marshall. It is not known if any of these latter certificates were subscribed in trust. After interest was calculated (£129 16s. 10d.), the total was rendered into a dollar value of $7,142.24. Vols. 1111 and 1113, RG 53, Natl. Arch. It is unclear what JM did with any state certificates issued in his own name, although he transferred one certificate for £75 1s., dated Dec. 10, 1784, to William Griffin. Vol. 1113, *ibid*.

For a history of the interest payments on, and transfer of, JM's holdings in federal stocks, see Receipts, July 4, and Oct. 10, 1792, and Sept. 30, and Oct. 3, 1793. By Nov. 30, 1793, JM had transferred his entire account of federal stock to his brother James Markham Marshall.

was filed and a general commission to take testimony was awarded. See Receipt, calendared at May 13, 1795, and Account Book, Receipts, May 21, 1790, Feb. 1792, and May 1795.]

Law Papers, February 1792

U.S. Circuit Court, Va.

Dobson and Daltera v. Fowler, answer, AD, U.S. Circuit Court, Va., Ended Cases (Restored), 1798, Virginia State Library.[8]

Donald, Scot & Co. v. Trevillian's Executor, answer, AD, U.S. Circuit Court, Va., Ended Cases (Unrestored), Va. State Lib.

Official Bond

DS, Executive Papers, Virginia State Library

[*March 17, 1792, Richmond.* JM, Harry Heth, William Foushee, and Daniel L. Hylton provide bond of £20,000 to Gov. Henry Lee upon the appointment of Heth as agent of the sinking fund. Daniel Call witnesses JM's signature.[9]]

8. See JM to William Marshall, *ca.* May 1792.
9. Heth (d. 1821) was a prosperous Chesterfield County landowner who counted among his property the Blackheath Coal Mines. He was also a partner in Nicolson, Heth & Co. in Richmond. He had acted earlier as special agent to dispose of the to-bacco paid the state as taxes in lieu of money, but in Nov. 1791 he asked the state to dissolve his agency. When Anthony Singleton (1750–1795) resigned as agent of the sinking fund, Heth was appointed by the Council of State on Mar. 14, 1792. JVCS, Jan. 24, 1789, Oct. 20, 1791, Mar. 14 and 21, 1792; *CVSP,* IV, 549–550, 552, V, 403, 418–419.
The sinking fund had been established in 1787 to provide funds to help retire the public debt. The fund was abolished in Dec. 1792. 12 Hening 452–454; 13 Hening 253, 525; E. James Ferguson, *The Power of the Purse: A History of American Public Finance, 1776–1790* (Chapel Hill, N.C., 1961), 223–224, 233.
Daniel Call (1765–1840), a Richmond attorney, married JM's sister-in-law Lucy Nelson Ambler (1776–1797) and later published *Reports of Cases Argued and Decided in the Court of Appeals of Virginia* (Richmond, 1801–1833), 6 vols.

To William Watts

ALS, Irvine-Saunders Collection, University of Virginia Library

Dear Sir   [Richmond, *ca*. March 1792]
   I receivd your letter by Mr. Scott. I have requested him to go
by Petersburg[10] & take out the subpoenas agreeably to your memorandum. If I can possibly attend the court I will for the purpose
of trying your cause. If I cannot attend I will engage Mr. Call[11]
to do the business for me. In the case of Wright & Baine I have
given an opinion formerly. The statement varied somewhat from
yours & I think upon that statement I was of opinion that there
had been an irregularity in the proceedings for which it was possible the decree might be opend but I am not sure that this was the
opinion I gave. I am very respectfully, Your obedt.

                                                    J MARSHALL

Opinion

Copy, Massie Family Papers, Virginia Historical Society[1]

                                       [Richmond, *ca*. March 1792]
   [Will.] "I Thomas Adams[2] of the Calf Pasture and County of Augusta
being About to take a perilous Journey to the Ohio River and being in my
perfect senses do make and ordain this my Last will and testament hereby
Revoking all others heretofore By me made Imprimis. It is my will and
desire that all my Just Debts be paid. I Give to my Dear wife Elizabeth[3]
the use of all my Slaves not hereafter particularly Disposed of with all my
Lands in Augusta and Amherst with the use of the Stocks thereon for an
during her natural Life in full Satisfaction Of her Dower and every Claim
She may have Agst. my Estate. I Give and bequeath to my Dear and only

   10. Watts's litigation was before the District Court at Petersburg.
   11. Daniel Call.
   1. This is item no. MssiM3855a5502–5503 in the society's collections. The will is
from Will Book, VI, 1778–1787, Augusta County, Virginia State Library.
   2. Adams (*ca*. 1730–1788), former clerk of Henrico County and former member of
the Continental Congress, moved to Augusta County about 1784 and served in the
House of Delegates from that county from 1784 until his death.
   3. Adams married Elizabeth Fauntleroy Cocke (1736–1792), the widow of his first
cousin, Bowler Cocke, Jr. There were no children of her second marriage, although
Elizabeth Adams had two children by her first husband.

Brother Richard Adams[4] after the Death of my wife all my Lands devised to my wife in the Counties of Augusta And Amherst Subject to the payment of my Debts in Exoneration of my Slaves. I Give and bequeath all my Locations of Lands on the western waters to my nephew William Adams Fry and William Smith a Son of my highly esteemed and much Lamented Nephew William Smith[5] Lately of the County of Essex deceased to Be equally Divided between them to hold to them And their heirs as tenants in Common and not as Joint tenants. Also after the Death of my wife I Give each of them One third of my Slaves the other third I Give to my Nephew William Adams[6] to them Respectively and their heirs and hope and trust they will Ever treat them with that kindness and humanity to which they have been Accustomed and not sell or barter them away as Cattle.

I Give and bequeath unto my honorable freind John Blair Esqr. Chancellor all the Lands he purchased of me in Arlbemarle County known by the name of the mountain Plains And for which he has Long since honestly paid me to him & his heirs forever. I Give to Ralph Wanlass[7] and his heirs the Lands and plantation whereon he now Lives Subject to be a house and home to his Mother during her Life In Case her necessity Should hereafter require it. After the Death of my dear wife I Give to my Neice Tabitha Epps[8] my Negroe Cooper Lemon. As there is no man whom I Consider myself under Greater Obligations than to my Slave Joe I hereby declare Joe a freeman And Give him full & Compleat Emancipation. Lastly I Constitute and appoint my worthy freind Majr. Thos. Massie[9] of Frederick And My Nephews William Adams and William Adams Fry Executors of this my Last will and testament written with my own hand and Signed & sealed with ⟨my⟩ own hand and Seal this fourteenth day of October in the year of our Lord 1785.

THOS. ADAMS (LS)

At a Court held for Augusta County Octr. 22nd. 1788.

This Last Will and testament of Thomas Adams deceased was presented in Court by Thomas And William Adams Fry Executors therein named

4. Adams (1726–1800), of Church Hill in Richmond, served in the House of Delegates from 1776 to 1778 and the Virginia senate from 1779 to 1782. He is referred to as "Col. Adams" in JM's opinion.

5. Fry was the son of Sarah Adams and John Fry of Albemarle County; William Smith was a grandson of Anne Adams (*ca.* 1731–1775), sister of Richard and Thomas Adams, and Col. Francis Smith (d. 1762), of Essex County.

6. Adams (1764–1787) was a son of Richard Adams.

7. Wanless (b. *ca.* 1757) was a long-time resident of Augusta County who had served in the county militia during the Revolution.

8. Mrs. Tabitha Eppes (b. 1728), the older sister of Thomas Adams, married Richard Eppes. The Tabitha Eppes mentioned here is presumably a daughter of that marriage.

9. Maj. Thomas Massie (1747–1834) married Sarah Cocke, Mrs. Elizabeth Adams's daughter, in 1780.

(the other executor being deceased) was proved by the Oaths of Thomas Hughart[1] and Archibald Stuart Esquires to be wholly in the hand writing of the testator And ordered to be recorded And on the Motion of the said Executors who made oath According to Law Certificate is Granted them for obtaining probat thereof in due form They having with Thomas Hughart and Archibald Stuart Esquires their Securities entered into bond in ten thousand pounds Conditioned as the Law directs

Teste J Lyle jr DC"

Queries on the Will of Thos. Adams decd.[2]

1st. Can the profits arising from the estate bequeathed to Mrs. Adams (while she enjoyed the sd. estate agreeable to the will) be considered as subject to the payment of the testators debts. If subject, in what case, and how ought the exr. of Mr. Adams, to proceed in order to make the estate which Mrs. Adams died seised of in fee, liable for the sd. profits?

2d. Whether the lands devised to Richd. Adams are subject to the payment of the debts in exoneration of the whole personal estate, or slaves only?

3d. Does it not appear to be the desire & intention of the testator to prevent the sale of the slaves, (in giving Richd. Adams the lands in exoneration of them) when we advert to the latter part of the clause in the will, that disposes of the slaves. Where the testator expresses his hopes, and seems to place a confidence in the legatees, that they will treat the slaves with the same kindness & humanity which they had received from him and not sell or barter them like cattle; and as there is a british debt far exceeding the amt. of the personal estate (exclusive of the slaves) Whether the exr. ought not to have power to proceed to immediate sale of the lands appointd by the testator to exonerate the slaves, or to hold the sd. lands as assets, or whether Richd. Adams can take possession, unless he does it under certain restrictions, and what those restrictions ought to be?

4th. The amount of claims against the estate neither foreign nor domestic, being ascertaind, & several considerable ones of the lat-

1. Thomas Hughart was sheriff of Augusta County in 1790 and later served as a justice of the county court.
2. The queries and answers are in an unknown hand. The document is undated; however, in Mar. 1792 JM received a fee of £1 8s. for advice "on Mr. T. Adams' Will." This fact, coupled with the evidence in the opinion that it was requested subsequent to the death of Elizabeth Adams (1792), leads to the editorial assumption that the opinion was prepared in Mar. 1792 or shortly thereafter. See Account Book, Receipts, Mar. 1792.

ter kind being at this time in litigation. Whether the exr. should proceed to a distribution of the slaves etc. as early as possible, the heirs and legatees being in a dispersed situation and some of them infants, in what manner is a division to be effected and how are the slaves to be disposed of in the mean time?

5th. If it is necessary that the exr. should hold the slaves till the debts are paid, can the hire of them (while held by him) be applied to the payment of the debts in exoneration of the slaves, or must the fund which the testator appoints in the will for their exoneration be exhausted, before the slaves or their hire can be charged with any part of the debts.

Should the fund named in the will be sufficient to pay all the debts, the hire of the slaves (while held by the exr.) will I presume, be divided among the legatees of the slaves?

6th. Has Miss Eppes, a fee simple, or life estate in Lemon?

Answers to the queries on the Will of Thos. Adam decd.

1st. From the manner in which the question is stated I presume Mrs Adams to be dead. The property bequeathed to her is certainly subject to the payment of the debts of the estate & the exr. if now possessd of it ought not to part with it, until a sufficient fund for the payment of the debts is secured. If the estate is not in possession of the exr. he will find a difficulty in acquiring it because he will be considered as having assented to the legacy. If any creditor would bring suit agnst. the exr. & legatees it would be the most certain mean of subjecting that estate, if no creditor will do so, & Mr. Smith the legatee refuses to deliver them up the exr must sue for them.

2d. I think the land devised to Colo Adams can only be applied to the payment of the debts in exoneration of the slaves. The exr. can not sell those lands, nor has he any thing to do with them. Colo Adams may if he pleases take immediate possession.[3]

---

3. The normal course of administration required that a testator's personal property constituted the primary fund for the settlement of his debts and the payment of legacies under the will. Should the debts exceed the assets in the executor's hands, the creditor might proceed against the testator's realty, either in the hands of his devisee or in the hands of his heir at law. It was the law in Virginia and in England, however, that a testator might, by clear expression of intent in his will, provide that his unencumbered real property might be sold in exoneration of debts, so as to permit his personal property to pass as designated in the will, independent of debts that were not a lien on the land, other legacies or charges, or both. JM's opinion here indicates that the testator's intentions should be given effect only so far as they specifically refer to the slaves. See Henry Swinburne, *A Treatise of Testaments and Last Wills* . . . , 5th ed. (London, 1728), 28, 29; William Nelson, *Lex Testamentaria* . . . (London, 1724), 98, 526; John

After the personal estate shall be exhaustd in payment of the debts, it is the duty of Colo Adams, either to sell the lands or pay the debts so far as may be necessary to exonerate the slaves. Shd. the personal estate & the lands be insufficient to exonerate the slaves Colo Adams will be liable for the rents of the lands while he holds them. He may be compeld to do so by a suit in Chanery brought either by a creditor, or by the legatees of the slaves.[4]

In the mean time the slaves are liable to creditors & therefore the exr. must not part with them. But if any of them shd. be sold for the payment of the debts, the legatees will have a right to come upon the land for them.

3. If the exr. proceeds to make distribution of the slaves, which I think he ought not to do, he must take bond & security from the legatees, to refund if it shd. be necessary for the payment of the debts.

Till a distribution they ought to be hired out, unless there are lands on which they may be workd to advantage. I presume Colo Adams wd. make no objection to their working the lands devised to him. But this would produce a difficulty in dividing the Crops. I am inclined to think the most eligible plan would be to hire them out.

4th. Miss Eppes has an absolute estate in Lemon.

J MARSHALL

Law Papers, April 1792

U.S. Circuit Court, Va.

Hanson v. Cowper, answer, AD, U.S. Circuit Court, Va., Ended Cases (Restored), 1794, Virginia State Library.[5]

T. Lomax, *A Treatise of the Law of Executors and Administrators*, 2d ed. (Richmond, 1857), II, 405, 408; Sir Samuel Toller, *The Law of Executors and Administrators*, 4th Am. ed. (Philadelphia, 1834), 415–418; and Thomas E. Atkinson, *Handbook of the Law of Wills and Other Principles of Succession* . . . , 2d ed. (St. Paul, Minn., 1953), 764–766.

Col. Richard Adams, as remainderman after the life estate of Elizabeth Adams, succeeded to the title in fee upon her death. Consequently, the only interest of the executor of Thomas Adams's estate was to have a right to bring a bill in equity to compel the sale of the land and the application of the proceeds in exoneration of debts otherwise chargeable against the slaves.

4. On the death of the life tenant, the lands and any increase in their value would pass on to the remainderman, Richard Adams. See Carter v. Webb, Jefferson (Va.) 123–132 (1772). He held the lands, however, subject to the charge under the will to exonerate the personal property of the testator in the slaves.

5. See Wills Cowper to JM, Nov. 21, 1793.

To William Marshall

ALS, U.S. Circuit Court, Va., Ended Cases (Restored), 1798, Virginia State Library

Dear Brother   [Richmond, *ca.* May 1792]
  If you are satisfied that the above is the signature of Mr. John Fowler & I beleive it is you will be authorized by it to deliver the certificates & file the order.[6] Your

J MARSHALL

Law Papers, May 1792

U.S. Circuit Court, Va.

Banks v. McCall and Shedden, bill in chancery, AD, U.S. Circuit Court, Va., Ended Cases (Restored), 1792, Virginia State Library.

Buchanan, Hastie & Co. v. Sullivant, answer, AD, U.S. Circuit Court, Va., Ended Cases (Restored), 1794, Va. State Lib.

Hill and Bryan v. Pearson, motion in arrest of judgment, AD, U.S. Circuit Court, Va., Ended Cases (Restored), 1792, Va. State Lib.

Hunter, Banks & Co. v. Sargeant and Constable, stipulation, ADS, U.S. Circuit Court, Va., Ended Cases (Restored), 1801, Va. State Lib.[7]

6. This letter is filed with the case papers of Dobson and Daltera v. Fowler and is related to the order of the court to take depositions. The suit was a British debt case in which JM represented Fowler. The U.S. Circuit Court ordered depositions taken in England on May 25, 1792. The case was then revived after the death of the plaintiff in 1797, and judgment was entered for the plaintiff on Nov. 27, 1798. U.S. Circuit Court, Va., Order Book, I, 96, III, 1, 123, Virginia State Library. See JM's answer in this case listed at Law Papers, Feb. 1792, and fee in Account Book, Receipts, May 1793.
  Documents in the U.S. Circuit Court, Va., Ended Cases, Va. State Lib., indicate that William Marshall was clerk of that court as early as June 3, 1790, and it is likely he was appointed in 1789. He signed the front of the court's Order Book, II, as clerk in 1795. Beveridge incorrectly states that he was appointed while JM was secretary of state. Albert J. Beveridge, *The Life of John Marshall* (Boston, 1919), III, 191, n. 1. This is the only known extant letter of JM to this brother.
  7. See JM to William Constable, July 11, 1789.

Petition

DS, Virginia Historical Society[8]

[Richmond, *ca.* July 1, 1792]

To The President and Directors of the Bank of the United States.

The Memorial of the Merchants and other Inhabitants of the City of Richmond, Town of Manchester & places adjacent in the State of Virginia, Most respectfully sheweth

That they conceive the establishment of a Branch of the Bank of the United States at the City of Richmond would be productive of reciprocal Advantage to the Stock Holders of the said Bank and to your Memorialists—For the following reasons

1stly. Because Richmond is the Capital of the State the place of greatest resort and the most centrical situation for Trade within the same, having also a direct communication within two days by means of Publick and private Posts with all the commercial towns in the State and more especially because the Payments are there made of the whole revenues of the State, as well as the Payments of Interest on the Loaned Debt of the United States; all of which Payments would probably be negociated through the Medium of a Branch of the Bank if it should be established there.

2ndly Because the Trade of Richmond and Manchester is very considerable, and both of these places being situated at the Falls of James River and supported by an extensive fertile and improving Back Country, may be expected rapidly to encrease, their Exports are already great, particularly in the Articles of Tobacco, Wheat, Flour, Indian Corn, Hemp and Coal, great part of which are purchased and paid for in Cash in consequence of orders from Europe, as well as from the middle, and Eastern States. From Richmond and Manchester (including places above the Falls which are naturally connected with them) about 20,000 Hhds. of Tobacco are annually exported which may be moderately estimated at 35 Dollars per Hhd. on an Average, above 300,000 Bushels of Wheat worth at least ¾ ths. of a dollar Per Bushel, considerable quantitys of Flour, Indian Corn, Hemp & Coal besides Articles of lesser Value Amountg. in the whole nearly to One Million, Two Hundred thousand Dollars. The Article of Tobacco which is the most Valuable production of the Country for Exportation and can always be

8. This is item no. Mss4R414a3 in the society's collections.

sold for Cash near to its Value, is subjected to the Inspection Laws of the State under strict regulations. The Notes of the Inspectors are considered by the Purchasers as a sufficient Security for the delivery of the Tobacco and the faith of the State is pledged by Law to reimburse any Losses occasiond by Fire in the Publick Ware Houses where the same must be deposited. These Notes would therefore furnish a peculiar and safe Subject of Security as a deposit for discount in addition to what is usually expected or required.

3dly. Because great convenience would arise from such an establishment to other places in the State, especially to Petersburg which has much commercial connexion and intercourse with Richmond & Manchester from which it is only distant 25 Miles, and which also carries on a very considerable Trade; also to the Port of Norfolk distant 110 Miles, and which has an easy communication both by Land and Water with the Capital as well as to Sundry other Towns on James, York and Rappahanock Rivers, the Commerce of which taken collectively extends over the greatest part of Virginia and comprehends a great part of the Trade of North Carolina.

4thly. Because a Scheme is now in agitation for the establishment of a State Bank in the said City[9] for which there would be no necessity if the measure now suggested should take place. And because this Measure would tend to Promote the Agricultural as well as the Commercial interest of the Country and to extend the bene-

9. After the Bank of the United States was chartered in Feb. 1791, stockholders outside Pennsylvania were determined that branches be established in their states. Opposition to the bank was strong in Virginia, however, and in December merchants in the Richmond area called a meeting for May 1, 1792, to consider petitioning the General Assembly to establish a state bank in the city. JM attended that December meeting. Whether the May meeting took place is not known, but by June it had become clear to Secretary of the Treasury Alexander Hamilton (1757–1804), at least, that a branch of the Bank of the United States would be approved for Richmond.

One of the signers of this petition, William Heth, had corresponded since Feb. 1792 with Hamilton on the relative merits of placing the branch in Richmond, Petersburg, or Norfolk. As late as June 28, Heth wrote Hamilton from Bermuda Hundred expressing his reasoned belief that Richmond should be preferred, although he had positive comments on other localities. It seems certain that had Heth signed this petition prior to writing Hamilton, he would have mentioned it. The editors therefore conclude that this petition was adopted between June 28 and July 10, when the directors of the bank authorized a branch to be located in Richmond. James O. Wettereau, "The Branches of the First Bank of the United States," supplement to *Journal of Economic History*, II (1942), 71–79; *Virginia Gazette, and General Advertiser* (Richmond), Dec. 7, 1791; and Harold C. Syrett *et al.*, eds., *The Papers of Alexander Hamilton* (New York, 1961–), XI, 49–50, 493–494, 584–588, XIII, 83–85. For information on JM's involvement with banking, see Bank Subscription Notice, Jan. 24, 1793.

ficial influence and promote the Wellfare of the General Government of the United States.

5thly. Because the Bills of the Bank of the United States do not pass at the said places at their proper Value being purchased by Brokers and other persons at a discount of One to Two Per Cent.

For all which reasons Your Memorialists respectfully request that you will take the Premisses into consideration and they hope that You will find it expedient to establish a Branch of the National Bank at Richmond under Proper regulations and restrictions.

J MARSHALL[1]

Opinion

ADS, Papers of John Norton & Sons, Colonial Williamsburg Foundation Research Archives

Richmond, July 2, 1792

[1782 Deed.] "KNOW ALL MEN by these preasents that I Mary Thruston of Norfolk County & Borough of Norfolk do by this Indenture made the first Day of June in the Year of our Lord Christ One Thousand Seven hundred & Eighty Two, give unto my nephew Charles Mynn Thruston, eldest Son of my Brother John Thruston, Deceased, late of Gloucester County & Town, in consideration of my great affection toward them, as well as of that Justice & Equity, which give him the said Charles Mynn Thruston, an equal claim to the property of his late Grandfather, to the bequeathed as any other person living can have, & because more than a Moiety of the Estate left by his said Grandfather Edward Thruston decd: has been given to other branches of his decendents, For these reasons, & in consideration also of Five Shillings current Money in hand paid, I do give & hereby convey all my right property, Interest & claim, in & to a Tract of Land called & known by the Name of Lintons, containing by estimation One hundred & fifty Acres be the same more or less, to him the said Charles Mynn Thruston to have & to hold (of Frederick Co) & his Heirs & Assigns for ever: Reserving to myself however, the Sole Use, rents profits & Emoluments thereof, for & during the term of my natural life & no longer, & of the aforesaid Tract of Land lying & being on Indian Creek, & bequeathed to me by the last will & testament of Edward Thruston decd: I confirm unto the said Charles Mynn Thruston his heirs & Assigns for ever the rights, the reversion & reversions, remainder & remainders, rents Issues & profits, reserving to myself as aforesaid, & for Divers other causes me thereunto moving, & in consideration of five Shillings of like

---

1. JM and 125 other individuals or businesses signed the petition.

Money in hand paid. . . . Finally in consideration of my advanced Years, & inability to superintend the renting out of my Lands & negroes & collecting the rents, I here by constitute & appoint my nephew Aforesaid, Charles Mynn Thruston, & my Friend & Brother in Law Cornelious Calvert, as my Agents & Trustees, to conduct & manage the Same, for & during my natural Life, for my sole use, behoof, benefit, & maintenance they Conducting them in such manner that no waste be made hereof, In witness whereof I Mary Thruston have hereunto set my hand & affixed my seal, the Day & Year first above written."[2]

I have been shewn by Mr. Grymes a deed from Mary Thruston in which in consideration of blood & of 5/ she conveys to Colo. Thruston a tract of land reserving to herself the sole use of it for her life.[3] It is objected that this is not a good deed because a freehold estate cannot commence in future without a particular estate to support it.[4] I think the deed good either as a conveyance to take effect immediately declaring the use to herself during life & to the grantee afterwards or as a covenant to stand seizd to the uses of the deed.[5] If however, as the case is not free from doubt, Mr Norton[6] wishes to try the title before he sells the land, an ejectment may

2. The opinion is enclosed with the deed and is endorsed on the verso "J Marshalls opinion, abt. Norfolk Land."

3. JM's analysis of the deed, which formed the basis of his opinion, does not appear to be accurate. He did not consider the relationship of the last paragraph to the other sections of the deed, yet if that paragraph were construed to create trustees for the transfer of the Linton estate, there would have been no question that a valid active trust had been created, with a lifetime use to Mary Thruston and a conveyance in fee after her death to Charles Mynn Thruston. On the other hand, the appointment of trustees might easily have been construed as a general appointment in relation to all real and personal property remaining in Mary Thruston's possession after the transfer of Linton to Charles Mynn Thruston. Obviously the document was poorly drawn and was subject to a variety of conflicting constructions.

4. The estate in Charles Mynn Thruston might have been held to be a springing executory interest, which could not be created at common law without the interposition of trustees. Blackstone, *Commentaries*, II, 165–167; William F. Walsh, *A Treatise on the Law of Property*, 2d ed. (New York, 1927), 428–429, 435–436.

5. JM was suggesting that the document might be construed either as a bargain and sale deed, supported by the five-shilling consideration, or as a convenant to stand seized, supported by the love and affection between individuals closely related by blood or marriage. However, the deed is not in the customary form of either of these documents. In the convenant to stand seized, the grantor became the trustee to hold for the use of the grantee or grantees, and he himself might be included within the latter group. In this conveyance, however, the grantor appears to have conveyed title to the grantee, reserving a use for life to herself. See Emory Washburn, *A Treatise on the American Law of Real Property*, ed. Joseph Willard and Simon G. Croswell, 5th ed. (Boston, 1887), II, 450–451, III, 376; Herbert T. Tiffany, *The Law of Real Property*, ed. Basil Jones, 3d ed. (Chicago, 1939), I, 400; Walsh, *Law of Property*, 427–428.

6. Probably John Hatley Norton.

be brought & a case agreed immediately so as to leave to the court, the question concerning the validity of the deed.

J MARSHALL

Receipts

DS, Vol. 1193A, B, RG 53, National Archives

[*July 4, 1792, Richmond*. JM signs two receipts of John Hopkins, U.S. commissioner of loans for Virginia, each for $59.351 for interest due on one to Mar. 31, 1792, and on the other to June 30, 1792, both on $2,923.33 assumed 6 percent stock and $2,067.01 assumed 3 percent stock.[7]]

Death of Mary Ann Marshall

Entry, Marshall Family Bible, Collection of Mrs. Kenneth R. Higgins, Richmond

[*August 1, 1792 (Richmond)*. A notation in JM's hand indicates that his daughter Mary Ann Marshall (born Nov. 24, 1789), died on this day. See Account Book, Disbursements, Aug. 1792.]

Lottery Notice

Printed, *Virginia Gazette, and General Advertiser* (Richmond), August 15, 1792, 1

[*August 2, 1792, Richmond*. JM, as one of the managers, publishes notice of a lottery to raise £450 for construction of a stone bridge across Shockoe Creek[8] on Main Street leading toward Rocketts landing. Depending upon the sale of tickets, the drawing was tentatively set for Oct. 29.]

7. On Mar. 3, 1792, JM transferred $251.00 in 6% assumed stock and $313.74 in 3% assumed stock to John Hopkins for a new balance of $2,923.33 and $2,067.01 in 6% and 3% stock respectively. Vol. 1134, RG 53, National Archives. See Receipt, Feb. 10, 1792, for an explanation of JM's holdings in federal stock.

8. The Richmond City Common Hall had been attempting to raise funds to build such a bridge since 1783, soon after the 1782 General Assembly authorized a lottery for that purpose. In Mar. 1783 the corporation appointed managers of a lottery, but in Jan. 1784 it was decided to erect a temporary wooden bridge while arrangements to pay for a stone one could be devised. A new lottery was planned in 1791 and 1792, when the wooden bridge was beyond repair. In June 1792 JM was among those appointed to draw the lottery and to petition the legislature for financial aid. The lottery notice printed here was authorized on Aug. 1, 1792. In September the Common Hall ap-

To Benjamin Rush

ALS, Library Company Manuscripts, Historical Society of Pennsylvania

Sir[9]   Richmond, August 6, 1792

I immediately transmitted to Mr. Turnbull the letter I receivd from your self & the other gentlemen namd with you as commissioners for the enquiry directed by the chancellor into Mrs. Turnbull's case.[1] He[2] has just enabled me to answer it. He declines calling on you on this business. Permit me sir to add that your request of compensation appeard to me to be reasonable & the sum moderate. With very much respect, I am Sir your obedt.

JOHN MARSHALL

proved a petition to be sent to the General Assembly after the justices of the peace in Henrico County had joined in its support. The House of Delegates rejected the petition on Nov. 10. 11 Hening 157; Richmond City Common Hall Records, I, 28, 34, 35, 37, 52, 85, 86–87, 94, 247, 256, 257–258, 259–260, 263, 266–268, 271, 272, Virginia State Library; *JVHD*, Oct. 1792, 113.

Construction of the bridge continued to present problems. Bids were let in 1793, but there were no takers until Feb. 1794, when Thomas Whitelaw agreed to undertake the job. JM, as grand master of the Masons' Grand Lodge of Virginia, laid the foundation stone at a ceremony on June 13, 1795. *Virginia Gazette, and General Advertiser* (Richmond), Jan. 16, and Apr. 24, 1793; *Richmond Chronicle*, June 16, 1795; Common Hall Records, II, 11, 44, 47, Va. State Lib.

JM was one of 10 managers who signed the notice, among whom were William Foushee, Andrew Ronald, and Robert Gamble. Gamble (1754–1810) had moved to Richmond from Augusta County in 1790 and immediately rose to prominence as a successful merchant.

9. Rush (1745–1813), the Philadelphia physician, had been appointed one of the examiners of the defendant by Chancellor George Wythe.

JM addressed the letter to "Benjamin Rush esquire, Philadelphia," and on the address leaf in another hand appears "Mr Marshall's letter informing of Col. Turnbull's declining to pay £50 for going to Baltimore to examine his wife."

1. The Rush to JM letter has not been found.

Robert Turnbull, of Prince George County, was attempting to divorce Sarah Buchanan Turnbull, of Baltimore, whom he had married in Mar. 1790. Mr. Turnbull had apparently taken his case to the High Court of Chancery, claiming Mrs. Turnbull was unable to consummate the marriage. It appears that sometime after this letter was written, Chancellor George Wythe decreed that his court could provide no relief under statutory or common law. Mr. Turnbull thereupon petitioned the House of Delegates for authority to file a bill against his wife in the High Court of Chancery. Patrick Henry was retained by Mr. Turnbull, and JM represented his wife. "The strange & indelicate case," as it was described in a letter to James Madison, came before the House of Delegates on Nov. 22 and 23. The legislature granted Turnbull's petition and enacted a procedure by which the High Court of Chancery could void the marriage if the facts were proved. *JVHD*, Oct. 1792, 135, 138; 13 Hening 301–302; John Dawson to James Madison, Nov. 7, 1791, Madison Papers, Library of Congress.

JM planned to represent Sarah Turnbull before the High Court of Chancery in Mar. 1794. See JM to Charles Lee, Dec. 28, 1793, and Account Book, Receipts, Apr. 1792 and July 1793, for entries of fees received in this case.

2. Turnbull.

Receipt

ADS, Tucker-Coleman Papers, Swem Library, College of William and Mary

[*August 27, 1792 (Richmond)*. JM receipts for £15 paid to him by James Brown, of Richmond, at the direction of St. George Tucker.]

To John A. Chevallié

Facsimile, Bruce Gimelson, Auction Catalog (Fort Washington, Pa., March 4, 1972), 34

Dear Sir[3]   Richmond, September 14, 1792
    I have receivd your letter by Mr. Richards together with your statements of Mr. Beaumarchais claims. You may be assurd of my particular attention to them. The Assembly will meet on the first of October & I think it woud be adviseable for you to be here so as to have the petition[4] ready to present very early in the session. Very respectfully, I am Sir your obedt. Servt.

                                              J MARSHALL

To Francis Walker

Transcript, William Cabell Rives Papers, Library of Congress

My dear Sir,   [Richmond, September 20, 1792]
    I have attended the taking some affidavits in your case with Syme. They prove positively that your Father was not entitled to a moiety of New Castle but that it descended on Colo Syme's wife after the death of her father so that it never formed any part of her

---

3. Chevallié (1765–1838) came to Virginia in 1778 as an agent of Caron de Beaumarchais (1732–1799). After the Revolution he remained in the state and helped Beaumarchais press his claims against Virginia for articles furnished during the war. Chevallié settled in Richmond and formed a partnership with Joseph Gallego (1758–1818). Both men became prominent residents of Richmond.
    4. The General Assembly convened on Oct. 5. See Petition of John A. Chevallié, Oct. 5, 1792; and Account Book, Receipts, July 1792, and Mar. 1795.

father's estate.[5] If you can give me any information on this subject, do so. I wait for it. Your,

J MARSHALL.

Petition of John A. Chevallié

DS, Legislative Petitions: Richmond City, Virginia State Library

[Richmond], October 5, 1792

To the Honble. the speaker & members of the house of Delegates the petition of John A. Chevallie agent in America for Monsieur Carron de Beaumarchais of France humbly sheweth[6]

That impeled by a strong desire to be serviceable in establishing the independence of these United States, Mr. de Beaumarchais very early in the late contest between America & Britain formd the dangerous & expensive plan of furnishing congress with those articles which were indispensably necessary & which were scarcely attainable by this country. In the prosecution of this plan after several efforts had been made, the Fier Roderique, a vessel fitted for war at great expense & laden with a very valuable cargo designd for the American Congress arrivd at York town in Virginia in the month of June in the year 1778. The Virginia lines both continental & state were then greatly distressed for absolute necessaries not to be procurd in this country & which if to be found, their scanty pay coud not purchase. The arrival of the Fier Roderique with her very valuable cargo was considerd by the Government of Virginia as a circumstance too fortunate to be neglected & immediate propositions were made for its purchase. After some treaty a contract was made by which one of the most valuable cargoes imported into America through out the war, a cargo loudly calld for by a suffering army was deliverd to the Government of Virginia which became indebted therefor to Mr. de Beaumarchais. Several partial payments were made towards the discharge of this debt & at length when paper ceasd to circulate it was referd by the Government to the sollicitor to ascertain in specie the sum remain-

5. Francis Walker was Thomas Walker's son. See JM to Thomas Walker, July 9, 1789, for information on this case with John Syme. See also Vol. I, 240, 372, n. 69, and JM to Francis Walker, *ca.* Oct. 1792, and Feb. 23, 1793.
 JM meant "Castle Hill," the Walker estate.
6. The petition is in JM's hand, although Chevallié arrived in time to sign it. See JM to John A. Chevallié, Sept. 14, 1792.

ing due. This was done & provision from time to time has been made to lessen the sum reported due by the sollicitor.[7]

Your petitioner humbly states that the agent of Mr. de Beaumarchais when he enterd into the contract which is before stated relied confidently on the honor & justice of the government. Convinced of the great importance of his cargo to the army of this State, he did not fear that the benefit coud be forgotten or the service uncompensated. Your petitioner has still the most entire reliance on the justice of the Commonwealth & is persuaded that if he can prove to the Honble the Legislature that Mr. de Beaumarchais has been really injurd in the original settlement as well as in the modes of payment since adopted that your Honble. house will look back to those times of danger when his aid was all important & will not permit him to sustain a loss by having put his whole fortune in hazard for the service of these United States. Your petitioner therefore humbly prays that the case of Mr. de Beaumarchais may be taken into consideration, that his claims may be accurately investigated & that he may have such relief as in justice ought to be afforded him.[8]

And your petitioner will ever pray etc.

JOHN A CHEVALLIÉ

7. Beaumarchais's claim had been laid before the solicitor in 1784. The Council of State sent the solicitor's report to the General Assembly in Dec. 1784, and Beaumarchais was notified.

8. The petition was referred to a special committee on Oct. 6, 1792. After the committee reported its findings on Nov. 27, the House of Delegates considered the report in the Committee of the Whole House on Nov. 30. A resolution to accept the solicitor's report and pay in specie the balance due Beaumarchais was tabled. On Dec. 1 a resolution passed whereby the House agreed only to honor the balance due Beaumarchais. A committee was appointed to draft a bill to that effect, but no bill was introduced before the session adjourned. Subsequent petitions in 1793 and 1794 were tabled. *JVCS*, III, 401, 406, 462, 506, 535; *JVHD*, Oct. 1792, 18, 144, 146, 155, 157, Oct. 1793, 8, 53, 93, Nov. 1794, 6.

Beaumarchais's claims against Virginia were plentiful, and the state made payments to him throughout the 1780s. From time to time, however, he contested the method of payment or the amount agreed on by the solicitor or state's auditor. Most of his complaints were caused by the enormous depreciation in currency, which had the effect of erasing his profits. By the time the state made a payment on a 1778 contract, for example, the value of the currency had declined so much that Beaumarchais demanded more. In an appeal of the auditor's decision in one such dispute in 1795, JM represented Beaumarchais before the High Court of Chancery. See Petition of John Warden, Dec. 15, 1809, Legislative Petitions: Richmond City, Virginia State Library. See also receipt from Chevallié in Account Book, Receipts, Mar. 1795.

Receipt

DS, Vol. 1193C, RG 53, National Archives

[*October 10, 1792, Richmond*. JM signs a receipt of John Hopkins, U.S. commissioner of loans for Virginia, for $59.35 for interest due to Sept. 30, 1792, on $2,923.33 assumed 6 percent stock and $2,067.01 assumed 3 percent stock.[9]]

Petition of James Markham

AD, Legislative Petitions: Fauquier County, Virginia State Library

[Richmond], October 15, 1792

To the Honble the speakers & Members of the Genl. Assembly the petition of James Markham humbly sheweth

That your petitioner was very early engagd in the service of his country during the late war & was employd in the hazardous & important business of bringing powder into Virginia at the commencement of the revolution in which he succeeded to the utmost hopes of the legislature & committee of safety.

Your petitioner was then commissiond as a captain & commanded one of the armd vessels belonging to this state untill he was taken prisoner & he continued a prisoner throughout the war.

Your petitioner therefore humbly prays that his case may be considerd & that the Honble. the Legislature may make him such compensation for his services as shall be thought adequate thereto. And your petitioner will ever pray etc.[1]

JAMES MARKHAM

9. See receipts, Feb. 10, and July 4, 1792, for an explanation of JM's holdings in federal stock.

1. JM had filed a similar petition for Markham in 1787. See Vol. I, 241–242. The 1787 General Assembly approved the petition but apparently never authorized payment to Markham, and JM filed this additional petition for him. It was referred to the Committee of Claims on Oct. 15, 1792, and never reported out. *JVHD*, Oct. 1792, 46. An endorsement on the petition, however, indicates action was taken. The state auditor's office paid Markham £950 15s. 2d. for "Pay & Depreciation," according to the endorsement signed by J. Pendleton.

Masonic Minutes

DS, Rough Minutes, Grand Lodge A.F. & A.M. of Virginia, Richmond[2]

Richmond, October 29, 1792

The Grand Lodge was opened in Ample Form.[3]

The proceedings of the Grand Lodge during the preceding year were read.

The Most Worshipful Grand Master being charged by the Lodge No 16 with having communed with the Expelled Mason Robert Borland,[4] the Grand Lodge debated for some time whether they could agreeably to law enter on an enquiry into the subject previous to the Election of Officers when it was,

Resolved that the Grand Lodge may constitutionally proceed to the enquiry.

After considering the charge exhibited by Lodge No 16 against the Grand Master,

Resolved Unanimously that the charge exhibited against the Grand Master by the lodge No 16 is unsupported, and that he stands honourably acquitted by the Lodge.

The Grand Lodge then proceeded to the election of officers for the ensuing year, when the Most Worshipful Thomas Mathews[5]

2. These minutes of the Grand Lodge are only one of several that JM signed as either grand master or deputy grand master. He signed the rough minutes, in possession of the Grand Lodge of Ancient Free and Accepted Masons of Virginia, on Oct. 28, 29, and 30, 1793. Rough minutes for subsequent meetings at which JM presided are not extant; however, a manuscript minute book for 1777 to 1796, also in possession of the Grand Lodge of Virginia, was apparently transcribed from the rough minutes, with only minor changes resulting from refinement of the language. JM signed the minute book copy of the proceedings only twice, on Nov. 25, 1794, and June 13, 1795. The transcriber signed JM's name to the minute book for the meetings of Oct. 31, 1792, Oct. 28, and Nov. 26, 27, and 28, 1794, and Nov. 24, 1795, presumably indicating that JM had signed the rough minutes on those dates. For a printed version of these Grand Lodge minutes, copied almost without change from the minute book, see Dove, *Proceedings*, 100–104, 120–132, 134–135, 139–140.

3. These minutes are preceded by: "At a Grand Communication, held at the Mason's hall in Richmond, on monday the 29th. of October 5792," and a list of 83 Masons present. See Dove, *Proceedings*, 97–99, where these minutes are printed in full.

The Masonic dating system begins with the year 4,000 B.C., the year Masons believe the world was created. The year 1792 A.D. therefore becomes the year of Masonic labor 5792.

4. Borland (d. *ca.* 1797), a carpenter from Norfolk, was a member of Portsmouth Lodge No. 16.

5. Mathews (1742–1812), a prominent Revolutionary soldier from Norfolk, represented that city in the state ratifying convention of 1788 and in the House of Delegates from 1781 to 1782, 1784 to 1793, and 1797 to 1800, serving as Speaker from 1788 to 1793.

was reelected Grand Master, proclaimed by the Grand Secretary, and congratulated agreeably to the custom of Ancient Masons.

The Most Worshipful Grand Master waved his privelige of appointing a Deputy, and the Grand Lodge going on to ballot, a majority of Votes appeared in favour of Brother John Marshall[6] (who was thereupon installed and congratulated by the brethren.)

Brother Robert Brooke was reelected Grand Senior Warden.

Brother William Bentley was reelected Grand Junior Warden.

Brother Alexander McRoberts was elected Grand Treasurer.

Brother James Henderson was reelected Grand Secretary.

Brother John Moody was elected Grand Senior Deacon.

Brother Alexander Yuille was elected Grand Junior Deacon.

Brothers Richard Wheelin and William Nicolson were elected Grand Stewards.

Brother Mathew Moody was reelected Grand Pursuivant.

Brother John V Kautzman was reelected Grand Tyler.[7]

Such Officers etc.

Resolved that a committee of the whole lodge or any five members thereof do meet in the Hall tomorrow at ten oClock, to take under consideration a variety of communications, and other business of the fraternity, and make report to the Grand Lodge on Wednesday evening to which time the Lodge stands adjourned.

THOS. MATHEWS G M

J MARSHALL D.G.M.

Witness J HENDERSON G S.

6. JM became a Mason during the Revolution, probably having joined one of the field lodges while he was serving in the Continental army. After he moved to Richmond in 1782, he became a member of Richmond Lodge No. 10. JM served as deputy grand master of the Grand Lodge of Virginia, the second most important position in the statewide organization, from 1786 to 1787 and was elected to that position again on Oct. 29, 1792. He was elected to the society's highest office, grand master, on Oct. 28, 1793, and was reelected on Nov. 25, 1794, serving until Nov. 23, 1795, when he resigned. *Ibid.*, 25, 99, 113, 121, 137. JM apparently no longer participated in Masonic activities after 1796, for in 1833 he wrote that "it [Masonry] soon lost its attraction & though there are several lodges in the city of Richmond, I have not been in one of them for more than forty years . . . nor have I been a member of one of them for more than thirty." JM to Edward Everett, July 22, 1833, Massachusetts Historical Society, Boston.

7. William Bentley (d. 1797), of Powhatan County, represented that county in the House of Delegates from 1791 to 1796 and served as a justice of the peace in 1794. James Henderson was also from Powhatan County, and John Moody (d. 1826), Alexander Yuille, William Nicolson (d. *ca.* 1804), Richard Wheelin (d. 1795), Mathew Moody (d. *ca.* 1804), and John Van Kautzman (d. 1798) were all from Richmond.

To Francis Walker

ALS, William Cabell Rives Papers, Library of Congress

[Richmond, *ca.* October 1792]

[   ]⁸ necessary that [   ] of your Father appear in McClungs suit.⁹ A motion is made to revive against him & the cause will probably come on in May. If any testimony exists in the case it shoud immediately be taken. As exr. you are not concernd unless you shoud be called on for back profits which I beleive cannot be in this particular case.

In those suits in which you are interested as exr. which is in Syme's suit if a bill of revivor shoud be fild [   ] suit, it [   ] any further act on your [*part*] other than taking any testimony which it may yet be in your power to obtain. I am dear Sir with much esteem, Your

J MARSHALL.

Law Papers, October 1792

U.S. Circuit Court, Va.

Williams v. Roberdeau, stipulation, DS, U.S. Circuit Court, Va., Ended Cases (Restored), 1792, Virginia State Library.

To James Webb

ALS, John Rutherfoord Manuscripts, Duke University Library

Sir¹   [Richmond], November 7, 1792

I have receivd yours of the 5th. inst.² The business you mention will certainly be attended to. If I can obtain leave to plead I may

8. The top portion of the manuscript has an uneven tear, making a few words on the front and back impossible to read. JM addressed the letter to Walker in Albemarle in care of Mr. Quarles.

9. For information on this case, see JM to Thomas Walker, July 9, 1789. See also Vol. I, 240, 372, n. 69, and JM to Francis Walker, Sept. 20, 1792, and Feb. 23, 1793.

1. Webb (b. 1762), an attorney living in Essex County, served in the House of Delegates in 1798. JM had earlier represented his brother-in-law, Albion Throckmorton, in the various suits against Hite's representatives in 1786. See Vol. I, 191.

2. Not found.

then take advantage of the declaration. At present it coud only be done by writ of error & that woud not stay the execution. It will I think be adviseable for the exr. to attend. Very respectfully I am Sir, Your obedt. Servt.

J MARSHALL

Law Papers, November 1792

U.S. Circuit Court, Va.

Ball's Executor v. Hill, declaration, ADS, U.S. Circuit Court, Va., Ended Cases (Restored), 1793, Virginia State Library.[3]

Brown's Executors v. Donald, Scot & Co., bill in chancery, AD, U.S. Circuit Court, Va., Ended Cases (Restored), 1796, Va. State Lib.

Smith v. Syme, declaration, AD, U.S. Circuit Court, Va., Ended Cases (Restored), 1796, Va. State Lib.

Van Bibber v. Green, declaration, ADS, U.S. Circuit Court, Va., Ended Cases (Restored), 1793, Va. State Lib.[4]

Masonic Dispensation

DS, Deputations and Correspondence, Grand Lodge A.F. & A.M. of Virginia, Richmond

Richmond, December 27, 1792

Virginia

In the name of the Holy Craft—[5]

I John Marshall Deputy Grand Master by order of the Grand Master[6] of the Commonwealth of Virginia do hereby authorise the Worshipful Master Wardens & other Officers of the Richmond Lodge No. 36 to initiate John Heth this evening into the Misteries of Masonry.

3. See Account Book, Receipts, Oct. 1792.
4. See Account Book, Receipts, Aug. 1791, and Jan. 1792, "Mr. Van Bibber."
5. According to Masonic regulations, a dispensation authorized a variety of Masonic activities and was issued by the grand master or deputy grand master when the Grand Lodge was not in session. It continued in force until the Grand Lodge could meet and officially approve the action or until a specified date. Dove, *Proceedings*, 28.
6. Edmund Randolph.

Given under my hand & Seal this 27th. day of December being the anniversary of our Saint John the Evangelist. A.D 1792. AL[7] 5792[8]

JOHN MARSHALL

Masonic Dispensations

DS, Deputations and Correspondence, Grand Lodge A.F. & A.M. of Virginia, Richmond

[*December 27, 1792, Richmond*. JM, as deputy grand master of the Grand Lodge, signs a dispensation authorizing Richmond Lodge No. 36 to initiate Charles Higbee as a Mason.[9]]

[*December 27, 1792, Richmond*. JM signs a dispensation authorizing Richmond Lodge No. 36 to initiate William Heth as a Mason.[1] Minute Book, 1777–1796, Grand Lodge A.F. & A.M. of Virginia, Richmond. Not found.]

Opinion

ADS, Baskervill Family Papers, Virginia Historical Society[2]

[Richmond, *ca.* December 1792]

[1767 Deed from Jefferson to Delony.] "THIS INDENTURE made this third day of January One Thousand Seven hundred and Sixty Seven Between George Jefferson of the County of Mecklenburg[3] of the one part

7. "A L" is the abbreviation for *anno lucis*, which means "in the year of light."
8. See *ibid.*, 110, where this action is recorded in the minutes of the Grand Lodge.
9. See Dove, *Proceedings*, 110, where this action is recorded in the minutes of the Grand Lodge.
1. See *ibid.*
2. This is item no. Mss1B2924a1788 in the society's collections.
The transcript of the deeds is not in JM's hand. Apparently it was presented to JM, and after reading it, he began his opinion at the end of the last deed. The signature and acknowledgments of each of the deeds have been omitted here.
An attached paper, containing entries dated Jan. 4 and Jan. 10, 1793, provides information concerning Henry Delony's payments on the deed of trust. Since these details were lacking when JM rendered his opinion, it is assumed that the opinion was prepared a short time before Jan. 4, 1793.
3. George Jefferson, brother of Peterfield Jefferson (b. 1735) and son of Field Jefferson (1702–1765), of Mecklenburg County, had patented 8,000 acres in Pittsylvania County by 1767. His father was a first cousin of the future president Thomas Jefferson.

and Henry Delony[4] of the same County of the other part WITNESSETH that the said Henry Delony at Special Instance and Request of the said George Jefferson entered into Bond to Matthew Marable[5] of the County of Charlotte Conditioned for the payment of four hundred and Eighty three pounds five Shillings and Eight pence farthing Current money of Virginia payable on or before the Eleventh day of September One thousand Seven Hundred and Sixty nine as Security for the said George Jefferson. Now THIS INDENTURE WITNESSETH that the said George Jefferson for and in consideration of the Sum of four hundred & eighty three pounds five Shillings and Eight pence farthing Current money of Virginia hath bargained sold aliened Enfeoffed Confirmed and delivered and by these presents doth give grant bargain sell Enfeoff Confirm and deliver unto the said Henry Delony his heirs Executors Administrators or Assigns Six Negroes TO WIT Chance, Hazozard, Pompey, Sam, old Tom, and Philis[6] Twelve head of horses Sixty head of Cattle Twenty head of hogs Twenty head of Sheep all his household furniture and all other his personal Estate whatsoever Together with one tract or parcel of Land lying and being in the County of Mecklenburg on both sides Roan Oak River Containing by estimation forty four and a half acres be the same more or less being the Land the said George Jefferson had of his father Field Jefferson deced. and of Peter Field Jefferson Known by the name of Jeffersons Ferry Reference to the Deeds from the said Field Jefferson and Peter Field Jefferson to the said George Jefferson of record in Lunenburg Court may more fully appear. To HAVE AND TO HOLD the said Land Slaves and other personal Estate above mentioned with their and every of their Appurtenances unto the said Henry Delony his heirs and Assigns to the only proper use and behoof of him the said Henry Delony his heirs and assigns forever IN TRUST nevertheless and to the Sole Intent and purpose that the said Henry Delony his Heirs etc. be Impowered to sell and dispose of the said Land Slaves and other estate above mentioned for as much as may be in the said Henry Delony's power to get in Ready money and to Insure to the purchaser or purchasers Their Heirs Executors Administrators or Assigns a good fee Simple Estate of in and to the premises at any time hereafter when the said Henry Delony shall be required to pay or cause to be paid to the said Matthew Marable the Sum of Four Hundred and Eighty three pounds five Shillings and Eight pence farthing as also to Indemnifie the said Henry his Expences costs of suits or other Incident Charges arising from his being Security for the said George Jefferson accruing or to accrue by the

4. Delony (d. 1785) was a member of the House of Burgesses from Mecklenburg County in 1765, 1766, and 1768.

5. Marable (d. 1786) was a member of the House of Burgesses from Mecklenburg County from 1769 to 1771.

6. With the exceptions of Hazard and Old Tom, the slaves mentioned were those taxed to George Jefferson in Pittsylvania County in 1767. See *Virginia Magazine of History and Biography*, XXIII (1915), 79.

Reason of the same and the sd. George Jefferson doth hereby Covenant and agree to and with the sd. Henry Delony his Heirs and Assigns that he the said George Jefferson for himself and his heirs and Assigns the above mentioned Land Slaves and other personal Estate above mentioned unto the said Henry Delony his Heirs Executors Administrators or Assigns for the purposes above mentioned against the Claim property or Demand of him the said George Jefferson his heirs Executors and Administrators and against the Claim and Demand of all other person or persons whatsoever shall and will warrant and forever defend by these presents In WITNESS whereof the said George Jefferson hath here un to set his hand and Affixed his Seal the Day and Year first above Written. . . ."

[1771 Deed from Delony to Burton.] "THIS INDENTURE made this Eleventh day of March One Thousand Seven hundred and Seventy one Between Henry Delony of the County of Mecklenburg of the one part and John Burton[7] of the same County of the other part WITNESSETH that whereas by a Deed of Trust of Record in the County Court of Mecklenburg from George Jefferson to the said Delony for the land herein after mentioned the Covenants and Conditions to be performed by the said Jefferson not being complyed with the said Delony became fully vested with a clear fee Estate in the premises. Now the said Henry Delony for and in the consideration of the Sum of One Hundred and fifty pounds Current money of Virginia to him in hand paid by the said John Burton the Receipt whereof he doth hereby Acknowledge hath given granted bargained sold Aliened Enfeoffed and confirmed and by these presents, doth give grant bragain sell alien Enfeoff an confirm unto the said John Burton his Heirs Executors Administrators and Assigns One certain Tract or parcel of Land lying and being in the County of Mecklenburg on both sides of Roan Oak River containing by Estimation forty four and half Acres be the same more or less being the Land whereon Jeffersons Ferry is kept and conveyed to the said Henry Delony as by the said Deed of Trust Reference thereunto being had will more fully and at large Appear Together with all woods underwoods ways waters and water courses to the same belonging and all houses outhouses and the Reversion and Reversions, Remainder and Remainders Rents Issues and profits thereof and all and every the Appurtenances to the said Tract of Land belonging or in any wise Appertaining. TO HAVE AND TO HOLD the said Tract of land and premises with all and every of its Appurtenances to the said John Burton his Heirs Executors Administrators and Assigns to the only proper use and behoof of him the said John Burton his Heirs and Assigns forever and the said Henry Delony for himself and his Heirs the said Tract of Land and Premises to the said John Burton his Heirs and Assigns against the Claim

7. Burton (d. 1789) was the son of Hutchins Burton (d. 1767) and Tabitha Minge Burton, of Mecklenburg County. See Francis Burton Harrison, *Burton Chronicles of Colonial Virginia* . . . (Darmstadt, Ger., 1933), 221–222.

and Demand of the said Henry Delony and his Heirs and against the Claim and Demand of all and every other person or persons whatsoever claiming under him shall and will warrant and forever by these presents Defend. IN WITNESS whereof the said Henry Delony hath hereunto set his hand and Seal the day and Year first above written. . . .

MEMORANDUM. That on the day and Year within written Quiet and peaceable possession and Seizen of the Lands and Tenements within mentioned was had and taken by the within mentioned John Burton according to the form and Effect of the within written Deed."[8]

[1785 Deed from Burton to Baskervill.] "THIS INDENTURE made this 22nd: day of September 1785 Between John Burton of the County of Mecklenburg of the one part and William Baskervill[9] of the same County of the other part. Witnesseth that the said John Burton for and in consideration of five hundred and two acres of Land to him conveyed by the said William Baskervill and fifty one thousand Seven hundred & Sixty five pounds of nett Inspected Petersburg crop Tobacco to him in hand paid by the said William Baskervill, Hath bargained and Sold, and by these presents doth give grant bargain and Sell unto the said William Baskervill and his Heirs forever a certain tract or parcel of Land Situate lying and being in the County of Mecklenburg on the North side of Roan Oak River containing five hundred and eighty Acres[1] more or less; and bound by the said River the Lands of John Baskervill, George Hunt Baskervill, Richard Swepson and Ray Moss[2] with all woods underwoods, ways, waters and water courses thereunto belonging, and the reversion and reversions, remainder and remainders, Rents, Issues and profits thereof To HAVE AND TO HOLD the said tract or parcel of Land with all and every of its Appurtenances to the said William Baskervill and his Heirs, to the said William Baskervill and his Heirs, to the Only use and behoof of the said William Baskervill his Heirs and Assigns forever; and the said John Burton the said Lands and premises against him the said John Burton and his Heirs to the said William Baskervill and his Heirs, and against the claim and demand of any person or persons whatsoever shall and will

8. This memorandum may indicate that a formal "turf and twig" feoffment was made. The memorandum became part of the record of title of the land and thus may have been considered presumptive evidence of actual possession.

9. Baskervill (1756–1814), of "Lombardy Grove," served as clerk of Mecklenburg County from 1784 to 1814. He was a brother-in-law of the grantor, John Burton, and a brother of John Baskervill (ca. 1745-1791), an adjacent landowner. The Mecklenburg County branch of the Baskerville family dropped the final "e" in their name about 1775. See Partick Hamilton Baskervill, *Genealogy of the Baskerville Family* . . . (Richmond, 1912), 54–55, 62, and table A.

1. In other words, the original Jefferson tract was consolidated into a larger parcel of land being conveyed by Burton.

2. George Hunt Baskervill (1765–1811) was William Baskervill and John Baskervill's brother and was also John Burton's brother-in-law. Richard Swepson had married Mary Tabb, widow of John Tabb, of Mecklenburg County, in 1779.

warrant and forever defend by these presents. IN WITNESS whereof the said John Burton hath hereunto Set his hand and Seal the day and Year above Written. . . ."

Que 1st. Did Delony convey a good right in fee simple to Burton? If not

2d. To whom must the money be tenderd by Jeffersons heir & how much must he tender in order to be entitled to repossess himself of this land?

3d. Does Delony warrant such a right as he states himself entitled to?

4th. Is Burtons estate liable for any incumbrance on the land?

5th. May Baskerville have recourse to Delonys estate?

A. 1st. This depends on a fact which is not stated. If Delony paid the debt to secure which the deed was made by Jefferson to him or so much thereof as the land was worth then his deed will pass the fee, otherwise I think it will not.[3]

A. 2d Jeffersons heir if no part of the money has been paid must, to entitle himself to the land pay the debt for which it was conveyd in trust to Delony & shoud by a suit in chancery bring all the parties interested before the court. The Chancellor woud then probably direct the representatives of Delony to account for the land to the present possessor.

3d. I do not think Delony's warranty extends beyond himself & those claiming under him but he may be liable on the fraud if he has misstated his title.

4th. Burtons estate is liable for the title to the land.

A. 5th. I think in case of the insolvency of Burtons estate Mr.

3. The 1767 instrument was a deed of trust to secure the £483 5s. 8d. advanced on behalf of George Jefferson by Henry Delony. Its legal effect as a conveyance of title was, on equitable principles, to be determined by the actual amount paid by Delony, or on his behalf, in satisfaction of the writing obligatory mentioned in the deed.

After JM delivered this opinion, the parties made inquiry in Jan. 1793 concerning payments on the bond. Records indicated that a total of £513 17s. 11½d. had been paid and that £14 2s. 3¼d. was payable as interest on the balance. Presumably some adjustment had been made for currency devaluations or some other monetary conversion. It is clear, however, that a substantial part of the indebtedness had been paid by Delony, and hence an equitable claim to the property had vested in Delony. Had the entire debt been paid, the deed would have operated as a conveyance of the fee simple estate in the land to Delony.

Since neither the terms of the deeds nor the opinion refer to the slaves as chattels, it is assumed that they were annexed to the lands covered by the deed of trust and hence treated as realty. See the discussion at Vol. I, 210, n. 2.

Baskerville might by a suit in chy. have immediate recourse to
Delony's estate but this is not certain.

J MARSHALL

Law Papers, December 1792

U.S. Circuit Court, Va.

Lyde v. Atkinson, answer, AD, U.S. Circuit Court, Va., Ended Cases (Restored), 1795, Virginia State Library.

McColl v. McDougall & Co., petition, AD, U.S. Circuit Court, Va., Ended Cases (Restored), 1792, Va. State Lib.

Opinion

Copy, Overton Papers, Swem Library, College of William and Mary

[Richmond], 1792

Question to John Marshall Esqr. in 1792[4]

Que 7th. How is the balance of the Estate to be divided?

Que 8th. What children of Francis Parrott are alluded to in that clause which gives her two shears all her Children or only those by her last husband?

A. 7th. This clause is so very darkly expressd. as to make any opinion on it a Meer conjecture. I should myself decide that Fran-

---

4. This copy was likely made sometime after 1801. On the verso appears the following, the first paragraph of which is in the same hand: "Observe Mrs. Thos. Yerby Will that thier was to be no division of his Estate untill the death his widow, except each Legatie was to have their Legacies. The provision in said will was more than the widow would accept of (& in concequence) ⟨she⟩ renounsed the will, & took the Negroes named in the will & devisd. to her, in consequence of that their was a necessity for a division to take place at the death of the said Thos. Mrs. John Parrott at that division drew for the two shears mentioned in the last clause of Said Thos. Will, agreeable to John Marshall, our present chief Justice opinion, that is to say one Shear in right of his wife & one Other Shear as Guardian to Peeds orphans. The lot drawn in right of his wife was a Negroe Named Lewis & Nine pounds 6/8 to make up his Negroe lot equal to the rest of the Legaties.

"John Parrott married Francis Yerby whose former husband Peed was dead & she had married Parrott she had 3 children by Peed & one by Parrott who survived had a child & died. A division took place after Yerby's death & John Parrott drew Lewis. J P's wife is dead, 11 years, she has children by Peed living."

cis Parrott took one part for herself & that one other part should be divided among her Children by Isaac Peed.

A. 8th. The words of the will woud limit & confine this Gift to the Children of Mrs. Parrott by her present Husband—unless She Should Survive them all. & I must give that opinion, but as their is reason to beleive that all her children were intended it is possible that a court might put that construction on the will.

Masonic Dispensation

[*January 17, 1793 (Richmond)*. JM, as deputy grand master of the Grand Lodge, issues a dispensation authorizing the formation of a lodge in Campbell County, designated Campbell Lodge No. 37.[5] Not found. Rough Minutes, Grand Lodge A.F. & A.M. of Virginia, Richmond.]

To Richard Henry Lee

ALS, Lee Family Papers, University of Virginia Library

Sir[6]   Richmond, January 18, 1793

I am just favord with yours of the 14th. inst.[7] The contract I enterd into with your deceasd Brother[8] was formd to enable me to make a very extensive & as I thought a very valuable purchase. Upon the faith of this negotiation my brother Mr. James Marshall is now in London with full powers to bind some other Gentlemen with myself[9] to the immediate payment of a sum of money which I cannot command without resorting to the stock I purchasd from Mr. Lee & which I shoud not have bound myself to pay but for that purchase. If then sir the expected engagements shoud be made

5. This dispensation was to be in force only until Oct. 28, 1793. See the subsequent dispensation, calendared at Oct. 31, 1793. Dove, *Proceedings*, 110.

6. The letter is addressed to Lee at "Chantilly" in Westmoreland County.

7. Not found.

8. Arthur Lee had died on Dec. 12, 1792. In an unknown hand on the address leaf, this letter was summarized as follows: "John Marshall's letter Jany. 18, 1793 stating his views for contracting with Mr. Arthur Lee for Bank Stock, and desiring to have the contract carried into execution." Apparently JM had agreed to buy stock in the Bank of the United States held by Lee before Lee's death. The stock obviously had appreciated, and JM counted on using his profits to help toward the purchase of the Fairfax lands.

9. Denny Martin Fairfax. See Fairfax Lands: Editorial Note, Feb. 1, 1793.

in London I shall be unfortunately so peculiarly circumstancd as to be compeld to request a performance of the contract which has been enterd into. If, as is more than possible, my brother shoud not enter into the engagements for which he is now in London, I shall feel real pleasure in relinquishing a contract the completion of which can produce the most remote inconvenience to you. For myself I have no apprehension of danger, because an immediate transfer of the stock to me woud I am firmly persuaded enable me so to dispose of the money it woud produce, as to compensate the loss in the purchase, before I shoud be calld on to apply it to its ultimate object. This opportunity will soon pass away not to return again. I shall not however wish to call on you to make the transfer unless forced to do so by the circumstance which producd the contract. I expect to hear decisively from London in March or April next.

Accept Sir my unfeignd thanks for the regard you express for me & beleive me to be with real respect & esteem, Your obedt. Servt.

J MARSHALL

Bank Subscription Notice

Printed, *Virginia Gazette, and General Advertiser* (Richmond), January 30, 1793, 3

Richmond, January 24, 1793

In pursuance of an act, intitled "An act for establishing a bank in the city of Richmond," books for receiving subscriptions will be opened on the first day of March, in the Capitol, at 12 o'clock, and at the same hour on each day thereafter until the 30th of March, on which day they will be closed.[1]

The superintendants will attend for one hour on each day.

J. MARSHALL,[2]

1. The act passed the General Assembly on Dec. 23, 1792, and followed a similar act establishing a state bank in Alexandria passed in November. JM had signed a petition dated *ca.* July 1, 1792, calling for the establishment of a Richmond branch of the Bank of the United States, but that branch had not yet been established, and prospects for its success appeared dim. That may have led JM to agree to serve as a superintendent of the subscription drive to establish a state bank in Richmond. This subscription was unsuccessful, however, and Richmond remained without a bank. 13 Hening 599; James O. Wettereau, "The Branches of the First Bank of the United States," supplement to *Journal of Economic History*, II (1942), 76–77.

2. JM was one of ten superintendents who signed this notice. Others included

To James Henderson

ALS, Henry E. Huntington Library[3]

Dear Sir   [Richmond, January 1793]
    I enclose you a dispensation[4] to which you will please to affix
the seal of the lodge with your attestation. I am very respectfully,
Your obedt. Servt.

                                                        J MARSHALL

Law Papers, January 1793

U.S. Circuit Court, Va.

Anderson & Co. v. Austin, declaration, ADS, U.S. Circuit Court, Va.,
Ended Cases (Restored), 1794, Virginia State Library.

Fairfax Lands

EDITORIAL NOTE

    Having lived the first twenty-five years his of life in Fauquier County, John
Marshall had a natural interest in maintaining tangible connections with that
region. When Thomas Marshall moved to Kentucky in 1785, he deeded his home,
"Oak Hill," to his eldest son.[5] At that time John Marshall did not expect to live
the remainder of his life in Richmond and in fact had not acquired any property
in that city until the day before his father gave him "Oak Hill." His intention to
follow his family into Kentucky did not materialize, but his interest in the Northern Neck of Virginia remained. In the 1790s he took advantage of the opportunity
to acquire large parcels of choice land there and joined with his brother James
Markham Marshall and his brother-in-law Rawleigh Colston to purchase as
large a portion of the lands claimed by the Fairfax family as possible.
    By 1786, when Marshall argued in *Hite v. Fairfax* that Thomas, Sixth Lord
Fairfax, had good title to the Northern Neck before the Revolution,[6] the propri-

---

William Foushee, James McClurg, George Pickett, and Robert Gamble, whose last
name was incorrectly printed "Garnett" in the newspaper notice.
    3. The letter was addressed to Henderson in Powhatan, and "Letter from D.G.M.,
Jany 1793:" appears on the verso in another hand.
    4. The dispensation from JM, who was then serving as deputy grand master of the
Grand Lodge, temporarily chartered Buckingham Union Lodge No. 38 and is printed
at Feb. 8, 1793.
    5. See Vol. I, 135–137.
    6. *Ibid.*, 153–164.

etor's title had been challenged significantly. After Lord Fairfax's death in 1781, the question of ownership of the 5.2 million acres in the Northern Neck had taken on a different character. When Fairfax's proprietary interest and his personal portion of the region passed by his will to British citizens who had never established Virginia residence, a lengthy political and legal struggle for the land began. The Fairfax interest in the proprietary fell into three divisions: lands appropriated to individuals who were to pay quitrents to the grantor; lands unappropriated, sometimes called the waste lands; and lands reserved for the private or personal use of the Fairfax family, sometimes referred to as the manor lands.[7]

In October 1782 the General Assembly had begun removing certain escheat exemptions and tax privileges that had been a central feature of the Fairfax proprietary. Beginning with a sequestration of the quitrents paid by tenants on the proprietary, the state had moved progressively to assert additional claims to the Northern Neck in the years following. By the end of 1785 Virginia had acquired the proprietary's land office papers and had assumed responsibility for all unappropriated lands within the grant, amounting to approximately 2.5 million acres. Governor Patrick Henry had begun granting title to portions of these lands before the close of 1786. In the next ten years the Commonwealth derived more than £100,000 from such land sales.[8]

Lord Fairfax's successor, Denny Martin Fairfax, disputed the state's right to these lands through a variety of lawsuits, all of which turned upon the legitimacy of his title as rightful devisee under Virginia law and the Treaty of Paris of 1783. In the course of litigation between 1786 and 1796, John Marshall acted as the attorney for Fairfax—first in the Hite case involving a colonial claim to part of the unappropriated lands, then in escheat proceedings brought by the state against the manor lands, and finally in a federal ejectment action he initiated for Fairfax against David Hunter, which tested the state's right to grant title to the unappropriated lands.

Even though the Court of Appeals had recognized in *Hite v. Fairfax* that Lord Fairfax's heirs held some property interests in the Northern Neck, the state was proceeding on the common law rule that aliens are unable to inherit land and that the land must escheat to the Commonwealth. Judge St. George Tucker clarified these points in *Hunter v. Fairfax* in the District Court at Winchester in April 1794. This was an ejectment action concerning a grant of unappropriated land by the state and was originally brought by Fairfax in the Frederick County Court. Judge Tucker ruled that under the common law an alien could take land by inheritance, although he could not hold it in fee simple. Fairfax could therefore hold the land until the Commonwealth took it, and it could only be taken by a formal inquest of office, which had not been held. Until the land escheated by an inquest of office, the courts would protect Fairfax's right to the land, and the Commonwealth could not grant it to Hunter or anyone else. Fairfax's attorneys, disagreeing with Tucker's reasoning, believed that the Treaty of Paris

7. John Alfred Treon, "*Martin v Hunter's Lessee*: A Case History" (Ph.D. diss., University of Virginia, 1970), 37–38, 75. For earlier studies of the Fairfax proprietary, see H. C. Groome, "Northern Neck Lands," Fauquier Historical Society, *Bulletins*, 1st Ser. (Richmond, 1921–1924), 7–65; and Stuart E. Brown, Jr., *Virginia Baron: The Story of Thomas Sixth Lord Fairfax* (Berryville, Va., 1965).

8. 11 Hening 112–129, 159–160, 289–291; 12 Hening 100–101, 111–113, 117; Treon, "*Martin v Hunter's Lessee*," 102.

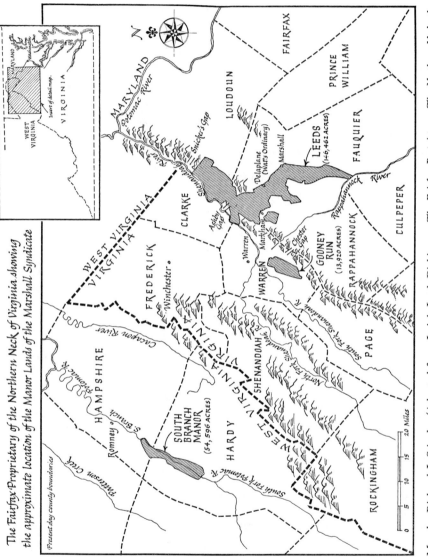

The Fairfax Proprietary of the Northern Neck of Virginia showing the approximate location of the Manor Lands of the Marshall Syndicate

Map by Richard J. Stinely. (Adapted from Josiah Look Dickinson, *The Fairfax Proprietary: The Northern Neck, the Fairfax Manors, and Beginnings of Warren County in Virginia* [Front Royal, Va., 1959], and the Deed Books of Hardy

secured clear title in Denny Martin Fairfax and that the land devised to him in 1781 was protected from escheat by Article 5, prohibiting future confiscations. They argued, therefore, that the common law had been consciously altered by this provision in the treaty and that Fairfax had held complete title after 1783.[9]

Denny Martin Fairfax did not want to establish fee simple ownership of the Northern Neck in order to settle there. At first he hoped to continue collecting rents from the appropriated lands while holding the manor lands for future personal use. Considering the increasing difficulty of holding the land while remaining a British subject, he began to think of selling it.[1] Having managed the defense of Fairfax's interests since 1786, Marshall was in an excellent position to know this. In a time when financial security was usually associated with land ownership, he recognized the possibility of organizing a group of relatives and close friends who would pool their resources to buy the best land. Marshall could then sell enough of his portion to pay for the land he wanted to retain. Because he had insufficient personal wealth at the time, this was in fact the only way Marshall could acquire a sizable estate. Firmly committed to the belief that Fairfax's title was good and that he could prove it in court, Marshall and his associates decided to purchase the manor lands. In addition to being the most valuable land, the manor lands had not yet been moved against by the state. In 1792 James Markham Marshall journeyed to London, where, on February 1, 1793, he entered into a contract with Fairfax, binding himself and the others to purchase the manors for £20,000 sterling. The articles of agreement stipulated that the lands to be included in the purchase were the Manor of Leeds, consisting of almost 160,000 acres in Fauquier, Loudoun, Frederick, and Shenandoah counties, and the South Branch Manor, containing almost 55,000 acres in Hampshire and Hardy counties.[2]

A few months after James Markham Marshall signed the original purchase agreement with Fairfax, the state increased its attack on the lands by instituting escheat action against portions of the Manor of Leeds in Fauquier, Frederick, and Shenandoah counties. County escheators held inquests of office following the procedure outlined in a November 1792 statute that conformed to the common law method of escheat. The jury's finding had to be forwarded to and recorded in the district court having jurisdiction over the county. If the jury found for the Commonwealth, individuals claiming title then would have twelve months to challenge the finding by entering a traverse. In Frederick County the office judgment found for the Commonwealth was quashed on a technicality by the District Court at Winchester in April 1794. The Shenandoah jury also found for the Commonwealth, and the Fauquier jury finally decided in favor of the Commonwealth after meeting three times between April and August 1794.[3]

9. St. George Tucker, "Notes on Cases in the General Court, District Courts, and Court of Appeals in Virginia, 1786–1811," Hunter v. Fairfax, Apr. 22, 1794, Tucker-Coleman Papers, Swem Library, College of William and Mary.

1. JM to Richard Henry Lee, Jan. 18, 1793; Carter Braxton to James Innes, Feb. 10, 1788, and Braxton to unknown, Dec. 31, 1792, both in Wykeham-Martin Papers, Kent County Archives, Maidstone, Eng.

2. See Articles of Agreement, following this editorial note.

3. 1 Shepherd 51–53; Robert Brooke to Henry Lee, May 4, 1794, Robert Page to James Innes, Aug. 11, 1794, Abram Davenport to Henry Lee, Sept. 5, 1794, and Robert Brooke to James Wood, Oct. 23, 1794, Executive Papers, Virginia State Library; James Wood to Speaker of House of Delegates, Nov. 13, 1794, Executive Letterbooks, *ibid.*; and Superior Court Order Book, 1794–1797, 45, Frederick County, *ibid.* See

When the Fauquier County finding was presented to the District Court at Dumfries in October 1794, Fairfax's attorney entered a traverse, or challenge, to the judgment. The court upheld the finding on October 24, 1794, whereupon an appeal was filed to the Court of Appeals, setting the stage for a ruling from the state's highest court on Fairfax's right to hold title. Ordinarily the Commonwealth's interest in the case would have been managed by the attorney general, James Innes, but John Marshall was acting as attorney general at the time this appeal was filed. Because of this development the Council of State asked Patrick Henry to prepare the state's case, stating that his experience "with the principles on which this claim is bottomed" made him "the most competent counsel." However, Henry refused to act as special counsel and the state therefore retained the services of John Wickham and Alexander Campbell, both of whom had experience in related cases.[4]

Marshall became convinced that the state intended to do everything possible to delay a final determination in the case. In March 1794 Congress had submitted to the states for ratification the Eleventh Amendment to the Constitution, and the General Assembly had ratified it promptly in November. The amendment was designed to deny the jurisdiction of the federal courts in any suit brought against a state by a person not a citizen of that state. When the amendment became effective, it was assumed Fairfax would lose the right of appeal to the federal courts, and the matter would thus end with the Virginia Court of Appeals.[5]

In the meantime, Marshall advised Fairfax to make contact with the ministers negotiating what became Jay's Treaty, hoping that they could be prevailed upon to include explicit recognition of Fairfax's title in the new treaty.[6] The 1783 treaty

---

also Tucker, "Notes on Cases," The Case of the Manor of Leeds, Apr. 22, 1794, Tucker-Coleman Papers, Wm. & Mary. JM attended the inquests in Frederick and Fauquier counties. See entries in Account Book, Disbursements, Feb. and Apr. 1794.

4. District Court Order Book, 1794–1798, 82, Prince William County, and Robert Brooke to Patrick Henry, Dec. 24, 1794, and Feb. 7, 1795, Exec. Letterbooks, and James Innes to Robert Brooke, Apr. 23, 1795, Exec. Communications, all in Va. State Lib.; Treon, "*Martin v Hunter's Lessee*," 78.

Campbell (d. 1796) was U.S. district attorney for Virginia from 1791 to 1796. He appeared with JM in Ware v. Hylton when it was argued before the U.S. Supreme Court in 1796. Later that year he committed suicide. See JM to Henry Lee, July 18, 1796, Sang Collection, Rutgers University Library.

5. Thomas Bryan Martin to Denny Martin Fairfax, Dec. 6, 1794, and Rawleigh Colston to Thomas Gregory, Dec. 4, 1794, Wykeham-Martin Papers, Kent Co. Arch., Eng. Colston wrote, "It is suggested by Mr. Fairfax's counsel [JM?], that the tryal has been delayed, as he conceives, until a certain amendment of the Federal Constitution shall be adopted by our State legislature now in session, in consequence of which Mr. Fairfax will be deprived of his right of appeal from the state to the Federal judicature."

The General Assembly ratified the 11th Amendment to the U.S. Constitution on Nov. 18, the House of Delegates having acted on Nov. 15, four days after convening. Although the amendment was later interpreted to apply to original jurisdiction only, it is clear that contemporaries, including JM, believed the amendment would encompass both original and appellate jurisdiction. See also Clyde E. Jacobs, *The Eleventh Amendment and Sovereign Immunity* (Westport, Conn., 1972), 82–87, 94–95, and arguments by defendant's counsel in Cohens v. Virginia, 19 U.S. (6 Wheat.) 264 (1821).

6. Thomas Bryan Martin to Denny Martin Fairfax, Dec. 6, 1794, and Rawleigh Colston to Thomas Gregory, Dec. 4, 1794, Wykeham-Martin Papers, Kent Co. Arch., Eng.

had prohibited future confiscations of land then held by British subjects, and Marshall believed the present escheat action legally constituted confiscation. Marshall was unaware, however, that Jay's Treaty had been initialed on November 14, 1794, and that it was too late to appeal to the negotiators to consider Fairfax's case. More important, though, was Marshall's decision to assert the equitable title he and his fellow purchasers now held to the manor lands. Since signing the contract to purchase this land in 1793, Marshall and his brother had contracted with Henry Lee, Rawleigh Colston, and John Ambler to join in the purchase of the Manor of Leeds. In February 1795, John Marshall prepared a bill for the High Court of Chancery that undoubtedly asserted the equitable title of the purchasers. He wanted the chancellor to issue a decree before the Court of Appeals considered the case in May, but the Council of State refused to waive the normal requirements of chancery process, which would take longer than the time remaining.[7] It remains unclear whether Marshall pursued his case in the High Court of Chancery. If he had won a decree there, the state certainly would have appealed it; but even if the Court of Appeals did reverse the chancery decree, Marshall, unencumbered by the Eleventh Amendment, would have had access to the federal courts, where he was confident the Treaty of Paris would be interpreted as securing Fairfax's title.

On another front, Marshall realized he had an opportunity to get the title question into the federal courts without waiting for the escheat appeal to be decided. David Hunter had declared his intention to bring before the Court of Appeals the ruling of the Winchester District Court in *Hunter v. Fairfax*, although the case had not yet been entered on the docket. Since the state was not a party, there was no question of sovereign immunity or the application of the Eleventh Amendment. Word that Jay's Treaty had been signed reached Richmond in March 1795, and Article 9's guarantee of title to British subjects then holding land in the United States reinforced Marshall's position. Accordingly, Marshall filed an ejectment action in the name of Fairfax against Hunter in the U.S. Circuit Court for Virginia in April 1795. The state, recognizing the significance of the case, employed counsel to support Hunter's claim that his title from the state was good. Judges Cyrus Griffin and James Wilson, however, ruled in favor of Fairfax on June 6, 1795, and Hunter, losing the state's support in January 1796, appealed to the U.S. Supreme Court.[8]

7. Samuel Flagg Bemis, *Jay's Treaty: A Study in Commerce and Diplomacy*, 2d ed. rev. (New Haven, Conn., 1962); JM to Charles Lee, *ca.* Dec. 1795; JM to Robert Brooke, *ca.* Mar. 2, 1795; Brooke to JM, Mar. 2, 1795; District Court Order Book, 1794–1798, 263–264, Prince William County, Va. State Lib.

8. JM's declaration and stipulation are calendared at May 30, and *ca.* June 1, 1795. See Treon, "*Martin v Hunter's Lessee*," 89; U.S. Circuit Court, Va., Record Book, III, 346–357, and Order Book, I, 536–537, Va. State Lib. See also David Hunter to Alexander Hamilton, July 7, 1796, Hamilton Papers, Library of Congress; Robert Brooke to Hunter *et al.*, Jan. 19, 1796, Exec. Letterbooks, Va. State Lib.

The case, Hunter v. Fairfax's Devisee, was scheduled for argument in Feb. 1796, the same term in which Ware v. Hylton was argued. JM was prepared to represent Fairfax before the court, but Hunter asked for a continuance in order to obtain counsel, and the court granted it over JM's objections. By July, Hunter had employed Alexander Campbell to represent him at the August term, but Campbell committed suicide shortly before he was to go to Philadelphia. Consequently, Hunter asked for and won another continuance. Apparently deciding to abandon his Supreme Court

The Court of Appeals continued to delay a decision in the escheat appeal, and Marshall continued to grow impatient with the dilatory tactics. Sometime during the 1795 session of the General Assembly, which JM attended, the issue was considered and debated, perhaps unofficially, but if a compromise was proposed by either side, the decision was to postpone official consideration until the 1796 session. Marshall decided to increase his attack in the courts in the meantime. Apparently realizing that a Court of Appeals decision against Fairfax would preclude an appeal to the federal courts in this case and that a decision of the U.S. Supreme Court upholding the decision in favor of Fairfax in the Hunter case might be restricted to the lands against which there had been no inquisition of office, Marshall decided to return to the District Court at Dumfries and file in the name of the purchasers of the Manor of Leeds a traverse contesting the office judgment found against Fairfax in Fauquier County. Because all the purchasers were citizens of Virginia, this would accomplish the goal he had sought in his attempted chancery action earlier that year. He instructed his attorney in the case, Charles Lee, to file the traverse and then demur to the state's reply, thus paving the way for an adverse ruling, which he would then appeal to the Court of Appeals, asking that it be joined with the appeal on the same issues filed in the name of Fairfax. This would give Marshall a clear avenue of appeal to the federal courts, should the Court of Appeals rule against Fairfax's title, and would thereby accomplish the same goal he had sought in his attempted chancery action earlier in 1795.[9]

As the General Assembly convened for the fall session in 1796, all the confusing strands of the dispute over the Northern Neck seemed to converge, and the ex-

---

appeal after the legislative compromise in Dec. 1796, Hunter failed to prosecute the action, and on Feb. 13, 1797, the court granted a motion of Charles Lee, representing Fairfax, for a *non prosequitur*, thus ending the appeal for good. This case never again appeared on the docket, and the 1795 circuit court decision therefore held. 3 U.S. (3 Dall.) 305 (1796); U.S. Supreme Court Minutes, Feb. 11 and 13, 1797, and Dockets, Mar. 14, 1796, RG 267, National Archives; and Treon, "*Martin v Hunter's Lessee*," 95–101.

The landmark case of Martin v. Hunter's Lessee, decided by the Supreme Court in 1813 and 1816, came from the case Hunter had lost in the District Court at Winchester in 1794. At the same time his appeal of the U.S. Circuit Court decision in Fairfax v. Hunter was pending before the Supreme Court, and while he was trying to obtain counsel for that litigation, Hunter filed an appeal of the Winchester decision with the Virginia Court of Appeals. That court heard argument in May 1796, but no decision was rendered at that time, probably because of the close relationship the case had with the escheat appeals from the Dumfries court. After the legislative compromise, attorneys for Fairfax asked in Oct. 1797 that Hunter's appeal be continued. It is unclear why they did not ask for a dismissal. The case lay dormant until 1803, when Hunter decided to revive it. The case name was altered to reflect the death of Fairfax and the inheritance of Philip Martin, becoming Hunter v. Martin's Lessee, and it was this case that the Virginia Court of Appeals decided in favor of Hunter in 1810 and that the U.S. Supreme Court reversed in favor of Martin's lessee in 1813. Although Treon is confused on numerous facts relating to the dates of the various actions involved, his account of the litigation is the only thorough review available. See Treon, "*Martin v Hunter's Lessee*," 112–248; 15 Va. (1 Munf.) 218 (1810); 10 U.S. (6 Cranch) 602 (1813); and 14 U.S. (1 Wheat.) 323 (1816).

9. See Brooke to Hunter, Jan. 19, 1796, Exec. Letterbooks, Va. State Lib., wherein Brooke wrote that the business "has been agitated in the Legislature and a decision on it postponed by them until their next meeting"; and JM to Charles Lee, *ca.* Dec. 1795.

pert attack engineered by John Marshall gained momentum, exerting strong pressure on the state. In February 1796 the U.S. Supreme Court had heard arguments in *Hunter v. Fairfax* on appeal from the U.S. Circuit Court. The Dumfries District Court had ruled in favor of the state in the traverse to the inquest filed in the name of *Marshall* et al. *v. Commonwealth of Virginia*, and Marshall's appeal destroyed the reason for the Court of Appeal's delay in rendering a decision.[1] Jay's Treaty had also been ratified in 1795, and its provisions guaranteeing full title to British citizens then holding land in the United States seemed to add weight to Marshall's case, in the federal courts at least. The state had good reason to fear that if the issue ever reached the U.S. Supreme Court, a ruling in favor of Fairfax's title would be likely. In its fall term the Virginia Court of Appeals adjourned without deciding *Fairfax v. Commonwealth* (it is unclear whether *Marshall v. Commonwealth* was joined) after four days of argument.[2] Certainly one reason for this continuance was the movement toward a legislative settlement in the General Assembly.

Marshall was at the 1796 General Assembly when it convened on November 8, representing the city of Richmond and sitting on all the significant committees. It is quite likely that by this time Marshall had devised a plan to settle the Northern Neck dispute by legislative compromise; it is certain that he was prepared to accept a plan if one were offered. On November 14, the day the Court of Appeals began hearing further arguments in the appeal from the Dumfries District Court, a petition from several Fairfax leaseholders in Hardy, Hampshire, and Shenandoah counties arrived at the House of Delegates and was referred to the Committee for Courts of Justice, of which Marshall was a member. The central features of a legislative compromise to the legal dispute were worked out in this committee while the Court of Appeals continued sitting. On November 18 the court adjourned the case until the next term, apparently confident the matter would be resolved in the legislature before then. On the following day Robert Andrews, of Williamsburg, introduced a resolution for the committee containing the outline of a compromise that was promptly adopted. The resolution called attention to the legal dispute, recognizing that one court had found for Fairfax and that in the case "now depending in the court of appeals of this state . . . a decision either way is likely to produce a great disquietude among a considerable body of the people, because it is probable that it will not prevent a resort to a repetition of legal efforts to revive it, that under this threatened uncertainty and uneasiness, there is reason to believe that a spirit of accomodation among those interested may prevail." One week later Marshall, in a letter to the Speaker of the House of Delegates, accepted the terms of the compromise on behalf of Fairfax and the purchasers of the manor lands. An act incorporating the exact terms of the settlement passed the Assembly on December 10.[3]

According to the plan, the purchasers would arrange for Fairfax to transfer title to the unappropriated lands to the Commonwealth, but in actual fact this would be initially accomplished by means of a deed between James Markham

1. District Court Order Book, 1794–1798, 263–264, Prince William County, Va. State Lib.

2. Court of Appeals Order Book, III, 150–152, Va. State Lib.

3. *JVHD*, Nov. 1796, 3, 4, 9, 10, 15, 24, 28, 41; 2 Shepherd 22–23 (1796). The Court of Appeals quashed the inquest in Fairfax v. Commonwealth on Oct. 10, 1798. Court of Appeals Order Book, III, 244–245, Va. State Lib.

Marshall, who was still in England, and Denny Martin Fairfax and then by a deed between Marshall and the Commonwealth. A proposed deed was submitted to the Council of State in January 1797. Edmund Randolph examined it for the Council and, except for minor details pertaining to relinquishment of dower rights, approved the draft.[4] On August 30, 1797, Denny Martin Fairfax transferred title to the unappropriated lands to James Markham Marshall for £2,625 sterling. The deed was recorded in the General Court in Richmond in June 1798, the General Assembly having acknowledged the completion of the Fairfax sale on December 23, 1797. The legislature directed the governor to honor the Fairfax title to the manor lands "as if he the said Denny had been a native citizen of this commonwealth, and as if no escheat or forfeiture thereof had ever taken place." To complete transfer of the other lands to the state, James Markham Marshall and his wife, Hester Morris Marshall, deeded "all Northern Neck lands recited in the Act of 1796" to the state on October 10, 1798.[5]

From the beginning of their negotiations with Denny Martin Fairfax, the Marshalls had focused their interest on the manor lands. As soon as the compromise was put into effect, John Marshall paid for South Branch Manor and gained legal title to that land. The state gained legal title to most of the Northern Neck lands that had remained "waste and unappropriated at the time of the death of Thomas Lord Fairfax" in November 1781. Denny Martin Fairfax was left with legal title to the Manor of Leeds, but he remained prepared to convey a deed to the Marshalls as soon as they could pay for it.

Sometime after John Marshall acquired South Branch Manor, his brother and Rawleigh Colston became coowners with him. This land was sold by them between 1797 and 1817, Marshall making 131 separate sales totaling 21,426 acres. From these sales Marshall earned £5,946 Virginia currency and $2,989.75. In 1802 Marshall divested himself of most of his remaining interest when he sold the "resurvey" to Isaac and Jacob Vanmeter. The "resurvey" was a 1,550-acre tract that had been part of the 1797 purchase of South Branch Manor. Marshall's share of this sale was £800. Finally, on December 13, 1802, John and James Markham Marshall sold the remainder of the South Branch Manor to Abel Seymour.[6]

4. E. Randolph to Brooke, Jan. 10, 1797, in Edwin Church, "James Markham Marshall," *Virginia Cavalcade,* XIII (Spring 1964), 29.

5. 2 Shepherd 23, 140; Deed, James Marshall and wife to Commonwealth of Virginia, Oct. 10, 1798, enclosed in Marshall's Lessee v. E. Foley, Land Causes, III, 1833–1850, 190–193, Fauquier County, Va. State Lib.

6. JM to James M. Marshall, Dec. 16, 1799, Marshall Papers, Lib. Cong.; JM to James M. Marshall, Apr. 4, 1800, Huntington Library, San Marino, Calif.; Hardy County Deed Book, A, 1797–1802, 187–190, 520–522, and Deed Book, V, 1800–1806, 187–190, West Virginia Department of Archives and History, Charleston.

The terms of the sale to Seymour were complex because of several uncertainties. The Marshalls claimed that the exact acreage could not be "properly ascertained" but estimated that there remained 11,000 acres, of which 9,371 were under lease and 1,629 were vacant. They also sold Seymour the rent arrearages, estimated at £1,112 Virginia currency. Seymour agreed to pay the Marshalls £2,284 Virginia currency in four equal annual payments beginning Mar. 1804. The Marshalls reserved the right to complete sales of tracts in the manor for which they had begun negotiations prior to Oct. 1802, but they agreed to pay Seymour the difference if the actual acreage and rents were short of their state's estimate. JM continued to sell tracts within the manor

It is likely that much of the money derived from the sale of South Branch Manor was used to pay for the more desirable Manor of Leeds, which the Marshalls had contracted to purchase for £14,000 sterling. Interest payments on this purchase price had to be maintained until legal title transferred, but assuming the Marshall syndicate collected rents on the Manor of Leeds from 1795 until 1806, this amount should have provided enough to satisfy interest requirements. On October 16, 1806, John Marshall, James Markham Marshall, and Rawleigh Colston paid £14,000 sterling to Philip Martin, Fairfax's successor, for 160,000 acres comprising the Manor of Leeds, thus terminating a thirteen-year effort to acquire that property. The partition of this acreage between the purchasers had been planned well in advance of this sale, and after a series of agreements and exchanges between 1808 and 1816, John Marshall's share amounted to approximately 50,000 acres.[7]

The long effort to acquire this property and to secure its title in the purchasers represented a great personal and professional success for John Marshall. His knowledge of the law and his skillful handling of the legal procedure had enabled him to maneuver Fairfax's, and his, case through the state and federal courts so successfully that the state in effect had been forced to compromise or perhaps lose all claim to the lands. Clearly, the Court of Appeals, submitting to the desires of the Council of State through their counsel, had employed dilatory tactics in an attempt to frustrate Fairfax's claim and to prevent him from appealing to the federal courts once the Eleventh Amendment became part of the Constitution. But Marshall had proved too astute; he had taken advantage of his technical position as equitable owner of part of the land in dispute and had thereby thwarted the state's attempt to keep the case out of the federal courts. Once he and his fellow purchasers became parties to the escheat action, the avenue of appeal to the U.S. Supreme Court was clearly open, and the state's case continued to weaken, especially after Jay's Treaty was approved. In short, Marshall's management of this case was brilliant; knowledge of the details contributes significantly to an understanding of his desire to remain in Virginia, close by the state government, until the outcome of the dispute was certain. Having won the fight by the end of 1796, he was freer to accept one or more of the increasing number of offers to enter national political affairs.

---

after the Seymour sale, transferring 2,798 acres for £629 Virginia currency and $207.50 between 1803 and 1817. By 1817 JM and his partners had sold all of South Branch Manor for a total of £16,234 Virginia currency and $3,404.50.

7. Hardy and Hampshire County Deed Books, 1797–1817, *passim*, W. Va. Arch., Charleston; Articles of Agreement, James M. Marshall, Rawleigh Colston, John Ambler, and JM, Sept. 11, 1801, Cornell University Library; Deed, Philip Martin to Rawleigh Colston, James M. Marshall, and JM, Oct. 18, 1806, Deed, R. Colston to JM and James M. Marshall, Oct. 5, 1808, and Deed, JM to James M. Marshall, Aug. 22, 1816, all in Land Causes, III, 1833–1850, 40–44, 200–203, 204–206, 206–208, Fauquier County, Va. State Lib.

Articles of Agreement

DS, Accession 24062, folder 70, Virginia State Library

[Maidstone, Kent], February 1, 1793

ARTICLES of AGREEMENT[8] made concluded & agreed upon the First Day of February in the Year of our Lord one thousand Seven hundred and Ninety Three BETWEEN The Reverend Denny Fairfax of Leeds Castle in the County of Kent and Kingdom of Great Britain Doctor in Divinity heretofore called Denny Martin Clerk of the one part and James Markham Marshall of the City of Richmond in the State of Virginia in America Esquire of the other part as follow VIZT:

FIRST the said Denny Fairfax for the Consideration hereinaftermentioned doth hereby for himself & his Heirs contract covenant & agree to sell grant & convey unto the said James Markham Marshall & to his Heirs or to such other person or persons as he or they shall direct or appoint[9] ALL THAT the Manor of Leeds in Virginia aforesaid with the Appurtenances AND ALL THOSE three several extensive Tracts of Land being part & parcel of the Northern Neck of Virginia situate ascertained bounded & described as appears in & by the three several Surveys following (that is to say) in & by one Survey of part thereof taken & made by John Warner on or about the Fifteenth Day of November one thousand Seven hundred and thirty Six and heretofore granted by Thomas late Lord Fairfax deceased as then proprietor of the said Northern Neck of Virginia to Thomas Bryan Martin[1] by a certain Instrument

---

8. The entire document is in the hand of Thomas Gregory, who added on the verso: "February 1793. The Revr. Doctor Fairfax and J.M. Marshall Esqr. Copy. Articles of Agreement. This To be delivered with the annexed notification to Thos. Bryan Martin Esqr. Also the Instrument for his Brother Denny taking the Name and using the Arms of Fairfax; But this last is to be kept, and only produced, but not parted with on the present occasion; as it may very probably be hereafter wanted to be produced on other occasions. Tho. Gregory."

This contract is printed in full because the details it contains are fundamentally important to the growing involvement of the so-called Marshall syndicate with the Fairfax lands. Although JM did not sign this document, it is clear that he considered himself a party to it and that Fairfax recognized that James M. Marshall meant to include others in the contract. See JM to Richard Henry Lee, Jan. 18, 1793, and Deed, Feb. 1, 1794, where JM actually carried out the terms of the contract by purchasing South Branch Manor in his name.

9. Namely, JM.

1. This Fairfax (1731–1798) was Denny Martin Fairfax's brother, who had settled in Virginia at the request of Thomas, Sixth Lord Fairfax. He had served in the House

of Conveyance dated on or about the Twenty First Day of August
in the Year of our Lord one thousand Seven hundred and Sixty
Seven And by him the said Thomas Bryan Martin afterwards reconveyed to the said Thomas late Lord Fairfax and his Heirs AND
ALSO as appears in and by a certain Survey of other part thereof
taken and made on or about the Twenty ninth Day of November
one thousand Seven hundred and thirty Six and heretofore also
granted by the said Thomas late Lord Fairfax deceased as then
proprietor as aforesaid to the said Thomas Bryan Martin & by
him in like Manner also afterwards reconveyed to the said Thomas
late Lord Fairfax & his Heirs AND ALSO as appears in and by a
certain Survey of the other and remaining part thereof taken &
made on or about the Tenth Day of March one thousand Seven
hundred and Forty Eight and heretofore likewise granted by the
said Thomas late Lord Fairfax deceased as then proprietor as
aforesaid to the said Thomas Bryan Martin & by him in like Manner also afterwards reconveyed to the said Thomas late Lord Fairfax & his Heirs All which said three several Tracts of Land and
premises before mentioned contain & comprise in the whole one
hundred and Fifty nine thousand Five hundred & Eleven Acres of
Land more or less and together form & constitute & are commonly
called or known by the Name of the Manor of Leeds situate lying
& being in the several Counties of Fauquier Loudon Frederick and
Shanandoah in the said State of Virginia or in some or one of them
AND ALSO ALL THAT the Manor of South Branch in Virginia aforesaid with the Appurtenances AND ALL THAT Tract or those Tracts
of Land other part & parcel of the sd. Northern Neck of Virginia
situate ascertained bounded & described as appears in and by two
several Surveys thereof taken & made by James Genn on or about
the thirty first Day of March one thousand Seven hundred and
forty Seven and the Seventh Day of April one thousand Seven
hundred and forty Eight and which said several last mentioned
premises were on or about the Twenty first Day of August one
thousand Seven hundred and Sixty Seven also granted by the said
Thomas late Lord Fairfax as proprietor as aforesaid to the said
Thomas Bryan Martin & by him afterwards in like Manner reconveyed to the said Thomas late Lord Fairfax & his Heirs All
which said several Land and premises last herein before mentioned

---

of Burgesses from 1756 to 1761 and continued to help protect the Fairfax interests after the death of Lord Fairfax.

contain & comprise in the whole Fifty four thousand Five hundred and Ninety Six Acres of Land more or less and together form
& constitute & are commonly called or known by the Name of the
South Branch Manor situate lying & being in the Countys of
Hampshire & Hardy or one of them in the said State of Virginia
AND ALSO all Manorial & other Rights & all Houses Buildings &
other Improvements And all Trees Timber Woods & Underwoods
to the said two Manors & each of them belonging AND all the Estate Right Title & Interest whatsoever of him the said Denny Fairfax how or by what Means soever derived & now vested in him of
into or out of the aforesaid two several Manors Lands & premises
& every part & parcel thereof respectively SAVE & EXCEPT nevertheless out of this present Contract & Agreement unto the said
Denny Fairfax & his Heirs All & such Tracts & parcels of Land
late of the said Thomas late Lord Fairfax as are not comprized &
comprehended within the aforesaid respective Surveys Bounds
Limits & Descriptions of the said several Manors of Leeds & South
Branch & all Benefit Advantage & Emolument whatsoever hereafter to arise accrue or be in any Manner derived from the Same
AND ALSO SAVE AND EXCEPT to all Grantees & Lessees of all or any
& every part & parts of the said premises hereby contracted for &
their respective Heirs or other Representatives the full & whole
Benefit & Advantage of all & every such his her & their several &
respective Grants & Leases whether made in the life Time of the
said late Lord Fairfax or at any Time since his Decease prior & up
to the Time of the notification of this present Contract as hereinafter mentioned AND SAVE AND EXCEPT also all Rents & Arrears
of Rent now at the Time of the Execution of this present Agreement due from all or any & every of the Grantees Lessees or Un-
dertenants of the said premises hereby contracted to be sold & for
which Rents or Arrears of Rent any Bond or Bonds or other Securities shall appear to have been actually taken either by the said
late Lord Fairfax in his Life Time or at any Time since his Decease
prior to the First Day of February which was in the Year of our
Lord one thousand Seven hundred and Ninety. It being hereby
agreed that all other Arrears of Rent not so secured prior to the
said First Day of February one thousand Seven hundred and
Ninety and all Rents and Arrears of Rent secured by Bond or
otherwise subsequent to that Day as well as all accruing Rents
(Except such only as that have been actually received at the Time

of the said Notification to be given as after mentioned) shall be considered as the property of the purchaser & shall pass to him with the said purchased premises So nevertheless that he shall not enter upon nor take or be entitled to have or take the proprietorship or possession of the said purchased premises till actual payment of his purchase Money and the Execution of the Conveyance as hereinafter agreed on.

AND the said James Markham Marshall doth hereby for himself his Heirs Executors and Administrators contract covenant & agree to purchase of the said Denny Fairfax All & every the said two several Manors Lands & premises before mentioned Subject nevertheless to all Grants or Underleases subsisting of or upon any parts of the said Estates at the Time of the said intended Notification at and for the price or Sum of Twenty Thousand pounds of lawful British Sterling Money & to pay the Same to or to the Order of the said Denny Fairfax or his Heirs at or in the Royal Exchange or elsewhere in the City of London as he the said Denny Fairfax or his Heirs shall direct or appoint at the Time or Times & in Manner hereinafter mentd.

AND it is hereby further mutually contracted & agreed That this present Contract shall be carried into Execution the said Sale & Conveyance completed and the said purchase Money paid as above stipulated on or before the First Day of February which will be in the Year of our Lord one thousand Seven hundred & Ninety Four at the farthest And that the said James Markham Marshall or such other person or persons to whom the said conveyance shall be made & executed shall & will in the mean Time & until the actual payment & Receipt of the said purchase Money well & truly pay & allow to the said Denny Fairfax & his Heirs from the Day of such Notification as before & after mentd. Interest at the Rate of Five pounds per centum per Annum for the said purchase Money PROVIDED nevertheless that the said Denny Fairfax shall be considered as bound to accept of any Sum or Sums not less than Five thousand pounds in part & on Account of such purchase Money at any Time or Times before the said First Day of February one thousand Seven hundred and Ninety Four if the same shall be proposed & ready to be paid at any such earlier Day & for which Sums or prompt payments if any shall be so made such Interest is thenceforth to cease But the said Denny Fairfax shall nevertheless not in any wise be compelled or compellable to execute the Conveyance of the said purchased premises before the said First Day of February one thousand Seven hundred and Ninety Four.[2]

AND it is hereby also farther mutually contracted & agreed by & between the said parties for themselves & their Heirs & hereby declared to be their true Meaning & Intention that in Consideration of such Arrears & accruing Rents as aforesaid being after the aforesaid Notification to be deemed the property of the purchaser the said James Markham Marshall or such other person or persons as aforesaid shall accept & take the said Estates charged (as they now are) under the Will of the said Thomas late Lord Fairfax with three several Annuities of One hundred pounds a year each to or in Favor of the three Children of Bryan Fairfax Esquire and which Annuities are to commence & accrue successively to them from & after the several successive Deceases of the present Sisters[3] of the said Denny Fairfax And shall and will from the Commenc-[ement] thereof respectively from Time to Time in future at his & their own Expence well & truly pay satisfy & discharge the same Annuities & every of them when & as the same shall become due & well & effectually exonerate indemnify & secure the said Denny Fairfax & his Heirs & all & every his Estates not included in the present Contract for Sale & all other his property real & personal as well in England as America of and from the payment of the same & all Claims Costs & Demands whatsoever for or on Account thereof And that he the said Denny Fairfax shall & will also in like Manner take upon himself & well & truly pay satisfy & discharge all Claims & Demands whatsr. which under & by Virtue of the said Will of the said late Lord Fairfax the Sisters of him the said Denny Fairfax have or may claim to have for or on Account of the Annuities of one hundred pounds a year each to them given by the said Will of the said late Lord Fairfax on the said Estates so contracted for as aforesaid & well & effectually exonerate indemnify & secure the said James Markham Marshall & such other person & persons as aforesaid & his & their Heirs & all & every his & their Estates & property of & from the payment of the same & all Claims Costs & Demands whatsoever for or on Account thereof AND ALSO that he the said Denny Fairfax shall & will immediately on the Execution of these presents give & deliver to the said

2. JM honored the contract by purchasing the least expensive portion, South Branch Manor, on Feb. 1, 1794, although no money was exchanged until the legal dispute with the state appeared resolved.

3. Frances (1727–1813), Sybella (1729–1816), and Anna Susanna (1736–1817).

James Markham Marshall to be [   ] conveyed to his Brother Thomas Bryan Martin now resident in Virginia & his Agent there a Notification in Writing of this present Agreement together with full Directions to him & his & their Agents immediately from & after the Receipt of such Notification to desist from the further Receipt of any of the said Arrears of Rent then due & outstanding & not secured as aforesaid and from letting out or making any farther Grant or Grants Lease or Leases of any part or parts of the said purchased premises or exercising any other Acts of Ownership thereon for or on Account or to the Use of him the said Denny Fairfax or his Heirs So nevertheless that possession of the said Estates or any part thereof is in no wise to be delivered to the purchaser until a further Notification shall be sent that the said purchase Money is actually paid & received in England according to the true Intent and Meaning of the Stipulations & Agreements herein before contained for that purpose PROVIDED also nevertheless and it is hereby further mutually contracted covenanted & agreed by & between the parties to these presents for themselves and their several Heirs That in Case the said Denny Fairfax or his Heirs shall by any legal Means whatsoever be rendered incapable of making the aforesaid Sale & Conveyance or of carrying the aforesaid Agreements on his part into Execution Then the same shall as to both the said parties be deemed to be from thenceforth absolutely null & void to all Intents & purposes whatsoever Or if the said Denny Fairfax or his Heirs shall be so rendered incapable as to any part or parts only of the premises so intended to be sold Then that a reasonable & proportionable part of the said purchase Money (to be settled by two indifferent persons to be named by each of the said parties) shall be deducted and allowed for such part of the premises which the said Denny Fairfax shall be so rendered incapable of conveying AND it is in like Manner agreed that in the Conveyance or Conveyances to be made in consequence of the present Contract the said Denny Fairfax shall not be called upon for any general Warranty or be expected to warrant or covenant for the Title of the said purchased premises any farther than against the Acts of himself & his Heirs & of all persons claiming through or under the said Thomas late Lord Fairfax deceased but not further or otherwise AND IT IS LASTLY AGREED that the Expence of this present Contract and agreement shall be borne and paid equally and jointly by and between the said James Markham Marshall and Denny Fairfax And the Expence of the future Conveyance by the said purchaser only IN WITNESS whereof each of the said parties have to these presents set their Hands and Seals the Day and Year first above written.

Witness   D. FAIRFAX
ROBT TOBY of Maidstone Gent.
GEO: BURR of Maidstone, Atty. at Law.

Masonic Dispensation

DS, Henry E. Huntington Library

[Richmond], February 8, 1793

JOHN MARSHELL Deputy Grand Master, To all and every, to whose knowledge these Presents shall come Greeting,[4]

WHEREAS it hath been duely represented that in the County of Buckingham in the Commenwealth of Virginia there reside a Number of the Brethern of the Society of Free Masons, and it appearing to be for the good and increase of that Ancient and noble Art that the said Brethern should be encouraged and enabled to proceed to work and be formed into a Regular Lodge under a Dispensation till the Twenty Eight day of October next then this said despensation to be null & Void,[5]

KNOW YE that I JOHN MARSHELL Esquire Deputy Grand Master of the Most Honorable and Antient Society of Free Masons within the aforesaid Commonwealth of Virginia.

Do hereby constitute and appoint the Worshipful Charles Yauncey[6] Master, Thomas Moseby Senr Warden, John Moseley Junior Warden, together with all such other Brethern as may be admitted to associate with them to be a just true and regular Lodge of Free Masons, by the Name Title and designation of the Buckingham Union Lodge N. 38, and further do hereby appoint and ordain all Regular Lodges to hold acknowledge and respect them as such,

4. This dispensation was enclosed with JM's letter to James Henderson of Jan. 1793.
5. Buckingham Union Lodge was officially chartered by the Grand Lodge at its meeting of Oct. 29, 1793. Dove, *Proceedings*, 115.
6. Charles Yancey (1770–1857), of Buckingham County, represented that county in the House of Delegates from 1796 to 1801, from 1810 to 1813, and from 1816 to 1838, and served in the Virginia senate from 1801 to 1805. Active in the Masons, he was grand master of the Grand Lodge of Virginia from 1822 to 1824. Alexander Brown, *The Cabells and Their Kin: A Memorial Volume of History, Biography, and Genealogy* (Boston, 1895), 301.

hereby granting and committing to them full power and authority to Assemble and convene as a regular Lodge to Enter, and receve Apprentices Pass Fellow Crafts, and raise Master Masons,[7] according to the known and established Customs, of Ancient Masonry and no otherwise.

IN TESTIMONY whereof I have hereunto set my Hand and caused the Seal of the Grand Lodge of Virginia to be hereto affixed this 8th Day February. AL. 5793 AD. 1793[8]

Witness   J MARSHALL
JAMES HENDERSON GS.   [SEAL]   Dep. Gd. M. of Virga.

To Francis Walker

ALS, Page-Walker Manuscripts, University of Virginia Library

Dear Sir[9]   Richmond, February 23, 1793
    Your messenger is but now ready to leave town.
    I think it woud do for you to take testimony shewing the relative value of the lands formerly in possession of Mr. Meriwether as far back as you can conveniently procure it & also stating the situation of the different tracts so that a rational conjecture may be formd of its value when the agreement was made.[1]
    In the suit against Cabell[2] an attachment must be executed on Wilkinson & it woud I think be proper to take some testimony to prove that Wilkinson was authorizd by the company to contract debts which were paid by your Father. Farewell, I am dear Sir your obedt.

                                                               J MARSHALL

    7. These are the first three degrees of the Masonic order, conferred on members by the local lodges.
    8. See Dove, *Proceedings*, 110–111, where this action is recorded in the minutes of the Grand Lodge.
    9. Addressed to "Francis Walker esquire, Albemarle."
    1. It is likely that the agreement was either a prenuptial agreement between Francis Walker's parents or a prenuptial agreement between Mildred Thornton Meriwether, his mother, and her first husband, Nicholas Meriwether. See JM to Thomas Walker, July 9, 1789, for further details.
    2. Walker v. Cabell was a suit brought in the High Court of Chancery in the autumn of 1790 that involved a partnership between Thomas Walker, William Cabell, Edward Carter, Alexander Trent, and John Wilkinson, formed on Dec. 28, 1770, for the purpose of operating an iron furnace, forge, gristmill, and sawmill. After the original scheme had been abandoned, Walker brought a bill in chancery requesting an equitable accounting. See Account Book, Receipts, May and Aug. 3, 1790, and bill in chancery listed at Law Papers, Sept. 1790.

Masonic Dispensation

Copy, Minute Book, Marshall Lodge No. 39 A.F. & A.M., Lynchburg, Va.

[*March 30, 1793, Richmond.* JM signs a dispensation³ for Robert Yancy, James Callaway,⁴ and Samuel Irvine to form Hiram Lodge No. 39 in Lynchburg.]

To William Branch Giles

ALS, Collection of the Association for the Preservation of Virginia Antiquities, on deposit at the Virginia Historical Society

My dear Giles⁵   [Richmond, *ca.* March 1793]

I enclose you several letters for your territory which I beg the favor of you to froward. Will you make one thing as publick as possible? Tis that the assembly have laid a dollar tax on judgements which the parties who are to obtain them must be prepard to pay.⁶ I forgot to mention it in my letters & tis a common concern. I am your

J MARSHALL

3. This lodge was officially chartered by the Grand Lodge on Oct. 29, 1793. At that time Hiram Lodge changed its name to Marshall Lodge in honor of JM, who had been elected grand master of the Grand Lodge on Oct. 28, 1793. Masonic Charter, calendared at Nov. 8, 1793; Dove, *Proceedings*, 113, 115; Rough Minutes, Oct. 29, 1793, Grand Lodge A.F. & A.M. of Virginia, Richmond; William Moseley Brown, *Marshall Lodge No. 39 A.F. & A.M.* . . . (Staunton, Va., 1953), 12, 134.

See Dove, *Proceedings*, 111, where this action is recorded in the minutes of the Grand Lodge.

4. James Callaway (1736–1809), a prominent resident of Campbell County, had built the first ironworks above Lynchburg and owned and operated lead mines in the area. Alexander Brown, *The Cabells and Their Kin: A Memorial Volume of History, Biography, and Genealogy* (Boston, 1895), 399–400.

5. Addressed to Giles, "atty. at law, P.burg." Giles was a member of Congress at this time but was in Petersburg practicing law between the Second Congress, which adjourned on Mar. 2, and the Third Congress, which convened on Dec. 2, 1793.

6. On Dec. 3, 1792, the General Assembly enacted a statute imposing a one-dollar tax on most processes of the courts. The only process not taxed appears to have been writs of capias ad respondendum issued by county courts. JM must have been referring to this tax, even though it is not specifically a tax on judgments. The same session of Assembly in fact imposed a fee of 18¢ for entering judgments, but this was a clerk's fee and not a tax. 13 Hening 336–337, 387 (1792); 1 Shepherd 224–226 (1793).

Write our client Jones[7] that he must come immediately to execute an appeal bond.

To James Henderson

ALS, Henry E. Huntington Library

Dear Sir[8]   [Richmond, *ca.* April 6, 1793]
    The bearer Mr. Yancy waits on you with a dispensation[9] to which you will please to affix the seal agreeable to the laws. I am yours respectfully

J MARSHALL

Masonic Dispensation

DS, Henry E. Huntington Library[1]

[*April 6, 1793, Richmond.* JM signs a dispensation for Nimrod Long, Charles Cowls, and George Latham to form Stevensburg Lodge No. 40 in Culpeper County.[2]]

7. David Jones (1736–1820) lived in Chester County, Pa. As a clergyman, he had served as a chaplain during the Revolution. He became a prolific author, writing primarily on theology and politics. He was a party in a legal action, Issac Williams and Joseph Tomlinson v. John Jeremiah Jacob and David Jones, that involved a disputed land claim. Jacob and Jones had lost the case in the High Court of Chancery in May 1792, and JM was planning an appeal to the Court of Appeals. See JM to David Jones, Jan. 16, 1794, and Account Book, Receipts, Nov. 29, 1789.
    8. Addressed to Henderson in Powhatan. "Letter from DGM., Feb. 5793," was written on the verso in another hand.
    9. The Masonic dispensation to Stevensburg Lodge No. 40, calendared at Apr. 6, 1793, was enclosed.
    1. This dispensation was enclosed in JM's letter to James Henderson dated *ca.* Apr. 6, 1793. On the verso JM wrote, "Dispensation for Lodge No. 40." "Dispensation of Lodge No. 40, Returned 5794," was written in another hand.
    2. This action was recorded in the minute book of the Grand Lodge, where it was also recorded that Stevensburg Lodge No. 40 was officially chartered on Oct. 29, 1793. Another dispensation was issued on Oct. 31, 1793, directing that Nimrod Long be installed as master of the lodge. Dove, *Proceedings*, 115; Masonic dispensation, calendared at Oct. 31, 1793.

To Charles Lee

ALS, Collection of the Association for the Preservation of Virginia Antiquities, on deposit at the Virginia Historical Society

Dear Sir[3]   [Richmond, *ca*. April 15, 1793]

You were so good as to tell me you woud attend to my business in Fredericksburg & I must rely upon you to do so. There is but very little remaining as I have made a point for some time past to engage in nothing new. There are two suits which are attended with some difficulty & to which I must beg your attention. The one is an action of trespass to which Mr. Warden[4] has fild the enclosd [*pleas*]. I have noted those to which I had thoughts of demurring & those on which I had designd to join issue. Will you look them over & alter them if you think proper. If you think it more adviseable take issue where I have demured. The inclosd paper is admitted as testimony to save the expense of attendance. This is a small suit but the plf. is poor & the costs are material to him. The other suit is one which Chew is interested in & will shew. The issue is joind on the plea of a former judgement & the [   ][5] replication of no such record. Do look into this & alter it if you think it adviseable. Mr. Washington[6] & Brooke have both been kind enough to say they woud aid me & I beg you to consult with them on this suit. I beleive any other suit [*I*] may have will turn out to be a plain business. There is one about a tobacco hoxhead or so which was lost & there was a new note issued. I must lose the cause unless the plaintiff will be so liberal as to give it up but I must get the favor of you to attend to it. I wish you a rich court & am with much esteem, your

J. MARSHALL

3. The letter is addressed to Lee "now at Fredericksburg" and is endorsed, in three different hands, "Ch. Justice, John Marshall's letter, Talbott v. Brooke." Action taken in that case before the District Court at Fredericksburg on Oct. 5, 1793, suggests one of the cases JM refers to in this letter. See District Court Law Orders, A, 1789–1793, 531, Fredericksburg, Virginia State Library. For other later references, see pps. 175, 236, 315, 357, 412, and Law Orders, B, 1794–1798, 149.

JM had apparently decided to go to Cumberland County, where an examination of murder charges against Richard Randolph was to be held on Apr. 29. See Commonwealth v. Randolph: Editorial Note, *ca*. Apr. 29, 1793, and "expenses travelling," in Account Book, Disbursements, May 1793.

4. John Warden (d. 1814), known as "Jock," was a prominent Richmond attorney who had begun his practice in Northumberland County in 1777.

5. A hole in the manuscript seems to have removed at least one word, although parts of two words had been crossed out by JM.

6. Bushrod Washington and Robert Brooke (1751–1799).

To James Brown

Printed, Walter R. Benjamin Autographs, Inc., *The Collector* (New York, February 1942), 58

[*April 21, 1793, Richmond*. JM requests payment for tobacco sold to Brown.[7]]

Commonwealth v. Randolph

EDITORIAL NOTE

During the winter of 1792/1793 a rumor swept across Virginia that caused the Randolph family great embarrassment and persisted for many years, even after a court exonerated the principal family members of any wrongdoing. The following document has been the primary source of information about the affair, but surprisingly historians have not questioned its authenticity or its value as evidence of Marshall's participation in what most have incorrectly termed a trial. Because this is the most important of the four documents that historians have used in describing the affair and the resulting court proceeding,[8] it deserves serious examination.

A description of what the editors believe the document to be raises only slightly fewer questions than their ideas of what it is not. It is a copy of what appear to be depositions, or summaries of depositions, and a concluding summary or argument by John Marshall. John Randolph of Roanoke, who prepared the copy from the original, labeled them "Jno Marshall's notes of evidence" on the verso of his copy, and on the first page he wrote the heading "Commonwealth vs. Randolph." Some of the questions raised by these incomplete and secondhand labels are answered by understanding how this case came into being as a result of the rumors that spread throughout the state.

7. See Account Book, Receipts, Apr. 1793, where JM entered, "Mr. Brown £7."
8. In addition to JM's notes of evidence, the Cumberland County Court Order Book for Apr. 29, 1793, has provided documentation of the court proceeding. Cumberland County Court Order Book, 1792–1797, 88, Virginia State Library. Two letters have also been used: John Randolph to Ann Randolph Morris, Oct. 31, 1814, and Ann Randolph Morris to John Randolph, Jan. 16, 1815, both of which are printed in William Cabell Bruce, *John Randolph of Roanoke, 1773–1833*, 2d ed. rev. (New York, 1922), II, 274–295.
Most writers have accepted and followed Bruce's account of the so-called trial, *ibid.*, I, 107–121, although he borrowed his account of Patrick Henry's involvement from William Wirt Henry, *Patrick Henry, Life, Correspondence and Speeches* (New York, 1891), II, 490–493. Other accounts are Robert Douthat Meade, *Patrick Henry, Practical Revolutionary* (Philadelphia, 1969), 417–420; H. J. Eckenrode, *The Randolphs: The Story of a Virginia Family* (New York, 1946), 171–187; Jonathan Daniels, *The Randolphs of Virginia* (Garden City, N.Y., 1972), 135–149; Francis Biddle, "Scandal at Bizarre," *American Heritage*, XII (Aug. 1961), 10–13, 79–82; Dumas Malone, *Jefferson and the Ordeal of Liberty* (Boston, 1962), 172–174; and Leonard Baker, *John Marshall: A Life in Law* (New York, 1974), 139–153.

Ann Cary Randolph, known as Nancy, daughter of Thomas Mann Randolph of "Tuckahoe," had come to live with her sister Judith and Judith's husband, Richard Randolph, stepson of St. George Tucker, sometime in 1791.[9] Richard Randolph had inherited "Bizarre," in Cumberland County, one of his father's plantations, and at nineteen had married seventeen-year-old Judith and decided to work the plantation rather than to pursue a career in law as his stepfather wanted. Two years later sixteen-year-old Nancy left "Tuckahoe" after refusing to accept her father's choice of a husband and moved in with the couple. Richard's younger brother, Theodorick, often visited "Bizarre," and he and Nancy planned to marry. Theodorick died in February 1792, however, only a few days after what Nancy later termed "the scene which began the history of my sorrows."[1] Nancy was now pregnant, and the child's father was dead. For a few months the secret stayed within the immediate family. Nancy was quite ill with her pregnancy, and Richard suggested that she was threatening to miscarry as Judith had done in 1790.

What actually happened in September or October 1792 is uncertain, though Nancy apparently miscarried or delivered a stillborn child on September 30, as she later insisted, or on the next night, when she, Richard, Judith, and a few others gathered at a relative's home for a visit. They had taken the short ride to "Glenlyvar," cousin Randolph Harrison's still unfinished home, on Monday, October 1, when Nancy was so unwell she went to bed soon after arriving. During the night she was in great pain and, as was observed the next day, lost some blood. She recovered in a few days, however, and seemed normal. For a brief time the immediate family must have thought the secret had been kept, as Richard had insisted it be, but talk soon spread from the slave quarters that during that first night at "Glenlyvar" Nancy had delivered a child and Richard had killed it. Soon it was said that the child was Richard's, adding incest to the accusations. In January 1793, Nancy, Richard, and Judith spent several days in Williamsburg with Richard's stepfather, St. George Tucker, who had moved from Cumberland County five years earlier, after Richard's mother died. The judge and law professor was obviously now told the secret. During visits in February and March the family discussed how to quiet the rumors.[2] Richard hoped to arrange an action of slander and finally asked Nancy's father, Colonel Thomas Randolph, to institute it. Richard planned to take Judith and Nancy north for the summer while

9. Richard Randolph (1770–1796) was the son of John Randolph (1742–1775), of "Matoax," and Frances Bland (1752–1788). After Richard's father died, Frances Bland Randolph married St. George Tucker in 1788. Judith Randolph (1772–1816) and Ann Cary Randolph (1774–1836) were daughters of Thomas Mann Randolph, Sr. (1741–1793), of "Tuckahoe," and Ann Cary Randolph, formerly of "Ampthill," and were also Richard's cousins.

Most of this paragraph is taken from letters recently discovered in the Tucker-Coleman Papers, Swem Library, College of William and Mary, written after Nancy married Gouverneur Morris. These documents permit a reinterpretation of the entire episode. See especially Ann Randolph Morris to St. George Tucker, ca. Dec. 13, 1814, Feb. 9, Mar. 2, and Mar. 20, 1815.

1. Ann Randolph Morris to John Randolph, Jan. 16, 1815, in Bruce, *Randolph*, II, 283. Nancy's father opposed her marrying Theodorick because his inheritance, as well as Richard's, was encumbered by a British debt. *Ibid.*, 282.

2. St. George Tucker to the public, May 5, 1793, in *Virginia Gazette, and General Advertiser* (Richmond), May 15, 1793.

the slanderers attempted to prove infanticide and incest. This plan was quickly dashed, however, probably by Colonel Randolph's refusal to bring suit.[3] Soon afterward Richard decided on the course that eventually brought the case into being. He no doubt made this decision with Tucker's help and perhaps with John Marshall's as well.

On March 29, 1793, Richard boldly announced to the public in several newspapers that he intended to appear before the Cumberland County Court when it met for its April term to become a prisoner "to answer in the due course of law, any charge or crime which any person or persons whatsoever shall then and there think proper to alledge against me." Randolph was in effect calling the alleged slanderers into the open. He begged them to appear and to attempt to bring about a conviction. If they were unwilling to appear in court, he asked them to publish their charges with direct or circumstantial evidence in the newspapers in order for the public to judge extralegally.[4] What followed has been mistakenly called a trial, even by contemporaries. That it be accurately termed an examination, and that the details of that examination be explained, is essential to an understanding of Marshall's notes of evidence.

On April 21 or 22 Richard Randolph appeared before one or more of the justices of the peace assembled for monthly court in Cumberland County. It is unknown how the charges were formally made, but a magistrate ordered him to be held by the sheriff for an official examination.[5] Virginia law provided that a free person charged with a crime would be brought before a magistrate who deter-

3. Richard Randolph to St. George Tucker, Mar. 14, 1793, in Bruce, *Randolph*, I, 116. That he quickly abandoned this plan is evident from a letter Judith wrote the next day to her sister Elizabeth. The letter is printed with Tucker's letter to the public, May 5, 1793, in *Va. Gaz., & Genl. Adv.*, May 15, 1793.

4. Richard Randolph to the public, Mar. 29, 1793, in *Va. Gaz., & Genl. Adv.*, Apr. 3, 1793.

Nancy wrote Tucker in 1815 regarding Richard's plans to defend himself from the charges: "In the spring of 93 Jack [John Randolph] shewed me at Matoax a letter from my brother T.M.R. [Thomas Mann Randolph, Jr.,] to Dick in which he says 'I defy you to transfer the stigma to your deceased brother.' My dear Sir, this caused silence on that subject then. He told Dick 'I will wash out, with your blood the stain on my family.' Jack's memory has lost all this. *Dick* exacted from *me Silence* by a promise which I kept . . . sacred. . . ." Ann Randolph Morris to St. George Tucker, Feb. 9, 1815, Tucker-Coleman Papers, Wm. & Mary.

The next month she told Tucker that as Richard set out for Cumberland Court on Apr. 21, 1793, she had given him a statement that Theodorick had fathered her child. She added, "He burnt it. My brother dared him to make that very attempt which he avoided by throwing the paper in the Fire. . . ." Ann Randolph Morris to St. George Tucker, Mar. 2, 1815, Tucker-Coleman Papers, Wm. & Mary.

5. John Randolph wrote Tucker on Apr. 21 that Richard had gone to Cumberland Courthouse that morning. Randolph to Tucker, Apr. 21, 1793, in *Va. Gaz., & Genl. Adv.*, May 15, 1793. Richard said he intended to appear before the court to become a prisoner on the first day of April court, which came on Apr. 22. Cumberland County Court Order Book, 1792–1797, 71, Va. State Lib.

Considerable evidence exists to indicate Richard was held in jail several days. Tucker says as much in his letter to the public and states that Richard was arrested on a magistrate's warrant. *Va. Gaz., & Genl. Adv.*, May 15, 1793. See also Cumberland County Court Order Book, 1792–1797, 161, Va. State Lib., where an order is given to pay six men for having guarded Randolph while he was in jail. Some of the men guarded him for seven days, suggesting he was jailed on Apr. 22.

mined whether an examination by the whole county court was necessary. If the magistrate so decided, he would order the accused held in jail, direct material witnesses to appear at the examination, and instruct the sheriff to summons the entire court to assemble for the examination on a given day not less than five or more than ten days from the arrest. The law contained no provision for bail at that point. If the offense was a capital crime, as in this instance, the examining court would decide whether the prisoner should be released or be held for trial in the district court having jurisdiction.[6] In what became known as *Commonwealth v. Randolph*, the examination resulted in dismissal of the charges; therefore, Randolph never went to trial.[7]

Little doubt remains that Marshall was indeed involved in this proceeding and that he was probably at Cumberland County Court on April 29. In 1814, on separate occasions, John Randolph of Roanoke, who had attended the court meeting, wrote that Marshall had been "misled" in 1793. The context of Randolph's reference strongly suggests Marshall played some official role in the proceedings.[8] It is clear from Marshall's Account Book that he traveled somewhere in late April or early May.[9] Marshall normally attended meetings of the Court of Appeals in late April and traveled to Fredericksburg District Court afterward. Both of these courts were meeting on April 29, but it is impossible to prove he was in Richmond or Fredericksburg, since all of the court's business could have taken place in his absence. Sometime in April 1793, moreover, Marshall wrote to Charles Lee asking him to take his cases in Fredericksburg.[1] His Account Book entry seems

6. 1 Shepherd 20–21 (1792).

7. The Cumberland County Court Order Book contains the following entry for Apr. 29: "At a court held for Cumberland county the twenty ninth day of April one thousand seven hundred and ninety three for the examination of Richard Randolph who stands committed and charged with feloniously murdering a child said to be born of Nancy Randolph, present . . . [sixteen justices]. The Court being thus constituted the prisoner was led to the bar in custody of the sheriff to whose custody he was before committed for the felony aforesaid and being charged with the same denied the fact, Whereupon, Sundry witnesses were sworn and examined touching the premises and the prisoner heard in his defence On consideration whereof and of the circumstances relating to the fact, it is the opinion of the Court that the said Richard is not guilty of the felony wherewith he stands charged and that he be discharged out of custody and go hence thereof without day." Cumberland County Court Order Book, 1792–1797, 88, Va. State Lib. The identical entry was made in the minute book. Cumberland County Court Minute Book, 1792–1794, Va. State Lib. (only in manuscript).

8. John Randolph to Ann Randolph Morris, Oct. 31, 1814, in Bruce, *Randolph*, II, 275, and Statement of John Randolph, Nov. 23, 1814, Tucker-Coleman Papers, Wm. & Mary.

9. See Account Book, Disbursements, May 1793, where JM entered "expenses travelling 35[s.]."

1. JM to Charles Lee, *ca.* Apr. 15, 1793. In the Court of Appeals on Apr. 29, one of JM's cases was "partly heard" and then continued for two days. On the last day of the term, May 1, "for reasons appearing to the Court," several other JM cases were ordered continued until October term. Court of Appeals Order Book, II, 227, Va. State Lib. The Fredericksburg District Court, where JM had been every spring since the court was established in 1789, convened on Apr. 29. In only one case, Hungerford v. Alexander on May 4, would one expect JM to be present. A commission to take depositions was issued to JM in that case, but that could have been the motion he refers to in the letter to Charles Lee, and it could have been introduced by Lee for JM.

to have been made early in the month, probably before the Fredericksburg court adjourned on May 9 and before Marshall would have returned to Richmond. He also normally spent a much greater sum of money in Fredericksburg.

Believing that Marshall was in Cumberland County on April 29, however, does not explain what role he played at the hearing. Evidence indicates that Patrick Henry was engaged by Richard Randolph, although documentation that he was offered 500 guineas for this hearing does not exist and has never been clearly cited by those accepting that story. Randolph undoubtedly paid Henry £140—a huge fee, if that was the total amount paid.[2] There is no record that Marshall received any fee in the case. Perhaps he was paid but failed to record the fee; perhaps he contributed his services to his cousins; or perhaps he was not retained by Richard Randolph after all. An examination of the notes of evidence offers some clues to Marshall's role.

One theory argues that the notes were taken during Richard Randolph's examination and represent an informal transcript of the trial.[3] If Marshall was present to help defend Richard at the hearing, however, it is unlikely he would have waited until the witnesses testified to take notes in order to prepare a closing argument for presentation immediately afterward. The entire procedure took place on April 29; it was the only business of record that day. Several extant court records show that charges were brought only against Richard. Nancy was never officially accused or brought before the whole court for examination of charges against her. A close analysis of Marshall's notes, however, suggests they were primarily prepared to prove Nancy's innocence, not to answer charges against Richard. When Marshall refers to Richard in his argument, he does so as if to defend Nancy. Of course, if he could have established doubt that Nancy were ever pregnant, the charges against Richard would have lost their foundation. This might explain his attention to her here. But there are other indications that he was concerned only with defending Nancy. Preceding John Randolph's statement in Marshall's notes is the heading "On the part of Mr. Randolph," and if this appeared on the original document and was not simply added by John Randolph,

---

In several other JM cases before that court, continuances were granted the opposing counsel. District Court Law Orders, A, 1789–1793, 440, 464, and *passim*, Fredericksburg, Va. State Lib.

2. The legend that Henry was offered 500 guineas began with William Wirt Henry, but has been accepted by Meade and most other writers as well. See Henry, *Henry*, II, 490, and Meade, *Henry*, 419. Meade also confused the record by stating in a footnote that the Cumberland County court records had disappeared. Meade, *Henry*, 518–519, n. 42. He used Bruce, *Randolph*, as a source, and the only records Bruce mentions are the court order books, which are extant and available on microfilm from the Va. State Lib. The court's minute book for the period as well as the clerk's fee book exist in manuscript at the Va. State Lib. They were transferred there in 1975.

Richard Randolph paid Patrick Henry £140 with a note due on May 30, 1793. Henry assigned the note to Nathaniel Anderson, probably immediately. On July 28, 1794, Anderson sued Randolph for payment in the Cumberland County Court and won a judgment. Cumberland County Court Order Book, 1792–1797, 217, Va. State Lib.

3. Bruce, Meade, Biddle, and Baker assume JM's notes represent an account of the proceedings as if they were taken in court. The notes have even been used as evidence of the order of testimony at the trial, but no documentation has been found that would substantiate this.

it probably refers to Richard rather than John and might indicate that testimony was taken on the part of someone else, namely, Nancy. Preceding Judith's testimony is the statement, "Upon the trial of Miss Nancy before the Magistrates, Mrs. Judith Randolph deposes." This allows for the supposition that Marshall prepared this document prior to the examination of Richard for use at the hearing and that he anticipated Nancy being called to testify. Judith's testimony as it applied to charges against her husband was not admissable under Virginia law, but a statement could be taken from her for use if charges were to be brought against Nancy. Also, if this document were to be handed to the magistrates, which is possible, it would be a shrewd way of getting Judith's testimony before the magistrates, just as inadmissible slave testimony was in effect introduced by a few of the deponents in their statements. One historian has interpreted the phrase "Upon the trial of Miss Nancy" to mean that Nancy did actually testify at Richard's examination;[4] but if that were the case, and if Marshall's notes represent an unofficial account of the proceedings, why did he omit notes on her testimony? It seems clear that Marshall did not in fact take these notes during the hearing but that he either prepared them prior to the hearing, at which Nancy did not testify, or the document was prepared after the hearing for use in defending Nancy later.

The argument that Nancy was separately questioned at some point and that Marshall perhaps wrote this document primarily for use at her interrogation is somewhat convincing. A few days after the April 29 hearing, Martha Jefferson Randolph wrote her father, "They have been *tried* and acquited,"[5] suggesting that both Richard and Nancy were heard. In a statement written in 1814, however, John Randolph said Nancy "underwent examination before a Justice of the peace in Virginia in 1793," implying she had been questioned by a single magistrate. Nancy wrote in 1815 that she had indeed been questioned, saying, "There was the strictest examination."[6] It is possible that a single magistrate visited Nancy at "Bizarre" between April 22 and 29, with Patrick Henry and Alexander Campbell in attendance, and that after her questioning, Judith gave a deposition to be used on Nancy's behalf if she were ordered held for examination. Marshall then could have put all the depositions together prior to the hearing. His comment that he did not hear Judith's testimony, however, suggests that he did hear the others and thus adds weight to the theory that he did in fact prepare the document on or after April 29.

If Marshall prepared the document after the hearing, why did he omit the testimony of Richard? It is possible that Richard's hearing was held in the morning, that everyone listed in the document except Judith testified then, and that the magistrates and the Randolphs wanted Nancy questioned by a magistrate separately in the afternoon to determine if she should be held for a similar examination. If the magistrate decided she should not be held, the rumors would

4. Bruce, *Randolph*, I, 114.
5. Martha Jefferson Randolph to Thomas Jefferson, May 16, 1793, in Edwin Morris Betts and James Adam Bear, Jr., eds., *The Family Letters of Thomas Jefferson* (Columbia, Mo., 1966), 117-118.
6. Statement of John Randolph, Nov. 23, 1814, Tucker-Coleman Papers, Wm. & Mary, and Ann Randolph Morris to John Randolph, Jan. 16, 1815, in Bruce, *Randolph*, II, 284.

certainly lose credibility.[7] Marshall might then have prepared the document between the two proceedings for presentation that afternoon to the one or more magistrates that would decide if Nancy should be arrested. He might have omitted Richard's testimony because it had not been given under oath,[8] or because Richard's release and the dismissal of charges against him was sufficient support of Nancy's innocence where he was concerned. Marshall's occasional parenthetical insertions of what he recalled a deponent having said supports the conclusion that he summarized their statements from rough notes when he prepared this document. The statement in his argument that "the person who came down stairs appears not to have been Mr. Randolph" implies that little doubt on that issue remained, and yet this point is not made in any of the depositions attached to Marshall's summary. Perhaps the question had been answered during the examination and was influential in the magistrates' decision not to try Richard.

A final theory that has some plausibility is that Marshall prepared this document after April 29 at the request of the family for unofficial use. This might better explain his lapses of memory as he summarized the statements of the deponents. He might have taken notes during the examination, or borrowed someone else's notes, and then, some days or even weeks later, prepared this document with his summarizing argument. This explanation would be consistent with the attention directed at Nancy's innocence, and is supported by the final paragraph of Marshall's summary. It is clear that many did not accept the finding of the court on April 29 and that rumors persisted.[9] It is also clear that St. George Tucker believed it necessary after the court's legal action to take the case before the public. He wrote on May 5, "The public mind is not always convinced by the decisions of *a court of law*. In cases where the *characters* of individuals are drawn in question, there lies an appeal to a *higher tribunal*: A COURT OF HONOUR!"[1] It is not challenging credulity to suggest that he or someone else asked Marshall to prepare a statement that might be distributed or published to help quiet rumors. In fact, it would have doubtless done more to convince the public than did St. George Tucker's publication of two letters of Judith respecting her husbands' culpability.

Even though additional court records and a better understanding of Virginia law at the time make clearer what occurred in April 1793, this document cannot be explained with certainty. Adding to the list of unanswered questions about

7. There would be no record of this interrogation, just as there had not been one made at Richard's appearance on Apr. 21 or 22. The matter would not become one of record until after the magistrate questioned the accused and issued a warrant for his or her arrest, holding the prisoner for examination by the entire court.

8. At the examination stage the accused was not sworn; only witnesses testified under oath. Theodore F. T. Plucknett, *A Concise History of the Common Law*, 5th ed. (London, 1956), 437, but see also 431–433. Notes were normally taken because they would be sent to the district court for use during the trial if the justices of the peace decided a trial should be held. For an example of such a case, see Commonwealth v. William Anglea, Cumberland County Court Order Book, 1792–1797, 146–147, Va. State Lib.

9. See for example Martha Jefferson Randolph to Thomas Jefferson, May 16, 1793, in Betts and Bear, eds., *Family Letters*, 118, where she wrote that only "a small part of the world and those the most inconsiderable people in it were influenced in there opinion by the dicision of the court."

1. *Va. Gaz., & Genl. Adv.*, May 15, 1793.

the entire episode is the loss of Marshall's own copy of this document. The original document would perhaps reveal something of the details of the examination and of Marshall's participation in the case. Its loss only enlivens the mystery and helps prevent the reconstruction of an accurate account of Virginia's most famous eighteenth-century criminal proceeding.

Commonwealth v. Randolph

Notes of Evidence

Copy, Virginia Historical Society[2]

Williamsburg, *ca.* April 29, 1793

CARTER PAGE[3] deposes,

That he has frequently seen Mr. Randolph and Miss Nancy[4] together, but knows of no criminal conversation between them; he has, however, seen them kissing and fond of each other. He had no other reason to suppose her pregnant, than an apparent alteration in her size, which he first perceived in May.

MRS. MARTHA RANDOLPH.[5]

In a conversation with Mrs. Richard Randolph, in presence of Miss Nancy; she spoke of Gum Guiacum[6] as an excellent medicine

2. This is item no. Mss2M3567a1 in the society's collections. The document is in the hand of John Randolph of Roanoke and is endorsed in his hand, "Respublica vs Randolph, Jno Marshall's notes of evidence." Randolph's stepfather, St. George Tucker, folded the paper and endorsed it "Resp: v. Randolph, Jno Marshall's notes of the Evidence, Copied from the original by Jno Randolph jr." A later transcript of Randolph's copy, with minor variations in spelling and punctuation and in an unknown hand, is in the Tucker-Coleman Papers, Swem Library, College of William and Mary.

At the end of the text Randolph wrote, "28 June, 1793, Wmsbg." It appears that Randolph copied the document at more than one sitting. He left "Bizarre" for Williamsburg on May 29 and remained there until July 7, 1793. William Cabell Bruce, *John Randolph of Roanoke, 1773–1833*, 2d ed. rev. (New York, 1922), I, 118. The editors have used the date of the court's examination as the best approximate date of JM's original.

3. Page (1758–1825), of "The Fork," Cumberland County, was an uncle of Richard Randolph. He had served as an aide to Lafayette during the Revolution.

4. Richard Randolph and Ann Cary Randolph.

5. Martha Jefferson Randolph (1772–1836), daughter of Thomas Jefferson, was married to Thomas Mann Randolph, Jr. (1768–1828), of "Tuckahoe." Her husband, a brother of Nancy and Judith Randolph, served as governor of Virginia from 1819 to 1822. For Martha's version of the scandal and court action, see Martha Jefferson Randolph to Thomas Jefferson, May 16, 1793, in Edwin Morris Betts and James Adam Bear, Jr., eds., *The Family Letters of Thomas Jefferson* (Columbia, Mo., 1966), 117–118.

6. Gum guaiacum. The drug was used for the treatment of chronic rheumatism, skin disorders, gout, and colic. William Cullen, *A Treatise of the Materia Medica*, ed.

for the cholic, but observed at the same time that it was a dangerous medicine, as it would produce an abortion. This conversation happened about the 12th. September. Miss Nancy was silent, but on the Friday following, about the 16th of september,[7] an application was made to her by Mrs. Page[8] for some gum guiacum for Miss Nancy. The medicine was not then sent, but it a few days afterwards it was sent to her, but not in a considerable quantity. She has known more to be given to a pregnant woman, without producing any mischief. She did suspect that Miss Nancy was pregnant.

MRS. PAGE.

For several months before she entertained any suspicion of a criminal correspondence between Mr. Randolph and Miss Nancy, she visited at Bizarre.[9] There appeared to be entire harmony in the family. She once heard Mrs. Randolph say, that Mr. Randolph and Miss Nancy were only company for themselves; but Mrs. Randolph added that Mr. Randolph was generally on his plantation and Miss Nancy up stairs in her Room. Her suspicions of a criminal intercourse between them, were founded on an apparent fondness for each other, and commenced about the last of March or first of April. In May she observed Miss Nancy's shape to alter. Miss Nancy generally appeared melancholy and complained of another disorder as well as the cholic. She appeared unwilling to undress and go to bed in her presence; but Mrs. Page had visited at Bizarre long before her suspicions commenced and did not recollect in the course of that time to have seen her undress and go to bed. Mrs. Page once heard a conversation between Miss Nancy and her maid, and being then suspicious of her situation and, on that account, desirous of hearing what passed, she approached the door. It was locked, but she could see through a crack Miss Nancy was in her undress and appeared to Mrs. Page to be pregnant.

Benjamin Smith Barton (Philadelphia, 1812), II, 139–142. Cullen comments, "Several physicians have apprehended mischief from the use of the guaiacum in a spirituous tincture; and I am certain that it sometimes happens," but he does not identify the nature of the mischief. *Ibid.*, 142.

7. In 1792, Sept. 12 came on Wednesday; thus Friday would have been the 14th. This was slightly more than two weeks from the night of the alleged infanticide.

8. Mrs. Carter Page (Mary Cary Page) (1766–1797), whose deposition follows, was a daughter of Archibald Cary and an aunt of Nancy and Judith. [Richard C. M. Page], *Genealogy of the Page Family in Virginia* (New York, 1883), 96.

9. This was the residence of Richard and Judith Randolph, located in Cumberland County on the Appomatox River near Farmville.

Mrs. Page heard her ask her maid whether she thought she was smaller; the maid replied she thought her larger; & Miss Nancy complained of ill health. Soon after Miss Nancy was said to have been delivered of a child, Mrs. Page informed her of the report which had been circulated to her prejudice, and told her she wished, she would put it in her power to contradict it; to which Miss Nancy replied, that if her denial would not satisfy her, she should give no further satisfaction. Mrs. Page recollects, once, to have seen Miss Nancy look down at her waist, & then cast her eyes up to Heaven in silent Melancholy.

RANDOLPH HARRISON[1]

had observed imprudent familiarities be[tween] Mr. Randolph and Miss Nancy, but had too high an opinion of them both to entertain any suspicion of a criminal correspondence. Mr. and Mrs. Randolph and Miss Nancy, accompanied by Mr. Archibald Randolph and Mr. John Randolph arrived at his House on Monday the first of october before dinner. He handed the Ladies out of the carriage. Miss Nancy had a close great [coat] buttoned round her. He observed no mark of pregnancy. She complained of being very unwell and soon after she came into the room, laid down on the bed. Soon after dinner Miss Nancy went up stairs to her Room, where she continued and appeared to be very unwell. After supper Mrs. Harrison went up with Mrs. Randolph to her bed, and he understood was in Miss Nancy's Room; she was very unwell and took the essence of peppermint, which she had been accustomed to take for the cholic. The House up stairs was unfinished, & was divided into two Rooms. The stair-case which was narrow, led into one called the outer Room, and from that, on the other side of the stair case, a door opened into the inner Room; so that they were divided by the width of the stair-case. Miss Nancy slept in the inner Room; Mr. and Mrs. Randolph in the outerroom. Late in the night Mr. & Mrs. Harrison were waked by loud screams which they supposed to proceed from Mrs. Randolph, but were presently informed that they proceeded from Miss Nancy, & were sent to for some Laudanum to be given her; the laudanum was sent, & Mrs. Harrison soon went up & remained in the Room

1. Harrison (1769–1839), of "Glenlyvar" and later referred to as being of "Clifton," after "Glenlyvar" was destroyed, was a son of Carter Henry Harrison and Susanna Randolph Harrison. His wife, Mary Randolph Harrison, was a cousin of Nancy, Judith, and Richard. Randolph Harrison represented Cumberland County in the House of Delegates from 1825 to 1827.

some little time and then returned, Miss Nancy being easier. They went to sleep again and while not completely awake, or very particular in their observation, heard some person come down stairs, whom they supposed to be Mr. Randolph, from the weight of the step on the stairs, and in some little time heard (as they supposed) the same person return. They imagined it to be Mr. Randolph, who had come down to send for a physician. Servants had frequently passed up & down stairs during the night. It was said that Miss Nancy had probably had an hysteric fit, to which she was subject; and that she had had one, two or three days before. The next day, which was Tuesday, Miss Nancy kept her bed. Mr. Harrison with Mr. Randolph went into her Room to lay the Hearth that she might have a fire. He observed about her nothing remarkable, except, considerable paleness, and a disagreeable flavor which he imputed to a cause, totally different from childbearing. He entertained no unfavorable suspicion concerning her, until information was given by a negro-woman, that she had miscarried. On the Wednesday Mrs. Randolph, Mrs. Harrison & Mr. Randolph rode out to a store where they all purchased some goods, and he knows not at whose instance they went. Some time after he heard a Report among the negroes that the Birth had been deposited on a pile of shingles between two Logs, & about six or seven weeks afterwards, he saw such a place, where there was a shingle which appeared to have been stained. On Wednesday Miss Nancy kept her Room but not her bed, and on Thursday he observed the flavor. On friday or Saturday, (I[2] believe on Saturday) they returned to Bizarre. The behaviour of the Ladies while at Mr. Harrison's, after this event, was the same as usual. Some time after (about three weeks) his family visited Bizarre; the behaviour of Mr. & Mrs. Randolph to each other was as usual, except that the deponent conceived that Mr. Randolph seemed somewhat crusty.

MRS. RANDOLPH HARRISON.[3]

Her testimony untill supper, precisely the same with that of her husband. After supper she went up with Mrs. Randolph, and they together enquired how Miss Nancy did? She appeared very unwell, & said she had taken her Gum guiacum (or Mrs. Randolph desired her to take, Her Gum guiacum as usual, I forget which)

2. JM.
3. Mary Randolph Harrison (1773–1835), wife of Randolph Harrison, was the daughter of Thomas Isham Randolph of "Dungeness" and Jane Cary Randolph.

after which, in some little time, Mrs. Randolph went to bed & Mrs. Harrison came down stairs to bed, also. Late in the night they were awaked by screaming. She supposed it at first to be Mrs. Randolph: she went up stairs and saw Mrs. Randolph sitting up in her bed, a candle I believe burning in the room; she asked Mrs. Randolph what was the matter with Nancy: Mrs. Randolph replied she did not know, but conjectured she had the hysterics as she had been subject to them; and she did not think that the cholic would make her scream so. Mrs. Harrison went to the door, which she found fastened by a Bolt, but this she supposed to be because the spring-latch was broken & the door could only be kept shut by being bolted. On knocking at the door it was instantly opened, & she was immediately desired by Mr. Randolph and Miss Nancy, as the candle shone on the eyes of Miss Nancy, not to bring it into the Room, as she had been taking laudanum, was in great pain, & could not bear the light, as it hurt her eyes. Mrs. Harrison put down the candle out side of the door & came into the Room. Miss Nancy, Mr. Randolph, a negroe girl of about fifteen & Virginia of about seven years of age were in the Room. Mrs. Harrison remained with them for some time, talked with them and found Miss Nancy getting easier, then apologized for leaving her, as she had a sick child who would not rest well without her. Miss Nancy replied that under those circumstances, she could not wish her to stay. The next day Mrs. Harrison was in the Room & saw some blood on the pillow case & some on the stairs. She did not see either sheets or bed quilt. The Blankets were drawn close around her. She looked very pale, but Mrs. Harrison entertained no suspicion which was unfavorable to Miss Nancy, untill she was told by a negroe-woman that she had miscarried. When she exa[mined] the Bed it appeared as if an attempt had been made to wash it, but it was still stained, & Mrs. Harrison found it necessary to take the feathers out in order to wash it perfectly. She did not discover in Mrs. Randolph that allarm or confusion, which might be expected if she supposed her sister was about to be delivered of a child, or that resentment which would arise from suspecting her husband of being the father of it; she only appeared uneasy at the illness of her Sister. Mrs. Harrison saw no appearances which might not be accounted for, without ascribing them to an improper cause. She visited at Bizarre some short time afterwards, and both there and at her House there appeared to be entire harmony between Mr. Randolph & his lady.

MRS. HARRISON. (the old Lady).[4]

Understood that Miss Nancy was unwell and came the next day (tuesday) to see her. She enquired of Mrs. Randolph how she did & was told that she had been very ill but was easier, that she had been kept awake very much in the night & had taken Laudanum with which she was now composed. Mrs. Harrison did not see her that day. On friday or Saturday (I forget which) Mrs. Harrison sat in the Room with her a considerable time. She discovered no mark (either by milk, fever, or otherwise) of her having been delivered of a child, nor did she discover any reason to suspect it. She had never seen Mrs. Randolph with a more chearful countenance.

MRS. WOOD.

examined the bed. There were appearances, which would justify the suspicion of a Birth or abortion, but thinks another cause might have produced the same effect.

MRS. BRETT RANDOLPH.[5]

visited in the family very frequently and without ceremony; she never saw any Marks of ill will or discontent between Mr. Randolph & his Lady or between the sisters. Mr. Randolph was very attentive to Miss Nancy, rather more so she thought than to Mrs. Randolph. Miss Nancy to the time of the visit to Mr. Harrison's, wore a close gown without any loose covering to conceal her shape. Mrs. Randolph thought her size so encreased as to admit of a *possibility* of her being pregnant, but there were instances of as considerable an alteration produced by ill Health: she saw Miss Nancy after her return from Mr. Harrison's & observed her & thought her size was diminished, but thinks that the removal of her ill Health might have produced that change in her size.

MR. ARCHIBALD RANDOLPH

about eighteen months past had entertained suspicions that Mr. Randolph & Miss Nancy were too fond of each other, but before this event is said to have happened, he had entirely relinquished those suspicions. He waited on the ladies to Mr. Harrison's & observed no change in the size of Miss Nancy. While at Mr. Harrisons (I believe on Thursday) she passed thro the room in which

4. This was most likely Susanna Randolph Harrison, mother of the host, Randolph Harrison.

5. Anne Randolph Randolph (1764–1820), of "Curles," was the daughter of Richard Randolph, Jr., of "Curles," a cousin of Richard Randolph of "Bizarre."

he was sitting & in a little time set out to go up stairs. She appeared
to be extremely weak, & as she began to ascend the stairs called
to him to assist her & rested for some time on his arm. He discovered a disagreeable smell, but had no unfavorable suspicion
untill he was informed by Mr. Peyton Harrison[6] that she had had a
child or miscarried. Miss Nancy did not go to her Brothers wedding,[7] nor did any of Mr. Richard Randolph's family.

PEYTON HARRISON

perceived in the spring a fondness for each other: was informed
by a servant that Miss Nancy had miscarried & thought himself
bound by his friendship for Mr. Archibald Randolph to inform
him of it.

BEVERLY LOYD, WILLIAM BRADLEY, JOHN KER & CHAND[LER]
SKRUGGS—severally deposed that they knew nothing of the matter.

ON THE PART OF MR. RANDOLPH.

JOHN RANDOLPH[8]

Had been told by his deceased brother,[9] while in Philadelphia,
that he was engaged to Miss Nancy. Was at Bizarre for some time
before this event happened, & was told by his brother Richard &
his wife that Miss Nancy was in low spirits in consequence of the
Death of his Brother Theodorick; & was requested not to mention
him to her. He once named him to her & she burst into tears. The
most perfect harmony subsisted in the family and he had often observed how much fonder Mrs. Randolph was of Miss Nancy than
of any other of her relations; & that that fondness had encreased.
Miss Nancy never wore stays: she continued to dress in her usual
way: he was much with her; frequently lounged on the bed both
with her and his Sister, & never suspected her of being pregnant.
He thought, himself, from her pallid & emaciated appearance;
from her complection, something of a greenish blue under her
Eyes that she laboured under obstruction. After this event is said
to have happened, while at Mr. Harrison's he sat in the Room
with her & thought he discovered the disagreeable smell which is
mentioned by the other witnesses: but on their return from thence

6. Harrison was a brother of Randolph Harrison.
7. The reference is probably to the *ca.* 1792 wedding of Nancy's brother, William
Randolph (1770–1848), to Lucy Bolling Randolph, daughter of Gov. Beverley Randolph.
8. John Randolph of Roanoke.
9. Theodorick Randolph (1771–1792) had died on Feb. 14.

he sat with her in the carriage and did not discover the smell. He observed no change in her after coming from Mr. Harrison's, but that her complexion was somewhat clearer than before.

BRETT RANDOLPH[1]

visited in the family without ceremony—saw the most perfect harmony prevail in it and saw no cause to suspect a pregnancy or criminal conversation.

Upon the trial of Miss Nancy before the Magistrates
MRS. JUDITH RANDOLPH deposed;

That she was awake the whole night, being kept up by her sisters illness; that being excessively fatigued and being otherwise unwell, she had but a short time before Mrs. Harrison came up, left the Room & waked up her husband, & desired him to go into Miss Nancy's Room & drop her some laudanum; that he at first expressed some reluctance, & said Nancy had the hysterics and would be soon easy, but on her repeating the request he got up & without putting on his coat, went into the Room. She says that a child could not have been born or carried out of the Room without her knowledge. That she is confident no such event happened. That her husband did not go down stairs untill after day.[2]

I did not myself hear the Testimony of Mrs. Randolph; it was delivered to me by Mr. Henry & Mr. Campbell.[3] The circumstances in the foregoing which would excite suspicion are

I. The fondness of Mr. Randolph & Miss Nancy for each other.

II. The appearances of pregnancy.

III. The application of Gum guiacum, knowing it to be a medicine to produce an abortion.

IV. The appearances at Mr. Harrisons, and

V. Her refusal to comply with the request of Mrs. Page for an examination.

Let us examine them without favor or prejudice.

1st. They were imprudently fond of each other.

I believe there is no man in whose house a young Lady lives, who does occasionally pay her attentions and use fondnesses, which a person prone to suspicion may consider as denoting guilt.

1. Brett Randolph (1760–1828), of Powhatan County, was the son of Brett Randolph and Mary Scott Randolph and was a cousin of Richard Randolph of "Bizarre."
2. This apparently ends JM's summary of the testimony, and what follows is his argument.
3. Patrick Henry and Alexander Campbell.

The sister of his wife is, perhaps, of all others the person for whom he would shew most fondness. But there was something peculiar to herself in the situation of Miss Randolph, which might well mingle, with a fondness for her an unusual degree of tenderness. She had been nursed in the lap of ease and indulgence; she had been accustomed only to wish, and to find her wishes complied with. At once her fathers House was no longer a home for her; she experienced, what was thought, a reduction of necessary supplies, and something of asperity among her relations. She had loved too the Brother of Mr. Randolph; that brother was no more and she felt his loss. Is it wonderful that the attentions of Mr. Randolph should be somewhat particular? But had they been conscious of guilt they would have suppressed any publick fondness and would have avoided all publick intercourse. This conduct to each other was under the eye of Mrs. Randolph, and never produced suspicion in her mind.

2d. Her appearances of pregnancy.

That there was a small increase in Miss Randolphs size is not denied: nor can it be denied that an increase of size is produced by another cause to which her appearances are ascribed. Let us then look into the testimony for truth. In may Mr. & Mrs. Page observed a change in shape which they thought indicated a pregnancy. She must then have been advanced three or four months, for every person knows that a fact of that sort is not discernable in a young woman, not seeking to conceal it until about that stage. By the first of october then she must have been eight or nine months gone, and must have been of the size of a woman about to be delivered. Was this so? Mrs. Martha Randolph saw her in September, and altho suspicious of her situation does not speak of any increase in size. Mrs. Page, herself saw her at the same time, so did Mr. Page, yet neither of them speak of an increased alteration of shape, Mr. and Mrs. Brett Randolph visited familiarly in the family, saw her without ceremony or disguise, they had heard the suspicions and saw nothing to warrant them. Mrs. Brett Randolph observed such an increase of shape, as Mr. & Mrs. Page observed in May, but says another cause was adequate to the effect. Mr. John Randolph who was continually in the House saw no cause of suspicion. Mr. Archibald Randolph who was a Lover[4] & one who had suspected an improper familiarity, did not suspect a preg-

4. He was courting Nancy Randolph.

nancy. Had she been near a delivery he could not but have observed it. Mr. Randolph Harrison who took her out of the carriage, declared that she had her usual close great coat buttoned round her, and that he had no suspicion of her pregnancy. This increase of size, then, observed by Mr. & Mrs. Page, in may, is to be ascribed to a cause which would leave the person stationary and not produce a continual growth.

3d. The Application for Gum guiacum.

This medicine was calculated, it was said, to produce abortion and also to remove obstructions. It might then be designed for the one purpose, as well as the other. If she was near a delivery, it would have been unnecessary to take this medicine to procure an untimely one; had she sought to procure abortion it would have been in the early state of her pregnancy. An application could have been made by means of her accomplice, without it's being known for whom, and medicine might have been procured which would have been infallible; she would have taken it at home, where the whole would have been concealed, and not abroad where discovery was inevitable.

4th. The appearances at Mr. Harrison's.

[*The*] illness might be produced by either cause; the screams were proof of pain, but not of pain sought be to concealed. Mr. Randolph's being in the Room is accounted for by the testimony of his wife. The request that the candle should not be brought in was natural from a person in pain, who had been taking laudanum. The person who came down stairs appears not to have been Mr. Randolph. The blood and all the appearances upon the bed, were to be produced by either cause, as those declare who saw it. The sight of it produced no suspicion untill a servant said there had been a miscarriage. Let it be remembered that suspicions had been propagated, and had probably reached the servants. In this situation any suspicious appearance would be considered by them as full proof. Had there been any appearance of a child it would have been shewn. The story of the shingles has no weight. Had the fact been as supposed, no person on earth would have deposited the birth on a pile of shingles. On the other hand Mrs. Randolph shewed none of that apprehension and extreme misery, which would have been the certain consequence of her knowing the situation of her sister. Her situation gave her the best opportunity of knowing the fact & she contradicts it. Old Mrs. Harrison saw her soon after and she had none of those marks which are consequent on child birth. She never kept her room as is usual on such occasions, but immediately on her return to Bizarre (which is not mentioned in the statement) resumed her usual exercise of riding on horse-back. The most perfect family harmony still subsisted. The smell which is mentioned would arise from either cause.

5th. Her refusal to be examined by Mrs. Page.

No person will deny the imprudence of this and if that unfortunate young Lady be innocent, she has abundant cause to regret her refusal. But the most innocent person on earth might have acted in the same manner. We all know that the heart conscious of it's own purity resents suspicion; the resentment is still stronger when we are suspected by a friend. The subsequent extent of the Report could not then have been resented, and the pride of conscious innocence was sufficient to produce the Refusal.

The friends of Miss Randolph cannot deny, that there is some foundation on which suspicion may build: nor can it be denied by her enemies but that every circumstance may be accounted for, without imputing guilt to her. In this Situation Candor will not condemn or exclude from society, a person who may be only unfortunate.

To John Cabell

ALS, Breckinridge Long Papers, Library of Congress

Dear Sir[5]   [Richmond, *ca.* April 1793]

I have receivd yours by your son. I do not think it worth your while to defend your suit with Campbell tho at the same time I must tell you that Campbell has applied to me as his counsel & therefore my opinion may be doubted by you, but I do really think you woud only increase costs by defending the suit.[6]

In your injunction against Cooper, nothing further is yet done. It will come on in the spring for final hearing & will certainly go against you if you do not in the mean time take testimony to es-

---

5. This is either John Cabell (*ca.* 1743–1815) of "Green Hill," Buckingham County, who served in the House of Delegates from 1777 to 1788 after attending the 1776 Virginia convention, or John Cabell (1772–1834), a Lynchburg doctor who owned a prosperous store.

6. See fee received in Campbell v. Cabell, Account Book, Receipts, Apr. 1793.

tablish your equity. Cooper has taken other depositions but you have taken none. I am dear Sir respectfully, Your obedt

J MARSHALL

Law Papers, April 1793

U.S. Circuit Court, Va.

Harwood v. Lewis, declaration, ADS, U.S. Circuit Court, Va., Ended Cases (Restored), 1794, Virginia State Library.

Harwood v. Throckmorton, declaration, ADS, U.S. Circuit Court, Va., Ended Cases (Restored), 1794, Va. State Lib.

Militia Duty

EDITORIAL NOTE

In the several years after the creation of the new national government, John Marshall refused offers of appointment to a federal office, even one that would allow him to remain in Virginia. Apparently he wanted to devote full time to his law practice and did not want to spend long periods away from Richmond or Fauquier County. He managed to remain uninvolved in national affairs during George Washington's first administration and displayed no ambition to broaden his political horizons. The events of 1793 and 1794, however, pulled Marshall into national affairs for the first time since the Virginia ratifying convention of 1788, and having once become involved, he never again limited himself to local affairs as he had during his first forty years.

Marshall's renewed involvement began only after he had avoided service for ten years following the Revolution. At the end of the war the state's militia had been restructured, and everyone between the ages of eighteen and fifty was required to serve. Marshall was exempted from this duty, however, because he was a member of the Council of State. Even when he resigned from the Council in 1784, he was able to avoid service, because the requirement of militia service was laxly enforced, especially in the case of former Revolutionary officers. As the militia was then organized, Henrico County contained only enough men for one regiment, and it is entirely possible that if Marshall was offered a commission, he refused to accept it. The head of the county's unit, referred to as the county lieutenant, Colonel Turner Southall, complained to the governor, "I am sorry to see that men better skilled in military knowledge (I mean the old officers) than some of those recommended, should have such an aversion to the appointment in the Militia, for this reason the Court was obliged to take the best they could find."[7] At the October 1785 session of the General Assembly a new arrangement of officers gave each county an additional colonel. Henrico County Court never recommended anyone to fill the additional position, however, and Southall apparently resigned his commission as county lieutenant between 1785 and 1787. On July 5, 1787, the Council of State commissioned Nathaniel Wilkinson and John Marshall colonels, Wilkinson being designated county lieutenant. Marshall, without explanation, resigned his commission immediately.[8]

During the next twelve months the question of how much power to grant the militia in the new government became a strongly debated issue. As a Federalist, Marshall shared the view that control of the militia should be placed in the central government, arguing that diversified state control was ineffective in a federal system. According to Richard H. Kohn, "Federalists argued, just as the nationalists had in the 1780's, that the state militias were useless in their present form."[9] The Antifederalists insisted on maintaining the state militia systems under the control of the state governments, arguing that this would be the best safeguard from the evils of a standing army. Once the Constitution was ratified, however, reform of the existing diversified militia system became important, because of an underlying and fundamental concern for the nation's defense. It is certain that John Marshall shared this concern, and it is clear that he favored an effective militia.

Having participated in the ratification debates and observing attempts to enact a national militia law, Marshall could hardly refuse service in an improved militia.[1] By 1790 the population of Richmond was sufficient to require its own regiment within the Henrico County militia, and in May 1791 the Henrico County Court recommended, presumably with his permission, that Marshall be named colonel of the newly authorized Richmond regiment. The commission issued from the executive on May 30, and Marshall took his oath before the Henrico Court on August 5, 1791.[2]

The new national government had begun attempts to reorganize the militia as one of its first orders of business. In August 1789, Congress had named a committee to prepare legislation for an improved militia system under some form of national control and regulation. It was not until 1792, however, that an acceptable bill was adopted, and it proved largely ineffectual as a reform measure.[3] Congress

7. Turner Southall to Patrick Henry, June 8, 1785, Executive Papers: Militia, Henrico County, Virginia State Library. See also George Webb, William Foushee, Daniel Hylton, and William DuVal to Patrick Henry, Feb. 8, 1785, *ibid.*

8. 12 Hening 10 (1785); *JVCS*, IV, 121, 141. For JM's resignation, see Vol. I, 234.

9. Vol. I, 274; Kohn, *Eagle and Sword: The Federalists and the Creation of the Military Establishment in America, 1783–1802* (New York, 1975), 85.

1. Kohn argues that Federalist theory was "clearly developed by 1788" and called for preparedness and centralization by improving the militia and giving control over it to the national government. Kohn, *Eagle and Sword*, 85, 86, 95, 281n. See also Vol. I, 274.

2. 13 Hening 200 (1790); "Recommendation of Militia Officers for the city of Richmond," May 1791, Executive Papers: Militia, Henrico County, and Henrico County Court Order Book, IV, 597, both in Va. State Lib.

3. Joseph Gales, comp., [*Annals of Congress*] *Debates and Proceedings in the Congress of the United States, 1789–1824* (Washington, D.C., 1849), 1st Cong., 1st sess., Aug. 8, 1789, 687–688; Kohn, *Eagle and Sword*, 128–138.

had passed a "milk and water" act and had "murdered an already dying militia system," according to Kohn.[4] The act nevertheless provided a framework for each state to follow in reforming its militia.

According to the Uniform Militia Act of 1792, each state had one year to arrange its militia into divisions, brigades, regiments, battalions, and companies. Officers were to be a major general for each division, a brigadier general for each brigade, a lieutenant colonel for each regiment, a major for each battalion, and for each company a captain, lieutenant, and ensign in addition to several subaltern officers.[5] At the following session of the Virginia General Assembly a new militia law was passed that conformed in most respects to the national act. The act divided the state into divisions and brigades. Each county, as well as the cities of Richmond, Norfolk, and Williamsburg, would have at least one regiment, but brigades and divisions were composed of several counties. In January the Council of State directed the governor to request nominations from the counties and cities so that commissions for regimental officers could be issued. Delays and disputes over the recommendations in the counties took several months, and the first commissions were not approved until May 1793.[6]

The May session of the Richmond City Hustings Court recommended officers for the city's regiment, designating Marshall as the lieutenant colonel. The following month, on June 10, Marshall took his oath of office before the Hustings Court with the governor's commission in hand. The Richmond regiment had been designated the Nineteenth and was one of six in the Second Brigade of the Fourth Division.[7] It was as commander of the Richmond militia that orders were directed to John Marshall by the executive during 1793.

Following the French declaration of war against Britain in February 1793 and the arrival of the news in the United States at the end of March, the administration pursued a policy of neutrality that was difficult to follow and that embroiled the governor of Virginia and the state's militia in the maintenance of neutrality. In 1778 the United States had signed two treaties with France: a treaty of alliance and a treaty of amity and commerce. The former bound the United States to protect French territory in America, that is, the West Indies. Two articles of the treaty of amity and commerce were especially important in 1793. Article 17 guaranteed each signatory the right of its ships of war and privateers to bring prizes into the ports, to keep them there without interference, and to take them out again at will. The article also forbade extending similar privileges to the enemy. Article 22 prohibited the fitting out of enemy privateers in either's ports, nor could enemy privateers "sell their prizes in the ports of either party." Because of these provisions and the French declaration of war, President Washington in 1793 requested the advice of the Cabinet on what the reaction of the United States should be. On April 22, following consideration of his Cabinet's advice, Washington issued a proclamation declaring the impartiality of the United States

4. Kohn, *Eagle and Sword*, 135, 137.
5. 1 Stat. 272.
6. 13 Hening 340–356 (1792); JVCS, Jan. 15, Feb. 7, Apr. 2, Apr. 12, May 6, and May 14, 1793.
7. "Recommendations of Officers," May 13, 1793, Executive Papers: Militia, Henrico County, and Richmond City Hustings Court Order Book, III, 123, both in Va. State Lib.

and prohibiting any American from "committing, aiding, or abetting hostilities against any of" the countries at war.[8]

As soon as news of the war had spread through the nation, sentiment for one side or the other was expressed, and it was certain Washington's proclamation would not be accepted without dissent. The arrival in May of French minister Edmond Charles Genêt and the subsequent outfitting of privateers in violation of the proclamation produced a series of events that involved Marshall and other Virginians in debate and further stimulated the growth of political parties in the state.[9] As colonel of the Richmond militia, Marshall had received the general orders regarding observance of neutrality that the governor had sent to commanders of all ports. Although it was a port, Richmond was not a likely place in which privateers would be outfitted. However, as the state capital, it was a center of debate on the issues. Reaction to Genêt's arrival and the growing political fervor against the administration's position induced Marshall and others who agreed with him to urge public meetings to express support for the president's attempts to maintain neutrality. Marshall helped organize the August meeting, chaired by George Wythe, and composed a set of resolutions of support, which were adopted. Following the meeting, he engaged in a brief newspaper battle with a leading Virginia Republican, James Monroe.[1]

In November 1793 the General Assembly discussed Washington's proclamation, and it is likely Marshall urged his Federalist friends in the legislature to support Governor Lee's recommendation that they adopt a resolution of support for the president's action. The Republicans, embarrassed by Genêt's conduct and the exuberance of pro-French support in Norfolk, were unable to prevent adoption of the resolution.[2] Soon thereafter the House of Delegates elected the major and brigadier generals for the state's militia, as provided for in the 1792 act. Henry Lee was named major general of the Fourth Division, and Marshall was elected brigadier general of the Second Brigade in this division.[3] From then until 1801 he was known by his contemporaries as General Marshall.

For several months Marshall's new duties were routine, concerned only with equipment and organization. He became directly involved in the diplomatic crisis, however, after Congress adopted the Neutrality Act in June 1794, prohibiting actions by American citizens that would violate the neutrality of the United States in the current European quarrels. Section 3 of the act specifically forbade the employment and outfitting of privateers to be used against foreign nations.[4] One month later the British consul at Norfolk reported to Governor Henry Lee that John Sinclair and other French sympathizers were fitting out a vessel as a priva-

8. Hunter Miller, ed., *Treaties and Other International Acts of the United States of America* (Washington, D.C., 1931), II, 3–41.

9. Richard R. Beeman, *The Old Dominion and the New Nation, 1788–1801* (Lexington, Ky., 1972), 133.

1. According to Beeman, "Up until the time of the Federalist meeting in Richmond, it had never been necessary for the Republicans to organize themselves within the state; they could always be assured of a majority in the legislature without the necessity of building a party structure. The decision of the Federalists to appeal directly to the people through the county meetings changed this." *Ibid.*

2. *JVHD*, Oct. 1793, 51, 69.

3. *Ibid.*, 102, 104; JVCS, Dec. 12, 1793.

4. 1 Stat. 381–384.

teer near Smithfield, on the James River. After receiving several conflicting reports, Lee sent David M. Randolph, a U.S. marshal, and Major George K. Taylor to Smithfield to investigate. Their orders were to determine Sinclair's intentions and to enlist the aid of the local militia to enforce the Neutrality Act if violations existed. Randolph and Taylor, with the help of about a dozen poorly armed men drafted from the Isle of Wight militia, took possession of Sinclair's ship, *Unicorn*, on July 19, after it had become apparent to them that he intended to violate the neutrality of the United States by using it as a privateer. After receiving threats of violence from Sinclair and his supporters and little cooperation from the local militia, Randolph and Taylor called on the Norfolk militia to send a ship to Smithfield to assist in retaining the *Unicorn*. They also informed Governor Lee of their precarious position and of Sinclair's intended violations of the Neutrality Act. Lee decided to send John Marshall and the Nineteenth Regiment of the Virginia militia to Smithfield to help enforce the prohibition of privateering.[5] Following Marshall's expedition to Smithfield and the militia's nonviolent suppression of any intended violations of American neutrality, Sinclair was arrested, and the commander of the Isle of Wight County militia was court-martialed for refusing to support Major Taylor's request for military assistance. Both men escaped conviction.[6]

Almost as soon as the Smithfield expedition ended, Marshall's brigade was called on to aid in quelling the Whiskey Rebellion. The division's major general, Governor Henry Lee, became the commander of the combined forces raised by the president. As early as September 4, 1794, Marshall received instructions for his troops from Lieutenant Governor James Wood. It is certain that Marshall did not go to Pennsylvania with the Virginia forces under Lee's overall command. All the state courts met in September and October, and Marshall apparently could not, or would not, neglect his practice. There was no real need for his presence with the troops in any case.

The failure of Marshall to accompany his troops on the expedition against the Whiskey Rebellion underscores his reluctance to accept a position that would require his absence from the state, at least until 1797. In 1795 he declined appointment as U.S. attorney general and in 1796 as ambassador to France. But militia duty offered him a means for involvement in many of the important issues of the young Republic without requiring his absence from Virginia, where his private affairs were demanding an ever-increasing amount of his time and attention.

From Henry Lee

Copy, Adjutant General's Record Book, War 10, Virginia State Library[7]

Richmond, June 8, 1793

The President of the United States having called on me[8] in my character of Commander in Chief of the militia of this State, to be

5. See JM's letters relating to the Smithfield expedition beginning at July 21, 1794.
6. U.S. Circuit Court, Va., Order Book, I, 405, 459, 464, 541, II, 10, 107, 338, 339, Va. State Lib.; *CVSP*, VIII, 262–264, 269–270, 276–277, 279, 310, 312, 321–323;

ready to suppress any attempt or attempts which may be made within the limits thereof to Violate the Neutrality he has declared in behalf of the people of the United States, towards the Belligerent powers, I consider it my duty to communicate the same to the Commandants of the militia of those Counties whose local situation may require it, together with the Sentiments expressed by the President on this occasion.

He has declared that the treaty existing between the United States and France, and the treaty existing between the United States and Holland,[9] do not authorize those powers to arm Vessels within our ports, therefore any attempt on the part of the belligerent powers, or their subjects so to do, will be a violation of the Neutrality.

In all such cases you will therefore be pleased to interpose with your militia, seizing and detaining any Vessel which you may find manned as a privatier on behalf of any of the belligerent powers or of their Subjects; and you will also interpose in all acts of hostility which may happen between the belligerent powers detaining the party first aggressing.

In any events of this sort, you will be so good without loss of

---

Claude O. Lanciano, Jr., *Legends of Lands End* (n.p., 1971), 23–62. See also report of court-martial in War 10, Va. State Lib.

7. The record book entry is preceded by the notation, "General Orders, Issued by the Commander in Chief of the Militia and the consequent Orders of the Adjutant General, (The following were addressed Specially to Commandants of Counties in Which are ports of Navigation.)"

8. In a private letter of Apr. 9, 1793, Gov. Henry Lee had informed Washington of the public alarm at the outfitting of French privateers in Virginia ports; his news arrived while the Cabinet was considering similar news from Charleston, S.C. On May 23, 1793, Henry Knox, secretary of war, submitted to Washington a proposed letter to the governors of the Atlantic states that had been approved by the members of the Cabinet. This may have been the circular letter of May 24, 1793, concerning the use of the militia to enforce the neutrality by denying the belligerent powers the use of American ports for equipping and arming their privateers. Washington Papers, Ser. 4, Apr. 9, and May 23, 1793, Library of Congress (microfilm ed., reel 103). The circular letter of May 24, 1793, which accompanied this letter to JM, is printed in *CVSP*, VI, 379.

9. The reference is to the treaty of amity and commerce with France, negotiated on Feb. 6, 1778. Arts. 21 and 24 might be construed to confer certain privileges upon French warships and privateers and to require the United States to deny similar assistance to British vessels. See Hunter Miller, ed., *Treaties and Other International Acts of the United States of America* (Washington, D.C., 1931), II, 17–18, 19–20. The Dutch treaty of amity and commerce, negotiated on Oct. 8, 1782, closely parallels the French treaty text; arts. 5 and 17 provide a similar basis for privileged treatment of Dutch warships and privateers. *Ibid.*, 64–65, 74. However, a strict construction of the terms of either treaty would not bind the United States to make its ports available for the arming of French or Dutch privateers or warships.

time as to communicate the Case to me with all the evidence legally taken in writing appertaining thereunto, that I may transmit
the same to the President of the United States, whose decision
when known to me will be forwarded to you. I have the honor etc.
HENRY LEE

Commissioners of Monongalia v. Warman

Argument in the General Court

Extract from Casebook, Tucker-Coleman Papers, Swem Library, College of William and Mary

Richmond, June 13, 1793
Commissioners of Monongalia vs. Warmer[1] Shff of Monongalia,
for Ballance of taxes under 1792, c. 43.[2]
Marshall said this Court has not Jurisdiction the Act of last
Session c. 13, requiring that Jurisdiction be *expressely* given concur-
rently with other Courts.[3] Here the Expression is *any Court of Rec-
ord.*
Per Cur: Unanimously. This necessarily implies that the Gen:
Court as a Court of record hath Jurisdiction.

1. St. George Tucker obviously misunderstood the sheriff's name, Francis Warman.
See 13 Hening 230 (1790), and *CVSP*, VII, 187, where a letter reveals that Warman
lost the case in the November General Court.
JM received two fees in this case. See Account Book, Receipts, June and Oct. 1793.
2. "An Act to Amend Several Acts for Opening a Waggon Road" provided that
taxes due from the sheriffs of Monongalia and three other western counties might be
collected by the commissioners of taxes obtaining judgments by motion in "any court
of record" in Virginia. *Acts Passed at a General Assembly of the Commonwealth of Virginia
... one thousand seven hundred and ninety-two* (Richmond, 1793), 92; 13 Hening 552 (1792).
3. JM referred to "An Act Reducing into One, the Several Acts and Parts of Acts
Concerning the General Court," enacted on Dec. 13, 1792. *Acts Passed at a General Assembly*, 40; 13 Hening 424. Sec. 3 of the act reads, "The jurisdiction of the [General]
court shall be general over all causes, matters and things at common law, as well
criminal as civil, except in such cases as by the constitution of the United States of
America or of this Commonwealth, or any statute made by the Congress of the United
States, or the General Assembly of this commonwealth, are or shall be vested in any
other tribunal, in any of which cases the jurisdiction of the General Court shall cease,
unless concurrent jurisdiction be thereto be expressly given by this act, or some other
statute." JM argued that the failure specifically to name the General Court in the act
for the collection of tax arrears precluded the General Court from exercising jurisdiction; in other words, the use of the term "courts of record" did not meet the requirements of the statute conferring jurisdiction on the General Court.

Commonwealth v. Tyler

Argument in the General Court

Extract from Casebook, Tucker-Coleman Papers, Swem Library, College of William and Mary

Richmond, June 17, 1793

Commonwealth v Jno. Tyler, as Security for Stith Hardyman[4] Sheriff of Charles-City County, an Exo. agt. Hardyman having issued & been returned "no property." This motion is made under the Act of 1787, c. 40, Sect: 6.[5]

Wickham Pro Deft. cited Virga Laws 1769, pa: 183, Ib: pa: 325, 326, and insisted the *present* Bonds were only pursuant to these Bonds. Rev. Code 181. Requires Sheriff to give Bond for the *faithful collecting, accounting for & paying the Taxes.*[6]

Marshall, on the same side insisted, that as agt. the Security, the Bond must be *shewn,* & shewn to be taken strictly pursuant to the Directions contained in the Rev: Code pa: 181.

Innes, Atty Gen:,[7] said here are words in these Bonds sufficient to comprehend the Case of taxes. The Duty of a Shff is to collect the public taxes. If he has given Security to perform *all the Duties*

4. John Tyler was a judge of the General Court at this time. His sister, Rachel, married Stith Hardyman about 1770.

5. The statute provided that when the lands, tenements, goods, and chattels of a sheriff were insufficient to satisfy his debts to the public, judgment might be obtained against the surety on the same summary basis as it might have been obtained against the sheriff. *Acts passed at a General Assembly of the Commonwealth of Virginia . . . one thousand seven hundred and eighty-seven* (Richmond, 1788), 11; 12 Hening 560–561 (1788).

6. John Wickham referred to a 1748 act "Prescribing the Method of Appointing Sheriffs," which required sheriffs to post a £1,000 bond for the faithful performance of their duties, and a 1753 act "to Amend An Act Declaring the Law Concerning Executions," which required sheriffs to post a bond of £2,000 for the performance of their duties in collecting and accounting for officer's fees. *The Acts of Assembly, now in force, in the Colony of Virginia* (Williamsburg, Va., 1769), 183, 325. The Revised Code was apparently the Chancellors' Revisal, which contained an act "Concerning the Appointment of Sheriffs" that required the posting of a £10,000 bond for "the true and faithful collecting, accounting, and paying the taxes imposed by law in his county." The Chancellors' Revisal was printed as *A Collection of all such Public Acts . . . of Virginia, passed since the year 1768 . . .* (Richmond, 1785), but the act mentioned was printed in 11 Hening 168 (1782).

7. James Innes served as attorney general of Virginia from Nov. 25, 1786, to Nov. 13, 1796. Jane Carson, *James Innes and His Brothers of the F.H.C.* (Williamsburg, Va., 1965), 156.

incidental to his Office of Sheriff, this will bind the Security in this Case. He cited Rev. Code 60, 204, 209. 1786, c: 19.[8]

NB. These Bonds were worded as the Virga Laws pa: 325, 326, direct.

Per totam Cur: Motion overruled.

Prentis & Company v. Braxton & Company

Argument in the General Court

Extract from Casebook, Tucker-Coleman Papers, Swem Library, College of William and Mary

Richmond, June 17, 1793

The cause being called for trial, Marshall moved to change the plea from payt. (this being an Action of Debt on a Bill of Exche:[9] & the plea put in by the Security) to nil debit,[1] waving the Benefit of the Act of Limitation, & admitting the Endorsors handwriting. The same motion was said to have been made last Court, but that the Court did not decide upon it.

Tucker & Winston[2] thought that this being somewhat in the nature of a *continued Motion* & offered in behalf of a Security for *Defts appe. only*,[3] this Motion was now admissible.

8. Innes referred to an act included in the Chancellors' Revisal that authorized county courts to require sheriffs to post a £3,000 bond before collecting duties and taxes within the county. 9 Hening 357 (1777). The reference to p. 204 of the Code is to an act repealing part of the 1782 statute mentioned by Wickham, printed in 11 Hening 168. Innes cited a more recent statute, which is reprinted in 11 Hening 277 (1783). "An Act to Amend the Several Acts of Assembly for Ascertaining Certain Taxes and Duties," on p. 209 of the Chancellors' Revisal, was adopted at the fall 1783 session of the General Assembly. It established a new schedule for sheriffs to follow in accounting and paying taxes into the state treasury. 11 Hening 305 (1783).

9. Bill of exchange.

1. "He owes nothing" was the plea that raised the general issue in an action of debt.

2. St. George Tucker and Edmund Winston (*ca.* 1735–1813), who became judges of the General Court in 1788.

3. Through this motion JM wished to amend the plea of payment, entered by the surety for the defendant's appearance. It would seem that JM was called to represent the defendant at trial, and in the course of doing so he discovered that the facts better supported the nil debet plea. The reasoning of Judges Tucker and Winston is not clear from the extracted passage; however, it is possible that they argued that the surety who had entered the plea of payment was acting outside the scope of his legitimate interests, since he was only bound for the defendant's appearance and not for his

Tyler, Henry & Roan, contra. Nelson[4] gave no opinion. Motion over-ruled.

Anonymous Case

Argument in the General Court

Extract from Casebook, Tucker-Coleman Papers, Swem Library, College of William and Mary

Richmond, June 21, 1793

Marshall affirmed, & Nelson Judge agreed that it had been determined in this Court, that where Judgement hath gone agt. a principal Defendant in the office & the Security for his appearance hath put in a plea, although the Security die, the suit shall proceed upon the plea put in by him, notwithstanding the abatement as to him.[5] The plea being in fact considered as the plea of the Defendant, although Judgement confirmd agt. him.

Opinion

Record Book Copy, Richmond City Common Hall, Virginia State Library

Richmond, [*ca.* July 15, 1793]

It is asked:[6]

1st. Do the Lots laid off and the squares appropriated by the directors under the Act of 1780, entitled "An Act for locating the

---

pleading. The material on "continuing motion" appears to relate to the court's cognizance of a motion that had been made to a previous term of court. They in effect argued that a motion of this nature might be heard in a subsequent term.

4. John Tyler, Spencer Roane, James Henry, and William Nelson, Jr. Henry (1731–1804) had been a judge in the Virginia court of admiralty and became a judge of the General Court on Dec. 4, 1788. It is not clear whether the judges who disagreed with the motion did so on its merits or whether they held it inadmissible on procedural grounds; from Tucker's transcript, however, the latter basis seems more likely.

On the policy of amending pleadings, see the 1785 attorneys' agreement printed in a note to JM to John Breckinridge, *ca.* May 20, 1791. See also Vol. I, 149, n. 2; Tabb v. Gregory, 8 Va. (4 Call) 225, 228 (1792); and Cooke v. Beale, 5 Va. (1 Call) 313, 318–319 (1794).

5. In other words, the defaulting defendant was bound by the plea entered by his surety, even though the death of the surety caused the action to abate as to him. The case referred to has not been found.

6. On July 2, 1793, the Richmond City Common Hall was presented with the

public squares to enlarge the Town of Richmond and for other purposes" form a part of the Town of Richmond?[7]

2d. If so do they form a part of the City of Richmond?

3d. If they do not form a part of the City of Richmond, have
the Common Hall or rather the Corporation power to regulate a
Market built on one of those squares?

To answer those queries it becomes necessary to examine the
different Acts of the Legislature on the subject. Those relative to
it which I have been able to find are

1st. The Act of 1742 ch. 20 which establishes the Town. This
Act bounds the Town to the westward by Shockoe Creek, and contains no power relative to Markets.[8]

2d. The Act of 1769 ch. 60. This Act enlarges the Bounds of
the Town so as to comprehend an Additional number of Lots at
Shockoe laid off by Wm. Byrd. It contains no clause concerning
Markets.[9]

3d. The Act of 1779. For the removal of the seat of Government.[1]
This authorizes the directors of the Public Buildings to lay off 200
half acre Lots and to appropriate six squares either of the former
Town or of the 200 additional Lots, or of adjacent ground to public
purposes and the Lots so laid off and squares appropriated shall
thenceforth form a part of the said Town. But a subsequent clause
postpones the Execution of this part of the Act until the further
provision of the Legislature. It is to be observed that on one of

---

problem of whether they possessed jurisdiction over 30 acres of land, once belonging
to Philip Turpin, that had been condemned by the directors of public buildings and
evaluated by a jury on Jan. 8, 1783. The mayor and recorder, on direction of the
Common Hall, referred the matter to JM and Andrew Ronald. Ronald's opinion co-
incided with that of JM, and upon reading these two opinions on July 15, 1793, the
Common Hall appointed JM and others to a committee to draw a legislative petition
requesting that the city limits be extended to include the land in question, since some
"suppose . . . [it] not to be within City limits." Richmond City Common Hall Records, II, 20, 25–27, Virginia State Library.

7. 10 Hening 319 (1780). This section is similar to sec. 2 of "An act for the removal
of the seat of government," 10 Hening 88 (1779). Both statutes provided that the lots
and squares involved "shall thenceforth be a part of the said town."

8. A 1742 statute provided for the establishment of semiannual fairs as one of the
privileges of the town of Richmond, but it did not mention construction of a public
market. 5 Hening 191–193.

9. Sec. 2 of this act added land at Shockoe Creek to the city of Richmond and gave
its residents the rights and privileges of the freeholders and inhabitants of the city of
Richmond. 8 Hening 421–422 (1769). On Byrd's relationship to the growth of the
city, see John R. Reps, *Tidewater Towns: City Planning in Colonial Virginia and Maryland*
(Williamsburg, Va., 1972), 267–269.

1. 10 Hening 85 (1779).

these squares, to be below the hill on the West of Shockoe Creek is to be erected a public Market, but this too is postponed.

4th. The Act of May 1780[2] which enacts, That the directors if it be found expedient shall cause two hundred additional Lots or half acres with necessary streets properly arranged, to be laid off adjacent to such parts of the Town as shall seem most expedient and they shall be at liberty to appropriate the six squares aforesaid or any part of them either from among the Lots now in the said Town or those to be laid off as before directed, or of the land adjacent to the former or latter Lots, and the six squares and two hundred Lots shall thenceforth be a part of the said Town.

5th The Act of May 1782 ch 65. "For incorporating the Town of Richmond and for other purposes."[3] This enacts that the Town of Richmond, bounded according to the Act of 1769 (afore mentioned) shall be stiled the City of Richmond. It proceeds to direct the freeholders and Housekeepers within the said City to elect a Common Hall, and makes the said Freeholders and Housekeepers a Body Politic & Corporate. After the passage of this Act the directors of the Public Buildings proceed to lay off several Lots and to appropriate certain squares to public purposes under the Act of May 1780. In 1787. The Legislature pass an Act ch 78.[4] The Legislature pass an Act stating that one of those squares, lying within the City of Richmond had been represented by the directors as being unnecessary for public purposes and therefore they authorize the directors to convey & release the right of the Commonwealth therein [to] Philip Turpin the original proprietor. This square is not within the Limits of the Town or described by the Act of 1769 but is annexed if at all under the Act of 1780.

There is I believe no other Law which elucidates the questions proposed.

A.1st. There can be no doubt but that the Lots and squares annexed in pursuance of the Act of 1780, become apart of the Town of Richmond; with respect to the Lots no act has passed from which it can be inferred that they have ceased to be a part of the Town. With respect to the squares I find no other Act but that which authorizes a conveyance of the right of the Commonwealth to Philip Turpin. Before this the squares had become a part of the Town and the Act does not expressly disfranchise it. I do not think the

2. 10 Hening 319 (1780).
3. 11 Hening 45–51 (1782).
4. 12 Hening 617–618 (1787).

square is by any implication either put out of the town, for the Commonwealth could have conveyed to any other person as well as to Mr. Turpin & the ground having been once annexed to the Town, I cannot think that its continuing a part of the town is in any manner dependent on its belonging to this or that person, to the Commonwealth or an individual.

2d. I confess that I consider this question as one of very much doubt indeed. Had the incorporating law been passed after the additional Lots were annexed to the town it would have been certain that those Lots were not included in the City because a part of a town may unquestionably be included within, and another part excluded from the Corporation; had the incorporating Law omitted to describe the boundaries of the town, I should have been equally clear that the additional Lots were within the City, but as the case stands, I feel very considerable doubts indeed on the subject. I must however give that opinion to which my judgment most inclines: It is, that the additional lots are without the City. My reasons are, that the City is only created by the law of 1782. That Law circumscribes and limits it to certain specified boundaries; those boundaries do not include the Lots in question. Although the lots were not then laid off, yet the Law authorising them to be laid off had passed. The incorporating Law by restricting the City to the bounds of the town as described by the Act of 1769 seems to have intentionally excluded the lots to be annexed to the town under the Act of 1780. It is a principle too, that an Act when compleated shall have relation to its commencement, and this would lead to putting the same construction on the Acts of 80 and 82, as if the lots annexed by virtue of the Act of 80 had been compleatly annexed at the passage of the Act. I am myself inclined to construe Acts literally and I am persuaded that upon a literal construction, the opinion I have given must be supported.

I do however admit that the case is by no means clear, and that there are strong arguments for a contrary construction.

Although the Legislature have a right to incorporate a part of a town only, there seems in this case to be no substantial reason for their doing so. Had the Act of 80 been subsequent to the incorporating Law and had annexed the lots to the City instead of the Town of Richmond, they would certainly have been within the Corporation. The same thing which was then stiled the town is now stiled the City, and it would seem that a change of the name could not be intended to alter the substance. The lots then being by the

Act of 80 to be annexed to the Town when they should be laid off, and the Town in the interim changing its name and being stiled the City, the lots when laid off should by the power of the Act of 1780 be annexed to the City. The framers of the Laws have themselves evidently thought so, for in the Act of 1787 they speak of the square to be conveyed to Turpin as being within the City. The Citizens themselves have uniformly thought so and have voted accordingly at all elections for the City. I think too the decision of the Court of Appeals on the subject of Executions on replevin bonds[5] rather favorable to this construction, because in that case they evidently departed from the letter of the Law, to carry its intention into effect.

My own Judgment however on the subject is that which I have given and if I am right the Legislature only can remedy the mischief.

3d. I find no clause in any Act which gives the Corporation powers beyond the limits of the City.[6] I think that body from the nature of its Constitution can only legislate for itself and control that which is within its own limits.

J. MARSHALL

Lease

Deed Book Copy, Office of the Clerk of the Fauquier County Circuit Court, Warrenton, Va.

[Fauquier County], July 25, 1793

THIS INDENTURE[7] made this twenty fifth day of July in the year one thousand Seven hundred and ninety three BETWEEN John Marshall of the City of Richmond of the one part and William Hume[8] of the County of Fauquier of the other part WITNESSETH that for and inconsideration of the Rents and Covenants herein after mentioned and for and inconsideration of the sum of five

5. Case not found.
6. The reference is to legislative jurisdiction; there was magisterial jurisdiction in the Richmond City Hustings Court extending beyond the boundaries assigned to the corporation and including the lands that formed part of the town of Richmond.
7. This lease is included as an example of the long-term leases of Marshall family lands in Fauquier County, measured upon the lives of the lessee and his descendants.
8. This was probably the William Hume (1734–1809) who studied law, served in the Revolution, and migrated to Campbell County, Ky., where he died.

Shillings to him the said John Marshall in hand paid: by the said William Hume at and before the sealing and delivery of these presents he the said John Marshall hath bargained sold leased and to farm let and by these presents doth bargain sell lease and to farm let unto the said William Hume one certain tract or parcell of land, being part of the tract of land called and known by the name of oak hill and bounded by the out line of the tract of oak hill by the line of John Rust[9] and by the road as it now runs. To HAVE & TO HOLD the said tract or parcell of land with all its appurtenances unto the said William Hume his heirs and assigns for and during the natural life of the said William Hume and for and during the natural life his son James Hume yielding and paying there for unto the said John Marshall his heirs Executors administrators or assigns on the first day of January one thousand Seven hundred and ninty one[1] and on the first day of January every year thereafter during the said term the annual Rent of Eight pounds and paying also to such persons as may be appointed to collect the same the taxes due or to become due from, or on the said tract or parcell of land and the said William Hume for himself his heirs Executors administrators and assigns doth covenant promise and agree to and with the said John Marshall his heirs Executors administrators and assigns in manner following that is to say that the said William Hume his heirs Executors administrators and assigns shall and will well and truly pay the rents and taxes herein before mentioned as the same shall become due and if at any time the Rents on any part of them shall remain unpaid for and during the term of one Calendar month after the same shall be due it shall and may be lawful for the said John Marshall his certain attorney his heirs Executors administrators or assigns to enter upon the premes and distrain for so much Rent as shall be in arrear and unpaid and sufficient property cannot be found on the premises whereon to make distress then it shall and may be lawfull for the said John Marshall to reenter upon the premises hereby bargained, Sold Leased and to farm let and to hold the Same in like manner as if these presents had never been made and the said William Hume his heirs or assigns will [on] or before the first day of January one thousand Seven hundred and ninety five plant on the said prem-

9. Rust (1755–1842) may have been a tenant of JM at this time. In 1797 JM sued him for rent due and payable. See Marshall v. Rust, Fauquier County Court Minute Book, 1797–1798, 154–155, Office of the Clerk of the Fauquier County Circuit Court, Warrenton, Va.

1. Perhaps a slip of the pen for "four."

ises one hundred apple trees sow down in timothy or clover meadow five Acres of ground, build one dwelling house at least twenty four feet by sixteen feet and one barn which shall be either thached or boarded at least thirty four feet by Sixteen feet which said orchard, meadow, house and barn shall be kept in good Repair during the said term there shall Remain on the said lott in one entire body at least twenty five Acres of uncleared land and it shall not be lawfull for the said William Hume his heirs or assigns to Sell or in any manner dispose of the said lott or any part thereof without the consent of the said John Marshall his heirs or assigns in writing first being had thereto. It shall not be lawfull for the said William Hume his heirs or assigns to [cut] any timber but such as may be necessary to be used on the said Lott nor shall the sd. Wm Hume his heirs or assigns Sell or carry away any timber but such as may be necessary to be used on the said lott nor shall the said William Hume his heirs or assigns sell or carry away or permit to be carried away from the said lott any timber for any purpose or by any person whatever and the said William Hume his heirs or assigns shall and will at the Expiration of this lease or whenever the same shall determine, deliver up the premises in good repair to the said John Marshall his heirs or assigns and will well and truly keep all the covenants in this Indenture specified according to the true intent and meaning hereof IN WITNESS whereof the parties to these presents have set their hands and affixed their seals the day and year first above written.

Signed Sealed & delivered⎱   JOHN MARSHALL (LS)
In presence of   ⎰   WILLIAM HUME (LS)
JNO. CLARK CHARLES L CARTER
WM SMITH   ⎱ JOHN RUST
EDWARD SHACKLETT ⎰ P MALLORY
CHARLES MARSHALL ⎰ THO SMITH

At a Court held for Fauquier County the 28th: day of October 1793 THIS INDENTURE was proved to be the act and deed of the said John Marshall and William Hume by the oaths of Charles Marshall and William Smith witnesses thereto and ordered to be Certified And at a Court Continued and held for the said County the 28th: day of April 1804 the Same was further proved by the oath of Charles L Carter another witness thereto and ordered to be Recorded.

Teste F. BROOKE C.C.[2]

Leases

Deed Book Copy, Office of the Clerk of the Fauquier County Circuit Court, Warrenton, Va.

[*July 25, 1793* (*Fauquier County*). JM executes separate bargain and sale deeds leasing to Benjamin Rector, Edward Shacklett, and Thomas Smith tracts of land in the Oak Hill tract of Fauquier County. The leases are for three lives and contain conditions and stipulations similar to those in the lease to William Hume, printed immediately above.]

Lease

Deed Book Copy, Office of the Clerk of the Fauquier County Circuit Court, Warrenton, Va.

[*July 25, 1793* (*Fauquier County*). JM executes a bargain and sale deed leasing to Thomas Simpson the tract of land in Fauquier County purchased by JM from Aquila Dyson on Oct. 18, 1787. The lease is for three lives and contains conditions and stipulations similar to those in the lease to William Hume, printed above.]

Deed

Deed Book Copy, Office of the Clerk of the Frederick County Superior Court, Winchester, Va.

[*August 5, 1793, Frederick County.* JM witnesses a deed from Philip Martin to Rawleigh Colston for land called Patterson's Creek or Philip Martin's Manor.]

2. Francis Brooke had succeeded his father, Humphrey Brooke, as clerk of Fauquier County in 1793 and continued in that office until 1805.

Masonic Dispensation

[*August 12, 1793, Richmond*. JM, as deputy grand master of the Grand Lodge, signs a dispensation authorizing Richmond Randolph Lodge No. 19 to initiate Samuel Greenhow as a Mason. Richmond Randolph Lodge No. 19 Records, 1787–1801, Grand Lodge A.F. & A.M. of Virginia, Richmond. Not found.]

Resolutions

Printed, *Virginia Gazette, and General Advertiser* (Richmond), August 21, 1793, 3

Richmond, August 17, 1793

At a numerous meeting of the Citizens of Richmond, and its vicinity, held at the capitol on Saturday the 17th of August, 1793, agreeable to notification;[3] and in order to take under consideration the late Proclamation of the President of the United States.[4]

The Proclamation of the President being read, the following resolutions were offered, discussed, and unanimously agreed to:

1st. That it is the interest and duty of these United states to conform to their several subsisting treaties, and to maintain a strict neutrality towards the belligerent powers of Europe, on the due and faithful observance of which the happiness and prosperity of our common country very greatly depend.

2dly. That our illustrious fellow citizen, GEORGE WASHINGTON, to whose eminent services, great talents, and exalted virtues, all America pays so just a tribute, has given an additional proof of his watchful attention to his own duty, and the welfare of his country, by his Proclamation notifying to all that these United States are in perfect neutrality with respect to the belligerent powers of Europe, and enjoining our citizens to an observance thereof.

3dly. That it is our duty as well as our interest to conduct ourselves conformably to the principles expressed in the said Proclamation, and to use our best endeavours to prevent any infringe-

3. This meeting was announced in the *Virginia Gazette, and General Advertiser* (Richmond), Aug. 14, 1793. For a description of the events preceding and following the meeting as well as an argument that JM organized the meeting, see Harry Ammon, *The Genet Mission* (New York, 1973), 135–140.

4. Washington issued the neutrality proclamation on Apr. 22, 1793.

ment of them by others; and we hereby declare that it is our firm intention to do so.

And a committee was appointed to draw up an address conformable to said resolutions, consisting of the following gentlemen: J. Marshall, C: Braxton, A. Ronald, J. M'Clurg, A. Campbell, and J. Steele. The Committee returned, and Mr. Marshall reported an address, which being read, was unanimously agreed to.

The meeting continuing to sit, the following Resolutions[5] were offered, discussed, and unanimously agreed to:

1st. That the constitution of our country has provided a proper and adequate mode of communication between these United States and foreign nations, or their ministers, whereby the sense of these United States or of foreign nations on any subject concerning either may be conveyed or received.

2dly. That if at any time this constitutional authority should be abused, & the Supreme Executive of the United States should misconstrue treaties, violate the laws, or oppose the sense of the union, there exists among the people of America, without the intervention of foreign ministers, discernment to detect the abuse, and ability to correct the mischief.

3dly. That any communication of foreign ministers on national subjects, with the citizens of these United States, or any of them, otherwise than through the constituted authority; any interference of a foreign minister with our internal government or administration; any intriguing of a foreign minister with the political parties of this country; would violate the laws and usages of nations, would be a high indignity to the government and people of America, and would be great and just cause of alarm, as it would be at once a dangerous introduction of foreign influence, and might, too probably lead to the introduction of foreign gold and foreign armies, with their fatal consequences, dismemberment and partition.[6]

GEORGE WYTHE, President.

A. DUNSCOMB,[7] Secretary.

---

5. JM wrote in 1827, "These resolutions and the address to the President which accompanied them, were drawn and supported by me." John Stokes Adams, ed., *An Autobiographical Sketch by John Marshall* . . . (Ann Arbor, Mich., 1937), 14.

6. Edmond Charles Genêt (1763–1834), who had been appointed minister plenipotentiary to the United States in Nov. 1792, arrived in Charleston from France in Apr. 1793. He fitted out several privateers and then started on a tour of the coastal states as he made his way to Philadelphia to present his credentials. He passed through Virginia in May 1793. Enthusiastic receptions led to indiscretions on Genêt's part, and anglophiles seized the opportunity to advance their cause by chastising the French

Address

Printed, *Virginia Gazette, and General Advertiser* (Richmond), September 11, 1793, 3

SIR,[8]   Richmond, August 17, 1793

IMPRESSED with a full conviction of the wisdom of your administration in general, and especially approving that system of conduct which you have adopted, and steadily observed towards the belligerent powers of Europe, we, the Inhabitants of Richmond and its Vicinity, in the Commonwealth of Virginia, are happy in an opportunity of conveying to you these our genuine sentiments.

When propitious Heaven had crowned with victory the efforts of your country and yourself, while rejoicing America enumerated the blessings to be derived from so important a revolution, it was not reckoned among the least of them that, in future, the people of this favored land might in peace pursue their own happiness though war and violence should desolate the European world, or drench

diplomat. See Richard R. Beeman, *The Old Dominion and the New Nation, 1788–1801* (Lexington, Ky., 1972), 126–128; Ammon, *Genet Mission*, 136.

James Monroe wrote to Thomas Jefferson on Sept. 3, 1793, "The party in Richmond was soon in motion, from what I have understood here have reason to believe they mean to produce the most extensive effect they are capable of. Mr. Marshall had written G[abriel] Jones on the subject & the first appearance threatened the most furious attack on the French minister, the pressure to it was ended in a manner honorable to the parties concerned (the mention of that character alone excepted) & he is only classed with Messrs. Jay & King." Stanislaus Murray Hamilton, ed., *The Writings of James Monroe* (New York, 1898), I, 274–276. JM's letter to Gabriel Jones (1724–1806) has not been found. Jones lived in Rockingham County and was of strong Federalist sentiment. After an active pre-Revolutionary political career, he refused election to the Continental Congress on two occasions and in 1788 refused election as a judge of the new district court. See fee entered in Account Book, Receipts, Jan. 1791.

James Madison wrote Jefferson on the same subject a day earlier than Monroe, reporting that Wilson Cary Nicholas could no longer be kept in confidence partly because of Nicholas's "communication & intimacy with Marshall. . . . It is said, that Marshall who is at the head of the great purchase from Fairfax, has lately obtained pecuniary aid from the Bank or people connected with it. I think it certain that he must have felt in the moment of the purchase an absolute dependence on the monied interest, which will explain him to every one that reflects, in the active character he is assuming." Madison to Jefferson, Sept. 2, 1793, Madison Papers, Library of Congress.

7. Andrew Dunscomb (*ca.* 1745–1802) had settled in Richmond after the Revolution when he was appointed by Congress to settle the accounts of the Confederation with Virginia. From 1792 to 1795 he served successively as common councilman, alderman, auditor-treasurer, and mayor of Richmond.

8. George Washington; his response to this address is also printed in the Sept. 11, 1793, issue of the *Virginia Gazette, and General Advertiser* (Richmond). JM claimed authorship of this address as well as the resolutions adopted at the public meeting. John Stokes Adams, ed., *An Autobiographical Sketch by John Marshall . . .* (Ann Arbor, Mich., 1937), 14.

it in human blood—so too, when the good genius of America had devised that change in our government, which her wisdom has since adopted, it was held an argument of some weight against the necessity of this change, and all in opposition to it with one voice declared, that, situated as this country is, no madness or folly could ever be so supreme as to involve us again in European contests. Nor was this opinion, so uniform and universal, in favor of peace, derived from any other source than a knowledge of the real situation and a conviction of the real interests of America. It is impossible for the eye of cool and temperate reason to survey these United States without perceiving, that, however dreadful the calamities of war may be to other nations, they are still more dreadful to us, and however important the benefits of peace to others, to us it must be still more beneficial.

From those whose province it is to make war, we expect every effort to avoid it consistent with the honor, interest and good faith of America; from you, Sir, to whom is assigned the important task of, "taking care that the laws be faithfully executed, we have already experienced the most active and watchful attention to our dearest interests."

Ever since the period when a just respect for the voice of your country induced you to abandon the retirement you loved, for that high station to which your fellow-citizens unanimously called you, your conduct has been uniformly calculated to promote their happiness and welfare: And in no instance has this been more remarkable, or your vigilant attention to the duties of your office more clearly discovered, than in your Proclamation respecting the neutrality of the United States.

As genuine Americans, with no other interest at heart but that of our country, unbiassed by foreign influence, which history informs us has been the bane of more than one republic, our minds are open to a due sense of the propriety, justice, and wisdom of this measure; and we cannot refrain from expressing our pleasure at its adoption.

We recollect too well the calamities of war, not to use our best endeavours to restrain any wicked citizen, if such indeed can be found among us, who, disregarding his own duty, and the happiness of the United States, in violation of the law of the land and the wish of the people, shall dare to gratify his paltry passions at the risk of his country's welfare, perhaps of his existence.

We pray Heaven to manifest its providential care of these states, by prolonging to them the blessings of your administration—and may the pure spirit of it continue to animate the government of America through a succession of ages.

Signed by desire and on behalf of the meeting,

(Teste) GEORGE WYTHE, *President.*

ANDREW DUNSCOMB, *Secretary.*

From James Wood

Copy, Executive Letterbooks, Virginia State Library

[*August 22, 1793, Richmond.* JM is instructed to take steps to remove any vessels fitted out as privateers that might enter any port within his jurisdiction. He is also told to seize any prize brought by such ships.[9]]

From James Wood

Copy, Executive Letterbooks, Virginia State Library

Sir,[1]   Richmond, August 23, 1793

You will be pleased to take the necessary Measures for calling into immediate and actual service, An Ensign, Sergeant, Corporal and twenty privates of your militia. They are to be employed as a Guard over the public Arms in this City. The House at present occupied by Mrs. Pearson is appropriated to the use of this detachment as a Guard–House. The Arms will be deposited in the Building near the Guard–House. Be pleased to give the officer instructions as to the mode of performing his duty. It is the desire of the Executive that besides guarding the Public Arms, you direct them to perform such duty as you may think conducive to the

9. The letter is addressed as a "Circular, To the Commanding officers of the Militia of the Several counties in which are Ports of Navigation." James Wood was writing the letter as the lieutenant governor, or president of the Council of State, in the absence of Gov. Henry Lee. On the day the letter was written, the Council ordered the action as the result of receiving an Aug. 16 letter from the secretary of war, Henry Knox. JVCS, Aug. 22, 1793.

1. Addressed to "John Marshall Esquire Lt Colonel Commandant, of the City Militia Richmond."

public safety of the City.[2] I have the honor to be with great personal respect etc.

JAMES WOOD

To Augustine Davis

Printed, *Virginia Gazette, and General Advertiser* (Richmond), September 11, 1793, 2

Mr. DAVIS,[3]   Richmond, September 8, 1793

WHEN a gentleman, whose style of composition is respectable, and who seems not to be impelled by the mere vanity of becoming an author, presses forward with a bold venture on the conduct of his fellow-citizens, his charge demands our consideration, under a title not to be overlooked.[4]

Persuaded that the present real disposition of our country differed essentially from the representations which had industriously been made of it; and, that much mischief had resulted, and more was to be feared from these misrepresentations, the citizens of Richmond and its vicinity deemed it proper that the people should

2. Following the revolt of Toussaint Louverture (1743–1803) in Santo Domingo in 1792, fear of slave conspiracies spread throughout the South. On Aug. 15, 1793, the Council of State heard reports that a slave insurrection was likely to occur in Richmond and in Norfolk, whereupon they ordered that extra weapons be brought to Richmond and placed under guard. The day before this letter was written, the Council directed that the arms be stored in "the house near the Capitol at present occupied by Mrs. Pearson (being public property)." JVCS, Aug. 15, 22, 1793. The Executive Letterbooks, Virginia State Library, contain many letters concerning arms and "internal security" in the summer of 1793.

3. JM, using the pseudonym Aristides, addressed this essay to Augustine Davis (d. 1825), Federalist editor of the *Virginia Gazette, and General Advertiser* (Richmond) from 1790 to 1809. Originally from Yorktown, Davis had published the *Virginia Gazette* in Williamsburg from 1779 to 1780, after which time he moved to Richmond, where he also published the *Virginia Independent Chronicle* from 1786 to 1790, the *Virginia Gazette, and Richmond and Manchester Advertiser* with Samuel Pleasants, Jr., from 1793 to 1794, and the *Virginia Patriot* from 1809 to 1820.

4. This essay is in response to one by James Monroe published under the pseudonym Agricola in the same newspaper on Sept. 4. JM wrote another Aristides essay on Nov. 20, and his two Gracchus essays appeared on Oct. 16 and Nov. 13. All four are printed in this volume. On questions of authorship and style, and for a discussion of the contents of the Agricola-Aristides-Gracchus exchange, see Harry Ammon, "Agricola Versus Aristides: James Monroe, John Marshall, and the Genet Affair in Virginia," *Virginia Magazine of History and Biography*, LXXIV (1966), 312–320; and Philip Marsh, "James Monroe as 'Agricola' in the Genet Controversy," *VMHB*, LXII (1954), 472–476. See also Harry Ammon, *The Genet Mission* (New York, 1973). For JM's only mention of the exchange, see John Stokes Adams, ed., *An Autobiographical Sketch by John Marshall . . .* (Ann Arbor, Mich., 1937), 14.

declare their own sentiments. Thus thinking they, as a part of the people, convened together to express their opinions on subjects all important to us,—the neutrality and complete sovereignty of these United States.[5] This proceeding has brought forth a criminating address signed AGRICOLA. The writer will not venture to say, that the people had a right peaceably to meet together and to declare their opinions on any political subject whatever, or that this right can only be properly exercised by calumniating public measures. His disapprobation, therefore, of those resolutions, goes not to the right of framing them, but to the matter they contain. To the public they are submitted, and the public will judge of them. They consist of two parts—the one approving the conduct of the President of the United States, towards the belligerent powers of Europe —the other declaring a detestation and abhorrence of any interference whatever of a foreign nation or minister with our political contests or internal government. Can the American exist who, like Agricola, professes himself the friend of neutrality, and yet does not most cordially unite with the citizens of Richmond and its vicinity in these sentiments? Is there a man among us who has so buried the love of country under a zeal for party or affection for a foreign nation, that he could stoop to be dictated to by the minister of that nation or could witness his dangerous efforts to create divisions among us, and opposition to our government, without feeling himself as the citizen of an independent republic, degraded and insulted? For what then is the conduct of the people of Richmond and its vicinity to be reprehended? This we are to learn from Agricola. Let us attend to him—He tells us that a game is playing by the enemies of the French revolution and of liberty, who under specious and wholesome appearances, cover from the view of those for whom the dose is intended, the poison it contains. That the French minister, in pressing the cause of his country, and of *liberty* upon the President, has in his zeal intimated a belief that the sentiments of the people were more favorable to his country and to her *cause* than our executive councils were; and that he would appeal to this sentiment. That the operations of the executive must be in some measure secret, and that a disagreement with a foreign minister, while there was a prospect of compromise, should be peculiarly so. That as the best interests of both countries required a secret discussion of these subjects, some object unfriend-

5. See JM's Resolutions and an Address, both printed at Aug. 17, 1793.

ly to both dictated the publication. This object is to effect the destruction of our present government, by dissolving all connection with France, and uniting with England. This was the true and genuine object of the publication of Mr. Jay and Mr. King.[6] That a train has been laid for disseminating the variance, and extending it to the community at large, is with certainty to be inferred. "How, (says Agricola) account for the prompt and correspondent publications at Richmond and Burlington,[7] if they were not dictated, or at least suggested from the same source." The citizens of these places are not more zealous than their countrymen for the national honor, nor have they exhibited stronger proofs of patriotism, that they should thus step forward to foment this unhappy division—they ought rather to have held aloof, and as impartial but afflicted spectators, deplored the occasion which gave birth to it. Agricola then prescribes to us the resolutions we ought to adopt.

These are the substantial parts of his publication. He will pardon me that I have not repeated his own words, and that I have totally omitted many insinuations which appeared to be entirely unfounded and unjust. To you, my countrymen, who have no object but the common good, whose happiness, whose existence perhaps, is staked upon your present conduct, who have only to be rightly informed to judge rightly, to you I submit this defence of the conduct of your fellow citizens, and this comment on the censure of Agricola.

If there be among us men who are enemies to the French revolution, or who are friends to monarchy, I know them not. If I might judge from the extent of my own information, I should disbelieve the assertion. If Mr. Jay, and Mr. King, entertain these opinions, Agricola would not censure them more severely than myself. I can only say, that however he may feel himself warranted to adduce so heavy a charge by the possession of other proofs, that which he vouchsafes to exhibit to the public will by no means authorise it. When a foreign minister shall dare to pursue measures calculated to raise a party to oppose our government under his banners, the men who give notice of such measures, are not for that only reason to be considered as the enemies of America. Much more is he to be suspected who looks on as an impartial spectator, and thinks

6. U.S. Chief Justice John Jay (1745–1829) and New York senator Rufus King (1755–1827) promoted the adoption of resolves supporting neutrality in New York City. Ammon, *Genet Mission*, 133–134.

7. New Jersey. *Ibid.*, 134.

himself unaffected by the efforts of a foreign minister to sow dis-
sention in his country.

These gentlemen are charged too with having improperly and for
vicious purposes divulged the secrets of the Executive. If the declaration alluded to was made in secret, if it was a private threat,
the secret must have been divulged to them before they could have
communicated it to others. But let it be, if this will gratify Agricola, that Mr. Jay and Mr. King, are foes to our happy government, that they have acted improperly in publishing the improper conduct of a foreign Minister—yet America is possessed of the
fact. We have it supported by the Minister himself. How ought we
to act upon it? Should we manifest our disapprobation of such
conduct, or should we hold aloof, as impartial spectators unconnected with our own government, and silently deplore the attempt to engage us against it, without censuring that attempt? The
first has been the conduct of the people wherever they have spoken
or acted, the last is recommended by Agricola.

When the people of Richmond and its vicinity, without naming
the Minister of France, or applying their resolutions to him, otherwise than as the fact they censured might be adopted by him,
proceed to declare that the interference of a Foreign Minister with
our internal government would be dangerous, alarming and de-
grading to us—Agricola is warm in his condemnation of them. He
attributes their resolutions, to the same source, if I understand
him rightly, to which he had before attributed the publication of
Mr. Jay and Mr. King; that is to an enmity to the French revolution and the cause of liberty, and to the desire of establishing a
Monarchy on the ruins of our present happy constitution. If this
be the idea of Agricola, the calumny grows not out of the fact, and
merits no other reply, than that Agricola himself, though he may
be less a friend to America, is not more attached to the cause of
France or the rights of mankind in general, than a great majority
of the meeting he ventures to defame. If, by saying the resolutions
at Richmond and Burlington were dictated or suggested from the
same source, he means that one common prompter moved the puppets at each place, and that the people think and speak not for
themselves, but as they are directed by a hand behind the curtain,
the slander is equally contemptible, and could never have been
fabricated, had no person in America been better versed in the
business of dancing puppets, than the people Agricola condemns.
But passing over these indecent insinuations, as unworthy of further

notice, I mean to shew that the conduct Agricola censures was highly proper, and that the strongest human motives urge you, my countrymen, to the adoption of similar measures.

Happily separated from the people of Europe, by an immence ocean, America is at peace with all of them. Almost every nation of that quarter of the globe is at war with France. We universally consider that gallant people as contending for the rights of human nature, and our best wishes attend their efforts. But we have treaties with her enemies not less obligatory on us, than those with France, and until it shall be the will of Congress to dissolve them by a declaration of war, it is not less the duty of the Supreme Executive of the United States, faithfully to observe them. No one of these treaties is offensive and defensive;—they place us in a state of perfect neutrality. With this situation Agricola professes himself to be content. A breach of this neutrality by individuals, if not disavowed and punished by the nation, would be a just cause of war, as being a breach of that faith which America has pledged to every power with whom she has a treaty. To attend to the observance of these treaties is the province of the President of the United States, and to notify their obligation and the penalties annexed to the violation of them, was surely his duty. A regard to this duty, produced his Proclamation. For this was he most industriously insulted and defamed. The public ear was every day offended by the most malignant charges against their beloved Chief Magistrate. He was treated in a scandalous paper (could you hear it Americans and be silent?) as if he had sacrificed the interests of his own country, to those of Britain, as if neutrality was pusillanimity, as if, while exerting his utmost powers to comply faithfully with all our engagements, he was dictated to by a nation, unfriendly to us, and feared to discharge our obligations to our best and most esteemed ally. An active, but I trust not a numerous party, incessant in their efforts to disgust America with the government of her choice, had the boldness to erect themselves into the proclaimers of the public opinion, and to declare that the people universally condemned the conduct of their President, and universally wished for those measures, which every reflecting man must know lead directly to war. Silence was misconstrued into approbation, and these hardy men already plumed themselves upon it. The minister of our beloved ally seems to have been credulous enough to believe them. They have seduced him into a conduct which his country must condemn, because his country is friendly to ours.

They have tempted him to measures, which if persisted in, must destroy that friendship, because they lead directly to the ruin of one of the parties. Weigh, I beseech you, the consequences of a foreign minister in a republic, appealing to the people from the constitutional decisions of their government. How is this appeal to be supported? Must it not be by raising a party to oppose the government? If one foreign minister may make the appeal, what shall restrain every other from making it? If one foreign minister may raise parties against the government, what shall restrain others? If foreign ministers be permitted to proceed thus, what must be the situation of our country? Attend to the effects of such proceedings in the antient world; attend to them in Sweden, in Holland, and above all, in Poland. Our safety, my fellow-citizens, as well as our honour, urges us to be prompt in discountenancing such dangerous measures. They are produced by an opinion, that the people will support them. This opinion can only be eradicated by the declarations of the people themselves. If the minister of France has been deceived, it is our duty to undeceive him, that he may pursue a conduct more worthy of the nation he represents, and more worthy of that to which he is deputed. He knows that the people of America love France, we all know it, we all feel and avow it; but it has become necessary for us to intermingle with such an avowal declarations of our respect for ourselves, and for our own government. It has now become necessary for us to say, that however devoted we may be to France, we cannot permit her to interfere in our internal government, nor can we allow her minister to set an example to others, so dangerous to our independence, and so destructive of our happiness. These motives impelled the people of Richmond and its vicinity to assemble together, and to pass the resolutions, which you my countrymen have seen, and which Agricola ascribes to such disreputable views. In expressing them they have condemned the act without ascribing it to any individual.

The people of Richmond and its vicinity, claim no pre-eminence of patriotism over their fellow-citizens—they only demand an equality with them. They pretend not to have rendered more signal services to their country than others, but they fear no comparison of character. They have acted like their countrymen, they think like their countrymen, and they claim an equal right to speak their sentiments. Every subject which begins at all, must begin with some one, and it is unjust to charge those who do begin, with assuming to themselves any superiority over others. The people of Richmond and its vicinity have spoken only for themselves. Agricola undertakes to prescribe to others. With much more propriety might his countrymen enquire, what Agricola have been your great achievements? What pre-eminent display of talents and patriotism have you ever made which shall authorize you thus to censure some, and dictate to others? What unbounded services have you rendered to the community, that may justify you in assuming that exalted seat in which you have placed yourself? Forbear, Agricola, forbear to indulge yourself in sarcasm and invective against your fellow-citizens! If your object be a worthy one, you should rather seek to convince, than to irritate.

ARISTIDES.

Petition

DS, Executive Papers, Virginia State Library

Richmond, September 12, 1793

To the Honble. the Governor & Council of Virginia

The undersigned petitioners beg leave to intercede with your honble. board for in behalf of Angelica Barnet, who is Confined in the public jail under sentence of Death for Murder.[8]

It seldom happens that Crimes of this high nature deserve the mercy of the pardoning power: but there are some circumstances in this Case, which seem to present it in a more favorable point of

8. Angella, or Angellica, Barnett, a free Negro, was convicted of murder at the Richmond District Court on Apr. 11, 1793. The day after her conviction the judges of the district court wrote the governor explaining the special circumstances of her case: the victim, Peter Franklin, broke into her house at night while on an unofficial search for runaway slaves, and after provoking her with various kinds of abuse and threatening or striking her with a whip, he received a blow to the head. Franklin died four days later, on Sept. 8, 1792, whereupon Angella Barnett was jailed. *CVSP*, VI, 337–338, 342–343.

On Apr. 13 the first of many subsequent petitions asking for mercy and pardon for Barnett was presented to the governor. The first was signed primarily by Richmond women, one of whom was JM's wife, Mary W. Marshall. On May 9 Barnett sent a petition to the governor asking for a pardon or a reprieve from her sentence to hang on May 17, claiming pregnancy by Jacob Valentine, a debtor who had been jailed with her. After a physician's examination confirmed her pregnancy, the reprieve was granted until June 21. Three subsequent reprieves moved the execution date to Sept. 13, a Friday. After receiving this petition on the eve of Barnett's execution, the Council of State granted her a pardon. The signers represent most of the Richmond bar. *CVSP*, VI, 344–345, 363–364, 372–373, 393; JVCS, May 14, June 14, July 16, Sept. 3, and Sept. 12, 1793.

view. It hath been said by many persons respectable for their Talents & veracity who were present at the Trial of the Prisoner, that the facts did not seem sufficient to justify a verdict of death. The situation of the Prisoner at the time when the offence was committed, deserves to be Considered. She was possessed of many of the rights of a free–Citizen, and among the rest the great right of personal immunity in her own house. This, unquestionably was invaded, by the Person who was unfortunately killed, and it is, perhaps to be regretted, at least it is reasonable to presume that many of the Circumstances alleged by the prisoner in her justification, might have been proved, if her associates were not, incompetent, by law to give Testimony against a White person.[9] Your petitioners think it probable, from what they have heard that the Venire might have Conceived prejudices against the Prisoner, which might have had too great an influence upon their decision.

Lastly, it is a Consideration of some weight with them, that the prisoner hath languished a long time in jail, in a situation which must have added to the miseries of imprisonment, & the horrors of an execution, which agony alone hath suspended.

Your petitioners for this act of mercy will hold themselves bound to pray.

ANDW. RONALD present at the trial, and thought her almost justifiable.

ALEX CAMPBELL—present at the greater part of the Trial, & impressed with the hardship of the prisoner's Case

CHAS COPLAND[1]—I heard part of the evidence at the trial and it appeared to me she defended herself agt the attack of the Man she killed.

WM. DUVAL I thought her Crime amounted to manslaughter only.

NATHL POPE JUNR. I was present during the whole Trial and did not think the Evidence sufficient to convict the [prisoner] of even manslaughter.

MATTHEW PAGE Jr I was present at the trial & thought from the evidence the prisoner was justifiable & that she acted only in her defence.

9. Existing law stated: "No negro or mulatto shall be a witness, except in pleas of the commonwealth against negroes or mulattoes, or in civil pleas wherein negroes or mulattoes alone shall be parties." 12 Hening 182 (1785).

1. Copeland (1756–1836) was a prominent Richmond attorney, considered a rival of John Wickham and William Wirt.

HENRY BANKS, present at the Tryal and thinks the Testimony did not authorise the verdict.

WILLIAM POPE[2]—present at the Tryal and thinks the verdict was a very uncontionable one, when he considers, the unfortunate circumstance hapned under the roof of the prisoner and in self defence.

J MARSHALL knows nothing of the case or testimony but having heard a favorable character of the prisoner is for that reason a meer petitioner for mercy.

J LYONS.

SAML. McCRAW[3]—present at the Trial, and humbly conceives the Verdict to have been a hard one, not justified by the Evidence, it appearing from the whole tenor thereof to have been in self defence, in a calamitous moment.

To Henry Lee

ALS, Executive Papers, Virginia State Library

Sir[4]   Richmond, September 23, 1793

Your letter of the 21st. was deliverd to me. I have written to the officer of the Guard on the subject it relates to.[5]

I take the liberty to state to you sir that if the guard be continued it will be necessary to adopt some mode for supplying them with rations. This I beleive may be effected without any other additional expense than the price of the provisions & I am not certain that the ration will cost more than the allowance to be made for it. It will also be necessary to erect a sentry box to protect the sentinel from inclement weather.[6] With very much respect, I am Sir your obedt. Servt.

J MARSHALL

2. Pope (1762–1852), of "Montpelier" in Powhatan County, had served as a Commonwealth's attorney and was now practicing law in Richmond.

3. McCraw (d. 1823) was a Richmond attorney who later served in the state senate from 1795 to 1798.

4. Addressed to "His Excellency, Governor Lee." A clerk wrote, "Colo. Marshals Letters," probably referring to this and JM to Henry Lee, Sept. 24, 1793. He also wrote, "Done Sep. 26, 1793."

5. These letters have not been found.

6. The reference is to the guard in Richmond, called out the previous month. See

From Robert Mitchell

ALS, Executive Papers, Virginia State Library

Dr. Sir[7]   Richmond, September 23, 1793

Give me leave to Give You a few hints, by desire of Some of the Worthey Inhabetants of this City.

That Mr. Nice[8] Commander of the Standing Guard Informed that he had a few men & Guns, but neither powder ore Shot, is this the defince of this City in Case of an Alarm from ———?[9] I thinke my Suspesions is now well Grounded By the Information from the County of Powhatan, that a number of negroes from Different parts of this Countrey had assembled at an Old Schoole house in P. County.[1] That Some of the whites, had taken Some and whipped them that they had Confesed that three hundred Was to meet there & had released them without makeing further enquirey not knowing at that time anything of the Information, we have had of this Intended Riseing, that Several of the negro foremen of the different Plantations had runaway, and that one belonging to a Mr. Baw had been Seen Since, with a Sworde he being one of the runaways, the people, (Say the planters) there are Surprised, that his Excy. the Governor had not Advised their L. Colo. of the County of the Suspicion of the negroes, that they be prepared against the Worst.

Takeing all matters of Information into Consideration I Cant

James Wood to JM, Aug. 23, 1793. JM's letter was presented to the Council of State, and that body ordered supplies for the guard. See JVCS, Sept. 26, 1793; and Henry Lee to JM, Sept. 26, 1793.

7. The letter is addressed to "Colo. John Marshal, Sho. Hill." JM enclosed this letter in his to Henry Lee of Sept. 24, 1793, and a clerk wrote on the verso, "Sept. 24th, 1793."

8. William Nice (d. 1808).

9. Mitchell drew a line here, probably assuming JM knew what he left unsaid.

Mitchell was mayor of Richmond for various terms between 1790 and 1804 and was a member of the Richmond City Common Hall when he wrote this letter. He no doubt wrote JM hoping he would bring the matter to the governor's attention.

1. Fear of slave insurrections was spreading throughout the state in 1793. See James Wood to JM, Aug. 23, 1793; Herbert Aptheker, *American Negro Slave Revolts* (New York, 1944), 209–219; Winthrop D. Jordan, *White over Black: American Attitudes toward the Negro, 1550–1812* (Chapel Hill, N.C., 1968), 391; and Robert McColley, *Slavery and Jeffersonian Virginia* (Urbana, Ill., 1964), 107.

In May 1794 a slave belonging to Mitchell was arrested and charged with having helped murder an overseer in Powhatan County; he was later acquitted. *CVSP*, VII, 191–193.

help thinkeing that the Intended Riseing is true. Therefore no harme Can arise, in prepairing for the Worst, relyeing much on your Good Conduct, as Colo. of this City meletia etc. Should I have mad use of any unproper expression in any part of this lettr. I am persuaded you will Excuse As I thinke you know me well & believe me, D Sir, To be Your Mo. Obd. Sert.

ROBT. MITCHELL

To Henry Lee

ALS, Executive Papers, Virginia State Library

Sir   Richmond, September 26, 1793
   I take the liberty to enclose you a letter I have just receivd from Mr. Mitchell[2] & beg leave to suggest the propriety of furnishing the guard with cartridges. With very much respect, I am Sir your obedt. Servt.

J MARSHALL

From Henry Lee

Copy, Executive Letterbooks, Virginia State Library

Sir,[3]   Richmond, September 26, 1793
   In answer to your letter of the 23d. instant I acquaint you that a continuance of the Guard is deemed proper, that Ammunition and provision will be furnished and with respect to the latter article suggest the mode most convenient and it shall be authorized.[4] I am etc.

HENRY LEE

   2. Robert Mitchell to JM, Sept. 23, 1793.
   3. The letter was written from the Council chamber and was addressed to JM as "Commandant of the militia of the City of Richmond."
   4. This action was authorized by the Council of State on Sept. 26, 1793. JVCS, Sept. 26, 1793. For JM's suggestions regarding provisions, see JM to Henry Lee, Oct. 5, 1793.

From Anthony Walton White

ALS, Anthony Walton White Papers, Rutgers University Library[5]

Dear Sir   New Brunswick, September 29, 1793

Permit me to introduce to you my Friend & Brother in law Judge Paterson[6] who visits Virginia in his official Character, any civilities you may please to shew him will be conferring an obligation on myself & his numerous friends in this quarter.

It is a very long time since I have had the satisfaction of receiving a line from you, your letters to me on the subject of my demands against *the very honourable Tobacco Gentlemen*[7] leads me to think it very extraordinary that the several sums due from them have not yet been received, the issue of these suits (as they have been along time commenced) ought to have been known years ago, perhaps my want of information may make this conclusion improper, I have drawn it from not having a doubt that those suits were commenced on your receiving the necessary proof & vouchers; & that the laws of every state would justify my believing a period far short of the one since that proof was in your posession would have carried the suits through the most extensive course of law, especially as it was my most pointed instructions to give no indulgence to those *very honourable gentlemen* but what the law would grant to them, do let me intreat you my dear Sir to have this business attended to & finished.

Permit me also to request the favour of you to call on my friend Shingleton[8] & ask him to give his deposition respecting 27,000

---

5. The address leaf is missing, and the endorsement in a hand other than that of JM reads: "Anthony W. White, New Brunswick, Sepr 29:93." On the same panel as the endorsement is a notation in pencil: "To John Marshall Esqr, Afterwards Chief Justice of the United States." Next to the salutation is another notation in pencil: "$25.00., wdwd, 60," suggesting the letter was once offered for sale.

6. William Paterson (1745–1806), an associate justice of the U.S. Supreme Court, was married to White's sister Euphemia. The autumn term of the Circuit Court opened on Nov. 22, 1793, at which time Paterson ceremoniously presented his commission and a certificate from Justice William Cushing proving that he had taken the necessary oaths upon becoming an associate justice. U.S. Circuit Court, Va., Order Book, I, 165, Virginia State Library.

7. See JM's letter of Mar. 15, 1789, to White concerning half-pay certificates and land warrants. On the other hand, a legal fee received on Jan. 23, 1787, might pertain to these collections matters. Vol. I, 369. If the litigation had in fact been in the courts for six and a half years, White was quite correct that some action might be expected.

8. Perhaps Anthony Singleton.

Dolls. that I left with him during the War to be delivered either to Captains Watts or Fauntleroy who were at that time in the State of Virginia on the recruiting service, Capt. Fauntleroy being the first that called on Capt. Shingleton for this money he gave it to him. Capt Fauntleroy's letter to me acknowledges this to be the case but his letter is without date, & he has neglected to mention for what purpose he received that sum of money, the last time I conversed with Captain Shingleton on this subject I think he told me that he recollected receiving the above mentioned sum of money from me with a request to deliver it to either Captains Watts or Fauntleroy for the purpose of recruiting, & if what I have said will strengthen Capt. Shingletons recollection sufficient to give his deposition that he did receive this sum of money from me and deliverd the same to Capt. Fauntleroy for the purpose of Recruiting it will give weight to Capt. Fauntleroy's letter as a voucher & serve me in a very particular manner.

As the Senate of your State have rejected the prayer of my petition[9] I must endeavour to make a settlement with the United States. I will therefore thank you to deliver Judge Paterson the Paper-money I left with you with Scotts & Boyers receipts for vouchers & money I put in their hands & every other paper etc. that may be of use to me in settling my public accounts. Have you ever procured from Mr Scott, Howells certificate? He certainly received it for the purpose of discharging that gentlemans proportion of the Tobacco Contract, & it ought in justice to be deliverd to me. Erskin I am told left landed property, can I obtain no part of it for my demand against him? Please to inform me if Boyer has settled with you, & If he is an Officer in the present service, if you have not recoverd the amount of my demand against him & there is no probability of doing it in Virginia will it not be best to send his account respecting the Tobacco to me? And I will put them in the hands of a Lawyer in Philadelphia with directions to sue him there should he visit that City.

Has old Mr Peyton had honour enough to pay his sons note? Or will he do it? I wish Coln. Hervie & yourself would award what sum of money David Leitch has to pay me on the deficiency of Land Warrants not accounted for by him, If Leitch is in Virginia

9. Not found. Apparently the application was for reimbursement of bounty money advanced for recruiting purposes. It is likely that the payment had been made for Virginia Continental Line troops and that since the state had refused legislative relief, White had decided to petition Congress for the $27,000.

sue him immediately for the amount of your award, & the small demand I had against him & left in your hands & if he has fixed his residence in Kentucky send this demand with your award & the power that justifies your giving the same to me & I will order him sued in that country for the amount of both.[1]

As you were so obliging to offer to send out my land Warrant for 6660 ⅔ Acres of land to your friend Colnl. Anderson,[2] & promised that it should be laid by him to my advantage, I take it for granted the Colonel has long ago accomplished my wishes & procured a Patent for the same, if he has not it will be adding to the very many difficulties & hardships I have experienced as a Virginia Officer, as such I have faithfully done my duty & the convincing evidence in my posession with those I have put in your hands will prove that I have advanced my money for the support & comfort of the Officers & Soldiers of that State, my reward has been a denial of Justice from the Legislature & base ingratitude from those individuals who experienced my friendship when they were in the greatest distress & from their homes & friends. I have ever supported Virginia against the attacks of her Enemy's but I am almost tempted to agree with them in believing it impossible for a debt to be recoverd of a Citizen of that State, if his Creditor should be unfortunate enough to reside in another. I have assigned my land warrant to two gentlemen in this Country who have given Judge Paterson a Power to dispose of the land. I shall be allways ready to satisfy you for the services you may have renderd me in the line of your profession & happy in having an opportunity of returning the attention & civilities you may please to shew to the bearer of this, I am Dr Sir, with great respect & Esteem, Your mo. obdt Humbl. Servt

ANTHY. W. WHITE

1. A fee concerning an "old appeal" in a case identified as White v. Letcher may pertain to this litigation. See Account Book, Receipts, Mar. 1789. The discussion indicates that the matter had been submitted for arbitration under the order of some Virginia court and that JM and "Coln. Hervie" served as arbitrators.

2. Richard C. Anderson, a Kentucky surveyor for the Virginia Continental Line.

Receipt

DS, Vol. 1194A, RG 53, National Archives

[*September 30, 1793, Richmond*. JM signs a receipt of John Hopkins, U.S. commissioner of loans for Virginia, for $30 for interest due to Dec. 31, 1792, on $2,000 assumed 6 percent stock.[3]]

Law Papers, September 1793

U.S. Circuit Court, Va.

Rucker's Executors v. Mercer, declaration, ADS, U.S. Circuit Court, Va., Ended Cases (Restored), 1794, Virginia State Library.

Masonic Dispensation

[*October 2, 1793, Richmond*. JM, as deputy grand master of the Grand Lodge, signs a dispensation authorizing Richmond Randolph Lodge No. 19 to initiate William C. Williams as a Mason. Richmond Randolph Lodge No. 19 Records, 1787–1801, Grand Lodge A.F. & A.M. of Virginia, Richmond. Not found.]

Receipts

DS, Vol. 1194B, C, and 1195A, RG 53, National Archives

[*October 3, 1793, Richmond*. JM signs three receipts of John Hopkins, U.S. commissioner of loans for Virginia, each for $30 interest due to Mar. 31, June 30, and Sept. 30, 1793, on $2,000 assumed 6 percent stock.[4]]

3. On Oct. 10, 1792, JM transferred all his assumed 3% stock, $2,067.01, to John O'Bannon, of Kentucky, and on Nov. 12, 1792, he transferred $923.33 in assumed 6% stock to James Markham Marshall, for a new balance of $2,000.00 assumed 6% stock and no assumed 3% stock. By Nov. 30, 1793, JM had transferred his entire account of federal stock to his brother James. See Vols. 1134, 1135, and 1147, RG 53, National Archives.

4. See receipts, Feb. 10, 1792, and Sept. 30, 1793, for an explanation of JM's holdings in federal stock.

To Henry Lee

ALS, Executive Papers, Virginia State Library

Sir[5]   Richmond, October 5, 1793
    I beleive the officer of the guard might contract with a butcher
for the rations necessary for the militia on duty. If this be approvd
of enquiry may immediately be made to ascertain the price at
which the ration is to be procurd. I am sir with very much respect, Your obedt. Servt.

                                                      J MARSHALL

To Henry Lee

ALS, Executive Papers, Virginia State Library

Sir   [Richmond, *ca*. October 8, 1793]
    I enclose a payroll of the company of Guards. The rations are
not estimated. I will with pleasure give any aid in my power to
ascertain their value. I transmit also an account of the officer of
the Guard which he prays the Honble Executive to direct the payment of.[6] I am Sir with very much respect, Your obedt. Servt

                                                      J MARSHALL

Masonic Dispensation

[*October 10, 1793, Richmond.* JM, as deputy grand master of the Grand
Lodge, signs a dispensation authorizing Richmond Randolph Lodge No.
19 to initiate William DuVal as a Mason. Richmond Randolph Lodge
No. 19 Records, 1787–1801, Grand Lodge A.F. & A.M. of Virginia,
Richmond. Not found.]

    5. Addressed to "His Excellency Governor Lee." A clerk wrote on the verso, "Colo.
Marshal's Letter, Done Oct. 8, 1793." The letter is in response to Henry Lee to
JM, Sept. 26, 1793.
    6. JM did not date this letter. On Oct. 8, 1793, however, the Council of State ac-
knowledged receipt of the account of Ensign William Nice, the officer of the guard,
and referred it to the auditor for settlement. The account was for locks on the doors of
the house where the arms were kept and for candles for the guard's use. On the same
day the Council ordered Ensign Nice's ration account paid. See JVCS, Oct. 8, 1793.

To James Breckinridge

ALS, Dartmouth College Library

My dear Sir[7]   Richmond, October 12, 1793
Your suit with McCraw[8] is at issue & I expect soon to obtain commissions for your depositions tho there is not yet an order for them. When do you intend to Richmond again? I think if you were here an arbitration woud be decided on. If anything shoud be necessary for you to do in order to obtain commission it will be to make an affidavit that the witnesses are material & reside in Kentucky. Make this affidavit & send it to me with the names of proper commissioners.

I am farming in the neighborhood & must buy plough horses. In consequence of this I woud take a stout able young plough horse for my claim on Norvel.[9] Will you take the trouble to tell him so & get him to contrive him to Richmond in the [   ] of the winter. Your

J MARSHALL

Affidavits

AD, Executive Papers, Virginia State Library

Richmond, October 13, 1793
The affidavit[1] of Edmund Potter of the sloop Phoenix taken the 13th. of October 1793.

7. The letter is addressed to "James Breckenridge esquire, Botetourt, Hond by Mr. Maize." Breckinridge (1763–1833), John Breckinridge's brother, had graduated from the College of William and Mary, was admitted to the bar, and practiced law for a time in Fincastle, Augusta County. He represented Botetourt County in the House of Delegates from 1789 to 1802 and at several sessions between 1806 and 1824. He was elected as a Federalist to the House of Representatives from 1809 to 1817.

8. Probably Samuel McCraw, a Richmond attorney.

9. Exactly where JM might have been farming is unknown, although it was common for areas of the city near the river to be used for this purpose. See entry for lucern in Account Book, Disbursements, Apr. 1793.

JM had represented James Norvell in an action before the High Court of Chancery and the Court of Appeals. See Norvell v. Ross in Account Book, Receipts, Dec. 20, 1789.

1. Except for the signatures, the entire document is in JM's hand. Word reached Richmond on Sept. 17, 1793, that "the plague or some other infectious disease" had

From whence have you saild last? [A.] From Wilmington.

What day did you leave Wilmington? A. The 2d of October.

What port did you sail from to Wilmington? A. From Milford on the 28th. of Septr.

What port did you sail from to Milford? A. Philadelphia.

How long was you at Milford? A. I had been about eight or ten weeks from Philadelphia to Milton but in that time had come up to Wilmington to refit.

Have you or your vessel been at or near Philadelphia for ten weeks? A. No.

Have you any goods on board from Philadelphia within ten weeks? A. No. I took my goods on board at Milford.

Have you landed any part of your cargo? A. No. Only a small trunk with cloaths brought from Milford.

Where did your passengers come on board? A. At Milford only.

Why did you go from Milford to Wilmington? A. It is the only port of entrance & clearance in the state of Delaware.

Were you acquainted with all your passengers? A. I was not.

Do you know that no one of your passengers was directly from Philadelphia? [A.] I understood that no one was, but this was from themselves. Three had livd in Philadelphia & I understood had left it for seven or eight weeks.

Was the female passenger who is Dead sick before she came on board? A. No. She only complaind at Norfolk this day week.

Are the rest of your passengers healthy? A. They are.

How long before you saild did this young woman apply for her passage? A. About ten hours.

Where did you take your hands on board? A. I have had two two or three years, and a third two or three months.

Where did you enter? A. At the hundred.

---

struck Philadelphia and some of the islands in the West Indies. The Council of State on that date subjected all vessels from the infected places to a 20-day quarantine off Craney Island, near the mouth of the Elizabeth River in Norfolk.

On Oct. 13 the governor received a message from "A Friend to Richmond" that a young woman had died of yellow fever after having arrived in Richmond a few days earlier from Philadelphia. The governor quickly learned that the woman had arrived on board the *Phoenix*, and he apparently ordered JM to visit the vessel, which was anchored in the James River off Manchester, across from Richmond. JM questioned the captain, Edmund Potter; a passenger, Duncan McInnes; and a boy, William Webb; and transmitted their affidavits to the governor. JVCS, Sept. 17, and Oct. 15, 1793; JM to Henry Lee, ca. Oct. 14, 1793. See *CVSP*, VI, 595, for the message alerting the governor.

Was any direction given you there or at Norfolk to receive a health officer? A. Not any.

The cargo consists of some boxes of Spanish hats, some dutch fans, & a pipe of port wine.

EDMUND POTTER

The affidavit of Duncan McGinnis passenger on board the said vessel.

Where did you come on board this vessel? [A.] At Milford about the 28th. of Septr.

Where did you reside before you came on board? A. I had resided in Philadelphia untill ⟨about⟩ seven weeks from wednesday last I then went into the country & came into the state of Delaware.

Did you bring with you any goods from Philadelphia? A. only some cloaths winter & summer.

When did the young woman passenger who is dead leave Philadelphia? A. About ten days after I did as I understood.

When did she first complain of being sick? [A.] This day week at Norfolk.

DUNCAN MCINNIS

The affidavit of William Webb a boy belonging to the said vessel.

When did you come on board? A. A day before we saild.

Did you belong to the vessel before? A. Yes.

How long had you been out of the vessel? A. About two weeks.

Where was the vessel when you left her? A. At Wilmington.

Where did she sail to from Wilmington? [A.] To Milford.

How long has it been since the captain the vessel or any of the hands have been in Philadelphia or higher of the Delaware than Wilmington? A. I think it has been three or four months.

WILLIAM WEBB

To Henry Lee

ALS, Executive Papers, Virginia State Library

Sir   [Richmond, *ca.* October 14, 1793]

You have receivd the examination of the Captain of the Phoenix, of a passenger, & of a boy belonging to her. Altho every person on board seems healthy she still appears to come under the description of those vessels which ought to perform quarantine & I have some reasons for thinking so in addition to those afforded by the examinations as transmitted to you. The Captain swore that his vessel had not been in the Delaware for ten weeks before she saild from Milford to Wilmington in order to clear out from Virginia. The boy swore that she was at Wilmington about a fortnight before she saild from Milford at which place he left her & came on board her again at Milford. The Capt. swore she receivd her cargo at Milford & there is reason to beleive this may be untrue as the boy came on board very soon after & found her laden at that time. The Captain too appeard very uneasy at the examination of the boy & seemd apprehensive that something might escape him which woud be unfavorable. He said after the affidavit of the boy that when he said the vessel had not been in the Delaware for ten weeks he misunderstood the question & had supposd it related to his being at or near Philadelphia. One of the crew was examind, not on oath, by a gentleman of the city (Mr. Brown) from whom it appeard that the vessel had gone to Philadelphia after the boy had left her at Wilmington. But admitting the statement of the Captain to be perfectly true it does not appear at what time the young woman who is dead was last in Philadelphia & therefore she may have had the infection & have communicated it to others on board who have not yet broke out with it. I am informd too by a Mr. Denny to whom I beleive the vessel was consignd that he receivd a letter by her from one of the owners dated Philadelphia the 26th of September, but one of the owners resided in Philadelphia & the other in Wilmington. I am Sir very respectfully, Your obedt. Servt[2]

J MARSHALL

2. The letter is addressed to "His Excellency Governor Lee" and is endorsed "Colo. Marshall, Letter, filed Oct. 15, 93." On Oct. 15, the first meeting of the Council of State after JM's investigation, Gov. Lee informed them that the *Phoenix* had eluded quarantine and that he had ordered a party of the Richmond militia to guard the vessel. The Council thereupon ordered JM to supervise the transfer of the vessel to the place of quarantine. JVCS, Oct. 15, 1793.

From Henry Lee

Copy, Executive Letterbooks, Virginia State Library

Sir   Richmond, October 15, 1793
A small escort of militia is requisite to conduct to Craney Island the Sloop Phoenix now lying off Manchester and directed to perform Quarantine. A vessel for their reception is provided at Rocketts.[3] I have etc.

HENRY LEE

To Augustine Davis

Printed, *Virginia Gazette, and General Advertiser* (Richmond), October 16, 1793, 2

MR. DAVIS,[4]   [Richmond], *ca.* October 16, 1793
IF in the political, as in the natural body, much real misery may flow from imagined ill, he can be no friend to the public happiness, who plays upon the public mind, and seeks without cause, to dissatisfy the people with that government to which their dearest interests have been willingly entrusted. In a republic, which united America is, and I trust will ever be the people, who are, and ought to be, the source of all power, chuse from among themselves the men who fill all the high departments of government. In the exercise of this important right, they can have no motive to balance against the general good, and it is therefore to be presumed, that they will endeavour to select those who are distinguished for their virtues and their talents. No human institution can be free from error, nor can human decisions be uniformly right; but a government thus constituted, affords the fairest prospect for general felicity, and the probability must ever be more in favor of, than against the patriotism of its measures. It is as possible that those who are

3. See Affidavits, Oct. 13, 1793, for background to this letter. The governor wrote to the superintendent of quarantine in Norfolk to alert him of the arrival of the vessel. Oct. 16, 1793, Executive Letterbooks, Virginia State Library.
An account of the expenses for the expedition was submitted by Samuel P. Duvall on Oct. 28. On Nov. 25, 1793, the Council revoked its general quarantine order after learning that the fever had subsided in Philadelphia and the West Indies. JVCS, Oct. 28, and Nov. 15, 1793.
4. In this essay JM responded to James Monroe's, published as Agricola in the same newspaper one week earlier, on Oct. 9. For an explanation of these essays, see notes to JM's first essay addressed to Augustine Davis, Sept. 8, 1793.

disgusted at not guiding the councils of their country, may be mistaken in the opinions they give as that those to whom this high trust has been confided, shall sacrifice the public interest to private or unworthy objects. It is not then to be admitted, that a public measure is wrong because it is censured, or that a government has adopted a vicious system, because a few angry men shall please to say so. Neither is a blind approbation of every governmental act to be countenanced. The public happiness may be alike affected by approving what is wrong, or condemning what is right. It becomes, therefore, the duty of a wise and virtuous people, mindful of their own welfare, to be attentive to the measures of their government, and to view them with a scrutinizing, but not a hostile, eye. If the conduct of the government be arraigned, (and arraigned it will be, so long as various minds shall be variously constructed) let us not condemn because an accusation is made, but let us look temperately into the charge, and exercise our best judgment upon it.

The attachment of America to France is warm and universal. We are bound to that nation by the strong ties of interest and affection. The flame glows in almost every bosom, and he would be considered as an apostate from American principles and opinions, who did not feel its influence. In this state of the public mind few things would more disgust the people with their government than a belief that it opposed the general wish, and was unfriendly to our favoured ally. Of consequence, if there should be a man among us inimical to our own government, he would, probably, as the most certain mode of subverting it, endeavour to impress an opinion that it was hostile to France. Accordingly some of the northern papers have teem'd with publications of this description, and at length Agricola has exhibited against the government a digested charge of systematic enmity to that much esteemed republic. If the charge be well founded, I shall deplore the fact; while my ardent wishes and best efforts will be united with those who may labour to correct it; if on the contrary it be a mere calumny, our confidence in the government should not be diminished thereby, and it should be a caution to us against giving swift and unlimited credence to other unexamined accusations.

The following facts are relied on as evidence to support the charge. 1st. Our commercial regulations. 2dly. The appointment of Mr. Morris as a minister to the Court of France.[5] 3dly. The

5. Gouverneur Morris had been named minister to France in 1792 prior to the

proclamation of the President of the United States. And 4thly. A publication in some of our papers signed Pacificus.[6] That these facts form a series of unprovoked offences, bordering on hostility itself, is very seriously asserted; and they are considered as outrages on the French nation, which, too obviously for controversy, give cause for throwing apart the two republics, and may even arrange them in hostile opposition to each other. It cannot be time misapplied, to enquire into the fairness of these deductions.

When we are told that our commercial arrangements are not merely irritating to France, but bordering on hostility itself, the mind is led immediately to search for discriminations unfavorable to that nation, and we are ready to infer that the treaties we have formed with her, have been violated on the part of America. But this so far from being proved is not even alledged. It is only contended that we have not sufficiently exceeded the stipulations between us in our concessions to France, or sufficiently shackled our commerce with Britain. As Agricola deals in the generals, and does not state precisely what he would ask us to give the one, or to impose on the other, it is not easy to know the point to which he would lead us, or which would rescue the legislature from his censure, we cannot therefore consider his position with so much accuracy as if he had defined his objection and his wish. Thus much, however, may I think safely be hazarded. Having a commercial treaty with France, the stipulations of that treaty ascertain and adjust the mutual commercial claims of the nations on each other. If this treaty be faithfully observed, and if each be as highly favoured in the ports of the other, as any nation whatever, neither can justly consider the other as taking even an irritating part against her. But the commercial regulations of America have been rather favorable to France. The duties on her wines and perhaps on her brandies, have not been so high ad valorem as the duties on the wines and spirits of other nations. It is true that no discrimination is made in the duties on her tonnage. Whether such a discrimination ought to have been made or not, is a question of policy to which I do not profess to be adequate. I confess the inclination of my own mind to be in its favor, but I am not sure that this is not produced rather by affection than judgment; for it must be admitted that too violent an effort to turn commerce out of the

---

execution of Louis XVI. He was recalled at the request of the French government in 1794.

6. Alexander Hamilton.

channel it has chosen for itself, may, at least for a time, very materially affect the cultivator of the soil. Nor is it certain that this measure would have protected the government from censure; for it has not unfrequently been urged by those who unite in condemning all its measures, and who for that reason term themselves the friends of liberty and of France, that the discrimination even in favor of American bottoms is a partial sacrifice of the interests of the many to the few, and ought to be reprobated by the people of the United States. To the legislature then on account of commercial regulation, no enmity to France is justly attributable; still less is the executive to be criminated for not having patronized measures more favorable to the trade of that nation. What patronage the executive can or ought to bestow on a subject brought before the Legislature, would be a question not unworthy of examination, if it was here necessary to enquire into it.

The second fact relied upon is the appointment of Mr. Morris, as minister from the United States to the court of France.

To encrease the odium of his appointment, this gentleman is very liberally abused; and we are told not only that he is wedded to monarchy, and opposed to the great principles of the French revolution, but that his morals and manners are hateful, and his understanding and information contemptible. The intimacy of Agricola with Mr. Morris may justify this abuse. Unacquainted with him myself, I can neither admit or deny it. It is not, however, readily to be believed, that any American is a friend of monarchy, nor ought we hastily, and without correct information, to decide, that the President of the United States has, without a motive, appointed to so important a trust, a gentleman liable to all the objections made to our minister at the court of France.

It is more probable that the picture has been coloured by the resentment of the artist, than that it is a just representation of the person for whom it is designed. But be this as it may, France must indeed seek for cause of quarrel with us, if this be laid hold of as matter of offence. It is well known that when Mr. Morris was appointed to that court, their government was a limited monarchy. It is not pretended that he would not have been well received by the then existing administration. It is even said, but of this I know nothing, that he would have been peculiarly pleasing to them.

We are not informed, nor have we reason to believe, that the present government has expressed to ours any disapprobation of this minister. Is it fair then to charge the President of the United

States for not having foreseen the changes which have happened in France? Or is it fair to charge our ally with such a promptness to quarrel with us, as, without a single representation on the subject, to think herself intentionally offended by the presence of a minister, of whom she has never complained, and who was deputed when the government bore a different form? Should a minister from France to America entertain political opinions in any degree variant from our own, we should not therefore consider his nation as hostile to ours. Should he even misconduct himself egregiously among us, we could not readily be prevailed on to criminate his nation for his errors, but should view with indignation any attempt to blend them together. We ought to count upon that rational friendship from France, which is exhibited by America; nor ought we to suspect them of the crime of renouncing their esteem for us, on account of a trivial accident not worth the serious attention of a moment.

When Agricola asserts, that "there was not a republican in the nation who did not feel himself wounded by the mission" I have only to say, that being unable to discern to which nation he alludes, or to ascertain the extent and correctness of his information, I forbear to make that comment which the assertion would too obviously justify. It is sufficient for the present purpose to say, that it is not easy for any man unconnected with party, and unstained by faction, to ascribe the appointment of Mr. Morris, whether proper or improper to an enmity to France, or to believe that France herself will entertain such an opinion. But these charges are too paltry to have been relied on even by the person who gave them an existence. Unwilling to confine his objections to the proclamation of the President, it is believed that he has introduced these as aids to his grand article, without thinking them possessed of intrinsic weight. I will proceed then to an examination of the proclamation which would seem to be considered by Agricola as consummating the vicious system he condemns. It is proper to recollect that the constitution of the United States prescribes to the President as a duty 'to provide that the laws be faithfully executed.' That our treaties are by the same constitution, declared to be the laws of the land. It is then the constitutional duty of the President of the United States (and I trust no motives will ever tempt him to swerve from it) to provide that our treaties be conformed to. It is admitted that these treaties place us in a state of perfect neutrality. Had the wishes of the people of America as well as Agricola been opposed to this situation still, until Congress should act upon the subject, we were bound to conform to it, and the President was bound by his duty to take care that it should be observed. It will not readily be believed by the people of America, who are remarkable for their intelligence and love of truth, that it shall be the duty of the President to provide that the treaties be conformed to, and yet that he is culpable for taking a single measure conducive to that end. If any measure might be taken, I am persuaded that we need only read the proclamation, instead of taking the representation others may make of it, to believe that one more proper and more unexceptionable could not easily have been adopted. But passing by the harshness of language applied to it, as masking rather the malignity than the attention, with which it has been considered, we will advert to the objections which are made by Agricola. These are, 1st. that it was unnecessary—2dly. that the time was unseasonable—3dly that the style is improper—and 4thly. that the matter is offensive.

It will not be denied that a neutral nation is accountable for the hostile acts of the individuals who compose it, unless those acts be disavowed, and proper means used to prevent the offence, and to punish the offenders. These means cannot be considered as unnecessary. It is not to be presumed that the people at large were acquainted with the extent of the obligation of the various treaties formed by the United States. It was then the duty of the executive to notify to them, that any hostile act committed by them or any of the belligerent powers, would be a breach of some one of the engagements of the United States. Many of our citizens were actually infringing the laws of neutrality, and it is to be supposed that they were not knowingly acting wrong. But admitting every citizen of the United States to have understood perfectly the duty of America towards all the belligerent powers, still many might suppose that the government would be slow in discovering, or punishing breaches of this duty, that it would act a double part, and wear the face of neutrality, while it countenanced acts of hostility. This opinion would have seduced many of our citizens into measures which might have subjected them to punishment, or involve their country in difficulties from which it could not easily have been extricated. It could not even under this view of the case have been unnecessary for the government to notify the conduct it meant to observe.

The second objection is, that the time was unseasonable. France had been engaged in war with the Emperor of Germany and the Kings of Prussia and Sardinia. Neither of those nations have much intercourse with America. Their territories are not in our neighbourhood, their vessels are not in our seas. There was no danger of violating the laws of neutrality with respect to them. A proclamation at that time would have been certainly unnecessary, and perhaps ridiculous. At length Britain and Holland are engaged in the war, and Spain is known to have actually acceded, or to be about to accede, to the dark confederacy. With these nations we have continual intercourse, their territories are in our neighbourhood, our ports are filled with their vessels, and our country with their merchants. Of consequence a breach of the laws of neutrality was easy to be committed, and was much to be apprehended. The time then for issuing the proclamation must be admitted to have been properly chosen.

I come next to the style of the proclamation.—Here too the charge is so vague, as not to ascertain the objectionable expressions. We are told that it declares to our ally, that we were neither bound to her by treaty or affection, otherwise than we were to the invading powers; but whether the whole proclamation, or if not, what particular part of it, conveys this idea, we are left to conjecture. I can find it in no part of that instrument. It is stated to be our duty to pursue a conduct alike friendly and impartial towards the belligerent powers, and this is a position neither to be controverted, or misunderstood, but it by no means will admit the construction of Agricola. It is the duty of a neutral nation so to act, as to observe a conduct friendly and impartial towards the powers at war, and a deviation from such conduct is well known to be a breach of neutrality; but it is as well known, that if a neutral nation be bound by treaties to one of the belligerent powers, to allow her privileges and advantages not to be allowed to any other power, the observance of such treaties, is her duty, and is by no means considered as a departure from neutrality, or from a conduct alike, friendly and impartial to all. Of this Agricola, cannot be ignorant, nor can it have escaped his notice, that the executive of the United States has discriminated between France and her enemies, in a manner very important to our ally. It would seem then that Agricola must have known the style of the proclamation to be exempt from the objection he makes to it. With respect to the matter of the proclamation, I do not understand Agricola as censuring that, unless it be construed, not as declaring the actual neutrality of the

United States, but as declaring that the United States shall be neutral; and as this is a construction which no man who reads it can make, it would be waste of words and time to say any thing concerning it.

The proclamation of the President of the United States then, declaring our neutrality, discloses no enmity to France, and must be admitted to have been a wise and a proper measure.

I shall pass lightly over the last subject of accusation against the government. His mind must be soured indeed who can give it consequence. It is the paper signed Pacificus. I am told it is a defence of the proclamation. Having never read it, I can neither approve, or disapprove of its reasoning. But for the present I will admit it to be proved, that Pacificus has resorted to unsound argument, in support of a measure demonstrably proper. Can this discontent France? Has our country already fallen to this? Are we so sunk, so degraded even in our own eyes, that we have become accountable as a nation for the false reasoning of any individual, who may chuse to publish his opinions? The papers of America teem with publications testifying our ardent attachment to France; while the press remains free (and Heaven forbid its freedom should be violated) every individual may reason on every subject, according to his own judgment. To suppose France can pass over the numberless proofs we have given of an affection unexampled between nations, and haughtily demand reparation for an injury supposed to be committed by the false reasoning of an unknown individual, is not less a libel upon that beloved nation, than it is unjust towards the government of the United states, to suppose that a proper measure has been adopted from improper motives.

This heavy charge then of systematic enmity to France stands totally unsupported, and must be considered as the mere creature of the imagination of Agricola. Remember my countrymen, that the government of the United States is created by yourselves, that those who fill its great departments are chosen by yourselves, that they are your friends, and not your enemies, that their measures must be intended to benefit, and not to injure you. With these impressions, watch every step it takes, Disapprove, I pray you, where upon a full and fair enquiry, reason would condemn, but do not censure where reason would approve.

GRACHUS.

Masonic Dispensations

DS, Grand Lodge A.F. & A.M. of Virginia, Richmond

[*October 31, 1793, Richmond*. JM, as grand master of the Grand Lodge, signs a dispensation for John Jones, Casper Wibber, and John Gardner to form Campbell Lodge No. 40 in Campbell County. The dispensation orders them to apply for a regular charter before the next meeting of the Grand Lodge, when the dispensation becomes void.[7]]

[*October 31, 1793 (Richmond)*. JM issues a dispensation directing that Nimrod Long be installed as master of Stevensburg Lodge No. 40 in Culpeper County.[8] Not found. Minute Book, 1777–1796, Grand Lodge A.F. & A.M. of Virginia, Richmond.]

Law Papers, October 1793

U.S. Circuit Court, Va.

Lidderdale's Executor v. Dejarnette, answer, AD, U.S. Circuit Court, Va., Ended Cases (Restored), 1794, Virginia State Library.

Petition

DS, Legislative Petitions: Richmond City, Virginia State Library

[Richmond], November 4, 1793

To the Honble., the Speakers & Members of the General Assembly, The Petition of yr. Memorialists humbly sheweth:

7. A regular charter was not issued at the next meeting, and on Jan. 3, 1795, another dispensation was issued to form Campbell Lodge No. 45. Before the official charter was issued by the Grand Lodge on Nov. 24, 1795, new officers were appointed and the name was changed to Aberdeen Lodge No. 45. An earlier dispensation to form a lodge in Campbell County is calendared at Jan. 17, 1793. Dove, *Proceedings*, 133, 141.

8. See the dispensation temporarily authorizing the formation of Stevensburg Lodge No. 40 calendared at Apr. 6, 1793.

That they together with a number of Citizens and inhabitants of the Town and City of Richmond, have erected at their private expence a large, elegant and commodius Market House in that part of the Town of Richmond calld Shockoe; the City Market being too remote and inconvenient for their resort. That the Citizens of Richmond have united in a Petition to yr. Honble. House for the passage of an Act Incorporating that part of the Town, in which yr. Petitioners & others have erected the said Market House, whereby they may be deprived of their said market, unless the same be establishd and recognized by the Legislature. Yr. Petitioners concur in the said Petition for Incorporating the said Town, provided a reservation and establishment of right as aforesd. be made, and the said market be placed under the Jurisdiction of the Body Corporate, to be Subject to such regulations as the other Market within the City, may from time to time, so as to give no preferrance, the one over the other, but what may arise from locality. Your Petitioners therefore pray that yr. Honble. House in acting upon the said Petition, for extending the Jurisdiction of the Common-hall & Court of Hustings, will by a clause in any Act to be passd on the Subject establish the said market under the controal of the Co. Hall, as aforesd. and yr. Petitioners shall ever pray and so forth.[9]

BUSHD WASHINGTON
JAS. INNIS
JOHN HICKS
JOHN MAYO
JOHN GREENHOW[1]
SAML. MCCRAW

Trustees appointed by the Subscribers.

JOHN MARSHALL[2]

9. In June 1793 a group of Richmond residents proposed building an additional city market on Shockoe Hill, asserting that the present market was inconvenient for residents living on the hill. A July 1782 ordinance had designated the existing public market, located on the east bank of Shockoe Creek where the Main Street bridge crossed, the only place where goods could be marketed in the city. The city rejected the proposal for a market on Shockoe Hill, but this document indicates that the group built one anyway, locating it just outside the city limits (which ran north and south one block west of JM's house and west along Broad Street). When proposals for annexing most of Shockoe Hill to Richmond were introduced in the legislature in the fall, the owners of the new market were placed in jeopardy of losing their business. They therefore submitted this petition to the General Assembly, which approved it and incorporated it into the act enlarging the city. Richmond City Common Hall Records, II, 18, Virginia State Library; 1 Shepherd 272 (1793); *JVHD*, Oct. 1793, 44, 54, 68, 69, 70–71, 73, 75, 96. The ordinance establishing the public market is in Common Hall Records, I, 136, Va. State Lib. For the boundaries of Richmond through-

Masonic Charter

Transcript, Marshall Lodge No. 39 A.F. & A.M., Lynchburg, Va.

[*November 8, 1793, Richmond.* JM, as grand master of the Grand Lodge, issues a charter to Lodge No. 39, to be known as Marshall Lodge, in Lynchburg.[3]]

To Augustine Davis

Printed, *Virginia Gazette, and General Advertiser* (Richmond), November 13, 1793, 1

MR. DAVIS,[4]   [Richmond, *ca.* November 13, 1793]

IN your paper, of the 16th of October, it was demonstrated,[5] so far as a political proposition will admit of demonstration, that the charge of enmity to France, exhibited against the government of the United States by its enemies, is the mere creature of a distempered imagination, and has not even the shew of probability to support it. But affection for France is not the only strong sentiment of America. It is not forgotten, that our long and hazardous contest for independence, was with Britain. It is believed that this is remembered on the part of Britain also, and that those haughty islanders might not be displeased at a fair occasion of reasserting their claim upon us. Their conduct is considered as manifesting a disposition unfriendly towards America; and this, connected with

---

out its history, see Mary Wingfield Scott, *Houses of Old Richmond* (Richmond, 1941), 28–29.

The city extended equal privileges to the new market on Shockoe Hill in Feb. 1794, but by that time the Common Hall had decided to erect a new market at the site of the old one on Shockoe Creek. The old wooden structure was destroyed in Apr. 1794, and a new brick building was under construction in June. Common Hall Records, II, 39, 42, 45–46, 48, 49, 54, 56, 72, Va. State Lib. The editors have been unable to locate exactly where and for how long the new market stood on Shockoe Hill, but for a plat of the land, see *ibid.*, 51–52. See also JM's "Subscription to market," Account Book, Disbursements, Mar. 1794.

1. Greenhow (1769–1795) was a Richmond merchant.

2. JM was one of 76 who signed the petition.

3. The dispensation signed by JM as deputy grand master, temporarily authorizing the formation of Marshall Lodge No. 39, is calendared at Mar. 30, 1793. The Grand Lodge officially approved the grant of a charter to Marshall Lodge at its meeting of Oct. 29, 1793. Dove, *Proceedings*, 115.

4. For an explanation of this exchange of essays with James Monroe, see notes to JM's first essay addressed to Augustine Davis, Sept. 8, 1793.

5. By JM in his first Gracchus essay.

the recollection of their former dominion over us, creates in the American bosom a disposition not more friendly towards them. To seize on this temper of the mind likewise, and turn it to use, the system of attack is now changed, and the government of the United States is charged with having exhibited, in its conduct towards Britain, the most mean and despicable pusillanimity. That we have cause of complaint against that imperious nation, is, I believe, known and felt by all, and therefore it is attempted, by a transition supposed to be practicable, to turn the resentment excited by the conduct of Britain upon our own government. As this can have no tendency to make us more respected, or to redress the injuries complained of, unless indeed the accusation be warranted by the fact, the object of this paper will be to enquire dispassionately into the truth of the charge.

It is stated by Agricola, that the present government found on its creation some interfering claims under the treaty, to be adjusted with Britain, which had already created much uneasiness, and been the subject of serious, though fruitless, discussion. "In fact, continues he, some stipulations had not been executed on either side." But the treaty was executed on the part of America, by the adoption of the constitution, since which our courts have been open for the recovery of British debts, for which verdicts and judgments have been rendered.

As Agricola rests his censure on the government, upon the perfect execution of the treaty on our part, it cannot be improper to examine the truth of his assertion.

In the year 1789, the foederal courts were constituted, and many suits for British debts were immediately instituted. Whether they were recoverable or not, is known to have been a question of serious doubt, and pleas in bar of the action were generally filed. Until the last term, no opinion of the court was given, and it is a known fact that to this moment not a single judgment has been rendered, where a plea has been filed.[6] It would seem then, that Agricola, in his statement of facts, has only consulted his passions, and that he has permitted his inferences to be drawn by rage rather than by reason; for it is not readily to be admitted, that the adoption of the constitution executed the treaty, while judgments were denied, nor could it truly have been stated by our executive, that

6. JM was of course attorney for defendants in many of these cases. Many legal papers he filed with the courts are listed in this volume. A volume devoted to JM's law practice will cover this topic in detail.

there was no bar to the recovery of British debts, while that very question was undecided, and seriously agitating in our courts. The pretexts then for not fulfilling the treaty on the part of Britain, which existed before the formation of the present government, are not entirely removed, and those interfering claims, which had occasioned much uneasiness, and which had been the subject of serious, tho' fruitless, discussion, still remain. At every session of the court, a decision of this question was expected, and then the remonstrances of America could no longer have been evaded, by retorting on us the charge of having broken the treaty. We cannot say that the government of the United States has not received assurances, that the western posts will be delivered to us, so soon as British debts shall be adjudged recoverable. On the contrary, we have reason to suppose, that some such assurances have been received—It is true, they have not been communicated to the public at large, but this is no proof of their non-existance. It is to be remembered, that Agricola himself contends, that the transactions of the executive must be in some measure secret, and that a difference with a foreign minister, or nation, while there was a prospect of compromise, ought to be peculiarly so. Agricola himself then has stated a position, which should have restrained his hasty censure on the measures of our government; but I have said that there is reason to suppose, the executive has received some assurances that the posts will be delivered up, when every impediment to the recovery of British debts shall be removed. I will state those reasons.

It is admitted that Britain has never claimed a right to the western posts, but has ever avowed that she held them only as pledges, to secure a compliance with the treaty on the part of America. This itself is a declaration that they are then to be surrendered. Again, the constitution declares it to be the duty of the President of the United States, to give Congress information of the state of the union. The state of our negociations with Britain would form an important part of these communications—Those made on this subject would for obvious reasons be secret: We know that secret communications have repeatedly been made, and we have therefore reason to suppose that Congress must be possessed of the state of the negociation. It will not be denied that many members of Congress are men of talents, and independent principles, that there are among them men, who are not distinguished for their attachment to the executive, or its measures, and who profess towards Britain as much antipathy as Agricola would require; yet no one of them has ever, on the floor of Congress, expressed a sentiment disapproving the conduct of the executive on this subject. If proper communications had not been made to Congress, we must suppose that they would have been moved for. A majority might have over-ruled the motion, but still the motion would have been made. Altho' then, I am by no means satisfied with the conduct of Britain, but feel resentment at the ill disposition manifested by that nation towards us, I can discover no cause for transferring that resentment to our own government.

But let us pursue Agricola somewhat further. He says, that "a dignified and magnanimous policy only could suggest a preference of two alternatives. First, either to take the posts by force, and risk the consequences; or, Secondly, to prevent the execution of the treaty on our part."

It is to be observed that these measures are recommended by Agricola, under an idea that judgment had been rendered on the claims contained in the antient and musty ledgers, which he informs us have been taken from the vaults in which they were deposited, and exhibited in our courts. As he has totally mistated the fact, on which his opinion is founded, the opinion itself may perhaps be changed. It is also to be observed, that the powers of the executive do not extend to either alternative. If either measure ought to have been adopted, it is the legislature only, and not the executive, which could have adopted it. If the charge of pusillanimity be supported, because the posts have not been taken by force, or reprisals made on the British debts, it lies not against the executive, but against every member of the senate, or house of representatives; because each member had a right to make the motion, and it was his duty to have done so, had he possessed sentiments like those avowed by Agricola: But Congress cannot justly be thought liable to this heavy charge. While there remained a probability that the posts would be given up, on an event not very distant, few men would have been willing to have taken them by force, and thereby have risked a war; and while it remained undecided whether British debts were recoverable or not, Congress could not be called on to pass a law forbidding their recovery. When that great question shall have been determined, if it be in favor of the creditors, a demand of the western posts may confidently be made; and if a surrender of them be refused, Congress may still either take them by force, or make reprisals on the British debts; if it be determined in favor of the debtors, it will afford proper subject of negociation, and the ground on which both nations stand will be clearly ascertained. It would seem proper, that the measures to be adopted by Congress should be postponed, until that question shall be decided, and then I trust that a dignified and magnanimous policy, a policy most conducive to the interests and honor of the United States, will be observed.

What Agricola means, when he asks whether even a line has been drawn between the two nations by a distant and dignified reserve on our part, I confess myself unable to discern. If he would consent to become intelligible, by stating in what that decent and dignified reserve has been departed from, or what procedure would in his estimation preserve it, some judgment might be formed on the subject and some answer given to the question. Till then, it can only be considered as a swelling sentence, which sounds well to the ear, but furnishes nothing for the mind.

Our attention is next called to the hostilities on our frontiers, and to the depredations committed on our commerce: These are subjects of serious importance, which demand our attention, and ought to be accurately investigated. It is said to be believed (and that there are circumstances which authorise the belief) that the Indian war has been fomented and supported by Britain; these are facts which ought not to be assumed without proof, altho' a suspicion of them may rouse indignant feelings in our bosoms, it would not justify hostilities. The government of the United States would be justly, as well as generally execrated, if, upon suspicion that Britain countenanced Indian hostilities, we should engage in war with her; we have no reason to suppose that proper enquiries, and proper representations on those enquiries, have not been made, and if cause of suspicion still remains, it is only an additional motive for a vigorous effort to close the Indian war; one victory would give us peace, or shew that the war was a British war. That the government is exerting itself for this object, is not to be questioned. If then the conduct of Britain, in fomenting the Indian war, has been unfriendly, the government is not chargeable with it; but is taking those measures, which on such an occasion sound wisdom would suggest.

But it seems, that in an attempt to treat with the Indians, our commissioners without an escort, or the usual gifts, took the route of Niagara and the Lakes, to meet deputies from the Indian tribes, under the British patronage, and in a British fort.[7] By doing so, we have voluntarily presented to the world an example of folly and self-degradation, without a parallel in the annals of nations. And this is urged as a mark of our complaisance and condescension to Britain.

This statement deserves to be considered.—That our endeavors to make peace with the Indians have proved abortive, is admitted; that the issue of the business might have been foreseen, and probably was foreseen, by the government, is not denied; nor can we feel a difficulty in assigning a proper motive for the embassy. The government of the United States is in its constitution popular. The opinion of the people at large must be respected, and its measures must be influenced by that opinion. A very numerous party in the United States considered the Indian war, as produced and continued by ourselves. With great zeal it was contended, that if peace was seriously sought for, peace was attainable. The government was calumniated for not endeavoring to treat with the Indians, and measures deemed proper for the prosecution of the war were clogged, and opposed upon the same principles. Against its own judgment, then, the government was compelled into the treaty, not by a disposition to crouch before Britain, but by a just respect for even the mistaken opinions of the people of America.

An effort to treat being resolved on, the place of negociation was to be fixed. This is said to have been in a British fort. Tho' I believe the contrary; yet as my recollection is not positive, I will suppose it to have been so. The treaty must have been held in our own territory, or in the Indian territory, or at some post occupied by the British. It is known that the Indians refused to meet within our own settlement. To have insisted on that which they would not assent to, was to have refused to treat with them on a mere punctillio. To dispatch our commissioners into their country, was neither more safe, nor more honorable, than to meet them on neutral ground. It is not true, that this was an unexampled instance of folly and self-degradation. To meet commissioners from an enemy in a neutral town, is not unusual, nor has it ever been considered as a mark of folly, or an instance of self-degradation. But they took the route of Niagara and the Lakes, without an es-

7. For a discussion of attempts to negotiate with the Indians and the resulting political debate, see Richard H. Kohn, *Eagle and Sword: The Federalists and the Creation of the Military Establishment in America, 1783–1802* (New York, 1975), 141–157.

cort, or the usual presents. Agricola does not tell us why they might not have taken this route, nor does he mark out the road he thinks they ought to have travelled. He does not shew that an escort was necessary, or what escort he would have recommended. To be accurate and definite in a censure is sometimes inconvenient, because the case will then admit of an accurate and definite defence. In fact, the event has shewn that an escort was unnecessary. Nor is it readily to be discerned, for what purpose an escort was to have been provided. If it was to have guarded the persons of the commissioners against the Indians, it is not yet certain that the whole American army would have been adequate to the object. That the usual presents were not in possession of the commissioners is admitted, but a regard for truth should have induced Agricola to add, that the presents could be drawn for by them, if the occasion required it. It is by no means certain, that the expence of purchasing, and conveying them to the place where the treaty was held, ought to have been incurred, before there was a probability that they might be required; and even admitting this, it would be difficult to prove from the concession, that it evinced a pusillanimous disposition with respect to Britain.

We are next to consider the depredations committed on our commerce. That they have been unwarrantable, and that they are in a high degree irritating, I am ready to declare. The question is not whether the British privateers have licentiously and illegally plundered our merchants, but whether our government has pursued wise and proper measures, to obtain redress for such injuries, and a suppression of the practice.

It will not be contended, that for the unlicensed conduct of some infamous individuals, America ought, without an explanation on the subject, or a demand of reparation, to declare war against Britain—Such is not the dictate of reason, or the usage of nations. The people of America would not thus have been dragged into a war, nor would they have supported one, so unnecessarily commenced. Those measures which were proper, and usual, have been adopted. It cannot be unknown to Agricola, that efforts have been made by the executive, in the most judicious and effectual manner, to collect proofs of the aggressions made by British privateers on our commerce; and that the avowed purpose of collecting them has been, to ground on a fair statement of authenticated facts, a demand of justice from the court of Britain. What effects that demand may produce, we do not yet know, but surely the government is not to be censured, because it has not anticipated a denial of justice, and acted on that anticipation.

The charge then of humiliating and pusillanimous conduct towards Britain, is as illy supported, as that of enmity to France. Its investigation will furnish the canded mind with additional inducements, to hear with caution the accusations of warm and angry men, who have not yet acquired sufficient respect for the opinions of their fellowmen, to suppose it possible, that a measure may be wise, and may proceed from upright motives, tho' disapproved of by them.

Altho' every just and honorable means of avoiding war should be used, it is more than possible that we may yet be engaged in one with Britain. Should the event take place, it is not by disgusting the people with their government, it is not by empty declamations to excite suspicions against that government, nor is it by a change in the executive that we are to be carried happily through it. The previous measures ought to be such as firmly to unite the people, by convincing them that the war was not sought for by us, but was inevitable, and when engaged in it, those who conduct it must have our confidence, or the wisest plans will prove unsuccessful.

GRACCHUS.

To Augustine Davis

Printed, *Virginia Gazette, and General Advertiser* (Richmond), November 20, 1793, 2

MR. DAVIS,[8]   [Richmond, *ca.* November 20, 1793]

FEELING as I do feel the most perfect conviction of the purity of motive which dictated the resolutions of the citizens of Richmond and its vicinity, and thinking the wisdom and propriety of those resolutions too well established to be now assailed, but for the mere purpose of imitation, I had hoped that they were not again to be arraigned at the bar of the public. But to have been forward in approving the pacific system of the government of the United States, and to have manifested a determination to support that system, tho' a bold and daring faction should enlist itself under the ban-

8. JM was responding to an essay James Monroe published as Agricola in the same newspaper on Nov. 13. For an explanation of this exchange of essays, see notes to JM's first essay addressed to Augustine Davis, Sept. 8, 1793.

ners of a foreign minister to force us out of it, was an offence too great to be forgiven. That respite which was considered as an abandonment of an unprovoked and unjustifiable attack upon the honest opinions of the people, was, it seems only a pause, for the collection of that virulent matter which has now burst forth with a violence proportioned to the time of its confinement. While Agricola was labouring by every species of misrepresentation, and by sophistry not to be dignified with the title of argument, to excite in the public mind a baneful irritation against the government of his country, I had not supposed that he was thus warring with his most sacred duties, solely to possess himself of advantageous ground from which he might renew his assault on a respectable body of his fellow-citizens, and display his malice against Aristides. In the notice I feel it now incumbent on me to take of him, I shall not pursue him through that circuitous route by which he has chosen to travel because the poison he has so industriously administered was quickly succeeded by its antidote, & he has been quickly followed by a writer who has sufficiently exposed the fallacy and weakness of those statements on which he professes to rely. It has been shewn that the charges exhibited against the government of the United States were as unfounded, as the wanton attack on the people of Richmond and its vicinity, was unprovoked and indecent. In his progress he has been as liberal of abuse as he has been parsimonious of reason and from the President of the United States to the supposed proposer of the resolutions in Richmond, no character has been touched but to be slandered. Where facts could not be directly alledged, the most foul and unwarrantable insinuations have been resorted to, and a degree of malice has been displayed in hinting calumnies, which could only be equalled by the infamy of fabricating them. If the opinions Agricola thought proper to combat had been really such as ought not to have been avowed, and he had thought it his duty to step forward, a volunteer for their suppression, arguments to prove their impropriety could not have been wanting, nor would those arguments have needed for their support the insinuation of an untruth concerning the source from which the resolutions were dictated or suggested. It is much to be regretted that a public question cannot be discussed without the introduction of private slander, nor is it an extenuation of the mischief that this forces a tartness of reply irksome to the injured person compelled to use it; but there will ever be a marked distinction between the instrument of faction and the person who writes for the honorable purpose of being useful to his fellow-citizens, and perhaps there is not a more certain criterion by which it is to be determined than the substitution of particular calumny for general reasoning.

Altho' so much of Agricola as seems to have been designed by himself for argument has been sufficiently refuted, it may not be improper to notice a principle which being unable to prove, he seems to have assumed. It is that those only (with the exception of a few who are deceived) wish well to the French nation who support the conduct of Mr. Genet in America, and that those who express their approbation of the government of the United States, and declare their determination to oppose the introduction of foreign influence, are bowing obsequiously to Britain and endeavoring to assimilate our government to her's. This it is true has not been in express terms asserted, but it seems to be the vital principle which animates every paper, and I know not how otherwise to account for his *crusade* against the people of Richmond in particular, and against that great body of people throughout the United States in general, whose only sin is, that they have avowed these sentiments. For the injustice of this principle I need only appeal to the judgment and feelings of my fellow-citizens throughout the community. To notice the conduct of Mr. Genet from his arrival in the United States to the present moment, would give me no pleasure, and would be unnecessary, because I believe the public mind is sufficiently impressed with its extreme impropriety. Even the *desperadoes* of his party but faintly support him, and after a very feeble defence, either declare that they do not mean to advocate his appeal to the people, or endeavour to turn our resentment on those who have first noticed his efforts to govern our politics, while they seek his apology in our love for his country and her cause. I ask each individual who is so much of an American as to resent the indignity offered to us by the minister of France, and to ward off the mischiefs which must result from it if submitted to, whether he connects in his mind the French people or the French cause with Mr. Genet? Whether his disapprobation of the conduct of that gentleman arises from, or has produced an enmity towards France? I am persuaded there is scarcely an individual who would not answer each question in the negative. If the publications on this subject be resorted to, It will, I believe, appear that those who have defended the measures of the government of the United States, and who have reprobated the intermeddling of foreigners with our political concerns, have in no instance, charged France with the conduct of her minister, or sought to weaken our attachment to that country. Our own safety made it necessary to manifest a firm determination to be guided only by ourselves, but in manifesting that determination, America has shewn and felt her affection for France to be undiminished. Notwithstanding the demonstration this procedure affords, we find it contended in the face of truth, and in opposition to the knowledge of those who read, that the public declarations on this subject proceed from a desire to separate these states from France, and unite them with Britain, in the hope of thereby wounding the cause of liberty and equality every where, and of paving the way for the establishment of the English form of government here, on the ruin of our own. If it could be justifiable to follow the example of Agricola in any thing, I would ask what can be the motive of such conduct? It cannot be to strengthen our attachment to France, because Agricola himself is not so miserable an advocate as not to discern, that, if any thing could impair the affection of America for that nation, it would be a belief that she countenanced the conduct of her minister, and sought, by leaguing herself with a faction, to distract or govern the politics of these United States. What then can be the motive? Is there a party determined to strengthen itself by foreign aid, for the establishment of its own views? Are they (still to follow Agricola) tho' not holders of, hunters after, public office? I do not myself believe there is such a party, because I do not believe that many can be found who will go through with Agricola; I am persuaded he will stand alone, the desperate advocate of such desperate measures. I believe the good sense and upright intention of my countrymen will every where prevail, and that with one voice we shall say, *we will govern ourselves, we will preserve our faith with all nations, and we will be at peace with the world.*

Enraged that these sentiments should be advocated, Agricola can spare none who have advanced them, and therefore condescends to think some parts of Aristides worthy of notice. He introduces his observations by saying "the contradictions and absurdities which appear in this essay obviously betray the embarrassment of the writer."

In the habit of saying rash things and of failing to support them, Agricola would not have been uniform, had he, with respect to Aristides, departed from this system. It would not be surprising, if, in this assertion, he should even think himself correct, for, as to a jaundiced eye every object seems tinged with yellow, it may be that to a confused mind every proposition appears embarrassed. But we will attend to his proofs. "It will be observed (says he) that instead of disproving the views of this faction he (Aristides) denies its existence." If I should admit this, it would be difficult to shew that it was either contradictory, absurd or embarrassed. To disprove the views of a party, whose existence is denied is a task I shall not undertake however Agricola may censure my declining it. But he is to support himself by quotation. In answer to his charge that a powerful faction in our government and country were seeking to embroil us with France, in order to establish a monarchy here, Aristides had said, "If there be among us men who are enemies to the French revolution, or who are friends to the monarchy, I know them not." By any but Agricola this would have been understood, rather as a declaration that Aristides knew of no such faction, than as an averment that none such existed. This was the more certain because he proceeds immediately to say, "If Mr. Jay and Mr. King be of this description, Agricola would not censure them more severely than myself." But he rushes on to comment on this quotation too precipitately to give himself time to understand it. He supposes that bitterness will be received in the place of justice, and that if an observation be sufficiently harsh it need not apply correctly. Agricola effects to understand this expression from Aristides as avering that he did not know a man in the United States, of any nation, who was either a friend to monarchy or an enemy to the French revolution, and having assumed this exposition, he triumphs in his supposed victory, as if he had proved thereby, that the Richmond resolutions were improper, or that the pacific system they approve, was a sacrifice of the honor and interests of the people of America. But as his triumph will be unenvied, neither, I believe, will it ever be imitated. It is impossible to understand this observation otherwise than as applying to Americans. In a neutral country there will ever reside persons born in and belonging to other nations who may be at war with each other. It is not to be supposed that such men do not retain some partiality for their native country and its government. When speaking of our own government and of those concerned in the administration of it, no general expression is understood as extending to them. Nor is it any proof when reasoning against the existence of a powerful and extensive faction, that a denial of it, or of a knowledge of men of such principles, is not seriously made, because there exists an individual, a foreigner, who pretends not to influence in the government or among the people, to whom Agricola or common fame may chuse to ascribe antirepublican opinions. Whether the person supposed to be alluded to, would wish to establish a monarchy, or to assimilate our government in any degree to the British, I do not to this moment, know, nor do I suppose Agricola could inform me. The observation as applied to the people of America is strictly true, nor do I know or believe that there exists in the government such a faction as Agricola has stated, or, that there are Americans within the circle of my acquaintance, who would support it if it existed. Is it possible that Aristides can be otherwise construed? Is Agricola the only reader who could mistake him? Or did he understand rightly the sentence quoted, but wished to impose a misconstruction on others? "Candor startles at the charge! Was his party zeal so violent as to hide so flagrant a truth from his eyes? This perhaps the best apology, but a bad one for a man who assumes the task he has chosen, and who imputes to others the same weakness." He forfeits however his apology by betraying his consciousness that he had in his own mind construed the assertion differently from his statement of it, when he says himself that he quotes this passage in order to prove that Aristides denied the existence of the faction he had spoken of. Nor is he more fortunate in searching for an idea contradictory to that which has been mentioned, or more correct in his statement of it. It has been said by Aristides that "Agricola, tho' he may be less a friend to America, is not more attached to the cause of France or the rights of mankind in general, than a great majority of the meeting he had ventured to defame"—having cited this, he asks what characters then composed the minority? That is if they were not as much attached to France, and the rights of mankind as Agricola, what must have been their characters? If I had said that they were not, I should have beg'd pardon of my fellow-citizens, I should probably have injured them. But I have not said so. I have vouched for a great majority, because I know them, but have not condemned those I did not know. For there were some among the American citizens with whom I am not acquainted. This perfectly consists with the former assertion, for there it is stated, that if the faction spoken of by Agricola, existed, I knew them not, and here it is avered, that I did know a great majority of the meeting defamed, and that in patriotism they yielded not to their accuser. I forbear to comment on these plain mistatements, or assign a motive for them. I will proceed to his further criticisms.

The state of the public mind when those resolutions were entered into, cannot be forgotten. No means were unessayed to induce an opinion that the constitution had been violated, and the honor and interests of the community sacrificed by the Executive of the United States. Measures which could not fail to produce a war, in which America would have been considered as, in some degree, the aggressor, were zealously supported in private and through the medium of the press. The public mind was supposed to have been prepared sufficiently for the condemnation of every act of the government, and for the support of the new system to be urged upon us. The appeal of Mr. Genet to the people was then announced. The fact was not then supported by that complete and ample testimony which he has since afforded, but there was too much cause to give it credence. Whether Mr. Genet had himself created the faction, or was imposed on by it—whether he had instigated the various libels which have appeared against the pacific system of the government, or had been really induced by them to suppose that the people at large were opposed to that system—it was alike necessary for the people to speak. If Mr. Genet had mistaken the sense of America, it was proper to undeceive him, and if he was about to form a party in opposition to the government, we could not be too early in telling him the American temper would not brook it. There was still a possibility that this gentleman might not have been criminal to the extent of the charge. The people of Richmond and its vicinity did not choose to aver that he was. It had however become necessary to assert the principle, and, if it applied to Mr. Genet, the principle was not the less true or the less proper on that account. This in the usual stile of Agricola is termed an uncandid and unbecoming evasion. But Agricola cannot do such violence to his propensities as to be just for a moment. By any but him it would be admitted, that an attempt to use the people as the instruments of their own calamity, could not be more properly repelled, than by a declaration that they would not be so used, and that this declaration could not be made with more delicacy, or less offensively, than by forbearing to mingle with it any assertion, that the attempt had actually been made, and that it had been made by the minister of France. The one perhaps can only be justified by actual conviction of guilt; the other is proper when there is just cause of fear; for I can never admit with Agricola, that it is time enough to guard against a mischief, when it has actually befallen us. What could have tempted Agricola to ask whether the resolutions are not vindicated on the ground of the certificate is only to be discovered by himself, since he could not have read Aristides and have considered him as supporting the resolutions by that testimony. In avering that this piece of evidence was relied on, it is difficult to believe that Agricola could either have imposed on himself, or could have hoped to escape detection in his attempt to impose on others. It might therefore have been treated as an idle enquiry, had he not in the succeeding paragraph assumed it as a fact.

It is painful to myself and tedious to others, in a discussion which ought only to contain matters useful and interesting to the public, to be compelled to waste so much of their time in correcting the mistatements of Agricola[—]mistatements, unimportant to the public because they do not in any degree affect the argument, but only concern the personal reputation of Aristides. Without reflecting that if the measures supported by Aristides, had even been defended with as much weakness and passion as they have been assailed, they would not be the less proper on that account; he has deserted the argument, and exerted all his talents at misrepresentation to shew contradictions and untruths in the writer he attacks, which would only affect the person, and not the subject. This compels me to ask the indulgence of noticing one other criticism of the same complexion. He charges Aristides with "advocating the resolutions on a supposition that they contain what in reality they do not contain, and for which they are censured." The quotation in support of this assertion is "he (the French minister) knows that the people of America love France, we all know it, we all feel and avow it, but it has become necessary for us to intermingle with such an avowal, declarations of our respect for ourselves and for [our] own government." Not choosing to hazard a denial of the truth of this proposition, Agricola contents himself with saying that a reader would suppose "that an avowal of our attachments to France, was the ground-work of these resolutions, and that the censure on her minister was only reluctantly intermingled with it." It is for Agricola alone not to discern that Aristides speaks of the continuing language of the people of America. It is for Agricola alone not to perceive that when the people of America are universally avowing their attachment to France, any declaration in support of our own government, must be intermingled with the avowals which are continually made of that attachment, altho' not expressed in the same resolutions.—But it is time to take leave, I trust forever, of such unessential criticisms, and to notice an argument which more deserves the public attention.

Agricola affects to consider the appeal of a foreign minister from the government to the people of America, as an event unimportant in itself, and not threatening, in its consequences, those dangers to our future welfare, which throughout the history of man, have invariably attended the introduction of foreign influence. This is not a mere invective against Aristides, but is the avowal of a political opinion seriously interesting to every citizen of the United States. It is impossible to divest this appeal of the means by which it is to be prosecuted. The mind cannot trace without shuddering at them. Upon this subject the good sense of America will not be misguided by the examples cited by Agricola, and, to our astonishment, said by him to be analogous to this. The two great revolutions of 1776 and 1788 are spoken of as cases where an appeal was made to the people, and the subjects proposed to them deliberately discussed, and I think wisely decided on. By whom were those appeals made? By whom were they prosecuted? By whom and by what were they or could they be supported? What interests or what motives did or could lead us to either important crisis and conduct us through it? The first was the united voice and united strength of America, appealing to the supreme director of all human affairs against foreign oppression. The second was the deliberate consultation of the people of America among themselves, unimpelled by foreigners, unsupported by foreign influence, foreign interests, or foreign force, on a subject uninteresting to them, but all important to us. It was the deliberate exercise of American wisdom, for the purpose of correcting those defects which experience had marked in our ancient system. In this there was and can be no danger while we exclude foreign influence. In such a case, whatever difference of opinion might prevail, there can be but one party, and that is the people of America; there can be but one object, and that is the happiness of our common country; there can be but one power exerted to produce or conduct us through the crisis, and that is the power of reason exerted in and on the American mind. How different the case this is cited to support. The person appealing to the people is a foreigner. The first proposition would be an attempt to seduce us into a violation of the constitution of our country. The interests to be discussed are foreign interests. The parties concerned are foreign nations at war with each other. The object is a foreign good. The power exerted in support of and opposition to the claims of the appellant, is a foreign power, aided by such factions as either might, by any means, be able to excite in the bosom of our country. To dilate on the obvious vice and folly of countenancing or admitting such an appeal would be an indignity to the common sense of my countrymen. What dangerous paths must he already have trodden, who cannot perceive them! But we are told that no mischief is to be feared from this measure of Mr. Genet, because his nation is republican. That is, that foreign influence may be admitted when conjoined with Agricola, and when they are to afford reciprocal aid to each other. Let it be remembered that Agricola has affirmed the existance of a powerful British faction in America. If this be true would not that faction call in the aid of British influence to oppose French influence so improperly applied? Admitting it not to be true (and I believe it is not) if the powers at war with France should perceive, that claims in which they were deeply interested, were to be decided, not by a reference to the constituted authority, but by parties among the people, they would certainly endeavor to strengthen themselves by the same means. Our country, instead of pointing its united efforts to the promotion of its own happiness, might be found divided into parties struggling under the direction, and for the views of foreigners. How incumbent then is it on those, who are unconnected with party and unstained by faction, who can have no object but the public good, no interest distinct from that of the community, to step forward and resist in its first advance, so baneful and so dangerous a measure. Foreign influence to be exerted on the people, in a republican government, can only be repelled by the conduct of the people themselves. Admit it once and it may be found too mighty for our best endeavors to exclude it.

ARISTIDES.

From Wills Cowper

ALS, U.S. Circuit Court, Va., Ended Cases (Restored), 1794, Virginia State Library

Dear Sir[9]   Portsmouth, November 21, 1793

I recd. your letter of the 15th. Inst.[1] only this evening. I sent you a few days past by Doctr. Slaughter of this place my affidavit in order to get Commissions to take the depositions of The Hon. Thos. Jefferson & John Cowper Senr. (the latter residing in No Carolina) in my suit with Hanson. Without their testimoney I should not wish by any means to go to trial, for reasons contained in my letter accompanying the affidavit.[2]

In consequences of full reliance that the Court would continue the Cause, I did not send up my Son Mr. John Cowper Jr,[3] the

9. The letter, postmarked at Portsmouth on Nov. 21 and addressed to "John Marshall Esquire, Attorney at Law, Richmond," is filed in the case papers of Hanson v. Cowper. Wills Cowper was a merchant, originally from Suffolk, who represented Nansemond County in the House of Delegates in 1782.

1. Not found.

2. Augustine Slaughter (d. ca. 1814), of Norfolk County, had served as a surgeon during the Revolution. Jefferson was secretary of state in 1793. John Cowper, Sr., was probably the individual who represented Nansemond County in the House of Delegates in 1783.

The case of Hanson v. Cowper began in the U.S. Circuit Court with the filing of a declaration in debt for £500 sterling in May 1791. While the litigation appears on the records to involve a debt to a British merchant incurred on June 22, 1775, it is also apparent that when the action was instituted, and for about a decade prior to 1791, Richard Hanson, the plaintiff, was doing business in Petersburg. Endorsements to the declaration indicate that the pleas, partially in JM's hand, were filed before Nov. 1793, when a jury was impaneled to try the issue. At the Nov. 1793 term the jury was withdrawn, and a commission was awarded to the defendant to take depositions of witnesses material to his defense. In May 1794 the case was continued upon the defendant's payment of costs.

The affidavits supporting the defendant's application for a commission asserted that Jefferson and the Cowpers were material witnesses to the facts alleged in the plea. Jefferson was involved as secretary of state, because JM's plea put in issue the validity of the 1783 peace treaty and various acts of the Virginia General Assembly sequestering British debts. Hanson v. Cowper, U.S. Circuit Court, Va., Ended Cases (Restored), 1794, and Record Book, III, 102–103, Virginia State Library. See JM's answer listed at Law Papers, Apr. 1792.

This case came on again for trial on Nov. 26, 1794, but after submission to the jury a juror was withdrawn by consent of the parties, and the defendant confessed judgment for $570. For the complete record see U.S. Circuit Court, Va., Record Book, III, 90–104, Va. State Lib.

3. This is probably the John Cowper, Jr., who served as a trustee of the Marine Hospital in Norfolk in 1790 and was appointed a trustee to sell state property in Portsmouth in 1792. In 1793 he was a ship builder in Norfolk, and in 1800 he was elected an alderman of the city of Norfolk. During the Revolution and in 1795 Cowper, his father, and his two brothers were engaged in privateering activities under the firm

greater part of his testimony being useless without the testimony of the above mentioned Gentlemen. I rely that the cause will not come on. I was this day served with a writ returnable to this Court, as a partner of Scott Irvin & Cowper at the suit of Graves agent of Stoneys Exors.[4] I shall thank you to stop any steps being had in it untill I see Mr. J. Cowper who manages the business of that Concern. I am very Respectfully Sir, Your ob. Servt

WILLS COWPER

Law Papers, November 1793

U.S. Circuit Court, Va.

Leroy v. Ross & Co., declaration, ADS, U.S. Circuit Court, Va., Ended Cases (Restored), 1794, Virginia State Library.

From Henry Lee

Copy, Adjutant General's Record Book, War 10, Virginia State Library

[*December 5, 1793, Richmond*. Gov. Lee issues general orders,[5] having received instructions from President Washington, outlining the conduct of British or French vessels or privateers that would be considered permissible in Virginia ports or within the three-and-a-half-mile limit along the coast.]

---

name of Wills Cowper & Co. The extant evidence indicates that Wills Cowper and John Cowper, Sr., of Nansemond County, were brothers; consequently John Cowper, Jr., was named after his uncle.

4. See Account Book, Receipts, Nov.–Dec. 1795, where JM received a fee in Stoney v. Cowper.

5. The neutrality proclamation was issued on May 2, 1793. The general orders are copied in the adjutant general's record book just after a copy of the orders sent by James Wood on Aug. 22, 1793. Wood's orders, issued as lieutenant governor in Henry Lee's absence, were also copied into the Executive Letterbooks, whereas Lee's were not. The date of this letter is puzzling and may be incorrect. Some of the letter is identical to one Henry Knox mailed to the governor of Pennsylvania on Aug. 7, 1793, and presumably to other governors as well. For Lee to have waited four months to transmit these instructions would have been negligent, but the date is clear in the record book. See Knox to governor of Pennsylvania, Aug. 7, 1793, Division of Archives and Manuscripts, Pennsylvania Historical and Museum Commission, Harrisburg.

To Charles Lee

ALS, Collection of the Association for the Preservation of Virginia Antiquities, on deposit at the Virginia Historical Society

Dear Sir[6]   Richmond, December 28, 1793
   I have receivd yours of the 22d. The presence of Mrs. Turnbull can not possibly be material, if however she wishes to attend the trial you may inform her that the cause will in all human probability [be] heard in March & if she will fix the day we will endeavor to bring it on at the time requested. The suit is brot. for a separate maintenance. Of consequence the subjects to which the testimony should point are the fortune of Mr. Turnbull, the injury done that of Mrs. Turnbull & the expenses she has incurd since the separation. If you can procure testimony to these points about Alexandria you may be useful while there otherwise you can only be serviceable in court. I am my dear Sir, Your

J MARSHALL

Opinion

ADS, Tucker-Coleman Papers, Swem Library, College of William and Mary[7]

[Richmond, ca. December 31, 1793]
   Colo. Thomas Mann Randolph departed this life in November or Decr. 1793 & devisd to his daughters a tract of land on which a crop of wheat was then growing.
   Que. Is that crop assetts in the hands of his exrs. or does it pass with the land to the devisees?
   A. The 47th. sec. of the act reducing into one the several acts concerning wills etc. seems to me completely to embrace the case stated.[8] I presume there can be no doubt but that the crop sown & growing on the 31st. of December passes to the devisees.

J MARSHALL

   6. The letter is addressed to Lee in Alexandria and bears a Jan. 2 Richmond cancellation stamp.
   For information on this annulment, see JM to Benjamin Rush, Aug. 6, 1792.
   7. An attached note suggests that JM's opinion was sent to St. George Tucker sometime after it was written.
   8. Sec. 47 of "An Act . . . concerning wills," adopted Dec. 13, 1792, provided that crops that belonged to one who died between Mar. 1 and Dec. 31 and that were har-

Law Papers, December 1793

U.S. Circuit Court, Va.

Burton's Executors v. Donald & Co., bill in chancery, AD, U.S. Circuit Court, Va., Ended Cases (Unrestored), Virginia State Library.[9]

To Archibald Stuart

ALS, Collection of Justice George M. Cochran, Staunton, Va.

My dear Sir[1]   [Richmond, *ca.* 1793]
I wrote to you some time past on the case of Mills & Bell. Have you receivd my letter? If you have I must beg the favor of you to sieze some liesure moment to communicate with me on the subject of it.

Our foreign affairs are becoming somewhat perplexd & I fancy the American Government will have occasion for all its wisdom to conduct it steadily through the threatend storm. I now begin to hope that we shall not encrease its embarassments by our indiscreet entemperance. Farewell with much esteem & affection, I am your

J MARSHALL

---

vested before Dec. 31 were assets in the hands of the executors or administrators; crops still growing on Dec. 31 and crops owned by one who died between Dec. 31 and Mar. 1 passed with the land to the devisees or heirs. 1 Shepherd 96. This provision was suggested as part of the revisal of the laws proposed by Thomas Jefferson, George Wythe, and Edmund Pendleton in 1779 and was first adopted in 1785. 12 Hening 151 (1785). It represents a clarification, and perhaps an alteration, of the procedure outlined in 1711 and 1748 whereby the law might be interpreted to mean that crops were assets in the hands of the executors or administrators regardless of the time of death of the owner. 4 Hening 23–24 (1711); 5 Hening 464 (1748). For a discussion of the 1779 revisal, see Julian P. Boyd *et al.*, eds., *The Papers of Thomas Jefferson*, II (Princeton, N.J., 1950), 305–324, 394–405.
9. See Jesse Burton to JM, Apr. 11, 1794, and Account Book, Receipts, Nov. 1793.
1. The letter is addressed to Stuart in "Stanton."

Certification

ADS, Collection of Justice George M. Cochran, Staunton, Va.

Richmond, January 6, 1794

I certify that I was employd by Mr. Stuart for Pickens in the appeal Pickens v Anderson & that he paid me my fee.[2] I further certify that there was obvious error in the record which renderd a reversal of the judgement of the county court inevitable. Mr. Lee[3] appeard for Anderson.

J MARSHALL

To David Jones

ALS, Collection of Henry N. Ess III, New York City

Sir[4]   Richmond, January 16, 1794

I have this moment receivd yours of the 9th. of January.[5] I shoud have written to you before this had I not supposd you to be in the western country. Your cause is decided entirely in your favor & the bill against You orderd to be dismissed.[6] Will you be so obliging as to pay the sum you directed me to draw on you for (100 dollars) to Mr. Pottinger[7] the clerk or agent of Mr. Robt. Morris. He will

2. Archibald Stuart had asked for certification that he had retained JM to handle an appeal for him to the General Court. See JM to Stuart, Jan. 22, 1794. Stuart paid JM £2 8s., which JM entered in his Account Book, Receipts, Oct. 17, 1789. After 1789 all appeals from county courts went to the new district courts. 13 Hening 11–17 (1789).

On the same paper below JM's certification, William DuVal wrote the following on Jan. 9: "I do certify that the Error in the Record was inspected by the General Court in the appeal of Pickens agt Mr. Anderson & that the Court reversed the Judgment of Rockbrige County Court, that all the Lawyers in the State could not support the Judgment of the County Court, the Error being notorious on the Face of the Record."

3. Probably Charles Lee.

4. The letter is addressed to "The revd. David Jones, Eastown, Chester County, Philadelphia, To be left in the post office," and includes the amount of postage, "20," on the address leaf. The leaf also bears a Richmond cancellation mark.

5. Not found.

6. See JM to William Branch Giles, ca. Mar. 1793. The case is Isaac Williams and Joseph Tomlinson v. John Jeremiah Jacob and David Jones, which was finished on Nov. 4, 1793. JM received his last fee, £30, in Mar. 1794. Account Book, Receipts, Mar. 1794.

7. JM's handwriting is clear, but he obviously meant Garrett Cottringer, Morris's bookkeeper and close business associate. Harold C. Syrett et al., eds., *The Papers of Alexander Hamilton*, XVIII (New York, 1973), 298.

apply to you with an order from me. I am Sir respectfully, Your obedt. Servt.

J MARSHALL

Bill of Exchange

ADS, Free Library of Philadelphia

[*January 17, 1794 (Richmond).* JM orders payment of $100 to Garrett Cottringer.[8]]

To Archibald Stuart

ALS, Collection of Justice George M. Cochran, Staunton, Va.

My dear Sir[9]   Richmond, January 22, 1794
   I was fortunate enough to recollect perfectly the fee you paid me for Pickens & have accordingly given a certificate which I hope will be satisfactory.[1] It is beyond measure grating to our feelings to be compeld even to resort to certificates to be cleard from a sneaking crime which no truely honest man woud suspect another of fair character & upright conduct to be capable of.
   I had the satisfaction to perceive the other day by a note passing under my eyes that you have some how or other God knows how establishd a credit with the bank of the United States. How have you effected this? I want to raise a great deal of money.[2] Can you put me in the way of doing the same thing? Farewell, I am your

J MARSHALL

8. This is the order referred to in JM's letter of Jan. 16, 1794. Drawn against David Jones, it was sent to Cottringer for negotiation. The bill is endorsed on the verso "Feby 11 1794 Recd Payment, Garrett Cottringer." In another hand there is a notation, "Cottinger's, Receipt, 100d Dol."
   9. The letter is addressed to Stuart in "Stanton."
   1. The certificate is printed at Jan. 6, 1794. JM was able to "perfectly recollect the fee" by looking in his Account Book under Receipts, Oct. 17, 1789.
   2. JM was in the process of purchasing the Manor of Leeds and South Branch Manor from Denny Martin Fairfax and in fact had a deed to the latter executed in England just ten days after writing this letter. See Fairfax Lands: Editorial Note, Feb. 1, 1793.

Deed

Deed Book Copy, Office of the Clerk of Hardy County, Moorefield, W.Va.

[London], February 1, 1794

THIS INDENTURE[3] made the first day of February in the year of our Lord one thousand seven hundred and ninety four BETWEEN the Reverend Denny Martin Fairfax of Leeds Castle in the County of Kent and Kingdom of great Britain Doctor in Divinity heretofore called Denny Martin Clerk Devisee in fee of (inter alia) the premises mentioned and intended to be hereby granted in and under the last Will and Testament of Thomas Lord Fairfax deceased of the one part AND John Marshall of the City of Richmond in the state of Virginia of the other part WITNESSETH that for & in consideration of the sum of six thousand pounds of lawful British Money to him the said Denny Martin Fairfax by the said John Marshall before the sealing and delivery of these presents in hand well and truly paid the receipt whereof he doth hereby acknowledge he the said Denny Martin Fairfax hath granted bargained and sold and by these presents Doth grant Bargain and Sell unto the said John Marshall and his heirs all that the Manor of South Branch in Virginia aforesaid with the appurtenances and all those two several Tracts of Land being parcel of the northern neck of Virginia situate ascertained bounded and described as appears by the two several surveys following, that is to say, in and by one survey of part thereof containing fifty four thousand five hundred and ninety six acres more or less taken and made by James Gunn on or about the thirty first day of March one thousand seven hundred and forty seven and in and by a Survey of other part thereof containing One thousand five hundred and fifty Acres more or less taken and made on or about the seventh day of April one thousand seven hundred and forty eight and which two several Tracts of Land and premises were heretofore granted by Thomas Lord Fairfax deceased to Thomas Bryan Martin and by him afterwards reconveyed to the said Thomas Lord Fairfax and his heirs and together form and constitute and are commonly called or known by the name of the South Branch Manor Situate lying and being in the Counties of Hampshire and Hardy or one of them in the said

3. This deed, dated the last day of the existing contract, kept the Fairfax-Marshall sales agreement alive. Most of South Branch Manor would be sold to help pay for the Manor of Leeds. See Fairfax Lands: Editorial Note, Feb. 1, 1793.

State of Virginia and also all manerial & other rights and all houses Buildings and other Improvements and all Trees Timber Woods and underwoods to the said Manor of South Branch belonging and all the estate right Title and Interest whatsoever of him the said Denny Martin Fairfax of into or out of the said Manor Lands and premisses and every part thereof save and except nevertheless out of this present grant unto the said Denny Martin Fairfax and his heirs all and every such Tracts and parcels of Land and other the Estates late of the said Thomas Lord Fairfax in Virginia aforesaid as are not comprized or comprehended within the aforesaid two several Surveys bounds Limits and descriptions of the said Manor of South Branch and also save and except to all & every Grantees and Lessees of all or any and every part and parts of the said premisses hereby granted and to their respective heirs or other representatives the full and whole benefit and advantage of all and every such his her and their several and respective grants and Leases whether made in the lifetime of the said Thomas Lord Fairfax or at any time since his decease prior to the seventeenth day of May now last past To HAVE AND TO HOLD the said Manor of South Branch Tracts of Land Houses buildings Improvements Trees Timber Woods and underwoods and all and singular other the premisses before herein mentioned and intended to be hereby granted and conveyed with their and every of their appurtenances (except as before excepted) unto the said John Marshall and to his heirs and assigns forever AND that free and clear of and from every encumbrance whatsoever except as aforesaid such grants and Leases of any part or parts of the said premisses which may have been actually and bona fide made prior to the said seventeenth day of May now last past AND ALSO except & subject liable and charged nevertheless to and with the payment of three several annuities of one hundred pounds a year each given by a Codicil to the said Will of the said Thomas Lord Fairfax deceased to the second third & fourth Children of Bryan Fairfax esquire for their respective lives as the same shall respectively commence and become payable by the said Will to such Children from time to time upon the several and successive deceases of Frances Martin Sybella Martin and Anna Susanna Martin the three Sisters of the said Denny Martin Fairfax and the said Denny Martin Fairfax for himself his heirs Executors and Administrators doth hereby covenant and agree with the said John Marshall his heirs Executors & Administrators in manner following that is to say that for and notwithstanding any act matter or thing by him the said Denny Martin Fairfax or by the said Thomas Lord Fairfax deceased in his lifetime done committed omitted or knowingly suffered to the Contrary he the said Denny Martin Fairfax is now seized of a good sure perfect and indefeasible Estate in feesimple of and in the premisses hereby and intended to be hereby granted and conveyed and hath full power and authority to sell and convey the same in fee simple subject and charged only as aforesaid and that he the said Denny Martin Fairfax and his heirs shall and will from time to time and at all times hereafter during the natural lives of his said three sisters the said Frances Martin Sybella Martin & Anna Susanna Martin well and truly pay or secure or cause to be paid and secured to them & each of them the said three several annuities of one hundred pounds a year to them given for their several lives under the Codicil to the said Will of the said Thomas Lord Fairfax deceased and from time to time well and effectually exonerate Discharge and indemnify the said John Marshall and his heirs and also the said hereby granted premisses of and from the same and the payment thereof respectively and all claims suits and demands for or on account of the same or the nonpayment thereof and shall & will also when thereto required by the said John Marshall his heirs or assigns or either of them make do and execute such further and other assurances for the more perfect conveyance of the premisses (subject and charged as aforesaid according to the true intent and meaning hereof as by the said John Marshall or his heirs or assigns shall be advised and required such further assurance to be at the proper expence of the party requiring the same and so nevertheless that the said Denny Martin Fairfax or his heirs required to make such further assurance be not compelled or compellable for the making thereof to go or Travel further than ten miles from his or their usual place of abode and the said Denny Martin Fairfax & his heirs shall and will warrant and forever defend the premisses hereby granted and conveyed to him the said John Marshall his heirs and assigns against all right Interest and claim of him the said Denny Martin Fairfax and his heirs and all other persons claiming under him them or either of them or from through or under the said Thomas Lord Fairfax deceased other than and except the said three Children of the said Bryan Fairfax claiming their said several annuities to commence as aforesaid AND also except such grantees Lessees or Tenants as are herein before excepted AND lastly the said John Marshall for himself, his heirs and

Assigns doth hereby Covenant and agree to and with the said Denny Martin Fairfax his heirs Executors and Administrators that he the said John Marshall his Heirs or assigns or some or one of them Shall & will from time to time and at all times from and after the first and other successive deceases of the said Frances Martin Sybella Martin and Anna Susanna Martin well and truly pay or secure or cause to be paid and secured to each and every of the said three Children of the said Bryan Fairfax the said Three several annuities of one hundred Pounds a year to them given for their several lives under the Codicil to the said Will of the said Thomas Lord Fairfax deceased to commence severally as aforesaid and from time to time and at all times well and effectually exonerate discharge & indemnify the said Denny Martin Fairfax his heirs Executors & Administrators and all and every his Estates, Lands and Tenements in Virginia charged with or liable to Answer the said Several Annuities of and from the same and the Payment thereof respectively and all claims suits and demands for or on account of the same or the nonpayment thereof. IN WITNESS whereof the said Parties to these presents have hereunto interchangeably set their hands and seals the day and year first above Written

Sealed & delivered by the above named Denny Martin Fairfax & by James Markham Marshall esq as attorney for the above named John Marshall in the presence of
THO. GREGORY
JOHN BARNES
JOHN JONES

D. MARTIN FAIRFAX [LS]

JOHN MARSHALL [LS]
by his atto. in fact
James M. Marshall.

all of Cliffords Inn, London

This deed was resealed and delivered by the above named Denny Martin Fairfax and the above named James Markham Marshall as the Attorney for the above named John Marshall the first day of February one thousand seven hundred and ninety seven in the Presence of

THOMAS GREGORY
JOHN BARNES
JOHN JONES.

RECEIVED the first day of February one thousand seven hundred and ninety seven by me the above named Denny Martin Fairfax of and from the above named John Marshall by his Attorney in fact James Markham Marshall the Sum of Six thousand

Pounds of lawful british Money being the Consideration Money above mentioned to be by him to me in hand paid.[4] I say received by me £6000
Witness hereto.

THO. GREGORY
JOHN BARNES.   }   D. MARTIN FAIRFAX
JOHN JONES

Official Bond

DS, Executive Papers, Virginia State Library

[*February 6, 1794, Richmond.* JM with Joseph Carrington, Edward Carrington, and Mayo Carrington, posts bond of £20,000 with Gov. Henry Lee upon the appointment of Joseph Carrington as agent to collect the arrears of taxes and duties in the Fourth Brigade district.[5]]

Law Papers, February 1794

U.S. Circuit Court, Va.

Maury v. Austin & Co., declaration, copy, U.S. Circuit Court, Va., Record Book, III, 259, Virginia State Library.

4. Significantly, JM did not actually pay the purchase price until after the legislative compromise of Dec. 1796.

The deed was recorded as follows: "At a Superior Court held for the District composed of the Counties of Hardy Hampshire and Pendleton at the Courthouse of the said County of Hardy the fifth day of September 1797 . . . and on the motion of the said John Marshall. . . ." JM was in France on that date, so the motion would have been made for him by someone else.

5. The document is a printed form on which Edward Carrington inserted the names of the obligees, the penal amount, the date, and the counties covered by the appointment.

Joseph Carrington (1741–1802) was a prominent resident of Cumberland County who had served on the county Committee of Safety. On Feb. 5, 1794, he was appointed agent for collecting taxes in the Fourth Brigade district. He had served as a member of the House of Delegates from 1777 to 1778 and from 1792 to 1793. Mayo Carrington (1753–1803), of "Boston Hill" in Cumberland County, was prominent in the Revolution and in the county militia after the Revolution. He represented Cumberland County in the House of Delegates from 1786 to 1788. JVCS, Feb. 5, 1794. See 1 Shepherd 229–231 (1793).

From Henry Lee

Copy, Executive Letterbooks, Virginia State Library

Sir,[6]   Richmond, March 14, 1794

The Executive have thought proper to distribute the brass field pieces belonging to the Commonwealth among the Artillery Companys of the City of Richmond the Borough of Norfolk, the towns of Alexandria, Fredericksburg and Petersburg and to place them under the controul of the Brigadier Generals of the Brigades to which the said companies are respectively annexed as to their use and safe keeping. You will be so good as to give directions on this subject as well as to designate the purposes for which only the pieces shall be used and to establish parade ground convenient to the Artillery Company and free from interruption and injury to the town and its inhabitants.[7] I am sir etc.

HENRY LEE

Advertisement

Printed, *Virginia Gazette, and General Advertiser* (Richmond), March 26, 1794, 1

Richmond, March 18, 1794

LAND *for* SALE.

BY virtue of a Deed of Trust to us made, will be sold on the premises, on the first day of April next, to the highest bidder,

A TRACT of LAND, lying in the County of Westmoreland, and containing by estimation six hundred acres, that being the tract of land which was sold and conveyed to ALEXANDER CAMPBELL by WILL. STARKS JETT.[8] The land will be sold on *a credit of twelve months*, and bond with *satisfactory* security will be required.

J. MARSHALL.
GEORGE PICKETT. } Trustees.
ANDREW DUNSCOMB.

6. The letter is addressed "To the Brigadiers General Mason, Williams, Mathews, Marshall and Jones, each." Stephens Thomson Mason was commander of the 6th Brigade, James Williams (1750-1821) of the 1st, Thomas Mathews of the 9th, and Joseph Jones of the 15th. The 6th Brigade included Alexandria; the 1st, Fredericksburg; the 9th, Norfolk; and the 15th, Petersburg. See "Establishment of the Militia . . . 1792 & 1793," Adjutant General's Record Book, War 10, Virginia State Library.

7. See JM to James Wood, May 20, 1794.

8. William Storke Jett (1763-1844), of "Walnut Hill" in Westmoreland County,

From James Wood

Copy, Executive Letterbooks, Virginia State Library

Sir,[9]   Richmond, March 21, 1794
   The System of discipline published by Baron Steuben,[1] and adopted by Congress in their resolution of the 29th March 1779, has been pretty generally diffused among the former militia officers and as public property ought not to be retained by them when out of office. I am therefore to request, that you will give to the officers commanding Corps in your Brigade, the most pointed orders to cause those books to be immediately collected and that returns of the numbers so reclaimed as well as those in the hands of the present militia officers, be made without loss of time to the Governor, in order that the deficiency may be supplied in conformity with the requisitions of the XXII Section of the militia law.[2] I have the honor etc.

JAMES WOOD

To Archibald Stuart

ALS, Stuart Papers, Virginia Historical Society[3]

My dear Sir   Richmond, March 27, 1794
   I enclose you a letter[4] to Bell which I wish you to seal & send to

---

was a brother-in-law of Lawrence Washington. In 1799 he served as sheriff of Westmoreland County.
   9. The letter is marked as a "Circular to the Brigadier Generals."
   1. Baron Friedrich Wilhelm Ludolf Gerhard Augustin von Steuben (1730–1794) came to this country from Prussia in 1777 with a long military career already behind him. He became inspector general of the Continental army and had great influence and popularity in the military. During the winter of 1778/1779 Steuben prepared his drill manual, which was published as *Regulations for the order and discipline of the troops of the United States* (Philadelphia, 1779), after gaining the approval of Congress. Worthington C. Ford *et al.*, eds., *Journals of the Continental Congress, 1774–1789*, XIII (Washington, D.C., 1914), 384–385.
   2. On Mar. 21, 1794, the Council of State ordered this action. The governor was Henry Lee, although he was out of Richmond from around Mar. 14 to early April. James Wood, the lieutenant governor, was writing as acting governor. The section of the militia law referred to is in 13 Hening 348 (1792). It provided that copies of the manuals were to remain public property, to be passed on to active officers only. JVCS, Mar. 14, Mar. 21, and Apr. 8, 1794. See JM to Samuel Coleman, *ca.* Apr. 1, 1794, and Coleman to JM, Dec. 19, 1795.
   3. This is item no. Mss1St91o2f41 in the society's collections. Addressed to "Archi-

him as soon as possible. I have examind the record & suppose it to be a full one. The errors suggested in the petition are 1st. That the value of the land ought to have been estimated by a jury, &

2dly. That so much of the original purchase money as remaind unpaid ought to have been deducted. If there is anything among the papers to cure these defects let me know it that I may apply for a certiorari. I am inclind to think the decree will be opend tho I am not certain of it & I suppose be it so or not the ultimate determination will be for Mills.

I am not employd for Matthews. He has chosen Counsellor Duval.[5] No person has appeard for Mrs. Burns. Unless the answer makes its appearance before the commencement of the next term a motion cannot be then made to dissolve the injunction. I cannot appear for Donaghoe. I do not decline his business from any objection to his *bank*: to that I shoud like very well to have free access & woud certainly discount *from* it as largely as he woud permit, but I am already fixd by Rankin & as those who are once in the bank do not I am told readily get out again I despair of being ever able to touch the guineas of Donaghoe.[6]

Shall we never see you again in Richmond? I was very much rejoiced when I heard that you were happily married but if that amounts to a ne exeat[7] which is to confine you entirely to your side of the mountain I shall be selfish enough to regret your good fortune & almost to wish you had found some little crooked rib among the fish & oysters which woud once a year drag you into this part of our terraqueous globe. You have forgotten I beleive the solemn compact we made to take a journey to Philadelphia together this winter & superintend for a while the proceedings of Congress. I wish very much to see you. I want to observe [   ][8] how much honester men you & I are [*than*] half our acquaintance. Seriously the[re ap]pears to me every day to be more folly, envy, malice & damnd rascality in the world than there was the day before & I

---

bald Stuart esquire, Stanton," the original manuscript is torn at the right margin, presumably by the removal of a wax seal.

4. Not found.

5. JM received a £5 fee in Matthews v. Burns. Account Book Receipts, Mar. 1794. The counsellor was William DuVal.

6. JM received a fee of £1 13s. 6d. in Rankin v. Donaghue in Mar. 1794. Earlier he had received an advice fee of £1 2s. 6d. from Rankin. Account Book, Receipts, Jan. 1793, and Mar. 1794.

7. A ne exeat regno is a writ compelling a party or witness to remain in the jurisdiction during the pendency of the litigation.

8. Torn.

do verily begin to think that plain downright honesty & unintriguing integrity will be kickd out of doors.

We fear & not without reason a war. The man does not live who wishes for peace more than I do, but the outrages committed upon us are beyond human bearing. Farewell—pray Heaven we may weather the storm. Your

J. MARSHALL

Law Papers, March 1794

U.S. Circuit Court, Va.

Lidderdale's Executor v. Harrison's Administrator, answer, AD, U.S. Circuit Court, Va., Ended Cases (Unrestored), Virginia State Library.[9]

To Samuel Coleman

ALS, Executive Papers, Virginia State Library

Sir[1]   [Richmond, *ca*. April 1, 1794]

Colo. Macon[2] has returnd to me the number of copies of Baron Steubens discipline in his Regiment & the number requisite for his officers. They have twelve & will require twenty six. I shall make a report so soon as I receive returns from the other Regiments. In the mean time if you can do so be pleasd to deliver to Colo. Macon so many additional copies as he may be entitled to receive. I am sir respectfully, Your obedt Servt

J MARSHALL

9. See Account Book, Receipts, Mar. 1794.

1. The letter is endorsed on the verso: "Letter B. General Marshall on the Subject of Steuben's Discipline, Found amongst the papers of 1794." See James Wood to JM, Mar. 21, 1794. Coleman had served as assistant to the clerk of the Council of State from 1786 until 1793, when he became assistant to Adj. Gen. Simon Morgan, whose office was receiving these returns for the governor. *JVCS*, IV, 17; JVCS, Dec. 1793. See also Samuel Coleman to JM, Dec. 19, 1795.

2. William H. Macon (1725–1813) was lieutenant colonel, or commander, of the New Kent County militia, designated the 52d Regiment of JM's brigade. When JM went to France in 1797, Macon was ordered to assume the brigadier's duties. Samuel Coleman to William H. Macon, June 26, 1797, Adjutant General's Record Book, War 10, Virginia State Library.

Commonwealth v. Cunningham & Company

Stipulation

ADS, Executive Papers, Virginia State Library

[Richmond], April 8, 1794

I release two shillings per hundred on the tobacco for which Samuel Baron Cuningham has obtaind a judgement against the commonwealth if no appeal be prosecuted thereon but if the appeal be prosecuted then this release is to be of no effect.[3]

J Marshall atty. for S. B. Cuningham

The Judgement obtained by Samuel Baron Cunningham against the Commonwealth is only exceptionable in that part of it which allows eighteen shillings pr centum for the tobacco lost. In every other respect it appears to be founded on the Decree of the Court of Appeals.

Jas Innes, pro republica

3. This stipulation of counsel relates to the amount of damages JM's client suffered after a Virginia county seized his ship during the Revolution. The Commonwealth had contended that the impressment was unauthorized and therefore illegal and that it was not obligated to Cunningham. In the Oct. 1793 term of the Court of Appeals, JM had argued in defense of a district court judgment in favor of Cunningham, but the higher court ruled the computation of damages incorrect and remanded the case for further determination. 8 Va. (4 Call) 331–337 (1793); *CVSP*, VII, 100–102.

The district court had reassessed the amount of damages on Apr. 5, 1794, and JM and Innes, acting as attorney general, then wrote this stipulation. They were apparently trying to compromise the amount of damages to avoid a second appeal. Despite this effort, later that day the Council of State ordered an appeal after receiving a note from the state auditor stating that this case might prompt many similar suits. The Court of Appeals upheld the district court's decision one week later. JVCS, Apr. 8, 1794; John Pendleton to Henry Lee, Apr. 8, 1794, Executive Papers, and Court of Appeals Order Book, II, 271, both in Virginia State Library. A copy of the district court's decision is in 8 Va. (4 Call) 337 (1793). For JM's fee, see Account Book, Receipts, May 1794.

From Jesse Burton

ALS, U.S. Circuit Court, Va., Ended Cases (Unrestored), 1797, Virginia State Library

Sir,[4]   [Lynchburg], April 11, 1794

I have enclosed the Loan Office Certificate[5] respecting the Payment made to James & R. Donald & Co al[s]o James Buchanans List of Credits which will shew that they Omited giving my Father Credit for a Bill of Exchange of 140£ made by Edward Carter,[6] I have also sent a Memo. of George Thompsons[7] who did a great part of my Fathers Business in his time—To shew that Mathew Woodson has paid a 100£. I expect Thompson will be at the Federal Court, tho he lives at present in Kentucky, he sent me word he would be in at that time & prove that point. The 4 Hogsds Tobo mentioned in his Memo. I suppose will be lost, as James Miller who received them is now out of the Cuntry & the inspectors Book Burnt by the British in the time of War, which puts it out of my power to fix that Matter. I hope Sir you'll do every thing in your power Respecting the Business as I cannot attend on account of the Smallpox.[8] You shall be thankfully rewarded for Your Trouble. Please to let me know if you receive the Certificates & whether

4. This letter is addressed to "John Marshall Esq., Attorney at Law, Richmond," and includes a notation in the same hand below the address lines that "Mr. Ball will please Deliver this & take Mr. Marshalls Receipt for the papers it contains." The letter is endorsed in JM's hand "To be filed in the suit of Burton's Exrs vs James & Robt Donald & Co." The chancery suit to which this pertains began when JM filed a bill requesting an injunction in the May 1794 term of the U.S. Circuit Court. After an exchange of pleadings, the suit was continued until May 1797, when the injunction was dissolved and the bill dismissed with costs. U.S. Circuit Court, Va., Ended Cases (Unrestored), 1797, and Rule Book, I, 116–117, 288–289, Virginia State Library. The bill is listed at Law Papers, Dec. 1793. JM received a £7 fee in the case. Account Book, Receipts, Nov. 1793.

5. The certificate was from the Virginia Loan Office and was issued under the terms of the sequestration statute of 1779. This certificate was undoubtedly pleaded as a partial defense to the action brought at common law by James and Robert Donald & Co. against Burton's estate. JM filed the suit in equity to enjoin the enforcement of the common law judgment in that case. 9 Hening 377–380.

6. James Buchanan (1737–1787), a Richmond merchant and alderman of that city in 1783, was the brother of Rev. John Buchanan and Alexander Buchanan. Carter was probably Edward Carter, Jr. (1750–1807), of "Blenheim" in Albemarle County.

7. Thompson (1748–1834), originally from Albemarle County, had married a Rebecca Burton.

8. Richmond was experiencing an outbreak of smallpox. JVCS, Feb. 5, 1794.

you think them Suficient; & in so doing You'll Greatly Oblige
Your, Most Obt Sev't

JESSE BURTON[9]

From Henry Lee

Copy, Adjutant General's Record Book, War 10, Virginia State Library

[*April 18, 1794, Richmond.* Gov. Lee issues general orders specifying designs for the militia uniforms, including one for general officers: "dark
blue coat, shirts lined with buff, capes, lapells and cuffs buff, buttons
yellow, Epaulets gold, one on each shoulder, black cocked hatt with black
cockade, black stock & boots."]

To James Wood

ALS, Executive Papers, Virginia State Library

Sir   Richmond, April 25, 1794
I am requested by several of the militia officers of this city to
aid them in an application to the executive for arms for their several companies.

In support of this application I beg leave to observe that the
possession of arms conduces exceedingly to the improvement of
troops in the usual evolutions & that it is hoped & beleived that
the public coud sustain neither inconvenience or loss from placing
muskets in the hands of the militia of this place, as they can with
great ease be re-collected shoud the occasion require it & as there
is every reason to beleive that they woud be kept safe & in good
order.[1] I have the honor to be sir with every sentiment of respect,
Your obedt. Servt.

J MARSHALL

9. Burton (1750–1795), of Campbell County, had been one of the original trustees
of Lynchburg in 1785.
1. JM addressed the letter to Wood, the lieutenant governor, rather than to Gov.
Henry Lee, because Lee had gone to Norfolk to supervise the fortification of that port
and was there from soon after Apr. 19 to mid-June. See JVCS, Apr. 19, 1794.
The Council of State had ordered 500 stand of arms moved from Point of Fork to
Richmond on Apr. 8. Apparently just after receiving JM's letter, the Council ordered
these arms distributed among the militias of Richmond, Fredericksburg, Chesterfield
County, and Prince George County. JVCS, Apr. 8, and 25, 1794.

Masonic Dispensation

[*May 2, 1794, Richmond*. JM, as grand master of the Grand Lodge, signs a dispensation authorizing Richmond Randolph Lodge No. 19 to initiate William Royall as a Mason. Richmond Randolph Lodge No. 19 Records, 1787–1801, Grand Lodge A.F. & A.M. of Virginia, Richmond. Not found.]

To James Wood

ALS, Executive Papers, Virginia State Library

Sir   [Richmond], May 20, 1794

It is stated to me by Captain Quarrier[2] that the field pieces in his possession coud be kept with great convenience & safety was he permitted to erect a small house on or near the parade ground which might protect them from the injuries they woud be exposd to if uncoverd. As the ground has been fixed on for the parade some distance out of town for general convenience to the citizens, it will be difficult to remove the pieces on every occasion from town to the place of meeting & it is hoped that the small expense (for it woud not exceed sixty dollars) of a house to cover the pieces might be usefully incurd, the more especially as it might protect all the artillery at this place.[3] I am Sir with very much respect, Your obedt. Servt.

J MARSHALL

2. Alexander Quarrier (1746–1827), captain of JM's artillery company, had moved to Richmond around 1787 from Philadelphia, to which he had migrated from Scotland in 1775. He was a coach maker and land speculator and later became the first captain of the Richmond Public Guard. [William] Meade, *Old Churches, Ministers and Families of Virginia* (Philadelphia, 1857), II, 345; E. M. Sanchez-Saavedra, "An Undisciplined Set of Vagabonds," *Virginia Cavalcade*, XVIII (Spring 1969), 41–47.

3. The request was promptly refused. A clerk wrote on the verso, "Genl. Marshall on the Subject of erecting a House for the Ordnance, Rejected, May 20th, 1794." No mention of the request appears in the minutes of the Council of State.

To Archibald Stuart

ALS, Stuart Papers, Virginia Historical Society

My dear Sir[5]   Richmond, May 28, 1794
I have considerd the record brought me by Mr. Clay & am really apprehensive that he is totally routed & has not a single rallying point left.

With respect to the errors in arrest of judgement, they woud be sufficient according to the great mass of authority collected in the books, but the principle which seems now to prevail tho' it is scarcely to be found in print is that where words are laid to be maliciously spoken & to be injurious to the plaintiff & the verdict has established them to be so, they are to be considerd as actionable unless it is plain that they coud not be slanderous.[6]

On the other point you woud certainly be right according to the law of England. The two pleas of not guilty & justification[7] are certainly inconsistent & in England a court woud not permit them but I have ever supposd the law to be otherwise here & this difference arises from the difference in the expression of the act of Assembly & act of Parliament.[8] By the act of Parliament the second

4. This is item no. Mss1Stg102f42 in the society's collections. The letter is addressed to "Archibald Stuart esquire, Atty at Law, Stanton," and bears the stamped impression "Richd June 2" in the left corner and "12/" in the right corner of the address leaf.

5. Not found.

6. Apparently Stuart's client, the defendant in a slander action, was contemplating appealing a verdict and judgment against him in a civil action for damages. At this time, when English common law courts were gradually asserting jurisdiction over slander, it was the general rule that the words were presumed not to be defamatory unless so proven by the plaintiff. Theodore F. T. Plucknett, *A Concise History of the Common Law*, 5th ed. (London, 1956), 495–496; S. F. C. Milsom, *Historical Foundations of the Common Law* (London, 1969), 332–344; William L. Prosser, *Handbook of the Law of Torts* (St. Paul, Minn., 1941), 777–809. JM indicated here that although the English cases still had validity, the rule in Virginia had been to assume that words spoken maliciously that were injurious to the plaintiff were in fact slanderous. See also Blackstone, *Commentaries*, III, 124.

Because JM referred to injuries, it is clear that this case was one in which the plaintiff had to allege and plead special damages. Slander per se, which defamed a plaintiff's reputation by accusing him of crime, of having a loathsome disease (usually a venereal disease), or which affected his business, trade, or occupation, did not require special pleading and proof of damages. See Prosser, *Torts*, 798–804.

7. Justification is the technical term for the defensive plea asserting that the matter uttered was true. Blackstone, *Commentaries*, III, 306. In contrast to the rules regarding criminal libel, truth was always a defense to a civil action for libel or slander. Prosser, *Torts*, 854.

8. The 1748 Virginia statute provided that "the defendant . . . may plead as many

plea is to be put in by the leave of the court & therefore the court may exercise a discretion concerning it in the exercise of which they have determind not to allow contradictory pleas, but under our act it is not necessary to ask the leave of the court but the defendant has a positive right to plead whatever he may think proper.[9] Whether the truth of a libel may be justified or not is a perfectly unsettled question. If in that respect if the law here varies from the law of England it must be because such is the will of their Honors for I know of no legislative act to vary it.[1] It will however be right to appeal was it only to secure a compromise.

We have some letters from Philadelphia which wear a very ugly aspect. It is said that Simcoe the Governor of upper Canada has enterd the territory of the United States at the head of about 500 men & has possessd himself of presque-isle.[2] As this is in Pensyl-

---

as several defenses as he shall think necessary for his defense, so as they not be admitted to plead and demur to the whole." 5 Hening 478. It was amended in 1785 to read, "The defendant may plead as many several matters, whether in law or fact, as he shall think necessary for his defense." 12 Hening 745. A comparable English statute, which provided a much more rigid rule but left discretion in the court to regulate pleadings, provided that "it shall and may be lawful for any defendant . . . in any action or suit . . . in any court of record, with leave of the same court, to plead as many several matters thereto, as he shall think necessary for his defense." 4 Ann. c. 16, sec. 4 (1705). By way of contrast to this Virginia practice, Massachusetts left discretion in the court; however, as a general rule, such an inconsistency between the plea of a general issue and special pleas, such as justification, was permitted. William E. Nelson, "The Reform of Common Law Pleading in Massachusetts, 1760–1830: Adjudication as a Prelude to Legislation," *University of Pennsylvania Law Review*, CXXII (1973), 130–131.

9. This line of reasoning was either commonplace among members of the Virginia bar, or, as is more likely, this opinion received wider professional attention and was not limited to Stuart as the recipient of this letter. Nearly the same phraseology appeared in an argument by Daniel Call, JM's brother-in-law, before the Court of Appeals a decade later. Stone v. Patterson, 10 Va. (6 Call) 74–75 (1806). While presiding over the U.S. Circuit Court for Virginia, JM used a similar statement in writing his opinion in Furniss v. Ellis and Allan, 2 Brock 16, 17 (Cir. Ct. Va. 1822).

1. This was the first mention of libel, or written defamation, in JM's discussion; the previous paragraph indicates that an oral statement constituted the defamation sued upon. JM asserted, somewhat tentatively, that the law of libel and slander was similar to that of England. As far as civil actions for slander were concerned, his opinion seems to have been substantially correct; however, certain significant alterations had begun to occur in the American law of criminal libel. See Leonard W. Levy, *Freedom of Speech and Press in Early American History: Legacy of Suppression* (New York, 1963), 176–309; James Morton Smith, *Freedom's Fetters: The Alien and Sedition Laws and American Civil Liberties*, 2d ed. rev. (Ithaca, N.Y., 1966), ix–xv; and Leonard W. Levy, "Liberty and the First Amendment: 1790–1800," *American Historical Review*, LXVIII (1962–1963), 22–37.

2. John Graves Simcoe (1752–1806), the first governor of Upper Canada, had commanded the loyalist provincial corps, the Queens Rangers (hussars), during the Revolution.

This rumor probably stemmed from two bases in fact. Simcoe moved into Ohio in

vania I hope the democratic society of Philadelphia will at once demolish him & if they shoud fail I still trust that some of our upper brethren will at one stride place themselves by him & prostrate his post. But seriously if this be true we must bid adieu to all hope of peace & prepare for serious war. My only hope is that it is a meer speculating story. Farewell, I am affectionately, Your

J MARSHALL

To James Wood

ALS, Executive Papers: Militia, York County, Virginia State Library

Sir   [Richmond], May 28, 1794
    I am informd that a company of Light Infantry is formd out of the 2d. battalion of the 68th. Regt. of militia. I beg leave to recommend as officers for that company Thomas Nelson jr. as Captain, Hugh Nelson jr. as Lieut. & Thomas Griffin as Ensign.³ I am Sir with great respect, Your obedt. Servt.

J MARSHALL

Apr. 1794 and built Fort Miami at the foot of the Maumee rapids and on the left bank of the Maumee River. Simultaneously the Pennsylvania government was raising a militia detachment to protect surveyors in the Presque Isle region on Lake Erie from hostile action by the Indians. These steps were taken against the wishes of the federal government, and President Washington ordered the operations halted on May 24, 1794. Harry Marlin Tinkcom, *The Republicans and Federalists in Pennsylvania, 1790–1801: A Study in National Stimulus and Local Response* (Harrisburg, Pa., 1950), 114–117.

    3. The 1792 militia law provided that a company of light infantry be attached to each battalion. The governor, with the advice of the Council of State, was to commission a captain, lieutenant, and ensign for each such company. 13 Hening 344.

    A clerk noted on the verso, "Commissions issued 28th May 1794." Thomas Nelson, Jr., of York County, was the son of Thomas Nelson, the former governor of Virginia. [Richard C. M. Page], *Genealogy of the Page Family in Virginia* (New York, 1883), 155. Hugh Nelson, Jr. (1768–1836), was Thomas's brother and apparently was referred to as "Jr." to distinguish him from his uncle. He moved in 1802 to Albemarle County, where he set up a law practice. From 1805 to 1809 he served in the House of Delegates and was elected a judge of the General Court, which position he resigned in 1811 to serve in Congress. In 1823 he was appointed U.S. minister to Spain. Thomas Griffin (1773–1837), an attorney, served in the House of Delegates from 1793 to 1800, the House of Representatives from 1803 to 1805, and the House of Delegates again from 1819 to 1823 and 1827 to 1830. From 1796 to 1820 he was an official of the York County Court.

From Henry Lee

Copy, Adjutant General's Record Book, War 10, Virginia State Library

[*June 17, 1794, Richmond*. Gov. Lee issues general orders "pursuant to advice of Council,"[4] after receiving a requisition from President Washington calling for a detachment of 11,377 men under the command of Maj. Gen. Hopkins assisted by Brig. Gens. Meade, Williams, Zane,[5] and JM. Quotas furnished by the adjutant general[6] were to be filled, and volunteers accepted and arranged into companies. All were to be "prepared to take the field at a moment's Warning."]

Law Papers, June 1794

U.S. Circuit Court, Va.

Southgate v. Winslow, declarations in two actions of debt, copy, U.S. Circuit Court, Va., Ended Cases (Restored), 1794, Virginia State Library.

4. Gov. Lee obviously issued the orders prior to the Council of State's consideration. The Council discussed the request for troops on June 18 and approved the orders. The orders are printed in *CVSP*, VII, 202–203, under date of June 30 and are headed "Rough General Orders." That document came from a different source and contains blanks not in the one calendared here.

Authority for the president's request for these troops was given in an act of Congress, May 9, 1794, providing for a total militia of 80,000. JVCS, June 18, 1794; 1 Stat. 367–368.

5. Samuel Hopkins (1743–1819) was major general of the First Division. A native of Albemarle County, he moved to Kentucky in 1796 and, after being admitted to the bar, served as a judge for a time before resigning to enter politics. After several terms in the state legislature, he served as commander of the western frontier in 1812. He ended his career with a term in the House of Representatives from 1813 to 1815. Everard Meade (1748–1802), of Amelia County, was commander of the Fourth Brigade. He had served in the House of Delegates from 1780 to 1783, but entered the state senate for four sessions beginning in 1794. James Williams was commander of the First Brigade. Isaac Zane (d. 1795), commander of the Seventh Brigade, was a merchant, miller, and distiller in Shenandoah County. He had served in the House of Burgesses from 1773 to 1775, attended the state conventions of 1775 and 1776, and was a member of the House of Delegates from 1776 until his death.

6. Simon Morgan (1755–1810) had been elected adjutant general by the House of Delegates on Dec. 2, 1793.

Power of Attorney

Deed Book Copy, Office of the Clerk of Fauquier County, Warrenton, Va.[7]

[Richmond], July 4, 1794

Know all men by these presents that I John Marshall have constituted & appointed & by these presents do constitute & appoint Charles Marshall to be my true and lawful Attorney for me and in my name to execute any bond or other instrument of writing as security for Denny Fairfax that he will account to the Common Wealth[8] for the rents of the Manor of Leeds in case the same should be escheated and will prosecute his suits with effect And I do hereby agree to be bound by whatever my said Attorney may do in the premises in like manner as if done by myself.

SEPTIMUS NORRIS[9]   JOHN MARSHALL

At a Court continued & held for Fauquier County the 27th. Day of October 1795. This Power of Attorney was proved to be the act and Deed of the said John Marshall by the oath of Septimus Norris a witness thereto and ordered to be recorded. Teste

F: BROOKE CC

To Henry Lee

ALS, Henry E. Huntington Library

Dear Sir   Richmond, July 7, 1794

An unfortunate contest has arisen in the 19th. Regiment of Militia between the Light Infantry & Grenadier companies concerning their rank. The officers of the Light Infantry having older commissions contend that the law establishes no superiority of the

7. In Box 93, Executive Papers, Virginia State Library, there is a notice by Charles Marshall executed on Oct. 30, 1795, indicating his intention to proceed immediately upon the collection of rents and threatening to distrain for arrears. Traditionally the tenants of the Fairfax manor lands had been slow and recalcitrant in paying rents; even today residents of Fauquier County refer to the territory of the former Manor of Leeds as "the Free State," because of this historical resistance to payment of rent or taxes. This power of attorney by JM placed the collections in the hands of his brother Charles, who resided in the county.

8. The bond to Denny Martin Fairfax has not been found; one to the Commonwealth is printed at July 10, 1795.

9. Norris (1763–1799) was a Fauquier County merchant.

one company over the other & that the senior commissions entitle them to the *right*.

The officers of the Grenadiers contend that according to military usage the Grenadiers are entitled to the right—that it is the priviledge of the company & is not dependent on the rank of the captain.

This controversy has already been attended with unpleasant effects which will encrease unless terminated by a decision of the respective claims of the parties. As the same causes of difference exist in other Regiments it woud seem proper that some general rule shoud be adopted which woud be observd throughout the militia. To procure this the present application is made to you.[1] With great respect & esteem, I am Sir your obedt. Servt.

J MARSHALL

Receipt

ADS, Minneapolis Public Library

[Richmond], July 10, 1794

Recd. from Mr. Brooking exr. of Mr. Isaac Holmes decd. ten pounds for prosecuting an appeal for the claim of Mr. Holmes to commutation for half pay through the district court & court of appeals.[2]

J MARSHALL

1. Gov. Lee responded to JM's application by ordering the major generals to have each brigadier general assemble a board of officers in each regiment to establish the officers' ranks. Reports of the decisions were to be finally registered in the adjutant general's office. General Orders, July 19, 1794, Adjutant General's Record Book, War 10, Virginia State Library. The problem of the ranks of colonels and majors, field officers, was ordered settled in August. See Henry Lee to JM, calendared at Aug. 15, 1794.

The question of which company was "entitled to the right" referred to which would march on the left or right in line formation. Gov. Lee responded in general orders: "In the formation of the militia by Battalion, the Grenadier, Light Infantry or rifle company, as the case may be, shall take the right—in formation by Regiment, the flank Companies to take post on the right and left, the Grenadiers having precedence of the light Infantry, and the Light Infantry having precedence of the rifle Company." General Orders, July 19, 1794, Adj. Gen.'s Record Book, War 10, Va. State Lib.

2. Vivion Brooking (1738–1808), a prominent Amelia County merchant, was the father-in-law of Isaac Holmes (1758–1793), who had served in the Revolution as a captain. Holmes's military service gave rise to this claim for half pay being prosecuted by JM on behalf of his estate. The District Court at Richmond had found in favor of Brooking on Sept. 12, 1793, whereupon the Commonwealth appealed. The Court of

From Thomas Jefferson

[*July 16, 1794*. Listed in Jefferson's "Summary Journal of Letters," Jefferson Papers, Library of Congress. Not found.]

From Alexander Quarrier

ALS, Executive Papers, Virginia State Library[3]

Sir   Richmond, July 19, 1794
I had the honor, Some time since to commumecat to you the offer of my Service together with the other officers of the artillery, and the Rest of the Company to make the first tour of duty that may be Requird from the President of the United States. The Company of artillery consists of 44 at Present and I have no doubt I Shall be able in a few days to complete the Company. I hope ther will be [*no*] difficulty in accepting it as it [*is*] at Present. [*I have*] the honer to be, [*Sir yo*]ur obt & Hl Set

A QUARRIER

From Henry Lee

Copy, Executive Letterbooks, Virginia State Library

Sir,   Richmond, July 21, 1794
You[4] will be pleased to proceed with all possible dispatch to Smithfield to support the Marshal of the United States in the Execution of his duty.

Appeals upheld the judgment on Apr. 24, 1794. Court of Appeals Order Book, II, 271, Virginia State Library.

JM recorded the receipt of this money in his accounts and indicated that the case was finished at this time. Account Book, Receipts, July 1794.

3. JM endorsed the letter "Quarriers Tender of Service." Capt. Quarrier was undoubtedly responding to a request for volunteers specified in orders to form a special detachment on June 17. JM was to be one of the brigadier generals assigned to the special detachment of 11,377 troops, and a company of artillery was called for. See Henry Lee to JM, calendared at June 17, 1794. JM apparently forwarded Quarrier's letter to the executive.

4. The letter was first begun in the third person, but JM's name was erased, and second person pronouns were substituted by the clerk. The orders are also copied in

The Cavalry of the 19th. Regiment will move with you, the Artillery and Light Infantry will follow by water.[5]

The Vessels in which they embark will be designated by white Colours on the Main Mast. This is done that you may if it shall become proper stop the Vessel and direct the return of her.

A company of Light Infantry from Petersburg under Captain Weiseger have orders to move immediately to Cabbin Point[6] and receive there your Commands. This force is to be augmented by General Marshal out of the contiguous Militia if requisite.

Major Taylor Aid de Camp to the Major General of the fourth Division was so good at my request as to accompany the Marshal and is now with him.[7]

He is advised of your approach and is desired to transmit to you such information as may have arisen since the date of the letters communicated to you this morning.

The Executive know that in your hands the dignity and rights of the Commonwealth will ever be safe, and they are also Sure that prudence; affection to our deluded fellow Citizens and marked obedience to law in the means you be compelled to adopt will equally characterize every step of your proceedings.

Collect every information respecting this daring violation of order and report the same to me and at the same time know exactly the conduct of the Lieutenant Colonel Commandant of Isle of Wight[8] as it will be necessary for me to understand the cause of his inattention to my instructions. I have etc.

HENRY LEE.

---

the Adjutant General's Record Book, War 10, Virginia State Library. For the background of these orders, see Militia Duty: Editorial Note, June 8, 1793.

5. See Henry Lee to William Richardson, July 21, 1794, Executive Letterbooks, Va. State Lib.

6. Joseph Weiseger was to proceed to Cabin Point in Surry County. See Henry Lee to Weiseger, July 21, 1794, Exec. Letterbooks, Va. State Lib.

7. George Keith Taylor (1769–1815), of Prince George County, studied law at the College of William and Mary and later became a leader of Federalists in Virginia, defending the Alien and Sedition Acts as a member of the House of Delegates in 1798 and 1799. He married JM's sister Jane (1779–1866) in 1799. Henry Lee was major general of the Fourth Division, and David Meade Randolph (1758–1830) was the U.S. marshal, appointed ca. 1791 and removed in 1801. Randolph was the son of Richard Randolph of "Curles" in Henrico County.

Gov. Lee wrote Taylor about steps being taken to respond to the situation in Smithfield. See Henry Lee to Taylor, July 21, 1794, Exec. Letterbooks, Va. State Lib.

8. See JM to Henry Lee, July 23 and 28, 1794. Col. James Wells was the commander of the Isle of Wight County militia.

To Henry Lee

ALS, Executive Papers, Virginia State Library

Sir   Smithfield, July 23, 1794

The troop reachd this place yesterday morning between six & seven oClock. The ship Unicorn (the supposd privatier) was in possession of a company of the Isle of wight militia & the revenue cutter lay below her with a detachment of militia from Norfolk commanded by Captain Wooside.[9]

Every idea of resisting with violence the execution of the laws seems to have been abandond. Immediately on my arrival the Marshal made a peaceable request on Captain Sinclair[1] to allow his house to be searchd for arms supposd to be containd in it, which he did not hesitate to permit. The search was made & thirteen pieces of cannon with some ball grape shot & powder were found. There were three pieces lying on the shore. A fatigue party is now employd in getting them on board the Unicorn after which the cutter will conduct her to Bermuda hundred or to Brodway.[2] I dispatchd a boat yesterday morning to stop the vessel which was proceeding down James river with the companies of artillery & infantry from Richmond & directed their return. I also orderd Captain Weisiger to return with the infantry of Prince George but as the Marshal entertains some apprehension of an attempt to rescue the vessel in the river I thought it adviseable to countermand the orders I had given & to direct Captain Weisiger to continue his march to this place with a view to his return in the Unicorn.

The situation both of Major Taylor & of the Marshal has been arduous & unpleasant. The Marshal has receivd personal insult & seems not to have been free from personal danger. Major Taylor has usd great & proper exertions to complete the business he was upon. He at first experiencd great difficulty in procuring aid of any kind but that difficulty is now removd. Since the arrival of distant militia those of the county are as prompt as coud be wishd in rendering any service requird from them. Indeed I am disposd

9. JM misspelled the name of Robert Woodside.
1. John Sinclair (1755–1820), of Smithfield. During the Revolution he was a very active privateer and apparently served for a period in the navy, being given the rank of captain. He moved to Gloucester County around 1800 and settled at "Lands End."
2. Bermuda Hundred was a port in Chesterfield County on the southern bank of the James River, across from Turkey Island and above present-day Hopewell. Broadway was on the Appomattox River where it meets the James River, near Hopewell.

to beleive that the original difficulty rested not with the men. The privates (except those residing in Smithfield) have manifested no disaffection to the government or reluctance to support the laws. But of this & of every circumstance which has occurred Major Taylor & the Marshal have taken memoranda & an ample report will be made to you so soon as they shall return to Petersburg.

Captain Sinclair declares that he never designd to violate the laws, that the ⟨cannon⟩ arms found in the house were not intended for the Unicorn but were purchasd for a gentleman to the Southward, that the ball will not fit the cannon, & that tho' she was originally designd for a privatier the intention was changd so soon as the act of Congress prohibiting vessels to be armd in our ports was known, in proof of which he says that a cargo is now engagd for her. These however are subjects proper to be discussd in court.

I am sorry to say that the surveyor of the port, who is considerd here as the informer,[3] seems to entertain great apprehensions from some of those who considerd themselves as interested in this business.

The vessel will I trust be ready to sail tomorrow & I shall then set out with the troop for Richmond. With very much respect I am Sir your obedt. Servt.

J MARSHALL

To Henry Lee

LS, Executive Papers, Virginia State Library

Sir,   Richmond, July 28, 1794

The troop of Cavalry ordered to Smithfield returned yesterday. A longer time than I had counted on was necessary to carry on board the different Articles libeled and to move the Unicorn and this has produced a delay more considerable than was at first expected. She is now on her way to Bermuda Hundred guarded by Captain Weisiger with his company of Light Infantry and attended by the revenue cutter.

3. Copeland Parker (1768–1830) was the inspector of revenue for the port of Smithfield. In 1796 he eloped with John Sinclair's daughter Elizabeth, whose father completely disowned and disinherited her. Claude O. Lanciano, Jr., *Legends of Lands End* (n.p., 1971), 20–22.

For Parker as "the informer," see Parker to William Lindsay, July 8, 1794, *CVSP*, VII, 214.

The additional expence of returning Captain Weisiger's Company in the Unicorn is very inconsiderable and is incurred at the request of the Marshal who did not think her safe unless guarded by armed men. His apprehension of a rescue seems to have arisen in Some measure from reports prevailing in Smithfield and received in a manner deserving some credit tho' not so as to be testimony, but principally from the boldness and decision of Captain Sinclair's character, from the high degree of irretation he manifested, and from the well known total inability of the Cutter to afford any effectual aid in case of attack. Captain Sinclair declares his perfect submission to the laws and avers that he had never meditated resistance to them. There were however strong circumstances which might readily induce an opinion that violence was contemplated. The night after the Unicorn was seized persons were heard for a considerable time loading fire arms in the house of Captain Sinclair. The drawing of iron ramrods and ramming down the charge were distinctly heard. When the search was applied for which I mentioned in my former letter he gave a list of the Arms in his possession and among them were fifteen muskets. These were found all charged. The situation of the house is such as completely to command the Deck of the Vessel. I do not think that one hund. men placed in the Vessel could have protected her ten minutes from fifteen placed in the House and at this time notwithstanding the application to Colonel Wells and the exertions of Major Taylor and the Marshal in Smithfield only a guard of six or seven badly armed men had been raised.

Captain Sinclair says that the only resistance he ever contemplated was against an unauthorized attempt which he understood was to be made to Search his house. This may be the fact but it would Scarcely Seem to be so since it was not unknown to him that the only search ever designed was under the Warrant of a Magistrate which was applied for but not obtained. This circumstance added to the evidence that the Vessel had been designed for a privatier did I own make such an impression on me that I should, had the Marshal requested it, have encreased the Guard. I had while in Smithfield frequent conversations with individuals of the Isle of Wight. So far as I can judge of their sentiments from their expressions I am persuaded that they feel no inconsiderable degree of mortification that a necessity should exist for calling militia from a distance to their neighbourhood to protect from Violence the laws of our common country and I am persuaded too

that this sentiment will so affect the commanding officers as to secure more activity from them on any future occasion than has
been exhibited on this. They seem not to have been sufficiently
impressed with the importance of maintaining the sovereignty of
the laws, they seem not to have thought it a duty of strong and
universal obligation to effect this object, but I do believe that a
more proper mode of thinking is beginning to prevail.

The militia on duty have so acted as not to have produced among
the citizens so far as my information extends a single murmur.

The chearfulness with which the troop submitted to labour not
usually imposed on Cavalry does them much honor.

It is with great regret I mention an accident which befel one of
the Prince George Infantry. The Unicorn almost touched the land.
The Company from Prince George was on board and was ordered
neither to go on Shore or to permit any person from the Shore to
come on board the Vessel. A militia man who had stolen out attempted to return and on being hailed by the sentinel attempted
to rush by him without an answer. It was so extremely dark that
the person could not be distinguished and the sentinel at the same
time pushed with his Bayonet & attempted to fire. The rain which
had fallen fortunately prevented the discharge of the musket but
a dangerous wound was received from the bayonet. Doctor Crawford[4] of the Richmond troop with great humanity dressed his
Wounds and attended him through the night but could not procure a probe to ascertain its depth.

I will send to you tomorrow an account of the monies expended
by me on the expedition. With very much respect & esteem I remain Sir, your obt. Servt.

J MARSHALL

From Henry Lee

Copy, Executive Letterbooks, Virginia State Library

Sir,[5]　　　　　　　　　　　　　　　Richmond, July 30, 1794
With very great satisfaction do I comply with the dictates of my
official duty in signifying to you my approbation of every part of

4. Probably Dr. Hugh J. Crawford, a medical officer for Richmond in 1795. JVCS,
Nov. 11, 1795.
5. The letter was addressed "To Brigadier General Marshall."

your conduct in the late necessary interposition of the militia to support the civil Authority.

The exemplary temper manifested on this occasion cannot fail to produce the happiest effects as it carries with it unequivocal testimony of the general determination to maintain inviolate the constitution and laws of the People.

I entreat you to express to the officers and soldiers detached from this city and from Petersburg under your orders how very much I admire the patriotic example exhibited by them and how sincerely I am gratified by your report of their orderly and soldier-like demeanor. With very great regard I am etc.

HENRY LEE.

To Militia Captains

Printed, *Gazette of the United States* (Philadelphia), August 22, 1794, 2

DEAR SIRS,   Richmond, August 2, 1794[6]

The approbation expressed by the Governor of the conduct of the militia in their late effort to preserve from violation the laws of their country, and which he requests should be conveyed to you, cannot be more properly communicated than by transmitting you a copy of his letter on that subject.[7]

It is with great pleasure I perceive that the commanding officer of the state is impressed with the same opinion of your conduct which is entertained by myself. With great regard, I am, your obedient servant.

J. MARSHALL

To Thomas Jefferson

[*August 2, 1794.* Listed in Jefferson's "Summary Journal of Letters," Jefferson Papers, Library of Congress. Not found.]

6. The newspaper mistakenly printed the date of this letter as 1792.
7. Henry Lee to JM, July 30, 1794, was also printed with this letter.

From Henry Lee

Copy, Adjutant General's Record Book, War 10, Virginia State Library

[*August 15, 1794, Richmond*. As part of his general orders calling for a special detachment to help quell the Whiskey Rebellion, Gov. Lee directs that in order "to complete the settlement of rank . . . a Board of General officers consisting of Major General Clark, and the Brigadiers Meade, Young, Marshall and Guerrant, assemble in the City of Richmond on the 26th. instant to ascertain the rank of the field officers, on which day, the Adjutant General is directed to attend, for the purpose of presenting every document and information in his possession relating to this subject. The report of this Board will be considered definitive and filed in the Adjutant General's office.[8]"]

Officers Rank Role

Copy, Adjutant General's Record Book, War 10, Virginia State Library

[*August 26, 1794, Richmond*. JM, Henry Young, John Guerrant, Jr., and Jonathan Clark, as members of a board appointed on Aug. 15, 1794, file their report of the rank of field officers in the Virginia militia.[9]]

8. Jonathan Clark was major general of the Second Division. Brig. Gens. Everard Meade, Henry Young, JM, and John Guerrant, Jr., were commanders of the 4th, 14th, 2d, and 3d Brigades respectively. Guerrant (1760–1813), of Goochland County, attended the 1788 Virginia ratifying convention, served in the House of Delegates from 1787 to 1796, and then sat on the Council of State, becoming its president in 1805.

These orders were printed in the *Virginia Gazette, and General Advertiser* (Richmond), Aug. 20, 1794.

Gen. Meade did not attend the meeting on Aug. 16. See the report of the board following.

9. James Wood received the report for the Council of State on Sept. 2, 1794. The report was later printed as a broadside. See Cabell Papers, University of Virginia Library.

Field officers were lieutenant colonels and majors. Curiously, out of 133 colonels listed on the roll, all but 15 had resigned, died, or been promoted. Of 182 majors, less than 75 were listed as active. This board was later reconvened to decide a challenge to one major's rank. See General Orders and Report of Board of Officers, Dec. 13, 1796, Adjutant General's Record Book, War 10, Virginia State Library.

From James Wood

Copy, Executive Letterbooks, Virginia State Library

Sir,   Richmond, September 4, 1794

It has been estimated that the sum of five hundred and fifty Dollars,[1] will be sufficient for the subsistence and transportation of the baggage of the militia from your brigade as far as Winchester the place of General rendezvous. This Sum you will be pleased to receive from the Treasury. If this sum should be found insufficient for the intended purpose, the deficiency will be paid immediately upon the accounts being rendered with proper vouchers. It is to be observed that one baggage Waggon to each complete company will be allowed for the transportation of the baggage, and also to carry forward any provisions which the Agent may find necessary to transport. As there are no tents, the baggage cannot be considerable.

You are authorized to employ an Agent to attend the Detachment for the purpose of procuring the necessary supplies on the march, and who is to make up his accounts with you immediately after his return. You are empowered to fix the compensation to be made to the Agent and to an Assistant if the appointment of one should be found indispensably necessary.[2]

As you are the person who will be made accountable for the expenditure, you will of course be particular in your instructions to the Agent as to the Application, and that proper Accounts be kept, accompanied with the necessary Vouchers. I have the honor etc.

JAMES WOOD.

1. The letterbook copy is addressed "To Brigadiers Young and Marshall, each," and is signed by Wood, the lieutenant governor, in Henry Lee's absence. Lee was away from Richmond from Aug. 20 to Sept. 10. JVCS, Aug. 20–Sept. 10, 1794. The amount stated here is the figure Henry Young's brigade was to receive; the letter JM actually received no doubt had the figure $350, the amount authorized for his brigade. For the authorization and amounts for every brigade, see *ibid.*, Sept. 4, 1794.

A similar letter was sent to the other brigadier generals at the same time, the only difference being the procedure for receiving their money. Circular to Brigadier Generals, Sept. 4, 1794, Executive Letterbooks, Virginia State Library.

For information on the Whiskey Rebellion, see Richard H. Kohn, *Eagle and Sword: The Federalists and the Creation of the Military Establishment in America, 1783–1802* (New York, 1975), 158–173; Leland D. Baldwin, *Whiskey Rebels: The Story of a Frontier Uprising* (Pittsburgh, 1939); and Militia Duty: Editorial Note, June 8, 1793.

2. The details of this mobilization came from Edward Carrington, the supervisor

From Alexander Quarrier

ALS, Executive Papers, Virginia State Library

[*September 6, 1794 (Richmond)*. Quarrier submits a request for supplies and ammunition and a detailed list of needs for outfitting his horses and wagons totaling £78.³]

To Henry Lee

ALS, Executive Papers, Virginia State Library

Sir⁴   Richmond, September 13, 1794

I enclose you a statement made by the captain of the artillery company of this town of the articles requird for the preservation or use of the artillery under his care. I have the honor to be with great respect, Your obedt. Servt.

J MARSHALL

Harrison v. Allen

Argument in the
High Court of Chancery

Extract from Casebook, Tucker-Coleman Papers, Swem Library, College of William and Mary

Richmond, September 1794

This Case is reported by Mr. Washington,⁵ as follows.

Washington for the plaintiffs. The question which arises in this

---

of revenue for the district of Virginia, and JM, who suggested alterations in the plan established by the Council of State. Edward Carrington to James Wood, Sept. 1, 1794, *CVSP*, VIII, 287.

3. Addressed "Genl John Marshall," the letter was transmitted to the Council of State by JM on Sept. 13. A clerk wrote on the verso, "Capt. Quarrier, 1794, Sept. 13th, On the Subject of equiping his Compy of Artillery. Postponed." The Council approved the expenditure on Dec. 3, and the clerk added a note to that effect on the verso. JVCS, Dec. 3, 1794.

4. Addressed to "His Excellency Governor Lee."

5. Although these notes are in St. George Tucker's notebook, they were copied from Bushrod Washington's notes by someone other than Tucker. A much shorter

Cause is, whether the Act of 1785[6] directing the Cource of Descents was in force or not in 1793, or whether the only Law upon
this subject at that time was the Common Law. If the former were
the case the plffs: must succeed, if the latter they must fail. It is I
contend merely a question of construction & not of legislation.
We do not call upon the Court by its fiat to make the Act of 1785
the law, but to say whether the Act of 1792 upon the true construction of it repealed the Act of 1785. I contend that the Act of 1792
is a reenacting of the Act of 1785 and not the substitution of a New
Law in its place and of cource that the repealing Clause applies
not to that act, or to so much of the act of 1790 as is collected into
that Act of 1792,[7] but to all other Laws upon the subject which

---

and less detailed report of the case is in Wythe 291 (1794). JM's fees for this case are
entered in Account Book, Receipts, Mar. 1794 and Nov. 1794.

At the end of the notes Tucker wrote, "From this Decree there was no Appeal."
Obviously he wrote that soon after the decree was handed down on Sept. 27, 1794,
because the case was in fact reopened, and a similar order was issued on Mar. 15, 1800.
That order was appealed and affirmed on Oct. 22, 1802. 7 Va. (3 Call) 288–305;
Court of Appeals Order Book, III, 209, Virginia State Library.

6. This statute provided for the partible descent of realty (as opposed to primogeniture) to children of the intestate decedent, permitted a descendant to inherit through
an alien ancestor, and permitted bastards to inherit from, or transmit their inheritance through, their mothers. It also provided for the legitimization of bastard children under certain circumstances. The act became effective on Jan. 1, 1787. 12 Hening
138–140 (1785). Virginia rules of inheritance, including the alterations made by the
1785 and 1790 acts, are discussed in Tapping Reeve, A Treatise on the Law of Descents
. . . (New York, 1825), 285–319.

7. Washington's argument is unclear without some knowledge of the legislative history of the statutes governing intestate succession to real property. The act of Dec. 8,
1792, as presented by the revisors and passed by the legislature, was originally to take
effect immediately upon enactment; however, at the same legislative session, its operation was suspended until Oct. 1, 1793. 13 Hening 534-535; 1 Shepherd 3, 99–101.
The problem seems to have been caused by an earlier amendment to the 1785 intes-
tacy law, contained in the act of Dec. 24, 1790, the substantive provisions of which
were also incorporated nearly verbatim in the 1792 statute. 13 Hening 122–124. Unfortunately sec. 7 of the 1790 act provided that "so much of all acts as comes within
the purview of this act, and particularly of the act intituled 'An act directing the course
of descents,' shall be and the same is hereby repealed." Narrowly construed, this repealing clause pertained only to secs. 3 and 16 of the 1785 act. Compare 12 Hening
138, 139, with 13 Hening 123. Broadly construed, the 1790 act would completely
repeal the statute of descents of 1785, permitting Virginia law to revert to the common
law pattern of intestate succession from 1785 to 1792.

Even if the broad construction of the 1790 statute were rejected, a much finer
point of statutory construction arose from the repeal in sec. 22 of the 1792 act of all
former law, which by the terms of the statute was effective immediately on enactment. 1 Shepherd 101. Did the subsequent suspension of the act also suspend the re-
pealer clause, leaving Virginia without a statutory rule concerning intestate descent
of land from Dec. 8, 1792, to Oct. 1, 1793? If so, the common law rules would be in
effect for that period of time.

are not so collected. Let me then premise some general rules in the Construction of Statutes.

1. The intention of a Statute is to be collected from the Cause of making it, or from other Circumstances; when this can be discovered, it should be followed with reason and discretion tho' contrary to the Letter 4. Bac: ab: 648.[8]

2. If the meaning be doubtful, consequences are to be attended to in the Construction otherwise if not doubtful. Hob. 97.[9]

3. The best mode of getting at the intention is to suppose the Legislature askd. at the time: do you mean this, or this?

Let me ask under the 2nd. rule what would be the Consequence of the Construction contended for? Two thirds of the Statute Law suspended during a year. It is unnecessary to say more than state the fact. The consequence can be more easily perceivd. at one glance, than expressd. in a day.

To get out of the mischief attending this Construction we must resort to the first maxim, and ask what was the Intention of the Legislative mind in passing the act of 1792? The act of 1789, ch: 9,[1] is compleatly expressive of that intention. The mischief stated in the preamble, is the multiplicity of Laws upon the same subject, or contradictory Laws dispersed throughout many volumes, copies of them with difficulty procured, many of them have been repealed, have expired or have had their effect, or have been reenacted in substance in the Laws taken from the Revisors' report etc.

The remedy provided for this mischief is by the appointment of persons whose duty amongst other things, is to report what Laws or parts of Laws shall remain in force, what of them are upon the same subject and ought to be reduced into single Acts, and what are unfit to be continued in force, or unnecessary to be published in any Code of the Laws, and to prepare a full Index to all the Laws, to note in order of time the titles of those Laws which may be omitted in a general compilation of the Laws. If the Legislature

8. Matthew Bacon, *A New Abridgement of the Law* . . . , 3d ed. (London, 1769), IV, 648.

9. Moore v. Hussey bristled with rules of construction, but this does not appear to have been one of them. Hob. 93–101, 80 Eng. Rep. 243–250 (K.B. 1610).

1. "An act concerning a new edition of the Laws of this Commonwealth," adopted Nov. 18, 1789, established a group of revisors that included JM. An amendment passed on Dec. 23, 1790, deleted his name, however. 13 Hening 8–9, 130–131. For a discussion of the problems created by this legislation, see Charles T. Cullen, "Completing the Revisal of the Laws in Post-Revolutionary Virginia," *Virginia Magazine of History and Biography*, LXXXII (1974), 89–95.

ever spoke their will in plain and explicit Terms they did so upon this subject, declaring that their object was to compile the old Laws into one body—not to enact new ones. The Compilors appointed by this Law in the prosecution of their Duty appear to have doubted whether their power was confined to the mere business of compiling, or might be extended to the introduction of new Laws, and a letter from them to the Legislature produced a second decleraration of the Legislative mind upon the subject, in the year 1791 (see the resolution of that Session page 37) which is too plain to be doubted.[2] They resolve that the power of the Revisors was confined to the single Business of compiling a new and concise Edition of the Laws and not to the forming of a new Code. After this explicite Decleration one would suppose that all doubts upon the subject were at an end—so in the Acts of 1792, p. 117, they are stiled the Republication of the Laws.[3] The result of these observations are that the former Laws were not enacted in 1792 by a new Decleration of the peoples will, but were collected together & sistamatised into a single Code and consequently the repealing Clause in question is not of the Acts of 1785 & 1790 as to descents, but of all other Laws on that subject, (if any there were) not brought into the new collection; it is certainly immaterial except for the sake of convenience whether the legislative will was found expressd. on one or twenty pieces of paper. It was still their Will, which remained unrevoked tho' the parts which might be found scattered in the chaos of Laws, were left in that dismembered situation, or gathered together & formed into a perfect & regular Body. When the intention then is thus plain, when all public inconvenience is thus easily prevented, why should we study to create difficulties & mischief. The repealing clause may be fully satisfied by leaving it to operate upon Laws not brought into the Code, and is therefore unnecessarily used when applied to the whole body of Laws.

I consider the Case of Williamson & Payne decided in the special Court of Appeals to be in point.[4] In that case an Execution

2. Cullen, "Completing the Revisal," *VMHB*, LXXXII (1974), 94–95.

3. "An act providing for the republication of the Laws of this Commonwealth" is in 13 Hening 531–534. In the session acts for 1792 this act appears on p. 85. Washington must have been referring to a manuscript version. See *Acts Passed at a General Assembly of the Commonwealth of Virginia . . . one thousand seven hundred and ninety-two* (Richmond, 1793).

4. The case apparently was never reported. An act of 1791 provided for a special Court of Appeals to meet on June 20 and Nov. 20 each year. 13 Hening 255.

was issued in   upon a replevy Bond taken   . Now
if the act of 1792 was a new Law then the old Law having expired
the new one could not without express words to that effect warrant an execution, but if it were merely the reenacting of the old
then the remedy was continued and this was the opinion of the
Court.[5]

But if the Law of 1792 is not to be considered as the reenacting
of the Law of 1785, then I contend that the Court will consider
the general suspending law in the same light as if it had been annexed to each particular law, which of cource will suspend the
whole Law as well the repealing as the enacting clause.

Wickham[6] for Deft. The Act of 1792 include all the Laws upon
the same subject. It is agreed that all others are repealed, and yet
it is contended against the express words of the Law, that all Laws
on the same subject are not repeald. By the mode of reasoning on
the part of the Plaintiff if another Law were to repeal the act of
1792 the act of 1785 would remain in force, tho' the Act of 1792
contains the Decleration of the public will, and all other Dec-
lerations of that will are here in express terms revoked, and this
Doctrine will lead us still further, for upon the same mode of reasoning all the old Laws which existed before the revision of 1769
are yet in force, and to the old Collections of these Laws we must
refer to discover the legislative will, tho it was expressly pronounced
to be contained in that revision.[7] The Laws of 1792 were enacted
for the purpose of preventing the inconvenience resulting from
the dispersed situation in which the Laws then were and the want
of repealing Clauses to some of the Laws is stated in the act of that
Session p: 117, to produce much inconvenience. Yet from the
construction now contended for, all those inconveniencies would
still continue. But it is said that the suspending Law is to be con-

5. The case would not appear to be directly in point, since the 1792 legislation on
replevy bonds was excepted from the suspension of legislation. 13 Hening 367–369,
535. The 1792 statute was a reenactment of the scheme of replevy bonds as contained
in the act of Jan. 4, 1788, which was to be in force for a three-year period ending on
Jan. 3, 1791. 12 Hening 458, 459. The act of Dec. 27, 1790, continued the 1788 act
for an additional year to Jan. 3, 1792, and the act of Dec. 15, 1791, continued the
1788 act in force until Jan. 1, 1793. 13 Hening 128, 244. Based on the foregoing and
on the action of the General Assembly in excepting the 1792 revised statute from the
suspension, it seems probable that the legislative intent was to continue the use of
replevy bonds and to incorporate the procedure into the permanent statutory law of
Virginia.
6. John Wickham.
7. Wickham was arguing that the revision was a codification with an attendant repeal of all other sources of statute law.

sidered as annexed to each Law so as to suspend the effect of the repealing as well as the enacting clause. If this argument be sound then the repealing clause never had effect, but I would ask: suppose a case had occurred & come to trial between the 8th. and 28th. of December[8] how would the Court have decided? Why surely that the former law was repealed. They could not have said that the repealing clause was suspended for the Legislature had not then declared their Will to suspended it. It can not therefore be considered as annexed to each seperate act. The truth is that the repealing clause had its effect for 20 days and effectually annihilated the former Laws which the suspending Law could not revive as it took effect from & after the passage thereof: and if the repeal of a repealing Law does not revive the first Law, which is a principle of construction fixed by the Law of 1789[9] a fortiori the old law is not revived by the suspention of the repealing law.

But why in a case like this where the words are plain and unattended with any ambiguity whatever shall we be exerting ourselves to find out doubts which can only be solved by recerrence to rules of construction. If the subject before the Court were less important than it is I am sure there would not be a question as to the operation of the Law under consideration.

Marshall for Plts. The Argument a fortiori as to the operation of a suspending Law upon a repealing Law I do not consider to be a sound one. There is a solid reason to be given why the old Law should not be revived by the repeal of a repealing Law and yet that it should by the suspension of the repealing Law. The principle in England as to the repeal of a repealing Law is directly the reverse of what it is in this country, since the Act of 1789. The old law is revived because it is considered not as being annihilated by the repealing Law but only suspended. The act of 1789 by destroying this principle admits its former existance. Of cource a suspending Law had the same effect, and not being within the Letter of the Law of 1789 still has the same effect.[1] It would be sufficient for

8. That is, between the effective date of the 1792 statute of descents and the effective date of the act suspending its operation, Dec. 8–28, 1792.

9. Sec. 2 of the act of Nov. 18, 1789, provided that "whensoever one law, which shall have repealed another, shall be itself repealed, the former shall not be revived, without express words to that effect." 13 Hening 9.

1. JM's subtle argument was based upon a strict construction of statutes in derogation of the common law of England and Virginia prior to 1789. The 1789 alteration of the rules concerning repealing statutes, he argued, did not apply to suspending statutes. He did not come to issue with Wickham's contention that the 1785 act was *repealed* on Dec. 8, 1792, but that the operation of the repealing statute was immediate,

me in a case like this to rely that it is not within the Letter of the Law, for if it be not, the Court would not extend it by construction so as to produce a great public calamity tho' they might to prevent it, but I repeat it, that it is not within the same reason.

The Chancellor.[2] A posterior Act will without any repealing Clause, repeal all former Laws inconsistent with it and therefore I can perceive no use for such a Clause unless the Legislature suppose that there were some other Laws upon the same subject omitted in the latter Law. In considering this Case it is unnecessary to recur to precedents. In 1785 the Law of decents was made compleatly arranging the Common Law upon that subject. This law was suspended until 1787 on the 8th. of Decr. 1792. The very same matter and in the very same words are again written as declarative of the public will with no other alteration except what was created by the Act of 1790. It is contended on one side that the Act of 1785 is repealed by the Act of 1792 and on the other that the repealing Clause applies only to those Laws or parts of Laws not brought into the Code of 1792. I shall consider first if the Act of 1785 be repeald, and 2ndly. if repealed, whether it was not revivd. by the suspending Law.

The more effectually to do this let us define 1st. What is a Statute? 2dly. What is a repeal? A Statute is a declaration of the Legislative will. The publication of that will is all that remains to give it energy, and whether this is done by writing on paper or parchment, by carving or by a public Trumpetor is totally immaterial. It is sufficient if by any means it be published. Its validity depends not on its being written. Various modes have been adopted by different countries & in different ages to make this Will of the Legislature known to those who are to observe it. It too often happens that the paper of parchment on which this Will is written is considered as the Will itself whereas it is only the simbol of it, and if the Arts of writing or printing were unknown, the people might nevertheless decree its Will & give it effecacy. Suppose then that the Legislature in 1785 had assembled and declared their Will to be (without committing to writing) that the Lands of an intestate should descend equally amongst all the Children and so on according to the Act of 1785. It would unquestionably have been a Law,

---

and its force was not suspended until Dec. 28, 1792. He did argue, however, that the suspension of a repealing statute revived the earlier law.

2. George Wythe.

and so continued until they revoked it. 2nd. What is a repeal? It is a deleartion made by the same body & in the same manner that the Legislative Will upon that subject is altered, but if the new Deleration and the old be the same the Legislative Will is not altered, but continuing. In such a Case then the Term repeal has no meaning for if it have it is repugnant to what the Legislature say. Apply these plain undenyable principles to this Case. In 1785 the Legislature declare their Will as to the Cource of Descents. In 1792 they again repeat the same Decleration. Does the latter declaration abrogate the former? Surely not, unless it appeared that the Legislative will was altered. The consequence of all this is, that the repealing clause in question applies to other Laws repugnant to the former and present declared will of the Legislature and of cource the Act of 1785 has never been repealed but is still in force: But if this were not so I am very clear that the suspending Law suspended the repealing as well as the enacting Clause.

Decree for the Plffs:

From James Wood

Copy, Executive Letterbooks, Virginia State Library

Sir,[3]   Richmond, October 4, 1794

I am advised by the Council of State to require that you will immediately institute the legal proceedings on all delinquencies under the late requisitions of the President of the United States[4] which have arisen within your Brigade district. I have enclosed you the opinion[5] of mr. John Marshall who acts as State Attorney in the absence of the Attorney General. I beg Sir, that you will be pleased to acknowledge the receipt of this letter by the earliest opportunity. I have the honor to be etc.

JAMES WOOD

3. The letter is addressed as a "Circular To the Brigadier Generals" and is written by Wood as lieutenant governor in Henry Lee's absence. Lee attended his last session of the Council of State on Sept. 16, before leaving for Pennsylvania. JVCS, Sept. 16, 1794. Since JM was a brigadier general, the editors assume he received a copy of this letter in order to carry out the order of the Council.

4. This refers to the requisitions of Aug. 7 and 25, 1794. See Militia Duty: Editorial Note, June 8, 1793.

5. See JM's opinion, Oct. 16, 1794.

Acting Attorney General

EDITORIAL NOTE

James Innes, attorney general for the Commonwealth from 1786 to 1796, notified the Council of State in August 1794 that President Washington wanted him to go to Kentucky to explain the current state of negotiations with Spain concerning navigation of the Mississippi River.[6] He assured the Council that if they approved his accepting the appointment, the work of his office would be continued in his absence. With a warning that state law prohibited simultaneous office-holding in both the state and federal governments, Governor Henry Lee informed Innes that the Council of State had approved his request, leaving it to his judgment whether he could legally accept the appointment. Lee also asked him to select a replacement if he did go to Kentucky.[7]

By October 3 Innes had determined at least to travel to Philadelphia to discuss the appointment with Washington, and he notified the Council that John Marshall had agreed to act as attorney general in his absence. After deciding that the terms of his appointment would not make him an official of the national government, Innes left Philadelphia for Kentucky in mid-November.[8] Marshall had assumed the duties of attorney general, which consisted primarily of rendering legal opinions for the state, soon after Innes's departure in October. The eight extant opinions printed in this volume indicate that Marshall acted as attorney general from October 16, 1794, to *ca.* March 21, 1795. It is quite possible that he performed these duties for a slightly longer time, although Innes was back in Virginia in April and presumably resumed advising the executive on legal questions.[9]

Marshall's first opinion was rendered several days after it was requested, because he was in Fredericksburg attending the fall session of the district court. On September 30 the Council of State had ordered a letter sent to the brigadier generals, demanding "immediate prosecutions against all Delinquents under the Militia law." Apparently the Council had decided to obtain the attorney general's opinion before transmitting the letter, but James Innes was about to leave

6. *CVSP*, VII, 374; *American State Papers. Documents, Legislative and Executive, of the Congress of the United States* . . . (Washington, D.C., 1832–1861), *Miscellaneous*, I, 926; Edmund Randolph to James Innes, Aug. 8, 1794, Domestic Letters, VII, 151–152, RG 59, National Archives. If Innes refused, Randolph asked him to inquire if JM would accept.

Randolph indicated later that the administration feared Kentucky might secede and that if Innes could help prevent this, he would in effect "save the preponderancy of federal power to the south. . . ." Randolph to Innes, Aug. 22, 1794, Domestic Letters, VII, 172–173, RG 59, Natl. Arch.

7. Henry Lee to attorney general, Aug. 14, 1794, Executive Letterbooks, Virginia State Library; JVCS, Aug. 14, 1794.

8. *CVSP*, VII, 373, 375.

9. *Ibid.*, 469–470. Innes signed for his salary on Apr. 9, 1795. The treasurer's records fail to list any salary for JM during this period. Innes's salary was recorded quarterly and was received for him by John Carter on Oct. 6, 1794; "part pay for the quarter past" was received for Innes by William Marshall on Feb. 2, 1795. Receipt Book, Oct. 1, 1794–Sept. 30, 1795, Treasurer's Office Records, Va. State Lib.

See Robert Brooke to JM, Mar. 21, 1795, for evidence that JM was still acting as attorney general.

the state and would not have had time to write an opinion. Consequently, the letter had to be held until Marshall returned from Fredericksburg. The Fredericksburg District Court adjourned on October 9, and Marshall's opinion was rendered on October 16.[1]

Opinion

ADS, Executive Papers, Virginia State Library

[Richmond], October 16, 1794

Que. 1st. Are those delinquents who have faild to obey the requisition lately made on the militia liable to the fine which is not to exceed one years pay by the Foederal law & also to ten dollars for not appearing at the place of rendezvous by the state law?[2]

2d. Are subjects or citizens of foreign powers liable to the penalties of our militia laws?

A. 1st. I rather incline to the opinion that only the fine imposd by the act of Congress ought to be collected. The words of our act of Assembly are general & I have no doubt of the power of the legislature to give additional penalties for the breach of any law of the union but I rather suppose the act of the Virginia assembly woud be construed to apply to cases to which the congressional act coud not apply.[3]

A. 2d. I do not think the subjects or citizens of foreign powers liable to the penalties of our militia law. The act of Congress plainly excludes them from the militia & the act of Assembly is expressd to be enacted for the purpose of carrying into effect the Militia System of the union.[4]

J MARSHALL

1. JVCS, Sept. 30, 1794; District Court Law Orders, B, 1794–1798, 106, Fredericksburg, Va. State Lib.

2. The federal act was adopted on May 2, 1792. 1 Stat. 264–265. The Virginia act passed on Dec. 22, 1792. 13 Hening 340, 354–355.

3. In addition to the May 2, 1792, federal statute, Congress also adopted a comprehensive militia bill on May 8. 1 Stat. 271–274. JM was repeating his belief, expressed earlier at the 1788 Virginia ratifying convention, that authority over the militia is concurrent. The Virginia act mentioned the federal law and stated the General Assembly's intention to "carry the same into effect," leaving little question that the state law was supplementary. 13 Hening 340.

4. Sec. 1 of the federal act of May 8, 1792, provided that "every free able-bodied white male citizen of the respective states" was subject to militia service. 1 Stat. 271.

Opinion

ADS, Executive Papers, Virginia State Library[5]

[Richmond], October 16, 1794

An agent appointed under the act for the more effectual collecting certain arrears of taxes & duties[6] has purchasd at a sale made in pursuance of that law a tract of land which he has since sold for a sum more considerable than he purchasd at & it is enquird whether the surplus is a gain to the commonwealth or ought to be credited to the sheriff.

The act of assembly is by no means explicit. It will admit of either construction & there is some weight in the argument in favor of either.

The object of the Commonwealth is not to speculate, but to secure the collection of debts due to itself. The purchase of the agent therefore may be considerd as a medium of collection. This idea derives aid from the clause directing the agent to sell for specie, commutables or certificates as the arrears of taxes coud or were to be dischargd by law. It woud seem probable that a discretion woud have been left with the agent to have sold for either article as shoud be most advantageous for the commonwealth if the produce of the sale was not to be credited to the sheriff.

But on the other hand if the sheriff shoud be credited with the profits of the sale he ought to be debited with the loss. It is by no means certain that this woud be the judgement of the court, for the act speaks of the purchase of the agent as an absolute purchase & not a meer substitution of himself in the place of the acting sheriff for the sole purpose of selling the property. The act too directs the amount of the sale to be indorsd on the execution. This forms an immediate credit to the sheriff & the law no where authorizes a recharge of the deficiency shoud one arise.

I am therefore of opinion that the agent ought not to credit the sheriff for the proceeds of the sale made by himself & I give that opinion with the less reluctance because, shoud the law be otherwise, the party can immediately bring it before the court & the

5. The document is endorsed "opinion, 1794, Oct. 16th, Genl. Marshall, On the Subject of Agent Davies's Letter." William Davies, of Prince George County, was appointed agent for collecting arrears of taxes for the Eighth Brigade district in Feb. 1794. JVCS, Feb. 5, 1794.

6. The act passed on Dec. 10, 1793. 1 Shepherd 229–231.

commonwealth will be aprisd on losing the profit of this sale that she is secure against loss on a future occasion where the property may sell for less than the sum given by the agent.[7]

J MARSHALL

From Edmund Randolph

Letterbook Copy, Domestic Letters, VII, 352, RG 59, National Archives

Dear Sir: Philadelphia, October 19, 1794
It is of great importance, that I should know the true state of the laws of Virginia, in relation to book debts. Be so good as to inform me by the return of the mail, whether the evidence of them stands upon any other footing, than it did, when I left Virginia; namely upon the law of October 1779, which commenced in force on the first of May 1780? You perceive, that my inquiry respects debts for goods, wares & merchandizes only.[8]

I wish also to know, whether any act has been passed in Virginia, *since the revolution war*, which changed the evidence of British debts from what it was *before the war?*[9] I am pretty confident, that none such has been passed. But accuracy is not to be dispensed with; and therefore I do not choose to trust myself after four years absence. I am dear Sir, Yr friend & servt.

EDM: RANDOLPH

7. JM was therefore advising the Council of State to use this as a test case so that the courts could interpret the law to protect the state from additional losses.

8. Randolph, U.S. attorney general from the beginning of Washington's administration, had been appointed secretary of state on Jan. 2, 1794.

9. By art. 4 of the 1783 peace treaty, debts between British subjects and American citizens were protected against "lawful Impediment." Hunter Miller, ed., *Treaties and Other International Acts of the United States of America* (Washington, D.C., 1931), II, 154.

At the time Randolph wrote this letter, John Jay was in England negotiating Jay's Treaty, which reaffirmed the debt provisions of the 1783 treaty and also provided for a commission to determine the claims of merchants unable to collect their debts in American courts. *Ibid.*, 249–251. While most federal courts proved adequate for the collection of British debts, collection in Virginia was uncertain because of the pending appeal of Ware v. Hylton. This circumstance undoubtedly led to Randolph's inquiry to JM, who was active in the defense of Virginia debtors against British merchants. In 1804, JM held for the Supreme Court that legal impediments to the recovery of British debts had existed in Virginia until 1793. Dunlop & Co. v. Ball, 6 U.S. (2 Cranch) 184. See Samuel Flagg Bemis, *Jay's Treaty: A Study in Commerce and Diplomacy*, 2d ed. rev. (New Haven, Conn., 1962), 356–358.

To Edmund Randolph

ALS, RG 59, National Archives

Dear Sir   [Richmond], October 27, 1794

Your letter of the 19th. has just reachd me. The evidence which will support an action for goods wares & merchandize sold & deliverd is precisely the same as when you left Virginia. The law upon that subject has sustaind no change since the close of the war.[1] To support an action for a British debt requires the same & no greater evidence than woud be requird from an American merchant instituting a suit of the same kind. Very respectfully, I am dear Sir your obedt.

J MARSHALL

Opinion

ADS, Executive Papers, Virginia State Library[2]

[Richmond, *ca.* November 3, 1794]
"A Statement of facts respecting the Land whereon Robert Craig late Sheriff of Washington County now lives and on which I did, as Agent,

1. An act prescribing the method of proving book debts, passed in Oct. 1748, established the admissibility of store book accounts and merchants books to prove indebtedness for goods, wares, and merchandise. A statute of limitations of two years after the transaction applied, unless the defendant had moved from the county of residence at the time of purchase, in which case the action might be brought within three years and the evidence would be admissible. 6 Hening 53–55. An act for proving book debts, adopted in 1779 but not effective until May 1, 1780, repealed the 1748 law and provided a six-month limitation for actions brought upon book debts, subject to a maximum enlargement by twelve months based upon the death of one or both of the parties. The defendant in such an action was protected by the terms of the statute even though he did not specially plead it as a defense. 10 Hening 133–134.

2. The statement signed by Taylor is in a clerk's hand; the opinion following is in JM's hand. The paper bears the endorsement "Agent Taylor's Report."

Attached to the document is a separate sheet in a third hand, reading: "The service of the execution vested the property in the sheriff, so that it became legally his for the purpose of satisfying the execution—In my opinion it passes to his representatives who may & is bound to sell—the question however came on before the last general court & was not decided. JM." The attached sheet is endorsed "Mr. Marshalls, Opinion, filed, Decr. 16. 94." These documents and some supporting information and correspondence are printed in *CVSP*, VII, 401–403. There they are dated Dec. 18, 1794, a date that appears nowhere on the document.

direct the now Sheriff of Washington to levy an execution for the arreages of taxes due from sd. Craig & Securities for the year 1788.[3]

In May 1792 this land is said to have been sold by Virtue of an execution issued against Robert Craig for arrears of taxes due from him as Sheriff for the year 1787.[4]

It is said this land contains about 180 Acres & has valuable improvements thereon & was sold at sd. Sale for eleven dollars; (which is less than three fourths of its value) & credit for three months was not offered at that time.[5]

It appeared from the oath of Alexr. Montgomery[6] that only about thirty days notice was given of the sale of sd land, that no commissioners attended to value sd Land; or were summoned to attend: he was then Sheriff of Washington.[7]

It appeared by the oath of Walter Preston that Robert Craig either advanced or offered to advance the purchase money then bid for sd. Land.

These proceedings I conceived were elegal & therefore I procecuted the business in the following manner which was put into my hands as Agent by the Commonwealth, viz:

I delivered the execution against sd Craig to Robert Campbell[8] now Sheriff of Washington & directed him immediately to levy it; which he did upon the aforementioned land; a claim was then set up to sd Land by David Carson, one of Robert Craigs securities, who called himself the purchaser; A Jury was then summoned to try the title of sd Land agreeable to law; witnesses were called on; the jury divided in opinion, seven & five, the majority for the Commonwealth.

I again appointed another day for a Jury to meet a second time viz the third of October, they accordingly meet; to ascertain the title; in the

3. John Taylor, of Montgomery County, had been appointed agent for collecting the arrears of taxes in the 17th Brigade district in Feb. 1794. JVCS, Feb. 5, 1794. The taxes left unpaid were from the 1787 levy, which were in arrears in 1788. CVSP, VII, 401.

4. Virginia had enacted several laws to compel sheriffs to settle their tax arrearages with the Commonwealth. 10 Hening 199–201 (1779), 255–256 (1780), 508 (1781); 12 Hening 474–475 (1787), 771–772 (1788). The statutory history of the problem of tax arrears seems to indicate that a variety of methods of collection had failed and that there had been a liberalization of the penal aspects of the law to encourage compliance by sheriffs and former sheriffs.

5. This was required by the 1781 statute. 10 Hening 516.

6. Alexander Montgomery was sheriff of Washington County in 1792 and 1793; his affidavit has not been found.

7. The commissioner was required to attend the sheriff's sale of lands for the settlement of tax arrears by the landowner. Presumably the same rules applied to former sheriffs whose lands were being sold to collect taxes withheld by them. The 1788 act required that eight weeks' notice of sale be given. 12 Hening 564, 565 (1787).

8. Campbell (ca. 1755–1831), brother of Col. Arthur Campbell, was a long-time magistrate of Washington County who later moved to Knoxville, Tenn. Joseph A. Waddell, Annals of Augusta County, Virginia . . . (Richmond, 1886), 397.

mean time, Alexander Montgomery the late Sheriff who sold the land executed a deed of conveyance for the same to David Carson in the Court of Washington; for the above consideration of eleven dollars & after the first execution was levied thereon; on the second meeting of a Jury on sd Land, but one witness appeared, tho several were directed to be summoned & he was objected to by some of the securities as being interested. The Case was stated however to the Jury, who were again divided, 8 to 4, a majority for the Commonwealth.

JNO. TAYLOR Agent
Novr. 3rd. 1794"

The sale made by the sheriff under the execution which was levied in 1792 seems to me to be void in consequence of the irregular procedure of the officer. He has in nothing obeyd the law. If no provision was made for the case I shoud feel no hesitation in advising the sale of the land under the second execution even altho a verdict of the jury had been renderd against the commonwealth. But the 22d. section of the 16th. Chap. of the acts of 1792 which is copied from the act of 1787[9] directs the Auditor where he shall suspect fraud in the service of an execution to make report thereof to the Executive whose duty it shall be to direct the attorney of the Commonwealth for the district county or corporation to file an information thereupon & if it shall appear that the sale was fraudulent the property shall not pass thereby. In this case the sale is in my opinion not only void through its fraud but its irregularity likewise. Yet as the irregularity seems mingled with fraud it may be most property to pursue the precise mode pointed out by the law.

J MARSHALL

Memorial

DS, Legislative Petitions: Richmond City, Virginia State Library

[Richmond], November 15, 1794

To the Honorable the Speakers & Members of the General Assembly

9. 13 Hening 474 (1792); sec. 11, 12 Hening 562 (1787).

The Memorial of Wm. F: Ast[1] and of sundry inhabitants of the City of Richmond and places adjacent most respectfully sheweth:

That the said Wm. F. Ast has suggested and drawn up a Scheme for mutual Assurance against fire. That the Subscribers being appointed a Committee to examine the same, conceive that the principles thereof are founded on a solid and equitable basis, and they are well satisfied that it will not only contribute to the Relief of Individuals by lessening the Calamities occasioned by the Ravages of fire, but will promote the public Welfare by keeping within the State considerable Sums of Money which are annually paid abroad for Insurance.

That as this institution is calculated for the benefit of the State at large it is necessary to have the approbation of the Legislature. Your memorialists therefore solicit the General Assembly to take into Consideration the annexed explanations of the plan, and pray that after such alterations therein as may be deemed proper are made that an act may be passed for incorporating the Subscribers to the mutual Assurance aforesaid under proper regulations and Restrictions.

Your memorialists think it just that the said Wm. F. Ast should have an adequate recompense for his trouble in suggesting forming & publishing the said Plan and that he should be allowed annually out of the funds of the Society one Cent for each hundred Dollars that may be insured as a Salary for which he offers to do the Duties of such Office as he may be appointed to by the said Assurance Society.[2]

J MARSHALL[3]

1. William Frederick Ast (1766–1807) was a native of Prussia who had recently settled in Richmond. W. Asbury Christian, *Richmond: Her Past and Present* (Richmond, 1912), 46–47.

2. The petition was accepted by the General Assembly, and an act "for establishing a mutual assurance society against fire in buildings in this state" was adopted with amendments on Dec. 22, 1794. *JVHD*, Nov. 1794, 12, 30, 74, 78, 96, 97, 108, 111; 1 Shepherd, 307–310. At a meeting of the society on Dec. 17, 1795, the legality of the society was questioned, and JM, as a member of the House of Delegates, was asked to present a bill prepared by a special committee to explain the act creating the society. This was done very quickly, and the bill was adopted on Dec. 23. 1 Shepherd 405–406; Minute Book, Dec. 17, 1795, Mutual Assurance Society, Richmond.

3. JM was one of 40 signers, among whom were Edward Carrington, George Wythe, Bushrod Washington, Andrew Leiper, Adam Craig, and Robert Mitchell.

Bounty Land Survey

ADS, RG 49, National Archives

November 25, 1794

Surveyed for John Marshall
1000 Acres of land on part of a
Military Warrant[4] No 30, on the
Waters of Caesars Creek beging.
at three Elms S.W. corner to
James Meriwethers survey No
1127, thence West 400 poles to
three Elms and an Ash, in the
line of Robert Roses Survey No
1079, thence North 400 poles to
a White oak Hickory, and Dog-
wood, thence East 400 poles to

No 1429.

1000 Acres

two Elms and an Ash, NW. corner to said Meriwether, thence
with his line South 400 poles to the beginning.

ISREAL COX   ⎰
GEORGE NAILOR ⎱ CC
JOHN EDGENTON M

NATHL. MASSIE[5] DS
November the 25th. 1794

Examined and Recorded May the 25th. 1795.

RICHARD C. ANDERSON.[6] S.

Bounty Land Survey

ADS, RG 49, National Archives

[*November 25, 1794.* This survey, No. 1,432, is for an additional 1,000
acres granted in military warrant No. 30 and was adjacent to the land
described in the other survey of the same date.]

4. The warrant came as a result of an act of Congress adopted on Aug. 10, 1790.
See 1 Stat. 182–184, and amendments adopted in 1794, 1 Stat. 394. JM submitted
this survey and obtained a grant for the land in 1796. Bounty Land Grant, Feb. 20,
1796, Collection of Clarence Dillon, Far Hills, N.J.
5. Nathaniel Massie (1763–1813) was a deputy surveyor in Virginia from 1780 to
1791, thereafter assigned to the Virginia military district north of the Ohio River. By
1800 he owned large tracts of land in the Northwest Territory, where he became active in Ohio politics. He was a delegate to the 1802 Ohio Constitutional Convention.
6. Anderson wrote on the verso, "I do certify that the warrant on which this Survey
was made was never before satisfied. Given under my hand and Seal of Office this
21st. day of January 1796."

Opinion

ADS, Executive Papers, Virginia State Library[7]

[Richmond], November 28, 1794

It is stated that Mr. White[8] was commissiond as sheriff on the 13th. of August 1794.

That the preceding sheriff[9] continues in office till the 6th. of Novr. so that the commission expresses that the power of Mr. White is to commence on the 6th. of November.

Several accidents prevented his giving bond & security according to law within two months after the date of his commission but in the third month he appeard in court & offerd to comply with the law.[1]

It is enquird whether under these circumstances the court ought to have receivd the bond or whether the executive ought to proceed to make another appointment.

The case of Mr. White is a hard one but the law seems to leave no discretion with the Executive to judge of those circumstances which shall dispense with a compliance with the law. The act admits of no dispensation, but positively requires the execution of the bond within a limited time or directs a new commission to issue. The circumstances then do not alter the case but the sole question seems to me to be whether the date of the commission or the commencement of the commission in effect, shall be considerd as the appointment. I think the date of the commission must be considerd as the appointment, because the appointment

7. The opinion is endorsed, probably much later, "Judge Marshall's opinion on Eli White's claim to Sheriffalty of Hanover."

8. Elisha White. See JVCS, Aug. 16, 1794.

9. John Syme. White had been trying to obtain the office at least since 1792. See JVCS, July 26, and Oct. 4, 1792.

1. A 1782 act substantially continued the colonial procedure for the appointment of sheriffs and their posting bond. The two-month limitation on filing bond, however, was not required until 1793. See 5 Hening 515–516 (1748); 11 Hening 168, 169 (1782); 13 Hening 534–535 (1792); 1 Shepherd 43 (1792).

When White failed to appear at the second meeting of the Hanover County Court after his appointment, the court notified the Council of State that another sheriff should be named. On Nov. 28, 1794, the Council ordered that another be appointed. Presumably after seeing JM's opinion, White petitioned the House of Delegates to lengthen the time required for posting bond, but that attempt failed. JVCS, Aug. 13, and Nov. 28, 1794; JVHD, Nov. 1794, 16, 30; Elisha White to the Council of State, Oct. 3, and Nov. 14, 1794, and White to the governor, Nov. 18, 1794, Executive Papers, Virginia State Library.

because every thing to be performd by the Executive is then completed.

J MARSHALL

Masonic Certificates

[*November 29, 1794 (Richmond)*. JM, as grand master of the Grand Lodge, issues two certificates directing the installation of officers of Fairfax Lodge No. 43 and Door to Virtue Lodge No. 44, in Charlottesville. Both lodges had been chartered by the Grand Lodge on this same day. Minute Book, 1777–1796, Grand Lodge A.F. & A.M. of Virginia, Richmond. Not found. See Dove, *Proceedings*, 132–133.]

Law Papers, November 1794

U.S. Circuit Court, Va.

Blane v. Archer, declaration, ADS, U.S. Circuit Court, Va., Ended Cases (Restored), 1795, Virginia State Library.[2]

Blane v. Hobday, declaration, ADS, U.S. Circuit Court, Va., Ended Cases (Restored), 1795, Va. State Lib.

Brown v. Jett, declaration, ADS, U.S. Circuit Court, Va., Ended Cases (Restored), 1795, Va. State Lib.[3]

Hatton v. Ker, declaration, ADS, U.S. Circuit Court, Va., Ended Cases (Restored), 1795, Va. State Lib.

Hunt v. Nelson, declaration, ADS, U.S. Circuit Court, Va., Ended Cases (Restored), 1795, Va. State Lib.

From William Price

ALS, Opinions of the Attorney General Related to Land Matters, Land Office Papers, Virginia State Library

Richmond, December 3, 1794

The Register of the Land Office To The Attorney Genl: Wishes to be informd if by the Act of Assembly passed the 10th of Decem-

2. See Account Book, Receipts, Jan. 1794.
3. See Account Book, Receipts, Oct. & Nov. 1793.

ber 1793, intitled "An Act giving further time to the Owners of Certificates and Plats of Survey on the Eastern Waters, to return the same to the Register of the Land Office,"[4] He (The Register) is debard from Receiving Surveys made on Treasury Warrants prior to the 15th of November 1792.

W PRICE

I think the survey may be receivd. It will be subject to a caveat.[5]

J MARSHALL

To Charles Simms

ALS, Simms Papers, Library of Congress

My dear Sir   [Richmond], December 12, 1794

I have receivd your letter of the 28th. of Novr.[6] & am very glad that the tobacco is in your hands. I had feared its miscarriage.

I am but little versd in marine law as I never practisd in the courts of admiralty & never turnd my attention to the subject. Of consequence my opinion on the case you state is not much to be relied on. If the vessel found at sea was a derelict & such she woud seem to be the subject is shortly taken up in lex mercatoria under the head of wrecks etc. & the property is declard to be in the finders.[7] I shoud myself however incline to the opinion that they woud only be entitled to salvage provided the owners of the ship &

4. 1 Shepherd 232. Price (1755–1808), nephew of Maj. William Price and son-in-law of William DuVal, was register of the Land Office from 1794 until his death in 1808.

5. JM wrote this opinion below Price's signature.

The 1793 law actually provided for a deadline of May 15, 1794, but a bill was pending in the General Assembly that would extend this period to Dec. 31, 1795. The bill became law soon after JM gave this opinion. See 1 Shepherd 296–297 (1794). For information on entering caveats against these surveys, see 1 Shepherd 70–71 (1792).

6. Not found.

7. JM was referring to Wyndham Beawes, *Lex Mercatoria Rediviva; or, A Complete Code of Commercial Law*. See 6th ed. (Dublin, 1795), 119, which indicates that if a vessel is totally forsaken by its master and crew and thereafter becomes a derelict, the first possessor who rescues it or any part of its lading "gains a Property" in the vessel or goods saved. The statement at the time JM considered it might be understood to bestow all of the saved property upon the salvor, but it is clear that no more than one-half of the value of the property would be subject to a salvage award. The remaining portion would be considered derelict property abandoned at sea, which under English law would be a droit of admiralty, payable to the crown. American law concerning

goods found shoud be discovered.[8] Whether the right be to salvage or to the whole property found it woud seem to me that the Gentleman of Alexandria, if the charter party be in the usual form, can have no claim to either. If I understand the custom rightly the person to whom a vessel is charterd acquires no right in her even for a time. He employs neither the master or hands but has meerly contracted with the owner of the vessel that she shall carry goods for him of a stipulated burthen to a certain port &, if she be charterd back again, shall bring back other goods.[9] If that be the nature of the contract in the present case it woud seem to me that the Freighters can acquire no interest in any casual acquisition of the vessel while on the voyage. I am dear sir with much esteem, Your obedt Servt.

J MARSHALL

From Robert Brooke

Copy, Executive Letterbooks, Virginia State Library[1]

[*December 16, 1794, Richmond.* Brooke transmits copies of a resolution adopted by the House of Representatives[2] and a letter from the secretary

---

droits of admiralty was unclear, but there was a growing tendency to award unclaimed derelict property to the salvor after waiting one year for the owner to claim it. See Theophilus Parsons, *A Treatise on Maritime Law* (Boston, 1859), II, 615–618, 619; Francis B. Dixon, *Abridgment of the Maritime Law . . .* (New York, 1857), 112–113; Martin J. Norris, *The Law of Salvage* (Mt. Kisco, N.Y., 1958), 219–222; and Grant Gilmore and Charles L. Black, Jr., *The Law of Admiralty* (Brooklyn, N.Y., 1957) 443–454, 514.

8. JM's supposition was correct. Salvage alone would be payable, and traditionally recovery in the case of a derelict would be higher. See Henry Flanders, *A Treatise on Maritime Law* (Boston, 1852), 316–319, 321; Herbert R. Baer, *Admiralty Law of the Supreme Court,* 2d ed. (Charlottesville, Va., 1969), 472–479. During the 18th and early 19th centuries there was an automatic rule that the salvor of a derelict was entitled to one-half of its value as his award, but that was changed by 1857. Dixon, *Abridgment,* 112–113; Norris, *Law of Salvage,* 219. For a discussion of the elements involved in the computation of salvage awards, see Gustavus H. Robinson, *Handbook of Admiralty Law in the United States* (St. Paul, Minn., 1939), 741*ff.* Robinson also indicates that from 1798 to 1828 the law of salvage in England assumed its present-day form. *Ibid.,* 710.

9. JM's distinction is one clearly recognized in modern admiralty law. A charterer is considered a demise, or bare boat charterer, only if he has exclusive possession, command, and navigation of the vessel during the voyage. Only such ownership would entitle him to participate in the salvage award. Flanders, *Treatise,* 152; Gilmore and Black, *Admiralty,* 170–171, 467–470.

1. The letter is addressed as a "Circular to the Brigadier Generals." Brooke became governor on Dec. 1, 1794, replacing Henry Lee. JVCS, Dec. 1, 1794; Richard R. Beeman, *The Old Dominion and the New Nation, 1788–1801* (Lexington, Ky., 1972), 136.

2. Joseph Gales, comp., [*Annals of Congress*] *Debates and Proceedings in the Congress of*

of war thanking the Virginia militia for its service in suppressing the Whiskey Rebellion. He asks that these copies be distributed within the brigade.]

From Robert Brooke

Copy, Executive Letterbooks, Virginia State Library

[*December 18, 1794, Richmond.* Brooke requests the dates of all military commissions held by JM in order to properly assign rank to the brigadier generals.[3]]

To St. George Tucker

ALS, Tucker-Coleman Papers, Swem Library, College of William and Mary

Dear Sir   [Richmond, *ca.* December 1794]
Mr. Roane is elected Judge of the court of Appeals![4]
Your causes or rather those of Mr. Randolph have been tried. Presentation of the bills to Mr. John Randolph in his life time was completely provd.[5] From a defect however in the procedure the plf. was nonsuited. Your

J MARSHALL

Law Papers, December 1794

U.S. Circuit Court, Va.

Buchanan, Hastie & Co. v. Sullivant, stipulation, ADS, U.S. Circuit Court, Va., Ended Cases (Restored), 1794, Virginia State Library.

---

the United States, *1789–1824* (Washington, D.C., 1849), 3d Cong., 2d sess., Dec. 4, 1794, 966.

3. The letter is addressed as a "Circular to the Brigadier Generals." The principles for determining rank among the brigadier generals are in JVCS, Aug. 13, 1794.

4. Spencer Roane was elected on Dec. 2, 1794, replacing Henry Tazewell, who had been elected to the U.S. Senate. *JVHD,* Nov. 1794, 58; Robert Brooke to Roane, Dec. 3, 1794, Executive Letterbooks, Virginia State Library.

5. Tucker had married the widow of John Randolph of "Matoax," father of John Randolph of Roanoke. Apparently he was trying to settle Randolph's estate, claims against which were sizable and not finally resolved until 1829. U.S. Circuit Court, Va., Record Book, XIX, 17–28, Va. State Lib. For a possible connection, see JM to Patrick Henry, Aug. 31, 1790.

Hunt v. Baylor, declaration, AD, U.S. Circuit Court, Va., Ended Cases (Unrestored), Va. State Lib.

Lynch's Administrator v. Donald & Co., bill in chancery, AD, U.S. Circuit Court, Va., Ended Cases (Unrestored), 1806, Va. State Lib.

Maury v. Austin & Co., declaration, ADS, U.S. Circuit Court, Va., Ended Cases (Restored), 1795, Va. State Lib.

Van Bibber v. Robins, declaration, ADS, U.S. Circuit Court Va., Ended Cases (Restored), 1795, Va. State Lib.

Vaughan v. Parker, declaration, ADS, U.S. Circuit Court, Va., Ended Cases (Restored), 1795, Va. State Lib.

From John Wayles Eppes

ALS, U.S. Circuit Court, Va., Ended Cases (Restored), 1797, Virginia State Library[6]

[Richmond, *ca.* 1794]

J W Eppes with his respects to Mr. Marshall encloses the papers which were lodged with Colo: Innes by his father.[7] If Mr. Marshall can spare Powel[8] on contracts he will be kind enough to send it by the bearer.

6. JM endorsed the letter "Wayles extrs ads. Farrel & Jones." It is filed with the case papers of Jones v. Wayles's Executors, an action on the case in assumpsit for the proceeds from the sale of a cargo of slaves. Also known as the "Guineaman case," this action was commenced in the circuit court in Nov. 1790 by Jerman Baker. The declaration was filed in Nov. 1791; JM's pleas filed in Nov. 1792 are missing. From Mar. 1794 to Nov. 1796 the parties were engaged in taking depositions upon open commissions and in preparing for trial. The editors have assumed that this letter, which transmitted to JM the accounts to be introduced into evidence, copies of bonds relating to the slave sales, and a certified copy of John Wayles's will, was sent sometime in 1794 in anticipation of an immediate trial. See JM's opinion, Apr. 1, 1791.

7. John Wayles Eppes (1772–1823), son of Francis Eppes, had attended the University of Pennsylvania and Hampden-Sydney College and was admitted to the bar in 1794. After representing Chesterfield County in the House of Delegates from 1801 to 1803, he was elected to Congress and served until he was defeated for reelection in 1810. He won election in 1812 for one more term. He went to the U.S. Senate in 1817 but resigned because of ill health in 1819.

8. John Joseph Powell, *Essay Upon the Law of Contracts and Agreements* (London, 1790); the first American edition was published at Walpole, N.H., in 1802. See Account Book, Disbursements, Mar. 1794.

Opinion

ADS, Executive Papers, Virginia State Library[9]

[Richmond, *ca.* 1794]

It is askd whether a magistrate who was in the commission of the peace[1] duely qualified under the existing laws previous to the 1st. of June 89 & who faild to take the oath prescribd by the act of Congress entitled "an act to regulate the time & manner of administering certain oaths" within the time limited by that act,[2] may resume his seat at this day upon taking the said oath?

The act of the United States directing the time & manner of administering the oath to the Government does not proceed to declare the office to be vacated by declining to do so. I shoud consider that law then rather as suspending the exercise of the duties of the office than as entirely ousting from the office, the person who has faild to take the oath. If so the oath may I think yet be administerd & the magistrate may on taking it resume the duties of the office.

J MARSHALL

Opinion

ADS, Executive Papers, Virginia State Library[3]

[Richmond, *ca.* 1794]

The following questions are stated to the Executive & an answer to them is requested.

The militia march out of the state under a requisition of the

9. The document is endorsed "Mr. Marshall, Opinion, On Oaths to be taken by Magistrates under the Act of Congress." In the absence of any indication of the date of JM's opinion, the editors have assumed that it was given sometime during 1794, when JM was serving as acting attorney general of Virginia.

1. That is, a magistrate duly appointed and commissioned under the laws of Virginia.

2. Sec. 3 of the federal act of June 1, 1789, required all state executive and judicial officers to take the prescribed oath to support the Constitution on or before Sept. 1, 1789. 1 Stat 23–24.

3. The opinion is endorsed "Marshalls Opinion on Militia Law," and the date "1794" was added in another hand. The internal evidence of the document supports this date, as does JM's service as acting attorney general for Virginia during that year.

President. The Executive of the state makes the requisition to the Officers of the Militia who have taken the oath to the commonwealth only.

Quaere. By what law are the officers to consider themselves bound as they are only acting under a state requisition & acting under this state law until the command is given to a Foedl. Officer?

2dl. Under these circumstances how are defaulters to be tried by state or Foedl. law while in the state & how are the fines to be appropriated to state or continental purposes?

3dly How are deserters to be punishd—I mean those who deserted after appearing at the brigade rendezvous & never joind their corps at the general rendezvous?

I presume the above queries are to be considerd not as abstract propositions but as applying to the late requisition on the Militia.[4] If they are so to be considerd then I think the real case widely differing from that supposd by the gentleman who makes the enquiries.

The requisition made by the Executive being in observance of a requisition made by the President is itself a continental requisition. The Officers are not to consider themselves as acting under a state ⟨commission⟩ requisition, nor is the command to be given to a Foedl. officer at all, but the militia officers of the state are to consider themselves as acting under the Foedl. government, in con-

---

4. On two occasions in 1794 Congress authorized the president to requisition state militias to serve out of their states of origin. The possibility of war with either France or Great Britain resulted in the act of May 9, 1794, that permitted 80,000 men to be called into federal service. The act of Nov. 29, 1794, authorized the calling forth of militia to deal with the Whiskey Rebellion in western Pennsylvania. The organic act of May 2, 1792, systematized calling forth the militia and included a provision that men so called into federal service would be subject to the articles of war applicable to federal troops. 1 Stat. 264–265 (1792), and 367–368, 403 (1794).

The confusion discussed in this opinion probably resulted from the form of the May 1794 statute, which restated substantial portions of the 1792 organic act but failed to include the provision that the militiamen were to be subject to the federal articles of war. This omission left congressional intent in doubt and permitted speculation that troops in service after May 1794 were not subject to the articles of war and were perhaps not actually called into federal service as the 1792 act provided.

By the time the Nov. 29, 1794, statute was enacted, Virginia militiamen were already in Pennsylvania on federal service. This authorizing statute resolved some of the confusion created by the earlier enactment, since it merely authorized the requisition without repeating any of the provisions of the 1792 organic law. For information on the Whiskey Rebellion, see Leland D. Baldwin, *Whiskey Rebels: The Story of a Frontier Uprising* (Pittsburgh, 1939); Richard H. Kohn, *Eagle and Sword: The Federalists and the Creation of the Military Establishment in America, 1783–1802* (New York, 1975), 139–173. See also James Wood to JM, Sept 4, 1794.

formity with the Foedl. law & as executing the orders of the President given through the Constitutional channel.[5]

2dl. The defaulters will be tried by the Foedl. law & the fines are to be collected by the Foedl. officer & appopriated as directed by the laws of the Union.[6]

3dly. I consider those who deserted after being deliverd up to the officer commanding the detachment as subject to martial law. They were properly tryable by a court martial composd of the officers belonging to the detachment[7] but as the service is over before a tryal has taken place there is great difficulty in saying how they are to be tryed. I rather suppose the law in this to be defective. If there is any mode of tryal it must be by a court calld by the Executive.[8]

J MARSHALL

Law Papers, 1794

U.S. Circuit Court, Va.

Hunter's Administrator v. Robb & Co., motion in arrest of judgment, ADS, in the file of *United States v. Walker*, U.S. Circuit Court, Va., Ended Cases (Restored), 1794, Virginia State Library.

5. In other words, federal service began immediately upon the issuance of the president's requisition to the governors, and thereafter the state authorities were acting pursuant to a delegation of the constitutional power from the president.
6. While sitting in the U.S. Circuit Court for Virginia in 1815, JM elaborated upon this point. A Virginia militiaman had failed to obey an order to take the field under a federal requisition during the War of 1812, and as a result of his refusal, he was court-martialed by a Virginia military tribunal convened under the state military law. JM held that since the offense was against federal authority and orders, it might only be punished by a federally convened court-martial. Meade v. Deputy Marshal, 1 Brock. 324–329 (Cir. Ct. Va. 1815).
7. Sec. 6 of the May 2, 1792, act required that militiamen in federal service be tried by courts-martial composed of militia officers. 1 Stat. 264.
8. In Meade v. Deputy Marshal, JM held that the proper procedure under Virginia law for the trial of privates not in actual service was in courts of inquiry and not in state courts-martial. 1 Brock 324, 328.

To Henry Tazewell

Printed extract, American Art Association—Anderson Galleries, Inc., Catalog
No. 3916 (New York, October 20, 1931), 41

[*January 11, 1795, Richmond.* "Our wheat is about three shillings per
bushel lower than it is in Philadelphia & New York. This some aristocrats
ascribe to proscription of money'd men & to the perseverence of the
legislature in refusing to permit a branch of the national bank to discount
in Virginia at six per cent but the good democrats & real friends of this
country are sure that it must be attributable to Hamilton, Jay & the
Devil. . . ." Not found.]

From James Wood

Copy, Executive Letterbooks, Virginia State Library

[*January 16, 1795, Richmond.* Having received word that the ship *Les
Jumeaux* had left Philadelphia in December partially armed as a cruiser,
Wood alerts JM that the ship might appear in one of the ports under his
jurisdiction in order to complete the outfitting. He instructs JM to seize
the ship if found.⁹]

Law Papers, January 1795

U.S. Circuit Court, Va.

Hunt v. Baylor's Executor, declaration, copy, U.S. Circuit Court, Va.,
Record Book, V, 569–570, Virginia State Library.

Hunt v. Nelson, declaration, copy, U.S. Circuit Court, Va., Record
Book, IV, 110, Va. State Lib.

9. The letter is addressed as a "Circular to the Commandants of the Counties in
which are Ports of Entry & delivery" and is written "In Council." Wood was writing
as lieutenant governor. The contents of the letter are taken from Timothy Pickering
to Robert Brooke, Jan. 6, 1795, *CVSP*, VII, 417–418.
Les Jumeaux, also known as *Le Casius*, apparently sailed directly to the West Indies.
For an account of the subsequent legal action taken against the vessel, see *State Papers
and Publick Documents of the United States . . .*, 3d ed. (Boston, 1819), II, 136–138.

High Court of Chancery

Morris v. Alexander & Co., interrogatories, AD, Arents Collection, Catalog No. S0826, Tobacco Documents, Robert Morris, 1785–1798, New York Public Library.

From Tench Coxe

Letterbook Copy, RG 58, National Archives[1]

Sir,   Philadelphia, February 1, 1795
The Supervisor of the Revenue for Virginia (Edwd. Carrington Esqr.) has been recently authorized to engage you on behalf of the United States, to maintain and defend, in concert with the attorney for the District, one or more Suits, or other law cases arising out of the act laying duties upon certain descriptions of wheel carriages.[2]

Your departure from Richmond before my letter arrived at that place may have prevented the necessary application of the Supervisor. Wherefore this is made. If no impediment to your engaging your co-operation exists you will permit me to refer on the subject of Fee to the Supervisor.[3]

There is a letter from the Attorney General of the United States, and another from the Secretary of the Treasury, which I should wish to subject to your inspection, if you are not preventing from

1. Transcribed in Letters Sent by the Commissioner of Revenue, 1794–1795.

2. Coxe wrote to Carrington on Jan. 14 asking that JM be retained, but by the time his letter arrived in Richmond, JM had left for Philadelphia to argue the case of Ware v. Hylton before the U.S. Supreme Court. Although the argument of that appeal was postponed to the next term, JM was admitted to practice before the Supreme Court on Feb. 2, 1795. Letters Sent by the Commissioner of Revenue, 1794–1795, RG 58, National Archives; U.S. Supreme Court Minutes, Feb. 2, 1795, RG 267, Natl. Arch.

Alexander Campbell was the district attorney.

The statute imposing a tax on carriages had been challenged by Daniel L. Hylton by an action in the U.S. Circuit Court for Virginia; it was subsequently appealed to the Supreme Court, which decided in favor of the constitutionality of the tax in Hylton v. U.S. 1 Stat. 373–375 (1794); 3 U.S. (3 Dall.) 171–184 (1796).

3. JM declined this appointment either orally or in an unfound letter on Feb. 1 or 2, informing Coxe that he was already engaged in the case against the United States. Coxe to Carrington, Feb. 2, 1795, Letters Sent by the Commissioner of Revenue, 1794–1795, RG 58, Natl. Arch.

engaging, and if I knew where I would have an opportunity to see you. I am, Sir, very respectfully, your most obedient Servant.

(Signed) TENCH COXE[4]

Commissr. of the Revenue

Masonic Summons

DS, Henry E. Huntington Library[5]

Richmond, [February 18, 1795]

To the Worshipfull N.W. Price, Grand Secretary you are hereby requested to order the Grand Tyler,[6] to Summon the Worshipfull W. Finnie, P.M., Ws.Burgh Lodge, John Groves, John Cunliff & Jos. Darmsdat, P.Ms. of Lodge no. 10, Cornelius Buck, Master, Lodge no. 14, Jacob Ege, P.M., Lodge no 19, William Bentley, P.M, Lodge no 20, Alexander Campbell, PM, Lodge no 36, William Nimmo, Master, Lodge no 36, Brothers John Lennox & James McMillan, William Austin, Lodge no 36,[7] To meet at the Masons Hall on Sunday morning 10'Clock, precisely. Then & there to take under consideration, a Certain matter, which will be laid before them. Herin fail not.

J MARSHALL G.M.

4. Coxe (1755–1824), a political economist and lawyer by training, had been a member of the 1786 Annapolis Convention and the Continental Congress. He served as commissioner of the revenue from 1792 to Dec. 1797.

5. The summons is endorsed on the verso, in a hand other than JM's, "The Warrant from the Most W G.M. to summons a Committee to investigate the difference between Jacob Abrahams & J K Read, 5795." See JM's letter of Feb. 18, 1795, to the men summoned in this letter, who constituted a Masonic trial commission, for a description of the dispute between Abrahams and Read.

6. John Van Kautzman was serving as grand tyler at this time.

7. William Finnie, of Williamsburg, had served as a quartermaster general during the Revolution and as mayor of Williamsburg in 1785. John Groves, John Cunliffe (a merchant, d. 1824), Joseph Darmsdat, Jacob Ege (1754–1795), Alexander Campbell, William Nimmo, John Lennox, James McMillan, and William Austin (d. 1807) were all members of Richmond lodges. William Bentley represented Scottsville Lodge, and Cornelius Buck represented Petersburg Lodge.

To Masonic Trial Commission

Copy, Minute Book, 1777–1796, Grand Lodge A.F. & A.M. of Virginia, Richmond

Richmond, February 18, 1795

To the Worshipfull William Finnie, P M, Wmsburg Lodge, John Groves, John Cunliffee & Joseph Darmsdatt, P. Ms, Richmd Lodge no 10, Cornelius Buck, Master, Lodge no. 14, Jacob Ege, P M, Lodge No 19, William Bentley, P M, Lodge No 20, The Worshipfull Alexander Campbell, P M, Lodge No 36, William Nimmo, Master, Lodge 36, Nathaniel W Price, Grand Secretary, Brothers John Lenox James McMillan & Wm. Austin, Members of Lodge No 36, Greeting

Whereas our Right Worshipfull John K Read Master of the Richmond Randolph Lodge No 19, hath this day made complaint to me that a certain Jacob Abrahams, a member of the Portsmouth Lodge No 16, hath unjustifiably impeached him, with having, contrary to the Known & established usage of worthy masons, had Carnal Knowledge of his wife, & as such conduct should it be *duly* proven, must lend to the destruction of the order of free and Accepted Masons, and bring the fraternity into contempt and disrepute. At the Especial desire and request of our aforesaid Brother John K Read, I hereby authorize and direct you, to meet in the Masons-hall on sunday morning precisely at 10 oClock, in order that you may investigate the said accusation, the charge being not only of great consequence to the Craft in general, but greatly important to our Brother Read, whose reputation has already suffered considerably, and whom if the charge is not *duly* and *unequivocally* proven, must have had great injustice done, not only to his Masonic, but to his private character. Trusting therefore to your diligent Circumspection in the case before you, I direct that you make due Report of your proceedings to me, and for so doing this shall be your sufficient Warrant. Given under my hand and seal this 18th. day of February 5795

(Signed) JOHN MARSHALL G M [LS]

From Masonic Trial Commission

Copy, Minute Book, 1777–1796, Grand Lodge A.F. & A.M. of Virginia, Richmond

[*February 22, 1795 (Richmond)*. The Masonic trial commission, appointed by JM as grand master of the Grand Lodge to investigate the charges made by Jacob Abrahams against John K. Read, returns to JM the report of their proceedings and their opinion that the charge is malicious and without foundation and that Read is innocent of the charges. The trial commission's report was accepted and confirmed by the Grand Lodge on Nov. 24, 1795. Minute Book, 1777–1796, Grand Lodge A.F. & A.M. of Virginia, Richmond.]

To Robert Brooke

ALS, Executive Papers, Virginia State Library[8]

Sir   [Richmond, *ca.* March 2, 1795]

The contest between the Commonwealth & Mr. Fairfax depending in the court of appeals will come on of course for decision at the next term. As I am not certain whether the title of citizen purchasers may be considerd as precisely the same with that of Mr. Fairfax I deem it incumbent on me as the counsel of that gentleman, & I hold it a duty to those purchasers not to be dispensd with, to assert their title.[9] I have therefore prepard the enclosd bill[1] which I mean to file in the court of chancery. As expedition seems to me to be unquestionably the interest as well of the commonwealth as of those who think their plain rights improperly suspended, I take the liberty to enclose the bill to you sir for your

8. Addressed to "His Excellency the Governor," the letter was endorsed on two occasions by two clerks as follows: "Mr. Marshall, On the Subject of Denny Fairfax, Postponed," and "Mr. Marshalls Letter on Subject of Fairfax's Land, Done 2d March 1795." In view of JM's desire for dispatch, it is likely that he wrote this letter only a day or two before the Council of State acted on it. JVCS, Mar. 2, 1795.

9. The citizen purchasers were JM, James M. Marshall, and others, who were now parties to the articles of agreement of Feb. 1, 1793, and who as such held equitable title to the land as purchasers under an executory contract of sale. JM was attempting hereby to add strength to the appeal of Fairfax v. Commonwealth. When this failed he adopted another line of attack by filing in the Dumfries District Court a traverse to the inquest of office found by the Fauquier County jury in the name of the purchasers. See Fairfax Lands: Editorial Note, Feb. 1, 1793, and JM to Charles Lee, *ca.* 1795.

1. Not found.

perusal, with a hope, that the officers of the commonwealth will be directed not to await the process of subpoenas & attachments but to bring the question to a fair decision on its merits at the next term.[2] I shoud not venture Sir to make this proposal if I did not suppose it to be the wish as well as interest of Governments to have the immediate use of the property in contest if its title shall be good. With very much respect I remain Sir, Your Obedt. Servt.

J MARSHALL

From Robert Brooke

Copy, Executive Letterbooks, Virginia State Library

Sir,   Richmond, March 2, 1795

In reply to your letter respecting the contest between the commonwealth and Mr. Fairfax now depending in the Court of Appeals, I have to inform you, that, although it is by no means the wish of the Executive to procrastinate the decision in that case, they do not see the propriety of dispensing with the usual Steps of prosecution in the suit you propose instituting in the Court of Chancery, but wish the common forms of the law to be observed, which perhaps may involve certain necessary delays; but I beg you will be assured that you will experience none but what are necessary. I am with much esteem etc.

ROBERT BROOKE

2. The normal preliminary process in chancery required the petitioner to file his bill with the court, requesting that a subpoena issue. In the absence of any objections on grounds of propriety, the subpoena would issue, and if the defendant was not present on appearance day, an attachment (a form of writ ordering the defendant's arrest) would be awarded, returnable to the next term of court. While Virginia procedure eliminated the English procedures leading to a commission of rebellion and an order of sequestration, the issuance of an order for an attachment might consume several months. Since the state was to be the defendant in JM's action, the Council of State was in the position to expedite the procedure by filing an answer soon after the bill was filed, making the lengthy process of subpoena and attachment unnecessary. On chancery procedures involved here, see Tucker, *Blackstone's Commentaries*, III, 442–445; 13 Hening 415–416 (1792).

From William Price

ALS, Opinions of the Attorney General Related to Land Matters, Land Office Papers, Virginia State Library

Sir   Richmond, March 3, 1795

A number of very large Surveys have been recd. in the Land Office, within six Months past, including a number of prior claims without mentioning the different quantities or Claiments. As the Grants will shortly be called for, I wish to be informed by you whether or not am I authorised to issue Grants on such Surveys. I am Sir, Yr. Obt. Sert.

WM. PRICE Regr.

The inconvenience which may result from such grants as are above describd is obvious but the Register seems to me to have no power to withhold the patent.[3]

J MARSHALL

From Robert Brooke

Copy, Executive Letterbooks, Virginia State Library

Sir,   Richmond, March 21, 1795

I will be much obliged to you to turn your attention to the enclosed and favor me with your opinion on them for the information of the Escheator of Fairfax.[4]

The inquisition[5] referred to in his letter is not in our possession it having been submitted to the consideration of the Attorney General and not returned to us.

As however it was not acted on or returned to the Court, in the

3. 1 Shepherd 72 (1792), but see also 1 Shepherd 361 (1795). JM wrote his opinion on the bottom of Price's letter.

4. The enclosed letter from Roger West, the escheator of Fairfax County, to Gov. Brooke has not been found. JM's opinion, also not found, was transmitted to West on Mar. 23, 1795. Robert Brooke to Roger West, Mar. 23, 1795, Executive Letterbooks, Virginia State Library.

5. This apparently refers to an inquisition of office found in Fairfax County against part of Denny Martin Fairfax's land. The law required that the judgment be filed with the district court having jurisdiction within one month of the inquisition. Since this had not been done, West wanted to repeat the procedure by holding a second inquest. JM was still acting as attorney general at this time.

time directed by law, might not a Second jury be impannelled. I am with much respect etc.

ROBERT BROOKE.

Masonic Dispensation

[*April 15, 1795, Richmond*. JM, as grand master of the Grand Lodge, signs a dispensation authorizing Richmond Randolph Lodge No. 19 to initiate Benjamin Colver as a Mason. Richmond Randolph Lodge No. 19 Records, 1787–1801, Grand Lodge A.F. & A.M. of Virginia, Richmond. Not found.]

From Robert Brooke

Copy, Executive Letterbooks, Virginia State Library

Sir[6]   Richmond, April 30, 1795

I send you enclosed a list of the Arms and Accoutrements furnished by the Commonwealth to the Brigade of Militia under your command, and have to request that you will appoint some proper person or persons to examine and cause to be reported to the Executive the particular number, state and condition of such Arms and Accoutrements. I am Sir etc.

ROBERT BROOKE.

Receipt

ADS, University of Virginia Law Library

[*May 13, 1795 (Richmond)*. JM witnesses a receipt of John Littlejohn, administrator of Michael Welch, from Christian and Stuffell Orandorf for £68 11s. 1d. on account of Henry Cookus's estate. See petition calendared at Feb. 18, 1792, and fees entered at Account Book, Receipts, Feb. 1792, and May 1795.]

6. The letter was addressed to "Brigadier Generals Williams, Marshall, Meade, Mason, Bradby, Mathews and Jones, each." James Bradby, of Surry County, was brigadier general of the Eighth Brigade. The substance of the letter was ordered written by the Council of State the day before. JVCS, Apr. 29, 1795.

Fairfax v. Hunter

Declaration

Copy, U.S. Circuit Court, Va., Ended Cases (Restored), 1795, Virginia State Library

[*May 30, 1795, Richmond.* JM, as attorney for Denny Martin Fairfax, files a declaration in ejectment in the U.S. Circuit Court for Virginia, claiming 788 acres of land in Shenandoah County.]

Fairfax v. Hunter

Stipulation

ADS, U.S. Circuit Court, Va., Ended Cases (Restored), 1795, Virginia State Library

[*(ca. June 1, 1795), Richmond.* JM as attorney for Denny Martin Fairfax submits a lengthy stipulation of the state of facts agreed to between counsel preliminary to argument before the U.S. Circuit Court for Virginia. The stipulation sets forth the title of Lord Fairfax, the text of his will, various acts of the Virginia House of Burgesses and General Assembly, and the provisions of the 1783 peace treaty with Great Britain.[7]]

Deed

DS, Edmund Jennings Lee Papers, Virginia Historical Society[8]

[*June 21, 1795, Richmond.* JM witnesses Henry Lee's signature on a warranty deed conveying "Belvidere," in Henrico County, to Bushrod Washington for consideration of £2,000. JM was one of the witnesses who later appeared before the General Court on Nov. 13 to prove the deed.]

7. The case was argued in the circuit court on June 6, 1795, and the court awarded judgment for the plaintiff. Hunter's appeal to the U.S. Supreme Court was nonprossed on Feb. 13, 1797. See Fairfax Lands: Editorial Note, Feb. 1, 1793.
8. This is item no. Mss1L5113a53 in the society's collections.

From Thomas Jefferson

[*July 9, 1795.* Listed in Jefferson's "Summary Journal of Letters," Jefferson Papers, Library of Congress. Not found.]

Bond

Deed Book Copy, Office of the Clerk of the Fauquier County Circuit Court, Warrenton, Va.

[Warrenton], July 10, 1795

Know all Men by these presents that we John Marshall Charles Marshall Martin Pickett & Septimus Norris are held and firmly bound unto Robert Brooke Esqr: Governor of this Common Wealth and to his Successors for the use of the Common Wealth in the just and full sum of ten thousand pounds current Money of Virginia to which payment well and truly to be made we and each of us bind our and each of our heirs Exors. & admrs. jointly & severally firmly by these Presents sealed with our seals & dated the 10th. Day of July 1795. Whereas John Blackwell in virtue of his office as Escheator did heretofore hold an office of Escheat upon that part of the manor of Leeds the property of Denny Fairfax which lies in the County of Fauquier and upon the said office the title was discussed in favor of the Common Wealth the said Denny being considered by the Jury as an alien[9] and upon which the said John Blackwell was directed by the Executive to take upon himself the collection of the rents and profits arising from the said Land until the final decision upon the said Escheat And whereas the said Denny by his Agents have applied to the said John Blackwell to take the collection of the said rents until the final decision he the said Denny claiming title thereto & upon which application the said John Blackwell hath agreed to give up the collection of the aforesaid rents Now the Condition of the above obligation is such that if the above bound John Marshall Charles Marshall Martin Pickett & Septimus Norris do and shall in all things well and truly indemnify & save harmless the said John Blackwell his heirs Exors. & adms. from all costs and Damages of every kind

9. See Fairfax Lands: Editorial Note, Feb. 1, 1793, for information on this escheat proceeding.

whatever that otherwise might ensue in consequence of the said Collection being given up to the said Denny Fairfax or his Agents and shall also without Delay pay or cause to be paid into the Public treasury all such rents and profits as may be collected by the said Denny Fairfax or his agents upon that part of the said Manor of Leeds upon which the said office has been found provided the final Judgment upon the said Escheat should be discussed in favor of the Common Wealth that then the above obligation shall be void otherwise to remain in full force & virtue

JOHN MARSHALL by L.S
CHARLES MARSHALLL his atto.[1]

Sealed & Delivered⎫
In presence of   ⎬
                      ⎭

CHARLES MARSHALL L.S
MARTIN PICKETT L.S.
SEPTIMUS NORRIS L.S.

At a Court held for Fauquier County the 26th: Day of October 1795 This Bond was acknowledged by the said Charles Marshall Attorney in fact for John Marshall Charles Marshall and Martin Pickett to be their act & Deed and ordered to be certified And at a Court continued & held for the said County the 27th: Day of October 1795 The same was acknowledged by the said Septimus Norris to be his Act & Deed and ordered to be recorded.

Teste F: BROOKE CC

To an Unknown Person

[*July 12, 1795, Richmond*. JM writes to an attorney about an action in the Supreme Court. Listed in American Art Association—Anderson Galleries, Inc., Catalog No. 2324 (New York, Feb. 27, 1929), 50. Not found.]

To Thomas Jefferson

[*August 1, 1795*. Listed in Jefferson's "Summary Journal of Letters," Jefferson Papers, Library of Congress. Not found.]

1. JM's power of attorney to Charles Marshall is printed at July 4, 1794.

To Mary Payne

Printed extract, Walter R. Benjamin Autographs, Inc., *The Collector*, LXXVII (New York, 1964), item E–74

[*August 5, 1795, Richmond.* "I was employd in your business & receivd a fee from Mr. Washington.[2] . . . From the representation of your case made me by Mr. Washington I thought it in your favor but I cannot now write you anything positive about it. On the return of that Gentleman I will give you the result of our consultation. . . ."]

Masonic Dispensation

[*August 15, 1795, Richmond.* JM, as grand master of the Grand Lodge, signs a dispensation authorizing Richmond Randolph Lodge No. 19 to initiate John Chisholm as a Mason. Richmond Randolph Lodge No. 19 Records, 1787–1801, Grand Lodge A.F. & A.M. of Virginia, Richmond. Not found.]

From George Washington

Letterbook Copy, Washington Papers, Library of Congress

Private
Dear Sir,   Philadelphia, August 26, 1795
The Office of Attorney General of the U States has become vacant by the death of Willm. Bradford esqr.[3]

I take the earliest opportunity of asking if you will accept the appointment? The salary annexed thereto & the prospect of a lucrative practice in this city, the present seat of the general Government, must be as well known to you—better perhaps—than they are to me, & therefore I shall say nothing concerning them.

2. Bushrod Washington. See Account Book, Receipts, July & Aug. 1795, for JM's fee from "Mrs. Payne."

3. Bradford (1755–1795) had died on Aug. 23. He had practiced law in York, Pa., after serving in the Revolution as a deputy muster-master general. In 1780 he became attorney general of Pennsylvania, and in 1791 he was appointed a justice of that state's supreme court. Washington had appointed him the second U.S. attorney general on Jan. 28, 1794.

If your answer is in the affirmative, it will readily occur to you that no unnecessary time should be lost in repairing to this place. If on the contrary it should be in the negative (which I should be very sorry for) it might be as well to say nothing of this offer. But in either case I pray you to give me an answer as promptly as you can. With esteem & regard, I am etc.

G. WASHINGTON

To George Washington

ALS, RG 59, National Archives

Sir   Richmond, August 31, 1795

I had the honor of receiving a few minutes past your letter of the 26th. inst.

While the business I have undertaken to complete in Richmond,[4] forbids me to change my situation tho for one infinitely more eligible, permit me Sir to express my sincere acknowledgments for the offer your letter contains, & the real pride & gratification I feel at the favorable opinion it indicates.

I respect too highly the offices of the present government of the United States to permit it to be suspected that I have declind one of them. I remain Sir with the most respectful esteem & attachment, Your obedt. Servt.

JOHN MARSHALL

Law Papers, August 1795

U.S. Circuit Court, Va.

Savage's Executors v. Govan, bill in chancery, AD, U.S. Circuit Court, Va., Ended Cases (Unrestored), Virginia State Library.

4. JM was referring to the Fairfax title issue. See Fairfax Lands: Editorial Note, Feb. 1, 1793. Washington appointed Charles Lee to the position on Dec. 10, 1795.

Birth of Mary Marshall

Entry, Marshall Family Bible, Collection of Mrs. Kenneth R. Higgins, Richmond

[*September 13, 1795 (Richmond)*. A notation in JM's hand indicates that his daughter, Mary Marshall,[5] was born on this day.]

From Thomas Jefferson

[*October 20, 1795*. Listed in Jefferson's "Summary Journal of Letters," Jefferson Papers, Library of Congress. Not found.]

Lease

Copy, Richmond City Deed Book, Office of the Chancery and Hustings Court Clerk, Richmond

[*October 22, 1795, Richmond*. JM,[6] among a committee of Edward Carrington, William Marshall, and William DuVal appointed by the Richmond City Common Hall, transfers for 21 years to Samuel Parsons, of Goochland County, a tract of city property known as the tanyard. Rent is to be $30 per year. Endorsements indicate Parsons assigned the lease to Benjamin Tate[7] on the following day. JM and William Marshall appeared before a Dec. 14, 1795, meeting of the Hustings Court to acknowledge the lease, but others delayed appearing, and the lease was not recorded until July 11, 1796.]

To Thomas Jefferson

[*October 29, 1795*. Listed in Jefferson's "Summary Journal of Letters," Jefferson Papers, Library of Congress. Not found.]

5. Mary, JM's only daughter to live past infancy, married Gen. Jacqueline Burwell Harvie (1788–1856), son of John Harvie, in 1813. She died in 1841.

6. JM had been elected again to the Richmond Common Council on July 1, 1794. He took his seat on July 12, after refusing the office of mayor. He was still serving in May 1795, when the extant records end, and was presumably a member when this lease was executed. Richmond City Common Hall Records, II, 58–59, Virginia State Library.

7. Tate (1764–1823), a local tanner and currier, was mayor of Richmond in 1811.

From Thomas Jefferson

[*October 29, 1795.* Listed in Jefferson's "Summary Journal of Letters," Jefferson Papers, Library of Congress. Not found.]

Law Papers, October 1795

U.S. Circuit Court, Va.

Buchanan, Hastie & Co. v. Sullivant, notice of taking deposition, AD, U.S. Circuit Court, Va., Ended Cases (Restored), 1794, Virginia State Library.

Fairfax v. Hunter, declaration (ejectment for 60 acres in Berkeley County), copy, U.S. Circuit Court, Va., Ended Cases (Restored), 1796, Va. State Lib.

From Robert Morris

Letterbook Copy, Morris Papers, Library of Congress

Dear Sir   Philadelphia, November 2, 1795

Your Brother & my Daughter Left us[8] this day two weeks and from the weather we judge they got to Sea soon after, as yet the Pilot has not returned so that I have not heard from them. I promised your Brother to remit you $3500 & should have done it the day of his Departure but disappointments put it out of my Power. You will receive enclosed herein Mr Wm Lytles note to me for $2000 dated 28th OUlto & payable on the 15th of this month. Mr Lytle will be in Richmond at or before that time when he will pay the money, and I will in a few days remit the remaining $1500.[9] I am Yrs Sir

                                    R M.

8. James M. Marshall and his wife, Hester (1764–1848), were traveling to England, where Marshall hoped to raise the funds necessary for the purchase of the Fairfax lands as well as for other enterprises. See Fairfax Lands: Editorial Note, Feb. 1, 1793, and Robert Morris to James M. Marshall, *passim,* Letterbook, Morris Papers, Library of Congress.

9. The editors have been unable to determine the reason for this remittance. James M. Marshall's account book, cited in Albert J. Beveridge, *The Life of John Marshall* (Boston, 1916), II, 210, may have contained an answer, but the book apparently

To Thomas Jefferson

[*November 2, 1795*. Listed in Jefferson's "Summary Journal of Letters," Jefferson Papers, Library of Congress. Not found.]

From Thomas Marshall

Printed, W. M. Paxton, *The Marshall Family* (Cincinnati, 1885), 22–23

Buckpond, Ky., November 6, 1795

The death of our dear Lucy is a heavy affliction—perhaps the more so on account of its being the first of the kind which has been felt by your mother and myself. I endeavor to forget it. I have not mentioned her name twice since your letter announced the unfortunate event. But alas, I frequently find myself sighing and moaning on account of her death, without realizing what I am grieving for. But why am I describing my affliction to you who must have felt the same more than once in all its bitterness. God send we feel it no more! Your sister Molly [Mrs. Humphrey Marshall], who had a long fit of illness, I believe knows nothing of our loss as yet. We were afraid to make it known to her. Make our kindest compliments of condolence to Mr. Ambler.[1] I feel for him sensibly, and make not the least doubt but he had his share of the affliction; but no person's can be equal to that of an affectionate father and mother, for the loss of a daughter who never till now was the cause of one painful sensation in the breast of either. Tell Mr. Ambler that we have the firmest confidence in his parental tenderness for the little son, the dear deceased has left with him. Tell him above all to be careful of its health and education—to be careful to sow the seed of virtue and honor early in its breast—to make it virtuous rather than learned, if he can't make it both. That part of what fortune I possess, which I intended for her, I shall

---

burned in a 1923 fire that destroyed many of the Marshalls' papers. Morris could well have owed the money to James M. Marshall and remitted it to JM in accordance with an agreement made between the brothers whereby JM would put the funds to use. It is also conceivable that Morris owed the money to JM, although the only apparent reason for a debt to JM would have been for JM's representation in Braxton v. Willing, Morris & Co., and $3,500 seems an excessive fee. For additional correspondence on these two subjects, see Morris to JM, Dec. 29, 1795.

1. The exact date of Lucy's death is not known. She and John Ambler had one son, Thomas Marshall Ambler (1792–1875), who later became an Episcopal minister.

leave to him; rather as acknowledgement of parental love and affection, than as an addition to his estate.

We are informed that you are appointed Attorney General for the United States, and that you have accepted the office.[2] Now I hope we may be informed why we have no Attorney in this State for the United States. I have complained of this in every letter I have written on the subject of revenue. I cannot possibly have the revenue collected, as no one will comply with the laws without compulsion, and the government has not put it in my power to compel compliance. This I have tried, but without success. What I can do, I know not. I should think that in the present situation of affairs there might be political reasons assigned for the neglect. But if that be the case, why am I repeatedly written to by the Commissioner of Revenue, as if it was expected that I could go on with the business in the same manner as if there were no impediment,[3] &c.

Opinion

ADS, Heth Papers, University of Virginia Library[4]

[Richmond], November 9, 1795

Some considerable time past Mr. Heth consulted me on the means of securing a gaming debt due from Mr. Carter to Mr. Cooper in such manner that, in case of the death of Carter his

2. JM had been offered the position in August, but he refused to accept. See George Washington to JM, Aug. 26, 1795, and JM to Washington, Aug. 31, 1795.

3. Thomas Marshall had been commissioned supervisor of the revenue for the district of Ohio on Dec. 18, 1794. He was complaining here about the difficulty of collecting taxes from residents of his territory, who had resisted payment since the tax was first imposed and who had continued to assist the insurgents in western Pennsylvania after the Whiskey Rebellion. Tench Coxe, the commissioner of revenue, had relayed Marshall's complaints to his superior, Alexander Hamilton. For information on the issue, see Harold C. Syrett et al., eds., The Papers of Alexander Hamilton (New York, 1961–), XVII, 418, 461, XVIII, 153–155, 167, 180, 193, 196–197, 204. Marshall's reference to "political reasons assigned for the neglect" probably referred to the difficult relations between Coxe and his new superior, Oliver Wolcott, for whom Coxe had been passed over when Hamilton resigned, although Marshall may have had larger issues in mind.

4. Following JM's opinion there is a notation by Henry Heth that "the Mr. Carter above alluded to is upwards of Seventy years of Age—after his Death his Executor is compeld to take notice of all gaming Debts—pay them—was the Debt bad or well Sold. H.H." The document is endorsed in a third hand "J. Marshalls, opinion on Gaming, debts."

representatives woud be unable to avoid the payment of it. I then gave him the opinion which I now give.

By the laws of Virginia a gaming debt is irrecoverable & every deed or obligation for the payment of it is void.[5] The representatives of Mr. Carter woud have it in their power to set aside any such deed or obligation. The only possible mode of avoiding this woud be to obtain a bond or other security to a person who shoud give a fair consideration & be totally unacquainted with the manner in which the debt was contracted.[6]

J MARSHALL

Certificate

ADS, Heth Papers, University of Virginia Library

[Richmond], November 9, 1795

I paid for Mr. Cooper in Jany. 94 five hundred dollars.[7] The manner in which I was drawn in to make this advance was such as inducd Capt. Cooper to shew vast solicitude to repay it. I was inducd to beleive from conversations on the subject that he woud use every exertion to repay me. Mr. Hunt is well acquainted himself with the circumstances & if[8] *I recollect rightly informd me that I shoud be paid from funds of Cooper in his hands or in the hands of Mr. Heth.* After Capt. Cooper left the country I applied to Mr. Heth

5. Virginia's gaming law was based on English statutes and laws enacted by the House of Burgesses. Tucker, *Blackstone's Commentaries*, IV, 173–174, n. 15; 6 Hening 76 (1748); 10 Hening 205 (1779); and see also Vol. I, 168–169. An act of 1792 declared all instruments based upon the consideration of a gaming debt to be "utterly void, frustrate, and of none effect, to all intents and purposes whatsoevered; any law, custom or usage, to the contrary thereof, in any wise, notwithstanding." 1 Shepherd 106. A bond to secure a gaming debt was void *ab initio* and could not vest any title in its original obligee, or in his assignee. See Judge Spencer Roane's comment concerning English law on this point, Norton v. Rose, 2 Va. (2 Wash.) 233, 248 (1796).

6. As a practical matter, even if a bond based upon a gaming debt was not void, but was merely voidable, the weight of Virginia case law indicates that it was not a negotiable instrument, and hence legal and equitable defenses might be pleaded, even against a subsequent assignee, without notice of the nature of the underlying transaction. Norton v. Rose, 2 Va. (2 Wash.) 233–255 (1796); Picket v. Morris, 2 Va. (2 Wash.) 255–276 (1796); Overstreet v. Randolph, Wythe 47–51 (1789).

7. The opinion of the same date, printed immediately above, indicates that Henry Heth was settling the affairs of Capt. Cooper, although that opinion is not directly related to this certificate. JM was obviously doing everything possible to avoid court action to recover the money lent to Cooper.

8. Heth placed an asterisk here and wrote on the verso, "This conversation between Hunt and Mr. Marshall past in April 94, after the desolation of Hill & Hunt. H H."

who said that he had not then in his hands any property belonging to Capt. Cooper but expected to have some (as I understood) on the receipt of the money for which Carters debt was sold. I assignd to him my claim on Cooper on his agreeing to pay me its amount when Coopers money shoud come into his hands. I told him that I woud bring an attachment to secure the money if necessary & woud have done so had I supposd it necessary. But knowing that the transfer of my claim to Heth with his assumpsit thereon was sufficient & that it woud & must be painful to Capt. Cooper to bring the subject into court I woud not bring a suit which coud only subject him to costs. I was confident too that Capt. Cooper woud be much gratified at my being paid. Independent of the 500 $ above mentiond I had advancd for the support of Capt. Coopers children who were left by him in Richmond about 40 dollars. I receivd from Mr. Heth of the sum he was to pay for Cooper £96.6.3. Virginia money & hold him acountable to me for the balance if he shall have so much money in his hands.

J MARSHALL

To Hudson Martin

ALS, Marshall Papers, Library of Congress

Dear Sir[9]   Richmond, November 16, 1795

I have receivd your letter of the 19th. of October[1] concerning the suits between Banks Clendinnen & Martin. You had notice when the report was made up & ought to have attended to the business. The duty of counsel at the bar is in court & not before the commissioner, in consequence of which notice is given to the party & not to the attorney, nor did I know when the commissioner was about to proceed on the business. Mr Anderson & yourself having notice woud neither attend yourselves or write to me concerning it. So soon as the present courts are over I will examine the report & endeavor to form such exceptions as may produce a resettlement. If you wish to charge Banks with any thing

9. JM addressed the letter to "Hudson Martin esquire, Albemarle." Martin (1752–1830), prominent in the affairs of Albemarle, Amherst, and Nelson counties, owned and managed a large estate in Albemarle County and married the granddaughter of Thomas Walker.

1. Letter not found.

on account of Clendinnen you ought to prove their connection. I
am dear Sir yours etc.

J MARSHALL

From William Farrar

DS, U.S. Circuit Court, Va., Ended Cases (Restored), 1795, Virginia State Library[2]

Sir   Richmond, November 19, 1795
    You will please allow Judgts. to be entered up against me in the
two Suits brought by Mr James Lyle agt. me in the Federal &
District Courts in the name of Geo Kippen & Co. etc.[3] on his
staying execution to the first April next, and taking off the interest
during the war (say Eight years). I am Sir, Yo Mo. Ob Se
                                            WILL: FARRAR
Test
THOS. HARDING
WM. MITCHELL

Lottery Ticket

Printed DS, Collection of Philip Gardiner Nordell, Ambler, Pa.

[*November 21, 1795, Richmond.* JM and George Pickett sign Richmond
bridge lottery ticket no. 846, for Lottery No. II.[4]]

Law Papers, November 1795

U.S. Circuit Court, Va.

McDougall & Co. v. Banks, answer, AD, U.S. Circuit Court ,Va., Ended
Cases (Unrestored), 1797, Virginia State Library.[5]

2. This authorization to confess judgment is filed with the case papers of Henderson, McCaul & Co. v. William Farrar, although it has no apparent connection with that case.
3. These cases are not identifiable with any pending cases in the U.S. Circuit Court for Virginia.
4. For details of the construction of a bridge across Shockoe Creek and JM's role in it, see the lottery notice, calendared at Aug. 2, 1792.
5. See Account Book, Receipts, Oct. 1795.

Scott v. Ware, bill in chancery, AD, U.S. Circuit Court, Va., Ended Cases (Restored), 1812, Va. State Lib.

From Samuel Coleman

Copy, Adjutant General's Record Book, War 10, Virginia State Library

Sir,[6]   Richmond, December 19, 1795

I beg leave to inform you that the Adjutant General has established an office in the Capitol, and hath requested me in his absence to execute those duties which are, by law, required of him; and that I am now, and shall hereafter continue to be ready to comply with his request according to the best of my abilities. I beg leave further to inform you Sir, that the proportion of Steuben's military discipline, allowed to your Brigade, is now ready for delivery. I have the honor to be Sir with due consideration and respect, your most obedt. Servant

                                        SAMUEL COLEMAN.

From Robert Morris

Letterbook Copy, Morris Papers, Library of Congress

Dear Sir   Philadelphia, December 29, 1795

I have postponed acknowledging the Rect of your letter of the 23d novr week after week in the Expectation of getting so far ahead of my pecuniary necessities, as to enable me to remit the Remaining $1500 of the sum directed by your Brother to be so Remitted, and sorry I am to say, that hitherto I have experienced Such constant disappointments in the Rect of money that it has

6. This letter is actually a composite of one written to the major generals notifying them of the establishment of the office in the capitol and another written to the brigadier generals. The second sentence was inserted in the latter. Both letters are on p. 48 of the Adjutant General's Record Book.

The Council of State had ordered Coleman to distribute these copies of Baron von Steuben's manual (*Regulations for the order and discipline of the troops of the United States* [Philadelphia, 1779]) on Nov. 11, 1795. JM's brigade was to receive 186 copies for its 222 officers. George Richardson, the inspector general of JM's brigade, received the copies on Feb. 5, 1796. JVCS, Nov. 11, 1795; Adjutant General's Record Book, War 10, Virginia State Library.

actually not been in my power to gratify my ardent desire of Re-
leiving your Engagements by that Remittance.[7] I hope however
that it will go enclosed herein. If not it will be owing to fresh Dis-
appointments. I will not however rest untill the business is accomplished. Nothing in this City ever equalled the scenes of General Distress occasioned by the demand for & want of money.

The decree in favor of mr Braxton is so entirely contrary to the
principles of Justice & every Idea I had on that Subject that I
cannot help attributing it to sinister Motives.[8] The Ship Pennsa[9]
was spoken with three days after leaving our Capes & I long to
hear of her safe arrival. As soon as I do you shall be informed
thereof by, Dr Sir Yrs

R M

To Charles Lee

ALS, Collection of the Association for the Preservation of Virginia Antiquities,
on deposit at the Virginia Historical Society

Dear Sir[1]   [Richmond, *ca.* December 1795]
I have transmitted to the clerk of Dumfries a traverse to the
Fauquier inquest drawn in the name of the purchasers. I wish if
possible that it coud be determind by means of a demurrer which
woud admit the conveyance to us, at the next term.[2] An argument
I presume woud be useless. My reason for wishing this is that the
Foedl. court is certainly open to us tho' it shoud be closd to Fair-

7. JM's Nov. 23 letter has not been found. For an earlier partial remittance, see
Morris to JM, Nov. 2, 1795.

8. JM no doubt notified Morris in his Nov. 23 letter of the Court of Appeal's ruling
in Braxton v. Willing, Morris & Co. The court rendered its decision on that day, reversing the High Court of Chancery decree of Oct. 1793 that had been in favor of
Morris. See Vol. I, 370, n. 62; 8 Va. (4 Call) 288 (1795); and Court of Appeals Order
Book, III, 102–107, Virginia State Library.

9. James M. Marshall and his wife, Hester, had sailed for England on board the
Pennsylvania.

1. Addressed to "Charles Lee esquire, Alexandria," the letter was later endorsed
in another hand "Fairfax v. Commonwealth, Letter," and in yet another hand "Send
E. R.'s opinion." Edmund Randolph had been asked by the Council of State to inquire into this new case. JVCS, Apr. 12, 1796.

2. See Henry Lee, Rawleigh Colston, JM, and James M. Marshall v. Commonwealth, May 20, 1796, District Court Order Book, 1794–1798, 263–264, Prince William County, Virginia State Library.

fax.[3] This reason however must be disclosd to no person. It woud certainly prevent a demurrer.

I some time past requested Mr. Patton of Fredericksburg to pay to the treasurer of the Potowmac company a sum of money on my account.[4] Will you take the trouble to ask if this has been done.

The legislature is considerd as growing worse & worse. It is to be hopd their session will soon determine.[5] With much esteem, I am your

J MARSHALL

Law Papers, December 1795

U.S. Circuit Court, Va.

Scott v. Ware, deposition, AD, U.S. Circuit Court, Va., Ended Cases (Restored), 1812, Virginia State Library.

3. JM believed at this time that the 11th Amendment, recently ratified by the Virginia General Assembly, would prevent an appeal to the federal courts in Fairfax's name. See Fairfax Lands: Editorial Note, Feb. 1, 1793.

4. Probably Robert Patton, a prominent resident of Fredericksburg. William Hartshorne (1742–1816), of Alexandria, was treasurer of the Potomac River Company.

5. The 1795 session of the General Assembly adjourned on Dec. 29.

Account Book

July 1788—December 1795

Account Book

EDITORIAL NOTE

This portion of John Marshall's accounts differs only slightly from that printed in Volume I. A full explanation and description of the entire Account Book appears on pages 289–292 in that volume, and little need be added here. The most significant change, also reflected in the correspondence, is in Marshall's law practice.

This portion of the Account Book reveals that Marshall limited his state court practice after 1788 to the courts meeting in Richmond, the High Court of Chancery, which continued to meet in Williamsburg until *ca.* 1790, and the district courts meeting at Fredericksburg and Petersburg. He also began receiving many cases from other district courts, sent by clients or attorneys who wanted Marshall's help in appealing a ruling to the Court of Appeals, which met only in the capital. As he wrote Charles Lee, *ca.* April 15, 1793, however, he had begun to concentrate only on the Richmond courts, apparently abandoning riding even to Fredericksburg or Petersburg twice a year. This is a reflection both of his prosperous practice before the Court of Appeals and the High Court of Chancery and of his increasing volume of litigation before the U.S. Circuit Court for Virginia.

After the passage of the Judiciary Act of 1789, British creditors began suing in the federal courts for recovery of debts owed them. Marshall probably had a great deal to do with an advertisement that appeared in Richmond newspapers in fall 1790, announcing that a meeting would be held on January 1, 1791, at Eagle Tavern, for "persons who are, or may hereafter be engaged or interested in any suits instituted by British Creditors, or their agents, in the federal courts against citizens of this state. As the sole object of this proposition is to provide for a fair and legal investigation of the several claims that may be exhibited, in order to an equitable issue, it is warmly recommended as essential to the welfare of a Common Cause, that those who cannot attend personally, may do so by deputation."[1] The number of federal cases for which Marshall recorded fees steadily increased from 1790 through 1795, although it is apparent from his receipts that he continued to maintain a heavy caseload in the High Court of Chancery, the Court of Appeals, and the U.S. Circuit Court for Virginia throughout the period covered by this segment of his Account Book.

The disbursements during this period indicate his continuing, and even increasing, social nature and sense of civic responsibility as well as his attention to family matters. Entries for family members continue with the same regularity as earlier. James Markham Marshall, having left Richmond, is replaced in his frequent receipts of money by his brothers Alexander and Louis. As in Volume I, each family member is identified only the first time he or she appears or in entries that are ambiguous. Several entries for John Smith suggest that Marshall supported a ward for some time. The occasional expenditure for a midwife and entries for son Tom's schooling remind us of Marshall's growing family, a side of his life not discussed in his extant correspondence. Marshall bought property and built a house in the years 1788 to 1790, and entries for taxes begin to reflect this

1. *Virginia Gazette, and General Advertiser*, (Richmond) Oct. 27, 1790.

growing prosperity. Interestingly, entries for whist or backgammon are missing after 1788, whereas they appeared frequently when Marshall first began keeping these accounts.

If Marshall continued keeping accounts after 1795, he must have done so in another book that has since disappeared. The sparse and apparently infrequent entries after October 1795 suggest that he simply ceased this kind of bookkeeping at the end of that year. Perhaps his successful practice and the time and energy required by his private affairs forced him to devote less time to recording receipts and expenditures. Perhaps, too, the introduction of dollars and cents well before the end of the Account Book provided the occasion to break the habit of keeping detailed accounts in pounds, shillings, and pence. It is also likely that with a lucrative law practice Marshall no longer felt compelled to watch his money so closely. It is unfortunate for the historical record, however, that this valuable source of information ceased at that time.

GUIDE TO ABBREVIATIONS

admr.	administrator
ads.	*ad sectam,* "at the suit of." When listing cases, ads. is used when it is desired that the name of the defendant should come first. Thus, *A* v. *B* would become *B* ads. *A*.
appl.	appeal
assee.	assignee
chy.	chancery
Comth.	Commonwealth of Virginia
ct.	court
cty.	county
dismd.	dismissed
dist.	district
Do.	ditto
eject.	ejectment
exn.	execution
exor, exr	executor
exx	executrix
fedl.	federal
G. Ct.	General Court
H. C.	habeas corpus
ha. cor.	habeas corpus
injn.	injunction
ld. wt.	land warrant
mo.	motion
pd.	paid
petn.	petition
rep.	replevin
retr.	retainer
sci. fa.	scire facias
Spe. ver.	special verdict

sups.   supersedeas
T.A.B.   trespass, assault and battery
ux   uxor, "a wife"
wt.   writ

AD, Marshall Papers, Swem Library, College of William and Mary

[Receipts]			
July 1st.	Powel v Carter Sci fa.	2	10	
	From Mr. Mayo		12	
	Tomlin ads. Kelly	5		
	Genl. Stephens[1] ads. Fleming & ux.	2	13	4
8th.	recd. from Mr. Dandridge exr. v. Hylton	7		
11th.	Clay v Coles supersedeas	2	11	
	Recd. from Mr. Faris for going to Wmsburg. on the Cyrus[2]	6	18	
17th.	Godwin v Pegram chy.	4	4	
19th.	From Colo. Peachy in three suits Craig v Fulton[3]	7	10	
	From Mr. Tyler in sundry suits	30	0	0
27th.	advice fee from corporation[4]	1	2	
30th.	Bowyer v Ramsays exrs. chy.	3		
		73	0	4

1. Edward Stevens.
2. See Vol. I, 354, n. 89.
3. William Peachy v. Samuel and Alexander Craig was probably on appeal from a county court to the General Court at this time. After the reorganization of the courts in 1788, the three cases, all with the same name, were transferred to the District Court at Staunton, and JM turned them over to Archibald Stuart. District Court Order Book, 1789–1793, 326, 329, 331, 334, Augusta County, Virginia State Library.
4. On July 22, 1788, the Richmond City Common Hall resolved that "the Mayor be requested at the expence of the City to take the advise of the Council, respecting the power or jurisdiction of the Court of Hustings of this City to summon a Grand Jury." Although no existing evidence indicates that JM acted as "the Council" to the city, his entry for just such a service so soon after this action by the corporation is too significant to ignore. The clerk would not have meant the Council of State, because there was no charge for the advice of that body. Richmond City Common Hall Records, I, 178, Va. State Lib.

[*Disbursements*]

		£	s	d
July 1	Market 12/1, fruit 5/		17	1
	Flour 30/, Brandy £10	11	10	
	Given Polly for looking glass	1	8	
	subscription for 4th. of July[5]		18	
	postage for letters at difft. times		6	
3d.	Market 25/6, Tea 14/	1	19	6
5	market 12/, given Villiers[6] 12/,			
	given old woman 6/	1	10	
8th.	expenses 4/6, paid in part for a			
	lott to Mr. Clay £50–10–2½	50	14	8½
	Chickens 4/, paid balance to			
	Mr. Clay	45	4	
9th.	Sugar 12/, paper 14/	1	6	
11th.	Gese 14/, sugar 7/6, given			
	Polly 3/ expenses 6/,			
	postage 7½, Glass 7/6, eggs 2/		16	1½
18th.	expenses going to & returning			
	from Wmsburg.[7]	4		
	market 13/, given away 6/8		19	8
20th	Apples Huckleberries & potatoes		3	5
22d.	wood 8/, fruit 2/3, pair of shoes			
	for self 12/	1	2	3
23d.	Paid P Lee[8] for Colo. Marshall	5	14	
24th.	Sugar 34/, barber 13/4, fruit 2/	2	9	4
27th.	bleeding Moes[9] 1/6, windows 2/,			
	soap & sugar 6/8		10	2
	market 9/; 31st. market 12/	1	1	
		133	13	7
	deduct £95 pd. for lott[10]	95		
		38	13	7

5. The July 4 celebration in 1788 included an early morning discharge of 13 cannon, an additional discharge of 13 at noon, and a dinner at the Eagle Tavern that evening. *Virginia Gazette and Weekly Advertiser* (Richmond), July 10, 1788.

6. R. Villiers, a Richmond author and bookseller, had advertised the showing of an Eidophusikon at the "Old Theatre" in late Aug. 1788. That showing had to be postponed when Villiers became ill with dumb ague. *Va. Gaz. & Wkly. Adv.*, Aug. 21, and Sept. 4, 1788.

7. See Receipts, July 11, 1788.

8. This was probably Philip Richard Francis Lee, who had been a captain in the Continental Line. JM had made similar disbursements to Lee on Apr. 2, 1788. Vol. I, 406.

9. Moses was a slave owned by JM. See Vol. I, 296.

10. The lot was purchased from Mr. Clay on July 8.

[Receipts]			
August 1st.	Jones v Johnston & al	2	10	
	same v Ransone (old suit in in chy.		10	
	Smith v Freith & al. (Heathcote & Fenwick) chy.	5		
2d.	From Means v Commonwealth supersds.[11]	2	8	
	From Hudson v Johnston (old appeal)[12]		14	
4th.	advice fee 22/6	1	2	6
5th.	advice fee 23/4	1	3	4
	From Alexandria corporation [13]	1	8	
	From Simons v Lee old suit[14]	2	8	
	From Murry & al (Yates McMaster) v Drewdiz	2	10	
6th.	Hartshorne ads. Hepbourne & al appeal	2	16	
	advice fee 22/6	1	2	6
8th.	Muse v Conway (not yet enterd)	2	8	
	Magann v Powell (old suit TAB.)	2		
	Mr. Savary de Valcolon[15] v Graves	1	8	
9	advice 18/		18	
25	From Goadsby vs. [Walker] Att. in Chy.[16]	2	4	0

11. See Certification, *ca.* Aug. 4, 1788.

12. Charles Hudson v. Thomas Johnson was a debt action that was almost immediately transferred from the General Court to the District Court at Charlottesville after the reorganization of the courts in 1788. JM reentered the case as attorney for Hudson when the decision of the district court was appealed to the Court of Appeals in 1791. 1 Va. (1 Wash. 10; Court of Appeals Order Book, II, 110–111, Va. State Lib.

13. Apparently JM had been employed by the city of Alexandria, perhaps for a legal opinion. There are no extant records for that city as early as 1788.

14. See Joseph Simon to JM, Mar. 25, 1791.

15. Savary de Valcoulon was agent for Coulougnac & Co., a firm of French merchants trying to collect their accounts from the Commonwealth. *JVCS*, III, 327, 413, 417, 436, 437, 506. Nothing is known about this particular suit against Graves, but see note at entry under Receipts, Dec. 26, 1788, "Rapicaut in Assembly," for JM's further connection with de Valcoulon.

16. This entry is in a hand other than JM's.

From Churchill ads. Courts (old suit)		2	8	
		33	18	4

[Disbursements]

August 2d.	eggs & butter 4/6		4	6
	gown etc. for Polly with Heathcote & Fenwick[17]		5	6
3d.	ducks 3/, fruit etc. 3/, Given Polly 19/6	1	5	6
5th.	fruit 2/, balance of acct. to Mr. Harrison[18] £5-10	5	12	
	Given Kned my brothers man 3/, do. 6/		9	
7th.	Given my brother Alexander[19] (for Colo. M)	6		
	blacksmith 2/6, given Polly 6/		8	6
9th.	fruit 1/9		1	9
25	Tax on a writ Storts v Lewes at the request of R. Brent[20]		6	
	expences going to & returning from Winchester	8		
	market 55/, do. 3/	2	18	
	Tea 15/		15	
	advancd my brother James for land warrant[21]	10	12	5½
	Mazai's book sur les etats unis[22]		18	
30	Market 2/, city tax 36/[23]	1	18	
		44	14	8½

17. JM must have applied the money received for the case of Smith v. Freith on Aug. 1 to this purchase.

18. Benjamin Harrison, a merchant in Richmond.

19. Alexander Marshall (1770–1825), who moved to Kentucky with his father, became a lawyer and settled in Mason County. He was a member of the Kentucky legislature from 1797 to 1800 and was appointed state court reporter in 1818.

20. This entry is in a hand other than JM's.

21. See additional entry at Disbursements, Nov. 13, 1788.

22. Philip Mazzei wrote the first French-language history of the American Revolution, *Recherches historiques et politiques sur les États-Unis de l'Amérique Septentrionale* (Paris, 1788). The three-volume set was advertised for sale in the *Va. Gaz. & Wkly. Adv.*, Sept. 11, 1788.

23. Richmond personal property records show that in June 1788, JM was listed as owning six tithable slaves, one horse, mare, or colt, and no taxable carriages. His tax was set at £2 4s. His real property was assessed at £200 and taxed at 10s. in the per-

deduct for land warrant for olly & tax on writ	17	16	5½	
	26	18	3	

[Receipts]

September				
2d.	from Mr. Johnston of Hanover town in an appeal on an attachment v Jones	4	4	
4th.	Easly ads. Burnet (John Allen) appeal[24]	2	16	
	Bently & Co. ads. Mayo appeal	2	10	
	Warington ads. Bolling do.	2	10	
	Southerland ads. Hill injn.[25]	3	16	
15	Braxton ads. Nelson	7		
17th.	From Mr. Maund	2	8	
	From Mr. Vernon for advice[26]	1	6	8
22nd.	From Anderson ads. Harris (old suit)	1	4	
	Advice 40/6	2	0	6
23	Hill v Brown assee. Hipkins (chy.)	7		
	Ball v Bough chy. injn.	1	10	
	Floods admrs. v Lee exr. of Lee[27]	2	10	
24th.	Meredith v May supersedeas	2	10	
	same v Walker appeal	2	10	
	Advice fee—Mr Southgate[28]	1	2	6

sonal property book. In the land book, however, his tax was £1 5s. These figures, of course, total 59s. It is unclear why JM only paid 36s. at this time. Richmond City Personal Property Book, 1788, and Land Book, 1788, Va. State Lib.

24. James Burnett v. Robert Easley was an appeal from Buckingham County Court that was transferred to the District Court at Prince Edward County almost immediately. JM represented Easley during the transfer. District Court Order Book, 1789–1792, 165, Prince Edward County, Va. State Lib.

25. See Vol. 1, 387, n. 30.

26. Abner Vernon. See entry for Noah ads. Hunter, Receipts, Oct. 6, 1788.

27. Walter Jones and John Shearman Woodcock, executors of William Flood, v. Richard Lee was a debt action brought in the General Court by JM for Jones and Woodcock. The case was transferred to the District Court at Northumberland County, where a series of actions occurred in Sept. 1789 and 1790. District Court Order Book, 1789–1793, 12–15, 92–93, 102, Northumberland County, Va. State Lib.

28. This entry is in a hand other than JM's.

	Street v Atkinson Colo. suit chy.	5	7	4
29th.	From Roan ads. Robinsons admr.	7		
30th.	From Mr. Vowles	3	10	9
	Warden ads. Beverly	2	10	
	Colo. Glenn for self & Watts	5	2	
	Lister ads. Ross & Co	2	8	
	Clayton v Comth. injn.	2	16	
		75	10	7

[*Disbursements*]

September

1st.	Market 6/8, do. 6/		12	8
	flour 36/, self 3/	1	19	
4th.	Market 19/, do. 6/, do. 5/	1	10	
9th.	Market 6/, do. 7/, Soap 3/		16	
	Paid Warrington[29] for sundries	5		
11th.	market 11/, do. 4/, wood 7/9	1	2	9
15th.	market 4/, postage 1/3, sugar 15/6	1		9
	Paid Betsy Munkus[30] 15/		15	
16th.	market 6/, do. 7/3		13	3
17th.	law books 20/	1		
18th.	market 5/, do. 6d., powder puff 2/6		8	
20th.	nails for enclosing lott[31] etc.	2	07	6
23d.	market 7/, do. 5/7½, do 4		16	7½
26th.	Sugar & thread 8/, painting porch 20/	1	8	
	paling in lott etc.	24	18	
	for presses	4	1	
27	market 4/, do. 11/		15	

---

29. James Warrington was a merchant in Richmond as late as 1787. "List of Merchants," Richmond City Hustings Court Order Book, II, 50, Va. State Lib.

30. See Vol. I, 371, n. 64.

31. JM began construction of his house in Richmond in Oct. 1788. See Construction Account, printed at Oct. 1788. When JM began keeping regular accounts on the construction, he transferred this and subsequent expenditures to that special account.

		49	3	6½
		30	5	6[32]
		18	18	0½
	Overpaid Mr. Deane[33]	4	2	

[Receipts]

October 1st.	Bates & Woodson v Boyd & White appl.	2	10	
	Wood ads. ⟨action⟩ Fitzpatrick[34]	2	10	
	Brown v Hewet (old suit)[35]	1	8	
2	Rudd assee. of Brown v Brown debt	2	10	
	Scott ads. Evans dismd.	10		
	Downman admr. v Payne admr.	2		
	George & Carr (from Carr) ads. Overton & Morris[36]	1	4	
3d.	Woodridge ads. Cheatham	2	12	
4th.	Brown ads. Johnstont (in part)	2	8	
	Glasscock ads. Stuart etc. (from Mr. Selden	2	10	
	Rice v Jones[37]	4	10	
	Blagrave ads. Baird & Co.[38]	2	10	

32. This represents the total JM paid for pailing, or fencing, his lot on Sept. 26, including the nails purchased on Sept. 20. JM added those two expenses at the bottom of the manuscript page before subtracting them from his month's disbursements.

33. James or Thomas Deane, Richmond merchants.

34. John Fitzpatrick v. Thomas Wood began in the General Court but was soon transferred to the District Court at Fredericksburg. The case was continued until May 1793, when it was submitted to arbitration, and an award was made on May 1, 1794. District Court Law Orders, A, 1789–1793, 174, 431, 449, 463, and Law Orders, B, 1794–1798, 13, Fredericksburg, Va. State Lib.

35. John Brown and John Cook v. William Hewett had been first filed in the General Court by JM for Brown and Cook in 1784. Hewett had rented a boat from JM's clients and failed to return it. The case was continued until after the reorganization of the courts in 1788, when it was transferred to the District Court at Fredericksburg. In May 1790 it was referred to arbitrators, and an award was made on May 6, 1793. District Court Law Orders, A, 1789–1793, 40, 106, 474, and Law Orders, 1790–1793, 105–106, Fredericksburg, Va. State Lib.

36. John Overton and Richard Morris v. John George, William Carr, and John Ramey was transferred to the District Court at Prince Edward County, where it was continued until Sept. 1791. District Court Order Book, 1789–1792, 94, 178, 210, Prince Edward County, Va. State Lib.

37. See JM's argument calendared in Vol. I, 186.

38. John Baird and Gray Briggs, surviving partners of John Baird & Co., v. Henry

5th.	McRoberts ads. Winston appeal	2	10	
	Urquhart v Manning appl. chy.	5		
	Same advice	1	2	6
	drawing deed	1	2	6
6th.	Call and v Cabell writ of error	2	10	
	Noah ads. Hunter[39]	2	8	
	Thomson ads. Hunter caveat[40]	5		
7th.	Staunton v Richards & Short appl.[41]	2	10	
	Price ads. Thomas appl.[42]	2	10	
	Brown ads. Rowzee	2	10	
		64	15	

[Disbursements]

October 1st.	Market 11/, expenses 3/		14	
2d.	expences 6/		6	
3d.	Market 9/, do. 3/		12	
4th.	Fish 15/, birds 3/, postage 2/8	1	0	8
6th.	Market 6/8		6	8
7th.	flour 28/	1	8	
	Tea 18/		18	
		5	5	4

Blagrove was transferred from the General Court to the District Court at New London. It was appealed from that court to the Court of Appeals in 1791, and JM again represented Blagrove. Judgment was given Baird and Briggs on Apr. 13, 1793. 1 Va. (1 Wash.) 170, 171; Court of Appeals Order Book, II, 210, 212, Va. State Lib. See Receipts, Nov. 1791, for additional fee.

39. Adam Hunter and Abner Vernon, executors of James Hunter, v. Basil Nooe was a debt action brought in the General Court that was soon transferred to the District Court at Fredericksburg. Judgment was given for Hunter on Oct. 8, 1794. District Court Law Orders, B, 1794–1798, 99, Fredericksburg, Va. State Lib.

40. JM entered a caveat for Joseph Thomson against David Hunter on July 2, 1788. Litigation over ownership of the land located in Hampshire County resulted in court action in 1790 and 1791. Land Office Caveats, July 2, 1788, 46, and Superior Court Order Book, 1789–1793, 69, 207–208, Frederick County, both in Va. State Lib.

41. William Staunton v. Humphrey Richards was an appeal from Culpeper County Court that JM filed with the General Court. The case was transferred to the District Court at Fredericksburg, where the county court judgment was affirmed on Apr. 30, 1791. District Court Law Orders, A, 1789–1793, 214, and District Court Records, 1789–1792, 448–450, Fredericksburg, Va. State Lib.

42. Phenehas Thomas v. Anne Price was an appeal from a Cumberland County Court judgment of Aug. 20, 1780, against Thomas in an action of detinue for the value of five slaves lost by Price. The case was transferred to the District Court at Prince Edward County, where the county court judgment was affirmed on Sept. 5, 1790, when Thomas failed to appear. District Court Records at Large, 1789–1792, 208–209, Prince Edward County, Va. State Lib.

[*Receipts*]

October

7th.	Reynolds ads. Duval (caveat[43]	1	12
8th.	Osbornes exrs. ads. Anderson		
	appeal	2	10
	Hunton ads. Tapscot sups.	2	10
9th.	Liliard ads. James (libel)[44]	2	10
	Clarke ads. Stockdale	2	10
	Graves ads. Commonwealth[45]	2	10
	[ ] ads. Same	2	10
	Ewing (Montgomery old suit)		
	v Cammel	1	8
13th.	Young v Byrd[46]	2	10
	Trueheart v Austin (old suit)	4	10
	Cammock ads. Cammock (chy.)	5	
	Dunn ads. Comth.	2	10
14th.	From Bourk ads. Foster &		
	ux £5	5	
	From Mr. Ruffin v Brown	2	13
15	From Mr. Joshua Howard in		
	the suits of Rhoddy in Genl.		
	court	2	8
	Colo. Fleming[47]	5	

43. JM filed a caveat for William Reynolds against Samuel Duvall, Jr., involving land in Henrico County. Land Office Caveats, Jan. 10, 1787, 15, Va. State Lib.

44. Joseph James v. Benjamin Lillard was a libel action that was transferred from the General Court to the District Court at Fredericksburg. Judgment was given James on May 8, 1790, but only one penny damages were awarded. District Court Law Orders, A, 1789–1793, 117, 119, Fredericksburg, Va. State Lib. See JM's plea listed at Law Papers, Aug. 1789.

45. Commonwealth v. William Graves was transferred from the General Court to the District Court at Richmond, where judgment was given for Graves on Sept. 9, 1791. That judgment was appealed by the Commonwealth to the Court of Appeals and was reversed. Court of Appeals Order Book, II, 167, 172, Va. State Lib.

46. This case was either Edwin Young v. Maurice Bird or Edwin Young v. Abraham Byrd, both of which were transferred to the District Court at Winchester. The former was dismissed by agreement on Sept. 2, 1790, whereas the latter, an assault and battery case, was abated by the death of Young in 1793. It is almost certain that JM participated in neither case after they were transferred to the district court in 1789. Superior Court Order Book, 1789–1793, 114, 502, Frederick County, Va. State Lib.

47. William Fleming (1729–1795) was a surgeon who settled in Botetourt County, where he entered politics. He served as a state senator and later as a member of the Council of State, acting as governor between June 1 and 12, 1781. In 1782 he became chairman of a committee to inquire into the western accounts, and in 1788 he represented Botetourt County at the state ratifying convention.

16th.	From Mr. Hughes (old suit)	1	8
	Wood v Thrift appeal	1	16
17th.	Pope ads. Taylor (old suit)	1	8
	From Mr. Eppes 14£	14	
		66	3

[*Disbursements*]

October				
8th.	Market 18/, do. 6/	1	4	
9th.	Butter 53/4, given Mrs. Knight 6	2	19	4
14th.	Market 15/, given Polly 12/	1	7	
16	Market 6/		6	
		5	16	4

[*Receipts*]

October 18	Johnston ads. Thompson & al Potties exrs.	5	2	6
	Clayborne in three suits	7	10	
	Belles exrs. ads. Hipkins	2	2	
21st.	Borne v Porter (old suit)[48]	2	16	
	Calloway ads. Hook (finishd)	2	8	
	Egmon v Barron (finishd)	1	8	
	Mr. Lightfoot in Allen v Sundries (finishd)	5		
22d.	Mr. Hayes ads. Parker	2	10	
	Brenard ads. Payne appeal	2	10	
	Williams exrs. ads. Mitchel[49]	2	10	
	Williams ads. Mitchel	2	10	
	Yancy ads. Mitchel & Co[50]	2	10	

48. Andrew Bourne v. Charles Porter abated by the death of Bourne after the case was transferred from the General Court to the District Court at Fredericksburg on Oct. 1, 1789. District Court Law Orders, A, 1789–1793, 16, Fredericksburg, Va. State Lib.

49. This and the following case were two debt actions filed in the General Court in Oct. 1788 against JM's client John Williams, executor of William Williams, by John Mitchell. Both cases were transferred to the District Court at Fredericksburg, where judgment was awarded Mitchell in both actions on Oct. 8, 1791. District Court Law Orders, A, 1789–1793, 29, 241, 302, 330, and District Court Records, 1789–1792, 622–624, 665–667, Fredericksburg, Va. State Lib. See JM's plea in this case, listed at Law Papers, Oct. 1789, and case agreed listed at Law Papers, Apr. 1791.

50. John Mitchell v. Robert Yancy was very similar to the case immediately above.

23	Lacy v Gardener (old suit)	1	8	
	Oldner v Nast etc. (old suit in chancery)	3		
	Sinclair ads. Hallings exr.	2	10	
	Gay ads. Ross appeal	2	8	
	Bells orphans & Legatees v Alcock	5		
24th.	Duke v Bournage & al. Chy.	5		
	Southerland ads. Hill (Chy.)[51]	1	8	
	Calloway ads. Hook (finishd)	1	8	
	Wharton & al ads. Spotswood	9		
	Baker ads. Lyons	5	10	
	Austin v Winston (finishd) 2 suits[52]	5		
		80	8	6

[*Disbursements*]

October 22	Market 24/	1	4	
	Market 2/, do. 15/		17	
24th.	market 8/6, sugar 12/8		12	8
		2	13	8

[*Receipts*]

October 24	Godwin v Pegram (balance)	1	6	
	Lucas v Coleman (appeal)			
	[ ] v Crawford etc. TAB	2	6	6
25th.	Pope v Tibbs (old suit)	2	8	
	Anderson ads. Hudson (motion)	2	2	
28th.	Kelso & Kincaid ads. Harris appl.	2	11	
	From Drinkal & Escridge[53] 2 motions	5		

See District Court Law Orders, A, 1789–1793, 30, 254, and District Court Records, 1789–1792, 511–512, Fredericksburg, Va. State Lib. See case agreed listed at Law Papers, Apr. 1791.

51. See Vol. I, 387, n. 30.

52. This case may be related to Chapman Austin v. William O. Winston and Bartlett Anderson, justices of Hanover County Court, in which JM appeared for Austin in 1797. Court of Appeals Order Book, III, 363, 365, Va. State Lib.

53. Drinkall and Eskrigge were merchants in Richmond as late as 1787. "List of Merchants," Richmond City Hustings Court Order Book, II, 50, Va. State Lib.

From Southgate v. Lee motion.		2	10	
From Pleasants ads. Armstead		5		
From Mr. Harrison (his balance)		19	10	2
From Christian for himself & Vaden		5		
		47	13	8

[*Disbursements*]

[October]

	Market		16	
25	do. 3/, do. 12/6		15	6
	do. 5/9, Candles 32/	1	17	9
27	flour 15/		15	
29th.	Market 4/, Sundries 2/6		6	6
	market 5/6		5	6
	rum £7–3	7	3	
	Sundries at Mr. Drinkals[54] for Negroes	5	7	3
	Stockings for self at Drinkals	1	16	0
	Mr Harrison[55] for wine	24	15	
	To Mr. Richeson[56] silver Smith	5		
		48	17	6

[*Receipts*]

November

1	Ballard v Jones injn. £4	4		
	Advice fee	1		
	do.	1	8	
	advice from Mr. Welbourne	2	5	
	Mr. Brooke ads. Yates & al. chy. (old suit)	5	12	
	Mr. Coupland £4–4	4	4	
2	Urquhart v Hamilton & Co. Chy. att[57]	5		

54. Richmond merchant. See Receipts, Oct. 28, 1788.
55. Benjamin Harrison, Richmond merchant.
56. George Richardson (b. *ca.* 1761). "Return of the Inhabitants," 1787, Richmond City Common Hall Records, I, 304, Va. State Lib.
57. Archibald Hamilton v. William Urquhart was a chancery suit involving the application of the depreciation statute of 1781 to debts secured by bonds before that

3d	Chichester ads. Bronaugh appl. chy.	5	2	
4th.	Mr. Ledly concerning riot etc. at Morgantown	2	8	
	White ads. Smith (old suit in Genl. ct)		12	
	Elliot v. Clopton injn. (in part)	1		
9th.	Dabny v Hawkins & al[58] (injn.	2	8	
	Hills exr. ads. Hill	4	19	6
11th.	Capt. Shepherd for Browning v Hite[59]	7		
12th.	From Mr. Lawson	7		
	Sea ads. Sea appeal chy.	5		
	Johnston & Scott ads. Minor injn.	3		
	Green ads. King	2	13	4
	Smithers ads. Noel (for Sullivan only old st)	5		
16th.	Ker v Webb motion on rep. bond	2	10	
	Page v Page (chy.)	7		
20th.	advice 22/6	1	2	6
	Cox ads. Johnston & ux chy.	5		
	Campbell & Woodlaugh v Nigly	2	16	
		88		4

[Disbursements]

November				
1	Market 19/6, Burn's poems[60] 5/	1	4	6
	corn 12/		12	

---

date. Chancellor Wythe ruled in favor of JM's client Urquhart in 1794. Wythe 295. See additional fee under Receipts, Aug. 3, 1790.

58. Samuel Dabney v. John Hawkins. See Vol. I, 145, for an earlier fee received in this case.

59. Thomas Shepherd. See bill in chancery signed by JM, Vol. I, 188, and additional fee entered at Receipts, Mar. 5, 1790.

60. Robert Burns's Poems, *chiefly in the Scottish dialect* was published in Philadelphia in 1788, and his Poems, *chiefly in the Scottish Dialect. To which are added, Scots poems, selected from the works of Robert Ferguson* was published that same year in New York. Thomas Brend, "Bookbinder & Stationer, near the Bridge," advertised one of these, probably the first, for sale in Richmond in Aug. 1788. *Va. Gaz. & Wkly. Adv.*, Aug. 21, 1788.

Date		£	s	d
	Cloak for Polly	7		
	Paid my brother James	6	12	
	candle box 5/, fruit 5/, do. 3/		13	
3d.	market 20/, do. 19/	1	19	
6th.	a breast pin for Polly sister[61]		12	
7th.	wood 7/, fruit 4/, bread 2/6		13	6
11th.	Market 6/8, Tea 18/	1	4	8
12th.	market 8/, do. 32/, corn 24/, oats 4/6	3	8	6
13th.	Given Polly 12/		12	
	Paid my brother James in full for ld. warrat.[62]	7	15	6½
15	potatoes 7/6, oysters 4/		11	6
20th.	wood 7/, paper 17/6, fodder 9/	1	13	6
	To my brother Alexander	1	8	
		35	19	8½
		15	15	6½ [63]
		20	4	2

[Receipts]

Date		£	s	d
November				
21st.	Wilkinson v Wilkinson & Clarke finishd	5		
22	Allday v Ward appeal	5		
	advice fee in suit Maynard & ux v Camps exr. chy. depending	1	8	
23d.	Singleton & White ads. Weeks	2	16	
	Hay ads. Baird & al.	4	16	
	Cox ads. Cary	2	10	
29th.	Jones v Galt[64] (appeal)	2	16	
	Burwell v Bealle (appeal)	2	16	
	Galt v Cuninghame & Co. & al.	5		
		32	2	

61. This was most likely Ann Ambler (1772–1832), whose 16th birthday was approaching on Nov. 16. Louise Pecquet du Bellet, *Some Prominent Virginia Families* (Lynchburg, Va., 1907), I, 33.

62. See entry at Disbursements, Aug. 25, 1788, for advance to James.

63. This figure represents the total amount JM gave his brothers in November. He added the amounts given them at the bottom of this manuscript page before inserting them here to be subtracted from the month's disbursements.

64. This entry and the one immediately following are in a hand other than JM's.

		88		4
	[*Total November Receipts*]	120	2	4
	[*Disbursements*]			
November				
23d.	Wood 7/, Turkies 7/, market 6/	1		
	chickens 1/3		1	3
26	American Museum[65]	1	16	
	Cloth for self at Galts[66]	7	6	6
	pd. Taylor for making up cloaths	1	4	
	Negroes 2/, salt 3/		5	
28th.	Market 50/	2	10	
		14	2	9
	[*Receipts*]			
December				
2d	McCraw v Pannil[67]	2	16	
	Slaughter exr. of Howison ads. Thomson[68]	2	10	
	Williams ads. Pope chy. (balance)	2	10	
	Advice fee	1	2	6
	From Mr. Henning in Houisons exrs. ads. Thomson	1	8	
	From Mr. Middleton in Houisons exrs. v Slaughter (finishd)	2	16	
8th.	From Powell v Quarles (dismd.)	2	16	
	advice from Mr. Hite	1	8	

65. The *American Museum, or repository of ancient and modern fugitive pieces, prose and Poetical* began publication in Philadelphia in 1787 and was edited and printed by Mathew Carey (1760–1839), prominent Philadelphia publisher, author, and economist. The magazine was very popular and, despite a claim of nonpartisanship, had a slight Federalist tone. It ceased publication in Dec. 1792. Frank Luther Mott, *A History of American Magazines, 1741–1850* (New York, 1930), 100–103.

66. Irving Galt was a Richmond merchant in 1787. "List of Merchants," Richmond City Hustings Court Order Book, II, 50, Va. State Lib.

67. James McCraw v. John Pannell was a trespass, assault, and battery action that was transferred to the District Court at Prince Edward County, where it was dismissed by consent on Sept. 2, 1789. District Court Order Book, 1789–1792, 6, 7, Prince Edward County, Va. State Lib.

68. See Vol. I, 395, n. 58.

9th.	From Brown v Watterson sups.	2	10	
11th.	Riply v McClelan Chy.	2	16	
	Loyal ads. Comth.	2	16	
	Hunnicutt v Pleasants exr. Chy.	5		
	Calvert ads. Comth.	2	10	
13th.	advice fee	1	8	
	from Anderson of Amelia [for] mo.	1	8	
16	Poythress (in Lacy ads. Ross & Co.	2	8	
	Geddy ads. Roane chy.	5		
22d	Langhorne v Brown	2	8	
	Bohannon v Littlepage	2	10	
	advice fee 22/6	1	2	6
26	Rapicaut in Assembly[69]	2	16	
	Lee v. Prosser & Wilkinson	2	16	
	Elliot v. Clopton £3-3-9 injn. in part	3	3	9
		57	18	9

[*Disbursements*]

December				
2d.	market 6/, sundries for house 6/		12	
	postage 6/, market 2/		8	
3	market 4/, do. 6/		10	
	Wood 7/6, market 25/	1	12	6
	Cushion for my sister 28/, for house 18/8	2	6	8
8th.	Market 6/, do. 2/6, sugar 12/	1	0	6
9th.	Tea 15/, Market 29/	2	4	
11th.	corks 2/6, sundries 6/		8	6
13th.	market 36/	1	16	

69. JM was probably being paid for drafting a petition for Savary de Valcoulon, agent for Réné Rapicault, who was attempting to collect interest on a liquidated debt that was possibly incurred for supplies furnished the Commonwealth on the western frontier. De Valcoulon presented the petition to the House of Delegates on Nov. 13, 1788, and on Nov. 21 the House resolved that the Council of State should examine the claim and issue warrants for any interest omitted from the time the debt originated until it was paid. On Dec. 18, however, the House rescinded the resolution, allowing that "when the said claim was liquidated, the said Rapicault did not claim the said interest, and was perfectly satisfied with the sum then allowed him." *JVHD*, Oct. 1788, 40, 57, 104; *CVSP*, VIII, 411, 525. See *CVSP*, IV, 53, for another petition of de Valcoulon for this interest.

		£	s	d
	Paid taxes for James 4–12–10			
	really	2	19	8
14th.	market 5/, wood 7/6		12	6
18	Shoes for negroes 3£–10,			
	market 6/	3	16	
	To Mr. Geddy for brandy	6		
	To do. for Virga. cloth	1	4	
22d.	market 8/3, Given Polly for			
	house 6/		14	3
	market 8/, do. 1/3, wood 7/6		16	9
25	Mutton 12/8, bread 2/		14	8
28th.	Muff for my sister 18/		18	
		28	14	0
		2	19	8[70]
		25	14	4

[Receipts]

		£	s	d
December	Tony ads. Stoval same			
	Henderson & McClure	3	0	0
29th.	From Mr. Hancock	24		
	Powel assee. v Eblin	2	10	
	Beale in order on Currie for			
	coal[71]	4	10	
	Cunlif v Temple injn.	5	0	
		39		
	Drinkal & Escridge in Stuart			
	& Hopkins two fees[72]	5		
		44		

[Disbursements]

		£	s	d
December				
28th.	Given Lucy 20/	1	0	0
	To Mr. Richeson[73] silversmith		6	

70. This is the amount JM paid for his brother James's taxes on Dec. 13.

71. Currie was no doubt of the firm Ross & Curry, which advertised that "any person wishing to be supplied with coal from Deep Run Pitts, The property of Messrs. Ross & Curry, may be supplied with any quantity wanted, on the shortest notice by making application to the subscriber residing at Rockett's." *Va. Gaz. & Wkly. Adv.*, Jan. 15, 1789. See entry under Disbursements, Dec. 31, 1788.

72. See other fees entered under Receipts, Oct. 28, 1788.

73. George Richardson.

	Sundries to Polly not before charged	16	18	8
	subscription to St. Johns[74]		15	
	Given Polly 6/, bread & market 3/6		9	6
	For Edie[75] 12/		12	
	Butter £3–10–9, bread 1/3, Tom 6/	3	18	
	linnen for Polly £4–15, lottery ticket 3	7	15	
31	Market & bread 3/, watch 12/, wood 8/	1	3	
	Given Polly for sugar 6/		6	
	To Cunlif[76] for coal	5		
	To Currie for do. in order from Beale[77]	4	10	
		42	13	2
	To Drinkal & Escridge[78]	1	6	
		41	7	2
		7		
		48	7	2

[79]31st of March 1789	Borrowd from Mr. J. A.[80]	£	81	18	8
June 29th. 89	Paid		31		
			50	18	8
			49	17	
			1	1	8

74. The festival of St. John the Evangelist was celebrated by the Masons in Richmond on Dec. 27 usually with a church service followed by a banquet or dance.

75. A slave owned by JM. See Vol. I, 308, n. 85.

76. John Cunliffe was a merchant in Richmond in 1787. "List of Merchants," Richmond City Hustings Court Order Book, II, 50, Va. State Lib.

77. See entry under Receipts, Dec. 29, 1788.

78. Drinkall and Eskrigge, Richmond merchants.

79. These entries appear in JM's Account Book directly below Receipts, Dec. 1788, and the listing of totals received and expended in 1788. The opposite page contains Disbursements, Dec. 1788, and the monthly totals of receipts and expenditures.

80. Jaquelin Ambler.

[*Receipts*][81]

Jany.	22	13	8
Feby.	4	18	6
March	111	14	10
Apl.	217	14	8
May	91	8	3
June	57	5	6
July	73	0	4
Augt.	33	18	4
Septr.	75	10	7
October	259		2
Novr.	120	2	4
Decr.	57	18	9
	1125	5	11
[*Disbursements*]	467	6	5
[*Balance*]	657	11	6

[*Disbursements*]

Jany.	41	15	7½
Feby.	36	0	4
March	41	16	3
Apl.	62	5	4
May	57	18	10
June	15	0	1
July	38	13	7
Augt.	26	18	3
Septr.	18	18	½
October	63	12	10
Novr.	20	4	2
	14	2	9
Decr.	27		4
	467	6	5

[82]Recd. in the year 1788	1169	5	11
expended in year 1788			
	467	6	5

81. Receipts and Disbursements for 1788 appear in double columns below Dec. Disbursements.

82. These figures appear on the page with Dec. Receipts.

		48	7	2			
		515	13	7	515	13	7
					653	12	4

[Receipts]

January 1st.	Advice fee	1	2	6
2	Swift v Goodman 2 Suits	2	8	
12th.	Malone & ux v Carters admr.[83]	1	8	
14th.	advice fee on Martins estate	1	4	
	do. on Saml. Gathrights will	1	2	
17th.	do. on Doctor Broddy's case	1	8	
22.	Shackleford v Baird & Co. exr. paid off	2	10	
23	Advice fee between Singleton & Wms.	1	2	6
29th.	Curries exrs. v Weaglesworth chy.	5		
	Same ads. Waugh do.	5		
		22	5	

[Disbursements]

January 1st.	Market 6/, pork £28	28	6	
	barber 31/, market 22/	2	11	
4th.	Given Polly 28/	1	8	
6th.	Market 6/, play[84] 9/, wood 7/6, shoes 2/6	1	5	0
	Market 2/, do. 9/, tape 1/		12	
12th.	Wood 8		8	
	Pd. my brother Alexander	4	4	
17th.	Market 27/, expences to Wmsburg	5	11	
22d.	Wood 7/, bread 1/3		8	3
23d.	corn 46/, Market 13/8	2	19	8
	expences at the play 6/		6	

83. George Malone and Lucy, his wife, v. William Edwards, administrator of John Carter. See JM's declaration listed at Law Papers, Apr. 1790.

84. There is no record of the appearance of a theatrical group in Richmond in Jan. 1789. This entry and the entry under Jan. 23 suggest the existence of a group or tour previously unknown.

27th	bread & market 4/6, sugar 9/, spade 6/		19	6
	Account with Drinkal & Escridge[85]	5	17	6
29th.	Wood 7/6, paid for Edie 12/, given away 6/	1	5	6
	boots & shoes for self 3£, shoes for Lucy 9/	3	9	
		59	10	5
	Paid my brother[86]	4	4	
		55	6	5

[Receipts]

February 4th.	Advice to Monsieur Cauvy[87]	2	8	
	Hatcher v Hatchers (chy.)	4	4	8
	Gilchrist ads. James att. chy.	5		
	Gilmore etc. I beleive Clarke v Brady	2	10	
	Titbald admr. of Gray ads Throckmorton appeal to be revivd[88]	2	10	
10th.	advice fee from Colo Baytop	1	8	
12th.	From Mr. Whiting (Gloster	2	5	
	Moore ads. Hannah appl.	2	10	
	Dorsey ads. Morgan do.[89]	1	16	
14th.	Parsons v Adams	2	7	
17.	Clayton ads. Moseby (Chy.)[90]	2	8	
27th.	drawing a deed	1		
		30	6	8

85. Drinkall and Eskrigge, Richmond merchants.
86. See entry under Disbursements, Jan. 12, 1789.
87. See Petition of John Peter Cauvy, Feb. 12, 1789.
88. This is most likely the case of Robert Throckmorton v. Titbald, administrator of Richard Gray. The appeal was from a county court to the General Court. After the reorganization of the courts, this case was transferred to the District Court at Winchester, where it abated upon the death of Throckmorton. Superior Court Order Book, 1789-1793, 92, Frederick County, Va. State Lib.
89. Morgan Morgan, sheriff of Berkeley County, v. Leakin Dorsey was an appeal from the Berkeley County Court that was transferred to the District Court at Winchester. JM, retained by Dorsey, handled the case during the transfer. *Ibid.*, 166.
90. This entry is in a hand other than JM's.

[*Disbursements*]

February 4	blankets for Ben & Moses[91] 12/		12	
	Market 6/, expences 20/, market 8/	1	14	
5th.	Given Lucy	1	10	
8th	wood 7/6, market 19/3	1	6	9
11th.	market 8/, wood 8/, hominy & bread 4	1		
	Subscription to Birth night[92]	1	4	
14th.	linnen for self £7.6, Shovel 4/6	7	10	6
	Paid Capt. Morgan for Colo. Marshall	23	3	6
20th	expenses going to & returning from Wmsburg.[93]	3	8	
	eggs 3/, wood 7/6, potatoes 7/6		18	
25th.	wood 8/, market 8/		16	
		43	2	9
	deduct £24–13–6[94]	24	13	6
		18	9	3

[*Receipts*]

March 2d	Pierce in Mollison & al. ads. Upshaw	5		
4th.	advice fee	1	2	6
7th.	advice fee	1	2	6
	From Mr. Beale[95]	4	11	8
	Dejarnet ads. Burton[96]	2	10	

91. Two slaves owned by JM.

92. George Washington's birthday was celebrated on Feb. 11 with a dinner party at the Eagle Tavern and a ball at the new capitol in the evening, accompanied by a supper catered by Serafino Formicola. *Virginia Independent Chronicle* (Richmond), Feb. 18, 1789; *Va. Gaz. & Wkly. Adv.*, Feb. 12, 1789.

93. JM probably went to Williamsburg to conduct business before the High Court of Chancery. George Wythe had become the sole chancellor in the reorganization of the courts late in 1788 but did not move to Richmond immediately. He continued his teaching duties at the College of William and Mary until his replacement was elected in Mar. 1790. 12 Hening 766–768 (1788); Charles T. Cullen, "St. George Tucker and Law in Virginia, 1772–1804" (Ph.D. diss., University of Virginia, 1971), 167–168.

94. This figure represents the total JM had paid Capt. Morgan for his father and the amount JM had given his sister Lucy.

95. Samuel Beale. See Vol. I, 404, for an earlier fee from Beale.

96. Daniel and Joseph Dejarnett v. Robert Burton was a debt action filed in the General Court in Oct. 1788. The case was transferred to the District Court at Fredericksburg, where judgment was entered against Messrs. Dejarnett on Apr. 29, 1790.

10th	Aylett v Ayletts representatives[97]	5		
	Askew v Smith & al.	2	16	
	Fowshee v Neilson	2	16	
14th.	Greenhow v Carter etc. &			
	Dandridge etc. old rep. bonds	5		
	Advice fee	1	8	
	do.	1	2	
16	Latil[98] v Alexander	5	2	6
	Advice fee	1	2	
20	advice fee	1	2	6
	Mr. Richeson (Thorpes will)	5		
	advice fee	1	8	
	Webb v Greer (to be dismd)	2	8	
25th.	Brownlow ads. Custis (chy.)	2	10	
	Nelson ads. Nelson (chy.)[99]	2	16	
	advice fee	1	8	
	Wells v Sundries appeals	5		
		60	5	8

[Disbursements]

March 2d.	Soap 3/, bread 1/3,			
	wheelbarrows /4		7	4
4th.	expenses 1/6, postage 3/4		4	10
	Given Lucy for my father		1	6
	Given my sister Marshall	1	8	
	Paid Ross & Corrie for coal[1]	6	11	8

The decision was affirmed by the Court of Appeals on Dec. 14, 1790. District Court Record Book, 1789–1792, 143–145, Fredericksburg, District Court Law Orders, A, 1789–1793, 72, 95, Fredericksburg, and Court of Appeals Order Book, II, 50–51, all in Va. State Lib.

97. Callohill Minnis *et al.*, executors of William Aylett,. v. Philip Aylett involved a contested will that was brought before the High Court of Chancery. JM may not have argued the case, but it is likely he took the appeal to the Court of Appeals after the chancery court decreed against Philip Aylett on May 21, 1793. The Court of Appeals reversed the decision on Oct. 21, 1794. 1 Va. (1 Wash.) 300, 301; Wythe 219; Court of Appeals Order Book, III, 8, Va. State Lib. See additional fee entered under Receipts, Mar. 1794.

98. Joseph Latile was the agent of Caron de Beaumarchais in the United States.

99. William Nelson v. Thomas and John Nelson was a suit in the High Court of Chancery. JM represented Thomas and John Nelson and won his argument in that court, whereupon William Nelson appealed to the Court of Appeals. That court affirmed the chancery court's decree on Oct. 25, 1792. 1 Va. (1 Wash.) 136; Court of Appeals Order Book, II, 192, 193, Va. State Lib. See also Receipts, Oct. 26, 1790, and Feb. 1795.

1. See note at entry under Receipts, Dec. 29, 1788.

	Market 9/, sundries 6/, ball² 15/	1	10	
	paid for stable rent	2		
	paid for breast pin for Lucy		14	
11th.	Market 6/, shovel 6/, wood 8/	1		
	beef £3–12–4, Hay £4–10	8	2	4
14th.	shoes for Polly 12/,			
	Oysters etc. 6/		18	
	sending Lucy to Fauquier³	3	16	
23d.	Market sundry times 9/,			
	postage 5/, wood 8/	1	2	
24th.	Sugar 6/, Tea 18/, eggs etc. 3/	1	7	
	To Mr. Collins for rum	8	10	
26	To Mr. Davies	3	9	
	Wood		7	
		41	8	8

[*Receipts*]

March	Brown v Short & al.⁴	4	16
	from Mr. Latil⁵ in Sundries v		
	Alexander	5	2
	Letcher ads. White (old appeal)⁶	1	8
		11	6

[*Disbursements*]

March 29th.	halfsoling Israels⁷ shoes	2
	soap 3/, fish & greens 2/,	
	pullet 1/	5

2. JM was likely paying part of his subscription to the Richmond Assemblies, annual social activities held every two weeks during the winter months. For earlier participation by JM, see Vol. I, 299, 320, 346, 372.

3. JM sent his brother Alexander to accompany Lucy on her trip. See entry under Disbursements, Apr. 8, 1789.

4. Bennett Brown & Co. v. Thomas Short was a debt action that JM took to the District Court at Fredericksburg, where it finally abated by the death of his client, Brown. District Court Law Orders, A, 1789–1793, 292, 364, 484, Fredericksburg, Va. State Lib.

5. Joseph Latile.

6. John Letcher, assignee of William Noll, v. Rawleigh White was an old debt action in the General Court. It was transferred to the District Court at New London, where it abated in Apr. 1793 by the death of Letcher. District Court Order Book, 1789–1793, 329, Franklin County, Va. State Lib.

7. One of JM's slaves.

31st	Paid for Hanibal[8]	70	
		70	7

[Receipts]

April 1st.	Samuel v Anderson	1	10
2d.	Williams & Pratt ads. Byrd appeal	2	16
3d.	Booker v Booker & al. chy.	5	
4th.	Colo. Taylors exrs. in full	11	6
	Colo. Peachy[9]	1	8
6th.	Elam v Gordon sups.	2	10
7th.	Allen ads. McCrea (issue from chy.)	2	16
	Graham v Harrison[10]	1	15
	Parks v Butler old suit[11]		12
	Clements v Bates	2	16
8	Turnbull (Ridly & Pringle v Ross	1	15
	Mr. Cockran 2 appeals[12]	4	16
	Gayle ads. Lee appeal[13]	2	10
13th.	Wharton v Syme (chy.)	7	
	Mordecai v Myers (Wt. error)	2	10
	Holland v Trents etc. (injn.)		15
15.	Cocke v Syme & al.[14]		15
	Field v Call	7	

8. This is the only mention of Hanibal, a slave, in JM's Account Book.

9. William Peachy.

10. John Graham v. William Harrison was a debt action in the District Court at Fredericksburg. See declaration listed at Law Papers, Apr. 1789.

11. John Butler v. Mary Parks was an appeal to the General Court from King William County Court that was soon transferred to the District Court at King and Queen County. That court's decision of Apr. 25, 1791, was taken to the Court of Appeals and reversed on Apr. 20, 1792. 1 Va. (1 Wash.) 76; Court of Appeals Order Book, II, 83, 164, Va. State Lib.

12. David Cochran v. John Street was an appeal to the High Court of Chancery from the Hanover County Court. The chancery court reversed the county court's decision on Oct. 28, 1791. Street later took the case to the Court of Appeals. 1 Va. (1 Wash.) 79, 80; Wythe 133; Court of Appeals Order Book, II, 166, Va. State Lib. See later fee at Receipts, June 19, 1790.

13. James Lee v. George Gayle was an appeal to the General Court from a Middlesex County Court decision of May 26, 1788. Because of the court reorganization, the case was sent to the District Court at King and Queen County, where the lower court was affirmed on Apr. 23, 1791. The Court of Appeals upheld the decision on Nov. 22, 1791. Court of Appeals Order Book, II, 140, Va. State Lib. See additional fee under Receipts, Jan. 1792.

14. This entry is in a hand other than JM's.

Peter Baird		I	8	
Barkeville ads. Hill—H. cor.		I	10	
		62	8	

[Disbursements]

April

1,2,3	Market 17/			17	
	paid my Taylor		I	18	6
7th.	postage 2/, market 7/			9	
8th.	oats 2/6, market 3/, potatoes 7/6			13	
	cheese 9/, paid Mr. Paine[15]				
	for sundries £7–1–4		7	10	4
	Sugar 6/, wood 8/, market 3			17	
	expences etc. at Pburg.[16]		4	4	
			16	8	10
	Given Alexander expenses in				
	going with Lucy to Fauquier[17]		I	8	

[Receipts]

April 20th.	Jamison & al ads. Allison				
	(Morrison)		5	12	
	Advice fee		I	2	6
22d.	McGavock ads. Campbell (old				
	appeal) see		2	10	
	Rispess ads. Gay appeal		2	10	
	Hunters exrs. in two rep. bonds		5		
	same ads. Spotswood[18]		2	4	

15. Samuel Paine was a merchant in Richmond.

16. The first meeting of the District Court at Petersburg occurred on Apr. 15, 1789. Under the scheme for reorganizing the courts this district included Prince George, Sussex, Dinwiddie, and Amelia counties. The district courts had almost the same jurisdiction as did the old General Court, and cases pending before the General Court when the reorganization took place were transferred to the dockets of the district courts beginning in Apr. 1790. New appeals were to go directly to the districts as soon as the 1788 act was adopted. JM decided to practice before the Petersburg District Court at its spring and fall terms, as well as the district courts at Richmond and Fredericksburg. 12 Hening 730 (1788); 13 Hening 11 (1789); JM to Archibald Stuart, ca. Mar. 1789. For a discussion of the court reorganization of 1788 and its consequences, see Charles T. Cullen, "St. George Tucker and Law in Virginia, 1772–1804" (Ph.D. diss., University of Virginia, 1971), 100–134.

17. Alexander and Lucy Marshall had left Richmond for Fauquier County on or about Mar. 14. See entry under Disbursements, Mar. 14, 1789.

18. Adam Hunter and Abner Vernon, executors of James Hunter, and Edward

	Major Jones—a hoxhead of tobo.			
	Chew ads. Eddy admr. etc.	2	10	
		21	8	6

[Disbursements]

April	flour £6, market 5/	6	5	
	coal to Cunlif & McCall[19]	7	5	10
22d.	Corn 45/, wood 7/	2	12	
	expences at the election[20]	1	8	
	going to Fredericksburg[21]	2		
29th.	market		6	
	expences at society		3	
		19	19	10

[Receipts]

May 4th	Calloway & Co. ads. Livesay	5		
	Beale ads. Braxton (Henrico court)[22]	4	4	
	Dicken ads. Dicken (from Lewis)	1	8	
	Finnie v Braxton (Robinson)	7		
	Grymes ads. Pendleton & al.[23]	5		

Herndon and James Lewis, executors of John Herndon, v. Alexander Spotswood was a chancery suit in which JM represented Hunter and Vernon. A decision was given for Spotswood on Nov. 24, 1790, but JM's clients appealed to the Court of Appeals. The decision was at first reversed on Nov. 26, 1792, but later affirmed on June 23, 1793. 1 Va. (1 Wash.) 145; Court of Appeals Order Book, II, 106, 146, 182, 204–205, 229, 231, 232, Va. State Lib. See later fees under Receipts, May 1791 and Nov. 1792.

19. John Cunliffe and John McCall were both merchants in Richmond. "Lists of Merchants," Richmond City Hustings Court Order Book, II, 50, Va. State Lib.

20. JM was a successful candidate for a seat in the House of Delegates at the election held on Apr. 27 in Richmond. He took his oath of office on Oct. 19, 1789, at the opening of the fall session of the General Assembly. Election Certificate, Apr. 27, 1789, Election Records, Va. State Lib.; *Va. Gaz. & Wkly. Adv.*, Apr. 30, 1789. See JM's oath of office, Oct. 19, 1789.

21. The spring term of the District Court at Fredericksburg convened on Apr. 29 under the plan for reorganizing the courts adopted in 1788.

22. The Henrico County Court submitted the case of Carter Braxton v. Samuel Beale to arbitration on May 6, 1788, but it was dismissed by agreement on Mar. 2, 1790. This case was not the same one that JM argued in Apr. and Oct. 1787, although there is little question the two are related. Henrico County Court Order Book, III, 308, IV, 171, Va. State Lib. See Vol. I, 221–230.

23. Philip Ludwell Grymes, William Thornton, and Daniel McCarty v. Edmund Pendleton and Peter Lyons, executors of John Robinson, was a suit before the High

8th.	Mr. Barrett ads. Hawkins (chy.)	2	8
	Lee ads. Field eject. Pburg.	1	10
	advice fee from Mr. White	1	4
9th.	Je[rdon] exx. v Potties exr.[24]	5	
11th.	Mr. Corbin in chy.	7	
	Dupriest ads. Ford	5	
12th	Hungerford ads. Pratt[25]	2	16
	Alexander v Dade[26]	14	
13	Halcomb ads. Wells	3	5
	From Mr. Giles[27] (district)	1	10
	Webb ads. Harvey	5	
14	Matthews exrs. ads. Puryear & al. appeal	2	11
21st.	Maeze v Hambleton[28]	2	8
	Swan ads. Hubert & ux.	2	16
	£	79	

[Disbursements]

May 4th.	Market 12/, do. 6/		18
9th.	Market 6/, fruit 9/		15
10th	Wood 7/, cabbage plants 6/		13
13	Market 6/, Tea & sugar 28/, market 4/	1	18
	postage 3/, Market 4/,		

Court of Chancery. A decree of Sept. 26, 1793, against JM's clients, Grymes, Thornton, and McCarty, resulted in an appeal to the Court of Appeals on Apr. 16, 1795. The case was then continued until Oct. 20, 1797, when it was remanded. Court of Appeals Order Book, III, 48, 50, 100, 115, 181, Va. State Lib. See later fee under Receipts, July 27, 1790.

24. Francis Jerdone, of Louisa County, apparently lost this case, for in 1793 he was advised to retain JM to handle an appeal. George Gairdner to Frances Jerdone, Apr. 4, 1793, Jerdone Family Papers, Swem Library, College of William and Mary.

25. Anne Hungerford v. Margaret Pratt and Thomas Bunbury was brought before the High Court of Chancery on appeal from the King George County Court, with JM representing Hungerford. The High Court of Chancery affirmed the county court's decree, but JM took the case to the Court of Appeals and won a consent decree on June 13, 1791. Court of Appeals Order Book, II, 76, Va. State Lib.

26. Vertina and Baldwin Dade v. Charles and Robert Alexander was a chancery suit on a devise of land and the sale of slaves. JM's clients, Charles and Robert Alexander, won in the High Court of Chancery on May 25, 1790, and the decree was affirmed by the Court of Appeals on June 17, 1791. 1 Va. (1 Wash.) 30; Court of Appeals Order Book, II, 78, 79, Va. State Lib. See later fee under Receipts, June 1791.

27. JM apparently worked with William Branch Giles in the District Court at Petersburg. See JM to Giles, Feb. 9, 1790.

28. See JM to Archibald Stuart, ca. Dec. 1789.

		£		
debates[29] 9/		16		
	£	5		

[Receipts]

May				
	Dabny ads. Powell	12	10	
	Buxton ads. Cary chy.[30]	2	8	
	Garth v Johnston appeal	2	10	
	Armstead ads. Pottie	2	8	
30th.	advice fee	1	2	6
	Dicken ads. Dicken	8		
	Humphries v Smith & Briscoe	5		
	H[all]onstale v Hamilton appeal chy	5		
	Lyles ads. Herbert	5	8	
	From the sheriffs	5		
		49	6	6

[Disbursements]

May 22d.	Market 20/	1		
	Paid Mr. Lee for potowmac compy.[31]	66		
24th.	Market 7/, do. 6		13	
	paid Barber 30/, Market 2/	1	12	
29th.	Market 5/, sugar 9/		14	
	Given my brother Alexander	3	16	
	beer 7/, paid for levelling cellar[32] 17/	1	4	

29. JM probably purchased *Debates and other proceedings of the Convention of Virginia, convened at Richmond, on Monday the 2d day of June, 1788, for the purpose of deliberating on the Constitution recommended by the grand Federal Convention*, vol. I of which was published in 1788 and vols. II and III in 1789 by William Prentis in Petersburg. It also is possible that JM was purchasing *Debates of the Convention, of the State of Pennsylvania, on the Constitution, proposed for the government of the United States*, I (Philadelphia, 1788). See Disbursements, Nov. 13, 1789, where JM recorded an additional purchase of debates.

30. Miles Cary v. Nathaniel Buxton involved a contested will. JM represented Buxton and won in the General Court, but Cary sought an injunction in the High Court of Chancery. The injunction was granted in 1792. Wythe 183. See entry under Receipts, Mar. 1792.

31. See Vol. I, 344, and additional entries under Disbursements, Jan. 21, 1790, and Mar. 1794. JM sold his three shares in 1796. JM and Mary W. Marshall to Charles Higby, July 22, 1796, Potomac River Company, RG 79, National Archives.

32. On a separate list of expenses incurred in building his new house JM entered, "Paid Mr. Duke for levelling the cellar 18/" on a line after his May 16 entries. These

30th	given Polly 14/		14	
			75 13	
			66³³	
			9	13

[Receipts]

June 2	From the Sheriff of Frederick³⁴	2	8	
	From Roane in Upshaw ads. Hord³⁵	3	10	
4th.	From Weir v Elliott & Co.³⁶	2	8	
	From Latil³⁷ in Beaumarchais v Smith	4	17	6
	Keeling ads. Rice Chy.	5		
6th.	Watkins ads. comth.	2	14	
7th.	advice fee	1	2	6
9th	Penn exrs. etc. ads. Wyat chy.	5		
	Hawkins exr. v Syme appeal	2	10	
10	Jones v Blakey	1	10	
	Jones ads. Wollers exrs. (finishd) John Corbin entitled to the money—Gilliam	2	10	
	Burrus exr. of Lipscomb ads. Booth	1		
10th.	From Mr. Bolling	1	8	
12	From Mr. Henry for advice	1	8	
	From Lyles on account of papers	2	8	
	Allen ads. Coutts appeal	2	10	
		42	4	

are certainly the same expenses, despite the difference of one shilling between the two entries. It is unclear why JM entered this expense twice. See Construction Account, Oct. 1788.

33. This is the amount JM paid for his Potomac River Company subscription, entered at Disbursements, May 22, 1789.

34. Joseph Berry. See *JVCS*, IV, 286.

35. John Hord and William Waring v. John Upshaw, Thomas Roane, and James Upshaw was an old chancery case that Upshaw, Roane, and Upshaw, JM's clients, had won in the early 1780s. It was appealed to the Court of Appeals but was sent back to the High Court of Chancery on Nov. 4, 1784. No additional records exist, but it must have returned to the Court of Appeals at this time. Court of Appeals Order Book, II, 33, 37, 38, 39, 44, 45, Va. State Lib. JM received fees in this case also on Oct. 18, 1789, and in June 1790.

36. See JM's declaration listed at Law Papers, Sept. 1789.

37. Joseph Latile.

[*Disbursements*]

June 4th.	Paid Doctor Currie[38]	11	
10th.	pair of shoes 12/, fruit 2/		14
11th.	Slides[39] for Polly 8/, Given		
	Polly 28/	1	16
	Ducks 6/, Market 20/	1	6
		14	16

[*Receipts*]

June 14th.	Colo. James	4	4	
15	The clerks	7		
	Mr. Binns (motion)			
	Conway v Harrison & al			
	(new exn.)[40]	2	10	
	advice fee from Mr. Bibb	1	2	6
	Jones v Blakey residue of fee	1		
	Cook ads. Lee Appeal[41]	2	10	
24	Jones v Verrel (appeals)[42]	5		
	Banks & al. ads. Lee	5		
	McRoberts—Carys exrs.	2	8	
30th.	Dandridge exr. v Lyons & al			
	exrs. etc.[43]	5		
		38	8	6

38. James Currie (1745–1807) was born in Scotland and studied medicine at Edinburgh before coming to Virginia, where he became a practicing physician. He lived at the corner of Broad and 10th streets in Richmond. Robert A. Rutland *et al.*, eds., *The Papers of James Madison* (Chicago, 1973), VIII, 495, n. 1.

39. A slide was a tongueless buckle or ring used as a fastener, clasp, or brooch; or a small perforated object sliding on a cord.

40. See notes on JM's argument in this case, June 16, 1789.

41. Charles Lee v. Thomas Cooke was probably first brought before the General Court, but it was transferred to the District Court at King and Queen County in 1789 after the reorganization of the state judiciary. After the district court decided in favor of Cooke on Apr. 19, 1793, Lee appealed. JM represented Cooke on appeal before the Court of Appeals on Oct. 21, 1794, and the judgment was affirmed three days later. 1 Va. (1 Wash.) 306; Court of Appeals Order Book, III, 9, 12, Va. State Lib. See additional fee under Receipts, Oct. 1793.

42. Peter Jones v. John Verell, Jr., and Martha, his wife, was an appeal from a decree of the High Court of Chancery issued on June 2, 1789. The Court of Appeals reversed the chancery decree on July 9, 1790, in favor of Jones, JM's client. Court of Appeals Order Book, II, 24, Va. State Lib.

43. In John Dandridge and William Armistead, executors of Bartholomew Dandridge, v. Thomas Lyon, JM asked the High Court of Chancery for an injunction against a judgment rendered in the James City County Court regarding the slaves in

[*Disbursements*]

June 16th.	sugar 12/, market 13/4	1	5	4
18th.	beer 7/6, fruit 6/		13	6
24th.	Given Polly 14/, fruits 5/, hat for Tom 3/	1	2	
	expences 15/, do. 18/	1	13	
26	paid off my account with Warrington & Keene[44]	11	8	
27th.	fruit sevl. times 3/, market 7/		10	
28th.	market 8/, fruit 4/		12	
		17	3	10

[*Receipts*]

July 1st.	From Mr. Shermer on account of Goadsby etc. v Wilkes & al.	7		
2d.	advice fee from Doctor Walker[45]	1	8	
3d.	Mr. John Scott	7	10	
	Mr. Rice (appeal Fluvanna)	2	10	
6th.	Mr. Williams v Chambers (appl. chy.)	5	12	
	Carter ads. Hall (old suit)	5	12	
8th.	Advice fee from Mr. Irving	1	2	6
10	From Mr. Royal ads. Anderson (appeal)[46]	2	10	0
	From Constable ads. Banks chy.[47]	6		

---

an estate. The injunction was allowed by the court on Oct. 31, 1791. Wythe 123. See JM to John Dandridge, Apr. 25, 1789.

44. Warrington & Keene was a mercantile firm in Richmond that had been advertising since May 12, 1789, "an extensive Spring & Summer Assortment of Goods . . . Fine Hyson Tea . . . A fresh supply of Law Books. . . ." *Va. Gaz. & Wkly. Adv.*, June 18, 1789.

45. Thomas Walker. See Vol. I, 240, 372, and JM to Thomas Walker, July 9, 1789.

46. This entry is in a hand other than JM's.

47. For information on Hunter, Banks & Co. v. Sargeant and Constable, see JM to William Constable, July 11, 1789. See also JM to William Branch Giles, July 8, 1789. In a letter of July 12, 1789, Benjamin Harrison, Jr., who had engaged JM for William Constable, wrote to Constable, "I have given Mr Marshall twenty Dollars with which I charge you. . . ." Constable-Pierrepont Papers, New York Public Library.

13th.	Davies ads. Jones appeal[48]	2	10	
17	Drawing conveyances	4	4	
	Cox v. Calloway (appeal old suit)		18	
20th.	Alexander v Gernon	5	12	
27th.	Thornton v Shackleford etc. chy.	5	12	
29th.	From Colo. Lynch concerning sheriff of Cammel	2	16	
30th.	From Mr. Beall[49]	10		
		70	16	6

[Disbursements]

July 1	House 28/, expences 18/	2	6	
3d.	coolers 15/; 4th. expenses[50] 6/	1	1	
5th.	Market 7/, Store £3-4, fruit 2/	3	13	
	tax on deed 12/, recording do.[51] 12/8	1	4	8
9th.	Given my brother Alexander	2	12	
11th.	Market 7/, do. 10/, sugar etc. 6/	1	3	
13th.	paid for military certificates	21	17	10
14th.	market 8/, materials for pickles			
17	market 8/, expences 6/		14	
20th.	Market 6/, taxes[52] £4	4	6	
22d.	For assignments in Ld. office for Colo. Marshall		15	

48. Orlando Jones and John Hudson v. Nicholas Davis was a district court case that was taken on appeal to the Court of Appeals. JM's client, Davis, won in the district court, and the judgment was affirmed by the Court of Appeals on Apr. 18, 1793. Court of Appeals Order Book, II, 161, Va. State Lib.

49. This could be Samuel Beale, who previously had been a client of JM's in Braxton v. Beale and Beale v. Cockburn. See Vol. I, 221-230, 404, n. 92.

50. On July 4 a large barbecue held in the country outside Richmond was attended by "a respectable body of Gentlemen." A flag was raised at dawn while cannons were discharged, and in the evening a dinner was held and toasts were drunk with the accompaniment of the usual 13 cannon shots. Va. Gaz. & Wkly. Adv., July 9, 1789.

51. JM was paying the tax on and recording the deed for the lot that he had purchased from Philip Turpin and on which he built his house. See Deed, July 7, 1789.

52. JM's personal property list for Richmond, received Mar. 18, 1789, indicates 2 tithable males in the household and ownership of 7 tithable slaves and 2 slaves below the age of 16. His real property was taxed at £1 5s. Richmond City Personal Property Book, 1789, and Land Book, 1789, Va. State Lib.

Date	Entry	£	s	d
23d.	Market 6/, postage 1/, sundries for pickles 24/	1	11	
24	Market 30/, Given Alexander 28/	2	18	
	cloths for myself	4	16	
		48	17	6
	deduct paid for certificates &	21	17	10
	given Alexander	2	12	
		24	9	10
		24	7	8

[Receipts]

Date	Entry	£	s	d
August 1st.	Jo Dameron ads. Duncan & Co.	5		
	Miller ads. Upshaw & al.	5	0	0
	Edmonds ads. Bakers exrs.	2	2	
3d.	Advice fee	1	8	
	Belsches exr. v. Massie appeal	5		
	Ballard ads. Grubb	5		
5	Pope v Taylor	5		
	Gordon v Jacobs & al	5	12	
5	Mr. Beale[53]	5	12	
6	Mr. Frazer Palmers exr. 5 aggregate fund			
8th.	Williams v Chambers	2	8	
	Taylors exrs. (Harvey) v Taylors exrs.	5	10	
12th.	Carter v Salle & al exrs.	2	1	
13	From Mr. Strother on account of a motion v Hites & Greene[54]		18	
14th.	Littlepage & Sydnor ads. Haynes	2		
	Boggus v Knight (Chy.)	2	8	
22d.	drawing a conveyance	1	8	
23	Hook ads. Ross	5		

53. See entry under Receipts, July 30, 1789.
54. Representatives of Jost Hite v. Christian Copp, Henry Snarr, Henry and Jacob Sellers, and William Strother involved a contested claim of land. The case was taken to the Court of Appeals, where the lower court judgment was affirmed on Nov. 16, 1791. Court of Appeals Order Book, II, 118, 127, Va. State Lib.

		£	s	d
	Riply v McClelan (old suit)	1	8	
	Middleton & Croughton (Mr. Warrington)	2	10	
	Corbin v Norton[55]	2	10	
		67	15	
30th.	From Sir Jonathan Becquith[56]	2	10	

[*Disbursements*]

		£	s	d
August 1st.	expences 3/, market 2/, fruit 2/		7	
8th.	Market 11/, expenses 8/		19	
9th.	Market 7/, fruit 2/, expenses 9/		18	
12	expences 6/, market 2/		8	
16	market 2/, do. 6/		8	
22	Market 10/, Tea 45/	2	15	
24	Market 9/, do. 12/	1	1	
	Given Alexander 6/		6	
	At Warringtons[57]	1	14	
	Given Alexander	5	10	
30th.	expenses 42/6	2	2	6
	market 12/		12	
		17		6

[*Receipts*]

		£	s	d
September	Cogbill ads. Walthall (finishd)	1	10	8
	Abny v Winston in part (old suit)		12	
2	Fontaine ads. Granberry	2	16	
	Wills v Ross (old appeal)	2	10	
	Machlin v Hunt eject.	2	10	
	McClurg v Ross 52/	2	12	
3d.	Walton v Fontaines exx.	2	14	
	Harris v Thompson	1	8	
4	Collins v Banks	2	16	
	Eject v Corbin (dismd.)		18	
	Payne ads. Oliver[58]	2	8	

55. See Charles M. Thruston to JM, Sept. 24, 1789.
56. See Vol. I, 336.
57. Warrington & Keene, a mercantile firm in Richmond.
58. Archer Payne v. Thomas Oliver was an action in the District Court at Richmond in which judgment was entered against Payne, JM's client, on Apr. 4, 1793. The appeal to the Court of Appeals was dismissed on Oct. 10, 1793, when neither

	Hawkins exx. ads. Gilberts exrs. new suit	2	8	
6th	advice	1	2	6
7th	Netherland ads. Badget	1	10	
	Graves ads. Winston	2	6	8
	Martin v Winston	1	8	
	Flournoy v Self	1	8	
8th.	Recd. from D. Cockran through Mr. Lewis[59]	5		
10	From Mr. Pearson	2	10	
		40	7	10

[Disbursements]

Septr.

1	a pen knife 6/, fruit 3/		9	
2d.	beer 7/6, market 15/, expenses 7/6	1	10	
	Given Alexr. (4 pr. stockings at Herons[60])	1	8	
10	expenses 9/, market 3/		12	
11th.	Market 6/8, Trunk 15/	1	1	8
		5		8

[Receipts]

Septr.

16	From Mr. Beverly vs Rennolds Exor. of Hipkins (Chy)[61]	5	5	0
18	From Robertson vs. Hall (chy) in part[62]	1	4	0
	Fowshee v Lea[63]	2	8	

party appeared. Court of Appeals Order Book, II, 240, Va. State Lib. JM entered an additional fee in this case at Receipts, Sept. 1, 1790.

59. JM also entered this under the same date on a separate account of the expenses of building his house. That entry indicates JM paid the money to Mr. Lewis. See Construction Account, printed at Oct. 1788.

60. James Heron's mercantile firm.

61. Robert Gaines Beverley v. John Rennolds, executor of Leroy Hipkins, was a petition for an injunction against a judgment awarded to Rennolds. The petition was granted on Oct. 26, 1791. Wythe 121. See additional fee entered under Receipts, Oct. 1789. This entry is in a hand other than JM's.

62. This entry is in a hand other than JM's.

63. Thomas Lea v. William Foushee was an action in the District Court at Fred-

Masterson v Turnbulls exrs (finishd)	2	10	
McClean v Taylor & Co. do.	5	12	
Brockenboro v Brockenboro	5	10	
Ross (advice)	2	8	
Collier v Jones	2	10	
Harrison v Hayes (new)	2	8	
Hardaway ads. Hardaway	1	8	
Lynch & ux v Cathcart (attend)	2	12	
Pegram ads. Compton (finishd)	2	12	
Jones ads. Hanson (do.)	3		
Booker ads. Field[64]	1	16	
Coleman v Eppes	2	10	
Lacy ads. Ross & Co.	9	12	
Call ads. Burwells exrs.[65]	3		
	56	5	

[*Disbursements*]

[September] expenses at Pburg.	8		
House expenses at Pburg. & Frburg.[66]	11	10	
	19	10	

[*Receipts*]

Octo. 1st	Walden—three suits[67] (Fburg)	4	4	
	Ragland ads. Pate[68]	1	00	0
	Pate ads. Pate	1	00	0

ericksburg in which JM represented Foushee. The case was transferred there by the High Court of Chancery. Judgment was given JM's client on Oct. 6, 1791. District Court Law Orders, A, 1789–1793, 12, 99, 312, Fredericksburg, Va. State Lib. The details of this complicated case are explained in 8 Va. (4 Call) 279–281 (1795).

64. See JM to William Branch Giles, Feb. 9, 1790.

65. See JM to William Branch Giles, Feb. 9, 1790.

66. JM had attended the District Court at Petersburg, which convened on Sept. 15, and the District Court at Fredericksburg, which began on Sept. 29.

67. One of these suits was no doubt Charles Walden's Executor v. David Payne. The District Court at Fredericksburg found against Walden, and JM filed an appeal. The Court of Appeals affirmed the decision on Nov. 20, 1794. 2 Va. (2 Wash.) 1; Court of Appeals Order Book, III, 36, 38–39, Va. State Lib. See additional entry under Receipts, Nov. 1794, and a plea listed at Law Papers, Mar. 1790.

A second suit, Allason v. Walden's Executor, was also before the same district court. See plea listed at Law Papers, Mar. 1790.

68. This and the following four entries are in a hand other than JM's.

		£	s	d
	Slaughter vs Slaughter (old suit)	2	10	0
2nd.	Pulliam ads. Glynn	2	16	0
3d.	Walton ads. Pate	1	00	0
11	Stoval v Tony (appl. G. Ct.)	2	10	
	Boggus v Knight (chy.)	1	12	
12	Joseph Curd v Pattison (injn.) Buckingham	5	2	
	Grantland ads. Richeson (chy.)	5		
	Morris v Jones (appl. Chy.)	5		
	Haddon admr. & al. ads. Hall & ux (chy.)	2	2	
	Haley ads. Powell & Shelton (appl. chy.)	5		
	Prices exrs. v Armstead (appl. chy.)[69]	5		
	Johnston ads Syme (chy.)[70]	5		
F.burg.	Scott ads. Terry eject. (referd[71]	5		
	Lewis v Dicken case[72]	2	10	
	Ritchie & Co. v Brown appeal[73]	2	16	
	⟨Doctor Fowshee⟩[74]	⟨2	8⟩	
		59	2	

69. This case, Robert Price, administrator of Thomas Price, v. William Nelson, executor, and Maria Armistead, executrix of William Armistead, was a debt action that was filed in the General Court and then was transferred to the District Court at Fredericksburg. JM's client won judgment on Oct. 7, 1789, but JM's entry, "appl. chy.," suggests the defendant was going to ask the High Court of Chancery to issue an injunction against the court's decision. No record of the case in chancery exists. District Court Law Orders, A, 1789–1793, 60, Fredericksburg, Va. State Lib. See a later fee under Receipts, June 1791.

70. John Syme, Jr., v. Thomas and William Johnston was a chancery suit in which JM's client, Syme, fought the Johnstons' request to dissolve an injunction issued in 1786 against a judgment of the General Court. The injunction was dissolved and Syme appealed. The Court of Appeals affirmed the decree on Dec. 15, 1790. 7 Va. (3 Call) 558–567; Court of Appeals Order Book, II, 14, 16, 53, Va. State Lib. See also JM to Archibald Stuart, ca. Dec. 1789; and 7 U.S. (3 Cranch) 92, 94 (1805).

71. Thomas Terry and George Booker v. John Scott was an ejectment action filed in the General Court in Oct. 1786. It was transferred to the District Court at Fredericksburg during the reorganization of 1788, and on Oct. 3, 1789, it was submitted to arbitration by consent of the parties. The report of the arbitrators was presented to the court on May 7, 1793. District Court Law Orders, A, 1789–1793, 37, 478, and Law Orders, 1790–1793, 111, Fredericksburg, Va. State Lib. See later fee in this case, Receipts, Mar. 1793.

72. See Henry Lewis to JM, Apr. 28, 1790.

73. James Ritchie & Co. v. Hezekiah Brown was an appeal of May 19, 1789, from Culpeper County Court. The District Court at Fredericksburg reversed the decision on May 10, 1791, and sent it back to the county court on May 5, 1792. District Court Law Orders, A, 1789–1793, 265, 363, Fredericksburg, Va. State Lib.

74. JM crossed out this entry and did not add it into his total receipts. He apparent-

[*Disbursements*]			
October			
2nd.	paid Carriage of a Trunk to Fredericksbg.		11
	Alexr. pd. Betsey Muncas in part for making his shirts[75]		16
12th.	Flour	7	5
		8	17

[*Receipts*]			
October	Ritchie & Minor ads. Madden (chy)	5		
	Jones v Hoomes & al[76]	2	8	
	Ashton ads. Gray[77]	1	16	8
	Towles ads. Wiley[78]	3		
	Lacoste & Glassel ads. Fletcher & Sunderland	2	8	
	Smith v Young & Stockdell[79]	2	16	
	Carters exrs. ads. Goodloe[80]	1	10	
	From Mr. Todd for advice to be given on papers to be recd.	1	8	
	From Doctor Mortimer[81]	2	8	

ly meant his entry under Receipts, Sept. 18, 1789, "Fowshee v. Lea," to cover this receipt.

75. Both entries under this date are in a hand other than JM's.

76. William Jones v. Joseph Hoomes and Abram Simons was an appeal to the District Court at Fredericksburg that was dismissed on Oct. 9, 1789, on the motion of Hoomes and Simons. District Court Law Orders, A, 1789–1793, 72, Fredericksburg, Va. State Lib.

77. George Gray v. Henry Alexander Ashton involved a claim of breach of agreement and was first filed in the King George County Court in Apr. 1789. JM apparently took the case to the District Court at Fredericksburg in the fall of 1789. Judgment was confessed on May 4, 1790. District Court Record Book, 1789–1792, 165–167, and Law Orders, A, 1789–1793, 66, 102, Fredericksburg, Va. State Lib. See JM's stipulation listed at Law Papers, May 1790.

78. John Wiley v. Thomas Towles was a debt action before the District Court at Fredericksburg. The case was continued from Oct. 2, 1789, until May 4, 1790, when it appears a motion to dismiss was granted following the plaintiff's failure to give security for costs on time. District Court Law Orders, A, 1789–1793, 34, 104, Fredericksburg, Va. State Lib.

79. See JM's declaration listed at Law Papers, Apr. 1790.

80. See Vol. I, 365, n. 41.

81. Dr. Charles Mortimer (d. 1801) came to Virginia before 1759 and settled in Fredericksburg. He was attempting to recover a debt from the estate of William Armistead and probably retained JM for that purpose.

Johnston v Gray (referd)[82]		18	
Wyat ads. Johnston (finishd[83]	1	4	8
Williams v Ralls exrs.[84]	1	8	
Beverly v Hipkins exrs. (chy.)[85]	5	12	
Calvert v Shropshire (finishd)	1	8	
Miller in eject.[86] & suit in chy.	14		
Ramsay ads. Daltons exrs.			
(old appl.	5	8	
Madison v Sheriff of Culpeper[87]	1	8	
	54	1	4

[*Disbursements*]

October	In house while I was at Petersburg & Fredericksburg	10

[*Receipts*]

October			
13th.	Alexander v Peyton (chy.)	5	
	Leftwich ads. Leftwich	4	16
	Herbert v Portlock (chy. appl.)	5	
14th.	Hughes v Clayton & ux (appl.)[88]	4	16
	Custis v Alexander	5	12

82. James Johnston v. William Fauntleroy Gray was originally filed before the General Court, with JM representing Johnston. After the reorganization of the courts in 1788, it was transferred to the District Court at Fredericksburg, where on Oct. 3, 1789, it was submitted to binding arbitration. Judgment was entered for Gray on Oct. 8, 1790. District Court Law Orders, A, 1789–1793, 34, 196, Fredericksburg, Va. State Lib.

83. See Vol. I, 395, n. 57.

84. Nathaniel Williams v. John Frisbie and Original Young, executors of John Ralls, Sr., was before the District Court at Fredericksburg, with JM representing Williams. On May 3, 1790, it was submitted to arbitrators. District Court Law Orders, A, 1789–1793, 36, 106, Fredericksburg, Va. State Lib.

85. See entry under Receipts, Sept. 16, 1789.

86. This is likely the case of James Miller v. Philip Johnston, an appeal from a Caroline County Court judgment against Miller in May 1789. The judgment was affirmed by the District Court at Fredericksburg on May 10, 1791. District Court Law Orders, A, 1789–1793, 267, and District Court Record Book, 1789–1792, 544–550, Fredericksburg, Va. State Lib.

87. Francis Madison v. James Pendleton, sheriff of Culpeper County, involved a judgment of the Caroline County Court rendered in Aug. 1789. The District Court at Fredericksburg awarded a writ of supersedeas on Oct. 9, 1789, and reversed the judgment on May 7, 1791. District Court Law Orders, A, 1789–1793, 72, 260, and District Court Record Book, 1789–1792, 534–535, Fredericksburg, Va. State Lib.

88. See Vol. I, 364, n. 30.

		£	s	d
	Williams & al ads. McClean (injn.)	4	4	
15th.	Newel ads. Pottinger (chy.)	5		
	Combs v Combs (appl. chy.)	2	15	
17th	Pickens v Anderson (appeal G. Ct.)[89]	2	8	
18th	Upshaw ads. Hord[90]	2	10	
	From Mr. Jo. Jones	2	10	
19th.	Walker ads. Syme[91] chy.	4	10	
	same v Thompsons exrs.	1	8	
20th.	From Mr. Love	27	13	4
	Roane ads. Hern (chy.)[92]	3		
	Clapham ads. Carlyles exrs.	5		
	Morris v Jones (appl. chy.)	2	16	
	Russel v Campbell	5		
21st.	Colo. C. Carter in Claybornes case	2	16	
		96	14	4

[Disbursements]

		£	s	d
October				
14th.	Market 12/, do. 2/, do. 21/	1	15	
	Butter 42/, market 18/	3		
16	beer 7/6, market 3/		9	
18th.	market 3/, do. 3/6		6	6
20	Market 6/10		6	10
	Given for negroe woman	38		
	expenses to & from Fburg[93]	8	15	
	personal expenses there	2		
		54	12	4

89. See Certification, Jan. 6, 1794, and JM to Archibald Stuart, Jan. 22, 1794.

90. See entry under Receipts, June 2, 1789.

91. See Vol. 1, 396; JM to Thomas Walker, July 9, 1789; and Receipts, calendared at Oct. 19, 1789.

92. Thomas and John Roane, James Upshaw, and William Latane, executors of William Roane, v. Frederick William Hearne and wife, Anne, widow of William Roane, involved a premarital agreement to transfer ownership of slaves in lieu of dower. The High Court of Chancery ordered the agreement enforced in Oct. 1790, but an appeal was taken by JM on behalf of his clients to the Court of Appeals, where the decree was affirmed on Nov. 21, 1791. Wythe 90; 1 Va. (1 Wash.) 47; Court of Appeals Order Book, II, 128, 136, Va. State Lib. See additional fee under Receipts Oct. 26, 1790.

93. These expenses were incurred in attending the district court session there.

		38		
		16	12	4

[Receipts]

October				
22d.	Thompsons exrs. v Spotswood (advice fee)[94]	3		
	Thomas v Kendal, to send exrs. to Satchel	2	10	
	From Crump (injn. v Comth.)	4	4	
	Overton v Ross[95]	2	10	
28th.	Oxly & Hancock[96]	14		
	From Mr. Groves in Banks ads. Lee	5	4	
30th.	From Mr. Winfry	1	8	
31st.	From Mr. Britain in Scott & al ads. Scot	4	5	
		27	1	

[Disbursements]

October				
22d.	Wine 28/, market 16	2	4	
23d.	Market 9/, beer 7/6, lanthorn 4/6	1	1	
	Market 16/, boot strops & tape 6/	1	2	
	Given Mrs. Burrus	1	8	
		5	15	

94. JM was apparently asked for advice in Francis Thornton, William Thornton, and Fielding Lewis, executors of Rev. John Thompson, v. Alexander Spotswood after the High Court of Chancery on Oct. 14, 1789, had reversed a decree of the Spotsylvania County Court against the appellants. They later took the case to the Court of Appeals, but there is no evidence JM participated further. 1 Va. (1 Wash.) 142; Court of Appeals Order Book, II, 36, 101, 146, 182, 204, 205, 206, Va. State Lib.

95. David Ross v. Elizabeth and Richard Overton involved damage to a mill near Richmond leased by Ross. It was before the District Court at Richmond but was not decided before JM stopped practicing there. It later went to the Court of Appeals. 7 Va. (3 Call) 268; Court of Appeals Order Book, IV, 208, 209, 224, Va. State Lib. See later fees under Receipts, June 1792, and Mar. 1793.

96. Oxley and Hancock v. John Short was a case in assumpsit before the District Court at Fredericksburg in which JM represented Short. Judgment was given the plaintiffs on May 7, 1790. District Court Law Orders, A, 1789–1793, 115, Fredericksburg, Va. State Lib. See Receipts, Nov. 3, 1789.

[*Receipts*]

		£	s	d
November	Mr. Charles Woodson, (2 appls.	5		
	Donald & Frazer & Joseph &			
	John Nicholson (I beleive for			
	Nicholson) appl.	2	16	
	Garth v Johnston (old appl. see)	2	10	
3	Oxly & Hancock ads Short[97]	7	00	0
4th.	Advice fee (Coleman)	1	2	6
	Rheling ads. Gabriels Chy.	5		
	Gootee ads. Henry chy.[98]	6		
12th.	Hall v Stratton (old appeal)	2	8	
16	advice fee on Winns will)	1	2	6
	Advice fee (Mosely's will)	1	16	
	Stuart ads. Donelly	5		
18	Brooks v Greenwood	5		
	Stith v Stratton[99]	11	16	
	Mr. Jerdon (appeal)	2	10	
20	Mr. Turner v Buchanan etc.			
	appeal	1	10	
	Buler ads. Williams	5		
24th.	Advice fee from Mr. Downman	1	8	
	Mr. Meredith	2	8	
		69	6	6

[*Disbursements*]

		£	s	d
November				
2d.	Meal 15/, Market 3/		18	
13th.	Market 15/, Stockings 28/	2	3	
	Market 6/, candles 38/3	2	4	3

97. See entry under Receipts, Oct. 28, 1789.

98. There was a case, James Henry v. John Gootee, in the District Court at Accomack and Northampton counties involving a debt action. It was decided in 1796; however, there is no evidence that JM practiced before that court. It is likely he participated in the case before it went to that court, perhaps on another issue before the High Court of Chancery. District Court Order Book, 1789–1797, 471, Accomack County, Va. State Lib. See his fee entered under Receipts, Sept. 1794.

99. Griffin Stith, Jr., v. John Stratton, Sr., was an action in detinue that ended in the District Court at Accomack and Northampton counties, as did the case above. JM could have participated in the cases when they were first brought before the General Court before the reorganization of the courts in 1788, or he could have been paid for solicited advice from the plaintiff's attorney. The latter possibility is remote, however. JM would have written the name of the attorney and "advice fee," if he had been so engaged in the case. *Ibid.*, 15, 40.

	debates of convention[1] 9/			9
	Subscription to assembly[2] £3	3		
	apples & potatoes 12/,			
	Oysters 4/			16
14.	Market 11/, do. 2/			13
	a hog 16/8, Meal 12/4	1		9
	a hiefer 25/, Market 23/	2		8
	Wine £14–2, Oysters 2/	14		4
21st.	Market 6/, sending for Mrs.			
	Crenshaw[3] 12			18
24	Market 38	1		18
	Sending for beef 12/			12
25	Brown sugar & coffee	1		8
	Taylor for making cloaths	1		10
	Given Mrs. Crenshaw	5		
	Sending her home 7/6, horse			
	hire 12/			19 6
29	market 9/			9
		40	10	9

[Receipts]

Novr. 29th.	Crow v Doherty	6
	Jacob ads. Williams & al[4]	5
		11

[Disbursements]

Novr. 29.	Beef from Mr. Burwell	5

1. JM probably purchased vol. II or III, which were both published in 1789 by William Prentis in Petersburg, of *Debates and other proceedings of the Convention of Virginia* . . . , or the constitutional debates of the Pennsylvania convention. See entry under Disbursements, May 13, 1789.

2. See Vol. I, 299, n. 37.

3. JM noted in his family Bible that a daughter, Mary Ann, was born on Nov. 24, 1789. A similar notation recorded her death on Aug. 1, 1792. See entry under Disbursements, Aug. 1792, where JM entered the purchase of a coffin. Mrs. Crenshaw was obviously employed to assist in the birth.

4. Isaac Williams and Joseph Tomlinson v. John Jeremiah Jacob and David Jones involved land claimed under a military warrant. The High Court of Chancery heard the case in May 1792 and decided for the plaintiffs. Jones appealed to the Court of Appeals, where the chancery decision was reversed on Nov. 4, 1793. Wythe 145; 1 Va. (1 Wash.) 230; Court of Appeals Order Book, II, 230, 249, 251, Va. State Lib. See JM to David Jones, Jan. 16, 1794; JM to William Branch Giles, *ca.* Mar. 1793; and additional fees at Receipts, Oct. 1791, May 1793, and Mar. 1794.

	Mutton from Mr. Lee	1		
	Sugar 6/, sugar 6, sundries 4/		16	
		6	16	

[Receipts]

December				
3d.	From Mr. John Dandridge[5]	2	16	
	For drawing deed	1	2	6
5th.	Dunn v Walker	2	8	
	Fairfax ads. Wormly[6]	5		
	Advice fee	1	2	6
	From Mr. Morris in Glass &			
	Wails	56	0	5
12th	Bowyer v Ramsay	4	4	
	In Leiper—Wilson v Hart[7]	4	16	
17	Keeble ads. Keeble	3	12	
	Custis v Fitchet (injn)	1	16	
	From Mr. Parsons (Carnes)			
	finishd	2	10	
	Mr. Jett—Sci. fa. v Ellzey etc.	5		
	Advice fee	1	2	6
	do.	1	4	
18th.	do.	1	2	
	May & Robinson v Wood &			
	Allison appeal (chy.	5		
	Wells ads. Banks chy.	2		
20	Advice fee	1	8	
	Fleet v Didlake drawing injn.	1	8	
	Norvell v Ross[8]	5		
		108	11	11

5. See JM to John Dandridge, Apr. 25, 1789.

6. This was probably a case between James Wormeley (d. 1830) and Denny Martin Fairfax. Wormeley had married the sister of Edmund Randolph and settled in Frederick County. After 1794 he exchanged his Virginia land for land owned by the Fairfax family in England, where he had moved. See additional fees under Receipts, Feb. 4, May, and July 20, 1790, Nov. 1791, and Apr. 1793.

7. See Vol. I, 388, n. 32.

8. James Norvell v. David Ross involved the ownership of slaves and was first argued before the High Court of Chancery, which decreed in favor of Norvell. Ross then appealed to the Court of Appeals, where the decree was affirmed on June 28, 1791. 1 Va. (1 Wash.) 14; Court of Appeals Order Book, II, 85, 89, 103, 104, Va. State Lib. See JM to James Breckinridge, Oct. 12, 1793.

[*Disbursements*]

December		£	s	d
3d	Waistcoat 15/, corn 6/, market 6/	1	7	
6	Turkey 4/, corn 10/, butter 3–3–7	3	17	7
9th.	Sugar, vinegar & mustard 17/4, Turkeys 5/	1	2	4
12th.	Paid for pork 6–14–8	6	14	8
17	Sugar 6/, market 18/, do. 6/	1	10	
20th.	market 3/, mats 1/3, oysters 3/		7	3
22	Corn 12/		12	
		15	10	10

[*Receipts*]

December		£	s	d
22d.	Conn v Treon & al.	3		
	advice fee from Mr. Overton	1	8	
	Roy & Garnett (appeals—not yet brought)	14		
23	Colo. Zane (retainer)	2	8	
24	Crow ads. Doherty	3	2	6
	McCampbell v Keys chy.	2	8	
28th.	Hollingsworth, Johnston & Co. v Ross (old suit)	7	4	
	Backhouse v Donald etc.[9]	2	8	
		35	18	
	Recd. [*1789*]	1114	2	
	[*Disbursements 1789*]	404	19	7
	[*1789 Balance*]	709	2	5

[*Disbursements*]

December		£	s	d
	Market 4/3, wood £8	8	4	3
25	lock 7/6, purse 5/		12	6
26	Wood 7/6, house 6/		13	6
	Market 6/, given away 9/		15	
	handkerchef 7/6, expences 4/		11	6

9. See JM's declaration, *ca.* June 1797, Backhouse's Administrator v. Donald's Executors, U.S. Circuit Court, Va., Ended Cases (Unrestored), 1798, Va. State Lib.

fodder 6/, given for taking the horse 6/		12	
Mr. McCol & Cunlif (coal)[10]	2	14	
Pork £22–13–8	22	13	8
	36	6	5
Expended in house[11]	404	19	7
Paid Gilliat[12] for Negroes clothing	10	1	4
Paid Mr. Heron[13] for sundries	10	7	3

[Receipts]

January			
6th.	drawing a conveyance	1	4
7th.	Advice fee	2	8
	Porter v Ailer & ads. Ailer— 3 suits[14]	6	14
14th.	advice fees 45/	2	5
	Mr. Latil[15] £4–4	4	4
21	Carter v Geddis eject.[16]	5	
22	Douglass ads. Woodson (appeal	1	8
23	Crenshaw v. Royster	2	8
	White ads. Johnston old appl.[17]	2	10

10. John McCall and John Cunliffe, Richmond merchants.

11. See entries for Dec. 1789 in Construction Account, printed at Oct. 1788, where JM listed the building expenses under "Money paid for my house." The figure on the separate list for Dec. 1789, however, is only £96 19s. 10d. Apparently JM's expenditure here was for items not recorded on the separate building expense list.

12. John and Thomas Gilleat were merchants in Richmond. "List of Merchants," Richmond City Hustings Court Order Book, II, 50, Va. State Lib.

13. James Heron, Richmond merchant.

14. Thomas Porter v. Henry Ayler and Ayler v. Porter were actions of debt and covenant before the District Court at Fredericksburg. After being submitted to arbitrators by agreement on May 9, 1791, the actions were settled on May 6, 1793. District Court Law Orders, A, 1789–1793, 263, 331, 405, 472, Fredericksburg, Va. State Lib. See JM's rejoinder listed at Law Papers, Sept. 1791.

15. Joseph Latile.

16. Jesse Carter v. Ann Gaddis was an ejectment action in Stafford County that JM brought before the District Court at Fredericksburg for Carter on Oct. 1, 1790. The action was dismissed by agreement on Oct. 6, 1791. District Court Law Orders, A, 1789–1793, 140, 307, Fredericksburg, Va. State Lib.

17. William White v. Thomas Johnson was an old appeal from a judgment of the General Court dated Oct. 1, 1783, against White, deputy sheriff of Louisa County. The Court of Appeals reversed the decision on Apr. 17, 1793, after hearing arguments the previous day. JM represented White. 1 Va. (1 Wash.) 158; Court of Appeals Order Book, II, 213, 217, Va. State Lib.

27th.	Jones in Moss & al ads. Dunlop	2	16	
	advice fee	1		
		31	17	

[*Disbursements*]

January 1st.	Corn 12/, Moses 3/, tray 1/3		16	3
	barber 3 £	3		
2d.	Market 12/, Shoes 12/	1	4	
3d.	Shoes for Tom 5/, buckles 2/		7	
	paid Taylor for making coat		12	
	Fodder 10/, paper 18/, ink 1/6	1	9	6
7th.	Market 15/, wood 7/6	1	2	6
12th.	Given old Jenny[18] 24/,			
	market 6/	1	10	
14	house 12/, blanket for Bob[19] 9/	1	1	
	Given for Negroe Bob 50£[20]	50		
	Given Doctor Turpin for a lott[21]	50		
18th	house 3/, Market 9/, paid for			
	Bob 12/	1	4	
	Subscription to a race		12	
19th.	a watch 5£, eggs 3/, soap 3/	5	6	
20th	load of wood 5/, Conscience 1/	0	6	0
	corn £8, oil 1/6, wine 22–10	30	11	6
21st.	Beef 38/4, tickets for play[22] 9/,			
	postage 10/	2	17	4
	paid the potowmack company[23]	30		
	Eggs 3/4, Tea kettle 15/,			
	Turin 8/	1	6	4

18. Jenny is mentioned only one other time in JM's Account Book. See entry under Disbursements, Feb. 1792, when she was paid for assisting Dr. William Foushee with the birth of one of JM's children.

19. This, the following entries for Bob, and an entry under Disbursements, Jan. 1792, are the only mentions of this slave in JM's Account Book.

20. See below where JM deducted this amount from his monthly expenditures.

21. This payment presumably was for the lot that JM had purchased from Philip Turpin and on which he built his house. See Deed, July 7, 1789, and entry under Disbursements, July 5, 1789. See also below, where he deducted the amount from his total monthly expenses.

22. In Oct. 1789 the Kenna family of actors performed in Fredericksburg and probably presented a series of plays in Richmond near the time JM recorded this expenditure. Suzanne Ketchum Sherman, "Post-Revolutionary Theatre in Virginia, 1784–1810" (M.A. thesis, College of William and Mary, 1950), 69.

23. See entries under Disbursements, May 22, 1789, and Mar. 1784, for other payments to the Potomac River Company.

	Making Bobs cloaths 4/3, pullet 1/	5	3
29.	Flannel 9/, corn 46/8, sundries 15	3 12	8
		184 3	4
	deduct £100 given for lott & negroe	100	
		84 3	4

[Receipts]

Feby. 1st.	Harris ads. Thompson	1	8
	advice	1	8
2d.	Mr. Buchanan for Sterling Douglass & Co.	6	9
	same on two bonds	3	6
	Mr. Fenwick (advice fee)	1	8
3d	Wormley ads. Steptoe (old suit	7	
	Clayton ads. Moseby	2	12
4th.	Pulliam ads. Jennings (finishd)	2	4
	Mr. James Wormly[24]	1	8
8	Yerby v Taff[25]	7	
	Field v Fields admrs.	5	
	Snickers v Ashby—appeal in chy.)	7	
11th.	Allison ads. Ross	5	
12	May for Beale ads. Mercer	12	
	Mr. Shore 30/	1	10
	advice concerning Pattons will to Mr. Howard	2	8
	do. to Mr. Brown[26]	2	16
16	Bassett v Newton & Taylor chy.	2	16

24. See entry under Receipts, Dec. 5, 1789.

25. There is a record of a case, Thomas Yerby v. Thomas Taff, in the District Court at Northumberland County, but no evidence indicates JM ever practiced before that court. This case appeared in the court's order book from Apr. 2, 1790, through Apr. 1, 1796. District Court Order Book, 1789–1793, 38, 156, 182, 1793–1802, 10, 56, 80, 109, Northumberland County, Va. State Lib. JM also entered an additional fee on Mar. 2, 1790.

26. JM apparently advised both parties in James Brown, executor of Hugh Patton, v. Charles P. Howard. The case came before the District Court at Fredericksburg on Oct. 6, 1792, when a second defendant confessed judgment. On May 3, 1794, the case was dismissed after the parties agreed. District Court Law Orders, A, 1789–1793, 420, 475, and Law Orders, B, 1794–1798, 34, Fredericksburg, Va. State Lib.

17	White & Whittle v McCollum	7		
23	advice concerning ship			
	Cleopatra	2	8	
	From Noel (finishd suit)	2	8	
		81	9	

[*Disbursements*]

February				
3d	Paid for the yard pailing	14	2	
	Milk 6/, market 2/, sundries 18/	1	6	
	wood 7/6		7	6
4th.	Market 8/9, postage 2/, wood 10/	1	0	9
	horse rack 7/6, Turkey 3/		10	6
9th.	Given Polly	1	8	
11th.	book for Tom 4/6, buttons 1/3		5	9
15	beef 49/4, hominy 3/	2	12	4
17th.	wood 6/, fish 9/3, buttons 4/		19	3
20th	expenses going to & returning			
	from Wmsburg.[27]	2		
	Given my brother Alexander	7	14	
24	Market 6/		6	
		33	12	1
		7	14	
		25	18	1

[*Receipts*]

February				
25	Hatcher & Chastain v Scruggs			
	exrs.	5		
	Anderson & al ads. Cloptons	5		
	Harris's exrs. ads. Yates[28]	5		
	Muse assee. v Stack	1	10	

27. It is very likely JM went to Williamsburg to conduct High Court of Chancery business. See entries under Disbursements, Feb. 25 and 26, 1790.

28. William and Sarah Yates v. Abraham Saltee, Bernard Markham, and Edward Moseley, executors of Benjamin Harris, was argued in the High Court of Chancery on June 1, 1792. JM represented Harris's executors against the charge of mismanagement of the estate while Harris's daughter, Sarah Yates, was a minor. The chancellor ordered the executors to pay part of the estate to Sarah Yates. The decree was appealed to the Court of Appeals, where it was reversed on Nov. 2, 1793. Wythe 163; 1 Va. (1 Wash.) 226; Court of Appeals Order Book, II, 244, 248, Va. State Lib.

	Graham v Hoomes & al.[29]	3	12
	Fleets exrs. ads. Paynes exrs.[30]	5	2
	Wingfield & Pate chy.	1	8
	Scott Fore & Britain ads. Scott	1	8
	Jones ads. Dunlop	2	16
		1	8
29th.	Rhulings ads. Gabriels	8	8
	Spratt v Dunlop chy.	4	16
		45	8

[*Disbursements*]

February			
25	For making out my chy. docket		18
	house expenses 18/, wood 6/	1	4
	presents to my mother & sisters	5	
	linnen & thread for self	7	
26	Market 6/, do. 13/		19
	Given for my chy. dockett		18
	Given away 6/, expenses 8/		14
29	Given my brother Alexander	8	8
		25	1

[*Receipts*]

March 1st.	Bell ads. Alcock	5	
2	Yerby v Taff[31]	2	5
	Smith ads. Stratton	5	
	Underhill v Yarboro	1	
	Willson v Wells	5	
	Dick Holland	2	8
3d.	advice fee	1	4
	Ashberry v Forrest & al	1	
	Smith v Duval etc.	5	12

29. See JM's declaration listed at Law Papers, Apr. 1790.

30. William Dudley and Henry Fleet, executors of Edwin Fleet, v. William and Joseph Elliott Payne, executors of John Elliott, was originally entered in the General Court by Edmund Randolph in Oct. 1784. The case was continued until after the re-organization of the courts in 1788, when it was transferred to the District Court at Fredericksburg. JM represented the plaintiffs on Oct. 3, 1789, when judgment was entered for them in the debt action. District Court Record Book, 1789–1792, 40–41, and District Court Law Orders, A, 1789–1793, 37, Fredericksburg, Va. State Lib.

31. See entry at Receipts, Feb. 8, 1790.

	Smallwood v Hansbro (Mercer)[32]	17		
4	Boush ads. Boush's exrs.	5	4	
	Pattisons admrs. ads. Wilson	5		
5	Browning v Hite[33]	14	8	
	Wingfield & Pate	1	8	
6	advice fee	1	8	
	From Underhill v Scarboro	4		
	From Cocke	4	10	
	Hill v Claiborne & al.[34]	5		
	Watts ads. Tucker & ux (Pburg.)	2	10	
	Carter v Trents etc.	4	16	
8th	advice fee	1	4	
		94	17	

[Disbursements]

March				
1	expenses at Formicolas[35]		6	
4	Market 10/6, do. 8/		18	6
	linnen for children £3–6/, milk 6/	3	12	
	house 24/	1	4	
	Oats £3–13–4	3	13	4
	house 12/		12	
		10	5	10

32. Peter Hansbrough v. William Smallwood was an ejectment action that was first filed in the General Court in Apr. 1786. It was continued until after the reorganization of the courts, when it was transferred to the District Court at Fredericksburg. Judgment was entered on May 8, 1790, for Hansbrough, but an appeal to the High Court of Chancery was registered. The case finally ended as Smallwood v. Mercer and Hansbrough in the Court of Appeals. 1 Va. (1 Wash.) 290, 292–293 (1794); Court of Appeals Order Book, III, 4, 5, 7, District Court Record Book, 1789–1792, 213–215, Fredericksburg, and District Court Law Orders, A, 1789–1793, 49, 63, 125, Fredericksburg, all in Va. State Lib.

33. See Vol. I, 188, and additional fee entered under Receipts, Nov. 11, 1788.

34. Edward Hill v. John Claiborne was a suit concerning the fraudulent conveyance of slaves. The High Court of Chancery held the conveyance to be fraudulent, which was what JM had argued as Hill's attorney. Claiborne appealed to the Court of Appeals, which affirmed the decree on Apr. 29, 1793. 1 Va. (1 Wash.) 177, 185; Court of Appeals Order Book, II, 221, 226, Va. State Lib. See additional fee entered under Receipts, Sept. 1792.

35. Serafino Formicola's tavern.

[*Receipts*]

March 8th	Taylors exrs. v Lawson	11	4
10	Reid & Burnsides[36]	9	
11	Harris ads. Thompson	3	
	Adkyns exrs. ads. Adkyns	2	8
	advice fee	2	8
12	Randolph ads. Banisters exrs.	2	8
	Thornton ads. Pendleton & al.	4	10
14	Wynn ads. Puryear appl. district	1	10
25	Panky ads. Woodson (old appl.)[37]	2	8
	advice 28/	1	8
	Branch v Cox & al (chy.)	3	10
28th.	Seabrooke ads. Byrd	10	
	Henly v & ads. Sundries	2	5
		55	17

[*Disbursements*]

March 10	wood 8/, newspaper 6/, market 6/	1		
	Given away 6, market 4/6		10	6
20th	expenses 6/, market 40/	2	6	
25	wood 7/6, Given Polly £4–10	4	17	6
	library annual subscription[38]	1	8	
	Wood 6/, corn 45/, market 6/	2	17	
	Given Polly 10/		10	
		13	9	0
		10	5	10
	[*Total March Disbursements*]	23	14	10

36. See JM to Andrew Reid, Apr. 26, 1790.

37. Anne Woodson v. John Samuel Pankey was a debt action in which JM represented the Pankeys. The case was no doubt first entered as an appeal from Buckingham County Court to the General Court. It was later transferred to the District Court at Prince Edward County, and JM would probably have given the case to someone else at that time. District Court Order Book, 1793–1799, 113, 128, 152, 174, Prince Edward County, Va. State Lib.

38. JM was one of the original subscribers to the Library Society in Richmond, formed Jan. 16, 1784. See Vol. I, 299, n. 34.

[*Receipts*]

April 1	Jones v Weiscart & Deneufville		
	sups.	2	10
	Garland ads. Claiborne	2	7
	Harris v Dandridge[39] 20/	1	
3d	Tate v Richardson (old eject)	3	
	Yancy ads. Strother (old		
	appeal)[40]	1	8
	Spencer v Harris (spe. ver.)	1	10
	Southerlands exrs. v Claiborne		
	sci. fa.	1	4
	Branch ads. Donald	1	10
6th.	Hampton v Syme (old suit)	2	10
	Graves ads. Winston	2	8
	Thurston ads. Daniel (appeal		
	district)	1	8
	advice fee	1	1
	Mr. Pierson	2	8
	Mr. Guerent	3	
	Mr. Claiborne		18
	Mr. Henly (suits referd)	4	4
	Elliot ads. McKenzie appeal	1	10
	Ruffin, Woodlief ads. Quesnie[41]	3	10
		37	6

39. Samuel Harris v. William Dandridge was an action in which Harris attempted to collect for repairing a mill for Dandridge. The case first was tried in the county court and was then appealed to the District Court at Richmond. The High Court of Chancery enjoined the district court judgment, and the case went to the Court of Appeals, in Oct. 1794. 1 Va. (1 Wash.) 326–330; Court of Appeals Order Book, III, 14, 17, Va. State Lib. See additional fees entered under Receipts, Sept. 1792, Mar. and May 17, 1793, and Oct. 1794.

40. French Strother v. Layton Yancey was an appeal from the Culpeper County Court to the General Court in 1787 involving the sale of certificates and horses. The case was continued until after the reorganization of the courts in 1788, when it was transferred to the District Court at Fredericksburg. The county court's judgment was affirmed on Oct. 6, 1790. District Court Record Book, 1789–1792, 302–305, 554, and District Court Law Orders, A, 1789–1793, 164, 275, Fredericksburg, Va. State Lib.

41. Neil Quesnel v. Thomas Woodlief, Edmund Ruffin, Jr., and Edward Harrison was first before the High Court of Chancery, where Quesnel asked the court to invalidate a contract he had made with JM's clients to purchase a tract of land. The acreage was almost 200 acres less than that contracted for, and Quensel claimed fraud and collusion. The chancellor dismissed the bill on Oct. 7, 1794, and Quesnel appealed the decree. Daniel Call represented the appellees in the Court of Appeals. 10 Va. (6 Call) 218 (1796); Court of Appeals Order Book, II, 146, 147, 152–153, Va. State Lib.

	[*Disbursements*]		
April 2d.	Market 20/, do. 6/	1	6
	sugar, beer & bread 16/		16
	Tickett for Polly 9/, given B.		
	Munkus 10/		19
		2	1

	[*Receipts*]		
[April] 15th.	Pride ads. Jones	4	16
	Clay v Greenhill	2	12
	Wrums exrs. v Mallory	2	6
	Woodward ads. Chappel	1	8
	Wilson ads. Munford (finishd)	2	4
	Lee ads. Field eject.	1	10
	Crump etc. & Dodson (advice		
	& retr.)[42]	5	12
	Moyler v Cocke	1	19
	Rogers & Manlove ads. Smart	2	8
	Farly v Gilliam & Skelton	2	10
	Bell v Roach injn. (in part)	1	8
	Craig v Hart admr.[43]	5	
	Ballard ads. Garland (appl.)	1	8
	Shore v Banisters exrs.[44]	5	12
	Fields legatees v Fields admrs.	5	

42. Dobson and Daltera v. Crump and Bates. This action in debt was brought upon a bill of exchange drawn by the defendants on Nov. 1, 1772, and protested for non-payment at Liverpool on June 11, 1773. The declaration, filed by Jerman Baker in the Nov. 1790 term of the U.S. Circuit Court, bears endorsements that indicate JM filed the answer in Feb. 1791. The plaintiffs demurred to certain pleas, and in early 1792 a commission was awarded to them to take depositions in Liverpool. The case was continued until Nov. 1794, when a nonsuit was entered against the plaintiffs, probably by virtue of a settlement of the dispute. The answer is listed at Law Papers, Feb. 1791. For an additional fee, see Account Book, Receipts, Mar. 10, 1791.

43. James Craig v. Robert Hart, an action to recover money, was filed in the General Court in 1785. After the reorganization of the courts in 1788, the case was transferred to the District Court at Fredericksburg, where judgment was entered for Craig, JM's client, on Oct. 7, 1790. District Court Records, 1789–1792, 377–381, and District Court Law Orders, A, 1789–1793, 41, 185, Fredericksburg, Va. State Lib.

44. Thomas Shore v. Neil Buchanan and Duncan Rose, executors of John Banister, was a suit before the High Court of Chancery to determine if Banister had been entitled to a parcel of land from his father-in-law as part of his wife's dowry. JM's client Shore won when the chancellor held that his court had no jurisdiction, but Banister's executors appealed to the Court of Appeals, where the decree was reversed on Apr. 24, 1793. 1 Va. (1 Wash.) 173, 175–176; Court of Appeals Order Book, II, 218, 222, Va. State Lib. See later fee at Receipts, Feb. 1793.

Smith etc. v Piper (from Vowles[45] finishd)	2	8
Glassel v Donald	2	8
Stuart ads. Fitzhugh[46]	2	16
Davenport ads. Almond & ux.[47]	2	8
Powell v Carr	1	8
	52	1

[*Disbursements*]

Apl.	expenses at Pburg.[48]	4	10
	empty bottles	4	
	expenses	3	
	stockings for self	1	8
		12	18

[*Receipts*]

May	Abbot ads. Wheeler	4	10
	Fairfax ads. Wormley[49]	5	12
	Downman ads. Downman (appls.)[50]	5	

45. Smith and Morton, assignees of Henry and Zachariah Vowles, v. Michael Wallace and William Piper came before the District Court at Fredericksburg on May 8, 1790, to recover a debt of more than £2,000. The court ordered payment by half that amount, and Wallace appealed to the Court of Appeals. That court heard the case on June 20 and 21, 1791, and affirmed the lower court's decision on June 23, 1791. Final judgment was entered on Oct. 7, 1791, in the district court. District Court Law Orders, A, 1789–1793, 122, 322, District Court Records, 1789–1792, 202–204, Fredericksburg, and Court of Appeals Order Book, II, 82, 88, 89–90, all in Va. State Lib.

46. John Stiles, lessee of William Fitzhugh, v. William G. Stewart was an ejectment action filed in the District Court at Fredericksburg in Sept. 1789, with JM representing Stewart. Judgment was entered for Stiles on May 6, 1791. District Court Law Orders, A, 1789–1793, 247, and District Court Records, 1789–1792, 501–502, Fredericksburg, Va. State Lib.

47. William and Mary Almond, administrator and administratrix of James Yarbrough, v. David Davenport involved a request for a writ of supersedeas from the District Court at Fredericksburg against a 1778 judgment of the Caroline County Court that required payment to Davenport of three slaves or £100 from Yarbrough's estate. JM, representing Davenport, suggested a diminution of the record whereby the court granted a writ of certiorari on Apr. 29, 1790. On Oct. 4, 1793, the court reversed the judgment and set aside the resulting proceedings. The court allowed an appeal to the Court of Appeals. District Court Law Orders, A, 1789–1793, 79, 303, Fredericksburg, Va. State Lib.

48. JM attended the session of the District Court at Petersburg that began Apr. 15.

49. See entry under Receipts, Dec. 5, 1789.

50. Rawleigh Downman, Jr., v. John Chinn, and Joseph B. and Rawleigh W.

Lawson ads. Hooe[51]	4	4
Walker (chy. finishd)[52]	3	
Bealer v Wyatt & Anderson (chy.)	5	
Same ads. Williams do.	5	
Blackburn (in Carr v Russel)	5	
Washington v Washington[53]	5	
Lawson, chy. to be brot.	7	
Triplett[54]	5	12
Keys ads. Boucher (chy. appl.)	5	
Washington v Hite[55]	6	
Mr. Mercer	4	16
Mr. P. Thornton ads. Robinsons admrs.	11	4
McCarty ads. same	5	12
Thompson v Banks	2	10
	80	

Downman, executors of Rawleigh Downman, was an appeal to the Court of Appeals from a judgment in favor of JM's clients, Downman's executors, in the District Court at Northumberland County on Apr. 3, 1790, involving a debt of £106. The Court of Appeals heard arguments on Dec. 14 and 18, 1790, and June 8, 1791, after which the district court judgment was affirmed on June 10, 1791. 1 Va. (1 Wash.) 26; Court of Appeals Order Book, II, 51, 60, 69, 72, Va. State Lib. See additional fees entered at Receipts, Feb. 1792. For later proceedings on the court's judgment, see 6 Va. (2 Call) 426, 507–508 (1800).

51. JM signed an affidavit in this case in Apr. 1787. Term Papers, Office of the Clerk of the Circuit Court, Fredericksburg, Va. See also District Court Law Orders, A, 1789–1793, 111, 264, 268, 278, Fredericksburg, Va. State Lib.

52. See JM's bill in chancery listed at Law Papers, Sept. 1790; additional fee entered at Receipts, Aug. 3, 1790; and JM to Francis Walker, Feb. 23, 1793.

53. James Quarles, executor of Henry Washington, v. Thacker Washington was an action involving a bill of exchange. JM represented Thacker Washington in the District Court at Fredericksburg, where judgment was entered for Quarles on Oct. 3, 1791. District Court Law Orders, A, 1789–1793, 292, and District Court Records, 1789–1792, 594–596, Fredericksburg, Va. State Lib.

54. Davenport and Daniel Triplett v. William Howe was an appeal from the Stafford County Court, which quashed an attachment sued out by Davenport and Triplett. The lower court judgment was affirmed by the District Court at Fredericksburg on May 6, 1790. District Court Records, 1789–1792, 167–170, 175–176, and District Court Law Orders, A, 1789–1793, 105, 110, Fredericksburg, Va. State Lib. See additional fees entered under Receipts, May 13, July 27, and Sept. 26, 1790, and affidavit signed by JM in Apr. 1787 in Term Papers, Office of the Clerk of the Circuit Court, Fredericksburg, Va.

55. See JM's stipulation listed at Law Papers, May 1790, and JM to Corbin Washington, Aug. 23, 1789. See also List of Fees, printed at 1791, where JM also recorded this fee.

[*Disbursements*]

May	expenses at Fburg[56]	8	
	lottery ticketts	9	12
		17	12

[*Receipts*]

May 11th	Bells exrs. ads. Patteson[57]	5		
13	Staples v Staples	5	12	
	Triplett v Howe injn. (in part)[58]	2	16	
	Frazer in part	1	16	
	Keeble ads. Keeble	2	4	
	Branch v Cox	1	8	
	Royster v Curd (apl. Goochld.[59])	2	8	
	same ads. Bolling	2	10	
	Mr. Machir (finishd)	5		
	Brother Wm. ads. Barrett	2		
	Jones v White (appeal chy.)[60]	5		
	Stainback & al ads. Ellington	2	16	
	Cockes exrs. ads. Branch exr. of Osborn	5		
	Walker ads. Spotswood injn.[61]	5		
	Iveson v Mills & Co.	5		
14	advice fee	1	10	
	Haden & al ads. Skipwith	2	1	4
	Hicks ads. Turnbul & Co.	5		

56. The session of the District Court at Fredericksburg that JM attended began Apr. 29.

57. Florence and Joseph Bell, executrix and executor of David Bell, v. John and Thomas Patterson was originally filed in the General Court in Oct. 1786, by Edmund Randolph. The case was continued until after the reorganization of the courts in 1788, when it was transferred to the District Court at Staunton and taken over by another attorney. Apparently the Pattersons, who lost in the district court, appealed the case, and the Bells retained JM at that time. District Court Order Book, 1789–1793, 1–3, 1789–1797, 8–9, Augusta County, Va. State Lib.

58. See entry under Receipts, May 1790, "Triplett."

59. This case was an appeal from Goochland County Court to the District Court at Richmond.

60. Wood Jones v. Elisha White was an appeal to the High Court of Chancery from the Charlotte County Court involving a disputed patent to land. The chancellor decreed in favor of JM's client Jones on June 1, 1791, reversing the county court. White appealed to the Court of Appeals, where the decree was affirmed on Oct. 13, 1792. Wythe 111–113 (1791); 1 Va. (1 Wash.) 116 (1792); 8 Va. (4 Call) 253–257; Court of Appeals Order Book, II, 182, 183, 184, Va. State Lib.

61. Alexander Spotswood v. William Walker was an appeal to the District Court

	Pierson	2	8	
		64	19	4

[Disbursements]

May	Market 10/, expenses 3/		12	
	Coffee	3	3	9
	Paid my subscription to Mr. Buchanan[62]	1		
	given away		12	
		5	7	9

[Receipts]

	Nottoway		
May 15th	Robinson v Prides exr	5	
	Taylor ads. Booker (review chy.)	6	6
16	Becquith v Batteo	10	
18th.	Ragsdale exr. v Batt exr[63]	5	
	advice fee	1	8
	Sterne & al ads. Ellington	2	
	Darke v Burnes[64]	5	
21st.	Orendorf v Cookus[65]	5	
	Oldner v Nast	3	

at Fredericksburg that was dismissed on Apr. 29, 1790. District Court Law Orders, A, 1789–1793, 76, Fredericksburg, Va. State Lib.

62. Although it is uncertain what subscription JM was paying, he was likely making the customary contribution to the salary of Rev. John Buchanan. See Vol. I, 313, and entries under Disbursements, Apr. 1792, Mar. 1794, and Jan. 1795, for other payments to Buchanan.

63. Edward R. Ragsdale, executor of Edward Ragsdale, v. William and John Batte, executors of William Batte, was founded on a General Court judgment of 1784. It seems likely that the Battes took the case back to court, and it was continued until after 1788, when it was transferred to the District Court at Brunswick County. It is unclear what JM did in 1790, if anything. The case was decided by the district court on Sept. 29, 1794, and appealed to the Court of Appeals in 1796, when the judgment was reversed. JM may have represented Ragsdale again before the Court of Appeals in 1796. 2 Va. (2 Wash.) 201–202; Court of Appeals Order Book, III, 120–121, Va. State Lib.

64. William Dark v. William Burns was an action that probably began in the General Court but was transferred to the District Court at Winchester after the reorganization of the courts in 1788. The case appears in that court's order book in Sept. 1790, but it would have been taken over by someone other than JM at that time. Superior Court Order Book, 1789–1793, 148, 172, 203, Frederick County, Va. State Lib.

65. See JM's petition of appeal in Orandorf v. Welch's Administrators, Feb. 18, 1972.

		£	s	d
	Riddick & ux v Carrs exr.	3		
	Hawkins exrs. v Sundries	4		
29th	Hansford ads. Francisco (chy)	2	16	
	Cobbs ads. Mosby[66]	2	10	10
		55	6	10

[*Disbursements*]

		£	s	d
[May]	market 36	1	16	
	Given Polly 28/	1	8	
	Given Polly 28/	1	8	
	market		6	
26	market 6/; 27th. do. 2/6		8	6
	Shoes		12	
27	market 3/, do. 1/, buckles 4/		8	
		6	6	6

[*Receipts*]

		£	s	d
June	Fairfax v Pendleton caveats	28		
	Hord & Upshaw[67]	1	8	
	Jones v Ransom (residue)	2	8	
	Keeble v Keeble	1	10	
	Hord & Upshaw	4	16	
3	From Mr. Leiper (old business)	2	16	
	From Harris ads. Thompson (residue)		18	
4	Wilcox v Calloway[68]	7		
	Webbs exr. ads. Donald etc.	5	12	
	Farly v Farly	7		
5th.	Sterling Douglass & Co. in addition	7		

66. Thomas Cobbs v. John Mosby was a bill in equity for relief against a verdict and was dismissed by the High Court of Chancery in Oct. 1791. Wythe 137. See additional fees entered under Receipts, Nov. 2, 1790, and Aug. 1794.

67. See entry under Receipts, June 2, 1789.

68. John Wilcox v. James Callaway was a suit before the High Court of Chancery involving the purchase of land patents. The court dismissed the bill on Nov. 1, 1790, but an appeal was taken to the Court of Appeals, where the decree was affirmed on Nov. 25, 1791. 1 Va. (1 Wash.) 38; Court of Appeals Order Book, II, 101, 113, 114, 115, 143, Va. State Lib. See additional fee entered under Receipts, Nov. 1791.

Stephens ads. Fleming & ux.				
do.		4	16	
Watson ads. Donalds		5	5	9
		83	9	9

[Disbursements]

June 2d.	market 22/	1	2	
	Market & sundries 18/		18	
	do. 2/, do. 1/3		3	3
		2	3	3

[Receipts]

June	Bibb v Vaughan, Strange etc.			
	sci. fa.	2	10	
	From Mr. Buchanan (for an			
	att. v Donald Frazer & Co.)	7		
	Slaughter ads. Comth.[69]	2	8	
	Massie, in sundries v Page &			
	Burwell	2	8	
	Miller v Baugh	1	10	
	Pride v Hoard	5		
	McDonald ads Moon	5		
19th.	Dabny v Powell (balance)	13	4	
	Carrington ads. Mayo			
	(finishd)[70]	10		
	advice fee—D. Cockran[71]	2	16	

69. Commonwealth of Virginia at instance of Gavin Lawson & Co. v. James, Robert, and Lawrence Slaughter, and William Ball was a debt action for £10,000 brought in the District Court at Fredericksburg on May 1, 1790. On Oct. 2, 1790, a judgment was entered ordering discharge of the debt by payment of approximately £215. District Court Law Orders, A, 1789–1793, 94, 99, 144, Fredericksburg, Va. State Lib. JM had earlier represented Gavin Lawson in other litigation. See Vol. I, 411.

70. Lessee of William Mayo v. Paul and Nathaniel Carrington was a writ of error to the Court of Appeals from a judgment of the General Court regarding a will making slaves a residuary legacy if they could not be freed. The heir claimed conditions prevented the residuary clause from operating. The Court of Appeals issued the writ of error on July 13, 1790, but later affirmed the General Court's judgment in favor of JM's clients, the Carringtons, on Dec. 1, 1791. 1 Va. (1 Wash.) 45; 8 Va. (4 Call) 472; Court of Appeals Order Book, II, 29, 147, 148, Va. State Lib. See additional fees entered at Receipts, June 1791, Apr. 1792, and Sept. 1794.

71. See entry under Receipts, Apr. 8, 1789.

25th.	part fee for victoriosa	7		
	old suits agt. Dunmoore	22	10	
	Colo. W. M. Cary[72]	5	4	
		86	10	
		83	9	9[73]
	[*Total June Receipts*]	169	19	9

[*Disbursements*]

June 8th.	Market 4/, postage 3/3		7	3
	Wood 6/, fruit 3/		9	
9th.	Stockings for self	2	12	6
	Oznabrugs	9	10	
	Stockings for Polly		14	
	waistcoats for self	1	2	
14	Market 6/, printer £3–18	4	4	
15	market 10/		10	
16	Market 30/, sugar & fruit 18/	2	8	
	Paid Mr. Braxton for bedstead etc.	50		
	Paid Mr. Latil[74] for press & kitchen furniture	26	6	6
	making copy of chy. dockett		18	
	Market 34/	1	14	
	market 7/, wood 6/		13	
	Given for Dick & others[75]	130		
	Paid county tax for my brother Market 7/	1	8	
	Paid Mr. Macon for flour	14	19	8
	market 9/, do. 24/, beer 7/, Tea 12/	2	12	
	Fruit 3/, milk 1/6		4	6
		250	12	5
		130		
		120	12	5

72. Wilson Miles Cary.
73. These entries are not in JM's hand.
74. Probably Joseph Latile.
75. Considering the total amount paid, JM purchased three or four slaves at this time.

[Receipts]

		£	s	d
July 9th.	opinion on Bollings case	1	16	
	Bolling v Bolling & Carys exrs.	5	18	
	Strup v Bull petn. for appl.	2	8	
	Buler	1	8	
14th.	Cocke v Nelson Heron & Co.	2	10	
15	advice fee	1	2	6
	Winston ads. & v Donald[76]	11	4	
	Coles ads. Wilkinson	2	8	
19	Barber v Donaldson	2	8	
	Harris v Jones & al att. chy.	4	16	
20	Opinion to Mr. Wormeley[77]	1	8	
22	Vowles		12	
	Lynham		30	
	Rhuling[78]	2	16	
	Mr. W Cary[79]	1	8	
27th.	Toler v Potties exr.	5		
	Mr. Grymes[80]	9	12	
	Triplet v Hooe[81]	4	3	2
30	Singleton ads. Westfall[82]	5	3	
	Bullock v Bullock exr. etc.	1	8	
31	Walker ads. Cuningham	15		
		122	16	8

[Disbursements]

		£	s	d
July 1	Paid barber	2	5	
2	Market 10/, sugar 3/9		13	9

76. Samuel Donaldson v. John Winston, of Hanover County, was a British debt case in which JM represented Winston. Judgment of one cent was awarded on Nov. 29, 1793. A later motion for a new trial was denied. U.S. Circuit Court, Va., Order Book, I, 214, 247, 362, and Record Book, IV, 1–4, Va. State Lib.

77. James Wormeley. See entry under Receipts, Dec. 5, 1789.

78. See JM to John Conrad Rhuling, listed at July 14, 1790.

79. Wilson Miles Cary.

80. See entry under Receipts, May 8, 1789, Philip Ludwell Grymes v. Edmund Pendleton.

81. See entry under Receipts, May 1790, "Triplett."

82. In Jacob Westfall v. John Singleton, Westfall asked the High Court of Chancery to enjoin an ejectment judgment against him obtained by Singleton in the Hampshire County Court. The chancellor dismissed the bill on May 18, 1792, but Westfall took the case to the Court of Appeals, where the ejectment was enjoined in perpetuity. 1 Va. (1 Wash.) 227 (1793); Court of Appeals Order Book, II, 227, 230, 234, 247, 250, Va. State Lib. See later fee under Receipts, Nov. 1792.

	Shirts for Dick		10	
	Market 5/		5	
9	expenses etc. to Williamsburg[83]	2	16	
	Market 5/		5	
	Corn £4–10	4	10	
	subscription to Mr. Blair[84]		14	
	Market 9/, do. while at Wmsburg. 15/, fruit 3/	1	7	
	Paid for Matrass	4	4	
	Spinning wheel		10	
16	Market, ducks, fruit etc.		14	
	chickens [17/], fruit etc. 2/		19	
	given away 6/, pd. for waistcoats 15/, fruit 4/6	1	5	6
	Sugar 9/, house 24/	1	13	
29th.	market 18/, do. 18/, sugar etc. 12/	2	8	
31	Rum & sugar	1 5		
		39	19	3

[Receipts]

August 2	Bowles v Toler (finishd)	5	
3	Jenkins v Michael injn.	5	
	Harrison ads. Harrison & al[85]	3	6
	Walker v Cabell & al Chy.[86]	4	4
	Dunton v Watson review	7	
	Keeble v Keeble	3	
	Allen v Walker appl. chy.	5	
	Dickie Admr. v Williams	3	
	Kidd v Johnston chy.	1	8
	Urquhart v Hambleton & Co.[87]	3	

83. See note to similar entry at Disbursements, Feb. 20, 1789.

84. This is probably a contribution to Rev. John D. Blair (1759–1823), a Presbyterian minister who came to Virginia from his native New Jersey in 1780. He taught at Washington-Henry Academy in Hanover County until the early 1790s, when he moved to Richmond. He became a friend of Rev. John Buchanan and held services with him in the capitol beginning in 1799. When he first moved to Richmond he supplemented his salary by teaching. Valentine Museum, *Richmond Portraits in an Exhibition of Makers of Richmond, 1737–1860* (Richmond, 1949), 18–19.

85. See fee entered under Receipts, Oct. 1794.

86. See JM's bill in chancery listed at Law Papers, Sept. 1790; JM to Francis Walker, Feb. 23, 1793; and earlier fee entered under Disbursements, May 1790.

87. See entry under Receipts, Nov. 2, 1788.

10	Hayes v Jenne	5		
	Brokenbro v Brokenbro	5		
	Kid	2	2	
	Carter	4	16	
	Opinion	1	10	
14	do.	1		
	Granberry v Granberry[88]	7		
	Glanvilles exr. ads. Evans	5		
	Cobbs v Allen	3		
	Chapman Austin	9	18	
		84	4	

[Disbursements]

August 2d.	Market 12/8, stuff for bag 2/		14	8
4	Market 6/, Shoes 12/		18	
6	Wood 6/8, hat for Tom 6/		12	8
10	Market etc. 24/	1	4	
	books £5–5, paper 20/, postage 6	6	11	
15	Linnen for Polly	5		
	house 14/, do. 12/	1	6	
	books 14/, hankerchiefs 21/6	1	15	6
	Saddlebags 24/, chickens 6/8	1	10	8
	Chair	10		
	expenses on my journey[89]	4		
	expenses at home	3	6	
	Newspapers		12	
	Horse & chair	40		
		78	10	6
		40		
		38	10	6

[Receipts]

Septr. 1.	Holland v Lepner & al.	1	10	
	Pulliam v Richardson	2	10	

88. JM was apparently involved in Josiah Granberry v. Josiah, Jr., and James Granberry, although others were listed as the attorneys of record. Little is known about the case before it was taken to the Court of Appeals from the High Court of Chancery in 1793. 1 Va. (1 Wash.) 246; Court of Appeals Order Book, II, 243, 244, 251, 254, Va. State Lib. See additional fee entered under Receipts, Oct. 1794.

89. JM normally traveled to Fauquier County each summer in July or August.

Pulliam ads. Richardson		18
Rudd ads. Huddleston	1	8
Branch v Sundries	7	4
Sadlier ads. Farley		12
Trabue ads. Almond (appl. Fburg.[90]	2	11
Advice	1	4
Cocke v Syme & al—old suit	1	15
Payne ads. Oliver[91]	2	12
Pearson 56	2	16
Hawkins exx.[92]	1	4
Neaves v Syme	2	
Advice	1	4
Wray & Co. v Pendleton	3	
Colo. E. Meade[93]	5	
Baily ads. Judkins (appeal)	2	8
Wigfal v Blow	1	14
Muir v Blair	5	
Sudbury ads. Cuzzins	1	10

(15 in left margin beside Colo. E. Meade)

	48

[Disbursements]

Septr. 1.	Market 9/4, wood 3/		12	4
3d.	market 3/, encyclopedia[94] 30/	1	13
4th.	expences		10
6.	market 3/, do. 2/, Hay 40/	2	5

90. John Almond v. John Tribue was an appeal from the Orange County Court in which JM represented Tribue. On May 2, 1791, JM appeared for his client before the District Court at Fredricksburg, but Almond failed to appear, whereupon the court affirmed the lower court's judgment. District Court Law Orders, A, 1789–1793, 225, Fredericksburg, Va. State Lib.

91. See entry under Receipts, Sept. 4, 1789.

92. John Hawkins's Executors v. Nelson Berkley was first before the Hanover County Court, but JM took it on appeal to the District Court at Richmond. That court affirmed the county court judgment on Sept. 12, 1792, at which time it was appealed to the Court of Appeals. On Oct. 17, 1793, the Court of Appeals affirmed the judgment. 1 Va. (1 Wash.) 204; Court of Appeals Order Book, II, 237, Va. State Lib. See also 9 Va. (5 Call) 118 (1804). Additional fees are entered under Receipts, Aug. 1791, Sept. 1792, and July 1793.

93. Everard Meade.

94. JM no doubt purchased vol. I of *Encyclopaedia; or a Dictionary of Arts, Sciences, and Miscellaneous Literature* . . . (Philadelphia, 1790–1798), 18 vols., which was advertised for sale in Richmond by subscription only. *Virginia Gazette, and General Advertiser* (Richmond), Sept. 1, 1790.

Paid taxes of city £3–3–8[95]	3	3	8
Paid tax for my brother James		13	4
bridle 42/, knives etc. 23/6	3	5	6
boot in a horse	20		
County taxes for 1789[96]	3	6	3
expenses going to & at Pburg.[97] etc.	4		
plates etc. 18/		18	
	40	17	1
	20		
	20	17	1

[Receipts]

September				
18	Advice	1	8	
	do.	1	10	
	do.	1	8	
	Gill v Ross[98]	4	4	
26	Alexander ads. Burnsides	5		
	Frazer ads. Elam[99]	3		
	Cohen & Isaacs v Thornly[1]	3		
	Advice	1	6	8
	Mercer ads. Dawson[2]	2	16	

95. Richmond personal property and land tax records for 1790 are not extant.

96. Fauquier tax records indicate JM owned an 842-acre tract as well as one of 268 acres. The tax on that land totaled £6 9s. 6d., almost exactly half of what JM recorded he paid. Fauquier County Land Book, 1789, Va. State Lib. Henrico County tax lists for 1789 are not extant.

97. JM attended the fall session of the District Court at Petersburg, which began Sept. 15.

98. David Ross v. Erasmus Gill and Sarah, his wife, began in the Richmond City Hustings Court when Gill sued Ross for rent. Gill lost the suit on Sept. 5, 1787, but appealed to the District Court at Petersburg, where the lower court judgment was reversed, with JM representing the Gills. Ross then appealed to the Court of Appeals, which affirmed the district court judgment on Apr. 28, 1792. 1 Va. (1 Wash.) 87; 8 Va. (4 Call) 250–252; Court of Appeals Order Book, II, 105, 110, 156, 169, Va. State Lib. See additional fees under Receipts, Apr. 1791, and Sept. 1793.

99. John Elam v. Burges Ball and Simon Frazer was a debt action that began in the General Court before the reorganization of the courts in 1788. It was transferred to the District Court at Fredericksburg, where judgment was entered for Elam on Oct. 8, 1790. District Court Law Orders, A, 1789–1793, 31, 188, Fredericksburg, Va. State Lib.

1. See JM's acknowledgement listed at Law Papers, Mar. 1791.

2. William Dawson v. James Mercer was an action for breach of contract originally filed in the General Court in 1785. A plea was entered in Apr. 1786, but the case was continued until after the reorganization of the courts, when it was transferred to the

Chapman v Chapman[3]	13	16	
Glassel v Graves	2	2	
Thornton v Fitzhugh (chy)	5		
Matson v Peyton	5		
Ball ads. Ewell[4]	2	10	
Hungerford v Alexander[5]	1	10	
Triplett v Howe[6]	3	16	
Advice	1	2	6
Richeson v Chandler (chy.)	2	10	
Thornly—dep. inspector ads Burnly[7]	2	8	
Alexander	4	10	
McHeny	1	10	
Page	2	8	
	71	15	2

[Disbursements]

September	painting chairs	1	4
	expenses at Fburg[8]	10	
	House	7	
		18	4

District Court at Fredericksburg. It was submitted to arbitration on Oct. 5, 1789, and on May 1, 1791, the plaintiff was nonsuited. JM represented Mercer. District Court Law Orders, A, 1789–1793, 47, 107, 186, 235, and District Court Record Book, 1789–1792, 475–477, Fredericksburg, Va. State Lib.

3. George Chapman v. George Chapman, infant, by Susanna Chapman was before the High Court of Chancery to construe a disputed will devising land. On June 1, 1796, the court dismissed the bill. Chapman appealed to the Court of Appeals, where the decree was affirmed on Apr. 19, 1799. JM was one of the attorneys for the appellants. 8 Va. (4 Call) 430; Court of Appeals Order Book, III, 186, 281–282, 286, Va. State Lib. See JM to George Chapman, July 23, 1788.

4. James Ewell v. Burges Ball was a debt action appealed to the District Court at Fredericksburg from Stafford County Court in 1791. JM represented Ball, for whom judgment on a special verdict was given on May 9, 1793. District Court Law Orders, A, 1789–1793, 324, 334, 490, Fredericksburg, Va. State Lib.

5. Thomas Hungerford v. William Thornton Alexander was filed by JM for Hungerford in the District Court at Fredericksburg, where he won a judgment on Oct. 6, 1794. District Court Law Orders, A, 1789–1793, 464, 522, and Law Orders, B, 1794–1798, 82, Fredericksburg, Va. State Lib.

6. See fee entered under "Triplett," Receipts, May 1790.

7. Hardin Burnley v. John Thornley, deputy inspector, was originally filed in the General Court but was transferred to the District Court at Fredericksburg after 1788. The case was continued until Sept. 30, 1791, when judgment was awarded JM's client Thornley after Burnley failed to prosecute. District Court Law Orders, A, 1789–1793, 55, 240, 274, Fredericksburg, Va. State Lib.

8. The session of the District Court at Fredericksburg began Sept. 29.

[*Receipts*]

October 12	Syme v Radford (chy.)	5	
	Grymes v Littlepage	1 16	
	Meux ads. Syme	5	
	Noel	2 8	
	Neal ads. Donald & Co.	2 16	
	Carter in Jaqueline ads. Claibornes exrs.	4 16	
	Thornton ads. Watlington	4 4	
	advice	1 1	
	Edmunds exr. etc. ads. Baker	2 18	
	Catlett v Thornton & al in part	5 12	
	Watson v Donald & Co	5	
	James[9] in Thomson & al ads. Seaton & ux	2 16	
	Powells exrs. v Cox appeal chy.	2 10	
	advice fee	1 2 6	
	Hadden admr. ads. Hall & ux (old)	1 8	
	T. Barnett & Co. v. Smith Young & Hyde[10]	5	
	Joyner v Blount	5	
	Advice fee	1 2 6	
	Cocke v Jordan	5	
	Brendt in Cartwright ads Byrd	5	
		69 10	

[*Disbursements*]

October 12	Market 6/, sheeting £8–1–10	8 7 10	
	Coat for Polly	2 8	
	Fenders, shovel & tongs	4	
	Wood 8/, Market 13–4	1 1 4	
	Taylor	1 8	
	Stockings for self	1 8	
	cloths for Tom & Jaquelin	1 14	

9. Richard James mentioned having paid JM this fee in a letter to John Breckinridge, Sept. 2, 1790, Breckinridge Family Papers, Library of Congress.

10. There is no record of Barnett & Co. v. Smith & Co. before 1804, long after JM had left the case. The original case resulted in judgment for JM's client, Barnett & Co., but it was brought to the Court of Appeals in 1804 to present new evidence. 9 Va. (5 Call) 98.

	Sundries for furniture	17	11	10
	Carpets	20	6	
	Market	1	3	
	Market 16, brush 3/6		19	6
	Market 7/, oysters 4/, market 9/	1		
		61	7	6

[*Receipts*]

October 26	Province ads. Rutherford	5		
	Terrel ads.	5		
	Bartlett & Stubblefield ads. Comth.	2	10	
	Hutcheson ads. Donnelly (appeal)[11]	5		
	Jones ads. Ross	4		
	McClanahan v the Comth. injn.	5		
	Nelson ads. Nelson[12]	25		
	Roane v Hearn[13]	2		
	Pulliam v Jennings	1	12	
		55	2	
		69	10	
	[*Total October Receipts*]	124	12	

[*Disbursements*]

Oct.	butter £3–2–6, tar 2£, oysters 4/	5	6	6
	Stuff for breeches, 20/, shoes for Tom 4/9	1	4	9
	Market 9/, plays[14] 30/	1	19	

11. Andrew Donally v. John Hutchison was an appeal from the District Court at Greenbrier County to the Court of Appeals in which JM represented Hutchinson. The lower court's judgment was affirmed on June 9, 1791. Court of Appeals Order Book, II, 71, Va. State Lib.

12. See entry under Receipts, Mar. 25, 1789.

13. See entry under Receipts, Oct. 20, 1789.

14. It was announced on Oct. 13 that the 1790 Richmond theater season would begin on Oct. 18 with a performance by the Virginia Company of *Know Your Own Mind* and *The Farmer*. However, the opening was postponed "till the Theatre be every way completed for the reception of the Audience," and the season opened on Oct. 21 with a performance of two comedies, *The Wonder* and *The Farmer*. *Venice Preserved*, a tragedy, and a comic opera, *The Poor Soldier*, were presented on Oct. 28. *Va. Gaz., & Genl. Adv.*, Oct. 13, 20, and 27, 1790; Sherman, "Post-Revolutionary Theatre," 264.

	£	s	d
Market 10/, corn £4–7–6	4	17	6
Postage 6/, Market 4/		10	
Great coat cloth etc.	3	6	
Cheese 11/5, plains £6	6	11	5
blankets £9–6	9	6	
	33	1	2
	61	7	6
[*Total October Disbursements*]	94	8	8

[*Receipts*]

		£	s	d
November 2d.	From Hunters estate	5		
	From Colo. Calloway	7		
	Mosby ads. Cobbs (chy.)[15]	2	2	
	Hawkins exx.	3	16	
16	Pritchard ads. Briscoe	14		
	Madison ads. Singleton	2	16	
	advice fee	1	8	
	Hopkins exr. of Bugg Hopkins[16] Crawly Robert[17] } ads. Robt. Donald & Co. Federal	7	10	
	Richeson ads. Syme	5		
	Hope ads. Hopkins	5		
	Ramsay ads. Bolling[18]	14		
	Scott ads. Comth.	16	16	
		84	8	

15. See entry under Receipts, May 29, 1790.

16. Hugh Colquhoun, surviving partner of Alexander Donald & Co., v. Samuel Hopkins, of Mecklenburg County, was a British debt case in which JM represented Hopkins. Pleas were entered on Nov. 28, 1791, and a judgment for the plaintiff was entered on Nov. 22, 1793. The judgment was set aside by consent on Nov. 30, 1793, and a consent judgment agreed to on Dec. 4, 1794. U.S. Circuit Court, Va., Order Book, I, 62, 165–166, 216, 456–457, and Record Book, II, 513–523, Va. State Lib.

17. Hugh Colquhoun, surviving partner of Alexander Donald & Co., v. Robert Crawley was similar to the case immediately above. Pleas and answers were heard on May 24, and Nov. 28, 1791, and judgment was entered for Colquhoun on Nov. 23, 1793. U.S. Circuit Court, Va., Order Book, I, 9, 10, 62, 85, 169–170, and Record Book, I, 468–477, Va. State Lib.

18. Mary Bolling v. Elizabeth Ramsey's Lessee was an ejectment action appealed from the District Court at Petersburg. JM represented the appellee, and on June 13, 1791, the case was dismissed for failure to prosecute. Court of Appeals Order Book, II, 77, Va. State Lib.

[*Disbursements*]

November				
2d.	Shoeing my horse 2/6		2	6
	Sugar £3–10–6, Market 24/	4	11	6
4	Market 16/, do. 42/	2	18	
	Spectacles for my Father	1	1	
	Shoes for house servants	3	2	6
	Waistcoats for self	1	1	
	Pd. Mr. Swann for tables & chairs	24		
	Market 22/, wood 7/	1	9	
	plate warmer 24/, sundries 18/	2	2	
	Knives & forks 52/, Market 6/8	2	18	8
	Market 3/, chairs £8–8	8	11	
	Straw 8/, do. 8/, wood 8/	1	4	
	Market 36/, oysters 4/3	2		3
	expences going to Williamsburg[19]	2	8	
	Corn	2	8	
	Market 18/		18	
		60	15	5

[*Receipts*]

Decr. 2.	Oxly & Hancock	42		
	Graves v Groves[20]	14		
	Carlyles exrs. v Alexander	14		
	advice fee	1	8	
	Stringer—Genl. court.	2	16	
	Advice fee	1	8	
	Ross v Pynes[21]	7	4	

19. On Nov. 26, 1791, JM was admitted to practice before the U.S. Circuit Court for Virginia. That court held its fall 1790 session in Williamsburg. Its spring session had met in Charlottesville. U.S. Circuit Court, Va., Order Book, I, 4, Va. State Lib.

20. John Groves v. Francis Graves was an appeal from a decree in the High Court of Chancery on a breach of contract. It is unclear whom JM represented. The decree was reversed on Dec. 18, 1790. 1 Va. (1 Wash.) 1; Court of Appeals Order Book, II, 33, 46, 59–60, Va. State Lib.

21. David Ross v. Benjamin Pynes was an appeal from a chancery decree dismissing an injunction against a judgment against Ross in the General Court. The Court of Appeals affirmed the dismissal and the judgment on Dec. 8, 1790. Wythe 71; 7 Va. (3 Call) 568–573; Court of Appeals Order Book, II, 42, 45, Va. State Lib.

Pauly v Commth.[22]	30	
Patteson v Smith & al	3	
Brackin v the college[23]	20	
Underwood ads. Miller (appeal)	1	8
Carringtons exrs. in Pleasants ads. Armstd.	5	
Gratz—for division of land[24]	5	
Scandland v Pattersons exrs.	5	
Breckenridge ads. Vaughan[25]	5	0
	157	4

[Disbursements]

[December]	Market 25/	1	5	
	Straw 8/, Market 36/	2	4	
	Fodder 20/, Market 10/6	1	10	6
	Plays at sundry times 8£[26]	8		
	Coal	13	8	6
	Chocolate 6/, market 7/		13	
	Advancd to my sister Lucy	8		
	Market 12/, do. at sundry times £6	6	12	
	Wood 12/, corn 20/	1	12	
	Coffee £4–19	4	19	
	Market 6/, sundries 6/		12	

22. Lewis Abraham Pauley began petitioning the House of Delegates and the Council of State as early as 1784 to receive payment on accounts the state had established during the Revolution. The Council added his name to a long list of creditors and made periodic token payments in the 1780s. Pauley, probably with the help of JM, petitioned the House of Delegates again in 1788 but was told to resort to the courts. At the fall 1790 term of the High Court of Chancery, Chancellor Wythe decreed in favor of Pauley after hearing arguments from Attorney General James Innes and JM. The state considered appealing the decree (JM in fact told Innes that the state should appeal) but decided against it, whereupon Pauley began drawing warrants from the solicitor. JVCS, III, 320, 356, 431, 461, 506, 535, IV, 91; JVCS, Nov. 19 and 20, 1790; Innes to Edmund Randolph, Nov. 20, 1790, Executive Papers, Va. State Lib. See also JVHD, Oct. 1788, 37, 56.

23. See Bracken v. College of William and Mary: Editorial Note, Dec. 7, 1790.

24. Probably Michael Gratz. See Joseph Simon to JM, Mar. 25, 1791.

25. See JM to John Breckinridge, Aug. 15, 1790.

26. JM had entered expenses for plays earlier in the winter season under Disbursements, Oct. 1790. Although there is no extant material indicating the performance of plays in Dec. 1790, this entry suggests that there was a continuance of the season. See entry under Disbursements, Jan. 1, 1791, for expenses for more plays of the winter season.

plays		I	7	
		50	3	

[*Receipts*]

	£			
Jany.	£	31	17	
Feb.		81	9	
March		150	14	
Apl.		99	7	
May		201	6	2
June		169	19	9
July		122	16	8
Aug.		84	4	
Sep.		119	15	2
Oc.		124	12	
No.		84	8	
Decr.		157	4	
		1427	12	9

I have taken Bland Ballards
  certificates for £145 9 10
  in dollars   457.52
interest computed to 31 Decr.
  1791   27.44
                                          484.96

	145	9	10²⁷
4			
	36	7	5½
	109	2	4½

sold for

£109   2   4½

[*Disbursements*]

	£			
Jany.	£	84	3	4
Feb.		25	18	1
Mar.		23	14	10
Apl		14	19	
May		29	6	3
June		122	15	8
July		39	19	3
Aug.		38	01	6

27. In addition to these figures, which JM wrote in the top right-hand corner of the
page, he also subtracted 129 from 168.6 and added 75 and 54 at the bottom of the
page. The addition and subtraction appear unrelated to other entries on the page.

Sep.	39	1	1
Oc.	94	8	8
No.	60	15	5
Decr.	50	3	
	623	15	1 [28]

[Receipts]

January 1st.	drawing a mortgage	1	8	
	Advice fee	1	4	
	Mr. Guy (fedl. Ct. Caroline)[29]	2	10	
	Grubb v chy.	5	12	
	advice fee	1	2	6
	Egglesten ads. Dob[son] etc.[30]	2	10	
	ads. Pate (district court)		15	
	Field v Taylor & al[31]	5		
	Mayo exr. ads. Davies & ux	1	10	
	Gilberts exrs. ads. Donald[32]	5	12	
	Anderson ads.[33]	2	10	

28. In the right-hand margin JM multiplied 44½ by 4 and added to the total 22, 11, and 6, for a grand total of 217. He then added £65 and £16. These computations appear unrelated to other entries on the page.

29. JM represented George Guy, of Caroline County, before the U.S. Circuit Court for Virginia in a debt action brought by James Dennistoun *et al.*, doing business as Donald, Scot & Co., Glasgow. JM filed an answer on Nov. 28, 1791, and on May 23, 1796, judgment was confessed. U.S. Circuit Court, Va., Order Book, I, 61, and Record Book, IV, 127–129, Va. State Lib.

30. Dobson and Daltera v. Joseph Eggleston, Sr., of Amelia County, was a British debt case in which JM represented the defendant. Pleas were made on Dec. 3, 1791, but the death of Eggleston abated the case on Dec. 2, 1793. U.S. Circuit Court, Va., Order Book, I, 79, 96, 224, Va. State Lib. See JM's answer listed at Law Papers, Feb. 1791.

31. Theophilus Field v. Richard Taylor and Edmund B. Holloway probably began in a district court and then went to the High Court of Chancery, for that court decreed against Field on May 12, 1798, at which time JM took an appeal to the Court of Appeals. The appeal was dismissed on May 11, 1799, when Field failed to appear. Court of Appeals Order Book, III, 323, Va. State Lib. See additional fee entered under Receipts, Sept. 1794.

32. James Dennistoun *et al.*, doing business as Donald, Scot & Co., v. Gabriel Penn and Daniel Gaines, executors of Henry Gilbert, of Amherst County, was a debt action in which JM filed papers in May 1791. Judgment was entered on May 22, 1795. U.S. Circuit Court, Va., Order Book, I, 16, 400, 461, and Record Book, III, 198–202, Va. State Lib. See JM's answer listed at Law Papers, May 1791.

33. This is likely the debt action of John Dobson v. Garland Anderson, of Hanover County. JM filed answers on Dec. 3, 1791, to which Dobson demurred. The demurrer was sustained, and judgment was entered for Dobson on Nov. 22, 1793. U.S. Circuit Court, Va., Order Book, I, 84, 166, and Record Book, I, 341–356, Va. State Lib. See additional fee entered under Receipts, Apr. 1792.

	advice fee	1	2	6
	Randolph v Markham	5		
	advice fee 24/, do. 2/6, do. £1–8	[2	14]	6
	From Jones[34] exr. of Ld. Fairfax	28		
	Willis ads. Askew[35]	5		
		74	4	

[Disbursements]

January 1	ink powder 3/, Market 3/		6	
	repairing a watch 9/		9	
	house servants		12	
	hominy 2/6, barber 47/	2	9	6
	flour £8–14–6, Salt 6/, Market 4/	9	4	6
	Straw 28/, coal 22/6	2	10	6
	Wood 8/, market 6/		14	
	Shoes for Dick 4/6		4	6
	pork £22–1–2, Salt 7/6	22	8	8
	Wood 10/, market £3–1, Salt 3/	3	14	
	Vinegar, pots, salt 18/, rum 4–10	5	8	
	Market 11/, beer 14/	1	5	
	play[36] 24/, cards 9/	1	13	
	Play 6/, market 5/		11	
	rum £4–10, Market 13/, apples 20/	6	3	
	Straw 8/, pork 2–14, do. 2–12	5	6	
	Market £1–15–11, do. 7/6	2	3	5
	play 9/, bed £3–12	4	1	
	Market 5/, do. 6/		11	

34. Gabriel Jones. For Fairfax's will, see *Virginia Magazine of History and Biography*, XXXIV (1926), 45–46. Jones had entered the payment on Dec. 10, 1790, in the Fairfax estate account book. Fairfax Family Papers, Library of Congress.

35. William Askew v. Francis Willis was an old case on appeal from the Berkeley County Court. After the reorganization of the courts in 1788, the case was transferred to the District Court at Winchester, where another attorney took the case. Superior Court Order Book, 1789–1793, 87, Frederick County, Va. State Lib.

36. JM's Account Book shows his attendance at several plays in Jan. 1791. The winter theater season continued with the Jan. 7 performance by the Virginia Company of *Busy Body*, a comedy, followed by several songs and the musical farce, *The Padlock*. The tragedy *Isabella; or the Fatal Marriage* and a farce, *The Citizen*, were presented on Jan. 12, with the evening concluding with an "Epilogue, and flying leap through a hogshead of Blazing Fire, by Mr. Hallam." *Va. Gaz., & Genl. Adv.*, Jan. 5 and 12, 1791.

Wood 7/6, tea 10/, jelly 6/, books 37/, linnen 5£	8	6	
shoes 6/, razors 12/, market 7/6, eggs 1/3	1	6	9
	79	11	4

[*Receipts*]

Feby. 1st.	From Colo. Baylor	5	12	
	Mr. Hatcher	2	8	
	Mr. Burton (federal)[37]	5		
	advice	1	2	
	Harris v Goodall	1	16	
	advice fee from Syme	1	8	
	advice fee Clarkes will	1	2	6
	Abraham v Scott injn.	4	10	
	advice	1	4	
	Bridgeforths exr. ads. Malones exr.	4	16	
	Governor Randolph[38] in three suits	15		
	From Mr. Hughes (finishd	25		
	From Mr. Walker (federal)	9		
	Legrand ads. Simmons	5		
	Davies ads. Batte & al.	5		
	Proudfit v Blane & al. chy.	5		
	Yates ads. Hite appeal[39]	4	16	
	Jerdones exrs. v. Kerr appl.	5		
	Davenport v Thompson[40]	4	10	

37. Donald & Co., Glasgow, v. Jesse and Robert Burton, of Albemarle County, was a debt action in which JM represented the Burtons. Answers were filed on Nov. 30, 1791, and judgment was given the plaintiff on Nov. 27, 1793. U.S. Circuit Court, Va., Order Book, I, 68, 185–186, and Record Book, II, 122–128, Va. State Lib. See JM's answer listed at Law Papers, Nov. 1791.

38. Beverley Randolph was governor until Dec. 1, 1791.

39. John Yates v. Jost Hite's Representatives was an appeal from an Aug. 5, 1790, ruling that was affirmed by the Court of Appeals on Nov. 15, 1791. Court of Appeals Order Book, II, 118, 126, Va. State Lib.

40. In James Davenport v. William Thompson, JM asked the High Court of Chancery to enjoin a Hanover County Court judgment against his client Davenport that involved a mortgage held with Thompson. On Oct. 24, 1791, the chancellor issued the injunction and reversed the judgment with amendments. Thompson appealed to the Court of Appeals, which reversed the decree and amended the order on Oct. 20, 1792. 1 Va. (1 Wash.) 125; Court of Appeals Order Book, II, 185, 188, Va. State Lib.

Brendt in Cartwright		4	4	
Robert ads. Southerland		4	10	
		112	18	6

[Disbursements]

Feby.	To Polly for house	4	8	
	to Lewis[41]	1	8	
	expenses 14, books 14/, market 6/	1	14	
	coal 26/4, shoeing horse 4/6	1	10	10
	market 3/3, wood 8/, market 13/4	1	4	7
	litter 26/, market 6/, stockings 7/	1	19	
	sugar £4–14–8, Tea £1–13–4	6	8	
	manure £3, Shorts 30/, market 12/	5	2	
	market 35/, wood 10/	2	5	
	varnishing carriage etc.	2	16	
	shoes for negroes in 89	4	2	6
	advancd my brother Lewis	3		
	Molasses 6/8, hominy & eggs 3/3		9	8
	Given Lucy 48/	2	8	
	postage 3/, additional for negroes in 89 £3	3	3	
		41	18	7

[Receipts]

March	Recd. from Macauly	60		
	Mosely v Mosely	2	16	
	advice fee	1	2	6
	Peytons exrs. ads. Mercer	5		

41. Louis Marshall (1773–1866) was one of JM's brothers who had moved to Kentucky with his father. Louis was apparently in Richmond at this time en route to Edinburgh, where he studied medicine. After finishing his studies there, he went to Paris and then returned to Kentucky, where he married in 1800 and took over the family home, "Buckpond." He excelled in the practice of medicine and conducted a school for a number of years. In 1838 he became president of Washington College in Lexington, Va., and in 1855 president of Transylvania University, in Kentucky. See William Buchanan, "Louis Marshall, M.D., His Administration as President of Washington College" (M.A. thesis, Washington and Lee University, 1941).

Mr. Pope in Innes v Linton & al	5	4
Cobbs v Allen (residue of fee)	1	16
Lee v Jones & al. exrs. of Flood	2	8
Grymes exr. ads. Robinsons & al.[42]	9	
Tate v Walker & al.	5	
Segougnee ads. Dormoy	2	10
Powells exrs v Cox (balance)	2	10
Boggus v Knight (balance)	1	
Winn & Johnston ads. Burrus	5	2
Fauntleroy exr. v Tomlin	1	8
advice fee from Winston	1	8
Burnet v Burnett	2	8
Wayles exrs. ads. Farrel & Jones[43]	7	
Payne	12	12
Harvey ads. Borden & ux.[44]	5	
advice fee	2	16
Hyat & al Bull etc. ads. Hite (appeal)[45]	5	
	131	6

[Disbursements]

March	Market 12, paid Mitchel[46] for carpet 15 £	15	12
	paid Macauly for wine	60	

42. In John Robinson, executor of Philip Grymes, v. Edmund Pendleton and Peter Lyons, administrators of John Robinson, JM argued for the Grymes estate before the Court of Appeals on Nov. 8 and 9, 1787. Reargument was heard on May 1, 1788, after which judgment was given for the Grymes estate on May 6, 1788. 8 Va. (4 Call) 130; Court of Appeals Order Book, I, 76, 1–2, 105, 112, 117, 120, 123, Va State Lib.

43. See JM's opinion in this case, Apr. 1, 1791.

44. Borden v. Harvie was a suit before the High Court of Chancery involving a contested will. JM represented Harvie and appealed the unfavorable decree of Mar. 11, 1794. The Court of Appeals heard argument on Oct. 21, 1795, and affirmed the judgment on Oct. 31, 1795. 2 Va. (2 Wash.) 156; Court of Appeals Order Book, III, 54, 79, 83, Va. State Lib. See additional fee entered under Receipts, June 1793.

45. In Robert Bull, John Grantham, Nicholas Schull, and Simon Hyatt v. Hite's Representatives, JM appealed a High Court of Chancery decree of Aug. 5, 1790, to the Court of Appeals, which affirmed the ruling on Oct. 24, 1793. Court of Appeals Order Book, II, 115, 189, 243, 244, Va. State Lib.

46. Mitchel & Lyle was a mercantile firm in Richmond as late as 1787. "List of Merchants," Richmond City Hustings Court Order Book, II, 50, Va. State Lib.

	£	s	d
Given Mr. Courtney	1	4	
	76	16	

[*Receipts*]

		£	s	d
March 10th	Clay ads. Greenhill	1	6	8
	Talbot v Welch etc.	2	8	
	Advice fee	1	8	
	Taylor & Carrington admrs. v Tindall appeal chy.	5		
	Brookes exrs. ads. Brookes	7		
	Trent Crump & Bates v Thomas	4	16	
	do. ads. Dobson[47]	9	12	
	Moulson (no suit brought)	2	8	
	Browns Heirs v Harrisons heirs	5		
	From Williams	5		
	Johnstons legatees v Johnstons exrs.[48]	5	12	
	Randolph & al ads. Masterson & al.	5	17	
	Fleming ads. Quesnel & Co.	1	4	
	Woodson v Harding	2	8	
	Martin v Rice	5	4	
	Mr. David Allison on account of advice on sundry subjects	2		
	Talbot ads. Duval appl. 50/	2	10	
	Same ads. Minnis	5		
		73	13	8

[*Disbursements*]

		£	s	d
March	Market	1		
	candles 6/, market 24/	1	10	

47. See JM's answer in Dobson and Daltera v. Crump and Bates, listed at Law Papers, Feb. 1791, and additional fee entered under Receipts, Apr. 15, 1790.

48. Gabriel Johnston v. John Johnston was an ejectment action before the District Court at Fredericksburg in which JM represented the plaintiff. The case was continued several times on motion of the defendant and on May 8, 1794, abated as a result of his death. The case was revived in the name of Elizabeth Johnston in 1796 but abated on her death in 1798. District Court Law Orders, A, 1789–1793, 113, 146, 152, 233, 249, and Law Orders, B, 1794–1798, 47, 266, 405, Fredericksburg, Va. State Lib. See additional fee entered under Receipts, Sept. 1794.

market £3–6–8		3	6	8
Market 6/8, city tax[49] £2–18		3	4	8
		9	1	4

[*Receipts*]

March	Beale ads. Mercer	33	
	Veal v de Francois[50]	5	
	Dandridge ads. Henry & al.	2	10
	Bates ads. Croxal[51]	2	9
	advice fee	1	8
	Tabb ads. Comth. & McCrea	2	9
		46	16

[*Disbursements*]

March	box of candles 49/1, market 1/6	2	10	7
	Museum[52] 15/, Mr. Nicholson[53] 17/6	1	17	6
	ploughing in clover 6/, market 6/		12	
	market 11/9, do. 4/, shoes for Tom 4/		19	9
	market 25/6, wood 10/	1	15	6
		7	15	4

To give my Father credit for three guineas recd. for my brother Alexander from Mr.

49. JM's personal property list for Richmond, received May 16, 1791, showed 2 male tithables in his household and ownership of 10 Negro slaves above and 1 below the age of 16 and 6 carriage wheels. His real property, assessed at £40, was taxed at 10s. Richmond City Personal Property Book, 1791, and Land Book, 1791, Va. State Lib.

50. Apparently Joseph Latile had an interest in this case. See entry under Receipts, July 1791.

51. James Croxall v. Thomas Bates was a debt action brought by a British firm against JM's client Bates. A Dec. 3, 1793, judgment was stayed by an injunction, which was dissolved on May 26, 1794, but chancery action was continued until Dec. 4, 1794. U.S. Circuit Court, Va., Order Book, I, 234, 369, 444, and Record Book I, 422–425, Va. State Lib.

52. JM purchased another volume of the *American Museum* magazine. See entry under Disbursements, Nov. 26, 1788.

53. Nicolson was probably of the mercantile firm Nicolson, Pennock, & Skipwith, which was operating in Richmond as late as 1787. "List of Merchants," Richmond City Hustings Court Order Book, II, 50, Va. State Lib.

Burwell which I request my
Father to pay to my brother.

[*Receipts*]

April	Elams exrs. ads. Newall		18	
	McGehee & al v Graves & al	5		
	Bullock exr. v Garland	5		
	Mr. Rcd. Morris	4		
	advice fee	1	8	
	advice fee	1	2	
	Baily ads. Verrel etc. Burton	5		
	Minor & ux & al v Taliaferro & al[54]	6		
	From Mr. Pollard	10		
	McRea ads. Harrison[55]	5		
	Graham ads. Graham[56]	7		
	advice fee	1	2	6
	Thomas & ux v Phillips	5		
	Bradford etc. v Wells (appeals)	2	8	
	Colo. Meade[57]	4	10	
	Field v Call	5	12	
	Eppes in eject.	7		
	Call ads. Burwell[58]	5		
	Mr. Booker	1	8	
	Grizard ads. Mason	1	4	
	Pride	2	8	
		74	2	6

54. William Minor and wife v. John Taliaferro was a chancery suit involving sale of land. The sale was affirmed by the High Court of Chancery on Sept. 15, 1795, and Taliaferro appealed. The Court of Appeals reversed the decree on May 9, 1799. 5 Va. (1 Call) 456, 460; Court of Appeals Order Book, III, 280, 318; but see also 335, 340, Va. State Lib.

55. Benjamin Harrison v. Christopher McRae was an appeal from the Cumberland County Court to the District Court at Prince Edward County, which affirmed the judgment on Apr. 6, 1791. JM represented McRae when the case was appealed to the Court of Appeals, where the judgment was affirmed on Nov. 23, 1791. Court of Appeals Order Book, II, 138, 141, Va. State Lib.

56. Elisabeth Graham v. Robert Graham was an ejectment action in which records appear in the District Court at Prince William County in 1794. JM never practiced in that court, but he may have handled the case earlier when it would have been on the General Court docket before the reorganization of the courts. District Court Order Book, 1794–1798, 69, 133, 162, 251, 334, 401, 403, 492, Prince William County, Va. State Lib.

57. Everard Meade.

58. See JM to William Branch Giles, Feb. 9, 1790.

[*Disbursements*]

April				
Market 16/, wheelbarrow 6/		1	2	
Market at dift. times 18/8			18	8
Cloaths for myself £4–18		4	18	
linnen for Lucy[59] £5–5–8		5	5	8
shoes for myself			12	
expenses at Pburg.[60] etc.		3	6	
Market 13/4, do. 6/,				
expences 6/		1	5	4
Beds		20		
		37	7	8

[*Receipts*]

April			
Tabb ads. Bolling		7	
Hardaway ads. Hardaway chy.		1	4
Gill v Ross[61]		4	4
Baird ads. Baird		4	16
		18	4

[*Disbursements*]

April		
Expenses going to		
Fredericksburg[62] etc.		6

[*Receipts*]

May			
Eddie v Winder[63]		4	4
Mr. Newton		3	
Brent ads. Oxly & Hancock[64]		2	8

59. The linen was probably purchased in anticipation of his sister Lucy's wedding on May 20, 1791, to John Ambler. *Va. Gaz., & Genl. Adv.*, May 25, 1791.

60. JM attended the session of the District Court at Petersburg, which began on Apr. 15.

61. See entry under Receipts, Sept. 18, 1790.

62. The spring session of the District Court at Fredericksburg, which JM attended, began Apr. 29.

63. Thomas Eddy v. Edmund Winder was a debt action in the District Court at Fredericksburg, which reversed a lower court decision on May 7, 1791. That reversal was appealed to the Court of Appeals, which affirmed the district court's decision on Oct. 25, 1792. District Court Record Book, 1789–1792, 518–520, and Law Orders, A, 1789–1793, 256, 268, 491, Fredericksburg, and Court of Appeals Order Book, II, 194, all in Va. State Lib.

64. Oxley and Hancock v. Robert Brent was a debt action in the District Court at

Bradford (in ct. of appeals)[65]	2	8
Herbert (chy.)	5	
McHany v George[66]	2	8
Turner v Scott[67]	2	8
Cammock (finishd)[68]	8	
Washington v Tillett (appeal chy.)[69]	4	4
Slaughter ads. Slaughter	5	
Spratt v Price	2	
Jones v Jett (in appeals)	5	
Herndens exr. v Spotswood[70]	6	
advice fee from Doctor Vass	2	8
Alexander v Cassons admr. chy.	6	
advice fee from Fox	1	
Richards exrs. (Federal[71]	5	
	66	8

[Receipts]

May 12th.	Asberry & al v Scruggs admrs.[72] appl.	4	4

Fredericksburg in which JM represented Brent. The case was continued on Oct. 3, 1791, and on May 9, 1792, the court ordered that an award to be determined by JM and Bushrod Washington would be made the judgment of the court. District Court Law Orders, A, 1789–1793, 291, 380, Fredericksburg, Va. State Lib.

65. See Vol. I, 388, n. 35, for an earlier fee in this case.

66. See JM's notes on argument, printed at May 4, 1791, and his plea listed at Law Papers, Sept. 1788.

67. George Turner v. Robert Scott was a debt action on a writing obligatory in which JM represented Turner in the District Court at Fredericksburg. The parties agreed on a settlement, and the case was dismissed on Sept. 30, 1791. District Court Law Orders, A, 1789–1793, 15, 125, 162, 166, 230, 273, Fredericksburg, Va. State Lib. See JM's replication listed at Law Papers, May 1790.

68. George Cammock v. William Drummond was an appeal from a consent judgment entered in the Caroline County Court. The District Court at Fredericksburg affirmed the judgment on May 7, 1791. District Court Law Orders, A, 1789–1793, 260, and District Court Record Book, 1789–1792, 531–533, Fredericksburg, Va. State Lib.

69. Edward Washington v. Samuel Tillett was before the High Court of Chancery, where a decree was issued on June 4, 1792. An appeal taken by JM to the Court of Appeals on behalf of his client Washington was dismissed on Apr. 27, 1793, for failure to prosecute. Court of Appeals Order Book, II, 225, Va. State Lib.

70. See entry under Receipts, Apr. 22, 1789.

71. See JM's answer in this case listed at Law Papers, Nov. 1791, and deposition consent listed at Law Papers, 1791.

72. George Asberry, John Chastain, and Jeremiah Hatcher v. Gross Scruggs's Administrators reversed a judgment of the District Court at New London on Apr. 18,

Petways exr. ads. Cox appeal chy.	5	2	
advice fee Southgate	2	8	
Kelso & Kincaid ads. Harris (appl.)	2	10	
Mr. Smith in contest for clerkship	7		
Richardson v Burnly	2	8	
Singleton	7		
Woodson ads. Woodson[73]	2	8	
Abraham v Robertson	4	16	
Allen (in old appeals in chy.)	5	7	
Owen ads. James & Robt. Donald 2 suits[74]	5		
Gathright ads. Neaves chy.	3	18	
Miller ads. McCall & Snodgrass British[75]	2	10	
Ware ads. Strange (assee.) fedl.	2	10	
Covington admr. ads.[76]	2	10	
Sampson ads. Drumright	2	16	
Massie v Burwells exrs.	7	4	
	69	11	

[Disbursements]

May	Wood 20/, Market 6/	1	6	
	Market at sundry times £3–6–8	3	6	8
	Coal 40/	2		

1792, after JM first had obtained a writ of supersedeas on Apr. 22, 1791. Court of Appeals Order Book, II, 158, Va. State Lib.

73. See Vol. I, 408, n. 4, for an earlier fee.

74. Robert Donald *et al.*, surviving partners of James and Robert Donald & Co., Glasgow, v. Thomas Owen, of Henrico County, was actually two debt actions brought in the U.S. Circuit Court in Nov. 1790. At the trial in Nov. 1793 a jury found for the plaintiffs, who had been represented by Andrew Ronald. See JM's answer listed at Law Papers, May 1791.

75. William Snodgrass, of Great Britain, v. Thomas Miller was a debt on a penal bond in which JM filed pleas for Miller on Dec. 3, 1791. The U.S. Circuit Court sustained the plaintiff's demurrer and awarded judgment on Nov. 26, 1793. U.S. Circuit Court, Va., Order Book, I, 77, 189, and Record Book, II, 343–351, Va. State Lib. See JM's answer listed at Law Papers, Dec. 1791.

76. This case was most likely William Snodgrass v. Sarah Covington, executrix of Luke Covington, an action to recover a debt on a penal bill, and was in all other respects identical to the case against Miller described in the preceding note. U.S. Circuit Court, Va., Order Book, I, 66–67, 180, and Record Book, II, 336–343, Va. State Lib.

To Lewis to bring my sisters from Fburg.[77]	3	16	
Market £3–14, wood 10/, butter 30/	5	14	
For house servants	15		
For self	3	5	7¾
	34	8	3¾

[Receipts]

June	Shelton ads. Shelton	14	
	Dew v Macclewhaine[78]	5	
	Gardener ads. Griffin	1	16
	Rhulings	7	
	Capt. Younghusband	5	12
	Davies ads. Wood[79]	2	16
	Hudnal ads. Hudnal (appeals)[80]	7	
	Alexander ads. Dade[81]	14	
	Nelson exr. of Armstead ads. Price[82]	5	
	Colo. Cole in Mrs. Anderson agt. her husband[83]	5	

77. They no doubt came to Richmond to attend JM's sister Lucy's wedding to John Ambler on May 20. *Va. Gaz., & Genl. Adv.*, May 25, 1791.

78. Samuel Dew v. William McIlwaine was an appeal to the Court of Appeals from a 1790 judgment in favor of McIlwaine before the District Court at Winchester. Representing Dew before the Court of Appeals, JM won a reversal and a new trial on June 20, 1791. Court of Appeals Order Book, II, 83, Va. State Lib.

79. JM represented Isaac Davis in an appeal brought by Josiah Wood on a judgment rendered by the District Court at Charlottesville in Apr. 1791. The appeal was heard before the Court of Appeals on Apr. 11, 1792, and the lower court's ruling was affirmed the following day. 1 Va. (1 Wash.) 69; Court of Appeals Order Book, II, 150, 152, Va. State Lib.

80. Thomas Hudnall v. Joseph Hudnall, Jr., was an appeal from a judgment of the District Court at Northumberland County. It was submitted to the Court of Appeals on Nov. 21, 1791, and the lower court's decision was affirmed two days later. It is impossible to determine which party JM represented. Court of Appeals Order Book, II, 139, 141, Va. State Lib.

81. See entry under Receipts, May 12, 1789.

82. See entry under Receipts, Oct. 12, 1789.

83. This is likely the case of Jane Anderson v. George Anderson, Mary Talley, and Nathaniel Anderson, representatives of John Anderson, about which little is known prior to the late 1790s. The case was first before the High Court of Chancery, and this is no doubt when JM became involved. Mrs. Anderson, who held a remainder interest in slaves, sought to have her husband's creditors enjoined from proceeding against her interest. The High Court of Chancery dismissed her bill, and the Court of

Robinsons admrs.	20		
Haley & al ads. Clendinnen	5		
Field v Kerr old appeal			
(Kentuck)	6	4	
Crow ads. Doherty[84]	4	16	
Johnston & Lindsay ads.			
Rhoddy & Taylor	7		
McDowal v Carpenter[85]	5		
Galt, two suits in fedl. court[86]	5		
Carrington & al ads. Mayo[87]	12		
	132	4	

[*Disbursements*]

June	Paid for kitchen chimney	2	14	7
	for enclosing the yard	8		
	do.	2	8	
	Market 30/, ploughing 6/	1	16	
	Market 24, do. 6/	1	10	
	Wood 20/, Hoes etc. 10/,			
	Market 12	2	2	
	paid the Taylor	6	12	9
	Market 7/6, Barber 45/	2	12	6
		46	15	10

Appeals affirmed that decree on Nov. 11, 1799. 6 Va. (2 Call) 163; Court of Appeals Order Book, III, 354, 360, Va. State Lib. See additional fee under Receipts, Mar. 1795.

84. John Daugherty v. William Crow was an appeal from a decree of the Supreme Court for the district of Kentucky made in Sept. 1787 that would have permitted Crow to initiate ejectment action against Daugherty. The appeal was partly heard on Dec. 17, 1790, but then continued until June 27, 1791. The decree was affirmed by the Court of Appeals on June 30, 1791. Court of Appeals Order Book, II, 57, 61, 104, 106, Va. State Lib.

85. Solomon Carpenter's Administrator v. James McDowell's Administrators was a debt action in which judgment had been given by the District Court at Staunton on Apr. 4, 1791. Apparently McDowell's administrators wanted to appeal the decision and retained JM for that purpose. There is no record of the case before the Court of Appeals. For the record of the case in the lower courts, during which time it is unlikely JM had any role in the litigation, see District Court Order Book, 1789–1793, 191, Augusta County, Va. State Lib.

86. Stephen Bagg, of Great Britain, v. John M. Galt was a British debt case in which pleas were entered on Nov. 29, 1791. The second case has not been found. U.S. Circuit Court, Va., Order Book, II, 205, 213, and Record Book, V, 218–221, Va. State Lib. See JM's answer listed at Law Papers, Nov. 1791.

87. See entry under Receipts, June 19, 1790.

[*Receipts*]

July				
advice fee from Mr. Harris[88]	1	2	3	
Latil[89] & de Francois ads. Veal	4	18		
Richeson & Quarles ads. Jones, Fedl.[90]	5	2		
Harris ads. Watkins[91]	5			
Donald & ux v McCallum & ux	5			
West v Roane	4	10		
advice fee	1	8		
Mr. Jones ads. Crawly	5	12		
Mr. Halcomb in Rice v Graves	4	10		
Advice fee	1	1		
	38	3	3	

[*Disbursements*]

July			
Market 18/, expenses 48/	3	6	
4th. of July[92] 34/6, tools 9/	2	3	6
Pd. Mr. Hay for beer[93]	2	14	6
boot in horses	7		
Market 24/, expenses going to Buckingham[94] 40/	3	4	

88. See JM to John Breckinridge, *ca.* July 1791.

89. Joseph Latile.

90. These were two British debt cases brought by John Tyndale Ware, executor of William Jones, surviving partner of Farrell & Jones, against John Quarles, Jr., and against Holt Richeson on Nov. 28, 1791. The case against Quarles was less typical than was Richeson's case and ended when the plaintiff was nonsuited on May 26, 1797, for failure to prosecute. Richeson's case followed the normal pleas and demurrers and ended on Nov. 25, 1795, when judgment was given the plaintiff. For Quarles's case, see U.S. Circuit Court, Va., Order Book, I, 63, 243, 249, II, 23, 143, 217, Va. State Lib.; and for Richeson's case, see *ibid.*, I, 63–64, 242, 401, 419, 457, III, 14, and U.S. Circuit Court, Va., Record Book, III, 429–436, Va. State Lib.

91. See JM to John Breckinridge, *ca.* July 1791, and an earlier fee in this case, Vol. I, 412.

92. Two social functions were held to celebrate July 4 in 1791. One group of men attended a dinner at the Eagle Tavern, while another attended a barbecue in the country. A 15-cannon salute greeted the rising sun, and the shots were repeated at noon. It is uncertain which meal JM attended. *Va. Gaz., & Genl. Adv.*, July 6, 1791.

93. William Hay, Richmond merchant.

94. JM purchased a tract of land in Buckingham County from Charles Mynn Thruston probably at this time, although he stated in 1803 that it was "in or about the year 1790." JM knew the title to the land was encumbered, but he bought it on the promise that the encumbrance would be removed. Failure to remove the encumbrance resulted in an interesting chancery suit that JM was forced to bring in 1803. See Albert J. Beveridge, *The Life of John Marshall* (Boston, 1916), II, 173, for a discussion of the case, although Beveridge incorrectly dates the chancery bill. Bill in

		£	s
	Wood 10/, market 12/, Oats 7/, sundries 7/	1	16
	Market 12/, fruit 3/		15
	paid for stable & paling	56	5
	Flour £9-9, Market 12/	10	1
		87	5

[*Receipts*]

		£	s
August	Mr. Van Bibber[95]	2	8
	Hawkins exrs.[96]	4	10
	Jones ads. Garland etc.	2	8
	Miller v Taylor[97]	5	
	Collier ads. Jones	2	12
	Brown ads.	3	
	Keeling v McCrea & al.	4	
	Fleming v Browns exrs.	1	8
	Mr. Roberts ads. Southeland	4	4
	Kidd v Donahoe & Bell	2	8
	Smith v Ewing (Rockingham appls.)[98]	4	11
	Massie v Cock	3	10
	Loving v Clough	1	4
	Draffen v Cheeseman & ux.	5	
	Elliott & al. ads. Davies district	2	10
	Colly ads. Alvis (district)	1	8

chancery, JM v. Charles M. Thruston *et al.*, Jan. 25, 1803, is in the Boston Public Library.

95. Andrew Van Bibber. JM's declaration in Van Bibber v. George Green is listed at Law Papers, Nov. 1792. The case was continued by the U.S. Circuit Court for Virginia, from Dec. 1792 to May 1793, when the defendant pleaded payment. In the Nov. 1793 term the matter came to trial, and the jury returned a verdict for the plaintiff for the amount claimed in the declaration plus one penny in damages. See U.S. Circuit Court, Va., Record Book, II, 352–353, Va. State Lib.

96. See entry under Receipts, Sept. 1, 1790.

97. Richard Taylor v. George Miller was a case in the District Court at Prince Edward County involving charges of extortion by Miller, former sheriff of Buckingham County. The district court rendered judgment against Miller on Apr. 7, 1791, and denied a motion for a new trial the following day. JM traveled to Buckingham County in July 1791, and perhaps Miller retained him to appeal the judgment to the Court of Appeals at that time. No further record of the case survives, however. District Court Records at Large, 1789–1792, 364–371, Prince Edward County, Va. State Lib. See entry under Disbursements, July 1791, for "expenses going to Buckingham."

98. JM obtained a writ of supersedeas to the District Court at Staunton in Benjamin Smith v. Mary Ewin, but the case was dismissed on Oct. 10, 1792, when Smith failed to prosecute further. Court of Appeals Order Book, II, 182, Va. State Lib.

		£	s	d
	Meredith v Johns & Benning	5		
		54	1	

[Disbursements]

		£	s	d
August	Market 9/, do. 20/	1	9	
	Raffling 36/, amicable society[99] 9/	2	5	
	Wine £14–5–8, expenses 9/	14	14	8
	Market 20/, do. 19	1	19	
	shoes 12/, hat 42/, expenses 11/	3	5	
	market 9/, watch 14	1	3	
	boots 48/	2	8	
		27	3	8

[Receipts]

		£	s	d
September	Hoomes v Lipscomb	5		
	Colo. W. Fleming[1]	10		
	Muir v Millers heirs & exrs. etc.	4	16	
		19	16	

[Disbursements]

		£	s	d
September	Market 22/			
	Market 9/	1	2	
	Given Lewis on account of my father[2]	15	1	
	expenses at Petersburg[3]	3		
	Given Lewis on account of my Father	37	12	9
		4	2	

99. The Amicable Society was organized by several prominent Richmond citizens on Dec. 13, 1788, to relieve strangers and travelers in distress. JM was elected to the society on Dec. 20, 1788. Contributions and subscriptions, such as JM's entry here, were most likely the method used to raise funds. [Samuel Mordecai], *Richmond in By-Gone Days* (Richmond, 1856), 188; W. Asbury Christian, *Richmond: Her Past and Present* (Richmond, 1912), 35.

1. William Fleming.

2. JM totaled the two sums he gave Lewis at the bottom of this page of the Account Book. The total, £52 13s. 9d., was omitted from the total of his September disbursements.

3. JM attended the fall session of the District Court at Petersburg that began on Sept. 15.

[*Receipts*]

October
12th.

Advice fee from McClanahan	1	16	
do. from Doctor Wilson	1	4	
Berry & al v Powell & al	2	16	
Advice from Mr. Garnet	2	16	
Hadens admrs. etc. ads. Hall	4	12	
Couts	5	12	
Draffen v Thomas (chy.)	5		
Hargraves exrs. ads. Goodall	3		
The clerk of Pendleton	3		
Mickies admrs. v Smith[4]	5		
Wilson ads. Corran admr.	2	8	
Speed exr. of Taylor ads. Harwood	5		
Edmiston ads. McCarrel	5		
Short v Edwards	5	12	
Homes v Kuhn[5]	5	12	
advice fee	1		
Barrie & al v Powell & al	1	16	
Harris in Federal court[6]	2	8	
Raine exr. of Marshall v Ross	5		
McCrea	7	10	
Spencer	5		
advice	1	2	6
	82	4	6

[*Disbursements*]

October

market 6/, postage 6/		12	
Market 19/, hay 24/	2	3	
market 4/, do. 2/, expenses 5/		11	

4. Daniel Smith v. John Mickie's Executors was an appeal to the Court of Appeals from an Apr. 1791 judgment of the District Court at Charlottesville that reversed an Aug. 1788 ruling by the Albemarle County Court in favor of Smith. The appeal was heard on Oct. 21, 1792, and the Court of Appeals reversed the district court judgment on Oct. 24, 1792. 1 Va. (1 Wash.) 135; Court of Appeals Order Book, II, 155, 189, 192, Va. State Lib.

5. See Vol. I, 183, 379, for JM's declaration in this case and an earlier fee.

6. Robert Donald v. John Harris, of Powhatan County, was an action to recover a 1774 debt. On May 28, 1792, pleas were made by JM to which the plaintiff demurred. On Nov. 29, 1793, the demurrer was sustained, and a judgment was entered for the plaintiff. U.S. Circuit Court, Va., Order Book, I, 93, 111, 209, and Record Book, I, 100–105, Va. State Lib.

	wood 10/, plays[7] 18/	1	8	
	market 12/, shoes 15/	1	7	
	market 12/, taxes[8] £1–13–6	2	5	6
		8	6	6
	plays 24/	1	4	
		9	10	6

[Receipts]

October	Gardner ads. Griffin	1	8	
	Dundass ads. Taylor[9]	7		
	Eppes ads. Fletcher	5		
	Fauntleroys exrs. v Tomlin	2		
	Browns exrs. ads. Donald Scott & Co.	2	16	
	advice	1	8	
	Nichols ads. or v. Nielson appeal	5		
	Jones ads. Williams & Tomlinson[10]	2	8	
	Hunter & Allason ads. Ross[11]	4	10	
	Lacost	10		
		41	10	

7. The fall theater season opened on Oct. 17 in Richmond when the Virginia Company presented *The Foundling; or Fortunate Soldier* (later billed as *The Foundling; or, Virtue it's own Reward*) and *Rosina; or Love in a Cottage*. Box seats were six shillings each. The casts included guest actors and actresses from London and Philadelphia. On Oct. 27 the players scheduled a tragedy, *Gamester; or, False Friend*, to which was added musical entertainment, *The Farmer; or, the World's Ups and Downs*. *Va. Gaz., & Genl. Adv.*, Sept. 28, and Oct. 19 and 26, 1791.

8. This entry may represent JM's payment of Henrico County property taxes, records of which are not extant. He had recorded full or partial payment of Richmond city taxes earlier in the year. See entry under Disbursements, Mar. 1791.

9. Jesse Taylor v. John Dundass was an appeal from the District Court at Dumfries to the Court of Appeals. JM's client Dundass had lost the case in the Fairfax County Court in 1790, but the district court reversed that judgment on Apr. 18, 1791. The Court of Appeals, after hearing arguments on Apr. 30, 1792, reversed the district court on May 3, 1792, affirming the county court decision. 1 Va. (1 Wash.) 92; Court of Appeals Order Book, II, 170, 179, Va. State Lib.

10. See entry under Receipts, Nov. 29, 1789.

11. There is an incomplete record of a case before the District Court at Prince William County in 1794 that could be related to this entry, although there is no indication JM practiced before that court. See David Ross and Thomas Pleasants v. William Hunter, Jr., and John Allison, District Court Order Book, 1794–1798, 8, 95, 151, 209, 351, 432, Prince William County, Va. State Lib.

	[*Disbursements*]		
October	market 30/, do. 18/	2	8
	encyclopedia[12]	1	10
		3	18

	[*Receipts*]		
November	Reid ads. Lidderdale fedl. chy.[13]	5	
	Tabb v Gregory appeals[14]	10	
	Baily v Justices exrs. chy. see	2	8
	Dunlop & al. v Pages	7	10
	Rob v Nelsons exrs. sci fa	2	10
	Calloway ads Wilcox[15]	28	
	Fallis ads. Richards	2	8
	Wormly (advice)[16]	1	8
	Trueheart (advice)	1	8
	Crane (murder)[17]	14	
	Mr. West of Maryland advice	5	4
	Archer ads. Ligon	2	10
	Kennon v McRoberts[18]	7	10

12. This entry records the purchase of a volume of *Encyclopaedia; or a Dictionary of Arts, Sciences, and Miscellaneous Literature*, to which JM had subscribed in Sept. 1790 with the purchase of vol. I. Vol. IV had been issued in 1791, and its arrival in Richmond was advertised in October. *Va. Gaz., & Genl. Adv.*, Oct. 12, 1791.

13. John Lidderdale's Executor v. George Butler and Thomas Reade was a chancery suit to recover the purchase price of two tracts of land in Charlotte County. Butler, a foreigner, had originally purchased the tracts and then sold one to Reade, JM's client. After publishing notices for Butler to answer in Dec. 1793 and May 1794, the U.S. Circuit Court ordered the sale of land to the plaintiff. U.S. Circuit Court, Va., Order Book, I, 230, 385, 446, and Record Book, III, 105–117, Va. State Lib.

14. In Tabb v. Gregory, JM represented Tabb on appeal from a judgment of the District Court at Brunswick County. Gregory had charged Tabb with slander uttered during Gregory's campaign for a seat in the House of Delegates in 1789. The court rendered a judgment in favor of Gregory on May 3, 1791, and Tabb then engaged JM to take the case on appeal. The Court of Appeals heard arguments on Apr. 13, 1792, and affirmed the judgment the following day. Further proceedings in 1794 resulted in a dismissal of the appeal in Apr. 1795. Court of Appeals Order Book, II, 153, 155–156, 264, III, 24, 49, Va. State Lib.; 8 Va. (4 Call) 225–229.

15. See entry under Receipts, June 4, 1790.

16. See entry under Receipts, Dec. 5, 1789.

17. See Petition of James Crane, *ca.* Dec. 2, 1791.

18. Richard Kennon v. Archibald and Elizabeth McRoberts was an ejectment action growing out of a will. The District Court at Brunswick County entered a judgment against Kennon on Oct. 4, 1790. JM filed an appeal for Kennon, and after JM argued before the Court of Appeals on Nov. 18, 1791, and Apr. 21 and 24, 1792, that

15	Wallace v Piper & al	5		
	Advice	1	2	6
	Peyton ads. Hendricks trustees	2	16	
	Kennedy & Wallace v Hervy			
	(not come)	5		
	Colo. Muter	6	15	
		100	9	6

[*Disbursements*]

November	Market	3		
	Candles 48/, stockings 23/	3	11	
	butter £3–9	3	9	
	Market 18/		18	
		10	18	

[*Receipts*]

November	Ham v Sale	1	4	
	Coleman v Turnbull	5	12	
	Coleman ads. Verrel[19]	4	18	
	Jefferies ads. Dunn admr. of			
	Young	5		
	Godwin ads. Buchanan etc.[20]	4	4	
	Buller Claiborne[21]	10		
	Blagrove admr. ads. Baird[22]	5		
	Bibb v Cawthorn[23]	2	8	

court reversed the district court's judgment on Apr. 30, 1792. 1 Va. (1 Wash.) 96; Court of Appeals Order Book, II, 132, 148, 165, 166, 170, Va. State Lib.

19. John Verell, Jr., v. John Scott Coleman was an appeal from a default in he District Court at Petersburg taken by Coleman on Apr. 17, 1790. JM represented Coleman before the Court of Appeals on Apr. 11, 1792, and on the following day the default judgment was affirmed. Court of Appeals Order Book, II, 150, 151, 152, Va. State Lib.

20. Buchanan, Hastie & Co., of Great Britain, v. Boswell Goodwin was a debt action in the U.S. Circuit Court in which JM represented the securities of Goodwin. Pleas were entered on May 26, 1792, and on May 25, 1795, judgment was entered for the plaintiff. U.S. Circuit Court, Va., Order Book, I, 109, 470, Va. State Lib.

21. Buller Claiborne (1755–post–1804) was a prominent resident of Dinwiddie County who served as justice of the peace there in 1782 and as sheriff from 1802 to 1804.

22. See entry under Receipts, Oct. 4, 1788.

23. Richard Bibb and John Watson v. Commonwealth for benefit of Catherine Cauthorne was an appeal to the Court of Appeals from a judgment rendered by the District Court at King and Queen County on Apr. 8, 1791, for the Commonwealth. JM represented Bibb on appeal. After arguments were heard on Apr. 25, 1792, the

	Simms ads. Harrison	2	
	Gibbs ads. Hastie & Co	2	8
	Clarkes exrs. ads. Donald & Co.[24]	2	16
	Mills v Johnston	2	8
	Fauntleroy ads. Brooke	7	
		54	18

[Disbursements]

November	Market 36/, books 40/	3	16
	Stockings 21/, market 9/	1	10
	Market 40/, butter 3£	5	
	Market 12, do. 3		15
	remitted Lewis in bills on Mr. Morris & Mr. Haslehurst[25]	41	
		11	1

[Receipts]

Decr.	Young v Skipwith[26]	7	
	Alcantana etc. v Bousquet	7	
	Smith in suit in chy. v Piper	4	4
	Advice	1	8
	Crump (New Kent)	5	
	Cary v Nicholas & al	5	
	Helm v Armstrong (finishd)[27]	5	

district court judgment was ordered reversed and amended on Apr. 30, 1792. Court of Appeals Order Book, II, 138, 167, Va. State Lib. See later fee under Receipts, Apr. 1792.

24. Robert Donald, surviving partner of James and Robert Donald & Co., of Glasgow, v. Charles Clarke's Executors was a British debt case in which JM represented Clarke's administrators. After pleas were filed in Nov. 1792, judgment was entered for the plaintiff on demurrer in Nov. 1793. U.S. Circuit Court, Va., Order Book, I, 124, 220–221, and Record Book, II, 81, Va. State Lib. See pleas listed at Law Papers, Dec. 1791.

25. Isaac Hazlehurst was a merchant and business associate of Robert Morris from Burlington County, N.J. E. James Ferguson et al., eds., The Papers of Robert Morris, 1781–1784 (Pittsburgh, 1973), I, 12.

26. JM had an early involvement in Samuel Young v. Sir Peyton Skipwith, an appeal from a decree of the High Court of Chancery involving specific execution on a contract to purchase land. The appeal was heard by the Court of Appeals in Oct. 1796 and was remanded to the High Court of Chancery. 2 Va. (2 Wash.) 300; Court of Appeals Order Book, III, 140, 146, 246, 279, 334, IV, 77, Va. State Lib. See later fee at Receipts, June 1794.

27. William Helm and Walter Clark v. William Armstrong was an appeal from a

Claiborne v Manable	5	2	
Duguid & al v Duguid & al— appeal chy.	2	10	
Powell v Keys	5		
Advice fee	1	2	6
Cropper v Linton[28]	5	14	6
Pitt v Pitt (separate maintenance)	3		
Savage v Conway	5		
Tibbs	2	8	
Corbin ads. Robins chy.	5		
Custis v Slocums exrs.	5		
Green exr. v Field exx.	5		
advice fee	1	2	
	80	11	
Niswanger ads. Regle	5		

[*Disbursements*]

Decr.	Wood 20/, Market 12/6	1	12	6
	Market 36/, shoes 12/, plays[29] 5£	7	8	
	plays £4–10, market £3–12	8	2	
		17	2	6
	Market 24/, Wood 30/	2	14	
	barber 46/	2	6	

Sept. 4, 1790, judgment of the District Court at Winchester in which JM represented Helm. The Court of Appeals affirmed the judgment on June 21, 1791. Court of Appeals Order Book, II, 84, Va. State Lib.

28. JM had represented John Cropper, Jr., when an action in detinue had been filed against him by Susanna Linton in Oct. 1788, before the reorganization of the courts. A separate action, but one holding importance for this case, was later litigated in the District Court at Accomack and Northampton counties in Oct. 1791. It involved conversion of several slaves, and judgment was entered for Linton. Perhaps JM was being paid to appeal this decision to the Court of Appeals. For the district court records, see District Court Order Book, 1789–1797, 177, 180, 182, 184, 186, 212, 244, 311, Accomack County, Va. State Lib.

29. Extant evidence reveals only one evening's theatrical entertainment in December. On Dec. 21 the Virginia Company scheduled for the benefit of Mr. Cleland, "from England," the comedy *He would be a Soldier*. Following a song by Mrs. Bignall, *Lash'd to the Helm*, by Mr. Courtney, was to be performed. A musical entertainment, *The Romp; or Love in a City* was to be followed by *Paddy Bull's Expedition*, by Mr. Bignall. *Va. Gaz., & Genl. Adv.*, Dec. 21, 1791.

[*Receipts*]

Jany.	74	4	
Feby.	112	18	6
March	131		6
do.	73	13	8
do.	46	16	
Apl.	74	2	6
do.	18	4	
May	66	8	
do.	69	11	
June	132	4	
July	38	3	3
Augt.	54	1	
Sept.	19	16	
oc.	125	12	6
Novr.	155	7	6
Decr.	85	11	
	1277	13	5

[*Disbursements*]

Jany.	£	79	11	4
Feby.		41	18	7
March		76	16	
do.		9	1	4
do.		7	15	4
Apl.		37	7	8
do.		6		
May		34	8	3¾
June		46	15	10
July		87	5	
Augt.		27	3	8
Septr.		4	2	
Oc		13	8	6
Novr.		21	19	
Decr.		19	16	6
		520	9	0¾
		2	6	

[*Receipts*]

January				
Madiras (Chy.)	2	2	
Draffen v Mills	4	9	8
Gayle ads. Lee Appeal[30]	2	10	
Advice fee	1	8	
Mr. Van Bibber[31]	7	10	
from Sundries v Currie in chy.	30		
Kidd v Donaghoe & Bell[32]	2	12	
Mason ads. Bassett	5		
Haptonstal ads. Hambleton	5		
	59	17	8

[*Disbursements*]

January				
Market 2/, plays[33] 12/, expenses 9/	1	3	
Sugar £3–10–3	3	10	3
Paid Mr. Fenwick[34] his account in full	21	11	9
a pair of stockings 7/, wood & hominy 5/		12	
to old woman for Rachael[35] 12/, play 9/	1	1	
expenses 3/6, given away £6–12	6	15	6
Given Bob 6/, pork £24–13	24	19	
corn 24/, wood 20/	2	4	
Library[36] 28/, buckles 57/, knife 2/6	4	7	6

30. See entry under Receipts, Apr. 8, 1789.

31. Andrew Van Bibber. See JM's declaration in Van Bibber v. Green, listed at Law Papers, Nov. 1792.

32. Daniel Kidd v. Hugh Donagho and Joseph Bell was brought before the High Court of Chancery after the Augusta County Court had rendered a judgment against Donagho and Bell in 1789. The High Court of Chancery affirmed the judgment on Sept. 20, 1792, after which the case was taken to the Court of Appeals. That court affirmed the judgment on Apr. 19, 1794. Court of Appeals Order Book, II, 263, 269, Va. State Lib.

33. There is no extant evidence of a theatrical group performing in Richmond at this time. This entry suggests an extension of the winter season or the existence of a performing group hitherto unknown. See entry under Disbursements, Dec. 1791.

34. W. Fenwick, Richmond merchant. *Va. Gaz., & Genl. Adv.*, Jan. 4, 1792.

35. This name appears only twice in JM's Account Book. For additional entry, see Disbursements, Mar. 1794.

36. JM paid his annual dues to the Library Society, which announced at its annual meeting on Jan. 7, 1792, that the share of any member in arrears for his annual

	£	s	d
raffling[37] 28/, expenses 18/	2	6	
Wood 20/, market 6/3, flour 9£	10	6	3
market 2/6, do. 7/3, corn 24/, wood 20/	2	13	9
Market 3/, straw 12/, beef £4–11–6	5	6	6
	86	16	6

[*Receipts*]

		£	s
February	advice fee	1	2
	Call ads. Buchanan (fedl.)[38]	6	14
	Downmans exrs. ads. Downman[39]	5	12
	Kit Branch (sundries)	11	4
	Orandorf v Cookus[40]	6	
	Edmundson v Webb	5	
	Claiborne ads. Willis[41]	5	
	Hanover justices (Claibornes exrs.) v Dandridge etc.[42]	2	16
	Bowyer v the Comth.	5	
	Advice	1	8

subscription would be sold at public auction. *Va. Gaz., & Genl. Adv.*, Jan. 25, 1792. See entry under Disbursements, Mar. 25, 1790, for an earlier Library Society payment.

37. Two lotteries were advertised in the Richmond newspapers at this time; one was for William Tatham's map and the other for a church in Manchester. *Va. Gaz., & Genl. Adv.*, Jan. 18 and 25, 1792. For JM's previous subscription to one of Tatham's maps, see Map Subscription, *ca.* Sept. 29, 1790.

38. John Buchanan, Jr., v. William Call, Richard Taylor, and John King, all of Prince George County, was a British debt case in which JM defended Call. The usual pleas were made on May 28, 1792, to which the plaintiff demurred. Judgment was given the plaintiff on May 25, 1795. U.S. Circuit Court, Va., Order Book, I, 112, 471, II, 69, and Record Book, III, 202–210, Va. State Lib.

39. See entry under Receipts, May 1790.

40. See JM's petition of appeal in Orandorf v. Welch's Administrators calendared at Feb. 18, 1792, and receipt calendared at May 13, 1795.

41. Francis Willis, Jr., v. William Dandridge Claiborne was an appeal from the District Court at Williamsburg in which JM represented Willis. Willis decided not to pursue the appeal, however, and on Apr. 14, 1792, it was discontinued. Court of Appeals Order Book, II, 156, Va. State Lib.

42. N. W. Dandridge had drawn and endorsed a bill of exchange that was involved in Carter Braxton *et al.*, surviving executors of Philip W. Claiborne, v. Beverley Winslow, Joseph Brock, and John Crane, surviving justices of Spotsylvania County, which came before the Court of Appeals in June and Nov. 1790 and again in June 1791. Apparently Hanover Justices (Claiborne's Executors) v. Dandridge grew out of the same dispute. 8 Va. (4 Call) 308 (1791); 1 Va. (1 Wash.) 31 (1791); Court of Appeals Order Book, II, 2, 34, 61, 62, 63, 64, 65, Va. State Lib.

Philips & al v Brock & al[43]	5		
Wooldridge v Wooldridge	5		
King ads. Clopton Dis. Ct.	2	2	
Advice fee	1	2	6
Hawkins exrs. ads. Smith	3		
Mr. Booker (old finishd suit)	2	16	
Haskins ads Harris (district)	1	10	
Mr. Downman (old appeal)[44]	11	10	
	81	5	6

[Disbursements]

February	Sundries for house 18/,			
	Wood 10/	1	8	
	postage 5/6, castors for chair			
	corn 12/, to Campiones for			
	Tom £5–12	6	4	
	To the Abbé[45] for Tom £2–16	2	16	
	Shoes for Israel 6/, beer 6/		12	
	Doctor Fowshee & Jenny for			
	birth of my son[46]	4	10	
	Milk 6/, Market 6/		12	
	postage 6/4, wood 15/, taking			
	up Israel 21/	2	2	4
	Market 4/, do. 18/	1	2	
	Caster oil 3/, Coal 20/7½	1	3	7½

43. William and Anne Phillips and Augustine and Betsy Lewis v. Joseph Brock involved a contested will before the High Court of Chancery. That court decreed in favor of JM's clients, Phillips and Lewis, on Sept. 21, 1793. The Court of Appeals affirmed the decree on Apr. 16, 1795. 2 Va. (2 Wash.) 68; Court of Appeals Order Book, III, 46, 47, Va. State Lib.

44. See entry under Receipts, May 1790.

45. Rev. John DuBois (1764–1842) was a Roman Catholic priest who fled his native France during the Reign of Terror in 1791 and, supplied with letters of introduction from Lafayette, came to the United States. DuBois settled in Richmond soon after his arrival and was permitted to celebrate mass in the capitol. DuBois announced that he would open in Jan. 1792 a "school for the French language," and would also "teach in private families, and . . . receive a small number of boarders, who will be instructed in the English, French, Latin and Greek languages, writing arithmetic, and book keeping." DuBois left Richmond in 1794, when he was sent to a clerical post in Frederick, Md. In 1826 he became the third bishop of New York. Va. Gaz., & Genl. Adv., Jan. 11, 1792. See entries under Disbursements, Feb. and Dec. 1793, for later payments to DuBois.

46. John James Marshall was born on Feb. 13 and died on June 10. See JM's recording of the birth and death of his son in his family Bible, calendared at Feb. 13–June 10, 1792.

		4	7	I
Wood 10/, beef £3–17–1				
		24	17	½

[*Receipts*]

March	Bridgeforth ads. Malone (old chy.)	I	10
	Briscoe ads. Morris & ux (old chy.)	2	10
	Randolph v Nicholas	5	12
	Foote ads. Alexander	7	
	Maese v Hambleton[47]	2	8
	Jerdone v Potties exrs.[48]	28	
	From Mr. Boucher	4	4
	Faris ads. Faris	5	
	Buxton ads. Cary[49]	4	10
	Mitchel ads. Tate & Brownlee	5	2
	Gordon v Crichton TAB	2	8
	Advice fee on Mr. T Adams will.[50]	I	8
	Scott v Trent[51]	2	8
	Wallers admrs. v Reynolds[52]	7	
	Flournoy	3	8
	Advice fee on the will of Mr. Fairfax	2	8
	Advice fee from clerks	3	14
	Conn v Treon	I	8
	Fallis ads. Richards	I	8

47. See JM to Archibald Stuart, *ca.* Dec. 1789.

48. See entry under Receipts, May 1789.

49. See entry under Receipts, May 1789.

50. See Opinion, *ca.* Mar. 1792.

51. John Scott v. Alexander and Peterfield Trent, merchants, was an appeal from a judgment in the District Court at Charlottesville in Sept. 1791. JM's appeal for Scott was based on a ruling that certain evidence was inadmissible in the district court. The Court of Appeals affirmed the judgment on Apr. 21, 1792. Court of Appeals Order Book, II, 158, 165, Va. State Lib.

52. Edward Waller's Administrator v. William Reynolds was an action before the High Court of Chancery involving fraud in obtaining military warrants. On May 30, 1792, the High Court of Chancery decreed that the warrants were sold fraudulently, a decision favoring JM's client, Waller's administrator. Reynolds took the case to the Court of Appeals, where the decree was affirmed on Apr. 24, 1793. 1 Va. (1 Wash.) 164; Court of Appeals Order Book, II, 218, 222, Va. State Lib. See later fees under Receipts, June 1792, and Apr. 1793.

advice		1	4	
		92	10	

[Disbursements]

March	Milk 6/, wood 10/, Market 12/	1	8	
	Market 18/, newspapers 9/	1	7	
	Market 24/, coal 28/6	1	8	6
	Wood 10/, shoes for Dick 7/3		17	3
	Given Mr. Blair[53]	2	16	
	Mauzy about the carriage[54] 6/		6	
	paid the Taylor	1	10	3
	Corn £3, Wood 20/, Tom 6/	4	6	
	market 6, oysters 4/,			
	subscription[55] 3£	3	10	
	Given away 6/, pd. Molly			
	Lawson 3£	3	6	
	Market 12/, Corks 6/		18	
	Seeds & clover £5–17–1	5	17	1
		27	10	1

[Receipts]

March	Murrays exrs. ads. Rose & Co.[56]	2	16
	Douglass ads. Bolling	7	
	Advice fee	1	8
	Trueheart v Duval	1	8
	For petn. v Comth.	7	
	Stuart v Matthews	5	
		24	12

[Disbursements]

March	Market 14/, do. 8/	1	2

53. Rev. John D. Blair. See entry under Disbursements, July 9, 1790.

54. Peter Mauzey (b. *ca.* 1751) was a coach maker in Richmond. "Return of the Inhabitants," 1784, Richmond City Common Hall Records, I, 334, Va. State Lib.

55. JM was probably subscribing to the Richmond Assemblies. See Disbursements, Mar. 4, 1789, for an earlier subscription.

56. See Thomas Peachy Account Book, 48, Tyler Papers, Swem Library, College of William and Mary, where Peachy entered under James Rose & Co., "To Cash Paid Mr. John Marshall 21 Mar 1792 in Suit in Chan vs. John Murray's Exrs. £2 16 0." Another fee was entered for Oct. 27, 1792, on the same page, but JM apparently did not record this fee in his accounts.

	£	s	d
Market 14/		14	
Market 3/9, do. 8/, do. 5/6, do. 6/	1	3	3
Wood 10/, do. 8/		18	
paid Mr. Blair for preaching[57]	4	4	
	10	1	3

[Receipts]

		£	s	d
April	Rudd v Clarke (appeal)	1	6	
	Eblin ads. Pleasants	1	10	
	defending Branch	14		
	From Austin	10	8	
	Ballinger ads. Lowry	1	16	
	two advice fees 43/	2	3	
	Belfield exr. of Lee v McCall (fedl. injn.)	5		
	Ferguson ads. McCausland	1	10	
	Bowles v Richardson (motion)	1	10	
	Hall ads. Reeves	5		
	Bibb v Comth. (old appeal)[58]	2	10	
	Smith ads. Evans[59]	8		
	Recd. from Mr. Burwell for Mr. H. Marshall[60] } 5 guineas			
	Watkins ads. Bolling chy.	4	12	5
	Miller v Smith exr. chy.	5		
	Watson v Dupey	5		
	Craig v Southall & al (chy.)	5		
		74	5	5

[Disbursements]

		£	s	d
April	black lasting for bag 5/8		5	8
	Market 6/, do. 7/6, do. 1/, do. 4/, do. 3/	1	1	6

57. See entry under Disbursements, July 9, 1790.
58. See entry under Receipts, Nov. 1791.
59. James and Thomas Evans v. William Smith was an appeal from a judgment rendered by the District Court at King and Queen County in Apr. 1791. JM represented the appellee Smith. The Court of Appeals dismissed the appeal on Apr. 13, 1792, for failure to prosecute. Court of Appeals Order Book, II, 154, 160, Va. State Lib. See entry under Receipts, Apr. 1793, for another fee in this case.
60. Humphrey Marshall.

Market 8/, Meal £2–13	3	1
Market 9/, house 54/	3	2
Milk 42/, wood 24/	3	6
paid Mr. Buchanan[61]	2	8
corn £4, market 2/	4	2
fodder 5/, shoes 12/, house 24/	2	1
Paid Mr. Campion for Tom	1	8
furkin butter £3–12	3	12
Milk 6/, Market 18/, delivering Edy 12/	1	16
Market 14/, coal £10–8–4	11	2	4
	37	5	6

[Receipts]

April	Keeling v Wilson & al (old suit)[62]	1	16
	Smith ads. Allen (fedl.)[63]	5	2
	Mrs. Turnbull[64]	14	
	Pettus's exrs. v Williams[65]	5	
	Tomkies v Fitzhugh[66]	5	

61. It is likely that JM was either making a contribution to the Amicable Society, of which merchant Alexander Buchanan (b. *ca.* 1760) was treasurer, or paying his annual contribution to the salary of Buchanan's brother, Rev. John Buchanan. See entry under Disbursements, Aug. 1791, for an earlier payment to the Amicable Society. See entries under Disbursements, May 1790, Mar. 1794, and Jan. 1795, and Vol. I, 313, for other payments to Buchanan.

62. Although no suits known as Keeling v. Wilson *et al.* that could be classified as "old" have been found in courts JM attended, the case of Wilson and McCrae v. Keeling was before the High Court of Chancery at this time and may be the one JM intended. This case involved a request for an injunction to prohibit Keeling from repaying Wilson and McCrae a 1788 debt in paper money. The High Court of Chancery granted the injunction on May 23, 1792, and the Court of Appeals affirmed the decree on Oct. 17, 1793. 1 Va. (1 Wash.) 194; Court of Appeals Order Book, II, 236, Va. State Lib.

63. Nathaniel Allen v. Isaac Smith, Littleton Savage, Peter Bowdoin, Griffin Stith, and William Stith was a debt action brought in the U.S. Circuit Court in equity. JM represented Isaac Smith when the case was first brought in Dec. 1792. The case was finally dismissed by the plaintiff on Nov. 27, 1794. U.S. Circuit Court, Va., Order Book, I, 140, 373, 411, Va. State Lib. See additional fee under Receipts, Nov. 1793.

64. Sarah (Mrs. Robert) Turnbull. See JM to Benjamin Rush, Aug. 6, 1792.

65. This was apparently a fee in anticipation of an appeal from a judgment in the District Court at Prince Edward County on Apr. 5, 1792, against Pettus's executors in Nathaniel Williams v. John Pettus's Executors. No record of appeal has been found, but see additional fee under Receipts, May 1795. District Court Records at Large, 1789–1792, 484–485, Prince Edward County, Va. State Lib.

66. The debt action of Robert Gilchrist, assignee of Benjamin Tompkins, v. Henry Fitzhugh's Executors had been decided in favor of Gilchrist in the District Court at Fredericksburg on May 6, 1790. Perhaps this fee represents an intention to appeal to

In Carrington ads. Mayo[67]	8		
Advice fee	1	2	6
Blackwell ads Haynes	5		
Appleberry v Anthony[68]	5		
Wilson ads. Corrans admr.	5		
Clay v Watkins	5		
Colo. Dark[69]	10		
Anderson ads. Dobson etc.[70]	2	10	
Alexander & al v Becquith & al[71]	12	10	
Pleasants v Page	5		
Johnston ads. Brown	4	10	
Harvey v Johns etc.	2	16	
Richeson v Burnly	2	12	
	98	18	6

[*Disbursements*]

April	Market 6/, do. 14/	1		
	Milk 6/, treating at muster[72] £4-5	4	11	
	Corn £5, Market 6/	5	6	
	Wood 10/, expences at Fburg[73] £5	5	10	
	Market 6/, sturgeon 9/		15	
	Market 6/, physic 1/6/, milk 6/		13	6
		17	15	6

the Court of Appeals, although no record of appeal has been found. District Court Record Book, 1789–1792, 171, and District Court Law Orders, A, 1789–1793, 109, Fredericksburg, Va. State Lib.

67. See entry under Receipts, June 19, 1790.

68. In the High Court of Chancery, James Anthony's Executors v. Elizabeth and Jane Applebury was on appeal from a county court, and the chancery court decreed in favor of Anthony's executors on May 24, 1793. JM may have represented Anthony's executors in the chancery suit, and he definitely represented them when the decree was taken to the Court of Appeals. That court affirmed the decree on Oct. 20, 1794. 1 Va. (1 Wash.) 287; Court of Appeals Order Book, III, 5, 7, Va. State Lib. See additional fees under Receipts, Oct. 1793, Oct. 1794, and Mar. 1795.

69. William Darke had served as a lieutenant colonel during the Revolution.

70. See entry under Receipts, Jan. 1, 1791.

71. See Vol. I, 351, n. 79, for an earlier fee in this case.

72. The law required a muster of each regiment in March or April. 12 Hening 11 (1785). JM was probably treating the Richmond militia, which he commanded. For information on his militia duty, see Militia Duty: Editorial Note, June 8, 1793.

73. JM attended the spring session of the District Court at Fredericksburg, which began Apr. 29.

[*Receipts*]

May	Govan ads. Quarles	5		
	Jones ads. Williams[74]	5		
	Allen ads. Middlemist	1	8	
	advice fee	1	2	6
	Lanier v Sturdivant	4	16	
	Hooe v Becquith[75]	3		
	Chandler v Donneville	5		
	Wright v Masons exrs.	5		
	Jett ads. Jordan	7		
	Wilson (Pburg)	3	16	
	Alexander v his tenants (appls.)[76]	7		
	Bowyer ads. Fedl.[77]	4	4	
	Smiths exr. v or ads. McCall & Co. fedl.[78]	5		
		57	6	6

[*Disbursements*]

May				
	postage 3/, market 6/		9	
	market 20/6, paling 36/, milk 1/6	2	18	
	Market 32/, wood 20/	2	12	
	milk 6/, Given Polly in Apl. &			

74. See entry under Receipts, Nov. 29, 1789.

75. See Vol. I, 351, n. 79, for an earlier fee in this case.

76. There was a series of ejectment actions brought by Charles Alexander in the General Court in 1782 and later transferred to the District Court at Dumfries. The district court found for Alexander in 1790, and most of the cases were then appealed to the Court of Appeals, where JM was retained to represent Alexander. Court of Appeals Order Book, II, 128, and District Court Land Causes, 1789–1793, 89, 91, 100, 101, 422, 451, 456, 466, 470, 489, 491, 492, 494, 498, Prince William County, both in Va. State Lib.

77. John Bowman, surviving partner of Spiers, Bowman & Co., Glasgow, v. William Bowyer, of Augusta County, was a British debt case. JM filed the appropriate pleas on May 29, 1792, to which the plaintiff demurred. The demurrer was sustained on Nov. 28, 1793. U.S. Circuit Court, Va., Order Book, I, 114, 120, 203, and Record Book, I, 395–403, Va. State Lib.

78. William Smith's Executor v. McColl & Elliott and John McColl & Co. was an attempt to enjoin a judgment against Smith's executor. JM represented Smith's executor when the petition was filed on Dec. 4, 1792. The injunction was granted and then later partially dissolved. U.S. Circuit Court, Va., Order Book, I, 136, 162, 539, and Record Book, I, 42–46, Va. State Lib.

May for the use of the house £9	9	6	
Flour £13–5–3	13	5	3
	28	10	3

[Receipts]

June

Waller ads. Reynolds[79]	5	12	
Williams ads. Bell	3	2	
Randolphs v Randolphs exrs.	5		
Calverts v Lenox	8		
Meaux ads. Syme	4	10	
Drewidtz v Matthews	2	8	
Patteson v Cobbs injn.	2	8	
Overton v Ross[80]	4	16	
Mr. Holt	1	10	
Mr. Carter (Shirley)	7		
Mr. Reid ads. Comth. motion	2	10	
Todd ads. do. do.[81]	2	10	
Haynes v Hamlin	7		
Wms. ads. Bell	2		
Wright v Wrights exrs.	5		
Walkers exrs. v Walke[83]	5		
advice fee	1	2	6
	78	8	6

[Disbursements]

June

house 38/, given 3/	2	1
market 12/, given 3/, market 6/	1	1

79. See entry under Receipts, Mar. 1792.

80. See entry under Receipts, Oct. 22, 1789.

81. George T. Tod was sergeant of Fredericksburg. It is uncertain why the Commonwealth was suing him at this time, although several months after this fee Tod killed a man while trying to serve him with process, and the grand jury indicted him for murder. He was acquitted on Apr. 30, 1793, but JM did not represent him in that case. District Court Law Orders, A, 1789–1793, 444, Fredericksburg, Va. State Lib., and *Virginia Herald, and Fredericksburg Advertiser* (Fredericksburg), May 2, 1793. See later fee at Receipts, Sept. 1795.

82. See JM to William Branch Giles, *ca.* 1790.

83. Thomas R. Walker's Executors v. Thomas Walke was an appeal from the Princess Anne County Court to the High Court of Chancery involving a guardianship account. The court affirmed the county court, and JM took the appeal to the Court of Appeals, where argument was heard on Apr. 26, 1796. The decree was then reversed in part on May 11, 1796. 2 Va. (2 Wash.) 195; Court of Appeals Order Book, III, 116, 130, Va. State Lib. See later fee at Receipts, Oct. 1795.

wood 10/, stockings 24/, cloaths 48/	4	2	
French books	3	14	
wood 10/, market 3/		13	
market 3/, virga. cloth £3–6, tin ware 24/	4	13	
Given away 6/		6	
Boots & shoes 3£, market 12/, masons ball[84] 12	4	4	
Market 6/		6	
Given Lewis	13	12	8
subscriptions on account of St. Johns[85]	1	4	
corn £6–7–6, given away 7/	6	14	6
expenses 6/, pd. the lodge[86] 40/	2	6	
given Polly 6/		6	
	35	3	2

[Receipts]

July	From Mr. Chevallier[87]	35	
	Newton v Wingfield	2	10
	advice	1	
	Mrs. Wilcox	14	
	Richardson ads. Jefferson (old appeal)	5	
	Toler v Woodson	5	
	From Colo. Green admr. of Davies	5	
	Daniel & al v Montague & al	5	
	Mr. John Calloway	5	
	McClanahan v McGeorge	2	8
	Daniels admrs. ads. Daniels	5	
	Davidson v Stephenson & ux.	7	4

84. A grand ball was probably the concluding event of the Mason's celebration of the festival of St. John the Baptist on June 24.

85. JM paid his annual expenses to celebrate the anniversary of St. John the Baptist, June 24. The schedule included a "Charity Sermon . . . by the Rev. John Buchanan," preceded by a procession of the Masons. *Va. Gaz., & Genl. Adv.*, June 20, 1792.

86. This entry represents JM's dues to his Masonic lodge.

87. See JM to John A. Chevallié, Sept. 14, 1792, and Petition of John A. Chevallié, Oct. 5, 1792.

		I	8	
	Advice fee 28/			
		93	10	

[Disbursements]

July	Market 7/6, wood 20/	1	7	6
	expenses 14/, barber 45/	2	19	
	subscription 4th. July[88] 6/,			
	postage 2/, given 2/3,			
	market 6/		16	3
	given 6/, pd. for waggon			
	£12–16–8			
	churn 2/, market 6/		8	
	a bonnet for Mrs. Marshall	1	4	
	Corn £4, china £25–11	29	11	
	expenses 50/, market 50/	5		
	market 18/, pd. Mr.			
	Elliot £7–1–6	7	19	6
	Lamb & butter 22/6	1	2	6
	cloaths for myself 48/	2	8	
		52	15	9

[Receipts]

August	Hunter v Miller Hart & Co	5		
	Dejarnet v Roes exrs.	5		
	Booker v Bacon & al	5		
	Mr. Richeson	3		
	Harris v Lyons	1	10	
	Mayos exrs. v Dixon etc.	5		
	Mayo v Braxton	5		
	Walker ads. Syme	5		
	do. ads. McClung	5		
	Swan ads. Clarke	5		
	Haken v Carter	5		
	King v Norton	5		
	Coleman ads. Henrico court	3		
	Sundry advice fees	3	15	

88. Extant sources do not reveal how July 4 was celebrated in Richmond in 1792. For descriptions of the celebrations of other years, see entries under Disbursements, July 1, 1788, July 3, 1789, and July 1791.

	Wishart ads. Blanchard (fedl. eject)[89]		5	
			66	5

[Disbursements]

August	barrel of flour from Colo. Gamble[90]	1	10	
	Shoes for Dick 6/8, Watermelons 2/		8	8
	Market 7/, wood 9/		16	
	Dallass's reports[91] 18/		18	
	Market 6/, given away 72/	3	18	
	Encyclopedia[92] 30/, Market 12/	2	2	
	Market 17/6, postage 6/	1	3	6
	Coffins for my son & daughter[93]	9	2	
	corn £4–10, coal £8	12	10	
	Gloves 7/6, market 7/6, expences 12/	1	7	
	coal £8–14–6, Mr. McKechne £4–4–3	12	18	9
	Hat 36/, fruit 6/, wood 10/	2	12	
	Taxes[94] & ticket for 1791	12	17	
	Vinegar 7/6, given 6/		13	
		62	15	2

[Receipts]

September 1	Winfrey v Wooldridge		3	6

89. James Blanchard v. Thomas and Mary Wishart was an ejectment action in the U.S. Circuit Court involving land in Princess Anne County. On Nov. 24, 1792, an order to make party defendants was entered. After several appearances, the court ordered Blanchard to pay court costs or the suit would be dismissed. U.S. Circuit Court, Va., Order Book, I, 123, 143, 237, 373, 423, Va. State Lib. See later fee at Receipts, May 1795.

90. Robert Gamble, Richmond merchant.

91. A. J. Dallas, *Reports of cases, ruled and adjudged in the courts of Pennsylvania, before and since the Revolution*, I (Philadelphia, 1790).

92. Vol. VI of *Encyclopaedia; or a Dictionary of Arts, Sciences, and Miscellaneous Literature*, to which JM subscribed, was advertised for sale in Richmond in Aug. 1792, after having been published earlier that year. *Va. Gaz., & Genl. Adv.*, Aug. 22, 1792.

93. See JM's notations of the deaths of his son John James and his daughter Mary Ann, calendared at Feb. 13–June 10, and Aug. 1, 1792.

94. JM's personal property list for 1792 indicated ownership of 9 Negro slaves over

Anderson & al v Breckenridge	2	
Starkees exrs. ads. McMurdo	5	
Blaydes ads. Richardson	2	16
Claibornes exrs. ads. Greenhill	3	18
Harris v appeal	2	2
Cooke v injn.	5	
Carver ads. Roses (appeal chy.)	2	8
Jones & ux v Buckner & al	4	16
Tyler v Tylers exrs.	5	12
Mr. Thomas for Mrs. Hawkins[95]	2	16
Miller v Bissett	1	16
Mr. Norton	50	
Corbin v Jenkins	5	
Fergusons v McCausland	5	2
Dandridge v Harris[96]	2	10
Harrison Carter exr. etc. (fedl.)	4	18
Guy v Thilman & al	4	16
Clarke v Jackson	2	8
Jett ads Bernard[97]	7	
	123	4

[Disbursements]

September			
Market 6/, market 12/, beer 6/	1	4	
Market 22/, meal 12/, books 14/	2	8	
Given Lewis	7	1	4
Wood 10/, market 12/	1	2	
Market 12/, to Granny 12/	1	4	
Wine	70		
Corn	3	6	
Shoes 12/, market 12/	1	4	
Given Peter Mauzy		7	6

---

the age of 16, 3 horses, and 6 carriage wheels. He also paid 12s. 6d. land tax. Richmond City Personal Property Book, 1792, and Land Book, 1792, Va. State Lib.

95. See entry under Receipts, Sept. 1, 1790.

96. See entry under Receipts, Apr. 1, 1790.

97. William Bernard v. William Storke Jett was before the High Court of Chancery and involved charges of misconduct in handling an estate that was too small to pay two legacies. JM represented Jett, and the court finally decreed on Sept. 28, 1798, that there had been no misconduct and that the legacies must abate proportionately. The Court of Appeals affirmed the decree on Apr. 23, 1801. 7 Va. (3 Call) 10; Court of Appeals Order Book, IV, 49, 64, Va. State Lib.

		£	s	d
	Market 24/, do. 18/	2	2	
	Buckingham taxes[98]	13	19	3¼
		103	18	1¼

[Receipts]

		£	s	d
September	Slater ads. Magnier (old genl. ct.)	2	10	
	Stroude v Hite & al[99]	5		
	Hoomes v Kuhn[1]	10		
	Watkyns ads. Moor	5		
	Hill ads. Claiborne[2]	2	8	
	Wilson v Happer	9		
		33	18	

[Disbursements]

		£	s	d
September	paid for Tom 6/, market 10/		16	
	Market 18/, chair 10/6	1	8	6
	Market 9/, do. 21/	1	10	
	market 2/6, play[3] 25/	1	7	6
	Cloth for myself £6-6	6	6	
		11	8	

[Receipts]

		£	s	d
October	Gregory ads. Hill[4]	7		
	Edwards ads. True	5		
	Mr. Jones	5		
	Daniel ads. Curtis	5		
	Advice fee	1	4	

98. See entry for the purchase of this land and related information under Disbursements, July 1791.

99. See first entry on JM's List of Fees, ca. Aug. 1786–1791, printed at the end of 1791.

1. See JM's declaration in this case, Vol. I, 183.

2. See entry under Receipts, Mar. 6, 1790.

3. The 1792 theater season opened in July with performances continuing through December. The performances JM viewed in September would likely have included the tragedy *Sorrows of Werter; or, The Disconsolate Lovers* and *Shakespeare's Jubilee*, both performed on Sept. 6, or a musical performance and a production of *The Quack, or, The Doctor in Petticoats* on Sept. 12. Sherman, "Post-Revolutionary Theatre," 103–104; *Va. Gaz. & Genl. Adv.*, Sept. 5 and 12, 1792.

4. See Vol. I, 387, n. 30, for an earlier fee in this case.

Bailey v Teacle[5]	2	14	
Mears v Custis (injn.	2	8	
Custis ads. Cowper	10		
Ball v Hill (fedl.)[6]	5		
Bab etc. ads. Lochart chy.	5		
	48	6	

[*Disbursements*]

October	Wood 12/, market 9/, glasses 12/	1	13	
	Market 3/, do. 22/, books 12/	1	17	
	paid Cary's paper[7]		18	
	expenses 6/, house 24/	1	10	
	Market 6/, do. 4/, wood 10/	1		
	Market 30/	1	10	
	Given Lewis	8	1	7
		16	9	7

[*Receipts*]

November	Roy exr. v Johnston (chy.)	2	2
	Advice fee 26/	1	6
	Hayes & ux v Jenney	2	8
	Dixon exr. v Willis[8]	4	10
	advice fee	1	8

5. Thomas and Anne Bailey v. Levin Teackle was a suit before the High Court of Chancery on a contested will. JM represented Anne Bailey. The court's decree was issued in Mar. 1793. Wythe 173. See later fee at Receipts, Apr. 1793.

6. Joseph Ball v. Edward Hill was an action on a penal bond brought before the U.S. Circuit Court for Virginia because JM's client, Ball, lived in Pennsylvania. The action was brought on May 24, 1793, and the court issued a judgment in favor of Ball on Dec. 3, 1793. U.S. Circuit Court, Va., Order Book, I, 142, 237, Va. State Lib. See JM's declaration in this case, listed at Law Papers, Nov. 1792.

7. James Carey, printer and publisher, began publication of the *Virginia Gazette: and Richmond Daily Advertiser* in Oct. 1792. That paper was issued only a short time, for in Jan. 1793 Carey moved to Charleston, where he published the *Star*, which was also short-lived. Carey moved again in 1793 and over the next seven years published newspapers in Savannah, Wilmington, Del., and Philadelphia. *Va. Gaz., & Genl. Adv.*, Aug. 29, 1792, Jan. 30, 1793; Clarence S. Brigham, *History and Bibliography of American Newspapers, 1690–1820* (Worcester, Mass., 1947), II, 1388.

8. John Dixon's Executors v. John Whitaker Willis was an old debt case from the District Court at Fredericksburg in which judgment was confessed for Dixon on May 3, 1790. This fee, coupled with a later fee in May 1793, suggests an appeal was being made, although no record of appeal has been found. For the early proceedings, see District Court Record Book, 1789–1792, 147–152, and District Court Law Orders, A, 1789–1793, 96, Fredericksburg, Va. State Lib.

Custis v Fitchet	2	16
Hethcote (retr.)	7	
Shepherd ads. Jackson chy.	2	16
Frazer v Moffett & al. chy appl.	3	8
Hunters exrs. v Spotswood[9]	14	
Moss exr. v Crump	2	8
Light ads. Wilson (fedl.)[10]	2	10
Singleton ads. Westfal (appl.)[11]	7	5
	53	17

[*Disbursements*]

November	wood 10/, do. 10/, market 18/	1	18	
	Matts 4/, expences 50/	2	14	
	Corn 24/	1	4	
	Market 28/, do. 6/, sugar 6/	2		
	hops 15/, Market 6/, straw 20/	2	1	
	paid for Lewis to Taylor, & to Mr. Mitchel	5	18	6
	pd. his barber		12	
	Given him to go to Philadelphia[12]	7		8
	Market 10/, do. 6/, do. 3/		19	
	Shoes for negroes	2		
	market 16/, wood 10/	1	6	
		27	13	2

[*Receipts*]

Decr.	Pettus's exrs. ads. Hastie & Co.[13] fedl.	5

9. See entry under Receipts, Apr. 22, 1789.

10. William Wilson v. Peter Light was brought before the U.S. Circuit Court on Nov. 29, 1794, with JM representing Peter Light. The case abated by the death of Wilson in 1797. U.S. Circuit Court, Va., Order Book, I, 421, II, 113, 219, Va. State Lib. See additional fee under Receipts, Nov. 1794. The case may have been revived in 1799. U. S. Circuit Court, Va., Order Book, II, 257, 382, IV, 373, Va. State Lib.

11. See entry under Receipts, July 30, 1790.

12. Apparently Louis went to Philadelphia at this time to begin studying medicine. William Buchanan, "Louis Marshall, M.D., His Administration as President of Washington College" (M.A. thesis, Washington and Lee University, 1941), 6.

13. Robert Hastie, surviving partner of John Lindsay & Co., Great Britain, v. John Pettus's Executor was a British debt case in which JM probably acted as a co-

	Fox ads. Ferguson & ux		5	
			10	

[Disbursements]

Decr.	Market 36/, wood 20/, plays[14] 30/	4	6
	Market 54/, pork £8	10	14
	Given John Smith for books[15] 12/		12
	Salt & saltpetre		12
	Market 40/, plays 18/	2	18
	Market 24/, plays 12/	1	16
	Market 15/, barber 45/, Corn £4–5	7	5
		28	3

[Receipts]

Jany.	£	59	17	8
Feb.		81	5	6
March		92	10	
do.		24	12	
Apl.		173	3	11
May		57	6	6
June		78	8	6
July		93	10	
Augt.		66	5	
Septr.		157	2	
Oc.		48	6	
Novr.		53	17	
Decr.		10		
[1792 Receipts]		973	4	1

---

counsel, although he may have taken the case over from the attorney of record, Richard Duval. Pleas were entered on May 29, 1792, and judgment was entered for the plaintiff on Dec. 2, 1793. U.S. Circuit Court, Va., Order Book, I, 118, 224, and Record Book, I, 457–468, Va. State Lib.

14. Among the plays performed in Richmond in December were a comedy, *The Road to Ruin*, and a comic opera, *No Song, No Supper; or, The Lawyer in a Sack*, both presented on Dec. 5, *Know your own Mind*, performed on Dec. 12, and *Comedy of Duplicity; or the Gamester*, on Dec. 19. *Va. Gaz., & Genl. Adv.*, Dec. 5, 12, and 19, 1792.

15. See additional entries for John Smith under Disbursements, Jan. 4, and Apr. 1793.

			571	2	¾
[*1792 Disbursements*]					
[*Balance*]			402	2	¼

[*Disbursements*]

Jany.	£	86	16	6
Feb.		24	17	½
March		27	10	1
do.		10	1	3
April		55	1	
May		28	10	3
June		35	3	2
July		52	15	9
Aug.		62	15	2
Sep.		115	6	1¼
Oc.		16	9	7
Novr.		27	13	2
Decr.		28	3	
		571	2	¾

[*Receipts*]

January	Baird v Dickies exrs.	5		
	Advice fee in Warrens case	1	2	4
	advice fee from Rankin[16]	1	2	6
	Towler v. Hastie & Co. chy.[17]	5		
	Advice fee from Brooke	1	8	
	do. on Ellis's will	1	2	6
	do. on Masons will	2	8	
	Mason v Davenport[18]	5		
	advice fee	1	2	6
	retaining fee from Burnly[19]	7		

16. See JM to Archibald Stuart, Mar. 27, 1794.

17. Elizabeth Towler v. James Jameson and Richard Cameron, surviving partners of Buchanan, Hastie & Co., was a suit in the High Court of Chancery in which JM represented Towler. The court decreed against Towler on May 12, 1795, and the case was taken to the Court of Appeals. JM did not represent Towler on appeal. The Court of Appeals reversed the decree on Oct. 15, 1798. 5 Va. (1 Call) 162; Court of Appeals Order Book, III, 193, 194, 246, 248, 249–250, Va. State Lib.

18. William Mason v. William Davenport was before the High Court of Chancery. JM, for his client Mason, asked for an injunction against a county court judgment. The injunction was granted, and Davenport appealed. The Court of Appeals affirmed the decree on Apr. 28, 1795. 2 Va. (2 Wash.) 200; Court of Appeals Order Book, III, 118, Va. State Lib.

19. JM was apparently being retained by Zachariah Burnley, against whom a case

Byrd exx. ads. (Fedl.)[20]	7		
Advice fee on Glovers will	1	2	6
Harris ads. Finnie	5		
Morris v Woods[21]	10		
Basset v Newton	4	16	
	57	4	

[*Disbursements*]

January

1	Market 22/, wood 20/, hay £7–10	9	12	
	quills 6/, market 12/		18	
4th.	blacking 2/6, postage for papers 3/6		6	
	Market 16/, beer 6/	1	2	
	Market 22/6, flour £10–16	11	18	8
	Coal 45/, market 6/, do. 3/	3	4	
	Market 28/3, expenses 15/	2	3	3
	market 6/, pd. Russel 15/	1	1	
	cutting lampreys 5/		5	
	For John Smith[22] 18/, market 11	1	9	
	market 12/, do. 18/	1	10	
	paid for slaves hird of Mr. Scott for canal	26		
	paid for corn	15		
	Given Polly	2	8	

had been brought by Charles Lambert in the District Court at Fredericksburg. The court decided against Burnley on May 3, 1793, and JM took the case to the Court of Appeals. That court affirmed the judgment on Oct. 22, 1794, after hearing arguments the previous day. 1 Va. (1 Wash.) 308; Court of Appeals Order Book, III, 9, 10, Va. State Lib. See additional fee under Receipts, July 1793.

20. John Lloyd v. William Byrd's Executrix was a debt action brought in the U.S. Circuit Court for Virginia. Judgment was entered for the plaintiff on May 27, 1794. U.S. Circuit Court, Va., Order Book, I, 372, Va. State Lib.

21. Several cases known as Benjamin and Nathaniel Morris and John Land v. James Wood were decided in the District Court at Prince Edward County. The amount of the fee indicates JM was retained to appeal several to the Court of Appeals, although record of only one such appeal survives. District Court Order Book, 1789–1792, 216, 222, 249, 1792–1795, 14, 1793–1799, 94, 117, Prince Edward County, and Court of Appeals Order Book, III, 53, both in Va. State Lib. See additional fee under Receipts, May 1794.

22. JM bought books for Smith in Dec. 1792 and shoes in Apr. 1793. See Disbursements for these dates.

shoes for Moses 6/		6	
	77	2	11

[*Receipts*]

February	Mr. Shepherd (balance of fee)	2	8	
	Cox v Mayo (in part	2	13	4
	Shore ads. Banisters exrs.[23]	5		
	advice fee in Semples suit	1	2	6
	advice fee on John Clarkes suit	1	2	6
	Smith v Hansford	2	16	
	Mr. Garnett	4	4	
	Douglass v Woodson	2	10	
	Cave v Cave & al[24]	5		
	From Lankford Hix & Booker ads. Booker, suit stands Taylor & al ads. Booker	3	4	
	Shelton ads. Johnston[25]	5		
	Harris ads. Gl[e]nn	4	18	
	Madeiras v district	1	4	
	advice	1		
	Jones ads. Pincham	2	10	
	Branch v Atkinson	5		
	Footes v Fitzhugh & ux	7		
	Smith ads. Anderson	5		
		66	12	4

[*Disbursements*]

February	paid for Candlesticks etc.	12	12	
	paid Mr. Dubois[26] for Tom	1	8	

23. See entry under Receipts, Apr. 15, 1790.

24. Richard Cave *et al.* v. Belfield Cave *et al.* was before the District Court at Fredericksburg upon an issue certified from the High Court of Chancery. The case was finally dismissed on May 5, 1796. District Court Law Orders, B, 1794–1798, 186, Fredericksburg, Va. State Lib.

25. Thomas Johnson v. Peter Shelton was before the High Court of Chancery, with JM representing Shelton. The court dismissed Johnson's bill of complaint on May 13, 1794, and the decree was appealed. The Court of Appeals affirmed the action on Oct. 23, 1795. Court of Appeals Order Book, III, 50, 69, 70, 74, Va. State Lib. See additional fees under Receipts, Sept. and Oct. 1794, and Oct. 1795.

26. Rev. John DuBois announced in January that his lectures on the French language would be held at the Richmond Academy. *Va. Gaz., & Genl. Adv.,* Jan. 23, 1793. See entry under Disbursements, Feb. 1792, for a previous payment to DuBois.

paid Mrs. Lawson[27] balance	1	16	
shoes for Jaquelin 4/6, letters 5/6		10	
expenses 6/, encyclopedia[28] 30/, [susp] 6/	2	2	
Grammar for Tom 2/3, market 34/	1	15	3
Dictionary for Tom 12/, shoes for do. 4/9		16	9
subscription for Cutler	3		
market 24/, straw 12/, given Rootes 18/	2	14	
market 22/, wood 9/, given away 3/	1	14	
dictionary for Tom 10/, given 6/, market 18/	1	14	
market 50/, given away 18/	3	8	
	33	10	

[*Receipts*]

March	Talbot v Buford	3	
	Mr. Branch	12	
	Gayle ads. Lee	3	4
	Eppes v Dobie	3	
	Lawrences exrs. & al v Littlepage	5	
	Winston ads. Pearson	5	13
	Andrews ads. Harrison	5	
	Wilcox's will	14	
	Burnet exr. of Johnston ads. Boswells exrs.	5	
	Scott v Booker injn.[29]	2	8
	Eppes exr. ads. Woodson & ux.	6	10
	advice fee	1	8
	Clayton exr. v Tyler exr.	5	
	Boyd v Robertson	5	

27. Molly Lawson.
28. As a subscriber to the series, JM no doubt purchased vol. VII of *Encyclopaedia; or a Dictionary of Arts, Sciences, and Miscellaneous Literature,* which had been issued in 1792 and had arrived in Richmond in Jan. 1793. *Va. Gaz., & Genl. Adv.,* Jan. 23, 1793.
29. See entry under Receipts, Oct. 12, 1789.

Petways exrs. v Cox	5		
Keler ads. Strachan	5		
Coleman exr. ads. Blount exr.	7		
Brown ads. Yates	2		
	95	3	

[*Disbursements*]

March	Wood 30/, market 18/,		
	sundries 12/	3	
	market 6/, brewing 6/		12

[*Receipts*]

March	From Mr. Overton[30]	2	8	
	Gordon v Nutt	5	8	
	Nance & ux v Green	2	10	
	Edmunds v Baker admr.	1	8	
	Gadberry ads. Baker & al	5		
	Fleming admr. of Deane v			
	Murry etc.	5		
	Russel ads. Howletts exrs.	5		
	Elam v Robertson	5		
	advice fee	1	8	
	McClain v Hamilton (finishd)	1	8	
	Jones exr. v Spears & Co.			
	Bowman	5		
	Mr. Hansbro (finishd)	4	16	
	Dandridge v Harris[31]		18	
	Fauntleroy ads. Brooke			
	(old suit)	7		
	Archer ads. Randolph	5		
	advice fee (Doctor Riddick	1	2	6
	Smith & al ads. Wallace[32]	3	10	
	Advice fee	1	2	6
		62	19	

30. See entry under Receipts, Oct. 22, 1789.
31. See entry under Receipts, Apr. 1, 1790.
32. Michael Wallace v. Isaac Smith involved a writ of right in the District Court at Fredericksburg. There were companion suits against two other defendants. The court issued several orders on Oct. 8, 1792, on a motion of the plaintiff. The case was continued several times until dismissed on Oct. 3, 1797. District Court Law Orders, A, 1789–1793, 429, and Law Orders, B, 1794–1798, 131, 237, 288, 353, Fredericksburg, Va. State Lib.

	[*Disbursements*]			
March	Market 24/	1	4	
	Market 12, given 6/, clover seed 5/	1	3	
	market 12/, paid Mrs. Lawson[33] 12/	1	4	
	box of candles	2	8	
	Given Polly 22/6	1	2	6
	market 6/, expenses 6/, postage 3/		15	
		7	16	6

	[*Receipts*]			
March 22d.	advice fee 22/6	1	2	6
	Bourn ads. Johnston (appeals)[34]	3		
	advice fee	1	8	
	Moore ads. Hudson[35]	1	10	
	advice fee 22/6	1	2	6
	Whitings exrs. v Lewis's exrs.	8	8	
		16	11	
		95	3	
		62	13	
	[*Total March Receipts*]	174	7	

	[*Disbursements*]			
March	Paid on account of Twinings lottery[36]	14	8	
	market 3/, given away 6/		9	

33. Molly Lawson.

34. In Johnson v. Bourn, JM represented Bourn when Johnson asked for a writ of error to a judgment of the District Court at Charlottesville on Sept. 21, 1791. The court found error, and a writ of supersedeas was issued on Apr. 13, 1792. On Apr. 13, 1793, the Court of Appeals reversed the district court judgment. 1 Va. (1 Wash.) 187; Court of Appeals Order Book, II, 154, 210, 211, Va. State Lib.

35. Charles and Elizabeth Hudson v. Robert Moore, Jr., was a debt action before the District Court at Richmond. The court found for Moore on Sept. 6, 1794, and the Court of Appeals affirmed the ruling on Oct. 30, 1795. Court of Appeals Order Book, III, 82, Va. State Lib.

36. See Lottery Notice, calendared at *ca.* Jan. 19, 1791.

Harrisons chy. practise[37]	1	16	
paid for wood 30/	1	10	
Market £2–16	2	16	
	20	19	
	7	16	6
	28	15	6
	3	12	
[*Total March Disbursements*]	32	7	6

[*Receipts*]

April	Logan ads. Paupers	2	12	
	Page exr. of Cary v Payne & Randolph (2 suits in district court)	5		
	Crump etc. v Smyth (old suit)	2	16	
	Fairfax ads. Wormley[38]	5	12	
	Barnes v Ramsay	1	16	
	McCallister & McAllister[39]	5		
	Lendsays admrs. ads. Smiths exrs. chy.	5	10	8
	Tabb etc. v Hill etc. (appeal)		15	
	Griffin v Bracken	4	16	
	Baily v Teacle[40]	5		
	Roy v Garnet[41]	7		
	advice	1	8	
	Finnie v Cureton	5		

37. Joseph Harrison, *The Accomplish'd Practiser in the High Court of Chancery*, 7th ed. (London, 1790).

38. See entry under Receipts, Dec. 5, 1789.

39. James McAlester v. John McAlester was an appeal from a judgment of the District Court at Winchester of Sept. 1791. The district court had reversed the Berkeley County Court and remanded the case. The Court of Appeals heard arguments on Oct. 11, 1793, after continuing the case from Apr. 1793. On Oct. 12, 1793, the court reversed the district court and remanded the trial. 1 Va. (1 Wash.) 193; Court of Appeals Order Book, II, 220, 233, 234, and District Court Order Book, 1794–1797, 36, 37, Frederick County, both in Va. State Lib.

40. See entry under Receipts, Oct. 1792.

41. James Roy v. Muscoe Garnett was an appeal from a judgment of the District Court at King and Queen County in an ejectment action. That court dismissed the bill of complaint brought by Roy on Sept. 25, 1792. JM represented Roy before the Court of Appeals, where the case was continued in Nov. 1793 and Apr. 1794. After hearing arguments on Oct. 29 and 31, and Nov. 1, 1794, the court affirmed the judgment. 2 Va. (2 Wash.) 9, 23–30; Court of Appeals Order Book, II, 248, 261, III, 20–22, 38, Va. State Lib. See additional fee under Receipts, Oct. 1793.

Paupers 5£, Mr. Brown[42] £7	12		
Taylor admr. ads. Baylor admr.	5	2	
Bowyer v Comth. appeal	5		
Bernard ads. Anderson appl.[43]	5		
Mr. Blair (Fedl.)	5		
Prescot	5		
	92	7	8

[Disbursements]

April	expenses 9/		9	
	fodder 14/, market 4/		18	
	given away 12/		12	
	given away 6/, shoes 12/		18	
	market 15/		15	
	John Smiths shoes 3/, tub 2/6		5	6
	Vinegar 7/, market 2/		9	
	market 6/, brewing 6/, corn £34/	2	6	
	paid Mrs. Lawson[44] 10 dollars	3		
	straw 9/, spent 6/		15	
	paid 12/, given B.M.[45] 12/8	1	4	8
	settled with Elliott his acct.	7	14	11
	market 24/	1	4	
		20	10	7

[Receipts]

April	Campbell v Cabell & al[46]	5		
	Mr. Hylton—retainer[47]	7		
	advice fee (Mrs. Buchanan)	1	8	
	Shelton ads. Sheltons exrs.	2	14	

42. See JM to James Brown, calendared at Apr. 21, 1793.

43. Thomas Anderson v. William R. Bernard was an appeal from a judgment of the District Court at Prince Edward County in a trespass case entered on Sept. 5, 1792. JM represented Bernard when arguments were heard in the Court of Appeals on Apr. 18, 1793, and on the following day the court affirmed the judgment. 1 Va. (1 Wash.) 186; Court of Appeals Order Book, II, 217, 218, Va. State Lib.

44. Molly Lawson.

45. Betsy Munkus.

46. See JM to John Cabell, ca. Apr. 1793.

47. See Jones v. Hylton and Eppes, answer, calendared at May 24, 1791. This case became Ware v. Hylton in May 1793.

Maxwell—chy.		5	
Waller v Reynolds[48]		3	
Smith ads. Evans[49]		5	
		29	2
		92	7	5
[Total April Receipts]		121	9	5

[Disbursements]

April	Lock 7/6, expenses 4/		11	6
	Lucern[50] 7/, biggin 12/,		
	market 14/, given 6/	1	19
	book 14/, market 6/, plants 7/	1	7
	Market 8/, book 14	1	2
	Maxwell chy.	1	
	corn £8–6–3	8	6	3
	Market 9/, subscription[51] 12	1	1
		15	6	9
		20	10	7
	[Total April Disbursements]	36	17	4

[Receipts]

May	Bell v Man	5	12
	Burk in Watts & al ads.		
	Henderson McCaul & Co.		
	(Fedl.)[52]	7	
	Eggleston ads. Worsham	3	
	Halcomb	3	19
	Mr. Hoop	2	8
	Hunter ads. Spotswood[53]	4	16

48. See entry under Receipts, Mar. 1792.

49. See entry under Receipts, Apr. 1792.

50. In the 17th and 18th centuries lucern was the name commonly given to the plant *medicago saliva*, which resembled clover and was cultivated for fodder. JM may have planted a crop in 1793. See JM to James Breckinridge, Oct. 12, 1793.

51. This expense was probably for social events connected with celebration of the festival of St. Taminy. See entry under Disbursements, May 1793.

52. Henderson, McCaul & Co. v. Edward Walls, Samuel Burke, and William Watts was a British debt case in which JM represented the defendants when pleas were entered on May 30, 1793. The U.S. Circuit Court sustained the plaintiff's demurrer on Dec. 3, 1793. U.S. Circuit Court, Va., Order Book, I, 146, 238, and Record Book, II, 301–309, Va. State Lib.

53. The District Court at Fredericksburg set aside an office judgment on May 2, 1793, in Mansanna Hunter v. Alexander Spotswood. A consent judgment was entered

	Advice Mr. Pendleton	2	16	
	Mitchel ads. Frith	5		
	Dixon v Hoomes	3	8	6
	v Willis⁵⁴		10	
	Loafman v Robertson	3		
17th.	Benson v Shepherd	5		
	advice fee etc. from Mr. Muse	2	16	
	Stone v Woolen chy.	5	4	
	Coleman ads. Markham	6	2	6
	Gilliam v Clarke	1		
	Dandridge ads. Harris⁵⁵	1	10	
	Hudson v Sundries	2	8	
	Brickhouse ads. H Banks & Co.	5		
		78	10	

[*Disbursements*]

May	Mr. Rutherford,⁵⁶ linnen	14	13	6¾
	Stockings for self	2	8	
	Wood 30/, market 18/	2	8	
	expenses travelling⁵⁷ 35/	1	15	
	expenses 3/, given Polly 6/		9	
	Market 4/, Scythe 4/6		8	6
	Market 12/, pamphlet 2/4		14	4
	Paid Moss for St. Taminy⁵⁸ 22/,			
	brushes 3/3	1	5	3
	Shoeing horses 4/6, putting			
	up Jack 9/		13	6

on Oct. 10, 1793. District Court Law Orders, A, 1789–1793, 454, 539, Fredericksburg, Va. State Lib.

54. See entry under Receipts, Nov. 1792.

55. See entry under Receipts, Apr. 1, 1790.

56. Thomas Rutherford was a merchant in Richmond as late as 1787. "List of Merchants," Richmond City Hustings Court Order Book, II, 50, Va. State Lib.

57. On Apr. 29 JM attended Cumberland County Court, called to examine Richard Randolph. See Commonwealth v. Randolph: Editorial Note, *ca.* Apr. 29, 1793. The entry four lines below this one, "Paid Moss for St. Taminy," suggests he was back in Richmond by May 2.

58. JM must have attended a dinner at Col. John Moss's Swan Tavern commemorating the festival of St. Taminy, humorously honored as the patron saint of America. The festival was celebrated in Richmond on May 2, 1793, and a parade and an evening ball accompanied the dinner. "The Old Swan," *Virginia Historical Register*, II (July, 1849), 158–169; *Virginia Gazette and Richmond and Manchester Advertiser*, May 2, 1793. See Vol. I, 303, n. 58, 329, and 357, for accounts of JM's participation in previous celebrations and more detailed information on the festival.

Market 12/, given for sending process 12/	I	4	
paid Mr. Heth £69–14–7	69	14	7
market 4/, given 12/, Market 18/	I	14	
	97	7	8¾

[Receipts]

May			
Turner ads. Watson	3		
Grymes ads. Fitzhugh (appeals)[59]	5	12	
Millers exrs. ads. Donalds exrs. (fedl.)[60]	5		
Harris ads. Finnie	5		
Carver ads. Rous	2	12	
Tate & Brownlee v Mitchel	5		
advice fee	I	2	
Harvey v Ross	5		
White ads. Grissett & Buckner	I	10	
Woodson v Woodson	5		
Adams's exrs. ads. Allason	5		
Hart ads. Parker	5		
Fowler ads. Dobson etc.[61]	4	10	
Carter & Carter (Frying pan)	I I		
	64	6	
	70	10	
[Total May Receipts]	134	16	

[Disbursements]

May			
Market 12/, do. 9/, coat for self 20/	2	I	

59. Hannah Fitzhugh v. Philip Ludwell Grymes was an appeal from a Sept. 18, 1792, decree of the High Court of Chancery in which JM represented Grymes. The Court of Appeals heard arguments on Apr. 14, 1794, and affirmed the decree on Nov. 19, 1794. Court of Appeals Order Book, II, 262, 273, III, 36, 37, Va. State Lib.

60. William Donald's Executor v. Simon Miller's Executors was a British debt case in which JM entered pleas for the defendants on May 27, 1793. The U.S. Circuit Court sustained the plaintiff's demurrer on Dec. 2, 1793. U.S. Circuit Court, Va., Order Book, I, 144, 227–228, and Record Book, IV, 4, Va. State Lib.

61. See JM to William Marshall, ca. May 1792, and JM's answer in this case listed at Law Papers, Feb. 1792.

Market 6/3, given Polly for			
house 24/7½	1	10	10½
Market 12/, given Polly 13/4	1	5	4
	4	17	2½
house 24/			
	97	7	8¾
[*Total May Disbursements*]	102	4	10¼

[*Receipts*]

June	Warman (motion in G. Ct.)[62]	2	16	
	Borden v Harvie & al[63]	7	12	8
	Monroe admr. ads. Lydes	5	12	
	Randolph (for county of			
	Nottoway)	12	4	
	Hall & Wilson (G. Ct.)	3		
	Briscoe v appl. Chy.	3		
		34	4	8

[*Disbursements*]

[June]	Wood 30/, Market 12/	2	2	
	Market 14/7, do. 6/	1	0	7
	Market 5/6, mending shoes			
	for Robin[64] 2/6		8	
	bonnet for Polly 30/, market 6/	1	16	
	market 24/, bruing 6/,			
	postage 4/	1	14	
	Corn 40/, Tea 12/,			
	barbacue[65] 6/	2	18	

62. See notes on JM's argument in the General Court in Commissioners of Monongalia v. Warman, June 13, 1793, and later fee at Receipts, Oct. 1793.

63. See entry under Receipts, Mar. 1791.

64. Robin Spurlock, a slave. In 1879 a former Richmonder wrote: "What the Chief Justice lacked in style was fully made up by his head servant, old Robin Spurlock, who dressed after the same fashion as his master, but in a much more elegant manner. Robin regarded his master as the greatest man in the world, and himself as the next. He stood at the head of the colored aristocracy of Richmond." C. M. S., "The Home Life of Chief Justice Marshall," *William and Mary Quarterly*, 2d Ser., XII (1932), 68.

65. This probably represents the cost of one meeting of the Quoits Club or the Barbecue Club. The club was organized in 1788, and according to an 1829 account, JM was one of the original members. This social club met on Saturdays between May and October at a spring on Rev. John Buchanan's farm, about one mile west of JM's house

	expenses to Buckingham[66]	2	16	
	Market 6/		6	
		14	4	7

[Receipts]

July	Brickhouse v & ads. Addeson	10		
	Roach & al v Wills exrs.	5		
	Turnbull v Turnbull[67]	9		
	Burnly v Lambert[68]	3		
	Overton ads. Webb	5		
	Bowdoin (Segoughnee) ads			
	Dormoy	2	10	
	advice fee	1	8	
	advice two fees	2	5	
	Hawkins exx.[69]	4	2	
	Bates ads. Harris exr. of			
	McKenzie	5		
	Stockslaters admr. ads.			
	Shermers exrs. (appl.)	5		
		52	5	

[Disbursements]

July	Corn	10		
	Whiskey	6	3	9
	barber 45/, market 18/, ice 6/	3	9	
	Subscription[70] £3, Wood 30/	4	10	

---

on Shockoe Hill. Its constitution limited membership to 30 men and forbade discussion of politics. Members ate, drank, and tossed quoits or played backgammon for entertainment. The club was still functioning when JM died in 1835. See Edmund Berkeley, Jr., "Quoits, the Sport of Gentlemen," *Virginia Cavalcade*, XV (Summer 1965), 11–21; "Chief Justice Marshall," *Southern Literary Messenger*, II (Feb. 1836), 188–189; and George Wythe Munford, *The Two Parsons; Cupid's Sports; The Dream; and the Jewels of Virginia* (Richmond, 1884), 326–341.

See additional entries for barbecue at Disbursements, Sept. 1793, Mar. 1794, May and July–Aug. 1795.

66. See entry under Disbursements, July 1791.

67. See JM to Benjamin Rush, Aug. 6, 1792, and JM to Charles Lee, Dec. 28, 1793.

68. See entry under Receipts, Jan. 1793.

69. See entry under Receipts, Sept. 1, 1790.

70. This was probably for activities held to celebrate July 4 or for the Mason's annual observance of the festival of St. John the Baptist. See Vol. I, 306, n. 71, 357, n. 7.

Subscription to French refugees[71]	9		
Dinner at Moss's[72]		11	6
postage 3/9, Market 7/6, expenses 12/	1	5	3
given 6/, expences 16/	1	2	
Coat 21/, Market 23/, fish 6/	2	19	
Market 22/, do. 6/	1	8	
Wood 30/, Market 46/, expenses 50/	6	6	
given away 18/, postage 8/,	1	6	
	48		6

[Receipts]

Aug.	Fletcher ads. Nicholas appl.[73]	2	4	
	Sherwin v Booker (district)	1	10	
	Johnston v Brown chy.	1		
	Booth v Hoge exx.	7		
	Advice 48/, do. 28/	3	16	
	Bevil etc. v Bevil & al £4	4		
	Jeter & al exrs. of Stoval v Leftwich & al[74]	1	16	
	Bibb ads. Overstreet	5		
	Douthat & ux & al v Prices exrs.	5	6	

71. JM contributed to a subscription campaign for the relief of several hundred French refugees who had recently arrived in Norfolk. They had fled Haiti during several days of intense racial fighting that began June 20 and culminated with the seizure of the capital by blacks and native insurgents. *Va. Gaz., & Genl. Adv.*, July 10 and 17, 1793; Thomas O. Ott, *The Haitian Revolution, 1789–1804* (Knoxville, Tenn., 1973), 69–72. For official correspondence about the care of the refugees, see *CVSP*, VI, 437–438, 444, 447.

72. JM probably attended the dinner held at the tavern of Col. John Moss to celebrate July 4. The dinner was attended "by a more numerous collection of the principal inhabitants of the town and its vicinity, than have for a long time attended to celebrate that auspicious day." Other activities to commemorate the anniversary of American independence included the firing of the federal salute at sunrise, followed by a procession of several militia companies to the capitol to hear an oration. The federal salute was repeated at noon, with a procession to Bloody-Run Spring for a dinner and oration, followed by a 15-cannon salute. *Va. Gaz., & Genl. Adv.*, July 10, 1793.

73. John Nicholas v. Nathan Fletcher was an appeal from a judgment of the District Court at Petersburg rendered on Apr. 20, 1793. The Court of Appeals affirmed the judgment on Oct. 25, 1794. 1 Va. (1 Wash.) 330; Court of Appeals Order Book, III, 15, Va. State Lib.

74. See Vol. I, 388, n. 33.

		£	s	d
	Bray ads. Dunn[75]	5		
	Hobson & ux v Archer & al	5		
	Lockhart v. Comth.	4	10	
	Hales v Carter	1	10	
	Loafman v Robertsons exrs.	2		
	Adkyns ads. Adkyns	4	10	
		54	2	

[*Disbursements*]

August	Flour £11–12	11	12	
	encyclopedia[76]	1	10	
	expenses 36/, do. 8/6,			
	market 3/4	2	7	10
	Shoes 12/, market 12/,			
	expenses 12/	1	16	
	Market 12/, Oats £4–11–9	5	3	9
	Corn 40/, expenses 18/	2	18	
	pd. Hanson & bond	1	7	
		26	14	7

[*Receipts*]

September	Wright v Arnold	1	10	
	Fleming & Randolph v			
	Nelson H. & Co.	2	16	
	Lawrence v Littlepage	2	16	
	Smith v West	5		
	Advice fee	1	2	
	Gill & ux ads. Ross[77]	5		
	Jones v Chamberlayne	5		
	Richeson v Drummond	5		
	Hamilton (Clerk)	3		
	Lewis v Comth.	3	12	
	Stockton v Lomax	1	10	

75. Thomas Dunn v. Charles Bray was an appeal to the High Court of Chancery from a judgment in favor of Bray rendered in the Essex County Court on Aug. 20, 1793. JM represented Bray in the High Court of Chancery, which affirmed the county court on Sept. 6, 1795. The Court of Appeals later affirmed the decree on Oct. 19, 1798. 5 Va. (1 Call) 294; Court of Appeals Order Book, III, 253, 254, Va. State Lib.

76. JM subscribed to *Encyclopaedia; or a Dictionary of Arts, Sciences, and Miscellaneous Literature* beginning in Sept. 1790, and this entry likely represents the purchase of vol. VIII, IX, or X, all of which were issued in 1793.

77. See entry under Receipts, Sept. 18, 1790.

	Wrights ads. Wright[78]	3	
	Clarke ads. Belfours heirs	2	12
	Jerdon v Johnston etc.	5	
	Eggleston ads. Worsham	2	
	Wrights exrs. ads. Wright	3	
	Mohun exx. v Logan Gilmore & Co.	5	
	Stanfield v the Comth.	4	10
	Semple v Robinsons admrs. & al	3	
		64	8

[Disbursements]

September	book for Tom 3/, expences 2/6		5	6
	paid Mr. Elliot 4–16–11	4	16	11
	Market 36/, peaches 6/	2	2	
	barbacue 6/, sugar & tea 24/	1	10	
	Heters for coffee 6/, expences 12/		18	
	Mahogany tables	10		
	Tea 18/, Market 3/, expenses 13/6	1	14	6
	Market 13/, expences 1/6, given Tom 1/		15	6
	Turkies 6/, market 12/		18	
	Given away 6/, market 7/6		13	6
	Cow £4–10, chickens 13/, market 15/	5	18	0
		29	11	11

[Receipts]

October	Blane ads. Sterling Douglass & Hunter	14	
	Walker, in Farley ads. Trent	5	
	Evert v Ward & al	4	10
	Marshall v Johnstons exrs.	6	
	Anthony ads. Appleberry[79]	5	

78. See JM to William Branch Giles, *ca.* 1790.
79. See entry under Receipts, Apr. 1792.

Cook ads. Daniels exrs. appeals[80]	5		
Finch ads. Thweats exrs. (appeals)[81]	5	8	
Maeze v Hamilton[82]	21		
Wilkinson v Apperson	5		
Wilson Campbell & Wheeler ads. Robinson etc.	5		
advice fee	1	10	
Murray v Austin & Co. (fedl.)[83]	5		
Dormoy v Lee	1	4	
Roy v Garnet[84]	7		
Wallace ads. Smith (in appeals)[85]	7	4	
Skipwith v Hanson	5		
advice fee		19	6
Reid v Burnsides[86]	3	13	
Advice fee	1	2	
Pendleton v Vandeveer[87]	7		
	75	10	6

[Disbursements]

October	Market 16/, shoes for Dick 6/, corks 3/6	1	5	6

80. See entry under Receipts, June 15, 1789.

81. Thweat and Hinton v. Adam Finch was an appeal from a 1789 judgment of the District Court at Petersburg. The judgment was affirmed on Oct. 23, 1793, but apparently there was subsequent action in other courts, perhaps the High Court of Chancery. Court of Appeals Order Book, II, 67, 151, 183, 209, 242–243, Va. State Lib. See additional fees under Receipts, Apr. and May 1795.

82. See JM to Archibald Stuart, ca. Dec. 1789.

83. James Maury, of Great Britian, v. Moses and Stephen Austin, doing business as Moses Austin & Co., was a suit to recover the value of goods sold to Austin & Co. JM represented the plaintiff before the U.S. Circuit Court and obtained judgment on June 5, 1795. U.S. Circuit Court, Va., Order Book, I, 530, and Record Book, III, 259–260, Va. State Lib.

84. See entry under Receipts, Apr. 1793.

85. Smith and Moreton v. Michael Wallace was an appeal from a decree of the High Court of Chancery of Mar. 12, 1793. The decree enjoined a judgment against Wallace in the District Court at Fredericksburg. The Court of Appeals heard argument on Apr. 15, 1794, and affirmed the decree three days later. 1 Va. (1 Wash.) 254; Court of Appeals Order Book, II, 263, 266, Va. State Lib.

86. See entry under Receipts, Mar. 10, 1790, and JM to Andrew Reid, Apr. 26, 1790.

87. Philip Pendleton v. Jacobus Vandevier was an appeal from a judgment of the District Court at Winchester granting an ejectment brought by Vandevier against

Cow 6/, house 6/		12	
Market 13/6, do. 3/3		16	3
Paid for Toms schooling to Mr. Harris[88] up to 1st Jany. 1794	18	3	8
paid for John Smith up to 13th. Novr. 1793	7		
Mending tea kettle 2/		2	
Market 8/, plays[89] 18/	1	6	
wood 30/, corn 57/	4	7	
Market 6/, do. 15/	1	1	
corn £4–10	4	10	
Dicks boots 3/6, bring Molly to bed[90] 12/8		16	4
Market 4/, do. 6/		10	
Market 12/, paid my Taylor 57/3	2	17	3
Market 7/, wood 20/	1	7	
	44	14	

[Receipts]

October & November	Hains & al shf. of Rockingham Comth.	2	10	
	Cabell v Bolling	1	10	
	Green & al v Appersons exrs.	2	16	
	Winston ads. Poindexter	2	6	
	Anderson ads. Comth.	2	14	
	Crittenden ads. Claiborne	3		
	Advice fee	1	2	6

Pendleton. JM represented Pendleton before the Court of Appeals on Nov. 3, 1794. The judgment was reversed on Nov. 7, 1794. 1 Va. (1 Wash.) 381; Court of Appeals Order Book, III, 22, 27, Va. State Lib.

88. JM's son Tom was taught by Eldridge Harris, a Richmond schoolmaster who announced in 1794 that he, along with several others, would reopen the Richmond Academy, offering instruction in Greek, Latin, bookkeeping, mathematics, and English grammar. *Va. Gaz., & Genl. Adv.*, Mar. 5, 1794, Dec. 23, 1795.

89. The 1793 Richmond theater season opened in October with the Virginia Company's presentation of *Young Quaker* and *Flitch of Bacon* on Oct. 24, followed by *A Day in Turkey, Poor Soldier, Provoked Husband,* and *Columbus* on Oct. 28. Sherman, "Post-Revolutionary Theatre," 117–118.

90. JM's sister Anna Maria (Mary) was known at this time as Molly. Married to Humphrey Marshall, she was visiting JM in October when apparently they believed she was about to deliver her baby prematurely. Her son, Thomas, was not born, however, until the following Jan. 15, at which time she had returned to Kentucky.

Pannell[91]	2	8	
Cowles v Walker	7		
Jones admr. v & ads. Ross	5		
Griffin v Lee	5		
Brown v Jett (fedl.)[92]	4	10	
Calland ads. Brough & ux	5		
Mr. Watts £9–16	9	16	
Mr. Laidly	2	8	
Jones ads. Comth.	2	10	
Hughes ads. comth. 5£, Warman[93] (old) 2–10	7	10	
Clarke v chy. 5£, Bell v Wms. 1–8	6	8	
Anderson (K. Wms.) Fedl.	2	16	
	77	2	6

[Disbursements]

October	Market 6/, given musick on genl. master[94] 12/		18
	Chair £18, given away 6/	18	6
	house 6/, market 12/		18
	wood 12/, market 12/	1	4
	market 2/, do. 36/, Grammer for Tom 6/	2	4
	Corn 15/, Market 18/	1	13
	fodder 15/, plays[95] 36/, expenses £4	6	11
	Market 20/, breeches for Dick 21/	2	1
	Market 42/, play 21/	3	3

91. The case of Alexander Spotswood v. Edmund Pendleton, John Campbell, Bernard Moore, Benjamin Pendleton, and Henry Field, with William Pannell et al., was before the High Court of Chancery some time prior to 1796, when that court dismissed Spotswood's bills of complaint. JM represented the defendants during this litigation. The decree was appealed to the Court of Appeals and affirmed on May 9, 1801. 8 Va. (4 Call) 514; Court of Appeals Order Book, III, 349, IV, 31, 32, 90, Va. State Lib. See later fee at Receipts, Mar. 1794.

92. See JM's declaration in Brown v. Jett, listed at Law Papers, Nov. 1794.

93. See notes on JM's argument in the General Court in Commissioners of Monongalia v. Warman, June 13, 1793, and an earlier fee entered under Receipts, June 1793.

94. In October a Mr. Garnet gave music lessons in Richmond. Va. Gaz., & Genl. Adv., Oct. 2, 1793.

95. See entries under Disbursements, Oct. and Nov. 1793.

Fodder 30/, market 6/	1	16	
	38	14	

[Receipts]

Novr.

Donalds exrs. Fedl.	5	2	
Bates ads. Croxal	3		
Jones v (I beleive Meade			
Walker) injn.	5	12	
Anderson v Demoss	5		
Joliff v Hite & al exrs.[96]	7		
Bates v Dobson etc. Chy. Fedl.	5	16	
Smith ads. Allen Fedl.[97]	3		
Hack ads. Custis	5		
Frazer v (finishd)	2	8	
advice fee 22/6	1	2	6
Nelson v Hunt	5		
Gouch ads. Kerr[98]	3		
Clarkes exr. ads. Freeland	5		
Boush ads. Whittle & wife	6	17	9
Bowler ads. Smith	3	12	
Burton v Donald & co.[99] (Fedl.)	7		
Taylor ads. Booker (Mr. Scott)	1	10	
Deane for conveyance	2	16	
	77	16	3

[Disbursements]

Novr.

expences £6–10	6	10	
Taylor	2	14	3
Pork	5	12	
Market 48/	2	8	

96. Amos Jolliffe v. Mary McDonald's and Isaac Hite's Executors was before the High Court of Chancery at this time. The court dismissed the bills of complaint on Sept. 6, 1796, and the Court of Appeals later affirmed the decree. 5 Va. (1 Call) 262 (1798); Court of Appeals Order Book, III, 216, 234, Va. State Lib.

97. See entry under Receipts, Apr. 1792.

98. Carr v. Gooch was an appeal from a Sept. 18, 1793, judgment of the District Court of Charlottesville for Gooch. JM represented Gooch before the Court of Appeals when arguments were heard on Apr. 22, 1794. The court affirmed the judgment two days later. 1 Va. (1 Wash.) 260; Court of Appeals Order Book, II, 270, 272, Va. State Lib.

99. See Jesse Burton to JM, Apr. 11, 1794, and bill in chancery listed at Law Papers, Dec. 1793.

venison 30/	I	10	
wood 30/	I	10	
Hay £4, plays[100] £3, market 54	9	14	
plays 24/, market 6/	I	10	
shoes £1–12–6, expenses 7/6	2		
	33	8	3

[Receipts]

Decr.	To three advice fees	3	7	6
	To three advice fees	3	18	6
	Southgate 2 fees in Fedl. ct.[101]	5	12	
	advice fee	1	10	
	Major Nelson £7-10	7	10	
	Messrs. Richesons	15		
	Green v Apperson	4	4	
		41	2	

[Disbursements]

Decr.	mats 2–6, expenses 13/6		16	
	market 6/, do. 12/, postage 7/6	I	5	6
	brewing 6/, expenses 7£	7	6	
	corn £10, Giliats store £60,[1]			
	market 6/	70	6	
	market 18/, hay 4–10,			
	venison 26/	6	14	
	barber 45/, Buckingham[2] £13–5	15	10	
	coal 4–5	4	5	
	Corn £7-10, expenses 30/	9		
	Wood 48/	2	8	

100. Among the plays performed in Richmond in November were *The Haunted Tower* and *Love-a-la-Mode*, presented on Nov. 7, and the comedy *The School for Scandal* and a musical farce, *The Son-in-Law*, on Nov. 27. Sherman, "Post-Revolutionary Theatre," 118–119; *Va. Gaz., & Genl. Adv.*, Nov. 27, 1793.

101. Miller Southgate v. William Winslow was the name of two cases brought by JM for the plaintiff. Pleas were entered before the U.S. Circuit Court for Virginia on May 28, 1794, and judgment was given the plaintiff in each case on Dec. 3, 1794. U.S. Circuit Court, Va., Order Book, I, 375, 433, 434, and Record Book, III, 168–169, 170–171, Va. State Lib.

1. JM was no doubt settling his account with John and Thomas Gilleat, Richmond merchants who had announced their partnership would be dissolved and their firm closed on Jan. 1, 1794. *Va. Gaz., & Genl. Adv.*, Dec. 4, 1793.

2. See entry under Disbursements, July 1791.

	£	s	d
To Mr. Dubois[3] for Tom	2	16	
	120	6	6

[Receipts]

	£	s	d
Jany.	57	4	
Feby.	66	12	4
March	174	7	
Apl.	121	9	5
May	134	16	
June	34	4	8
July	52	5	
Aug.	54	2	
Septr.	64	8	
Octobr	152	13	
Novr.	77	16	3
Decr.	41	2	
	1030	19	8

[Disbursements]

	£	s	d
Jany.	77	2	11
Feby.	33	10	
March	32	7	6
Apl.	36	17	4
May	102	4	10¼
June	14	4	7
July	48		6
Aug.	26	14	7
Septr.	29	11	11
Oc.	83	8	
No.	33	8	3
Decr.	120	6	6
	637	16	11¼

[Receipts]

		£	s	d
January	Turner ads. Watson	2		
	Shelton v Sheltons exrs.	5		
	Smythe ads. Reynolds	7	10	

3. Rev. John DuBois. See entry under Disbursements, Feb. 1792.

	advice fees	2	6	6
	Claiborne v Comth.	11		
	advice fee	1	8	
	Advice fees etc. Mewburn & Fenwick	7		
	Eckols v Hoover chy.	5		
	Blane v Archer[4] & same v Hobson	7		
	Randolphs exrs.	7		
	Miller v Hog	5		
	Digges ads. Muschett (finishd)	5		
	Shackelford & al v Bronaugh & al	1	4	
	Stephen ads. Hite[5]	5		
[February]	Campbell v Carlton	5		
	Smith & al ads. Wrae (district	2	16	

[*Disbursements*]

January	Flour	12		
	Market six dollars	1	16	
	Market 19/, do. 6/, expenses 25/	2	10	
	house 24/, Given away 12/	1	16	
	Salt 20/, pork 39£, market 20/	41		
[February]	house £6–12, expenses to Frederick[6] 6	12	12	
	repairing chair £1–10, saddle 4–17–6	5	7	6
	Wood £4–4, butter 4	8	4	

4. See JM's declaration listed at Law Papers, Nov. 1794.

5. Lewis Stephens v. Isaac Hite was a motion for a writ of supersedeas from the District Court at Winchester to the Frederick County Court. The case was continued to Apr. 22, 1793, when the district court reversed the county court in favor of Stephens. No evidence survives that would indicate JM practiced in this district court. The appearance of a fee here, however, suggests Hite planned an appeal to the Court of Appeals, and JM was being retained by Stephens. No record of appeal has been found. JM may have been retained when he traveled to Frederick County this month. Superior Court Order Book, 1789–1793, 302, 383, 505, Frederick County, Va. State Lib.

6. JM went to Frederick County to attend the inquest of office held on Feb. 19 to determine if Denny Martin Fairfax's land in that jurisdiction had escheated to the state. It is possible JM represented Fairfax at the inquest, although JM's brother Charles filled that position before the District Court at Winchester in April, when he succeeded in having the inquest quashed. See Fairfax Lands: Editorial Note, Feb. 1, 1793, and Robert Brooke to Henry Lee, May 4, 1794, *CVSP*, II, 130–131.

[Receipts]			
March	Pemberton & al ads. Levels	2	10	
	Ratcliffe ads. Hawkins	7	10	
	Harrison & uxr. v Allen[7]	6		
	Advice fees	2	5	
	Pendleton Pannel & al ads. Spotswood[8]	50		
	Clarke & al ads. Belfour & al	2	8	
	Willing & Morris surviving partner of Samuel Inglis & Co. v. Patteson	7		
	Carver ads. Roush (finishd)	10		
	Rankin v Donaghoe[9]	3	6	6
		1	13	6
	Whitings exrs. ads. Loyd exr. (fedl.)[10]	6	4	
	Jones ads. Tomkies	1	4	
	Crenshaw v Duval eject	2	8	
	Dormoy v Lee	1	16	
	Randolph (Harrison & al) ads. Lydderdale[11]	5		
	Taylor exr. v Cock & Godwin (find.)	10		
	Jones v Williams (finishd)[12]	30		
	Bowles v shf. of Hanover	1	4	
	Ferguson v Moore (appeals)[13]	4		

7. See notes on JM's argument before the High Court of Chancery, Sept. 1794, and later fee at Receipts, Nov. 1794.

8. See entry under Receipts, Oct.–Nov. 1793.

9. See JM to Archibald Stuart, Mar. 27, 1794.

10. John Lloyd, executor of Osgood Hanbury, v. Robert Cowne, executor of Thomas Whiting, was an action entered in the U.S. Circuit Court for Virginia sometime before 1796. The case was continued until 1797, when orders for depositions to be taken in England were issued. The court found for Whiting's executor on Nov. 29, 1798, although by this time JM was probably no longer connected with the case. U.S. Circuit Court, Va., Order Book, II, 122, 239, III, 3, 129, Va. State Lib.

11. See JM's answer in Lidderdale's Executor v. Harrison's Administrator, listed at Law Papers, Mar. 1794.

12. See entry under Receipts, Nov. 29, 1789.

13. James, Walter, and Dougal Ferguson v. Daniel Moore was an appeal to the Court of Appeals after the District Court at Petersburg affirmed a Dinwiddie County Court judgment against the Fergusons. The district court judgment was entered on Apr. 20, 1793, after which JM was retained by the appellants. The Court of Appeals reversed the district court on Apr. 17, 1795. 2 Va. (2 Wash.) 54; Court of Appeals Order Book, III, 46, 49, Va. State Lib.

Aylett ads. Ayletts exrs. (appeals)[14]	3			
Hacket v Allcock—1100 wt. Tobo.[15]	7			
Telford v Pope Chy.	1	4	6	
Burns ads. Matthews[16]	5			
Brown v Gardner & al	5			
Barr & ux v Wailes admrs.	5	4		
Advice fee	1	8		
Marshall v Finney & al	5			
Advice & drawing answer	2	8		

[*Disbursements*]

[March]	Market 6/, postage 12/6	18	6
	given away 9/, Manure 3/6	12	6
	Given for Rachael 12/, market 3/	15	
	Market 6/, whip for Polly 12/	18	
	Corn 12 £, hay £3–16	15	16
	Given to the poor of Richmond	3	
	Paid Potowmack company by Mr. Wash.[17]	20	
	Market 24/, taxes[18] £13,		

14. See entry under Receipts, Mar. 10, 1789.

15. After the Caroline County Court ruled in favor of Thomas Alcock on Mar. 14, 1794, Martin Hackett retained JM to seek an injunction against the judgment in the High Court of Chancery. That court dismissed the bill on May 15, 1795, and JM appealed to the Court of Appeals on behalf of Hackett. That court first affirmed the dismissal and then in 1799 reversed itself after a rehearing. 5 Va. (1 Call) 463; Court of Appeals Order Book, III, 122, 125, 128, 255, 256, 283, Va. State Lib.

16. JM was probably retained to represent Burns's executrix in the Court of Appeals after the District Court at Staunton rendered a judgment on Apr. 6, 1792, against the defendants in Robert Burns's Executrix v. Richard Mathews and William Chambers. No record of appeal has been found, but JM did not normally practice in the District Court at Staunton. District Court Order Book, 1789–1793, 427, 1789–1797, 169, Augusta County, Va. State Lib. See JM to Archibald Stuart, Mar. 27, 1794.

17. Potomac River Company stockholders were advised that they must pay to treasurer William Hartshorne, in Alexandria, £5 sterling per share on or before Mar. 1, 1794. *Va. Gaz., & Genl. Adv.*, Jan. 29, 1794. For JM's previous payments to the company, see entries under Disbursements, May 22, 1789, and Jan. 21, 1790.

18. The taxes paid probably included JM's personal property tax for Richmond, the list for which was recorded Mar. 29, 1794, and indicated JM owned 8 tithable Negro slaves, 3 horses, 1 coach, chariot, or post chaise, and 1 riding carriage. His real property was assessed at £50 and taxed at 16s. 8d. Richmond City Personal Property Book, 1794, and Land Book, 1794, Va. State Lib. JM's Fauquier County property tax for 1794 was £2 15s. 10d. for 520 acres. Fauquier County Land Book, 1794, Va.

	Encyclopedia[19] 30/	15	14	
	Subscription to market[20] 3£,			
	laws[21] 24, Powell[22] 18/	5	2	
	Market 8/, Store £20	20	8	
	Market 12/8, wood 24/	1	16	8
	Sugar £12–11, expenses to			
	Hanover 7/7	1	0	6
	Ball[23] 18/, barbacue 30/	2	8	
	expences 7/6, shoes for Dick 7/		14	6
	house 36/, expenses to			
	Fauquier[24] 4£	5	16	
[April]	Market 40/, corn £3–15,			
	book for Tom 4/6	5	19	6
	Corn £8, Market 12/	8	12	
	Subscriptions & regementals 48/	2	8	
	paid subscription to Mr.			
	Buchanan[25]	2	8	

[Receipts]

May	Hite	12	
	Nelson v Davies admr.	5	

State Lib. The amount of this entry suggests he may also have been paying property tax for Henrico County, the records for which are not extant.

19. This entry suggests JM purchased vol. X, issued in 1793, or vol. XI, issued in 1794, of *Encyclopaedia; or Dictionary of Arts, Sciences, and Miscellaneous Literature*, to which JM subscribed.

20. JM subscribed to the building of the new market house in Shockoe Valley. See Petition, Nov. 4, 1793.

21. *Acts passed at a General Assembly of the Commonwealth of Virginia . . . one thousand seven hundred and ninety-three* (Richmond, 1794).

22. JM owned a copy of John Joseph Powell, *Essay Upon the Law of Contracts and Agreements* (London, 1790), and this entry could represent the purchase of that volume or of Powell's *An Essay on the Learning respecting the Creation and Execution of Powers* . . . , 2d. ed. (Dublin, 1791). See John Wayles Eppes to JM, *ca.* 1794. See also entry under Disbursements, Apr. 1795, for JM's purchase of another work by Powell.

23. It is possible that a ball concluded the celebration of the festival of St. Patrick held in Richmond on Mar. 17 and that JM attended those festivities. *Va. Gaz., & Genl. Adv.*, Mar. 19, 1794.

24. JM no doubt attended the inquest of office held on Apr. 19 to determine if Denny Martin Fairfax's land should escheat to the Commonwealth. It is possible that JM represented Fairfax at the hearing, where the jury voted 11 to 5 in favor of the state. Because the vote was less than the number required, the state asked for a second hearing to be held in June. See Fairfax Lands: Editorial Note, Feb. 1, 1793, and Robert Brooke to Henry Lee, May 4, 1794, *CVSP*, VII, 130–131.

25. See Vol. I, 313, and entries under Disbursements, May 1790, Apr. 1792, and Jan. 1795, for other payments to Buchanan.

Lunceford ads. Glasscock[26]	5		
Holland exr. of Hyslop v			
Floyd genl. ct.	2	16	
advice fees	2	16	
Lindsay v Donalson	7		
Cuningham[27]	150		
Jarvis ads. Wilkins[28]	5		
Taylor v Dandridge	5		
Glasscock v Mitchells exrs.	5		
Graves ads. Madison	5		
advice fee	2	8	
Tabb	7	10	
Carrington	5		
Mr Morris[29]	10		
Farrar ads. Henderson McCall			
& Co.[30] fedl.	2	16	
Dormoy	3		
advice fee 22/6	1	2	6
Parke ads. Russels exrs.	7		
Bernard ads. Jordan	5	12	
Advice fee	1	2	6
Falken	5		
Mills	5		
Price exr. ads. Campbell[31]	4	9	6

26. John Lunsford v. George Glascock, Jr., had been decided in the District Court at Northumberland County on Sept. 2, 1793, in favor of the plaintiff. This fee apparently represents Lunsford's retainer of JM in an appeal brought by Glascock before the Court of Appeals. No record of appeal has been found, but JM did not normally practice in the District Court at Northumberland County. For the record of the case there, see District Court Order Book, 1789–1793, 167, 196, 1793–1802, 2, Northumberland County, Va. State Lib.

27. See a summary of the case Commonwealth v. Cunningham & Co. at Stipulation, Apr. 8, 1794.

28. John Wilkins's Executor v. William Jarvis was heard in the District Court at Accomack and Northampton counties on appeal from the Northampton County Court. The court affirmed the county court's judgment in favor of Jarvis on Oct. 18, 1792. Any fee JM received would represent additional action before the state courts in which he practiced, most likely the Court of Appeals. No record of appeal has been found. For the record in the lower court, see District Court Order Book, 1789–1797, 212, 232, and Record Book, 1791–1794, 302–305, Accomack County, Va. State Lib.

29. See entry under Receipts, Jan. 1793.

30. Henderson, McCaul & Co. v. William Farrar, of Goochland County, was a British debt case in which JM represented Farrar. JM undertook bond for Farrar and filed pleas on June 6, 1795. Judgment was confessed on Dec. 1, 1795. U.S. Circuit Court, Va., Order Book, I, 537, II, 38, and Record Book, III, 451–453, Va. State Lib.

31. John Campbell v. George Brooke's and Robert Page's Executors, one of whom

	Mr. Dixon 42/	2	2	
	Rogers v Waggoner	4	16	
	Colo. Powell	5		
	D. Claiborne	25		
	Ferguson v Tabb	5		
	Levy ads. (Fedl.)[32]	5	5	
	[*Disbursements*]			
May	Market 19/, wood 48/	3	7	
	James river company	11	17	8
	Manure 6/, market 2/, briddle 12/	1		
	rum & brand	6	4	
	market 18/, postage 9/, given Dick 6/	1	13	
	Oznabrugs £9–15	9	15	
	Mrs. Lawson[33]	3	12	
	Cart 6/, do. 9/9, market 6/	1	1	9
	house expences 36/	1	16	
	race[34] 24/, spent 6/	1	10	
	shoes for Robin 6/		6	
	Mending the waggon		15	9
	conveyance of Shares		6	
	market 5/, house 30/	1	15	
	shoes 12/, self & wife £4–11	5	3	

---

was Robert Price, was before the High Court of Chancery and involved the sale of securities by Carter Braxton to Campbell. The High Court of Chancery decreed in favor of Campbell on Mar. 14, 1797, but JM took the case to the Court of Appeals on behalf of his clients, the defendants. The Court of Appeals did not hear arguments until Nov. 11 and 12, 1799, and on Nov. 15, the chancery decree was affirmed. 6 Va. (2 Call) 92; Court of Appeals Order Book, III, 361–362, 363, Va. State Lib. For subsequent litigation, see 9 Va. (5 Call) 115 (1804) and 17 Va. (3 Munf.) 227 (1811).

32. Bank of North America v. Ezekiel Levy was before the U.S. Circuit Court for Virginia, with JM representing Levy. Pleas were filed on Dec. 4, 1793, and the case was continued several times before judgment was entered for Levy on May 28, 1798. JM had left the case by then. U.S. Circuit Court, Va., Order Book, I, 139, 245, 442, 479, II, 214, III, 2, 108, 209, Va. State Lib.

33. Molly Lawson.

34. JM was a member of one of Richmond's Jockey Clubs, which set the rules and raised the purses for horse races held every May and October. This figure probably represents the subscription levied JM by his club. *Va. Gaz., & Genl. Adv.*, May 7, 1794. See Vol. I, 315, n. 20, for more information on the Richmond horse races.

[*Receipts*]

June				
Young ads. Skipwith[35]	5		
Advice fee 22/6, do. 48/	3	10	6
Osbornes exrs. ads. Spiers & Co.	2	16	
Fontaines secys. ads. Comth.	2	14	
Preston shf. of Washingtons secy.	2	10	
Whiting exr.	10		

[*Disbursements*]

June				
Fruit 6/, expenses 6/		12	
Market 6/, brewing 6/		12	
Market 6/3, do. 12/6, Gowns to Polly 4£	4	18	9
Sugar 48/, Circus[36] 24/	3	12	
Market 12/8, do. 24/	1	16	8
expenses £3–6	3	6	
Sundries for house £9	9		

[*Receipts*]

July			
advice & drawing agreements	1	10
Brooking exr. of Munford (Fedl.[37]	5	
Same exr. of Holmes[38] (finshd)	10	
Woodson & ux ads. Leake (chy.)	5	
Advice fee	1	10
Wilkinson 5£	5	
Miller ads. Barham	5	
Jones in Crawly & Garland	4	10

35. See entry under Receipts, Dec. 1791.

36. A circus was performing in Richmond at this time, for it was announced that Mr. Picketts, the equestrian performer, had arrived in town, and "after a day or two's rest, the public will be favored with a variety of feats in Horsemanship at the new Circus on the Richmond walk." *Va. Gaz., & Genl. Adv.,* May 21, 1794.

37. John Bowman, surviving partner of Spiers, Bowman & Co., v. Vivion Brooking, executor of Robert Munford, was a British debt case in which JM filed pleas for the defendant on Dec. 4, 1794. Judgment was entered for the plaintiff on May 30, 1795. U.S. Circuit Court, Va., Order Book, I, 442, 512, Va. State Lib.

38. See JM's receipt for fees in Holmes's Estate v. Commonwealth, July 10, 1794.

[*Disbursements*]

		£	s	d
July	barber 45/, postage 11/	2	16	
	Encyclopedia[39] 30/	1	10	
	Wood 24/, chickens 6/, ducks 6/	1	16	
	Whortleberries 4/, beer 7/6		11	6
	Flour £11	11		
29	Pd. Mr. Harris[40] for Tom	2	7	4
	Sundry expenses 7£	7		

[*Receipts*]

		£	s	d
August	advice fee	1	2	6
	Cruth & ux etc. v. Brimms exrs. chy. (see Mr. Clavel)	2	10	
	Mr. Tabb	8		
	Dandridge v Toler & al.	3		
	Goode ads. Hayes	5	18	
	Trents & Trent	5		
	Bell ads. Lewis[41]	3		
	Voss v Loyal	2	16	
	Doctor Selden	2	8	
	Mosby—Appeal finishd)[42]	1	10	
	Jacob & al v Winston & al.	5		
	Clarke & ux v Coleman	5		
	Winston exr. of Harris v Lyons	1	10	
	Mr. Mayo ads. Coleman	2	10	

[*Disbursements*]

		£	s	d
August	Taylors accounts £6-7-9	6	7	9
	Wood 12/, fruit 5/, chickens 21/	1	18	
	brandy £10-5-6	10	5	6

39. JM no doubt purchased vol. XI or vol. XII, both issued in 1794, of *Encyclopaedia; or a Dictionary of Arts, Sciences, and Miscellaneous Literature*, to which he had subscribed since Sept. 1790.

40. Eldridge Harris, Richmond schoolmaster.

41. The case of John Lewis v. William Bell and Richard Morgan was pending in the District Court at Winchester, and it is conceivable this fee represents payment for advice. There is no evidence JM practiced in that court. A consent judgment was entered in this debt action on Apr. 20, 1795. Superior Court Order Book, 1794–1797, 147, Frederick County, Va. State Lib.

42. JM apparently appealed the chancery decree of Oct. 1791 in Thomas Cobbs v. John Mosby to the Court of Appeals. No record of appeal has been found, however. See entry under Receipts, May 29, 1790.

Rum £5–6, meal & hominy 18/	6	4
fruit 18/, market 7/	1	5
Corn £4–10, Market 3–7	7	17
expences £2–16, wood 24/	4	
brewing 6/		

[Receipts]

September	Field ads. Taylor & al chy.[43]	5	
	Craig ads. Donald	1	10
	Advice	1	6
	do. 3 fees	3	5
	appeal about a mill	2	10
	Blount ads. Kimbro		18
	Eustace ads. Eustace[44]	5	
	Rudd v Clarke	3	
	Grymes v Berkeley	1	10
	Keys exrs. ads. Harmen	4	10
	Keenes v Smith	30	
	Smith ads. Smith (old Suit)[45]	5	
	White Whittle & Co v McCallum (find)	7	
	Archer ads. Frazer dist ct.	1	10
	Johnston ads. Johnston[46]	5	
	Wards admrs. ads. McCallum	6	
	Lambkin ads. Fallen appeal	5	
	Shelton ads. Johnston[47]	4	5 · 6
	Hooper ads Curd (appeals)[48]	3	
	Woodson v Payne chy.[49]	1	14

43. See entry under Receipts, Jan. 1, 1791.
44. William Eustace v. John Eustace's Executor was an appeal from a decree of the High Court of Chancery on May 4, 1792. JM represented William Eustace in the Court of Appeals on Apr. 18, 1793. On Apr. 20, the court reversed the High Court of Chancery and the Lancaster County Court, from which the chancery appeal had come, and ordered a new trial. 1 Va. (1 Wash.) 188; Court of Appeals Order Book, II, 217, 219, Va. State Lib. See additional fees under Receipts, Mar. 5, and July–Aug. 1795, which suggest JM continued with the case, perhaps in the High Court of Chancery.
45. See Vol. I, 382, n. 4.
46. See entry under Receipts, Mar. 10, 1791.
47. See entry under Receipts, Feb. 1793.
48. Joseph Curd v. George Hooper and Henry Bell was an appeal from an Apr. 2, 1793, judgment of the District Court at Prince Edward County to the Court of Appeals. JM represented Hooper, the sheriff of Buckingham County. On Oct. 29, 1795, the appeal was dismissed for failure to prosecute. Court of Appeals Order Book, III, 81, Va. State Lib.
49. JM sought an injunction against a county court judgment from the High

	Land ads. Curd[50]	5	
	Mr. B. Randolph	14	8
	Crenshaw ads. Duval	5	
	Molloy v Hudson	5	
	Gootee ads. Henry[51]	6	
	Randolphs exrs. v Ferguson & ux	3	
	Carringtons v Mayo & al[52]	5	
October	Darby ads. Armstead	5	
	Granberry v Granberry[53]	9	
	Cazenove ads. Dade (appeals)[54]	6	
	Southcomb v Croughton	6	
	Shelton ads. Johnston[55]	2	14
	Anthony ads. Applebury[56]	4	16
	Shelton v Barbour (appeal)[57]	5	
	Underwood ads. Underwood	5	
	Grymes ads. Curtis	5	
	Jett v Jetts exrs. (chy. to be brought)	5	
	Comth. v Newel[58]	12	

Court of Chancery in Samuel Woodson v. Thomas Payne. The court refused the bill for injunction on Oct. 3, 1796. Woodson then took his appeal to the Court of Appeals, but JM did not represent him there. 5 Va. (1 Call) 495 (1799); Court of Appeals Order Book, III, 263, 271, Va. State Lib.

50. Joseph Curd v. John Land was taken to the High Court of Chancery after the Buckingham County Court entered a judgment against Curd on Mar. 13, 1793. JM represented Land in the High Court of Chancery, which reversed the county court on May 20, 1795. Land then appealed to the Court of Appeals. See additional fee entered under Receipts, July–Aug. 1795. Court of Appeals Order Book, III, 163, 247, 249, Va. State Lib.

51. See entry under Receipts, Nov. 4, 1789.

52. See entry under Receipts, June 19, 1790.

53. See entry under Receipts, Aug. 14, 1790.

54. Baldwin Dade v. Peter Cassanave was an appeal from a May 14, 1794, judgment of the District Court at Dumfries to the Court of Appeals in which JM represented Cassanave. The judgment was affirmed on Oct. 12, 1795. Court of Appeals Order Book, III, 50, Va. State Lib.

55. See entry under Receipts, Feb. 1793.

56. See entry under Receipts, Apr. 1792.

57. William Shelton v. Sherod Barbour was an appeal to the Court of Appeals from the District Court at Charlottesville. The district court held against Shelton on Sept. 17, 1794. Barbour was a slave held by Shelton, and he was attempting to gain his freedom. The Court of Appeals reversed the district court on Apr. 13, 1795, and Barbour remained in slavery. JM and Bushrod Washington represented Shelton on appeal. 2 Va. (2 Wash.) 64; Court of Appeals Order Book, III, 43, 45, Va. State Lib.

58. Commonwealth v. Newill was an action in the District Court at Washington County. Newill was a justice of the peace who was charged with accepting a bribe and was found guilty on Oct. 4, 1793. At the time this fee was entered JM was acting attorney general and represented the state on appeal. The Court of Appeals heard ar-

Wooldridge ads. Wooldridge[59]	15		
Dandridge v Harris[60]	5		
Smith v Bolling	5		
Harrisons exrs. ads. Harrison[61]	2	8	
Hicks v Turnbull	7		

[*Disbursements*]

September	Market 35/	1	15	
	Salt 6/, Breeches 3£	3	6	
	Market 12/, Market 30/	2	2	
	Corn 36/, bran 6/, Market 12/	2	14	
	Tea 24/, Market 12/	1	16	
	Tea for my Mother 30/	1	10	
	Market 12/, boots 48/	3		
	Given Polly 6£, Meal 12/	6	12	
	house 40/, Coat for Dick 28/	3	8	
	expences travelling[62] £6–4	6	4	
	Club at Moss's 31/	1	11	
	Meal 13/6, Market 33/3½	2	9	3½
	house 12/, market 6/,			
	whisky £9–12	10	10	
	Market 48/, given 12/, Tom &			
	Johnny 12/	3	12	
	Wood 24/			

[*Receipts*]

November	Boggus v Humphries	2	8

guments on Apr. 21, and Oct. 15 and 16, 1795, and reversed the district court on Nov. 2, 1795. 2 Va. (2 Wash.) 88; Court of Appeals Order Book, III, 52, 66, 71, 72, 85, Va. State Lib.

59. Thomas Wooldridge v. Joseph Wooldridge was an appeal from the High Court of Chancery to the Court of Appeals in which JM represented the appellee. The Court of Appeals heard argument on Apr. 29, 1796, and affirmed the judgment the following day. Court of Appeals Order Book, III, 120, 121, Va. State Lib.

60. See entry under Receipts, Apr. 1, 1790.

61. Collier and Braxton Harrison v. Henry Harrison was a suit in the High Court of Chancery involving an inherited mortgage on slaves. JM represented Henry Harrison, and the court decreed in his favor on Sept. 28, 1796. An appeal was taken to the Court of Appeals, where JM appeared for Henry Harrison. The decree was reversed on Oct. 18, 1799. 5 Va. (1 Call) 419–429; Court of Appeals Order Book, III, 335, 337, 339, 341, Va. State Lib. See additional fee at Receipts, Aug. 3, 1790.

62. JM probably had traveled in August to Fauquier County, where the final inquest of office was held to determine if Fairfax's land should escheat to the Commonwealth. See Fairfax lands: Editorial Note, Feb. 1, 1793.

Hooe & Alexander v Becquith[63]	20	
Christian v Rogers	5	
Walden v Payne & Allison[64]	10	
Fearne ads. Comth.	4	16
Tatham ads. Macky	3	
commrs.	6	12
Gardner ads. Brown	5	
Jerdone v Dabny & ads. Same[65]	10	
Genl. Darke[66]	14	
Peyton ads. Comth	2	16
Stuart ads. Gray & Co. (Fedl.)	3	
Colo. Calloway (Fedl.)	20	
Miller ads. Grills	5	2
Page exr. ads. Loyd	5	2
Ascue v Miller	5	
Light ads. Wilson & v Maxwell[67]	7	
Andrews exr. of Beall	15	
Robinsons admrs.	20	
Harrison v Allen[68]	24	
advice fees 3£	3	

[*Disbursements*]

Novr.	Market 8 dollars, given 6, knives for Tom & Johnney 6/, brewing 6/	3	6

63. See Vol. I, 351, n. 79.

64. See entry under Receipts, Oct. 1, 1789.

65. This entry indicates JM represented Sarah Jerdone in the case of Francis Jerdone's Executrix v. James Dabney before the High Court of Chancery. That court decreed in favor of Jerdone on Oct. 4, 1794. JM's notation "& ads. Same" indicates he continued to represent Jerdone when Dabney appealed to the Court of Appeals. JM argued against reversal on Oct. 31, 1795, and the court affirmed the judgment that day. Court of Appeals Order Book, III, 83, Va. State Lib. See later fee at Receipts, Nov. 1794.

66. William Darke.

67. For information on Wilson v. Light, see entry under Receipts, Nov. 1792. Peter Light v. James Maxwell was an appeal from a Sept. 1794 judgment against Light in the District Court at Winchester. The case was docketed in the Court of Appeals on Apr. 12, 1796, but was dismissed and remanded on Nov. 4, 1796. Court o Appeals Order Book, III, 109, 145, 274, IV, 40, Va. State Lib.

JM may also have been involved in Maxwell v. Light, appeals from a Sept. 1795 district court judgment. See 5 Va. (1 Call) 100 (1797); Court of Appeals Order Book, III, 145, 185, 187, Va. State Lib.

68. See entry under Receipts, Mar. 1794.

market 48/, wood 36/, tongues 27/		5	12	
paid Mr. Heron[69] £3–3–11, market 21/		4	4	11
shedes £3–15, market 6/		4	1	
sundries at Vendue[70]		26	6	8
Market 3£, spoon 3–12–8, postage 1/6		7	14	3
Shoes £3–6		3	6	
Ship £27–4, market £3		30	4	

[*Receipts*]

Jany.	advice fee 22/6, Edwards exr.	1	2	6
	advice fee—Mr. Price	1	4	
	advice fee (Mr. Preston)	1	16	
	drawing a deed (Mr. Berkeley)	1	2	6
	Moore v Mimms	5		
	Carrington vs. Jefferson etc.	2	9	
	Bird (v Pollard & al.	5		
	advice fee 22/	1	2	6
	Douglass & Prentis ads. Lorell Fedl.[71]	30		
	Calvert v Loyal (old suit)	15		
Feby.	Duke & al. v Dukes exrs. & al.	5		
	Minnally ads. Meredith	3	19	10
	Dickins v Lee	5		
	Tomkies & ux. v Booths exrs. & al.	2	12	
	advice fee 22/6	1	2	6
	Batt exx. v Baily	5		
	Minton ads. Buxton	6		
	Cummock & Co. ads. Godwin	6		
	Nelsons ads. Nelsons[72]	5		
	Hewlet v Glenn	3		

69. James Heron, Richmond merchant.

70. The Vendue was a public auction held regularly in Richmond. *Va. Gaz., & Genl. Adv.*, Feb. 25, and Apr. 15, 1795.

71. Joseph Larelle v. William Prentis and Larelle v. William Douglass were brought before the U.S. Circuit Court for Virginia in 1795. On May 30, 1796, the cases were dismissed when Larelle failed to give security as ordered by the court. U.S. Circuit Court, Va., Order Book, II, 66, 134, Va. State Lib.

72. See entry under Receipts, Mar. 25, 1789.

	[*Disbursements*]			
Jany.	books 42, venigar 6/, bran 24/	3	12	
	beef £7–10, mutton 34/	9	4	
	corn £40, cloaths basket 3/	40	3	
	Oats 50/, books 9/	2	19	
	Cards 6/, Jaquelin 6/		12	
	Shoes for J Smith 7/6, hominy 2/9, postage 2/		11	3
	paid subscription to Mr. Buchanan[73]	3		
	Cambrick for self 50/	2	10	
	Mr. Nicholson printer[74] 30/	1	10	
	Saddle for Polly £5–10–6	5	10	6
	fitting out myself £7–10	7	10	
	hat for Tom 9/, Encyclopedia[75] 30/	1	19	
	beef 52/3, pork £12–10, market 6/	15	8	3
	lock 6/, market 9/8, given 7/6	1	3	2
	Mrs. Lawson[76] £10, Stockings 13/4, 1/6	10	14	10
	bran 6/, spade 6/8, beef 3–8–8	4	1	4
	taxes for county & city,[77] bran 6/	9	18	4

73. See entries under Disbursements, May 1790, Apr. 1792, and Mar. 1794, and Vol. I, 313, for earlier payments to Buchanan.

74. Thomas Nicolson (*ca.* 1758–1808), a Richmond printer and publisher, published the *Virginia Gazette* in Williamsburg from 1779 to 1780. In 1780 he moved to Richmond, where he published the *Virginia Gazette* until 1781 and the *Virginia Gazette and Weekly Advertiser* from 1781 until 1797. "Return of the Inhabitants," 1787, Richmond City Common Hall Records, I, 347, Va. State Lib.; Brigham, *American Newspapers*, II, 1460.

75. JM had subscribed to *Encyclopaedia; or a Dictionary of Arts, Sciences, and Miscellaneous Literature* since Sept. 1790, and this entry suggests the purchase of vol. XII, issued in 1794, or vol. XIII, issued in 1795.

76. Molly Lawson.

77. JM's personal property list for Richmond, recorded Apr. 16, 1795, indicated ownership of 9 tithable Negro slaves, 4 horses, and 1 coach, chariot, or post chaise. His real property was taxed at 10d. Richmond City Personal Property Book, 1795, and Land Book, 1795, Va. State Lib. It is unclear why JM would be paying city tax in January, for he usually paid it in the spring or early summer. It is possible, however, that this entry was for his 1794 city taxes. See entry under Disbursements, Mar. 1794, for information on JM's 1794 city taxes. JM's 1795 property tax for Fauquier County was £2 15s. 10d. for 520 acres. Fauquier County Land Book, 1795, Va. State Lib. Henrico County tax records for 1794 and 1795 are not extant.

	bringing two women to bed[78]	1	4	
	[Receipts]			
March 2d	Talbot v Buford	1	8	
	Baskerville & Gadberry	5		
	Baskerville & Woodson (appl. dist. ct.)	1	12	8
	Boggus v Humphries	2	8	
	Selsur v Osborne	5	8	
	Dowdale v Crap[79]	3	16	
	Yerbys ads. Yerbys[80]	5	12	6
3d.	Ward ads. Webber & ux[81]	4	2	6
	Duke v Meriwether	3	12	
	Marquis v Grigsby & al (old suit)	2	13	
4	advice fee	1	2	6
	Scott Thomas v Price	4	16	
	Hall (an old suit in ct. appeals finishd)	18	2	
	Mr. Brough (finishd)	4	10	
5th.	Eustace ads. Eustace[82]	2	16	
	Campbell & Wheeler ads. Robinson[83]	2	8	
	Hancock & al ads. Bott & al.	5		

78. This entry is probably for two slaves who were giving birth.

79. Several cases known as James Dowdall v. James Crap came before the District Court at Fredericksburg, and it is uncertain which action JM recorded a fee for here. One action ended in a judgment for Crap on Oct. 2, 1794. Another was dismissed on Oct. 5, 1796. District Court Law Orders, B, 1794–1798, 42, 63, 96, 245, Fredericksburg, Va. State Lib.

80. JM may have been involved in early proceedings of Mary and William Yerby v. George Yerby's Administrator. The High Court of Chancery issued a decree on May 17, 1800, and that was appealed to the Court of Appeals. JM was no longer involved, however. 7 Va. (3 Call) 289 (1802); Court of Appeals Order Book, IV, 243, 249, Va. State Lib.

81. Ward v. Webber and wife was an appeal from a decree of the High Court of Chancery of May 14, 1792, that refused to review a judgment of the General Court. JM represented Ward in arguments before the Court of Appeals on Oct. 13, 1794. The decree was affirmed on Oct. 17, 1794. 1 Va. (1 Wash.) 274; Court of Appeals Order Book, II, 261, III, 4–5, Va. State Lib. See additional fee under Receipts, Sept. 1795.

82. See entry under Receipts, Sept. 1794.

83. JM represented the defendants before the High Court of Chancery in William Robertson v. James Campbell and Luke Wheeler. The court dismissed Robertson's bill on May 13, 1797. JM left the case before it reached the Court of Appeals. 6 Va. (2 Call) 354; Court of Appeals Order Book, IV, 4, 17, Va. State Lib.

Ryder ads. Smith	2	8	
Hook ads. Ross	5	12	
Chevallie in Beaumarchais v			
Comth.[84]	15		
Mr. Bernard[85]	3	18	
Ragland v Goodall & al	2	2	
Shelton (caveat finishd)	2	8	
	105	15	2

[Disbursements]

March	paid Mr. Dixon his gazette			
	to this day[86]	1	4	
	Brown v Pleasants £6			
	bran 6/, given away 12/		18	
	Coal 49/8, market 6/,			
	postage 15/	3	10	8

[Receipts]

March	Anderson & al ads. Anderson		
	& al.[87]	5	
	Goode & al ads. Hayes	7	10
	Skipwith ads. Hanson £10–10	10	10
	Fitzhugh v Peytons exr.	7	10
	Ewing v Donald	5	12
	Noble v Taylor	5	
	Littlejohn v Cookus (in		
	Orandorf v Cookus)	3	
	Rankin v Donaghoe	1	4
	Burfoot v Littlepage	3	

84. See entry under Receipts, July 1792.

85. This fee probably represents a retainer from William Bernard in Bernard v. Richard Brewer. The District Court at Northumberland County had affirmed a Richmond County Court judgment against Bernard on Apr. 9, 1794. The case was submitted to the Court of Appeals on Oct. 14, 1795, and on the following day the district court judgment was reversed. 2 Va. (2 Wash.) 76; Court of Appeals Order Book, III, 70, 71, Va. State Lib.

86. JM was settling his account with John Dixon, Jr. (d. 1805), Richmond printer and publisher who issued the *Virginia Gazette and Richmond Chronicle* from 1793 to 1795. Dixon had previously published the *Virginia Gazette, and Public Advertiser* in Richmond from 1791 to 1793. He later issued the *Richmond Chronicle* from 1795 to 1796, the *Observatory* (Richmond) from 1797 to 1798, and the *Examiner* (Richmond) from 1798 to 1799. Brigham, *American Newspapers*, II, 1403.

87. See entry under Receipts, June 1791.

Anthony ads. Appleberry[88]	2	8	
Advice fees 45/	2	5	
advice 28/, Mr. Nicholas			
£6–12	8		
advice 52/	2	12	
Taylor v Deneufville	2	10	
Dabny v Thompson[89]	5		
	71	1	

[*Disbursements*]

March	Beef 42/, market 6/	2	8
	coal 50/, bran 12/	3	2
	Market sundry times 6£	6	

[*Receipts*]

April	Phillips ads. Brock	4	10	
	Mayo ads. Saunders appeal	1	10	
	advice fee 22/6	1	2	6
	Harris ads. Trents	3		
	Atkinson ads. White (appeals)[90]	5		
	advice fee 22/6	1	2	6
	Booker v Bookers admr.	5	2	
	Parish ads. Claiborne[91]	7		
	Watson ads. Donald	2	10	
	Ramsay ads. Burter	3	10	
	Fauntleroy ads. Brooke	6	15	
	Mr. Kerr (Fedl.)	10		
	Colo. Peachy[92]	5		
	Gatewood ads. Bowman[93]	5		

88. See entry under Receipts, Apr. 1792.

89. JM was retained by Robert Dabney in Dabney v. Anderson Thompson, William DuVal, Martin and James Hawkins, and Nelson and Waddy Thompson to appeal a Mar. 18, 1795, decree of the High Court of Chancery. The appeal was dismissed by agreement on Nov. 10, 1795. Court of Appeals Order Book, III, 92, Va. State Lib.

90. See Vol. I, 373, n. 72.

91. JM represented Parish in Buller Claiborne v. John Parish, an appeal from a May 8, 1794, judgment of the District Court at Williamsburg affirming a New Kent County Court judgment in an ejectment action. The Court of Appeals reversed the judgment and ordered a new trial on Nov. 7, 1795. 2 Va. (2 Wash.) 146; Court of Appeals Order Book, III, 89, Va. State Lib.

92. William Peachy.

93. John Bowman, surviving partner of Spiers, Bowman & Co., Great Britain, v.

Triplet v Wilson[94]	6		
Wade v Geddy (appeal chy.)	5		
Mrs. Peyton (by Mr. Bolling)	2	3	
Finch ads. Thweat (old appeal)[95]	4	16	

[Disbursements]

[April]	Tar 16, Coal 25/	1	1	
	Market 36/, mutton 28/, bran 18/	4	2	
	market 18/, quils 14/	1	12	
	bottles 30/, given away 30/	3		
	market 7/3, Coal 18/, given away 6, market 6/	1	17	3
	market 12/, shoes for Dick 6/		18	
	Powell on devises[96] 15		15	

[Receipts]

May	Clements ads. Shaw & Moore[97]	5		
	Old ads. Ross	2	3	7
	Advice fee 22/6	1	2	6
	from Cogbill ads. Pleasant (friendly)	1	10	
	Tucker & ux v Washington	5		
	Orandorf[98]	30		

Dudley Gatewood's Administrator was a British debt case in which JM represented Gatewood's administrator, James Gatewood. Pleas were filed on June 3, 1795, and the U.S. Circuit Court for Virginia entered a judgment for Bowman on June 3, 1796. U.S. Circuit Court, Va., Order Book, I, 528, II, 62, 168, and Record Book, V, 67–74, Va. State Lib.

94. JM represented the appellant in Simon Triplett v. Cumberland Wilson and Alexander Campbell, an appeal from a Sept. 1793 decree of the High Court of Chancery. The Court of Appeals affirmed the decree on Nov. 19, 1796, conforming to the U.S. Supreme Court's decision in Ware v. Hylton. Court of Appeals Order Book, III, 56, 134, 154, Va. State Lib. See also 10 Va. (6 Call) 47 (1806).

95. See entry under Receipts, Oct. 1793.

96. John Joseph Powell, *An Essay upon the Learning of Devises, from their inception by writing, to their consumation by the death of the devisor* (London, 1788).

97. JM was retained by the appellee in Robert Shaw v. Abraham Clements, an appeal from a Sept. 1794 judgment of the District Court at Staunton in favor of Clements. The appeal was submitted on Apr. 13, 1796, and on Nov. 1, 1798, the court affirmed the judgment. 5 Va. (1 Call) 373; Court of Appeals Order Book, III, 109, 132, 255, 263, Va. State Lib.

98. See fee, Orandorf v. Cookus, under Receipts, Feb. 1792.

	from Mr. Hite	10	6	
	Pleasant v Christian	6		
	Allen (Cumberland)	3	2	
	Whitings exrs. ads. Nortons[99]	5	2	
	Finch ads. Thweat chy.[1]	5		
	Pasteur v Burwell & al (friendly)	5		
	Corbill ads. Mitchel	5		
	Advice fee	1	2	6
	Clay v Poythress & al	5		
	Clay ads. Tucker	5		
	Beasly v Winfry	6	5	
	Calloway v Comth.	7		
	Fowler ads. Dow	5	2	
	Jeter v Sharp & al	3		
	Dandridges exrs. ads. Farrel & Jones	7		
	Foote v Fitzhugh	5	5	
	Massie v Burwells	5	12	
		134	12	7

[Disbursements]

May	barbacue 48/	2	8	
	Virga. laws[2] 3£, 1st. May 18/	3	18	
	market 24/, expenses 1/6	1	5	6
	linnen £7–10, goods for self 58/	10	8	
	market 6/, whisky £6–16	7	2	
	shoes 13/6			

[Receipts]

May	Callaway & Co. chy. employd by Mr. Munke	7		
	Bedford ads. Moore	4	4	
	Simmons exrs. v Simmons exr.	5		

99. JM was probably being retained by the appellee in an appeal of John H. Norton v. Francis Whiting's Administrator, a debt action from the District Court at Winchester, where judgment had been confessed on Sept. 6, 1791. No record of appeal has been found, however. For the district court action, see Superior Court Order Book, 1789–1793, 239–240, Frederick County, Va. State Lib.

1. See entry under Receipts, Oct. 1793.

2. *Acts passed at a General Assembly of the Commonwealth of Virginia . . . one thousand seven hundred and ninety-four* (Richmond, 1795).

Smith Fedl.	9		
Duke v Meriwether	1	10	
Stuart v Garnet etc. (chy)	2	8	
Pettus's exrs. ads. Williams[3]	5		
Jerdone[4]—motion	5		
Minors exrs ads. McCall & Sheddan	3		
Wishard ads. Blanchard[5]	9		
Maeze v Hamilton[6]	2	8	6
Rawlins ads. Cuningham & Co.[7]	5	4	
Johnston & al ads. Treasurer	2	10	
Bowyer ads. Jackson[8]	4		
Edwards ads. Robinson[9]	5		
Marshall ads. Meredith	5		
Armstead etc. v McCargo	5		
	80	4	6

[Disbursements]

[May]	Store for sundries £14–12	14	12
	given away 6/		6
	Market 36/	1	16

[Receipts]

June	Porterfield ads. Kinnerly[10]	5

3. See entry under Receipts, Apr. 1792.
4. See entry under Receipts, Nov. 1794.
5. See entry under Receipts, Aug. 1792.
6. See JM to Archibald Stuart, *ca.* Dec. 1789.
7. Andrew Cockran, William Cunningham & Co., Great Britain, v. Benjamin Rawlings was a British debt case in which JM filed pleas for Rawlings on Dec. 8, 1795. Judgment for the plaintiff was entered on June 4, 1796. U.S. Circuit Court, Va., Order Book, II, 64, 173, and Record Book, V, 76–78, Va. State Lib.
8. In John Jackson, of Great Britain, v. William Bowyer, the plaintiff was suing for the value of goods sold and delivered to the defendant in 1772. The case was continued until after the time JM could have represented Bowyer. Final judgment was entered on May 30, 1799. U.S. Circuit Court, Va., Order Book, II, 144, 248, III, 129, 187, 224, and Record Book, VI, 193–197, Va. State Lib.
9. The case of Thomas Robinson v. Gilbert Edwards had been filed in the District Court at Northumberland County in 1794, and on Apr. 1, 1795, a default judgment had been entered. Apparently JM was being retained for subsequent litigation in either the High Court of Chancery or the Court of Appeals. District Court Order Book, 1793–1802, 59, 81, Northumberland County, Va. State Lib.
10. The District Court at Staunton entered a default judgment against the de-

Caldwell ads. Watson	5		
Wilson v Kelly appeal	5		
Loyal & Wilson	6	6	
Advice	6		
Batte & al ads. Davies	7	4	
Advice 24/	1	4	
Smith in Hites exr. ads. Stevens	5		
Emmerson ads. McMeken, fee recd. by Mr. Colston & Colo. Magill[11]	5		
Motion on rep. bond in Genl. Ct.	2	10	
White ads. appeals	3	13	
Francisco ads. Winston (appeals)[12]	2	8	
Fenwick & Co. v North	5		
Threlkeld v Triplett	3	17	8
Hicks & al ads. Bibb	5		
Pendleton v Coutts	5		
Telford v Pope	3	15	6
Advice fees	4	10	
Cowles v Brown[13]	5		

[Disbursements]

June	Market 12/, given away 18/	1	10	
	Saddle for Tom 36/, expences 14/	2	10	
	Market 32/9	1	12	9
	Market 14/6, lost 13 £	13	14	6
	Stable 12/, Vendue £15[14]	15	12	

---

fendants on Apr. 2, 1795, in Robert Porterfield v. William and James Kinnerly. This fee indicates JM was being retained to appeal, although no record of appeal has been found. District Court Order Book, 1789–1797, 376, Augusta County, Va. State Lib.

11. Rawleigh Colston and Charles Magill.

12. Edmund Winston v. Peter Francisco was an appeal from an Apr. 1795 judgment of the District Court at Prince Edward County that affirmed a Buckingham County Court's judgment against Winston. JM represented Francisco on appeal when the case was submitted on Apr. 19, 1796. The Court of Appeals affirmed the judgment on Sept. 6, 1796. 2 Va. (2 Wash.) 187; Court of Appeals Order Book, III, 119, 123, Va. State Lib.

13. JM represented Cowles in the early proceedings of Edmund Cowles v. William Browne before the High Court of Chancery. The chancery decree was issued in 1800, and an appeal was filed in the Court of Appeals afterwards. 8 Va. (4 Call) 477 (1791).

14. See similar entry under Disbursements, Nov. 1794.

	Market 5£, expenses 3£	8		
	Flour £16–4	16	4	

[Receipts]

July, Aug.	Wade v Jackson & al	4	18	20
	White v Sundries trespass	1	10	
	Advice fees	2	16	
	Mrs. Payne[15]	6		
	Norton v Cary & al	5		
	Bell & al v Lewis & al	4	14	
	Pemberton	9		
	Motion in Cty. Ct. 7£,			
	Morris ads. Berkelley 2–13	9	13	
	Land v Curd[16]	5		
	Fulgham v Lightfoot[17]	13		
	Bullock ads. Goodall[18]	5		
	Edwards & al ads. Tooms	5		
	Kelsie v Wormeley & al	5		
	Eustace v Eustace[19]	3	12	
	Advice 30/	1	10	
	Webster ads. Staples[20]	6	18	

[Disbursements]

July, Aug.	chickens 6/, barber 45/,			
	market 18/	3	9	
	Oats 36/, also 10/, Sundries			
	£11–1–6	13	7	6
	paper 26/, book 12/	1	18	

15. See JM to Mrs. Mary Payne, calendared at Aug. 5, 1795.

16. See entry under Receipts, Sept. 1794.

17. The case of Charles Fulgham v. Lemuel Lightfoot was determined in Isle of Wight County Court on Aug. 15, 1795. It is unclear why JM received a fee at this time; it is certain he did not practice in that court. The case next went to the District Court at Suffolk, where the county court judgment was affirmed and where it is certain JM also did not practice. The case was finally appealed to the Court of Appeals, but there is no record of JM's participation in that court either. 5 Va. (1 Call) 250 (1798); Court of Appeals Order Book, III, 232, Va. State Lib.

18. JM represented Bullock in early proceedings of Bullock v. Goodall and Clough. The case was appealed to the High Court of Chancery from the Hanover County Court in May 1795 and to the Court of Appeals in 1800. 7 Va. (3 Call) 39; Court of Appeals Order Book, IV, 27, 43, 94, 99, 100, Va. State Lib.

19. See entry under Receipts, Sept. 1794.

20. The dates of Staples v. Webster are not known through all of its stages, but it is known that the case came to the Court of Appeals from the High Court of Chan-

Taylor for self	15		
Mr. Crutchfield for adding			
new causes	1	10	
letters 12/, expences £5	5	12	
Sundries at store	11	1	6
Butter 12/6, Watermelons 4/5		17	
barbacue 6/, postage 15/	1	1	
expences going to Hanover	1	16	
paid 36/, postage 24/,			
dinner 18/	3	18	
Table cloths £5–8	5	8	
Mrs. Lawson[21]	2	8	

[Receipts]

Septr.	Sundry fees	30		
	Colo. Lynch	21		
	Chiles ads. Wortham	3	12	
	Golston v Gist	5		
	Todd v Comth.[22]	5		
	Ward ads. Webber[23]	3		
	Willis ads. Williams	5		
	Catlett v Quarles	2	16	
	Stuart v Garnett & al	2	12	
	Murchie	13		
	Armstead v Armstead	5		
	Stottslager ads. Keller	7		
	Advice	1	2	6
	Anderson ads. Robinsons	5		
	Alexander ads. Alexander	5	5	
	Rose	5		
	Garratt ads. Ruffin	6	16	
	Claiborne ads. Hamberrys			
	representatives	5		
	Donalson v Markham	9		
	Cobourn v Stevens (Chy.)[24]	5		

cery. JM was probably involved in the chancery proceedings, although he did not participate in the Court of Appeals litigation. 9 Va. (5 Call) 261 (1804).

   21. Molly Lawson.

   22. See entry under Receipts, June 1792.

   23. See entry under Receipts, Mar. 3, 1795.

   24. JM represented James Cobun in the High Court of Chancery in Cobun v. George Stephens. Cobun was appealing a county court decree that ordered him to

	Mosby v Johnstons exrs.	5		
	[Disbursements]			
Septr.	Wine	31		
	Market 36/, given Doctor Foushee 4–10	6	6	
	market 24/, vinegar 6/	1	10	
	Charlotte Keith 16/6, market 6/	1	2	6
	Market 12/, given Tom for paints 24/	1	16	
	Market 18/			
	[Receipts]			
October	Leprade exr. v Glassells	2	8	
	Cunninghame v Foster	2	8	
	Advice	1	2	6
	Walke exr. ads. Walker[25]	2	12	
	Colo. Pryor[26]	5		
	Shelton ads. Johnston[27]	2	8	
	McCrea v Woods[28]	5	4	
	Advice	3		
	advice	1	2	
	Austin v Whitlock	5		
	Lawson v	10		
	Booker exx. ads. Cuningham Fedl.[29]	7		

convey land to Stephens. The court reversed the decree on Mar. 14, 1798. After JM left the case, it was appealed to the Court of Appeals and affirmed on May 8, 1800. 6 Va. (2 Call) 371; Court of Appeals Order Book, IV, 26, 32, Va. State Lib.

25. See entry under Receipts, June 1792.

26. This was probably the Pryor who lost in Adams v. Pryor in the High Court of Chancery on Oct. 2, 1795. JM represented Pryor in the Court of Appeals, and the chancery decree was reversed on Oct. 25, 1798. 5 Va. (1 Call) 332; Court of Appeals Order Book, III, 169, 257, 259, Va. State Lib.

27. See entry under Receipts, Feb. 1793.

28. JM represented Philip McRae in McRae v. Richard Woods, an appeal from a Mar. 1794 decree of the High Court of Chancery. The Court of Appeals affirmed the decree on Oct. 22, 1794. 2 Va. (2 Wash.) 80; Court of Appeals Order Book, III, 56, 69, 74, Va. State Lib.

29. William Cunningham v. Richard Booker's Administratrix was a British debt case before the U.S. Circuit Court for Virginia in which JM filed pleas for Booker on Dec. 8, 1795. Judgment was entered for the plaintiff on June 4, 1796. U.S. Circuit Court, Va., Order Book, II, 64, 176–177, Va. State Lib.

Banks exr. of Rubsamon ads. McDougal[30]		5		
Massie admx. of Cobbet v Chamberlayne		5		
2 advice fees		2	16	
Colo. Peachy[31]		5	4	
Cabell & al v Hardwick[32]		2	11	4
Advice fees		2	5	
Anderson ads Downing		5		
Craigen & Crouchman v Thorn & al		6		
Scot (Fedl.)		4	16	
Minor v Jones		14		
Randolph v Tuckers exrs		5		

[*Disbursements*]

[October]	Market 18/, do. 12	1	10	
	boots & shoes	3	7	3
	Schooling boys	5		
	Taylor for boys	2	9	3
	Wine 12£ 17–6	12	17	6
	Market	24		
	do	3		
	Mrs. Lawson[33]	10		
	Market 12/		12	
	Market	3	13	

[*Receipts*]

Nov., Decr.	Clay v Williams & al	5	14
	Blow ads. Wigfal	12	

30. Peter McDougall & Co. v. Thomas Banks, executor of Jacob Rubsamon, was filed on Oct. 2, 1795. Rubsamon had been security for a debtor of the plaintiff, and this action was brought in an attempt to collect on a 1792 judgment for £900. On June 7, 1797, the U.S. Circuit Court found for Banks, JM's client, on evidence that Rubsamon had died prior to the 1792 judgment. U.S. Circuit Court, Va., Order Book, II, 119, 330, and Record Book, IV, 283–289, Va. State Lib. See JM's answer listed at Law Papers, Nov. 1795.

31. William Peachy.

32. William Cabell, Jr., *et al.* v. John Hardwick was an appeal from a Sept. 18, 1795, judgment of the District Court at New London for Hardwick in debt. The Court of Appeals affirmed the judgment on Oct. 23, 1798. 5 Va. (1 Call) 301; Court of Appeals Order Book, III, 254, 257, Va. State Lib.

33. Molly Lawson.

Cowper ads. Stoney[34]	6		
Dolby v. Price[35]	2	14	
Jett exr. ads. Ellzey	6		

[*Disbursements*][36]

Borrowed from[37] [ ]			
The account about £5 £	54		
Combs & Tape 4/6,			
Flowrs 7/6, Gauze 3/6		15	[6]
White silk gloves 7/6,			
Ribband 4/		11	[6]
Cat gut thread & sewing silk 3/		3	
one Lustring £5–17,			
Calicoe £1–12–6 £	7	9	6
2 yds. ¼ green silk 18/		18	
For cloak £3–12–6, for Shoes 8/	4	0	6
For Calicoe Gown	1	15	
For one salmon Silk			
To 3 yds. linnen @ 2/6 per yd.			
8 yds. white ribband			
3 yds. black Ca[*licoe*]			
2¼ yds. mu[*slin*]			

[*Receipts*]

In hand	35	16
	1	16
	37	12
Recd. from the Treasury	20	
Recd. from Mr. Wm. Nelson		
one fee	3	

34. See Wills Cowper to JM, Nov. 21, 1793.

35. John Dalby v. Thomas Price was an appeal from a June 1795 decree of the High Court of Chancery in which JM represented Dalby in the Court of Appeals. Arguments took place on Apr. 30, 1796, and on May 4, 1796, the court reversed the decree. Court of Appeals Order Book, III, 121, 125, Va. State Lib.

36. The remaining Account Book entries were written on two sides of a piece of paper that has been bound at the end of the accounts, following the page containing Receipts, Nov.–Dec. 1795. It obviously was inserted there during binding, and physical evidence indicates it did not belong there originally.

The total of £63 1s. 3½ d. at the bottom of these receipts is the amount JM carried forward to Receipts, Oct. 1783. See Vol. I, 295. It appears therefore that these entries were made ca. Aug.–Sept. 1783 and that this page should have been bound as the first page of JM's restored Account Book.

37. The top and bottom right-hand corners of the page are missing.

Recd. from the Treasury	20		
Recd. for warrants from T M	7	4	
Recd. for my Father from			
Mr T. Austin	12		
Recd. for my Father from			
Mr. T. Austin	10	7	6
	110	3	6
	47	2	2½
	63	1	3½

LIST OF CASES
IN THE ACCOUNT BOOK

Each case title in John Marshall's Account Book is listed here twice, once under the plaintiff and again under the defendant. Italics indicate cases commented on in the editors' notes. Generally names in the case titles are spelled as Marshall entered them in the Account Book.

The page references in this list are to the Account Book only. Any other mentions of these cases in the volume are given in the Legal Index (see p. 527), which contains case titles that appear in Marshall's correspondence and papers.

INDEXES

LEGAL INDEX
GENERAL INDEX

LEGAL INDEX

The Legal Index contains both legal digest entries and case titles that appear in John Marshall's correspondence and papers. When a case title additionally appears in Marshall's Account Book, those page references are given here also. However, for case titles appearing only in the Account Book, see the list of cases following that document. For names of individuals and general subject entries, see the General Index, which begins on p. 535.

GENERAL INDEX

The General Index contains names of individuals that appear in this volume, as well as general subject entries. Dates of individuals, if known, may be found at their first page reference; if in an earlier volume, the volume number and page reference will follow the name in parentheses. For legal digest entries, see the Legal Index, which begins on p. 527; for case titles, also see the Legal Index and the List of Cases in the Account Book (p. 499).

Beckley, John (I, 243 n. 4), 5, 13
Becquith, Sir Jonathan (I, 336 n. 11), 369
"Belvidere," 316
Bentley, Richard, 80, 81
Bentley, William, 129, 310, 311
Bermuda Hundred, 275
Berry, Joseph, 364
"Bizarre," 60 n. 5, 162, 169
Blackheath Coal Mines, 111 n. 9
Blackwell, John (I, 22 n. 5), 317
Blair, James, 69
Blair, John (I, 140 n. 9), 113
Blair, Rev. John D., 398, 436, 437
Bland, Frances, 162 n. 9
Bland, Theodorick, 82 n. 6
"Blenheim," 264 n. 6
Bloody Run Spring, 463 n. 72
Booth, Mary, 23
Booth, Thomas, 23
Booth, William, 105
Borland, Robert, 128
"Boston Hill," 258 n. 5
Bracken, Rev. John, 67–81
Bradby, James, 315 n. 6
Bradford, William, 319
Bradley, William, 174
Braxton, Carter (I, 370–371 n. 62), 197, 329
Breckinridge, James, 217
Breckinridge, John (I, 182 n. 2): letters to, 25–26, 33, 52–53, 54, 55, 59–60, 91–92, 94–95, 96, 97, 103
Brend, Thomas, 347 n. 60
Brent, R., 338
Briggs, Gray, 98
British debts, 248–249, 293 and n. 9, 333; discussed by JM, 232–235; and E. Randolph, 293 and n. 9, 294
Broadway, Va., 275
Brooke, Francis, 194, 271, 318
Brooke, Humphrey (I, 138 n. 7), 99, 100, 195 n. 2
Brooke, Robert, 129, 160, 317–318; letters from, 302–303, 313, 315; letters to, 312, 313
Brooking, Vivion, 272
Brown, James, 86, 124, 161, 457
Buchanan, Alexander, 264 n. 6, 438
Buchanan, Andrew, 39
Buchanan, James, 264
Buchanan, Rev. John (I, 313 n. 11), 264 n. 6, 398 n. 84; and insanity hearing, 14 n. 1, 15; money paid to, 393, 438, 475, 485; and Quoits Club, 461 n. 65

Buck, Cornelius, 310, 311
Buckingham County, 156, 422 and n. 94, 446, 462, 470
"Buckingham Lodge," 40 n. 8
Buckner, Mr., 36
"Buckpond," 412 n. 41
Bull, Robert, 106
Bullitt, Cuthbert, 54
Burnley, Zachariah, 63
Burns, Robert, Poems, 347 and n. 60
Burr, George, 156
Burton, Hutchins, 134 n. 7
Burton, Jesse, 264–265
Burton, John, 134–137
Burton, Rebecca, 264 n. 7
Burton, Robert, 83–84, 411
Burton, Tabitha Minge, 134 n. 7
Butler, Percival, 36
Byrd, William, 102 n. 7, 189

C

Cabell, John, 178–179
Cabell, William, 157
Cagneau, Henry, 15, 16 n. 8
Call, Daniel, 71, 75 n. 7, 111; as attorney, 112, 268 n. 9, 388 n. 41
Callaway, James, 158
Calloway, John, 442
Calvert, Cornelious, 121
Camm, Rev. John, 69 n. 2, 81
Campbell, Alexander, 144, 197, 208, 259; as attorney, 144, 145 n. 8, 166, 175, 309 n. 2; as Mason, 310, 311
Campbell, Arthur, 295 n. 8
Campbell, Robert, 295
Campbell County, Va., 229
Carey, James, 447
Carey, Mathew, 349 n. 65
Carrington, Edward (I, 117 n. 1), 258, 297 n. 3, 321; as supervisor of revenue, 281 n. 2, 309
Carrington, Joseph, 258
Carrington, Mayo, 258
Carrington, Paul, Sr. (I, 149 n. 1), 52 n. 6
Carrington, Paul, Jr. (I, 184 n. 4), 52, 53, 92 n. 1
Carson, David, 296
Carter, Charles L., 194
Carter, Edward, 157 n. 2
Carter, Edward, 264
Carter, John, 290 n. 9
Cary, Wilson Miles, 46, 396, 397
"Castle Hill," 30 n. 9, 125 n. 5